Google Cloud Associate Cloud Engineer Certification and Implementation Guide

Master the deployment, management, and monitoring of Google Cloud solutions

Agnieszka Koziorowska

Wojciech Marusiak

BIRMINGHAM—MUMBAI

Google Cloud Associate Cloud Engineer Certification and Implementation Guide

Group Product Manager: Preet Ahuja

Publishing Product Manager: Preet Ahuja

Content Development Editor: Sujata Tripathi

Technical Editor: Rajat Sharma

Copy Editor: Safis Editing

Project Coordinator: Prajakta Naik

Proofreader: Safis Editing

Indexer: Tejal Daruwale Soni

Production Designer: Prashant Ghare

Marketing Coordinator: Rohan Dobhal

First published: September 2023

Production reference: 1010923

Published by Packt Publishing Ltd.
Grosvenor House
11 St Paul's Square
Birmingham
B3 1RB

ISBN 978-1-80323-271-3

www.packtpub.com

I am dedicating this book to the loving memory of my dad, Janusz Baum (1959-2022), who was a beloved electrical engineering teacher with a unique talent for explaining complicated concepts in a way his students could easily understand. Writing this book has given me solace by channeling my grief into something he always valued: sharing knowledge with others. I have come to appreciate just how difficult yet fulfilling it can be.

– Agnieszka

This book is dedicated to my beloved daughters – Emilia and Liliana, who will forever be the most important parts of my life, and to my wonderful wife, Ewelina. Without her support and encouragement, this book would have never existed.

I love you all.

– Wojciech

Contributors

About the authors

Agnieszka Koziorowska is an experienced systems engineer who has been in the IT industry for 15 years. She is dedicated to supporting enterprise customers in the EMEA region with their transition to the cloud and hybrid cloud infrastructure by designing and architecting solutions that meet both business and technical requirements. Agnieszka is highly skilled in AWS, Google Cloud, and VMware solutions and holds certifications as a specialist in all three platforms. She believes that although it can be challenging for individuals to keep up with ever-evolving technological advancements, by sharing our knowledge and expertise with one another, we can come up with innovative ideas and solutions that will greatly benefit the IT industry as a whole.

I want to say thank you to the people in the tech industry who helped me transition from an infrastructure engineer to a cloud architect. Your support meant a lot to me and helped me reach my goals.

Wojciech Marusiak, with over 16 years of experience in the IT industry, is a seasoned and innovative IT professional with a proven track record of success. Leveraging extensive work experience in large and complex enterprise environments, Wojciech brings valuable knowledge to help customers and businesses achieve their goals with precision, professionalism, and cost-effectiveness. Holding leading certifications from AWS, Alibaba Cloud, Google Cloud, VMware, and Microsoft, Wojciech is dedicated to continuous learning and sharing knowledge, staying abreast of the latest industry trends and developments.

About the reviewers

Marcelo Marques is a cloud engineer with over 10 years of experience in the technology industry. He specializes in cloud computing and has a wealth of knowledge and experience with large organizations in the technology, financial, manufacturing, and public sectors. Marcelo is driven by knowledge and is always looking to learn and grow. He has all the GCP certifications and is also pursuing knowledge of other cloud providers such as AWS and Azure. He is passionate about cloud computing and is always looking for new ways to use it to solve complex problems.

I would like to thank everyone who helped me in some way along my journey. I will mention a few names, but that doesn't mean they are the only ones. Anderson "Vaka" Leite, Katuchi Iseki, Patrick Lynch, Tiago Algodas, Adelson Smania, and Leonardo Morales, thank you for all your support and help. As I always say, we keep rising.

Mona Mona currently works as an **Artificial Intelligence/Machine Learning** (**AI/ML**) specialist at Google Public Sector. She was a senior AI/ML specialist solutions architect at Amazon before joining Google. She earned her master's in computer information systems from Georgia State University. She is a published author of the books *Natural Language Processing with AWS AI Services* and *Google Cloud Certified Professional Machine Learning Study Guide*. She has authored 19 blogs on AI/ML and cloud technology and was co-author of a research paper on CORD19 Neural Search, which won an award for Best Research Paper at the prestigious **Association for the Advancement of Artificial Intelligence** (**AAAI**) conference.

Table of Contents

Part 2: Configuring and Implementing Google Cloud

3

Planning and Managing GCP Resources   37

4

Implementing Compute Solutions – Google Compute Engine   81

5

Implementing Compute Solutions – Google Kubernetes Engine (Part 1)   153

6

Implementing Compute Solutions – Google Kubernetes Engine (Part 2)   191

7

Implementing Compute Solutions – Cloud Run, Cloud Functions, and Infrastructure as Code   259

8

Configuring and Implementing Data Storage Solutions   311

9

Configuring and Implementing Networking Components   367

Part 3: Data Analytics, Security, Operations, and Cost Estimation in Google Cloud

10

Data Processing Services in Google Cloud   411

Preface

Welcome to Google Cloud Associate Cloud Engineer Certification and Implementation Guide. This book is designed to help you prepare for the Google Cloud Associate Cloud Engineer (ACE) certification exam and teach you how to implement Google Cloud solutions in real life.

We both took the ACE exam, and we found it to be very hands-on and practical. There were a few theoretical questions, and all of the questions required us to have hands-on experience with Google Cloud. This made the exam very challenging, but it was also very rewarding.

We hope that you find this book helpful in your preparation for the ACE exam. We also hope that you find the knowledge that you learn in this book to be rewarding and useful in your work with Google Cloud.

We also know that you might be at the very beginning of your cloud journey or very experienced with the cloud. Therefore, we start with an overview of the technology and service first and then move on to practical implementation. This should give you confidence and experience with Google Cloud and prepare you well to face the ACE exam.

We hope you will enjoy reading the book as much as we enjoyed writing it for you while exploring and having fun with Google Cloud services.

You can connect with us, as well as other like-minded professionals, on this Slack channel – `bit.ly/ace-gcp-book-slack`.

Who this book is for

Google Cloud Platform Associate Cloud Engineer Certification and Implementation Guide is intended for individuals preparing for the ACE certification. It can be used by IT system administrators, DevOps personnel, or cloud architects as it covers all Google Cloud Platform topics. The book is ideal for those who want to start working with Google Cloud, gain practical knowledge, and pass the certification.

This guide is a great opportunity for those who are looking for their first technical certification in Google Cloud. It's a comprehensive guide that covers all Google Cloud Platform topics and daily activities. With this book, individuals can gain practical knowledge, get started with Google Cloud, and successfully pass the certification exam.

What this book covers

Chapter 1, Associate Cloud Engineer Certification Essentials, will help you gain a deep comprehension of the ACE certification and what is involved in the exam. We will provide you with essential details, including exam objectives, registration procedures, and useful insights for obtaining certification.

Chapter 2, Google Cloud Platform Fundamentals, discusses Google Cloud's market position, core services, unique solutions, management interfaces, and command-line tools. Additionally, we will explain the advantages of using public cloud computing over traditional on-premises solutions.

Chapter 3, Planning and Managing GCP Resources, provides an overview of Google's Cloud Computing Services, including how to plan your resource hierarchy, manage users, assign roles and identities, and utilize organizational policies. You will also learn about billing and how to create and manage budgets. Finally, the chapter concludes with a discussion on API management.

Chapter 4, Implementing Compute Solutions, aims to provide a comprehensive understanding of Google's computing options and guide readers on when to use specific services. By giving an overview of compute solutions, we hope to equip readers with the necessary skills to implement them using different deployment options such as the Google Cloud console, command-line tools, and Infrastructure as Code.

Chapter 5, Implementing Compute Solutions – Google Kubernetes Engine – Part 1, aims to help you understand the containerized compute deployment option – Google Kubernetes Engine. We will delve into the architecture of Kubernetes and Google Kubernetes Engine, explore various application deployment methods, and discuss the different types of deployment available on Google Kubernetes Engine

Chapter 6, Implementing Compute Solutions – Google Kubernetes Engine – Part 2, provides an understanding of different operational tasks in Google Kubernetes Engine, such as managing clusters and node pools, as well as the Pod life cycle. Additionally, we will explore how to deploy applications on Google Kubernetes Engine and how users can access them via the available networking services.

Chapter 7, Implementing Compute Solutions – Cloud Run, Cloud Functions, and Infrastructure as Code, discusses the remaining part of Google's Cloud Computing services. Our focus will be on Google Cloud Run and Google Cloud Functions, their distinct features, and the appropriate scenarios for their usage. We will also guide you on deploying these options using the web interface or command-line tools. Additionally, we'll provide insights on Infrastructure as Code and how to leverage available solutions on the Google Cloud Marketplace.

Chapter 8, Configuring and Implementing Storage Solutions, discusses the various ways to store data in Google Cloud. Google Cloud offers fully managed storage and database services that cater to different application requirements. Each section will focus on a different storage type, its features, security measures, and availability. We will also examine the use cases for each category. It is important to design a storage and database strategy for cloud workloads to ensure that every application performs well, is resilient, and has a quick response time.

Chapter 9, Configuring and Implementing Networking Components, explains why it is important to understand how Google Cloud's network services portfolio can be utilized to construct dependable and secure architectures. In this chapter, we will guide you on how to configure network services for your workloads in Google Cloud. We'll cover important topics such as **Virtual Private Cloud** (**VPC**), connecting to VPC from an on-premises location, securing VPC with firewall services, the DNS service in Google Cloud, and which network load balancers to choose for different workload types.

Chapter 10, Data Processing Services in Google Cloud, talks about data processing in today's world where data is as valuable as oil. However, it is often scattered and difficult to understand. In this chapter, readers will learn how to use Google Cloud Data Analytics products to efficiently extract and manipulate data. This knowledge and skills will help them derive meaningful insights from it.

Chapter 11, Monitoring, Logging, and Estimating Cost, discusses the Google Cloud Operations Suite, which offers various tools such as Cloud Monitoring for monitoring the health of your applications and Google Cloud services, Cloud Logging for real-time log management, and diagnostic tools to enhance your service's performance while reducing costs and latency. Furthermore, we will also go over cost estimation in Google Cloud.

Chapter 12, Implementing Identity and Security in Google Cloud, aims to give you a better understanding of identity and access in Google Cloud. Our focus here is on preventing unauthorized access and keeping track of user actions on Google Cloud resources to enhance security. In this chapter, we'll cover key areas such as establishing a Cloud Identity for an organization, granting access to Google Cloud resources, handling service accounts, and utilizing Cloud Audit Logs for security and compliance purposes.

Mock Test 1

Mock Test 2

To get the most out of this book

To fully maximize the benefits of this book and engage with its content effectively, there are a few key requirements that users should have. The primary essentials are a web browser and a supported operating system. Here's what you need:

- **Web browser**: It is essential to have a modern web browser installed on your device. Popular browsers such as Google Chrome, Mozilla Firefox, Microsoft Edge, or Safari are recommended. Make sure your browser is up to date to ensure optimal compatibility with the online resources and tools mentioned throughout the book.

- **Supported operating system**: This book assumes that readers have access to a supported operating system. This may include but is not limited to Windows, macOS, Linux, or ChromeOS. The specific operating system requirements for each tool or platform discussed in the book will be highlighted when relevant.

By having a compatible web browser and supported operating system at your disposal, you will be well equipped to navigate through the various concepts, tools, and resources presented in this book, enabling you to make the most out of your learning experience.

Software/hardware covered in the book	Operating system requirements
Google Cloud SDK	Windows, macOS, or Linux

Download the example code files

You can view the answer explanations for the mock tests on the GitHub repository of this book at `https://github.com/PacktPublishing/Google-Cloud-Associate-Cloud-Engineer-Certification-and-Implementation-Guide`. If there's an update to the material, it will be updated in the GitHub repository.

We also have other code bundles from our rich catalog of books and videos available at `https://github.com/PacktPublishing/`. Check them out!

Conventions used

There are a number of text conventions used throughout this book.

`Code in text`: Indicates code words in text, resource name, folder names, filenames, file extensions, pathnames, dummy URLs, or user input.

Here is an example: "As described in the Kubernetes components section, we interact with clusters using a YAML file called `kubeconfig` in the `$HOME/.kube/config` directory."

A block of code is set as follows:

```
apiVersion: apps/v1
kind: ReplicaSet
metadata:
  name: frontend
  labels:
    app: guestbook
    tier: frontend
spec:
  replicas: 3
  selector:
    matchLabels:
      tier: frontend
  template:
```

```
    metadata:
      labels:
        tier: frontend
    spec:
      containers:
      - name: php-redis
        image: gcr.io/google_samples/gb-frontend:v3
```

When we wish to draw your attention to a particular part of a code block, the relevant lines or items are set in bold:

```
apiVersion: apps/v1
kind: ReplicaSet
metadata:
  name: frontend
  labels:
    app: guestbook
    tier: frontend
```

Any command-line input or output is written as follows:

```
gcloud components install kubectl
sudo apt-get install kubectl
```

Bold: Indicates a new term, an important word, or words that you see onscreen. For instance, words in menus or dialog boxes appear in **bold**. Here is an example: " You can check your Google Cloud expenditure and remaining days in **Billing Account Overview**."

> **Tips or important notes**
> Appear like this.

Get in touch

Feedback from our readers is always welcome.

General feedback: If you have questions about any aspect of this book, email us at customercare@ packtpub.com and mention the book title in the subject of your message.

Errata: Although we have taken every care to ensure the accuracy of our content, mistakes do happen. If you have found a mistake in this book, we would be grateful if you would report this to us. Please visit www.packtpub.com/support/errata and fill in the form.

Piracy: If you come across any illegal copies of our works in any form on the internet, we would be grateful if you would provide us with the location address or website name. Please contact us at copyright@packt.com with a link to the material.

If you are interested in becoming an author: If there is a topic that you have expertise in and you are interested in either writing or contributing to a book, please visit authors.packtpub.com.

Share Your Thoughts

Once you've read *Google Cloud Associate Cloud Engineer Certification and Implementation Guide*, we'd love to hear your thoughts! Scan the QR code below to go straight to the Amazon review page for this book and share your feedback.

https://packt.link/r/1803232714

Your review is important to us and the tech community and will help us make sure we're delivering excellent quality content.

Download a free PDF copy of this book

Thanks for purchasing this book!

Do you like to read on the go but are unable to carry your print books everywhere? Is your eBook purchase not compatible with the device of your choice?

Don't worry, now with every Packt book you get a DRM-free PDF version of that book at no cost.

Read anywhere, any place, on any device. Search, copy, and paste code from your favorite technical books directly into your application.

The perks don't stop there, you can get exclusive access to discounts, newsletters, and great free content in your inbox daily

Follow these simple steps to get the benefits:

1. Scan the QR code or visit the link below

https://packt.link/free-ebook/978-1-80323-271-3

2. Submit your proof of purchase
3. That's it! We'll send your free PDF and other benefits to your email directly

Part 1:
Overview of Google Cloud Platform and Associate Cloud Engineer Certification

The first part of the book is dedicated to the Associate Cloud Engineer certification itself. In the upcoming chapters, we will focus on the exam details and registration process. We will then cover the Google Cloud Platform fundamentals, its building blocks, its position in the market, and how Google Cloud compares to on-premises data centers.

This part of the book comprises the following chapters:

- *Chapter 1, Associate Cloud Engineer Certification Essentials*
- *Chapter 2, Google Cloud Platform Fundamentals*

1

Associate Cloud Engineer Certification Essentials

This book's first chapter will focus on the Associate Cloud Engineer Certification exam. We will focus on the registration process, resources outside of the book, passing the exam, and additional certification resources.

There are many places outside of the book to learn about Google Cloud. Some of them are more useful than others based on our experience, so we will share them with you here.

In this chapter, we're going to cover the following main topics:

- What you will learn
- Exam registration
- Exam resources
- Certification tips
- Additional certification resources

What you will learn

Google Cloud has a comprehensive portfolio of certifications. On the `https://cloud.google.com/certification` website, **Associate Cloud Engineer** (**ACE**) is one of the first certifications suited for people who would like to validate their knowledge and skills of Google Cloud. This chapter will guide you through the registration process, provide helpful certification resources, and offer certification tips.

Exam registration

Google Cloud uses an external company, **Kryterion**, to proctor exams. Using the `https://webassessor.com/googlecloud` website, we will create an account required to take an exam. Kryterion allows taking the Associate Cloud Engineer exam onsite and online.

Account creation

Regardless of where and how the exam will be taken, account creation is necessary. To register, you will require just an email address.

Once you are ready to create an account, visit `https://www.webassessor.com/wa.do?page=createAccount&branding=GOOGLE` and provide all the necessary details.

Onsite exam

During an onsite exam, the candidate needs to present two different forms of identification. At least one of the documents must be a government-issued ID with a photograph.

The following documents can be used as primary identification:

- Government-issued (local, state, province, or country) driver's license or identification card
- Passport
- Military identification
- National identification card

The following documents can be used as secondary identification:

- Student identification from an accredited school
- Credit card
- Check-cashing card
- Bank debit card
- Employee identification card
- Retail membership card
- Wholesale membership card
- Health insurance card
- Green card/Visa

Those requirements might change over time, so it is essential to double-check the provider's website before the exam.

To find the nearest test center, you can use this link: `https://www.kryteriononline.com/locate-test-center`.

Online exam

For those who prefer an online certification, Kryterion allows them to do this. One of the main requirements is to install software that Kryterion secures. We have a critical hint from our online exam taking. Please use your personal laptop and not a business one. The main reason is that some additional security software might be installed on many business laptops, and you might not be able to run Kryterion software at all.

Before the exam, installing the software and testing whether it will run is recommended. This allows you to save some time and reduce stress.

System readiness check

A system readiness checker can be found at the following link: `https://www.kryteriononline.com/systemcheck/`. It tests your operating system, microphone, webcam, and Internet speed. Once everything is checked, it informs you about possible problems.

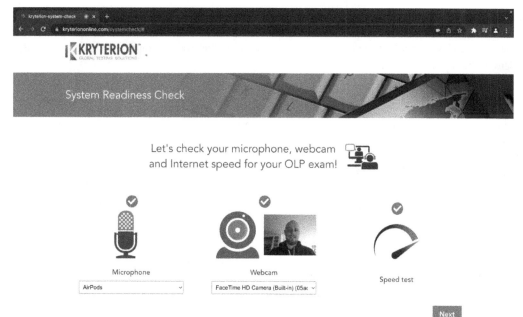

Figure 1.1 – Kryterion System Readiness Check

Once the test is performed and you click **Next**, you will see the web page displaying a **Congratulations!** message:

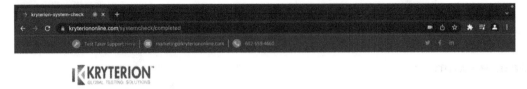

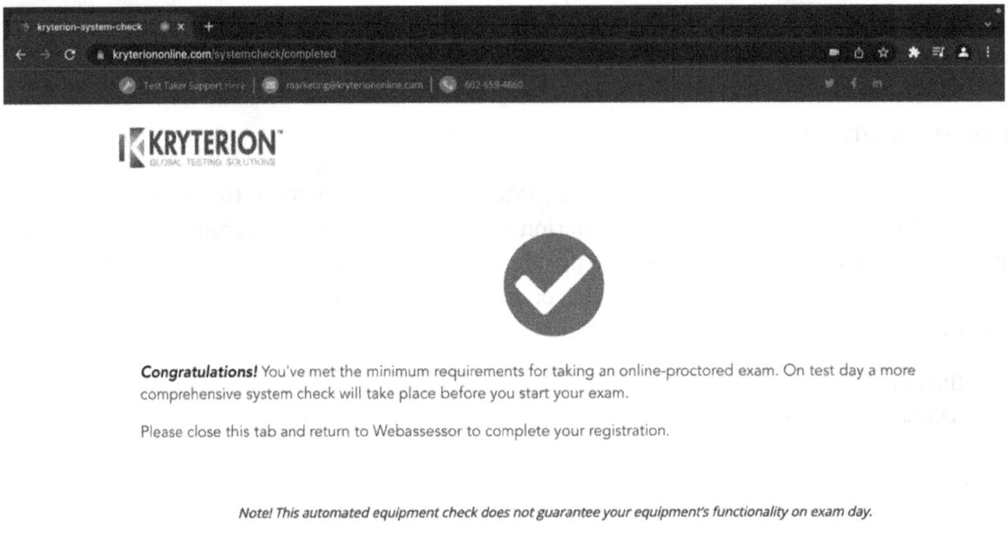

kryterion-system-check
kryteriononline.com/systemcheck/completed
KRYTERION
Congratulations! You've met the minimum requirements for taking an online-proctored exam. On test day a more comprehensive system check will take place before you start your exam.
Please close this tab and return to Webassessor to complete your registration.
Note! This automated equipment check does not guarantee your equipment's functionality on exam day.

Figure 1.2 – Successful pass of the system readiness check

This confirms that your device is ready to be used during the exam, and you shouldn't face any issues.

If your test wasn't successful, or you faced some issues, you can check the minimum system requirements, which can help you narrow down the issue.

System requirements

Your computer needs to fulfill the following requirements before you run Sentinel Secure, the Kryterion software:

System Requirements for OLP Exams		
	Windows	**Mac**
Hardware	Minimum 50 MB available space	Minimum 50 MB available space
Screen Resolution	1024 x 768 or greater	1024 x 768 or greater
Webcam and Mic	Internal or external USB	Internal or external USB
Internet Access	Recommended minimum of 1.0 Mbps upload / 1.0 Mbps download (*ping must be below 200 ms*)	Recommended minimum of 1.0 Mbps upload / 1.0 Mbps download (*ping must be below 200 ms*)

Operating System	Windows 8.1 or 10 (Touch screens require the use of a mouse and keyboard)	OS X 10.13 High Sierra 10.14 Mojave 10.15 Catalina 11.1 Big Sur
Browser	The latest version of Google Chrome or Firefox	The latest version of Safari, Google Chrome, or Firefox
Additional Considerations	Local Administrator rights You must disable all software that might interfere with your online proctored exam. This includes, but is not limited to, pop-up blockers, antivirus software, firewalls, VMware/Bootcamp, Skype, Photobooth, and TeamViewer. On Windows 10 systems, you can disable active applications in the **Task Manager | Startup** tab. Right-click the item and select **Disable** from the local menu.	Local Administrator rights You must disable all software that might interfere with your online proctored exam. This includes, but is not limited to, pop-up blockers, antivirus software, firewalls, VMware/Bootcamp, Skype, Photobooth, and TeamViewer.
Chromebooks are not supported at this time.		

Table 1.1

The requirements mentioned in the preceding table can be found here: https://www.webassessor.com/wa.do?page=certInfo&branding=GOOGLECLOUD&tabs=13#OLPSysReqs.

Installation process

Kryterion provides a detailed installation guide for Windows and macOS operating systems which can be found here: https://kryterion.force.com/support/s/article/Installing-Sentinel-Secure?language=en_US.

Test-taker checklist

Once you have checked and prepared your computer, review the following requirements about the place in which you will take the exam and its surroundings, as follows:

- Review and meet all system requirements as mentioned in the *System requirements* section.
- Review and meet all requirements for the testing environment.
- Secure a quiet, well-lit room to take the exam.
- Bring a reflective surface (for example, a phone or mirror) to perform a room scan.
- No person other than the test taker is allowed in the testing area.
- No item other than your computer is allowed in the test area. This includes all papers, writing instruments, and different devices.
- Disconnect external computer monitors from your laptop and close all applications.
- Food and drink, and headphones/earbuds are not permitted during the exam.
- Be prepared to sit for the entire length of the exam. You cannot take a break or step away from the camera's view. A good idea is to use the restroom prior to the test.
- Have your government-issued photo identification ready for verification (must match the legal first and last name in Webassessor).

As you see, those requirements are quite strict and must be adhered to. Otherwise, your exam might be stopped and graded as failed.

Retake policy

Google clearly states what happens if you do not pass the exam (if you read this book carefully, you most certainly won't fail), and it is valid across all Google Cloud exams.

After the first failure, you must wait 14 days; after the second failure, you must wait 60 days, and 365 days after the third failure before retaking the exam.

The retake policy is valid for both onsite and online Google Cloud exams.

Available languages

As of writing this book, the Associate Cloud Engineer certification is only available in English.

In the next section, we'll look at some helpful tips to follow while taking the exam.

Certification tips

In our professional career, we have cleared a lot of certification exams, and so, we have some useful tips that may come in handy for you. We are listing some essential certification tips as follows:

- **Clear the area around you**: Kryterion staff will review your surroundings to ensure that you are alone in the room in which you will take the exam. Keep your desk clean, disconnect extra monitors, and remove photos and notes.

- **Think positively**: You studied hard, and you know the material. Just imagine yourself holding a nice and shiny ACE certificate and proceed with positivity.

- **Get enough sleep before the exam**: It will help you focus, and you will be energized.

- **Eat healthily**: Don't try to experiment with new dishes. You never know how your body will react while taking an exam. we recommend something sweet (candy bar or chocolate) to fuel the brain.

- **Read a question two or three times**: It will help you to find the answer that is being asked in the question.

- **If you don't know the answer**: Mark it **to review** and move on to other questions. You can always review the tricky ones at the end.

- **Be strategic**: In almost all exams, there are multiple questions. Try to exclude two that don't make sense in the context of the question.

- **Relax**: The day before the exam, try to relax in the best way you can.

- **Keep the focus on the timer**: You must manage your time well.

We are sure that these tips will help you to get the best possible certification score.

Additional certification resources

Apart from this book, we recommend several resources that might help you prepare better. Some of them are free, and some of them must be paid for:

- *Qwiklabs – Google Cloud Essentials Quest*: `https://www.cloudskillsboost.google/quests/23`, or *Cloud Engineering Quest*: `https://www.cloudskillsboost.google/quests/66`.

- Create a new Google Cloud account with 20+ free products and $300 in free credits.

- Familiarise yourself with Google Cloud documentation.

- Read Google Cloud best practices.

Summary

In this chapter, we covered how to create an account to register for the exam. We covered onsite and online exam requirements. In addition to that, we shared some certification tips and provided you with some extra certification resources.

In the next chapter, we will focus on Google Cloud itself, its position in the market, its core, and its unique services. We will briefly list some public cloud benefits compared to on-premises.

2

Google Cloud Platform Fundamentals

This second chapter will focus on Google Cloud Platform fundamentals. We will describe all the core layers of Google Cloud, how they relate to each other, and their core components. We will find out the benefits of each Google Cloud layer and learn when to use them. We are going to cover the following main topics:

- Why Google Cloud Platform?
- Choosing the right cloud solution
- An overview of the core services offered by Google Cloud
- Management interfaces and command-line tools

Why Google Cloud Platform?

Google and Google Cloud are well-known and established parts of the leading company *Alphabet*. You must have used Google's products such as Gmail, YouTube, or the Google search engine at some point in time. But have you ever used Google Cloud Platform? You might be asking yourself the following questions:

- Why should I try it out?
- What is in it for me?
- Why should I learn another cloud when I have already learned the other ones?
- Is it worth investing the time in learning it?

We asked ourselves these questions as well, not only before studying for the certification but to also think about whether or not it is worth spending the time to be a Google Cloud expert.

Google 1 billion users experience

We mentioned Gmail, YouTube, and the Google search engine, Google Chrome, as some of the products that Google invented and that are used daily around the world. You might ask yourself why.

Google as a technological company faced tremendous growth and many challenges along the road. During this growth, Google engineers and Google products evolved, fixed many problems never tackled by anyone else, and constantly improved their products.

In 2004, Google invented the MapReduce programming model, which was inspired by Apache MapReduce and the **Hadoop Distributed File System (HDFS)** filesystem. The Bigtable NoSQL database in 2006 inspired Apache HBase and Cassandra, as some of the best-known open source projects that were modeled after Bigtable. The Borg cluster controller in 2015, with the Omega scheduler, was announced in 2016, which became the open source project well known as Kubernetes.

To learn more about Google Cloud and its contribution to open source projects, you can visit the following link: `https://cloud.google.com/open-cloud`.

The history of Google Cloud

Monday, April 7, 2008, was the day when Google announced the preview release of Google App Engine, and this date is considered the beginning of Google Cloud. App Engine was a tool used to easily run their web applications on Google-grade infrastructure. Service became generally available in November 2011.

Google Cloud today

At the time of writing in April 2023, Google Cloud is currently available in 37 regions, with a total of 112 separate zones and 176 network edge locations, and it operates in 200+ countries and territories.

By the time you read this book, Google Cloud will have expanded into other regions. You can visit the following URL to check where it operates at a given time: `https://cloud.google.com/about/locations`

As a global cloud provider, Google Cloud ensures to locate the resources closest to its users and their businesses. Google Cloud is heavily investing in its global presence and its expansion plans into new regions confirm this. At the time of writing, Google Cloud offers at a minimum the following products at launch:

- Google Compute Engine (GCE)
- **Google Kubernetes Engine (GKE)**
- Cloud Storage
- Persistent Disk
- Cloud SQL

- **Virtual Private Cloud** (**VPC**)

- Key Management Service

- Cloud Identity

- Secret Manager

Other Google Cloud products will continue to evolve based on the demand from customers.

In the following figure (the original image can be found here: `https://cloud.google.com/images/locations/regions.png`), we can see Google Cloud's global presence, including the existing and planned regions for 2023. It is worth mentioning that Google Cloud splits each region into three separate zones:

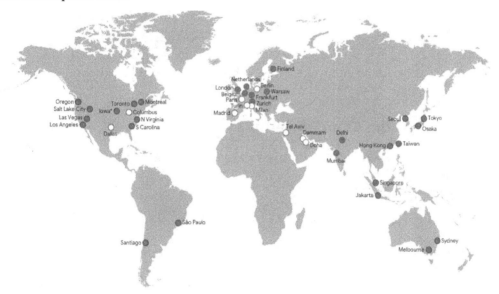

Figure 2.1 – Google Cloud regions across the world

Regions are just part of the Google Cloud presence. All regions are connected with each other via global networks and **Content Delivery Network** (**CDN**) points of presence.

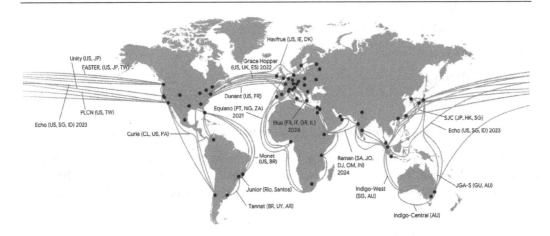

Figure 2.2 – Google Cloud Edge points of presence across the world

To view current Google Cloud locations, visit the website `https://cloud.google.com/about/locations`.

What makes Google Cloud different?

There is no right answer to this question because every customer and business is different and has different requirements. We have gathered differentiators that might be the most common ones. Let's have a look at them:

- Google-grade security

  - Google has managed their infrastructure for more than 15 years and this experience has allowed them to keep customers safe when using applications such as Gmail or Google Apps. Google Cloud is based on this experience and provides additional security products for customers.

- Billing by the second

  - GCE instances use a 1-second billing feature that allows customers to only pay for used resources.

- Big data

  - Innovation is the core principle of Google and this has led not only to technological innovations such as MapReduce, Bigtable, and Dremel but also next-generation services for cloud data warehousing (BigQuery), advanced ML (AI Platform), batch and real-time data processing (Dataflow, Pub/Sub, and Dataproc), and visual analytics (Google Looker Studio). Google Cloud big data solutions are serverless, which removes complexity and increases the ease of use.

- Global network

  - Google Cloud networks have global availability by default and are scaled according to software-defined solutions, instantly responding to users' needs.

- Environment friendly

  - Google Cloud data centers run on 100% renewable energy where it is available. Since 2017, Google has been carbon neutral and has set the goal to run all its data centers carbon free 24/7/365 by 2030.

Recently, Google Cloud released carbon footprint tools, which allow customers to choose **virtual machines (VMs)** with low CO_2 emissions, resulting in a lower carbon footprint.

In the following figure, we have an excellent example of this commitment. When creating a **GCE** VM, users can choose the Google Cloud region with the lowest CO_2 consumption:

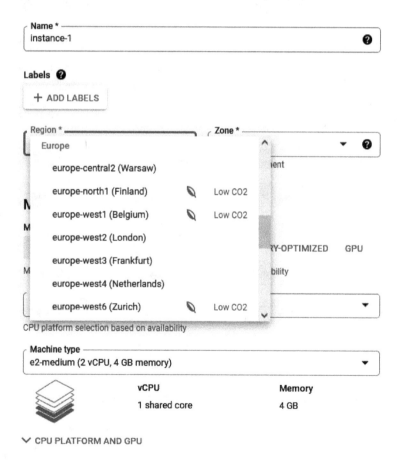

Figure 2.3 – The creation of the VM with a selection of regions with a low CO_2 footprint

Google provides cloud sustainability reports at the following website: `https://cloud.google.com/sustainability`

This website is a great resource for anyone who would like to learn more about what Google did in the past to work toward carbon neutrality, and how Google wants all their data centers to be carbon free by 2030.

Choosing the right cloud solution

To have a better understanding of which cloud solution might suit your requirements, we have created a diagram with an overview of services and their corresponding customer and provider responsibilities:

Figure 2.4 – An on-premises versus IaaS versus PaaS versus SaaS comparison

Let's dig into the four different types of resource consumption with varied usage and responsibilities.

On-premises

On-premises service usage is the classical deployment and management of resources. The whole responsibility lies with the data center or service owner at all layers – the OS, storage, data, and applications. You must ensure service availability, provision resources, and manage them. In addition, you are responsible for any maintenance activities, and you must plan well in advance, for not only the purchase but also the capacity of the infrastructure.

Infrastructure as a service

Now, we move to the **Infrastructure as a Service (IaaS)** cloud consumption model where the cloud provider is responsible for hardware – the servers, storage, networking, security, availability, cooling, electricity, and infrastructure capacity. By offloading this to the cloud provider, customers have already gained some advantages in comparison with on-premises services. Customers can focus on delivering the applications and managing resources while still having full access to the OS, applications, and data.

Some of Google Cloud's IaaS services are as follows:

- GCE
- Cloud Storage
- VPC
- Persistent Disk

The preceding list is not comprehensive and we will discuss IaaS services in further detail in upcoming chapters.

Platform as a service

The layer above IaaS is **Platform as a Service (PaaS)**. Customers who are using the PaaS model benefit from all services that are included in the IaaS model. However, in contrast to IaaS, they no longer need to patch OSs or update SQL databases.

What they need to take care of is planning the deployment type (whether using a single database or a replicated one), in which region to deploy Cloud SQL, and how to design their database schema. The cloud provider takes care of patching, building the database, and making it highly available. On-premises deployments of such a service might take a massive amount of time, consume countless hours, involve many teams, and most importantly, consume a huge amount of funds.

Some of Google Cloud's PaaS services are as follows:

- App Engine
- Cloud SQL

The preceding list is not comprehensive and we will discuss the PaaS service in further detail in upcoming chapters.

Software as a service

The final cloud consumption model is **Software as a Service (SaaS)**. It is a way of delivering without installing and maintaining any software, and there is no need to patch OSs or applications. We focus solely on software consumption and usage. One great analogy of SaaS is by thinking of a bank that takes care of simply providing access to us as customers. How a bank is doing it is irrelevant to us – we simply consume bank services.

If we go back to cloud services, IaaS and PaaS are managed by a cloud provider, and we simply focus on consuming services or applications.

Some of Google Cloud's SaaS services are as follows:

- Cloud DNS
- Cloud Armor
- Cloud CDN
- Cloud IAM

The preceding list is not comprehensive and we will discuss SaaS in further detail in upcoming chapters.

We have covered all the types of cloud services consumption and compared them to traditional on-premises service consumption. Each type of cloud consumption has different layers and responsibilities divided between cloud users and cloud providers. This will allow you to choose the best solution based on your requirements and needs.

An overview of the core services offered by Google Cloud

Google Cloud offers more than 100 products to their customers. It is very hard to list all these products and it doesn't bring much value to our Associate Cloud Engineer certification journey. Therefore, we have decided to list the core services from computing, storage, networking, security, and AI and ML.

A full list of Google Cloud products can be accessed by visiting the following web page: `https://cloud.google.com/products`

Compute services

We start with a list of core compute services:

- App Engine
  - A managed application platform

- Bare Metal

  - Dedicated hardware for specialized workloads

- Cloud Run

  - A serverless solution for containerized applications

- GCE

  - VMs from Google Cloud

- Spot VMs and preemptible VMs

  - Google Compute instances with a short lifetime, ideal for batch jobs and fault-tolerant workloads

- Shielded VMs

  - Hardened Google Compute VMs

- Sole-tenant nodes

  - Dedicated hardware designed for workloads that require compliance and licensing

- SQL Server on Google Cloud

  - A managed SQL Server solution to run MySQL, PostgreSQL, and Microsoft SQL Server

- VMware Engine

  - A fully managed VMware as a service solution

The preceding list is very comprehensive and not all products are relevant to the Associate Cloud Engineer certification.

Storage services

We have listed the core storage services that complement compute services from Google Cloud as follows. Very often, both services are used together, but some products such as Cloud Storage can be consumed separately:

- Storage Transfer Service

  - A service for transferring a large amount of data to Google Cloud with the usage of storage appliances

- Cloud Storage

  - Secure object storage with high durability and scalability

- Filestore

    - A managed NFS service

- Local SSD

    - Highly performant, locally attached to GCE instances, NVMe disks

- Persistent Disk

    - Block storage for Google Compute VMs

The most popular storage services are Cloud Storage and Persistent Disk. We will focus on them in the upcoming chapters of the book.

Networking services

Another set of services that are used daily in Google Cloud are networking services, from Cloud CDN or DNS to a core service, which is VPC:

- Cloud Armor

    - A DDoS and web application firewall service

- Cloud CDN

    - A global CD

- Cloud DNS

    - A managed domain name resolution service

- Cloud IDS

    - A Cloud **Intrusion Detection System (IDS)** that provides network threat detection

- Cloud Load Balancing

    - A multi-region load balancing solution

- Cloud NAT

    - A managed NAT service for GCE VMs

- Hybrid connectivity

  - Cloud VPN, Interconnect, and Partner Interconnect for connecting with Google Cloud

- Network Service Tiers

  - Tier-based network options

- Network Telemetry

  - Monitoring of the Google Cloud network with VPC flow logs

- Private Service Connect

  - A secure connection between your VPC and other Google Cloud services

- Traffic Director

  - A service with a traffic control plane and management for open service mesh

- VPC

  - A global virtual network for Google Cloud resources

Network services from Google Cloud are unique in the market and are one of its key differentiators.

Security and identity services

Security and identity services are another set of services from Google Cloud that are crucial to every customer. The most important ones are listed as follows:

- Access Transparency

  - A service for customers to use to audit cloud provider access to resources

- Assured Workloads

  - Allows customers to use Google Cloud in compliance with the requirements

- Binary Authorization

  - A service for deploying trusted containers on GKE

- Chronicle

  - Security insights from telemetry

- Cloud Asset Inventory

  - An asset management service to view, monitor, and analyze Google Cloud resources

- Cloud Data Loss Prevention

  - A service for classifying, inspecting, and redacting sensitive data

- Cloud Key Management

  - A managed security keys offering

- Confidential Computing

  - Fully encrypted VMs

- Firewalls

  - Global firewall solutions for protecting cloud resources

- Cloud IAM

  - A service for managing resources and access

- Secret Manager

  - Securely stores API keys, passwords, or certificates

- Security Command Center

  - A bird's-eye view into the security of your Google Cloud services

- VPC Service Controls

  - API-based security controls

- VM Manager

  - Provides a OS patch management, OS configuration management, and OS inventory management service

Google Cloud offers a comprehensive set of services with a core focus on security based on many years of experience and its customers' requirements.

AI and ML services

We'll finish detailing the core services by listing AI and ML services. This list includes the newly released Vertex AI platform, which combines many AI capabilities into one product:

- Vertex AI

  - A managed platform for ML

- AutoML

  - A custom low-code ML model training and development service

- Vision AI

  - Pre-trained models for detecting emotion, text, and more from images

- Video AI

  - Video analysis that recognizes objects, places, and actions in videos using ML

- Cloud Natural Language

  - A service for extracting from, analysing, and classifying unstructured text

- Cloud Translation

  - Detects and translates languages with dynamic translation

- Text-to-Speech

  - Speech synthesis in 220+ voices and 40+ languages

- Speech-to-Text

  - Speech recognition and transcription supporting 125 languages

- Dialogflow

  - A platform for designing and integrating user interfaces into mobile applications, web applications, or bots

- AutoML Tables (beta)

  - A service for building and deploying ML models using structured data

- Recommendations AI

  - AI product-based recommendations for any customer interfaces

- AI Infrastructure

  - A service to use to train deep learning and ML models

- Cloud **Tensor Processing Units (TPUs)**

  - TPUs for ML applications

Google Cloud is well known for its advanced and best-on-the-market AI and ML products. Although Associate Cloud Engineer focuses more on computing, storage, networking, and security, it is still worth mentioning the best products on the market.

Management interfaces and command-line tools

There is no one right or wrong way to use Google Cloud services. Every customer or company has a different way of using Google Cloud and all of them are good. Developers use the cloud via API calls or code execution and security officers might simply use the Google Cloud console from the browser.

In the following sections, we've described all the interfaces that can be used to manage and use Google Cloud.

Google Cloud console

For most users, the Google Cloud console will be the primary tool that they use to interact with Google Cloud. It uses a modern interface, with the possibility to customize the dashboard, allowing users to pin services and organize them for ease of use. The following figure shows a typical Google Cloud console. The Cloud console can be configured according to your requirements and what you want to see there. To do it, use the drag-and-drop functionality on the widgets:

Figure 2.5 – The Google Cloud console main screen

Typically, it can be accessed from computers as well as mobile devices.

Cloud Shell

Cloud Shell is a Linux shell provided for every Google Cloud user. It has a set of pre-installed development tools such as the gcloud CLI, kubectl, Terraform, and Git. Users can access it directly from the browser and it provides 5 GB of Persistent Disk storage.

Figure 2.6 – The Cloud Shell main screen

Cloud Shell is the ideal solution for users who don't want to use a locally configured command-line interface or who want to always use the same pre-configured terminal, which is ready in a few seconds.

The gcloud CLI

The gcloud CLI is a set of command-line tools for managing Google Cloud resources. With the gcloud CLI, you can perform all the actions that can be done in the browser-based Google Cloud console. The gcloud CLI can be installed on many OSs, including the following:

- Generic Linux
- Debian/Ubuntu
- Red Hat/Fedora/CentOS
- macOS
- Windows

In *Figure 2.7*, you will find the Google Cloud SDK installed on Windows. Although it might look different on your OS, the functionality is the same:

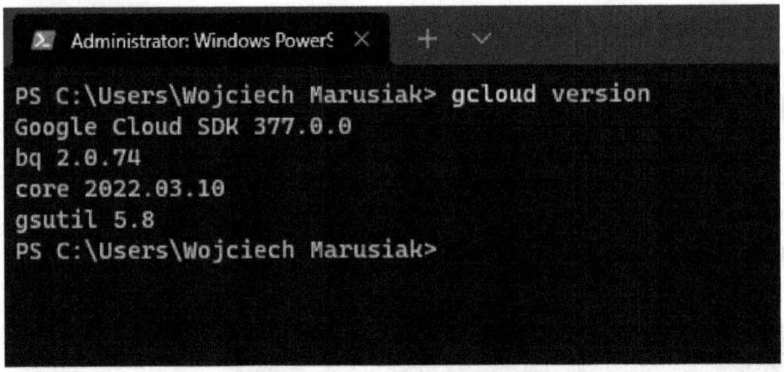
Administrator: Windows PowerS
PS C:\Users\Wojciech Marusiak> gcloud version
Google Cloud SDK 377.0.0
bq 2.0.74
core 2022.03.10
gsutil 5.8
PS C:\Users\Wojciech Marusiak>

Figure 2.7 – The gcloud CLI installed on Windows 10

To review the installation instructions, visit the following link: `https://cloud.google.com/sdk/docs/install-sdk#installing_the_latest_version`.

Cloud APIs

Cloud APIs allow users to interact with Google Cloud directly from your code. Cloud APIs provide a similar functionality to Cloud SDKs and the Google Cloud console. Integrating Cloud APIs with REST calls or client libraries is possible in many popular programming languages. For example, GCE can be accessed from client libraries written in C#, Go, Java, Node.js, PHP, Python, and Ruby.

The following is a JSON-formatted example of a GCE API with an IP address:

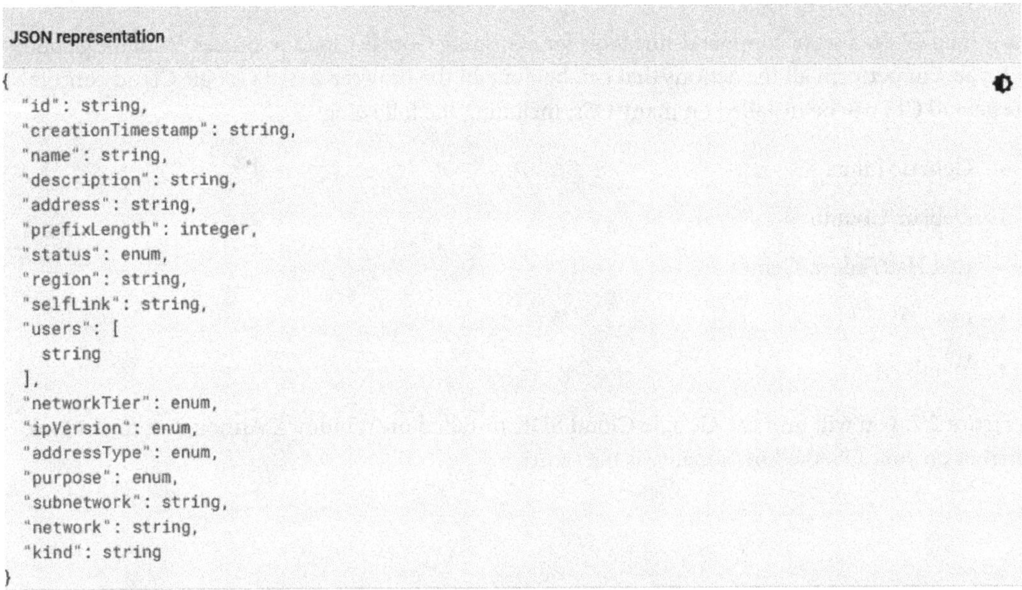
JSON representation
{
"id": string,
"creationTimestamp": string,
"name": string,
"description": string,
"address": string,
"prefixLength": integer,
"status": enum,
"region": string,
"selfLink": string,
"users": [
string
],
"networkTier": enum,
"ipVersion": enum,
"addressType": enum,
"purpose": enum,
"subnetwork": string,
"network": string,
"kind": string
}

Figure 2.8 – A sample representation of an IP address resource in the JSON-formatted GCE API

Google Cloud API resources can have different descriptions and use many different values.

Config Connector

For those who are familiar with Kubernetes and would like to manage Google Cloud resources the *Kubernetes way*, Google Cloud offers the Config Connector tool. It is very similar to managing Kubernetes resources in the YAML format. Config Connector provides a collection of Kubernetes **CustomResourceDefinitions** (**CRDs**) and controllers, which eventually reconcile your environment with your desired state:

```
# configconnector.yaml
apiVersion: core.cnrm.cloud.google.com/v1beta1
kind: ConfigConnector
metadata:
  # the name is restricted to ensure that there is only one
  # ConfigConnector resource installed in your cluster
  name: configconnector.core.cnrm.cloud.google.com
spec:
 mode: cluster
 googleServiceAccount: "SERVICE_ACCOUNT_NAME/@PROJECT_ID/.iam.gserviceaccount.com"
```

Figure 2.9 – A sample configuration file in YAML format in Config Connector

The preceding figure shows the Config Connector configuration file that is required for its initial usage.

Google Cloud Deployment Manager

Google Cloud Deployment Manager is a deployment service that allows automation and Google Cloud resource management. It uses the concept of a configuration file with YAML-based syntax that can import one or more template files used during the deployment. Templates can be written in Jinja or Python.

```
# Copyright 2016 Google Inc. All rights reserved.
#
# Licensed under the Apache License, Version 2.0 (the "License");
# you may not use this file except in compliance with the License.
# You may obtain a copy of the License at
#
#     http://www.apache.org/licenses/LICENSE-2.0
#
# Unless required by applicable law or agreed to in writing, software
# distributed under the License is distributed on an "AS IS" BASIS,
# WITHOUT WARRANTIES OR CONDITIONS OF ANY KIND, either express or implied.
# See the License for the specific language governing permissions and
# limitations under the License.

resources:
- name: vm-created-by-deployment-manager
  type: compute.v1.instance
  properties:
    zone: us-central1-a
    machineType: zones/us-central1-a/machineTypes/n1-standard-1
    disks:
    - deviceName: boot
      type: PERSISTENT
      boot: true
      autoDelete: true
      initializeParams:
        sourceImage: projects/debian-cloud/global/images/family/debian-9
    networkInterfaces:
    - network: global/networks/default
```

Figure 2.10 – A sample configuration file in YAML format in Deployment Manager

You can visit the Google Cloud GitHub repository to find more examples in Jinja and Python: `https://github.com/GoogleCloudPlatform/deploymentmanager-samples`

Deployment Manager can only be used to deploy Google Cloud resources.

Terraform

Terraform is an **Infrastructure as Code (IaC)** software tool created by HashiCorp. Terraform use its own declarative language, **HashiCorp Configuration Language (HCL)**, or JSON.

Terraform abstracts underlying resources with its own programming language and allows users to focus on deployment, rather than learning each deployment target-specific language. In simple words, if you learn how to use HCL, you no longer need to learn how to deploy specific cloud provider features and you use the necessary Terraform provider. The following is a sample code part written in HCL, which describes a Cloud SQL instance deployment:

```
resource "google_sql_database_instance" "main" {
  name             = "main-instance"
  database_version = "POSTGRES_11"
  region           = "us-central1"

  settings {
    # Second-generation instance tiers are based on the machine
    # type. See argument reference below.
    tier = "db-f1-micro"
  }
}
```

Figure 2.11 – Terraform sample configuration code describing a Cloud SQL instance deployment

Similar to Cloud APIs, Terraform's IaC approach allows for the use of software-deployment-like techniques with infrastructure.

Service Catalog

Service Catalog is a product intended for cloud administrators who manage Google Cloud organizations where control distribution, internal compliance, and solution discoverability are needed.

It allows us to curate available products in Service Catalog and allows easy resource visibility and deployment at the organization, folder, and project levels. It is a go-to tool for ensuring internal compliance and governance.

The following figure shows the creation of a link-based solution:

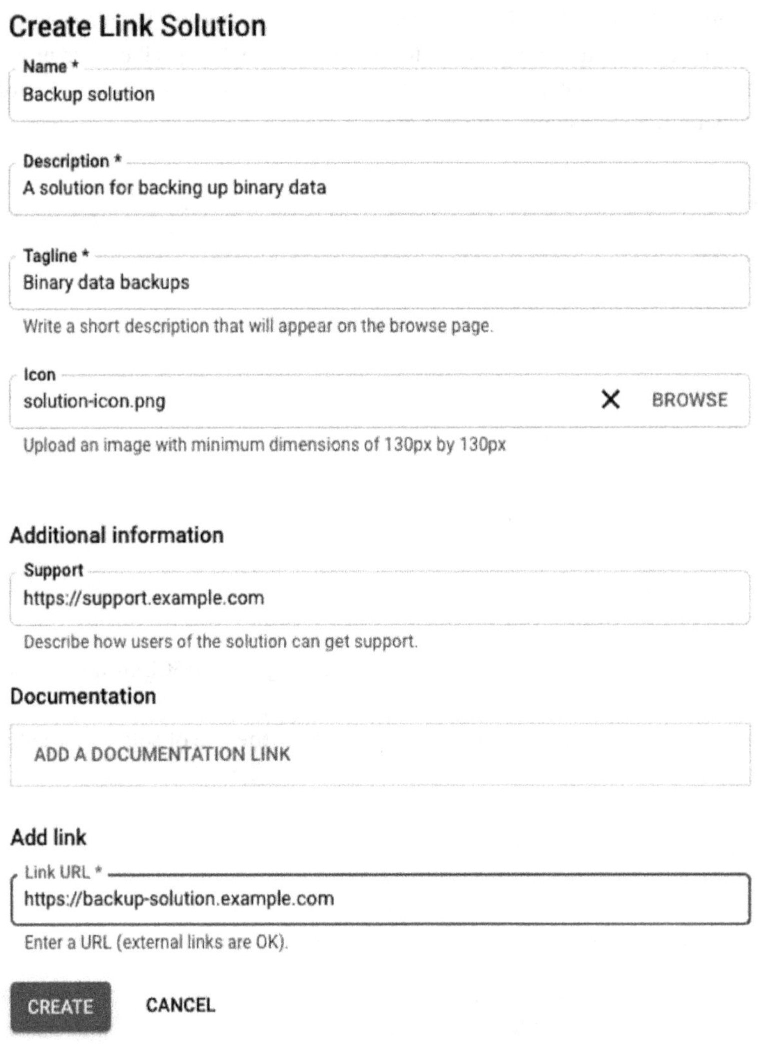

Create Link Solution

Name *

Backup solution

Description *

A solution for backing up binary data

Tagline *

Binary data backups

Write a short description that will appear on the browse page.

Icon

solution-icon.png   ✕   BROWSE

Upload an image with minimum dimensions of 130px by 130px

Additional information

Support

https://support.example.com

Describe how users of the solution can get support.

Documentation

ADD A DOCUMENTATION LINK

Add link

Link URL *

https://backup-solution.example.com

Enter a URL (external links are OK).

CREATE   CANCEL

Figure 2.12 – A sample configuration of Service Catalog

Once a solution is created, it will appear in the **Solutions** table.

Mobile applications

Google Cloud offers mobile applications for both Android and iOS, which give users the ability to monitor and make changes to Google Cloud resources. You can manage resources such as projects, billing, an App Engine app, or GCE VMs.

You can use the following features:

- Incident management

  - Open, assign, acknowledge, and resolve incidents

- GCE

  - Start, stop, and turn SSH into instances and view logs from each instance

- App Engine

  - Troubleshoot errors, roll back deployments, and change traffic splitting

- Alerts

  - Get alerts on production issues

- Dashboard

  - View the health of your services, view graphs, and key metrics

- Cloud Storage

  - View and delete Cloud Storage data

- Error reporting

  - Understand crashes of your cloud services

- Billing

  - See up-to-date billing information and get billing alerts for projects

- Cloud SQL

  - View the health of, start, and stop Cloud SQL instances

With all the features provided in the mobile application, you can view your most important resources from your smartphone as well.

The following figure shows multiple sections that can be viewed in the application, such as the dashboard, resources overview, billing, and monitoring:

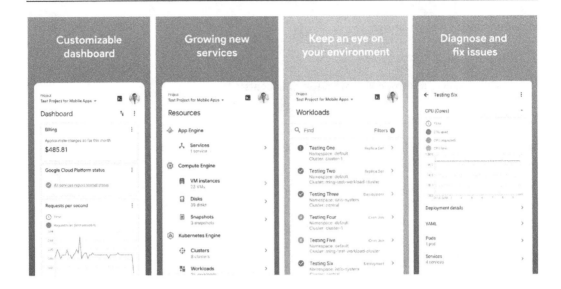

Figure 2.13 – An overview of the mobile application

Mobile applications can be installed on Android or iOS, allowing simplified cloud management on the go.

Summary

This chapter focused on bringing Google Cloud closer to us. We learned how and when Google Cloud started its business, and we tried to understand what makes it different within the market. Later on, our focus was on choosing the right cloud solution. We learned about the different types of services and when to use them. We then listed the essential Google Cloud services necessary to ace the exam and core services within IaaS, PaaS, and SaaS solutions.

At the end of this chapter, we learned different ways to interact with Google Cloud.

In the next chapter, we will learn how to plan and manage Google Cloud resources.

Questions

Answer the following questions to test your knowledge of this chapter:

1. In the IaaS cloud delivery model, who manages servers, storage, and networks?

    A. You

    B. The cloud provider

C. You and the cloud provider together

D. Managed Service Provider

2. Which *as a service* model offers the most flexibility in the operating system and application configuration?

A. SaaS

B. PaaS

C. IaaS

D. IDaaS

3. In the PaaS model, who will install a new database patch?

A. It will be you, as you have full access to the database

B. The cloud provider, as this is its responsibility

C. It will be a joint effort between you and the cloud provider

D. None of the above

4. Which tools can be used to manage Google Cloud resources?

A. Config Manager, the gcloud CLI, and the Google Cloud console

B. Terraform, Cloud APIs, and Cloud Shell

C. Cloud Shell, Service Manager, and the Google Cloud console

D. Cloud Shell, the gcloud CLI, and Cloud APIs

5. What is the name of the Google Cloud service to run VMs?

A. Google Compute Engine (GCE)

B. Google Kubernetes Engine (GKE)

C. Google Storage (GS)

D. Google Elastic Compute (GEC)

6. Which components are the base of a VM?

A. The operating system

B. The compute disk

C. The processor and RAM

D. All of the above

7. You have been asked to store millions of small files on a cheap but powerful storage solution. What will you choose?

   A. Persistent Disk

   B. Google Cloud Storage

   C. Cloud Filestore

   D. Storage Transfer Service

8. You are tasked to choose the best solution to host containerized applications with node control, scale, and cluster configuration. Choose the correct answer.

   A. Cloud Run

   B. Spot VMs

   C. GKE

   D. Cloud Armor

9. Google Cloud VPC is which of the following by default?

   A. Configured with pre-defined IP ranges

   B. Global

   C. Software-defined

   D. All the above

10. What are the benefits of cloud computing?

    A. Billing by the second, easy resource allocation, and security

    B. Paying only by usage, no commitments, and a broad product portfolio

    C. No need for upfront investment in the hardware and managed services such as Cloud SQL or Cloud Run

    D. All of the above

Answers

The answers to the preceding questions are provided here:

1D, 2C, 3B, 4B, 5A, 6D, 7B, 8C, 9D, 10D

Part 2:
Configuring and Implementing Google Cloud

The second part of the book focuses on understanding, planning, and managing Google Cloud resources. We will learn how the most popular Google Cloud services work, the benefits they offer customers, and how to implement solutions using them, such as Google Compute Engine, Google Kubernetes Engine, Cloud Run, Cloud Functions, and Infrastructure as Code. We will also gain a deep understanding of the storage and networking solutions, as they are all interconnected and cannot function independently.

This part of the book comprises the following chapters:

- *Chapter 3, Planning and Managing GCP Resources*
- *Chapter 4, Implementing Compute Solutions*
- *Chapter 5, Implementing Compute Solutions – Google Kubernetes Engine – Part 1*
- *Chapter 6, Implementing Compute Solutions – Google Kubernetes Engine – Part 2*
- *Chapter 7, Implementing Compute Solutions – Cloud Run, Cloud Functions, and Infrastructure as a Code*
- *Chapter 8, Configuring and Implementing Storage Solutions*
- *Chapter 9, Configuring and Implementing Networking Components*

3

Planning and Managing GCP Resources

Welcome to the third chapter. In this chapter, we will focus on planning and managing GCP resources. Our focus lies mainly on planning Google Cloud resources, describing use cases for specific solutions, and learning what the benefits of the different application types are. We will dive into billing and budgets, which are essential in terms of the financial aspect of Google Cloud and a reporting point of view. The last topics covered in this chapter are API and quota management.

We are going to cover the following main topics:

- Planning Google Cloud resources
- Billing and budgets
- API management
- Quota management

Planning Google Cloud resources

The configuration and implementation of Google Cloud resources is an easy process. You create a project, enable an API, deploy virtual machines (VMs), and complete the task. This process is simple and looks like it is easy to implement. But is it really?

Did you consider all the possible options for your use case? Did you configure your VM or resource optimally? Is your deployment secure?

We could explore these questions in different dimensions and we can end up discussing this for a long time. However, there is a reason we brought them up here. It's because planning is far more important than implementation.

If a cloud deployment is planned and architected well, its implementation and extension are faster, repeatable, easier to maintain, secure, and optimized.

The architecture of Google Cloud isn't the main topic of the **Associate Cloud Engineer (ACE)** certification, but it is important to remember it. Perhaps after passing the ACE exam, you might want to pursue the Professional Cloud Architect exam, and that exam covers the architecting of Google Cloud resources.

The book *Professional Cloud Architect – Google Cloud Certification Guide*, by *Konrad Cłapa and Brian Gerrard, Packt Publishing*, is an excellent resource for learning more about Google Cloud architecture and deploying and configuring Google Cloud resources.

Google Cloud has prepared excellent resources for all those interested in planning and configuring.

Google Cloud setup checklist

The Google Cloud setup checklist is a step-by-step guide for anyone who wants to have scalable, well-architected production and enterprise-ready workloads. It is essential to mention that like identity configuration, role and permission assignment, or resource hierarchy organization, some tasks can be done differently, as every company and environment is different.

The following link covers the initial aspects of the Google Cloud setup checklist – `https://cloud.google.com/docs/enterprise/setup-checklist`. You should be able to see the following list items:

1. Cloud identity and organization
2. Users and groups
3. Administrative access
4. Set up billing
5. Resource hierarchy
6. Access
7. Networking
8. Monitoring and logging
9. Security
10. Support

The checklist consists of various tasks that have step-by-step procedures. Some tasks can be accomplished in multiple ways depending on the desired way to implement them – be it programmatically or in Cloud Console.

Checklists help with following Google Cloud's best practices but feel free to use them according to your needs.

Google Cloud's best practices

Best practices are a set of methods or techniques that have been generally accepted as superior to other alternatives. Best practices are called this because the outcome that is produced by using them is better than those produced by using other methods. A best practice may be a feature of accredited management standards such as ISO 9000 and ISO 14001.

Google Cloud's best practices are resources that Google has identified and recommends to customers who want to achieve the best possible cloud architecture and follow Google's recommendations. Google has developed best practices by working with many customers and those repeatable best patterns have helped to ease initial cloud setup and speed up configuration and implementation.

We must ask ourselves one question – *Should I always follow the best practices?* There is no right or wrong answer to this question. Our answer is – *It depends*.

Following the best practices solely because somebody asked us to do so doesn't make sense. Omitting a set of best practices or implementing only part of it is fine – we just need to make those decisions consciously and know what it means for us when we skip or apply different practices.

If you want to read more about Google Cloud's best practices, visit the following links:

- `https://cloud.google.com/architecture/framework`
- `https://cloud.google.com/security/best-practices`

In the next section, we will dive into blueprints, which are one of the best ways to implement Google Cloud's best practices and start the journey with Google Cloud.

Google Cloud blueprints

We've covered the setup checklist and best practices of Google Cloud. All those steps bring us closer to the deployment of Google Cloud in a practical, secure, and well-designed way.

Fortunately for us, Google Cloud has prepared many different methods of implementation for its customers. A Google Cloud implementation blueprint is based on Google Cloud best practices. Again, you don't need to follow all of them; you can choose parts that make the most sense for you and your organization:

- **Kubernetes Resource Model (KRM) blueprints**: KRM blueprints use **Config Connector**, part of **Anthos Config Management**, which allows us to deploy Google Cloud resources using the KRM. The KRM makes it easy to select resources with YAML or JSON declaratively.

    To learn how to implement blueprints using the KRM, visit the following link – `https://cloud.google.com/anthos-config-management/docs/concepts/blueprints#krm-blueprints`.

- **Terraform blueprints**: For those who prefer to use Terraform and want to use **HashiCorp Configuration Language** (**HCL**) to deploy Google Cloud resources, this is also possible. Policies for Terraform blueprints are written as Open Policy Agent constraint templates. Terraform Validator enables client-side policy validation by converting Terraform plans into Cloud Asset Inventory asset metadata, then validates them with OPA policies. This allows the detection of misconfiguration earlier in the deployment pipeline.

  To learn how to implement blueprints using Terraform and its HCL language, visit the following link – `https://cloud.google.com/anthos-config-management/docs/concepts/blueprints#terraform-blueprints`.

We continue our journey with Google Cloud. We started with a high-level overview of the best practices and then we moved on to implementation with various blueprints. In the next section, we will jump into planning compute resources.

Planning compute resources

Google Cloud offers a variety of compute options to choose from. Ultimately, it depends on what kind of workload you will run and what type of control over the resources you or your team require.

The following figure provides an overview of the Google Cloud compute options. The more we move to the right, the more highly managed and less customizable services are. Services on the left-hand side of the figure are highly customizable and less managed by Google Cloud:

Figure 3.1 – Compute resource options

One thing to remember – you can mix different types of computing resources according to your needs.

We will now describe all Google Cloud compute options:

- **Google Compute Engine** (**GCE**): VMs are a commodity, and GCE allows you to choose from various predefined T-shirt sizes and create desired VM sizes according to your requirement. You can select different disk options, attach GPUs, and decide which operating system you want to use.

- **Preemptible and spot VMs**: Both preemptible and spot VM instances are highly discounted (from 60% up to 91% compared to regular VMs). The difference between preemptible and spot VMs is their lifetime. Preemptible VMs live for up to 24 hours (preemptible) and spot VMs don't have a maximum runtime. Google Cloud offers them to all customers, and they have one characteristic in common – they can be terminated with a notification sent 30 seconds prior to the termination. Preemptible instances use excess GCE capacity, so their availability varies across Google Cloud regions. The ideal workload for this type of VM is stateless applications, containerized workloads, web apps, or test and development workloads.

- **Custom VM sizes**: One of the features in GCE we like a lot is the possibility to create custom VM sizes. Google Cloud offers the opportunity to configure VMs according to your needs. Whether you need a powerful VM with many CPUs and you don't need a lot of RAM, or you want to choose between 1 or 2 vCPUs per core to select a different CPU family type – you are covered.

In the following figure, we can see the process of custom VM creation:

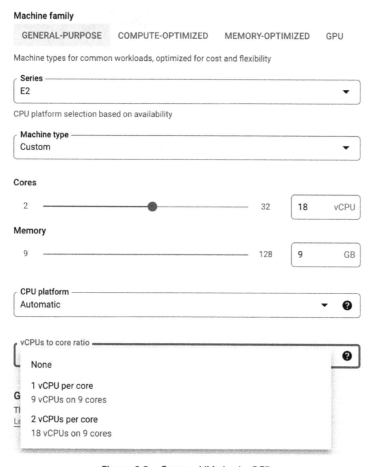

Figure 3.2 – Custom VM size in GCE

Let's move on to the next set of compute options in Google Cloud:

- **Google Kubernetes Engine (GKE)**: Google Cloud offers managed Kubernetes, which is the best choice for containerized applications that require orchestration, managed scaling, updates, and connectivity. GKE creates Kubernetes master nodes and manages them for end users, as well as allowing node pool creation. Also, autoscaling nodes allow you to monitor resources.

- **Cloud Run**: Cloud Run is a fully managed serverless platform to run containers. In comparison to GKE, you provide your application's code, and Cloud Run hosts the application and autoscales it according to the workload.

- **Google App Engine**: Google App Engine is a fully managed serverless platform for web applications. App Engine is responsible for the application and database autoscaling and providing networking connectivity. It allows you to update applications on the fly, host different versions, and enable diagnostics.

- **Cloud Functions**: For those who require event-driven serverless functions, Cloud Functions is the best choice. You write code and decide what will happen when the event is triggered, and the rest is done automatically.

- **Firebase**: If you're building an application that relies on a backend for synchronization and/or storage, Firebase is a great option. It allows you to store complex NoSQL documents and files using an API and client available for iOS, Android, and JavaScript.

We covered planning all the computing options in Google Cloud. We will now focus on planning database resources and choosing the right database for your workload.

Planning database resources

Similar to compute options, Google Cloud offers a variety of database products in which you can store the data. Each product has its unique features and can support various application options:

- **Cloud SQL**: This is a fully managed MySQL, Microsoft SQL Server, or PostgreSQL database service for traditional workloads such as CRM, ERP, e-commerce, or web applications.

- **BigQuery**: This is a serverless, highly scalable, and cost-effective multi-cloud data warehouse designed for business agility and offers up to 99.99% availability. It's best to use for multi-cloud and real-time data analysis with built-in, ready-to-use machine learning models.

- **Firestore**: This is a serverless document database with built-in features such as high scalability and high availability (99.999%) that supports ACID transactions against document data. It's best to use Firestore for mobile, web, or IoT applications with real-time or offline synchronization requirements.

- **Cloud Spanner**: This is a fully managed relational database with global, unlimited-scale, robust data consistency synchronization across regions and continents with up to 99.999% availability. Cloud Spanner customers use it for gaming, global financial ledger, or supply chain/inventory management use cases.

- **Cloud Bigtable**: This is a fully managed NoSQL (non-relational) database service with consistent sub-10 ms latency access, which can handle millions of requests per second and offers up to 99.999% availability. It can process more than 5 billion requests per second at peak and more than 10 exabytes of data under management. The ideal use case for Cloud Bigtable is applications such as personalization, AdTech, recommendation engines, or fraud detection.

This concludes our discussion of the database options in Google Cloud and when you should choose a specific database for your workload. In the next section, we will review options for storing data in Google Cloud.

Planning data storage options

This section covers various data storage options – object, block, and file storage. Every product and use case is different, and different product selections apply. The most important thing for us to understand is that block storage is required for VMs to be able to install the operating system of choice. In comparison, object storage cannot be used to install operating systems and cannot be used as a boot device for GCE VMs.

Let's start with storage options for compute in Google Cloud.

Compute storage options

We have two options to choose from with GCE. We can use either a persistent disk or local **solid-state drives (SSDs)**.

Like other planning considerations for computing or database workloads, choosing the appropriate storage options should be done carefully. We need to identify the desired storage size, performance requirements, and availability.

The Google Cloud storage advisor web page can guide you through different storage options and assess your requirements. The following links will help you to navigate through other storage options:

- `https://cloud.google.com/architecture/storage-advisor#review_the_storage_options`
- `https://cloud.google.com/compute/docs/disks#introduction`
- `https://cloud.google.com/storage/docs/storage-classes#descriptions`

Persistent disk

A standard disk is attached to every VM in GCE. Persistent disk offers us a variety of options that can be precisely mapped to our requirements. It is a block device used with every Compute Option VM utilized as a boot device:

- **Zonal persistent disk**: Zonal persistent disks provide durable storage and data location in one zone.

- **Regional persistent disk**: Regional persistent disks have storage qualities that are similar to persistent zonal disks. However, persistent regional disks provide durable storage and data replication between two zones in the same region.

- **Standard persistent disk**: Standard persistent disks (pd-standard) are backed by standard **hard disk drives (HDDs)**.

- **Balanced persistent disk**: Balanced persistent disks (pd-balanced) are backed by SSDs. They are an alternative to SSD persistent disks that balances performance and cost.

- **SSD persistent disk**: SSD persistent disks (pd-ssd) are backed by SSDs and offer high **input/output operations per second (IOPS)** and throughput.

- **Extreme persistent disk**: Extreme persistent disks (pd-extreme) are backed by SSDs. Extreme persistent disks are designed for high-end database workloads with consistently high performance for both random access workloads and bulk throughput.

Local SSDs

A local SSD is an ephemeral, locally attached form of block storage for VMs and containers. Compared to other block storage options, it offers superior performance, very high IOPS, and very low latency. The typical use cases for local SSDs are flash-optimized databases, hot caching layers for analytics, or application scratch disks.

Google Cloud Storage

GCS is ultra-low-cost, highly reliable, and secure object storage with high-speed access speeds where customers can store any amount of data. Object storage cannot be used as a boot disk for GCE VMs. GCS offers multiple types of storage classes.

The following GCS concepts are common in all classes:

- Object: Pieces of data uploaded to GCS.

- Storage class: This is a piece of metadata that is used by every object.

- Bucket: Buckets are the primary containers that store your data. Everything that is stored in GCS must be contained in a bucket.

- Unlimited storage with no minimum object size.

- Worldwide accessibility and worldwide storage locations.

- Low latency (time to the first byte is typically tens of milliseconds).

- High durability (99.999999999% annual durability).

- Geo-redundancy if the data is stored in a multi-region (more than two regions) or dual-region (exactly two regions).

- A uniform experience with GCS features, security, tools, and APIs.

Google Cloud describes in detail and keeps documentation up to date about exact locations of multi-region and dual-region pairs. Visit the following URL to learn more about exact multi-region and dual-region locations: `https://cloud.google.com/storage/docs/locations#available-locations`

Now that we know all the common features in GCS, we need to understand when to use each type of storage and their main features:

- **Standard**: Standard storage is best for frequently accessed data ("hot" data) and stored for brief periods. The ideal use cases for standard storage are "hot" data that's accessed frequently, including websites, streaming videos, and mobile apps.

- **Nearline**: Nearline storage is low-cost storage. It is suitable for data stored for at least 30 days, including data backup and long-tail multimedia content.

- **Coldline**: Coldline storage is a very low-cost storage option. It is suitable for data that can be stored for at least 90 days, including disaster recovery.

- **Archive**: Archive storage is a good choice for data that can be stored for at least 365 days, including regulatory archives.

With all the options described in this section, we can find the right storage options with the desired functionality and best price range.

Conclusion

The choice of three storage categories already shows us how complex cloud products can be. In this section, we focused on each product's main options. We could multiply these selections by various dimensions, and would still be able to find something tailored to us.

Billing and budgets

A Cloud Billing account is one of the prerequisites for consuming any Google Cloud resource. Without it, we can't create any VM, utilize the free trial period, or use resources under the Google Cloud Free Tier.

One aspect that might be of interest to those leaning toward the ACE certification is the free trial.

Free trial

Google Cloud offers a 90-day, $300-worth free trial for every newly created Google Cloud account. Once registered, $300 worth of credits is added to the bill, which can be used with all products. During the free trial period, resources used from the Free Tier do not get charged against your free trial credits:

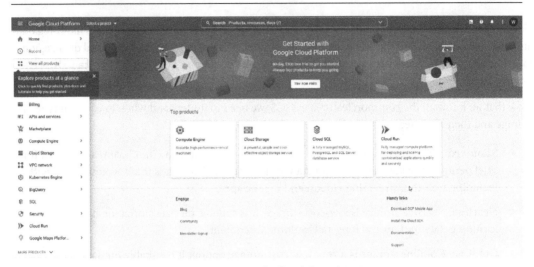

Figure 3.3 – First visit to Google Cloud Console as a new user

In *Figure 3.3*, we see the option to activate the free trial. After clicking **TRY FOR FREE**, we need to verify our account. We need to add a mobile phone number, provide some information about ourselves, and add a credit card:

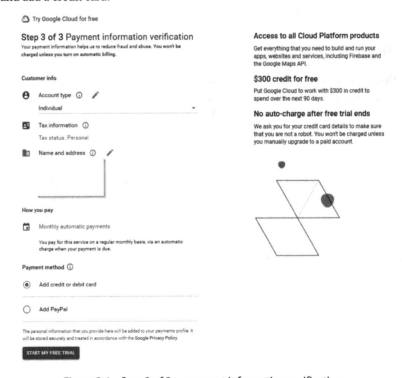

Figure 3.4 – Step 3 of 3 – payment information verification

Once we add a credit or debit card and confirm our identity, we are welcomed into the free trial:

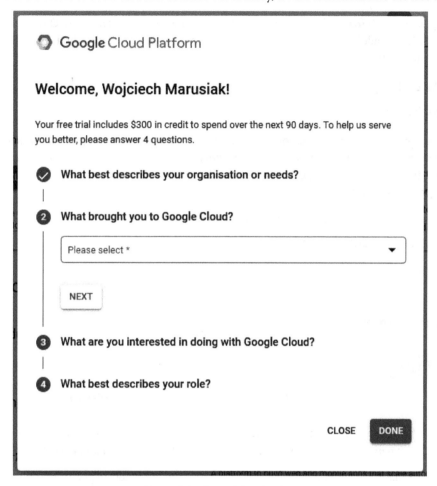

Figure 3.5 – Free trial activation

After providing some required data, we can finally start using Google Cloud.

Program eligibility

A free trial program is created under the following conditions:

- You have never been a customer of Google Cloud, Google Maps, or Firebase.
- You have never previously signed up for the free trial.

Let's review how can we start the free trial program at Google Cloud.

Program start

The 90-day, $300-worth free trial starts automatically when the sign-up is completed. One prerequisite required to finish it is adding a valid credit card or another acceptable payment method. Other payment methods, which vary per country, are as follows:

- Debit card
- A bank account

Google Cloud provides an extensive list of supported and unsupported payment methods, which might change over time. If you wish to find out which payment methods are supported and unsupported in your country, visit the following URL – `https://cloud.google.com/billing/docs/how-to/payment-methods`.

The following figure shows the possibility of adding a credit or debit card:

Figure 3.6 – Example of adding a payment method in the Google Cloud portal

Please remember that payment options may vary between countries. We are located in Germany, and the following payment options were available for users: credit or debit card and PayPal.

For companies, there is the option to receive invoices, which isn't available to private users. To review the payment options for companies, please visit the following link: `https://cloud.google.com/billing/docs/how-to/get-invoice`.

The payment step is very important for private persons and companies and shouldn't be underestimated because one small error can lead to a temporary account blockage or suspension.

Program limitations

Newly created Google Cloud accounts that use a free trial have some limitations, which are temporary and will be removed if you use your account for an extended period of time.

Some initial limitations are as follows:

- You can't add GPUs to your VM instances.
- You can't request quota increases

- You can't create VMs with Windows server-based images.

- You can't create Google Cloud VMware Engine resources

With the limitations in mind, we will now focus on the program duration and its features.

Program duration

The free trial program ends when you spend your $300 in credits or 90 days have passed since you signed up.

You can check your Google Cloud expenditure and remaining days in **Billing Overview**:

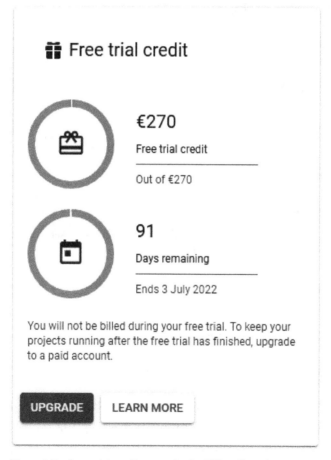

Figure 3.7 – Free trial credit status in the Billing Overview section

Please note that the initial $300 is converted into the currency used where you reside.

Upgrading to a paid Cloud Billing account

As you progress with learning about Google Cloud, your free trial might end, or you might have already used all $300 in credit. There might be a case where even if your free trial is not yet finished, you would like to create a Windows-based VM or increase your quotas.

To do so, you need to upgrade to a paid Cloud Billing account. You remove some initial restrictions and ensure that your resources won't be deleted by upgrading.

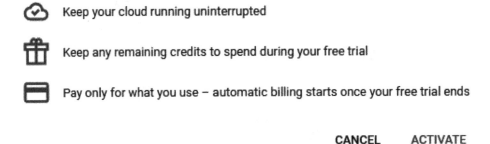

Activate your full account

⊘ Keep your cloud running uninterrupted

🎁 Keep any remaining credits to spend during your free trial

💳 Pay only for what you use – automatic billing starts once your free trial ends

CANCEL   ACTIVATE

Figure 3.8 – Activation of a complete account

As you can see in the preceding figure, activation is done just by clicking the **ACTIVATE** button.

Once our account is fully activated, we can start using all Google Cloud services. In the next section, we will describe the Google Cloud Free Tier offering.

Google Cloud Free Tier

Free Tier is an offer from Google Cloud where users can use services for free. One difference between a free trial and Free Tier is that Free Tier is available to all Google Cloud users. Free Tier is available to users monthly, and its limits are calculated per billing account. In the next section, we will understand the Free Tier usage limits and which products can be used in the program.

Free Tier usage limits

Google Cloud offers more than 28 products included in the Free Tier program. The range of products is broad: from Google App Engine, BigQuery, Cloud Functions, GCE, or GKE up to reCAPTCHA Enterprise and Pub/Sub.

Please visit the following page to review details about Free Tier usage limits per available product: `https://cloud.google.com/free/docs/gcp-free-tier#free-tier`.

If the usage of the product exceeds the Free Tier limits, the user is billed for the product at standard rates.

Billing

Billing in Google Cloud is quite an important topic. Without a billing account with an associated payment method, you can't run any cloud resources. This is critical if you have production workloads and don't want interruptions. Payment method issues might cause account suspension, and you certainly want to avoid that.

In the next section, we will guide you through the process of creating a billing account.

Creating a billing account

If a Google Cloud organization manages your account and you are a member, you must have **Billing Account Creator** permissions:

1. From Google Cloud Console, click on **Billing**.

2. Select the Google Cloud organization if you are part of one; otherwise, proceed with account creation:

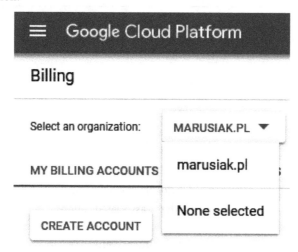

Figure 3.9 – Selection of an organization when creating a billing account

3. Click **CREATE ACCOUNT**.

4. Enter a name in **Name**, choose an option for **Country**, and click **CONTINUE** to proceed.

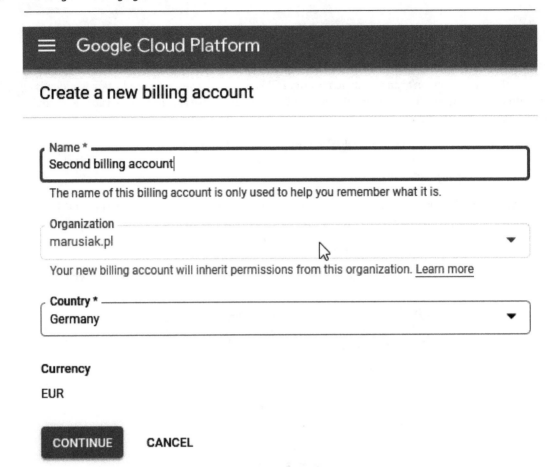

Figure 3.10 – We need to provide the billing account name and
choose a country with the associated currency

5. We are at the last stage of creating a new billing account. We can select an existing payment profile or create a new one. If we already have a payment profile associated with the payment method, we need to click **SUBMIT AND ENABLE BILLING**.

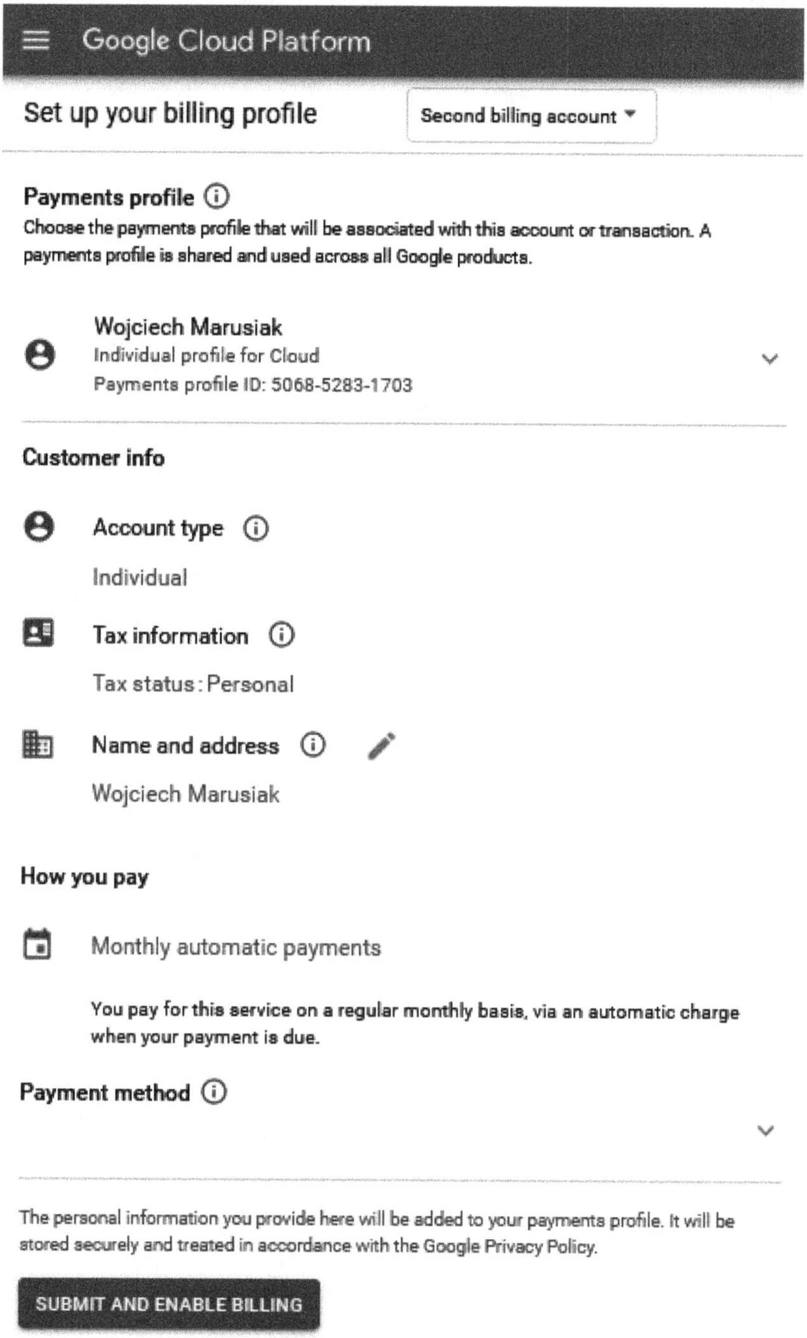

Figure 3.11 – Final step to complete the new billing profile creation

6. The new billing profile is ready to use:

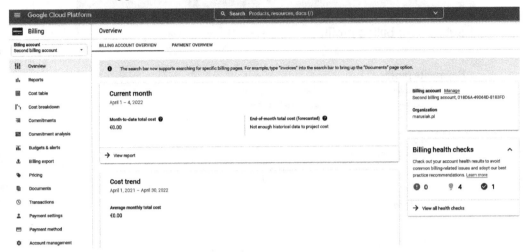

Figure 3.12 – Newly created billing profile is active

Once the billing profile is created, we can link it to a project.

Linking a new project to a billing account

Our billing account is created, and we are ready to use it. We will guide you through the new project creation process and associate it with the billing account.

The following are the steps to link a new project to an existing billing account:

1. From the main screen, click **NEW PROJECT**:

Figure 3.13 – Initial phase of new project creation

2. The next and final step in the new project creation process is to provide a **project name** and select the **Billing account**, **Organization**, and **Location** values:

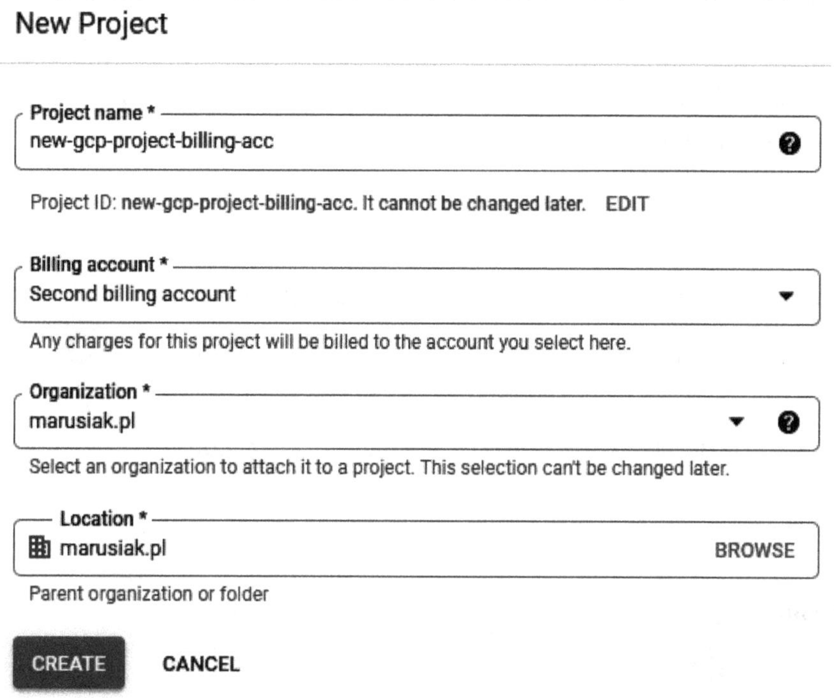

New Project

Project name *
new-gcp-project-billing-acc   ❓

Project ID: **new-gcp-project-billing-acc**. It cannot be changed later.   EDIT

Billing account *
Second billing account   ▼

Any charges for this project will be billed to the account you select here.

Organization *
marusiak.pl   ▼   ❓

Select an organization to attach it to a project. This selection can't be changed later.

Location *
⊞ marusiak.pl   BROWSE

Parent organization or folder

[CREATE]   CANCEL

Figure 3.14 – A new project can be created with a selected billing account

3. You can place it in a specific folder or root organization tree:

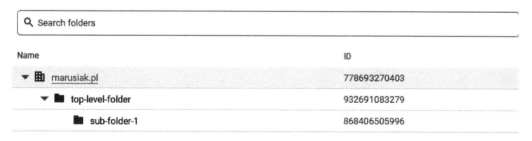

Figure 3.15 – Optional placement selection of project within the organization

This step concludes how to link the new Google Cloud project to a billing account.

Linking an existing project to a billing account

Migrating a Google Cloud project to different billing accounts is a straightforward procedure.

We will now link the existing Google Cloud project to a billing account:

1. On the main Google Cloud Console screen, click **Billing**.

2. As we have multiple billing accounts, click **MANAGE BILLING ACCOUNTS**.

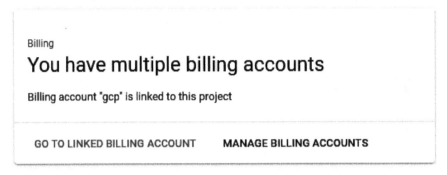

Figure 3.16 – Multiple billing accounts in Google Cloud Console

3. In the **Billing** section, we have an overview of existing billing accounts.

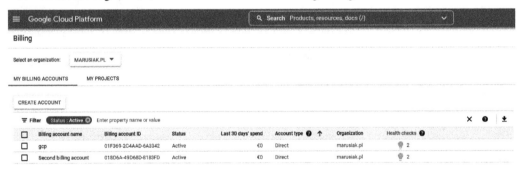

Figure 3.17 – Billing accounts overview

4. To change the billing account for a project, click **MY PROJECTS**:

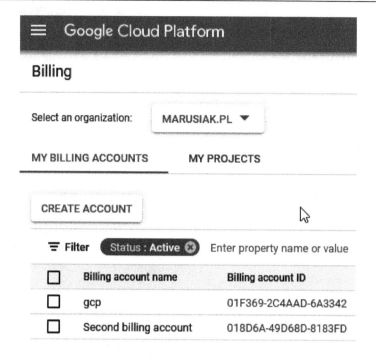

Figure 3.18 – The MY PROJECTS section in the billing account overview

5.   To change the billing account for a project, choose the **Actions** button:

Figure 3.19 – Change the billing action in the MY PROJECTS section of Billing

6.   From the drop-down menu, choose the desired billing account:

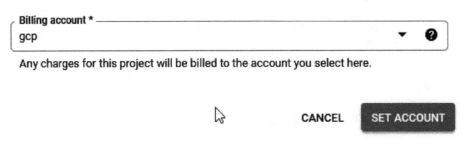

Set the billing account for project "new-gcp-project-billing-acc"

This project pays for both Google Cloud Platform and Maps Platform. Select a billing account that supports both Google Cloud Platform and Maps Platform. Learn more

Billing account *
gcp

Any charges for this project will be billed to the account you select here.

CANCEL   SET ACCOUNT

Figure 3.20 – Billing account selection

7. To finalize the process, click the **SET ACCOUNT** button.

8. Once the process is completed, you will see a change in the billing account associated with your project.

Linking an existing project to a billing account is a straightforward process.

We will pivot from linking projects with billing accounts into budgets and alerts.

Budgets and alerts

Like our life outside the cloud, budgets play a crucial role in everybody's lives. A budget helps create financial stability, allows us to track expenses, and helps us to plan our expenses.

The budget in Google Cloud plays a similar role to that in our daily lives. Some may say that it is even more critical because if we make a mistake during the learning phase, the cost of it might be high.

Google Cloud offers excellent flexibility and elasticity. If the setup of your resources is misconfigured, or your code is miswritten, you might end up paying thousands of dollars for resources you never needed. The budget and alerts should be configured before any cloud activities.

Google Cloud allows us to create budgets, set thresholds, and send notifications using a selected notification medium.

Budget creation

To create a budget for a Cloud Billing account, we need to have **billing.budgets.create** permissions. To view all budgets, **billing.budgets.get** and **billing.budgets.list IAM** permissions are required.

One way of assigning this permission could be the IAM role assignment of **Billing Account Administrator** or **Billing Account Costs Manager**.

Let's create our first budget in Google Cloud Console:

1. Navigate to the **Billing** section of Cloud Console.

2. Choose **Budgets & alerts** from the **Cost management** section.

3. Click the **CREATE BUDGET** button:

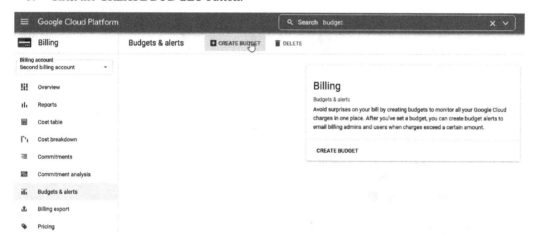

Figure 3.21 – Initial budget creation dialog

4. We need to provide a budget name, choose a time range (a **Monthly**, **Quarterly**, **Yearly**, or **Custom** range), specify how many projects to include (one, more, or all), and select the desired services:

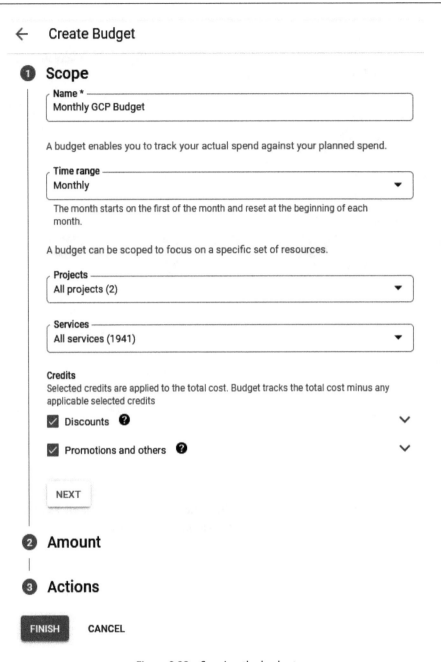

Figure 3.22 – Scoping the budget

5.   In the **Amount** section, choose **Specified amount** if your budget should be compared against it. Choose **Last month's spend** if your budget should be dynamically compared to the last calendar period's spend:

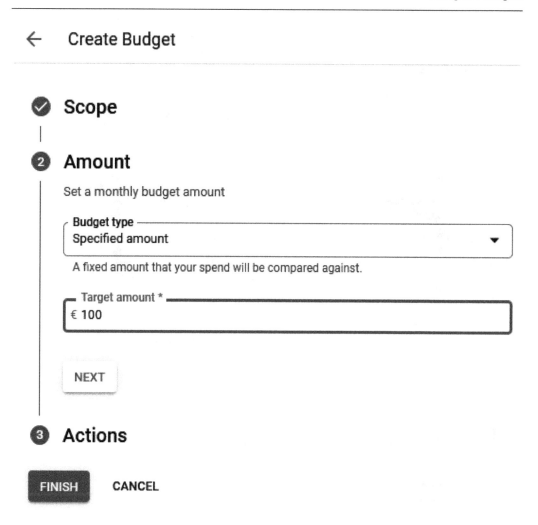

Figure 3.23 – Selection of the type of budget and the amount

6. In the last section of budget creation, we need to enter threshold rules. We can add more thresholds if we want more granular notifications. By default, we have three points, but more can be added:

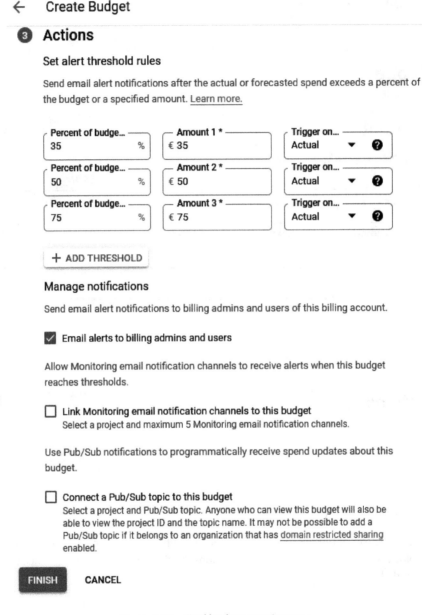

Figure 3.24 – Final budget creation page

7. To complete the budget creation, we need to select one of the notification channels. It can be an email alert to billing administrators and users, linking the monitoring email notification channel to the budget, or connecting the Pub/Sub topic to the budget once the selected budget creation is completed.

8. It is important to mention – *budget creation doesn't stop the usage of your resources or block the creation of new ones.* Once you reach 100% of your budget, you can still create new cloud resources, but you will be charged for them.

Budgets can be edited and deleted, but the essential task is to create one and not miss the notifications when exceeding the configured thresholds. To learn more about Google Cloud budgets, visit this link: `https://cloud.google.com/billing/docs/how-to/budgets-notification-recipients`.

Viewing billing and cloud usage

Billing is configured and we created alerts so we are well prepared to consume Google Cloud resources. The **Billing** section allows us to view detailed reports and break down costs at the project or service level:

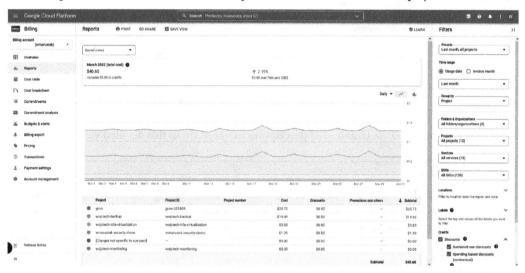

Figure 3.25 – Sample last month's report view

You see an example of a monthly report for our account in the preceding figure. On the right-hand side, we can filter the views by projects, folders and organizations, services, and more:

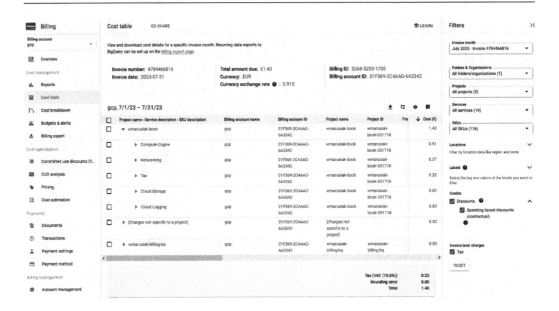

Figure 3.26 – Cost table breakdown filtered on the project level

We can view the project ID, SKU, and SKU description information in this detailed view.

Billing exports

Google Cloud offers additional possibilities for those whose existing billing and cloud usage reporting isn't enough. Billing exports allow customers to export billing data into the Google Cloud data warehouse called **BigQuery**.

We will learn about BigQuery in upcoming chapters, but in the context of billing exports, BigQuery can be used to export all billing data automatically. It can be helpful if an organization uses external tools to analyze or visualize data. The following documentation explains how to configure billing exports to BigQuery: `https://cloud.google.com/billing/docs/how-to/export-data-bigquery-setup`.

We configured a billing export into BigQuery for one of our projects.

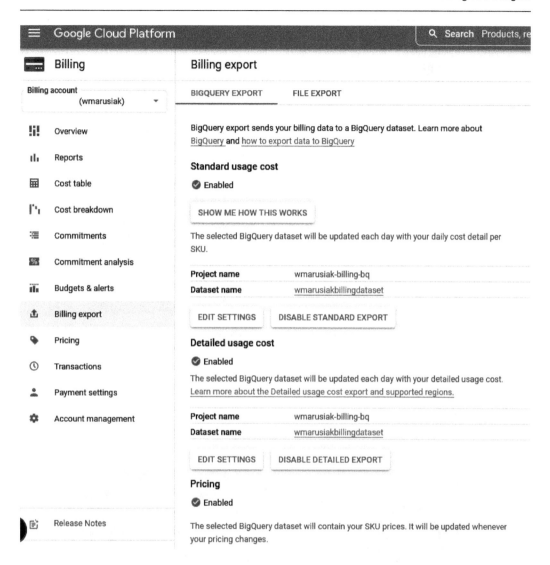

Figure 3.27 – Billing account configured to export all billing data into BigQuery

It may take up to 24 hours to see the data from the billing account in BigQuery. Once the data is in the BigQuery dataset, we can query it.

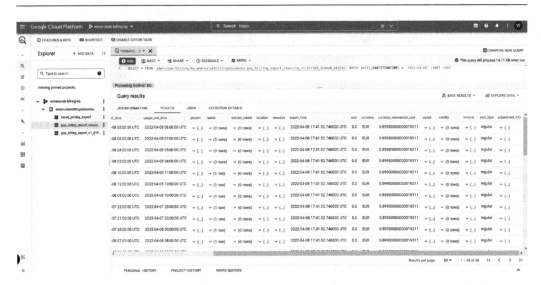

Figure 3.28 – Sample query in BigQuery with billing data

Looker Studio is a free product offered to Google Cloud users. We can store up to 10 GiB of data with the Free Tier and query up to 1TiB data.

Once the export is finished, we can work with the data. For example, we can visualize it in Google Cloud Data Studio, as shown in the following figure (image from `https://lookerstudio.google.com/u/0/reporting/64387229-05e0-4951-aa3f-e7349bbafc07/page/p_l3qef1s8rc`):

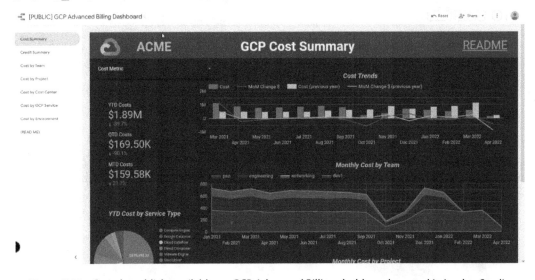

Figure 3.29 – Sample publicly available on GCP Advanced Billing dashboard created in Looker Studio

Billing exports allow users to analyze their cloud expenditure further and visualize it in Looker Studio.

We can drag and drop dimensions from the available fields in the following screenshot:

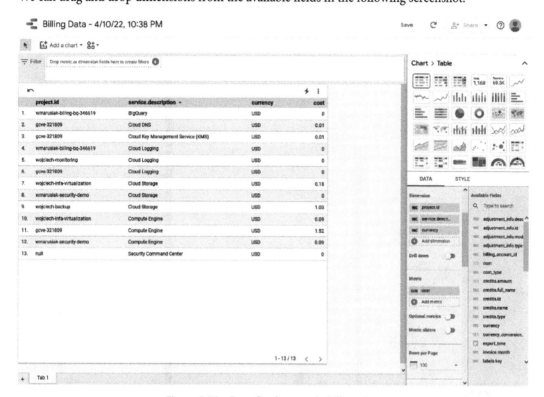

Figure 3.30 – Data Studio sample billing data

We can add charts to visualize our data better as well:

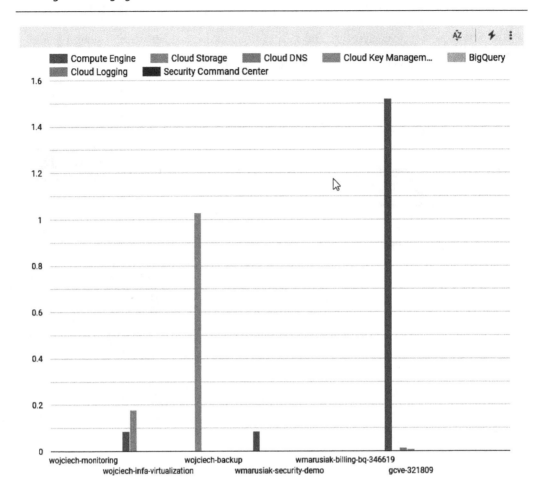

Figure 3.31 – Cloud Billing data exported into BigQuery and visualized in Data Studio

Visualization is quite a straightforward process and we can configure charts to our liking or business requirements.

API management

All Google Cloud services can be used only if the correlated API has been enabled. API enablement occurs at the project level. For example: if you used GCE and GCS in your existing project and created a brand-new task, you will need to enable both APIs.

There are three options for us to enable an API in the Google Cloud project:

- Ask a security admin to create an API key for you.
- Ask a security admin to grant you access to the project so that you can create an API key in the same project that the API is associated with
- Ask a security admin to grant you access to enable the API in your own Google Cloud project so that you can create an API key

In the next section, we will learn how to enable a Google Cloud API.

Enabling an API

We can enable an API in two places – Cloud Console or Google Cloud Shell. Let's start with Cloud Console.

Enabling an API in Cloud Console

To enable an API in Cloud Console, we need to go to **APIs & Services** in our project:

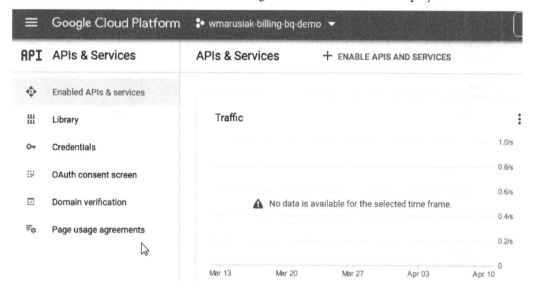

Figure 3.32 – Overview of APIs & Services

Simply type the product name or choose it from the categories to enable a particular API. Once selected, click **ENABLE**:

Pub/Sub Lite API

Google Enterprise API

A zonal messaging service optimized for cost

Figure 3.33 – API enablement for Pub/Sub

API enablement usually takes just a few seconds. Now, let's look at how to enable an API in Cloud Shell.

Enabling an API in Cloud Shell

Similar to Cloud Console, APIs can be enabled in Cloud Shell. The steps are as follows:

1. To list all projects, type the following command:

    ```
    gcloud projects list
    ```

2. The next step is to choose our desired project:

    ```
    gcloud config set project PROJECT_ID
    ```

3. Before we enable the API, we need to list all available services by running the following command:

    ```
    gcloud services list --avialable
    ```

4. Choose the desired service and enable it:

    ```
    gcloud services enable SERVICE_NAME
    ```

Once we enable the API, it is good to know where to check which APIs are enabled to have an overview. This is the topic of the next section.

Overview of an enabled API

To check which APIs are enabled, we can view this information in the **APIs & Services** section, shown as follows:

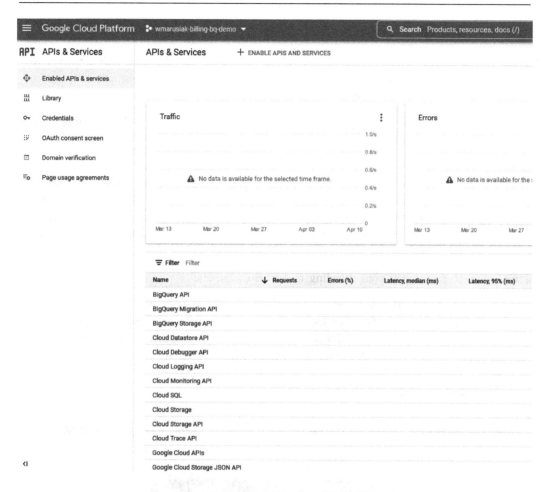

Figure 3.34 – Overview of enabled APIs

In addition to information on enabled APIs, we can view the number of requests, error percentage, and latency.

API management is a straightforward process, but it is essential to remember that APIs are already enabled every time we use the Google Cloud service. If we have never used a service, we need to have sufficient permissions to allow it to use it.

The fact that API management is a straightforward process is especially important to remember if we want to run services in newly created projects. The next section focuses on quota management, which is an important topic for day-to-day cloud usage and the certification.

Quota management

Another part of using Google Cloud services is quotas. Together with APIs, they fully allow you to manage how you will use Google Cloud services. While APIs enable us to control whether the service is in an enabled or disabled state, quotas will allow us to control how many resources can be used.

Different products may have various quantifiable resources such as the number of API calls or requests per time period, or be as simple as CPU and RAM space or disk storage number.

You might wonder why cloud providers limit you from spending however much you want on cloud resources. First and foremost, Google Cloud wishes to protect you from unexpected spending. We all make mistakes, and some code deployment, script, or even GUI errors happen. If there is no protection, your credit card could be quickly charged with thousands of US dollars. Some cloud resources are more expensive than others – for example, GPUs or high-CPU and RAM VMs. They can max out your credit card very quickly.

All this is done to protect you, your spending, and other customers.

The longer you use the cloud and have a more extended spending history, the possibility of creating more cloud resources increases. Google Cloud evaluates many factors such as previous spending or abuse penalties. Customers might have different quotas based on these aspects and some other factors. In the next figure, we can see the **Quota** section of Google Cloud Console:

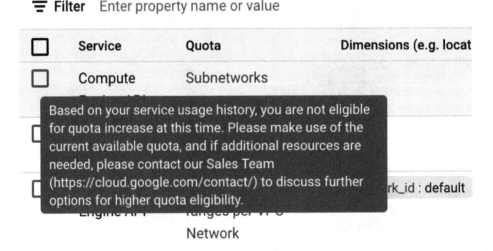

Figure 3.35 – Unable to change quota notification

The preceding screenshot shows precisely that the quota can't be changed yet.

The final word is to remember that quotas are project resources. In the next section, we will focus on the quota increase process and factors.

Quota increase

Quota increase is an automated process where many pre-existing factors such as project longevity, how long you have been using Google Cloud, and whether the account is newly created are evaluated. Some quotas might be denied now for you but approved later.

Fortunately, it is not a fully automated process, and Cloud Customer Billing works on those requests. Usually, it takes 2-3 business days to process a request. In our experience, quota increase requests have been processed much faster.

Quota increase permissions

To view your project quota in Google Cloud Console or access the project quota programmatically, you must have the following IAM permissions:

- **resourcemanager.projects.get**
- **resourcemanager.folders.get** (if you want to view the quota for an entire folder)
- **resourcemanager.organizations.get** (if you want to view quota for an entire organization)
- **serviceusage.quotas.get**

To change your quota at the project, folder, or organization level, you must have the following permission:

- **serviceusage.quotas.update**

These permissions allow you to manage quotas in Google Cloud.

Quota increase process

To increase a quota, follow these steps:

1. To view all quotas and available resources in your project in Cloud Console, go to **Quotas**:

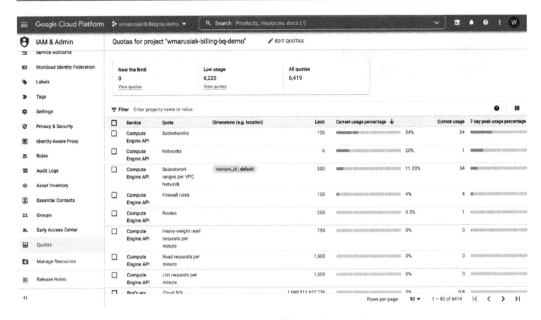

Figure 3.36 – Overview of Quotas in a project

2.   Choose the desired quota to change. Click the **EDIT QUOTAS** button.

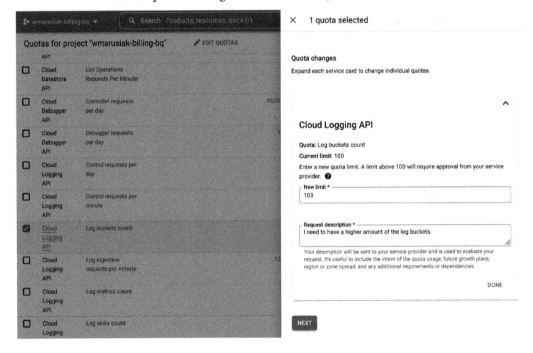

Figure 3.37 – Editing the desired quota with the request description

3. Once you have added a new limit and request description, you need to provide your details such as an email address and a phone number:

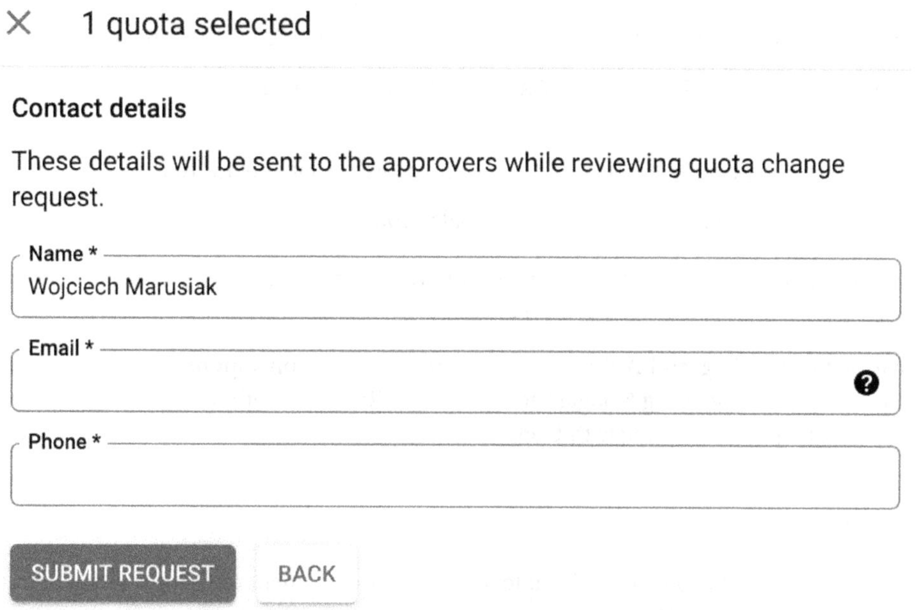

✕   1 quota selected

Contact details

These details will be sent to the approvers while reviewing quota change request.

Name *
Wojciech Marusiak

Email *   ❓

Phone *

SUBMIT REQUEST   BACK

Figure 3.38 – Quota increase request with contact details

4. After we click **SUBMIT REQUEST**, we receive a ticket number, and will receive updates by email:

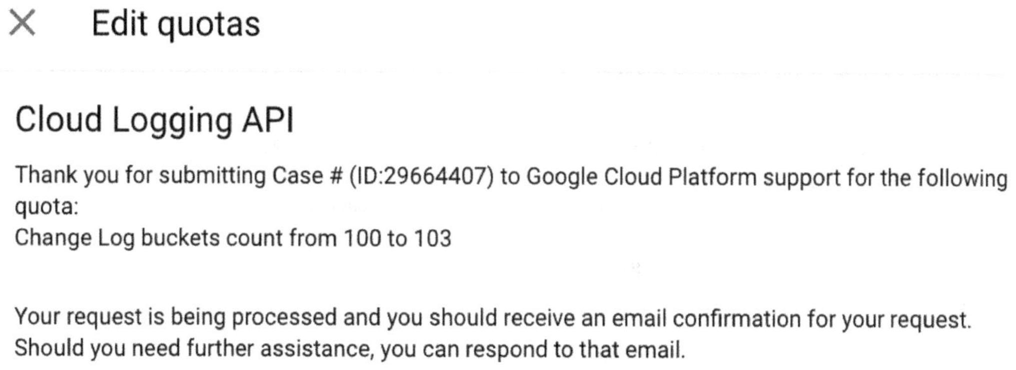

✕   Edit quotas

Cloud Logging API

Thank you for submitting Case # (ID:29664407) to Google Cloud Platform support for the following quota:
Change Log buckets count from 100 to 103

Your request is being processed and you should receive an email confirmation for your request. Should you need further assistance, you can respond to that email.

Figure 3.39 – Quota increase request with ticket number

This concludes the process of increasing a quota in Cloud Console.

Sometimes, a quota increase fails, and we will cover possible causes and errors you might encounter.

Quota errors

You might encounter the following quota errors:

- `429 TOO MANY REQUESTS` – An HTTP error when the HTTP/REST request is exceeded
- `413 REQUEST ENTITY TOO LARGE` – An HTTP error if you exceed a quota with an API request
- `ResourceExhausted` – The HTTP error if you exhaust a quota with gRPC
- `1` – If you exceeded the quota using the Google Cloud CLI

Hopefully, by reading this section, you will not encounter quota errors, and if you do, you will know what caused them and be able to fix them very fast.

Quota management, billing, and API management are day-to-day operations that some of you will do programmatically or by using Google Cloud Console. Regardless of how they will be executed, they are an integral part of working with Google Cloud.

Summary

After reading this chapter, you should be able to plan the deployment of Google Cloud compute, database, and storage options. We covered various types of persistent disk options for GCE, different types of object storage, and various database options. We created new billing accounts and created budgets and alerts. We learned how to enable an API and increase the quota for a specific GCP service.

In the next chapter, we will focus on the implementation of Google Cloud compute resources starting from VMs up to Cloud Run or infrastructure as code.

Questions

Answer the following questions to test your knowledge gained from this chapter:

1. Which permissions are required to increase the quota in a project?

    A. **resourcemanager.projects.get**

    B. **resourcemanager.folders.get**

    C. **resourcemanager.organizations.get**

    D. **serviceusage.quotas.get**

    E. All the above

2. Which product would you use for a workload that requires full access to the underlying operating system?

   A. GKE

   B. Cloud Run

   C. GAE

   D. GCE

3. What is the main difference between persistent disk and cloud storage?

   A. Cloud Storage is used mainly for object storage

   B. A persistent disk is a default boot device for VMs

   C. Cloud Storage objects can be accessed from VMs

   D. The persistent disk has an unlimited size

4. A Compute Engine VM can have which of the following disks?

   A. A zonal persistent disk

   B. An extreme global disk

   C. A regional bucket disk

   D. A local SSD

5. To use Google Cloud products, I need to _____:

   A. Have a billing account

   B. Attach a payment type

   C. Create a project

   D. Enable a specific product API

   E. All of the above

6. What is the durability of Cloud Storage?

   A. 99.999999999% annual durability

   B. 99.9% weekly durability

   C. 99.9999999999999999999% monthly durability

   D. 99% annual durability

7. Select a product that uses event-driven serverless functions:

    A. Cloud Run

    B. Cloud Serverless

    C. Google Serverless Run

    D. Cloud Functions

8. Select all that apply:

    A. The project must have an associated billing account

    B. One billing account can be associated with multiple projects

    C. A billing account requires a payment method

    D. There can be numerous billing accounts

    E. All of the above

9. Which product fits best to the requirements of autoscaling applications and databases with high availability and integrated monitoring and A/B testing?

    A. GKE

    B. GCE

    C. GAE

    D. Cloud Run

10. Select a database for an application that requires high scalability and high availability and will be deployed as a mobile application:

    A. Cloud Bigtable

    B. Cloud SQL

    C. BigQuery

    D. Firestore

11. Which type of persistent disk provides the highest availability?

    A. A global extreme disk

    B. A local SSD

    C. A zonal persistent disk

    D. A regional persistent disk

12. Who can use the Google Cloud Free Trial?

   A.   Any new customer

   B.   Existing and new customers

   C.   Customers who use invoicing

   D.   Only Free Tier customers

13. Why is it recommended to create billing alerts?

   A.   It provides visibility into existing cloud expenditure

   B.   It informs us about cloud expenditure

   C.   It prevents excessive cloud expenditure

   D.   It protects our budget

   E.   All of the above

14. Select as suitable type of Google Cloud Storage for backups that will be stored for more than 10 years and retrieved once per year:

   A.   Standard

   B.   Nearline

   C.   Performance

   D.   Archive

15. You have been asked to advise on a data warehouse solution that can query complex datasets interactively with sub-second query response time and high concurrency. Which option would you go for?

   A.   Google Cloud Run

   B.   BigQuery

   C.   Cloud Bigtable

   D.   Cloud SQL

16. Choose a computing option for a containerized application with complete control over the nodes with the ability to fine-tune and run custom administrative workloads:

   A.   Cloud Run

   B.   Cloud Spanner

   C.   GKE

   D.   GAE

17. Choose the compute option for a stateless or batch-processing application:

    A. n1-ultramem-160

    B. Preemptible/spot VM

    C. GCE

    D. Cloud Run

18. Who can use Google Cloud Free Tier?

    A. Free Tier ends after 30 days and cannot be used afterward

    B. Free Tier is available after the free trial

    C. Only enterprise customers can use it

    D. It is available to all Google Cloud users

19. Select all that apply to budget exports:

    A. They provide greater flexibility than Google Cloud Billing

    B. They allow you to integrate with other billing tools

    C. They provide greater visibility into the billing data

    D. Data can be visualized in other tools

    E. All of the above

20. GCS cannot be used _____:

    A. As a boot disk for compute VMs

    B. For high-performance object storage

    C. For archival storage

    D. For database storage

    E. Answers A and D

Answers

The answers to the preceding questions are as follows:

1E, 2D, 3B, 4A, 5E, 6A, 7D, 8E, 9C, 10D, 11D, 12A, 13E, 14D, 15B, 16C, 17B, 18D, 19E, 20E

4

Implementing Compute Solutions – Google Compute Engine

The aim of this chapter is to familiarize ourselves with the implementation of various compute solutions.

We will cover the **Google Compute Engine (GCE)**.

We will try to create each computing solution, in this and the upcoming chapters, by using the Cloud console and the command line with the `gcloud` CLI. We will learn how to edit and manage each specific resource. In our experience, which we gained by clearing the Associate Cloud Engineer exam twice, the compute solutions from the Google Cloud portfolio are some of the most important ones.

Let's dive into the different compute solutions.

Computing options

In the previous chapter, we had an overview of which compute solutions should be used and when. For the exam itself, we need to remember which solutions can be easily implemented based on the scenario, how much time we might need to do it, and how to estimate the total cost and choose the best solution accordingly.

GCE

Let's start with GCE, one of the core Google Cloud products.

The base resources for **virtual machines (VMs)** are a processor, memory, storage, and a network. We have many ways to configure VMs, based on our requirements and how to implement them, be it through the Cloud console, command line, or code implementation.

It might not come as a surprise to you that Google Cloud utilizes a hypervisor that is responsible for virtualization – hosting many virtual servers on one or more significant servers. Google Cloud uses a KVM-based hypervisor secured and hardened by Google itself: `https://cloud.google.com/blog/products/gcp/7-ways-we-harden-our-kvm-hypervisor-at-google-cloud-security-in-plaintext`.

Throughout the chapter, we will refer to a *VM* as an *instance*, so please do not be confused when we switch between the two phrases. Similarly, we will refer to **Google Compute Engine** as **GCE**.

GCE machine families

Before we actually create our first GCE instance, it is important to learn about the different types of machines – so-called machine families.

Generally speaking, Google Cloud offers machine families for different types of workloads.

Here is the general summary of different machine families:

- **General-purpose**: This offers the best balance between price and performance for a wide range of tasks.
- **Compute-optimized**: This delivers the highest performance per core on Compute Engine and is specifically designed for compute-intensive workloads.
- **Memory-optimized**: This is perfect for tasks that require a large amount of memory, providing more memory per core compared to other machine families, with a maximum capacity of 12 TB of RAM.
- **Accelerator-optimized**: This is specifically tailored to massively parallelized **Compute Unified Device Architecture** (**CUDA**) compute workloads, such as **machine learning** (**ML**) and **high-performance computing** (**HPC**). This machine family is the optimal choice for workloads that require GPUs.

GCE machines are further classified by series and generation. For example, the N1 series is the older version of the N2 series. Typically, a higher generation or series indicates newer CPU platforms or technologies.

Every machine series has predefined machine types with a set of resources available for the VM. If that predefined machine type doesn't meet your requirements, you can create a custom machine type.

Google Cloud offers several workload-based machine families:

- General-purpose workloads:
  - **E2**: Day-to-day computing at a lower cost. Typical use cases for E2 machine types can be low-traffic web servers, back office apps, containerized microservices, virtual desktops, and development and test environments.

- **N2, N2D, and N1**: A balanced between price and performance. Typical use cases can be low- to medium-traffic web and application servers, containerized microservices, CRM applications, and data pipelines.

- **C3**: Consistently high performance for a variety of workloads – high-traffic web and application servers, databases, in-memory caches, ad servers, game servers, data analytics, media streaming and transcoding, and CPU-based ML training.

- **Tau T2D and Tau T2A**: Best per-core performance/cost for scale-out workloads. Typical use cases include scale-out workloads, web servers, media transcoding, large-scale Java applications, and containerized microservices.

- Compute-optimized:

  - **C2, C2D,** Ultra-high performance for compute-intensive workloads. Typical workloads include compute-bound workloads, high-performance web servers, game servers, ad servers, HPC, media transcoding, and AI/ML workloads.

- Memory-optimized:

  - **M3, M2,** and **M1**: The highest memory-to-compute ratios for memory-intensive workloads. Typical applications deployed include medium-to-extra-large SAP HANA databases, in-memory data stores such as Redis, simulations, high-performance databases such as Microsoft SQL Server or MySQL, and electronic design automation.

- Accelerator-optimized:

  - Optimized for accelerated HPC workloads. Typical workloads include CUDA-enabled ML training and inference, HPC, massively parallelized computation, natural language processing, the **deep learning recommendation model** (**DLRM**), video transcoding, and a remote visualization workstation.

To learn more details about each machine family, including a detailed description and the recommended settings for each type, visit the following URL: `https://cloud.google.com/compute/docs/machine-resource`.

Having learned about different machine families, we are now ready to start with our first GCE machine creation.

Creating GCE

Let's create a VM running Ubuntu Linux as the operating system.

Console

1. In the Cloud console, open **Compute Engine** and click **CREATE INSTANCE**:

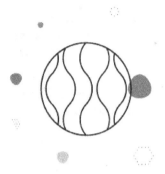

VM Instances

Compute Engine lets you use virtual machines that run on Google's
infrastructure. Create micro-VMs or larger instances running Debian, Windows,
or other standard images. Create your first VM instance, import it using a
migration service, or try the quickstart to build a sample app.

CREATE INSTANCE   TAKE THE QUICKSTART

Figure 4.1 – Creating an instance in the Cloud console

2. We can now specify multiple options for the VM. Pick the instance name, and then choose the desired region and zone:

Figure 4.2 – The first part of instance creation – an instance name and instance region with a zone

3. We have several options under **Machine family** in the **Machine configuration** section. We selected the **GENERAL-PURPOSE** type of the VM, and for the **Series** option, we selected **E2**:

Machine configuration

Machine family

GENERAL-PURPOSE   COMPUTE-OPTIMIZED   MEMORY-OPTIMIZED   GPU

Machine types for common workloads, optimized for cost and flexibility

Series ─────
E2   ▼

CPU platform selection based on availability

Machine type ─────
e2-medium (2 vCPU, 4 GB memory)   ▼

	vCPU	Memory
	1 shared core	4 GB

Figure 4.3 – The Machine configuration section with several machine family options to choose from

4. Some more options from the **Machine family** section include **CPU platform**, **vCPUs to core ratio**, and **Visible core count**:

CPU platform ─────
Automatic   ▼   ❷

vCPUs to core ratio   ▼   ❷

Visible core count   ▼   ❷

Figure 4.4 – Optional configurations for the VM

5. If the application on the VM instance requires a display device, you can enable this when creating the instance:

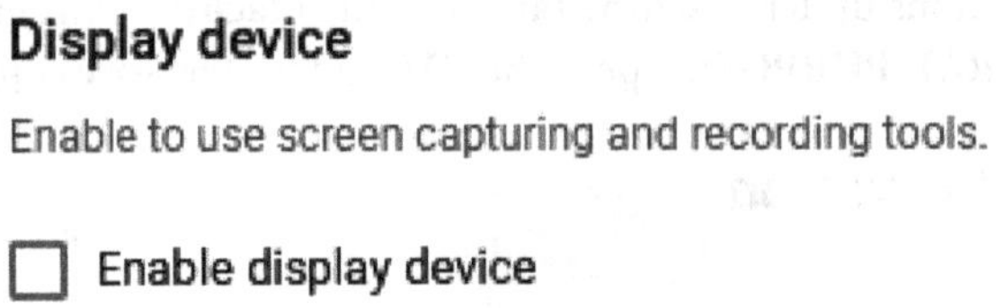

Display device

Enable to use screen capturing and recording tools.

☐ Enable display device

Figure 4.5 – The Display device option when creating the VM

6. In the following sections, we can enable a confidential VM service, which allows us to encrypt VM memory by leveraging a **Virtual Trusted Platform Module (vTPM)**. This feature is available only in a specific type of the VM – the N2D series type of VMs. You can deploy a container image to the VM instance if you wish:

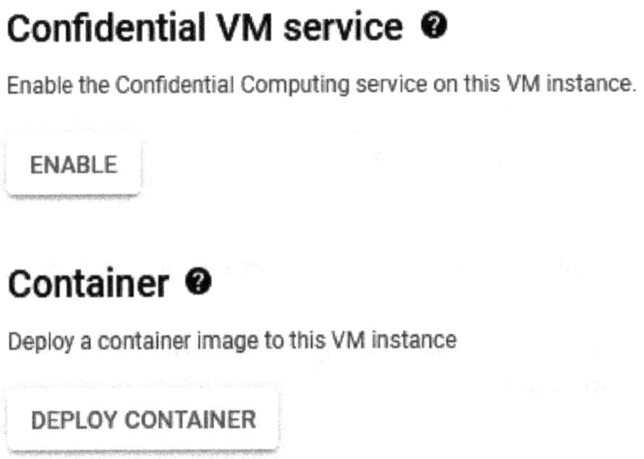

Confidential VM service ❷

Enable the Confidential Computing service on this VM instance.

ENABLE

Container ❷

Deploy a container image to this VM instance

DEPLOY CONTAINER

Figure 4.6 – Confidential VM service and container deployment options when creating the VM

7. In the **Boot disk** section, we have the freedom to choose any operating system available:

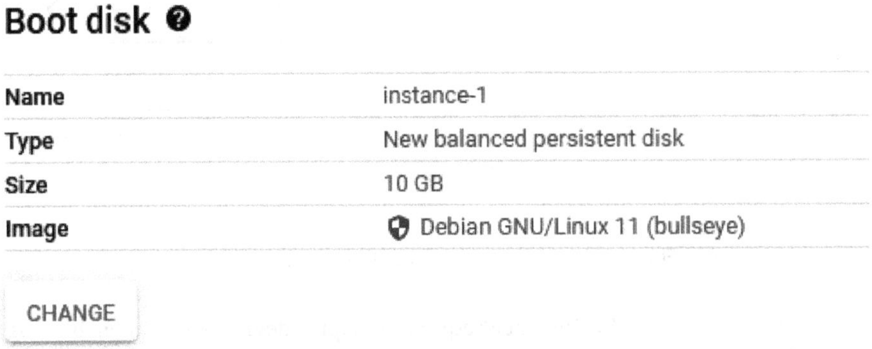

Boot disk ❷

Name	instance-1
Type	New balanced persistent disk
Size	10 GB
Image	🛡 Debian GNU/Linux 11 (bullseye)

CHANGE

Figure 4.7 – The Boot disk section from the new VM creation wizard

8.   We changed the operating system to Ubuntu 20.04 LTS, and we selected the boot disk type as **SSD persistent disk**, with a size of 5 0 GB:

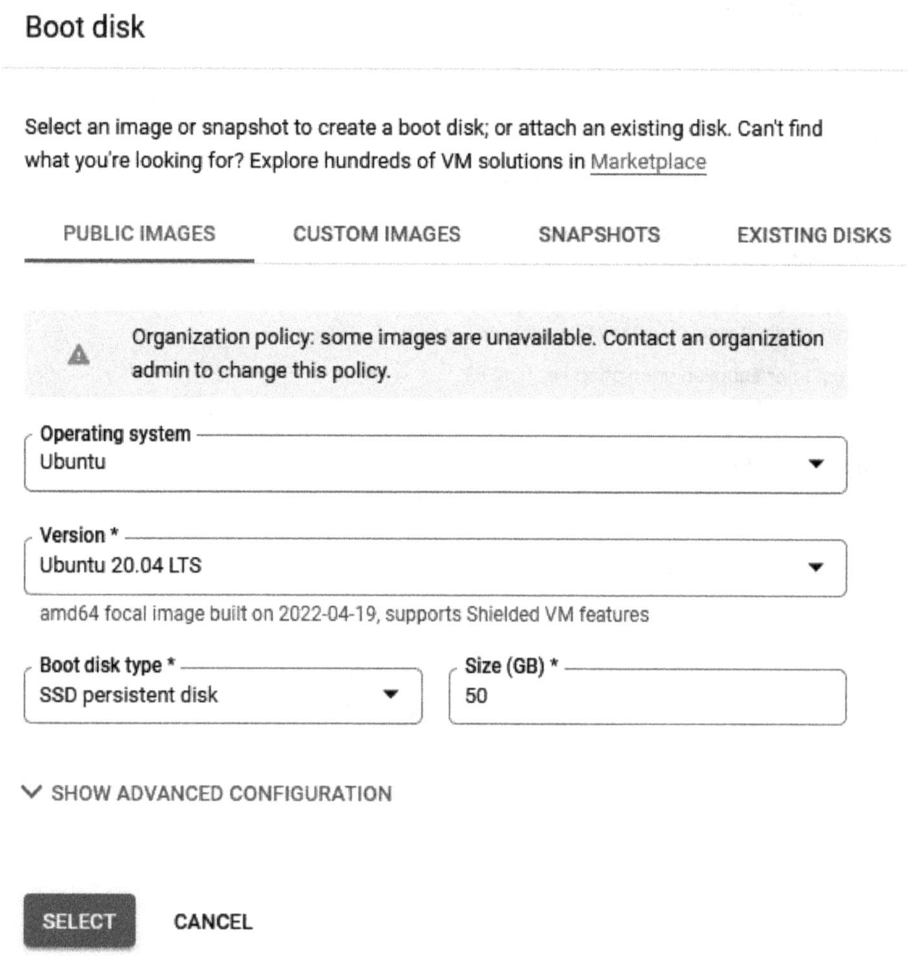

Boot disk

Select an image or snapshot to create a boot disk; or attach an existing disk. Can't find what you're looking for? Explore hundreds of VM solutions in Marketplace

PUBLIC IMAGES   CUSTOM IMAGES   SNAPSHOTS   EXISTING DISKS

⚠   Organization policy: some images are unavailable. Contact an organization
       admin to change this policy.

Operating system
Ubuntu   ▼

Version *
Ubuntu 20.04 LTS   ▼

amd64 focal image built on 2022-04-19, supports Shielded VM features

Boot disk type *   Size (GB) *
SSD persistent disk   ▼   50

∨ SHOW ADVANCED CONFIGURATION

SELECT   CANCEL

Figure 4.8 – The boot disk, operating system selection, and boot disk type option with its size

9.   In the advanced configuration section, we can configure a deletion rule, encryption, a snapshot schedule, and custom device naming, as shown in the following screenshot:

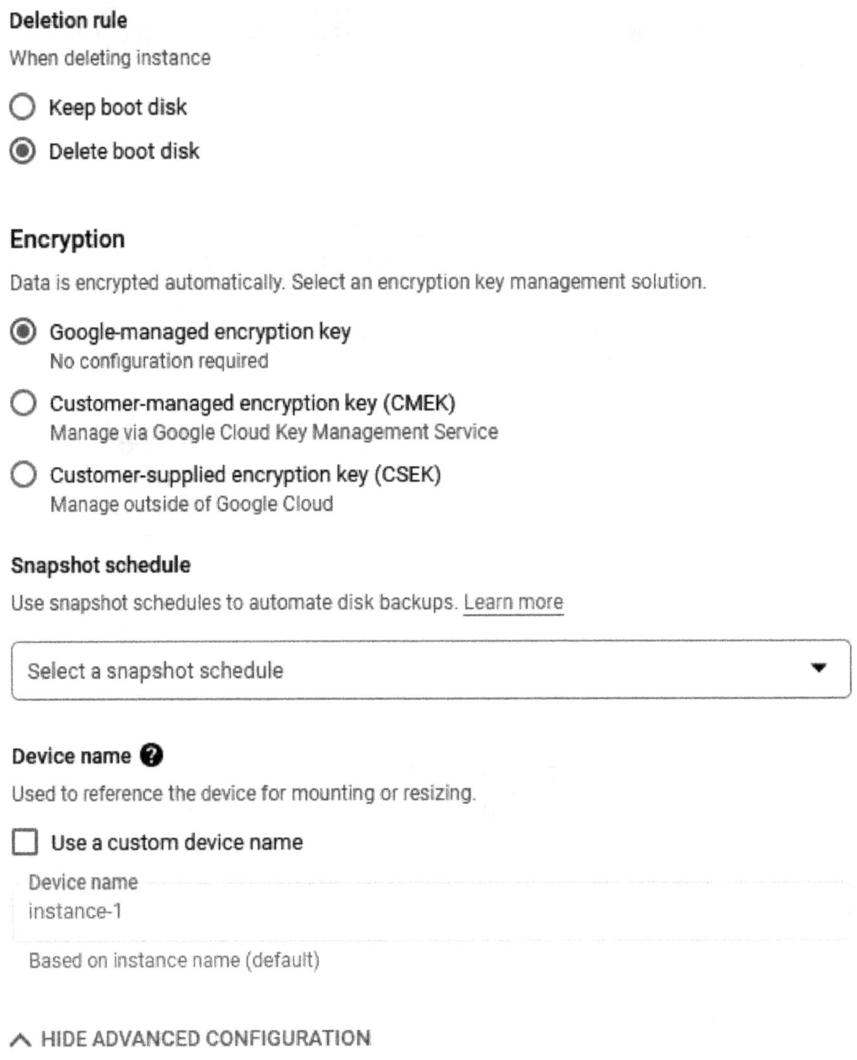

Deletion rule

When deleting instance

○ Keep boot disk

◉ Delete boot disk

Encryption

Data is encrypted automatically. Select an encryption key management solution.

◉ Google-managed encryption key
No configuration required

○ Customer-managed encryption key (CMEK)
Manage via Google Cloud Key Management Service

○ Customer-supplied encryption key (CSEK)
Manage outside of Google Cloud

Snapshot schedule

Use snapshot schedules to automate disk backups. Learn more

Select a snapshot schedule ▼

Device name ❓

Used to reference the device for mounting or resizing.

☐ Use a custom device name

Device name
instance-1

Based on instance name (default)

∧ HIDE ADVANCED CONFIGURATION

Figure 4.9 – Disk deletion rule and VM encryption options during VM creation

10. On the **Identity and API access** screen, we can choose a service account and configure access scopes to Cloud APIs:

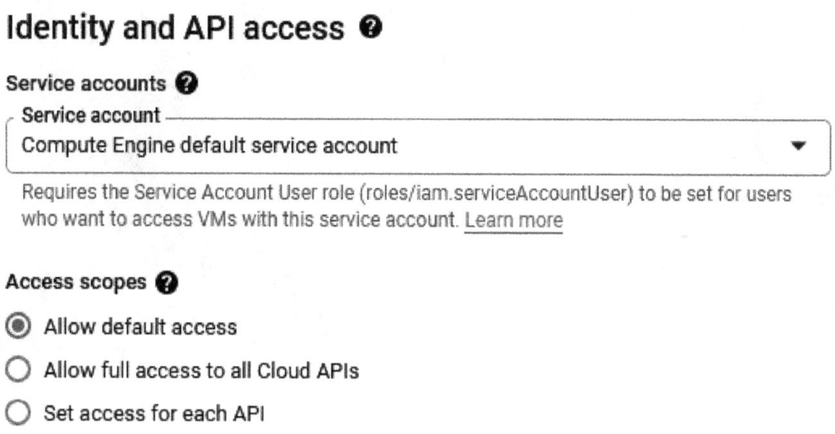

Identity and API access ❷

Service accounts ❷

Service account
Compute Engine default service account   ▼

Requires the Service Account User role (roles/iam.serviceAccountUser) to be set for users who want to access VMs with this service account. Learn more

Access scopes ❷

◉ Allow default access

○ Allow full access to all Cloud APIs

○ Set access for each API

Figure 4.10 – The Identity and API access configuration screen

11. In the last section, **Firewall**, we can allow HTTP and HTTPS traffic in our newly created VM instance:

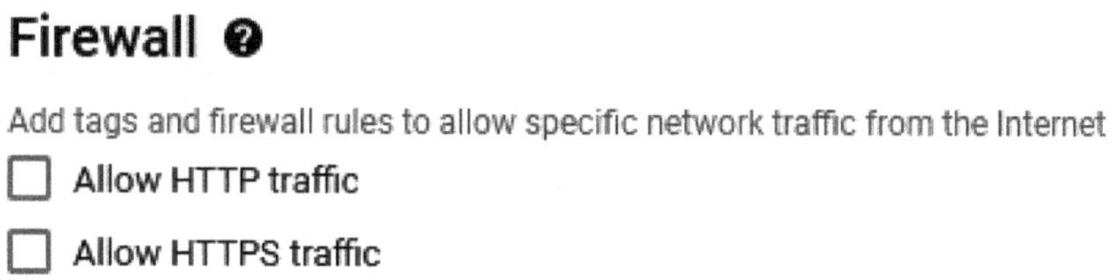

Firewall ❷

Add tags and firewall rules to allow specific network traffic from the Internet

☐ Allow HTTP traffic

☐ Allow HTTPS traffic

Figure 4.11 – Allow HTTP/HTTPS firewall rules configuration screen

12. Further options, such as networking, disks, security, and sole tenancy, will be discussed later in this chapter. By clicking the **Create** button, we can create the VM. Next to the **Cancel** button, the **Equivalent Command-Line** button can help us learn the `gcloud` commands.

13. After a short period, `instance-1` will be successfully created, and it is reachable via the **Secure Shell (SSH)** protocol, as shown in the following screenshot:

```
PS C:\Users\Wojciech Marusiak> ssh wojcieh@35.195.153.173
The authenticity of host '35.195.153.173 (35.195.153.173)' can't be established.
ECDSA key fingerprint is SHA256:aacC6WsB+GoD7KpJTz4J1HAEuotJBLE5Xo+yJrBXrE8.
Are you sure you want to continue connecting (yes/no/[fingerprint])? yes
Warning: Permanently added '35.195.153.173' (ECDSA) to the list of known hosts.
Linux instance-1 4.19.0-21-cloud-amd64 #1 SMP Debian 4.19.249-2 (2022-06-30) x86_64

The programs included with the Debian GNU/Linux system are free software;
the exact distribution terms for each program are described in the
individual files in /usr/share/doc/*/copyright.

Debian GNU/Linux comes with ABSOLUTELY NO WARRANTY, to the extent
permitted by applicable law.
wojcieh@instance-1:~$
```

Figure 4.12 – A successful login to the instance via the SSH protocol

Command line

VM creation can be achieved using command-line tools. The equivalent of the previously described instance creation using Cloud Shell can be achieved using the following command line:

```
gcloud compute instances create instance-1 --project=wmarusiak-
book-351718 --zone=europe-west1-b --machine-type=e2-medium
--network-interface=network-tier=PREMIUM,subnet=default
--maintenance-policy=MIGRATE --provisioning-model=STANDARD --create-
disk=auto-delete=yes,boot=yes,device-name=instance-1,image=projects/
ubuntu-os-cloud/global/images/ubuntu-2004-focal-v20220419,mode=rw
,size=50,type=projects/wmarusiak-book-351718/zones/europe-west1-b/
diskTypes/pd-ssd
```

The preceding command specifies the following options:

- --project: The project in which we want to create the instance.

- --zone: The exact zone from the desired region.

- --machine-type: This can either be one of the pre-defined machine sizes (vCPU and RAM) or a custom one.

- --network-interface: This specifies the network tier and subnet.

- --maintenance-policy: This specifies what should happen with the VM if a maintenance event happens. Migrate causes live migration of a VM. Terminate stops a VM instead of migrating it.

- --provisioning-model: If you wish to use spot VMs, you should choose spot instead of a standard.

- --create-disk: This specifies what should happen with the instance disk when the instance deletion occurs. In this example, we can see the size of the disk as well as its type (HDD, SSD, or a balanced one).

The aforementioned options have multiple switches and allow for precise VM specification and configuration.

In the next section, we will edit the Google Compute instance to familiarize ourselves with options and command-line options.

GCE management

Once an instance is created, we can start using it, install any application, and configure it to our needs. However, sometimes, we need to change some settings, add disks, or change the network to which our instance is attached.

For example, let's start with some information about a running instance.

The running VM inventory

The easiest way to find out the details of an instance is to navigate to the Cloud console and view its details.

Console

In the Cloud console, we can click on the desired instance and view various details about the instance.

We have visible four sections on the instance details page, which are listed as follows:

- **Details**: The screen that displays the main information. We can see basic information (name, instance ID, creation time, and so on) as well as machine configuration, disks, and networking information.

- **Observability**: Initial monitoring information about the instance, which is live-updated. By default, we see metrics such as CPU utilization and network traffic. It is possible to collect and visualize even more metrics by installing the **Ops Agent**.

- **Os Info**: This is a part of VM Manager, a suite of tools that can be used to manage operating systems at scale. It requires **OS Config Agent** and **VM Manager API** enablement to be installed on the instances. Once enabled, it displays information about available patches, vulnerabilities, and installed packages.

- **Screenshot**: This can be used to see a screenshot of the instance in the Cloud console, provided that the display device setting is enabled on the instance.

By viewing this information in the Cloud console, we can easily find details about the instance, its configuration, and possible issues.

Command line

Similar, if not even more, detailed information about an instance can be retrieved by executing the following command:

```
gcloud compute instances describe INSTANCE_NAME --zone=INSTANCE_ZONE
```

The output of this command is long and detailed, so we encourage you to run the command yourself and try to find information about the boot disk, image, instance type, and networking.

Starting and stopping a VM

Let's now focus on start and stop activities, which are a great introduction to working with the Cloud console and the gcloud command line. You might ask yourself, why do we need to stop an instance? If resources aren't consumed, you don't need to pay for them. Running instances that you don't need might increase your bill significantly. This might not be the case if you have only two or three instances, but it might make a difference if you have hundreds or thousands of instances. Enterprises can stop development and acceptance instances that are needed only during working hours to save thousands of dollars.

Console

Once logged in to the Cloud console, in the **Compute Engine** section, select the desired GCE instance and click the **STOP** button:

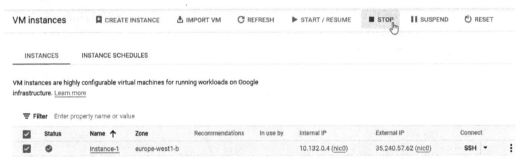

Figure 4.13 – Stopping the GCE instance using the Cloud console

Similar to stopping the instance, we can start it by clicking on the **START / RESUME** button when it is selected:

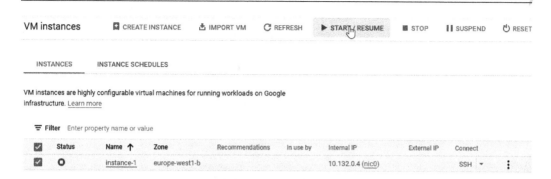

Figure 4.14 – Starting the GCE instance using the Cloud console

Command line

An instance can also be started by using the command line:

```
gcloud compute instances start INSTANCE-NAME --zone=ZONE-NAME
```

Here's an example – gcloud compute instances start instance-1 --zone=europe-west1-b.

To stop the instance, we need to execute the following command-line commandlet:

```
gcloud compute instances stop INSTANCE-NAME --zone=ZONE-NAME
```

Here's an example – gcloud compute instances stop instance-1 --zone=europe-west1-b.

Adding a public SSH key to a VM

GCE allows us to add SSH keys to Linux VMs during VM creation or to an existing VM. SSH keys are a popular way to administer Linux servers because they are more secure than passwords. Passwords can be easily guessed or stolen, but SSH keys are much more difficult to compromise. This makes SSH keys a more secure way to access Linux servers.

In addition, if the organization policy allows or configures it, it is possible to add a public SSH to project metadata to access all VMs in a project. This setting can be overridden during VM creation.

To learn more about creating SSH keys, visit the following link: https://cloud.google.com/compute/docs/connect/create-ssh-keys#linux-and-macos.

Console

To add an SSH key to a VM when it is created, we need to add it in the **NETWORKING, DISKS, SECURITY, MANAGEMENT, SOLE-TENANCY** section.

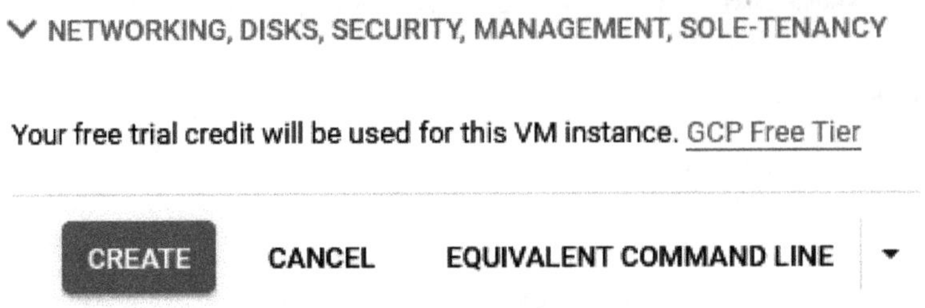

Figure 4.15 – Advanced options available when creating the VM

Once we open this menu and navigate to the **Security** option, we can click the + **ADD ITEM** button and add the public SSH key:

Security
Shielded VM and SSH keys

Shielded VM ❓
Turn on all settings for the most secure configuration.

- ☐ Turn on Secure Boot ❓
- ☑ Turn on vTPM ❓
- ☑ Turn on Integrity Monitoring ❓

VM access
Manage how users connect to the VM

> ✔ By default, when you connect to a VM using this console or gcloud, your SSH keys are generated automatically. Learn more

- ☐ Control VM access through IAM permissions ❓
  Link VM access to the user's IAM role. Enables OS Login. Learn more

  - ☐ Require 2-step verification
    Require a second form of user authentication. Learn more

- ☐ Block project-wide SSH keys
  When checked, project-wide SSH keys cannot access this instance. Learn more

Add manually generated SSH keys
Add your own keys for VM access through a 3rd-party tool. You cannot use these keys when IAM-based access (using OS Login) is enabled. Learn more

+ ADD ITEM

Figure 4.16 – The Security part of the advanced VM configuration

Once added, we can continue configuring VMs and creating them:

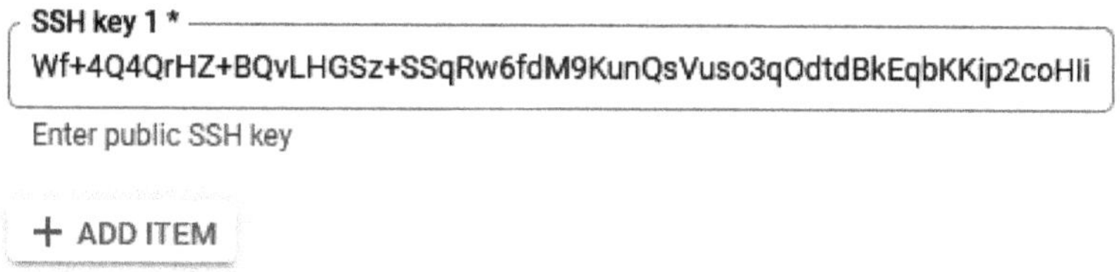

SSH key 1 *
Wf+4Q4QrHZ+BQvLHGSz+SSqRw6fdM9KunQsVuso3qOdtdBkEqbKKip2coHli

Enter public SSH key

+ ADD ITEM

Figure 4.17 – The SSH key added to the VM configuration during the creation process

We could also add it later if the VM were created without SSH keys during the creation process.

Click on the instance name and use the edit button to add the SSH key:

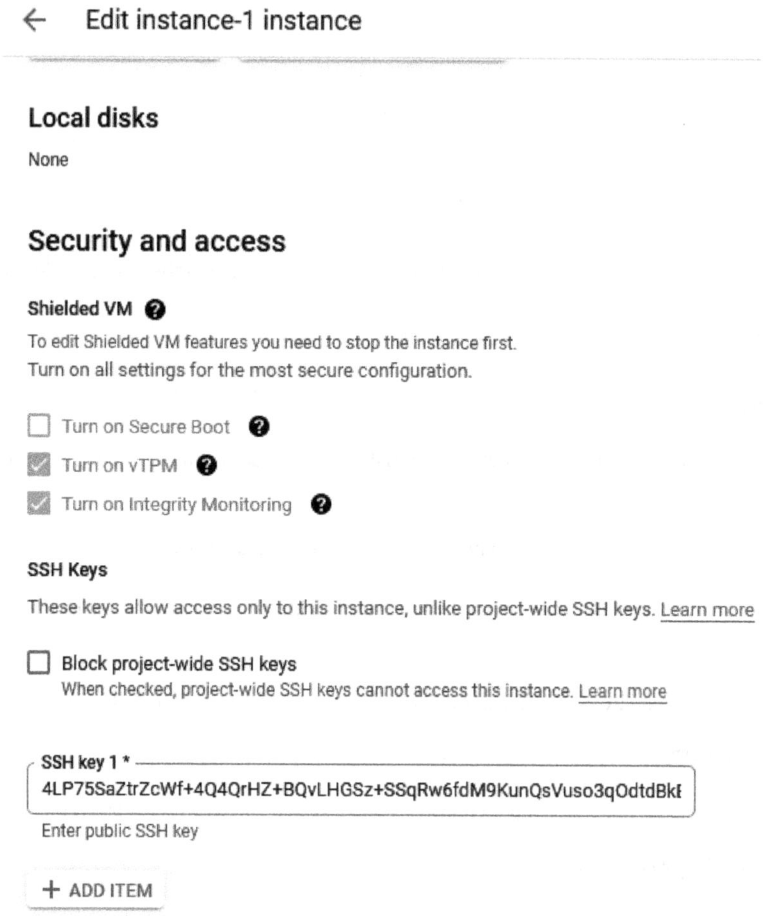

← Edit instance-1 instance

Local disks

None

Security and access

Shielded VM ❓

To edit Shielded VM features you need to stop the instance first.
Turn on all settings for the most secure configuration.

☐ Turn on Secure Boot ❓

☑ Turn on vTPM ❓

☑ Turn on Integrity Monitoring ❓

SSH Keys

These keys allow access only to this instance, unlike project-wide SSH keys. Learn more

☐ Block project-wide SSH keys
When checked, project-wide SSH keys cannot access this instance. Learn more

SSH key 1 *
4LP75SaZtrZcWf+4Q4QrHZ+BQvLHGSz+SSqRw6fdM9KunQsVuso3qOdtdBkł

Enter public SSH key

+ ADD ITEM

Figure 4.18 – The SSH key added to the running VM configuration

Once the SSH key has been added, confirm the change by clicking the **Save** button.

The SSH key will be visible in the **DETAILS** section of the VM:

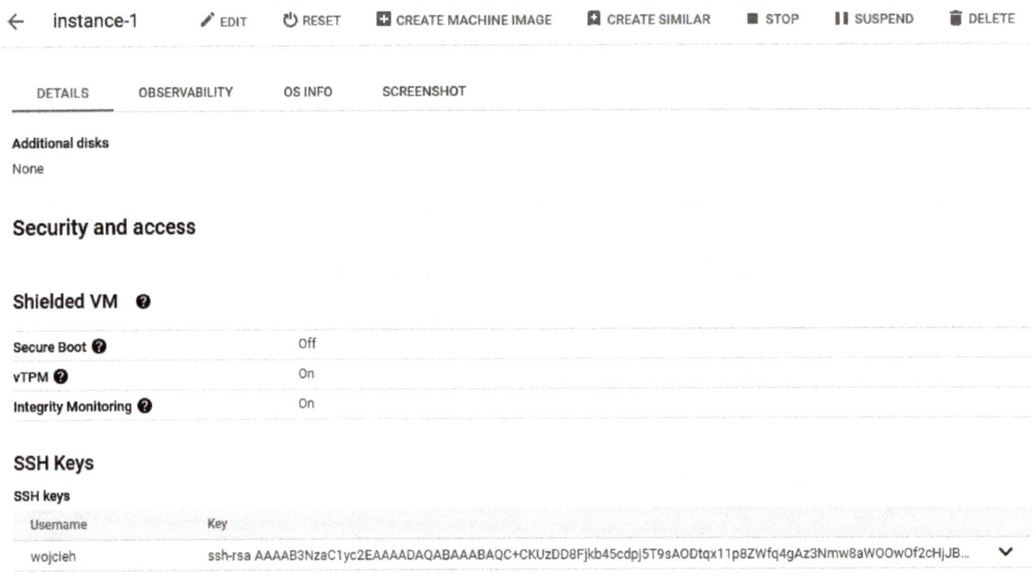

Figure 4.19 – The SSH key added to running VM configuration visible in the instance details page

Now, let's add the SSH keys using the command-line interface.

Command line

To create a VM and add the public SSH key to the instance metadata during the creation process, use the following command:

```
gcloud compute instances create VM_NAME --metadata=ssh-keys=PUBLIC_KEY
```

Once the VM has been created, we can update its metadata with the public SSH key using the following set of instructions:

1. First, we need to get the VM metadata. To do so, we need to use the following command:

    ```
    gcloud compute instances describe VM_NAME
    ```

2. Create an empty file, and add a username and key using the following format:

    ```
    USERNAME: KEY_VALUE
    ```

3. Save the file.

4. Use the following command line to update the instance metadata:

```
gcloud compute instances add-metadata VM_NAME --metadata-from-
file ssh-keys=KEY_FILE
```

The VM metadata will then be updated:

```
admin_@cloudshell:~ (wmarusiak-book-351718)$ gcloud compute inst
ances add-metadata instance-1 --zone=europe-west1-b  --metadata-
from-file ssh-keys=ssh-key.txt
Updated [https://www.googleapis.com/compute/v1/projects/wmarusia
k-book-351718/zones/europe-west1-b/instances/instance-1].
```

Figure 4.20 – The SSH key added to the running VM configuration using the command line

Once the changes are done, we can log in to the VM using SSH keys.

The next section focuses on deleting instances by using both the Cloud console and the gcloud command.

Deleting a VM

Deleting a VM is a very straightforward process. Let's try first to delete the VM in the Cloud console. In order to do that, you don't have to stop the VM in advance; the deletion can be done while it is running.

Console

Select the VM from the list and then click on the three dots:

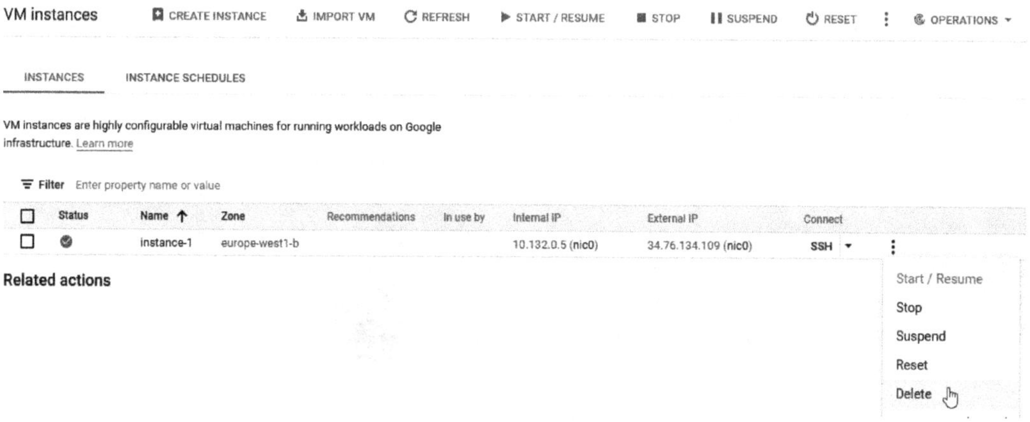

Figure 4.21 – The three dots menu with the option to delete the VM

Choose **Delete** as an action, and then confirm the deletion process:

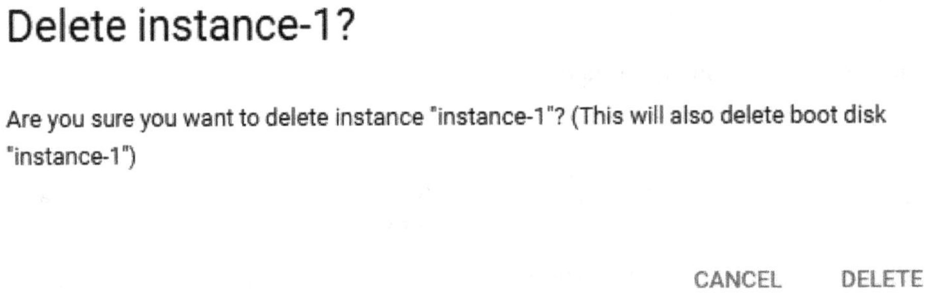

Delete instance-1?

Are you sure you want to delete instance "instance-1"? (This will also delete boot disk "instance-1")

CANCEL   DELETE

Figure 4.22 – Confirmation of the VM deletion

Once confirmed, the VM deletion process executes. Remember that this action can't be stopped.

Command line

The deletion process using the command line is straightforward. Use the following command to initiate the deletion process in the command-line interface:

```
gcloud compute instances delete VM_name
```

With each `gcloud` command, it might be necessary to add the zone where the VM runs. You can append the zone to each `gcloud` command. Otherwise, you might be asked to specify a zone.

To specify a zone, use `--zone=us-central1-a` in your `gcloud` command.

You will be asked whether you wish to proceed, and then the process will start:

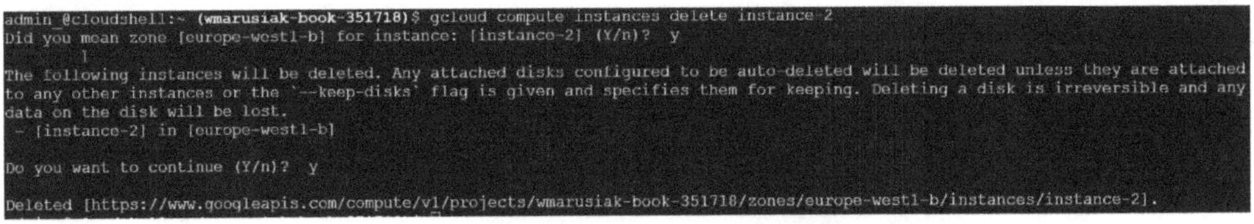

```
admin_@cloudshell:~ (wmarusiak-book-351718)$ gcloud compute instances delete instance-2
Did you mean zone [europe-west1-b] for instance: [instance-2] (Y/n)?  y
    ]
The following instances will be deleted. Any attached disks configured to be auto-deleted will be deleted unless they are attached
to any other instances or the `--keep-disks` flag is given and specifies them for keeping. Deleting a disk is irreversible and any
data on the disk will be lost.
 - [instance-2] in [europe-west1-b]

Do you want to continue (Y/n)?  y

Deleted [https://www.googleapis.com/compute/v1/projects/wmarusiak-book-351718/zones/europe-west1-b/instances/instance-2].
```

Figure 4.23 – VM deletion using the command-line interface

You can confirm that the instance has been deleted by executing the following command:

```
gcloud compute instances list
```

Once the command executes, you shouldn't see the instance you wanted to delete.

Adding a GPU to a VM

Graphical Processing Units (GPUs) can be added to the instances of a VM. GPUs can help render graphics-intensive workloads such as 3D visualization, 3D rendering, virtual applications, and ML computations. It is possible to add them to VMs to support those workloads.

Google Cloud offers many GPU platforms. The details can be found on this website: `https://cloud.google.com/compute/docs/gpus`.

To locate GPU models available in a specific region or zone, use the following link: `https://cloud.google.com/compute/docs/gpus/gpu-regions-zones`.

Console

Adding a GPU when a VM is created isn't any different from creating a *normal* VM.

To add a GPU to the VM, choose the **GPU VM under Machine family**. Once selected, you can specify the VM type and choose the desired amount of vCPUs, RAM, and GPUs:

Machine configuration

Machine family

GENERAL-PURPOSE   COMPUTE-OPTIMIZED   MEMORY-OPTIMIZED   GPU

Optimized for machine learning, high performance computing, and visualization workloads

GPU type
NVIDIA Tesla A100

Number of GPUs
1

☐ Enable Virtual Workstation (NVIDIA GRID)

Series
A2

Machine type
a2-highgpu-1g (12 vCPU, 85 GB memory)

	vCPU	Memory
	12	85 GB

CPU platform
Automatic

vCPUs to core ratio

Visible core count

Figure 4.24 – A GPU added to the VM during the creation process

Once the VM is created, you can check in the VM settings that the GPU has been added, and then you can start using it:

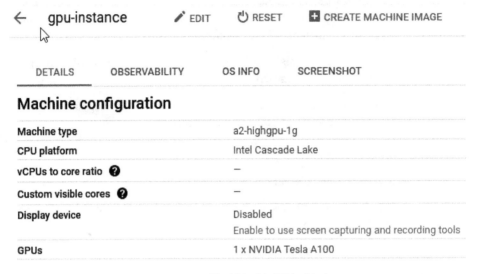

Figure 4.25 – The VM with GPU added

It is recommended to check the GPU quota in the desired region and increase it to meet your demands.

Command line

The following commandlet allows us to create a GPU-based VM:

```
gcloud compute instances create VM_NAME \
    --project PROJECT_ID \
    --zone us-central1-c \
    --machine-type a2-highgpu-1g \
    --maintenance-policy TERMINATE --restart-on-failure \
    --image-family centos-7 \
    --image-project centos-cloud \
    --boot-disk-size 200GB \
    --boot-disk-type pd-ssd
```

After creating the VM instance, installing the NVIDIA and CUDA drivers might be necessary in order to allow us to fully use the GPU's power.

Creating an instance template

An instance template is a resource that can be used to create individual instances or used in managed instance groups. It defines lots of information such as the machine type, the boot disk image, labels, start-up scripts, and other properties.

Console

The creation of an instance template is very similar to the creation of a single instance.

Please refer to the *Creating GCE section* for the details. The only difference between a single instance and a template is that the template is free and can be used with managed instance groups.

Command line

The command used to create an instance template differs from the one used to create a single instance:

```
gcloud compute instance-templates create INSTANCE_TEMPLATE_NAME
```

The instance-templates namespace has many switches and configuration options, so we highly recommend reading through the Cloud SDK reference and trying to make a one-instance template by using a command-line interface.

The following link describes the gcloud command switches and allows us to choose appropriate options to create an instance template: https://cloud.google.com/sdk/gcloud/reference/compute/instance-templates/create.

Connecting remotely to a VM

Remote management of instances is a critical topic. It is not only complex but also important from a security point of view. We have all heard about big companies having their clouds hacked, so we should try to ensure that we access instances securely.

We will connect to two types of instances – Linux and Windows. We will access Linux instances using SSH keys (no username and password access) and the SSH protocol, which uses network port 22. Windows Server instances can be accessed using a native protocol called **Remote Desktop Protocol (RDP)**, which uses network port 3389.

We must allow the required network port in the firewall table to access instances remotely. Firewalls will be discussed in more detail in upcoming chapters, but we must remember to allow network traffic in the VPC Firewall table to connect.

Bastion hosts

Bastion hosts are VMs that provide secure access to other VMs in a GCP network. They should be hardened to be more secure than other VMs in the network. This includes using strong passwords and SSH keys, keeping the software up to date, and disabling unnecessary services. The idea is to restrict their access to your on-premises networks or specific narrowed-down network ranges.

Sometimes, bastion hosts are called jump boxes or jump servers. Regardless of the name, the idea is the same. They are secure and allow you to access your cloud infrastructure.

To learn more about bastion hosts and how to securely connect to the Google Cloud instances, visit the following link: https://cloud.google.com/solutions/connecting-securely.

Identity-Aware Proxy

Although **Identity-Aware Proxy (IAP)** isn't a part of the Associate Cloud Engineer exam, I'd like to introduce this Google Cloud product as something that'll be a significant security improvement to your infrastructure.

IAP allows you to securely connect to your instances without a public IP address to both Linux and Windows operating systems. IAP provides a single point of control for managing users and access to systems with just HTTPS access, as can be seen in the following diagram (for more details, refer to `https://cloud.google.com/iap/images/iap-load-balancer.png`):

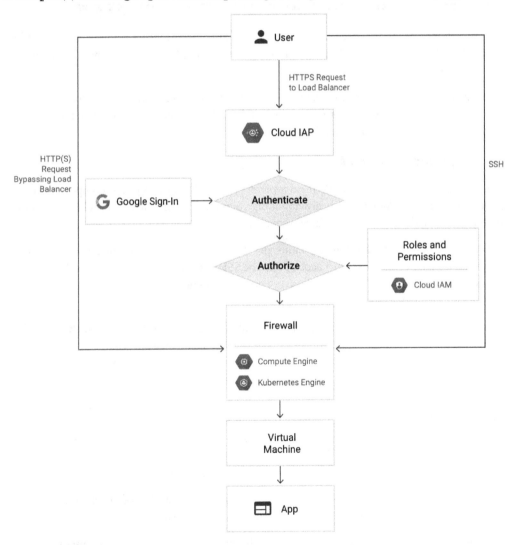

Figure 4.26 – Access to VMs with IAP

To learn more about IAP, visit the Google Cloud documentation: `https://cloud.google.com/iap/docs/concepts-overview`.

Linux instances

For our purposes, we will not use IAP or OS login, which is available to connect to Linux instances. Still, we encourage you to try to connect to both possibilities using both options.

Console

Instances can be accessed from within the Cloud console itself by using Cloud Shell or any other software of your preference available on your operating system.

The following screenshot shows the different ways to connect to a Linux instance:

Figure 4.27 – A Linux instance with options to connect via SSH

We have many options on how we can connect to the instance. They are as follows:

- Open an SSH connection in the browser window
- Open an SSH connection in the browser window on a custom port
- Open SSH connection in the browser window using a provided private SSH key

The most straightforward connection can be achieved by clicking on the SSH button, and a new window will open where we have full access to the instance:

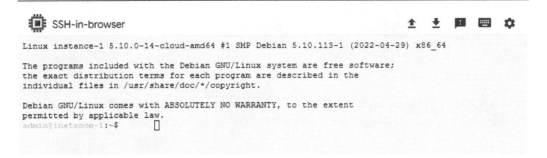

Figure 4.28 – In the browser, an SSH connection to the instance

This connectivity is effortless to establish and use.

Command line

To access an instance from the Cloud Shell, we need to execute the following command:

```
gcloud compute ssh --zone "zone_name" "instance_name" --project
"project_name"
```

The following screenshot shows that the connection to Cloud Shell using the `gcloud` command is very easy to establish.

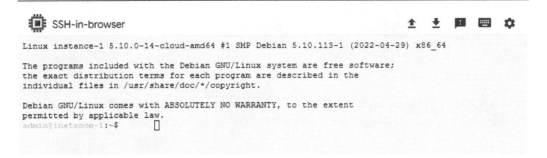

Figure 4.29 – An SSH connection to the instance from Cloud Shell

As many SSH clients are available for many operating systems, it is impossible to cover them all in this book.

The following screenshot shows the SSH session established with the instance, using its public IP address and the PuTTY SSH client from the Windows operating system:

```
rsa-key-20220529@instance-1: ~                                    —    □    ×
 Using username "rsa-key-20220529".
 Authenticating with public key "rsa-key-20220529"
Linux instance-1 5.10.0-14-cloud-amd64 #1 SMP Debian 5.10.113-1 (2022-04-29) x86
_64

The programs included with the Debian GNU/Linux system are free software;
the exact distribution terms for each program are described in the
individual files in /usr/share/doc/*/copyright.

Debian GNU/Linux comes with ABSOLUTELY NO WARRANTY, to the extent
permitted by applicable law.
rsa-key-20220529@instance-1:~$ w
 21:21:26 up 11 min,  1 user,  load average: 0.00, 0.00, 0.00
USER     TTY      FROM            LOGIN@   IDLE   JCPU   PCPU WHAT
rsa-key- pts/0    94.114.144.78   21:21    0.00s  0.00s  0.00s w
rsa-key-20220529@instance-1:~$     ~ ~~=^Z^C
rsa-key-20220529@instance-1:~$ []
```

Figure 4.30 – An SSH connection to the instance from Cloud Shell

Connecting to instances is quite an important topic, and we strongly advise trying out connectivity via the SSH protocol.

Windows Server instances

Google Cloud allows us to use Windows Server images alongside Linux ones. Before initiating the RDP connection to the Windows Server-based instance, we need to change our initial password.

To do this, click on your Windows Server instance and choose **Set Windows password**:

Figure 4.31 – Setting the Windows instance password

You can either reset a password for the existing user or create a new user by typing a new username in the **Username** field:

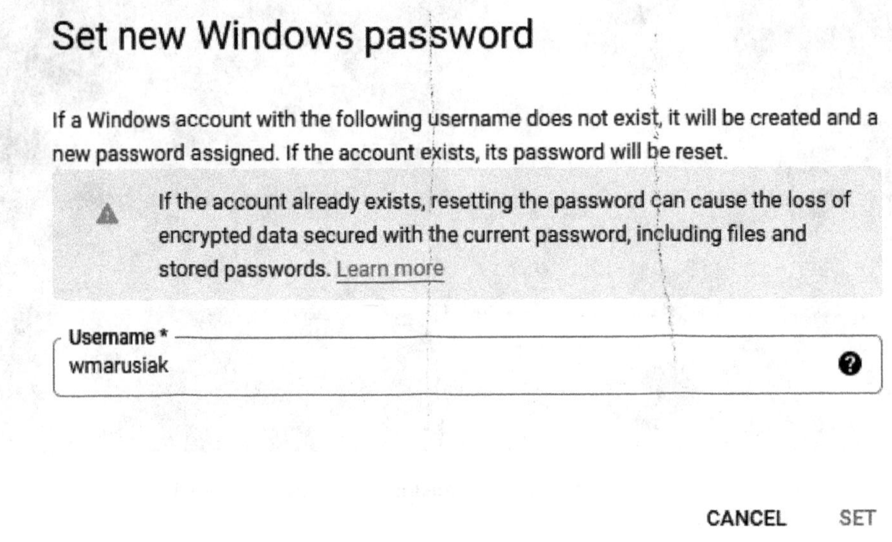

Set new Windows password

If a Windows account with the following username does not exist, it will be created and a new password assigned. If the account exists, its password will be reset.

⚠   If the account already exists, resetting the password can cause the loss of encrypted data secured with the current password, including files and stored passwords. Learn more

Username *
wmarusiak   ❓

CANCEL   SET

Figure 4.32 – The Set new Windows password screen

After a moment, a new password for the specified user will be displayed:

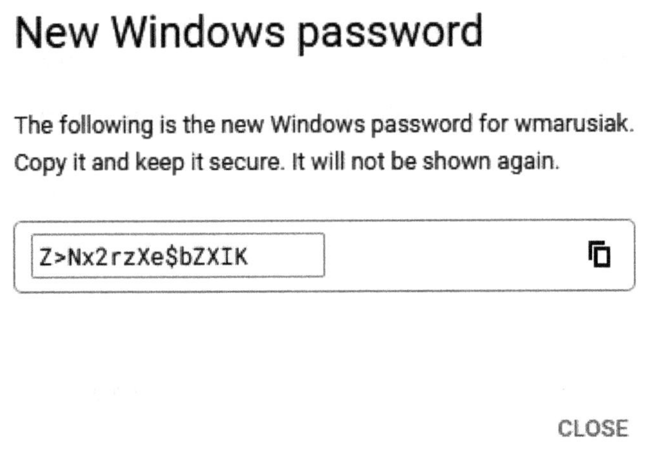

New Windows password

The following is the new Windows password for wmarusiak. Copy it and keep it secure. It will not be shown again.

Z>Nx2rzXe$bZXIK

CLOSE

Figure 4.33 – The password for the user displayed in the console

If the port TCP 3389 is open and the firewall rule is created, we can connect using the RDP client of our choice:

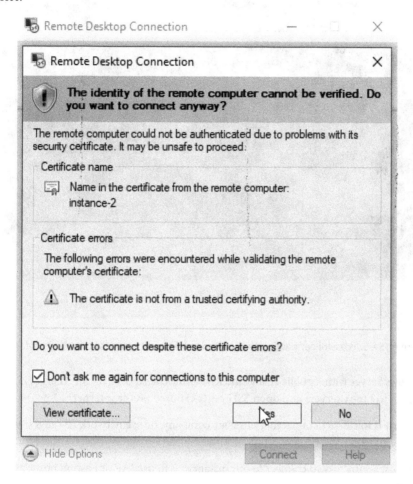

Figure 4.34 – Connecting to the Windows Server instance

After a moment, we are connected to the instance:

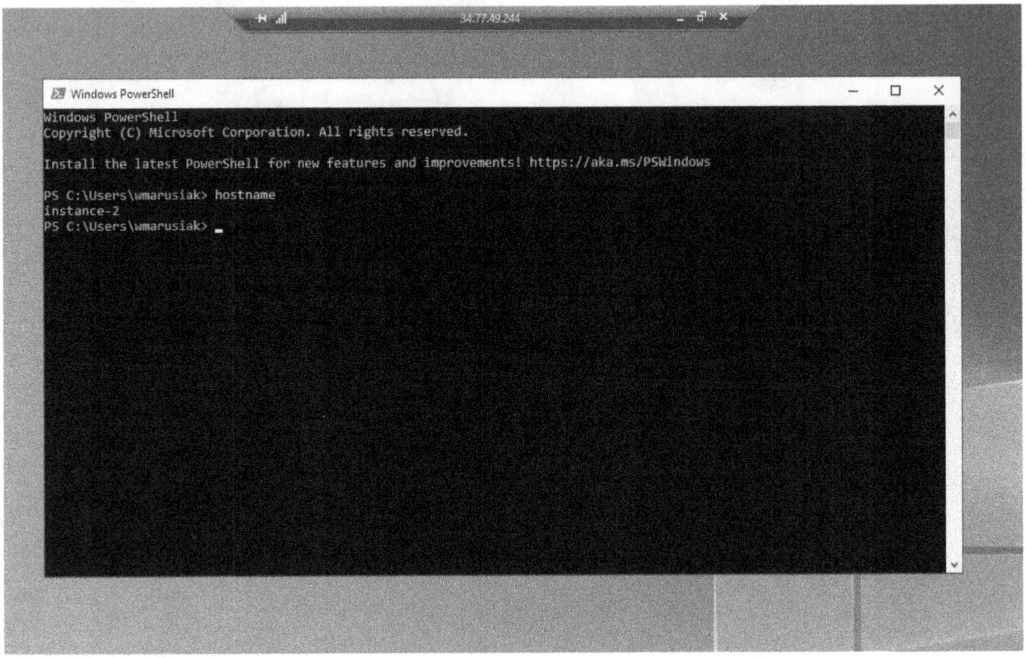

Figure 4.35 – Successful connection to the Windows Server instance via the RDP protocol

Having Windows Server with a public IP and the RDP protocol exposed on the internet is a bad idea. This also applies to Linux servers and open SSH ports exposed on the internet.

The best solution is to restrict connectivity to your company, or use network IP ranges to minimize security breaches.

The best and most secure way to connect to our instances is to use IAP or bastion hosts, as described earlier in the chapter.

GCE storage

An essential part of using Compute Engine is storage-related operations. It is impossible to cover all combinations of tasks, so we will list the most important ones that will help you gain practical knowledge and confidence when taking the Associate Cloud Engineer exam.

GCE Storage options

Compute Engine offers several storage options for VM instances. Each of the following storage options has unique price and performance characteristics:

- Persistent Disk volumes provide high-performance and redundant network storage. Each Persistent Disk volume is striped across hundreds of physical disks:

  - By default, VMs use zonal persistent disks and store data on volumes located within a single zone, such as us-west1-c

  - It is also possible to create regional persistent disks, which synchronously replicate data between disks located in two zones and provide protection if a zone becomes unavailable

- Hyperdisk volumes offer the fastest redundant network storage for Compute Engine, with configurable performance and volumes that can be dynamically resized.

- Local SSDs are physical drives attached directly to the same server as your VM. They can offer better performance but are ephemeral.

Google Cloud has prepared a great overview of each storage option with information about minimum and maximum capacity, the scope of access, and maximum capacity per instance. To read in detail about each disk type, visit the following URL: https://cloud.google.com/compute/docs/disks#introduction.

Adding a disk to a VM

We will start with one of the most straightforward tasks – adding an additional disk to an instance.

Console

In the Cloud console, we will start by adding an additional disk:

1. To add a disk to the existing instance, click on its name in the Cloud console.

2. Once the instance is selected, click **EDIT**:

Figure 4.36 – Editing the instance in the Cloud console

3. Navigate to the **Additional disks** section and choose to add a new disk. This will open a new window where we can create and attach a disk to the instance:

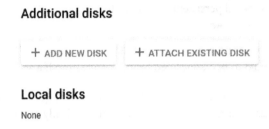

Figure 4.37 – The Additional disks section in the EDIT section of the instance

4. In the new window, we have many options to choose from:

    • **Name**: The name of the disk.

    • **Description**: We can describe what the purpose of the disk is or why we want to add it.

    • **Source**: This can be a blank disk, image, or snapshot.

    • **Disk type**: We have the following options: a balanced persistent disk, an extreme persistent disk, an SSD persistent disk, and a standard persistent disk. If you click the **Compare disk types** button, a comparison will help you choose the best disk based on the workload:

Compare disk types

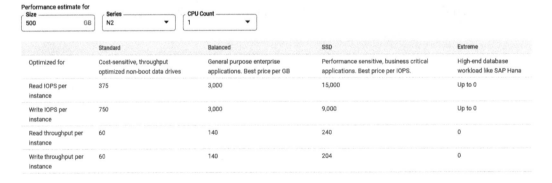

Figure 4.38 – A table with a comparison of all available disk types in Google Cloud

    • **Size**: We can enter disk sizes between 10 and 65,536 GB.

- **Snapshot schedule**: If a snapshot schedule was previously created, we can use it to enable automatic snapshots on the disk we create.

- **Encryption**: Google Cloud allows us to pick from three encryption options – a Google-managed encryption key, a **customer-managed encryption key** (**CMEK**) where we leverage Google's Cloud Key Management Service, and a **customer-supplied encryption key** (**CSEK**) where encryption keys are managed outside of Google Cloud.

- **Labels**: This allows us to organize projects and resources easily by adding key-value pairs to the resources – for example, we could label a newly added disk with a key and its value (e.g., key = department and value = infrastructure). Labels allow us to easily organize resources and use filters.

- **Disk attachment mode**: We can attach disks in read/write or read-only mode.

- **Deletion rule**: We can decide to keep the disk or delete it when we delete the instance that the disk is attached to

- **Device name**

5. Once all parameters are selected, click the **Save** button to attach the disk to the instance. This doesn't mean that we can put files on it right away. There's another step that involves formatting and mounting the disk in the operating system itself:

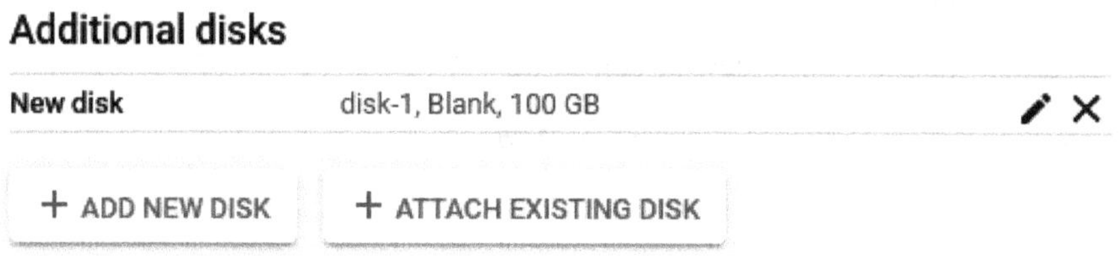

Additional disks

New disk	disk-1, Blank, 100 GB	✏ ✕

+ ADD NEW DISK   + ATTACH EXISTING DISK

Figure 4.39 – A new disk is added to the instance

6. After a moment in the storage section of the VM, both disks (the boot disk) and the newly added disk are visible:

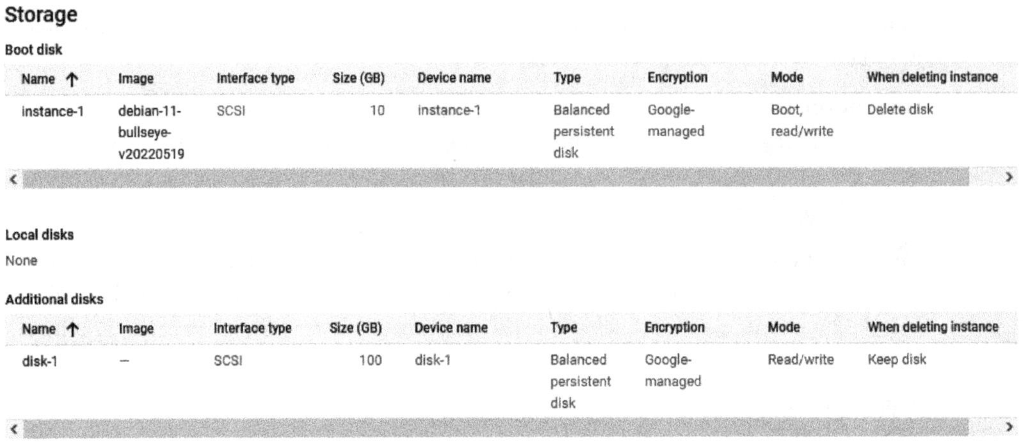

Storage

Boot disk

Name ↑	Image	Interface type	Size (GB)	Device name	Type	Encryption	Mode	When deleting instance
instance-1	debian-11-bullseye-v20220519	SCSI	10	instance-1	Balanced persistent disk	Google-managed	Boot, read/write	Delete disk

<   >

Local disks

None

Additional disks

Name ↑	Image	Interface type	Size (GB)	Device name	Type	Encryption	Mode	When deleting instance
disk-1	—	SCSI	100	disk-1	Balanced persistent disk	Google-managed	Read/write	Keep disk

<   >

Figure 4.40 – A new disk is visible in the instance configuration section

We will perform the same operation in the next section using the command-line interface.

Command line

The command-line interface consists of two steps. The first step is to create a disk, and the second is to attach it to the instance.

To create a disk, we will initiate the following command:

```
gcloud compute disks create additional-disk \
      --zone=europe-west1-b\
      --size=200GB \
      --type=pd-balanced
```

The next step is to attach the newly created disk to the instance:

```
gcloud compute instances attach-disk instance-1 \
   --disk additional-disk \
   --zone=europe-west1-b
```

The commands were executed successfully, and we can check whether the disk was attached by running the following command:

```
gcloud compute instances describe instance-1 --zone=europe-west1-b
```

The output of the gcloud command shows the disk attached to the instance, as shown here:

```
index: 0
interface: SCSI
kind: compute#attachedDisk
licenses:
- https://www.googleapis.com/compute/v1/projects/debian-cloud/global/licenses/debian-11-bullseye
mode: READ_WRITE
source: https://www.googleapis.com/compute/v1/projects/wmarusiak-book/zones/europe-west1-b/disks/instance-1
type: PERSISTENT
- autoDelete: false
boot: false
deviceName: disk-1
diskSizeGb: '100'
index: 1
interface: SCSI
kind: compute#attachedDisk
mode: READ_WRITE
source: https://www.googleapis.com/compute/v1/projects/wmarusiak-book/zones/europe-west1-b/disks/disk-1
type: PERSISTENT
- autoDelete: false
boot: false
deviceName: persistent-disk-2
diskSizeGb: '200'
index: 2
interface: SCSI
kind: compute#attachedDisk
mode: READ_WRITE
source: https://www.googleapis.com/compute/v1/projects/wmarusiak-book/zones/europe-west1-b/disks/additional-disk
```

Figure 4.41 – A new disk is visible in the instance by using the command line

After learning how to add the additional disks to the instance, we will move on to the next section, which involves deleting the disk from the instances.

Deleting a disk from a VM

We will now demonstrate how to remove a 10-GB disk from an instance using the Cloud console and command-line tools. We want to mention one crucial piece of information here – we can't delete a disk attached to an instance.

Console

In the console, navigate to **Compute Engine**, click on the desired instance, and choose **Edit**.

Once the instance details load, scroll to the storage section and remove the additional disk from the instance by clicking the **X** button.

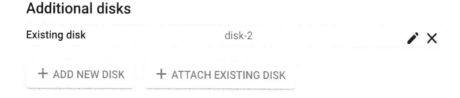

Figure 4.42 – Removal of the additional disk from the instance by clicking the X button

After clicking the **Save** button, the disk deletion is in progress. The deletion process depends on the setting in the deletion rule. When the disk is added, it can either be kept or deleted instantly.

Command line

Like adding a disk to the instance by using the command line, deleting the disk from the instance is a two-way process.

First, we need to edit the instance and detach the disk from it, and then we need to delete the detached disk.

In the command-line interface, we need to find the name of the disk device that we want to remove. Use the following command to find it out:

```
gcloud compute instances describe instance-1 --zone=europe-west1-b
```

The following screenshot shows the output of the preceding command:

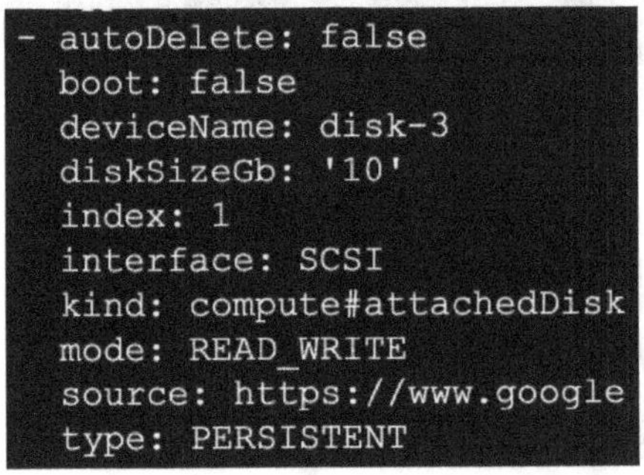

```
- autoDelete: false
  boot: false
  deviceName: disk-3
  diskSizeGb: '10'
  index: 1
  interface: SCSI
  kind: compute#attachedDisk
  mode: READ_WRITE
  source: https://www.google
  type: PERSISTENT
```

Figure 4.43 – The additional disk with its deviceName information

With the information about the deviceName flag, we can initiate a command to detach it from the instance:

```
gcloud compute instances detach-disk instance-1 --zone=europe-west1-b
--device-name=disk-3
```

After a short period, removing the disk from the instance is finished.

To completely delete the detached disk, we need to execute the following command:

```
gcloud compute disks delete deviceName
```

The following figure shows the output of the command:

```
admin_@cloudshell:~ (wmarusiak-book)$ gcloud compute disks delete disk-3
Did you mean zone [europe-west1-b] for disk: [disk-3] (Y/n)?  y

The following disks will be deleted:
 - [disk-3] in [europe-west1-b]

Do you want to continue (Y/n)?  y

Deleted [https://www.googleapis.com/compute/v1/projects/wmarusiak-book/zones/europe-west1-b/disks/disk-3].
admin_@cloudshell:~ (wmarusiak-book)$
```

Figure 4.44 – The additional disk with its deviceName information

Disk deletion was completed.

Resizing a disk

A typical operation when working with instances is resizing a disk. We do it mainly when the disk is full and needs more capacity.

Console

To increase the disk size, we need to go to the storage section of the Cloud console and click **Disks**. Choose the desired disk you want to increase by clicking its name and then clicking on the three dots. Choose **EDIT** to increase the disk size:

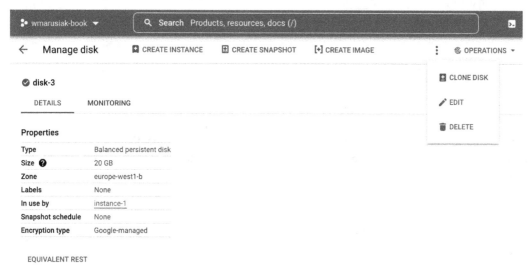

Figure 4.45 – Detailed information about the existing disk attached to the VM

Enter a new disk size and click **SAVE**:

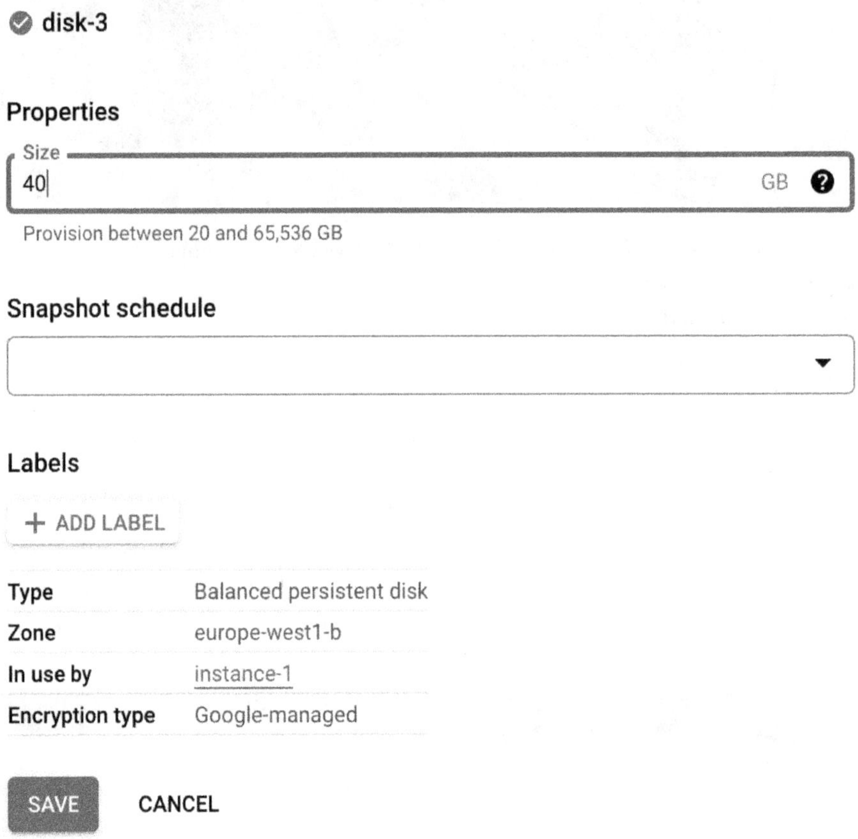

✅ **disk-3**

Properties

Size

| 40| | GB | ❓ |

Provision between 20 and 65,536 GB

Snapshot schedule

| ▼ |

Labels

+ ADD LABEL

Type	Balanced persistent disk
Zone	europe-west1-b
In use by	instance-1
Encryption type	Google-managed

[SAVE]   CANCEL

Figure 4.46 – Change of disk size in cloud console

After a moment, the disk size will be increased to the desired size. Remember that increasing the disk size in the Cloud console doesn't update the filesystem in the instance itself. You must extend the filesystem itself to use increase the capacity.

Command line

To increase the disk size, we need to get its name first. Utilize the command from the task, Deleting a disk from a VM .

Once you have the disk name, use the following command to resize it:

```
gcloud compute disks resize DISK_NAME --zone=ZONE_NAME --size=XXXGB
```

One thing to remember is the disk size limit for instances. The size limit for a single disk is 65,536 GB, and the maximum capacity for a local SSD is 375 GB. The maximum storage capacity per instance is 257 TB and 9 TB for local SSDs.

Creating an instance snapshot

An instance snapshot allows us to capture the state of a disk at a snapshot creation point in time. Snapshots can be used to go back in time to when a snapshot was created. Snapshots are the easiest feature to utilize if you want to revert to a different state quickly.

Snapshots use cases are as follows:

- Quickly reverting to the previous state of the disk
- Operating system patching
- Application patching
- Operating system changes

One important thing to remember is that snapshots aren't a backup. Although they provide similar functionality, snapshots aren't backups for the following reasons:

- Backups should be independent of the source VM
- Snapshots don't provide a capability for granular restore options such as file restoration

Let's create our first snapshot of the disk.

Console

In the Cloud console, navigate to **Snapshots** and click **Create a snapshot**.

We need to provide a name for the snapshot, (optionally) add a snapshot description, and choose a source disk:

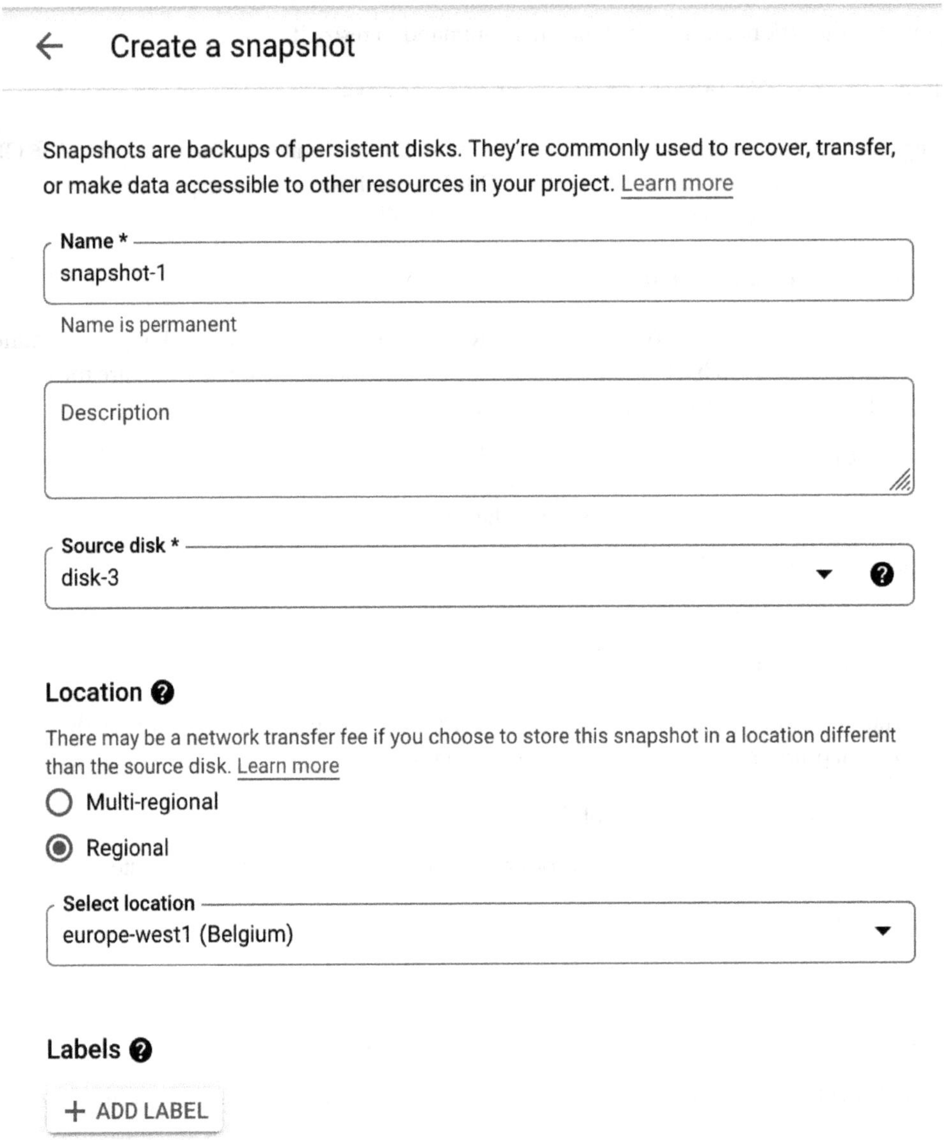

← **Create a snapshot**

Snapshots are backups of persistent disks. They're commonly used to recover, transfer, or make data accessible to other resources in your project. Learn more

Name *

snapshot-1

Name is permanent

Description

Source disk *

disk-3   ▼   ❷

Location ❷

There may be a network transfer fee if you choose to store this snapshot in a location different than the source disk. Learn more

○ Multi-regional

◉ Regional

Select location

europe-west1 (Belgium)   ▼

Labels ❷

+ ADD LABEL

Figure 4.47 – The initial snapshot configuration section

We can use multi-regional or regional snapshot locations, add labels, choose encryption, and use application-consistent snapshots:

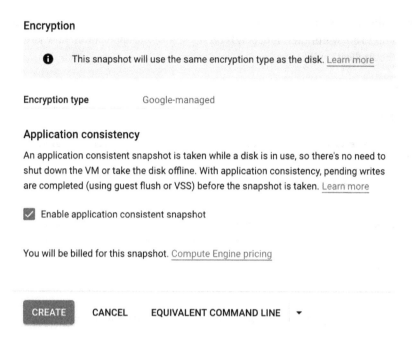

Figure 4.48 – Section two of the snapshot creation

An application-consistent snapshot allows us to preserve application consistency and uses operating system features such as the **Volume Shadow Copy (VSS)** Service in Windows.

If you want a 100% consistent snapshot without any application or data corruption, we highly suggest powering off the instance before taking a snapshot.

In the last step, click **CREATE** to initiate snapshot creation. Remember that when creating a snapshot, we do so for just one selected disk:

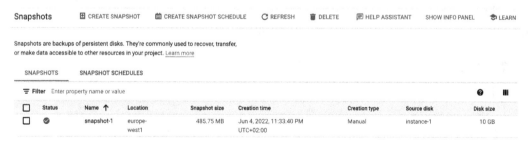

Figure 4.49 – Newly created snapshot visible on the Snapshots page

After a moment, the snapshot of the disk is created and can be used. Snapshot creation can take from several seconds up to a few minutes. It depends on the size of the application, how large the disk is, and how **busy** the application is.

Command line

To perform a disk snapshot, we can run the following command:

```
gcloud compute snapshots create SNAPSHOT_NAME --source-disk=SOURCE_
DISK_NAME --source-disk-zone=DISK_ZONE
```

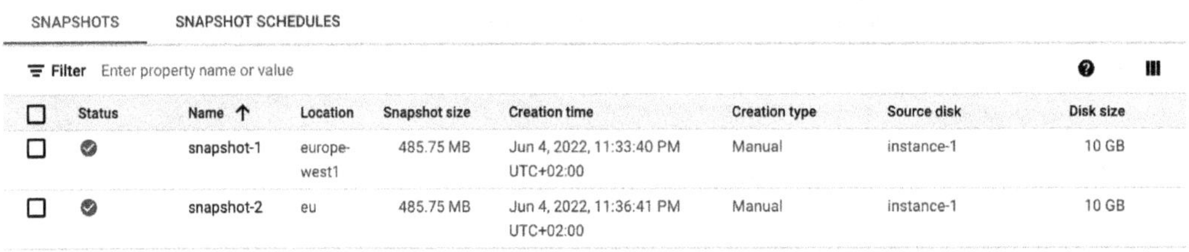

SNAPSHOTS	SNAPSHOT SCHEDULES							
⇒ Filter Enter property name or value							❷	Ⅲ
□	Status	Name ↑	Location	Snapshot size	Creation time	Creation type	Source disk	Disk size
□	✓	snapshot-1	europe-west1	485.75 MB	Jun 4, 2022, 11:33:40 PM UTC+02:00	Manual	instance-1	10 GB
□	✓	snapshot-2	eu	485.75 MB	Jun 4, 2022, 11:36:41 PM UTC+02:00	Manual	instance-1	10 GB

Figure 4.50 – A command-line snapshot is created

Snapshot creation takes a moment.

After successfully creating the snapshot, we can proceed to delete snapshots.

Deleting an instance snapshot

Deletion of the snapshot is a straightforward process.

Console

In the Cloud console, navigate to the **Snapshots** section of **Storage**. Select the desired snapshot and click **DELETE**:

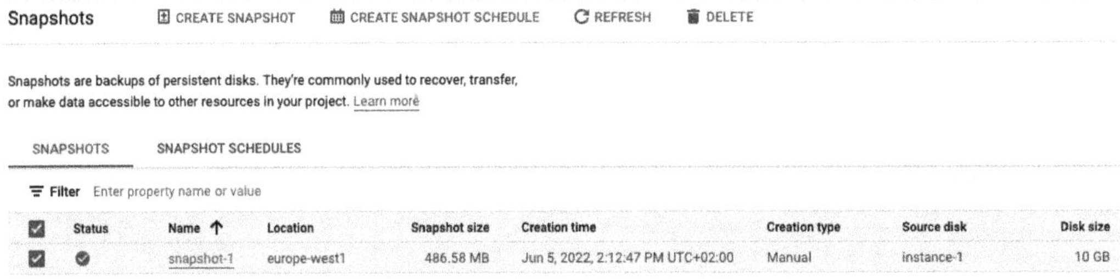

Snapshots	⊞ CREATE SNAPSHOT	⊟ CREATE SNAPSHOT SCHEDULE	↻ REFRESH	🗑 DELETE

Snapshots are backups of persistent disks. They're commonly used to recover, transfer, or make data accessible to other resources in your project. Learn more

SNAPSHOTS	SNAPSHOT SCHEDULES						
⇒ Filter Enter property name or value							
☑	Status	Name ↑	Location	Snapshot size	Creation time	Creation type	Source disk	Disk size
☑	✓	snapshot-1	europe-west1	486.58 MB	Jun 5, 2022, 2:12:47 PM UTC+02:00	Manual	instance-1	10 GB

Figure 4.51 – Snapshot deletion in the Cloud console

After clicking **DELETE SNAPSHOT**, the deletion takes place.

Command line

Before we can delete a snapshot, we need to know its name and refer to it in the command-line interface.

To list existing snapshots, we need to execute the following command:

```
gcloud compute snapshots list
```

Once we have a list of existing snapshots, we can delete them by executing the following command:

```
gcloud compute snapshots delete SNAPSHOT_NAME
```

The following screenshot shows the deletion of the snapshot:

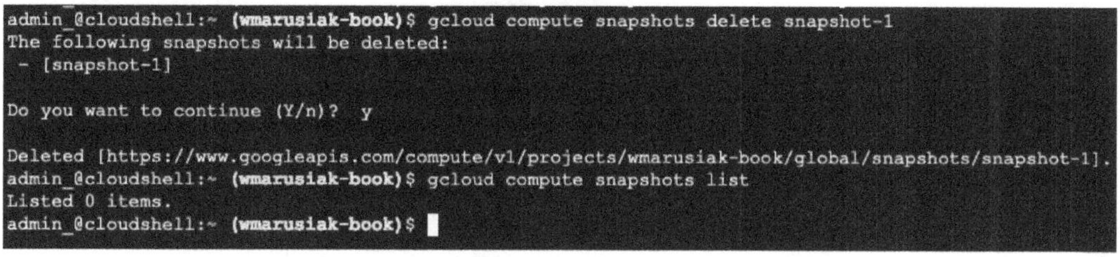

```
admin_@cloudshell:~ (wmarusiak-book)$ gcloud compute snapshots delete snapshot-1
The following snapshots will be deleted:
 - [snapshot-1]

Do you want to continue (Y/n)?  y

Deleted [https://www.googleapis.com/compute/v1/projects/wmarusiak-book/global/snapshots/snapshot-1].
admin_@cloudshell:~ (wmarusiak-book)$ gcloud compute snapshots list
Listed 0 items.
admin_@cloudshell:~ (wmarusiak-book)$
```

Figure 4.52 – A screenshot of the snapshot deletion

As we see in the previous screenshot, the snapshot has been deleted and is no longer present.

Creating an instance snapshot schedule

As we saw, manual snapshot creation works and can be done in the Cloud console and by using command-line tools. There is another possible method, which is to create a snapshot scheduler. This allows us to configure certain things, similar to when we use snapshots:

- The schedule location
- The snapshot location
- Frequency
- The deletion rule
- Application consistency
- Labels

Having the necessary information about the requirements, we can now proceed to create a snapshot schedule in the Cloud console.

Console

In the Cloud console, we need to add details to all the aforementioned necessary fields, and once the snapshot schedule is created, we need to add the disk that to the schedule:

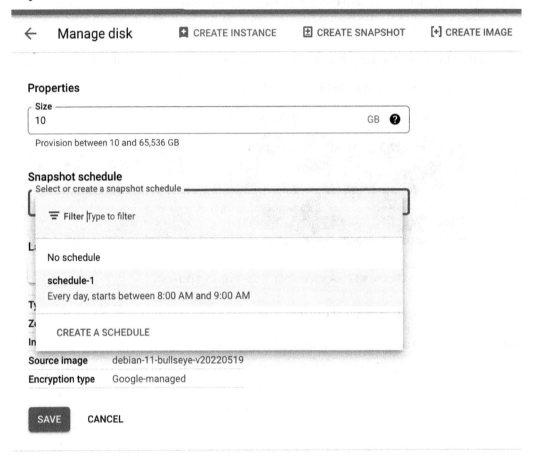

Figure 4.53 – Attaching a snapshot schedule to the disk

Once the disk is added, the snapshot will be executed as per our configuration.

Command line

Similar to the Cloud console, we need to first create a snapshot schedule:

```
gcloud compute resource-policies create snapshot-schedule SCHEDULE_
NAME --project=PROJECT_NAME --region=REGION_NAME --max-retention-
days=XX --on-source-disk-delete=keep-auto-snapshots --daily-schedule
--start-time=08:00 --storage-location=REGION_NAME
```

After creating the snapshot schedule, we need to attach it to the instance disk to utilize the feature. Use the following command to do so:

```
gcloud compute disks add-resource-policies DISK_NAME
--resourcepolicies=SCHEDULE_NAME --zone=ZONE_NAME
```

After initiating the command, the disk will be attached to a snapshot schedule.

Creating an instance image

Custom images are the best solution if you want to reuse the fully preconfigured operating system with custom applications and settings. It is possible to create custom instance images from source disks, images, snapshots, or images stored in Cloud Storage and use these images to create VM instances.

Console

Let's create a custom instance image based on the existing disk. We encourage you to test other image sources as well.

In the Cloud console, navigate to the **Disks** section in Compute Engine. Select the desired disk image used as the source image:

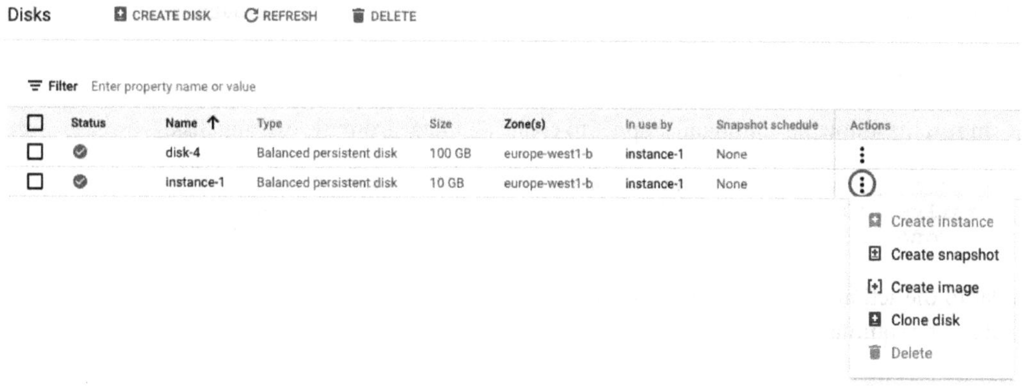

Figure 4.54 – Choosing a disk as a base for a new custom image

Before clicking **Create image**, it is recommended to stop the instance to guarantee that filesystem consistency is preserved. You can force image creation while the instance runs, but you must be aware of the possible consequences.

We need to provide the following information to create an image:

- Name
- Source: This can be a disk, snapshot, image, cloud storage file, or virtual disk in the VMDK or VHD format

- `Source Disk`
- `Location`: Multi-regional or regional
- `Family`
- `Labels`
- `Encryption`: This can be a Google-managed encryption key, a CMEK, or a CSEK

After a moment, the image is created, and then we can utilize this image to create new instances.

Figure 4.55 – A newly created custom image, visible in the Images section of the Cloud console

Images can be imported and exported – both operations are available in the **Images** section.

Command line

We can run the following command snippet to create an image from the existing disk:

```
gcloud compute images create IMAGE_NAME --project=PROJECT_NAME
--family=IMAGE_FAMILY_NAME --source-disk=SOURCE_DISK_NAME --source-
disk-zone=SOURCE_DISK_ZONE --storage-location=STORAGE_LOCATION
```

Similar to the actions performed in the Cloud console, an image created from the disk is made after initiating the commands.

Deleting an instance image

Deleting an instance image involves a few steps in the Cloud console and two stages in the command line.

Console

To delete an instance image in the **Images** section of Compute Engine, we need to select the desired image. Remember that it isn't possible to delete the images provided by Google Cloud. We can only delete the images that we created.

To delete an image, select it and click **DELETE**:

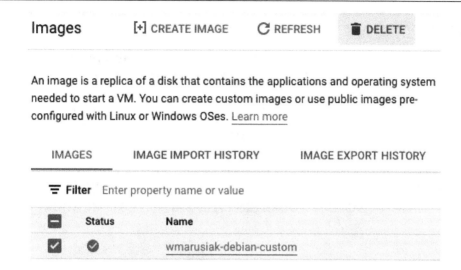

Figure 4.56 – Deletion of an image in the Cloud console

Image deletion takes a moment and cannot be reversed.

Command line

Before we can delete an image, we need to know its name. To list all images and omit the ones from Google Cloud, run the following command:

```
gcloud compute images list --no-standard-images
```

If we don't use the -no-standard-images switch, we will receive a list of all images available.

To delete the image, execute the following command:

```
gcloud compute images delete IMAGE_NAME
```

On the command line, we will receive confirmation that the image is deleted. You can execute the previous command to list all the images again and check whether it is listed.

In the next section, we will perform network-related activities.

The GCE network

Network-related activities are as important as overall management and storage activities – not only in real life when working with Google Cloud but also for the exam.

The following tasks represent Compute Engine networking activities. The upcoming chapter is dedicated to covering VPC, VPN, and Load Balancer networking resources.

Configuring an instance with a static internal IP address

Reserving a static internal IP address before creating a VM is possible. Alternatively, we can create an instance with an ephemeral internal IP address and convert it in to a static internal IP address.

Console

To reserve a static internal IP address in the Cloud console, follow these steps:

1. Go to the VPC networks.
2. Choose the desired VPC network where you want to reserve a static internal IP address.
3. Click **STATIC INTERNAL IP ADDRESSES** and then **RESERVE STATIC ADDRESS**.
4. We need to enter the details for the following fields in the form:

    *   **Name**
    *   **Description**
    *   **Subnet**: The subnet where we want to reserve the static IP address
    *   **Static IP address**: Select to assign it automatically or manually
    *   **Purpose**: Shared or non-shared

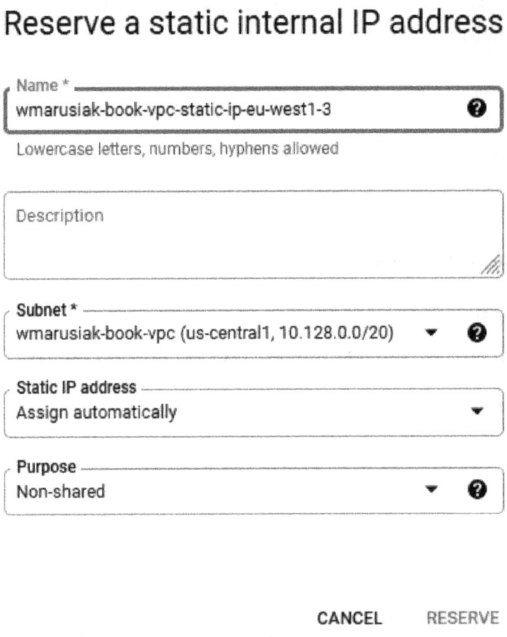

Reserve a static internal IP address

Name *
wmarusiak-book-vpc-static-ip-eu-west1-3   ❷

Lowercase letters, numbers, hyphens allowed

Description

Subnet *
wmarusiak-book-vpc (us-central1, 10.128.0.0/20)   ▼   ❷

Static IP address
Assign automatically   ▼

Purpose
Non-shared   ▼   ❷

CANCEL   RESERVE

Figure 4.57 – Reserving a static internal IP address

You have the option to choose a static IP address automatically, or you can enter it manually, and if you select the **Shared** option for the purpose, it can be shared by 50 frontends:

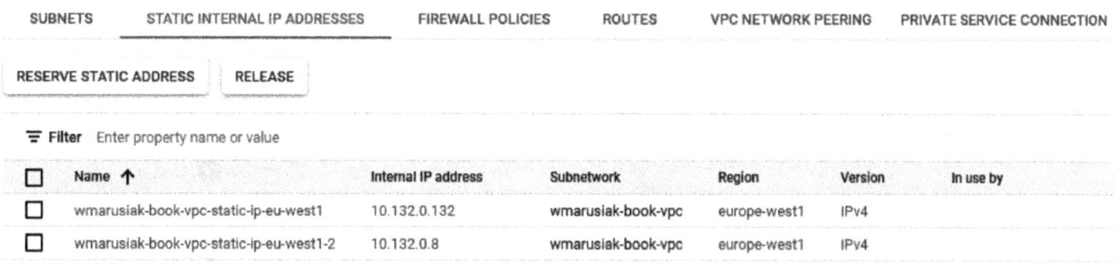

SUBNETS	STATIC INTERNAL IP ADDRESSES	FIREWALL POLICIES	ROUTES	VPC NETWORK PEERING	PRIVATE SERVICE CONNECTION

RESERVE STATIC ADDRESS   RELEASE

≡ **Filter**   Enter property name or value

	Name ↑	Internal IP address	Subnetwork	Region	Version	In use by
☐	wmarusiak-book-vpc-static-ip-eu-west1	10.132.0.132	wmarusiak-book-vpc	europe-west1	IPv4	
☐	wmarusiak-book-vpc-static-ip-eu-west1-2	10.132.0.8	wmarusiak-book-vpc	europe-west1	IPv4	

Figure 4.58 – An example of reserved static IP addresses assigned automatically and manually

In Google Cloud, part of the network IP ranges is reserved. These reservations are essential for management.

The following is the list of used IPs from the network range:

- `Network`: The first address in the primary IP range for the subnet – for example, `10.11.12.0` in `10.11.12.0/24`

- `Default gateway`: The second IP address from the IP range – for example, `10.11.12.1` in `10.11.12.0/24`

- `Second-to-last-address`: the IP address reserved by Google Cloud for potential future use – for example, `10.11.12.254` in `10.11.12.0/24`

- `Broadcast`: The last address from the IP range – for example, `10.11.12.255` in `10.11.12.0/24`

To learn more about IP ranges in Google Cloud, visit the following link: `https://cloud.google.com/vpc/docs/subnets#ip-ranges`.

Reserving the static IP address is just the first part of configuring the instance with this IP. We need to go to the end of instance settings and change the IP address from **Ephemeral** to a previously created one:

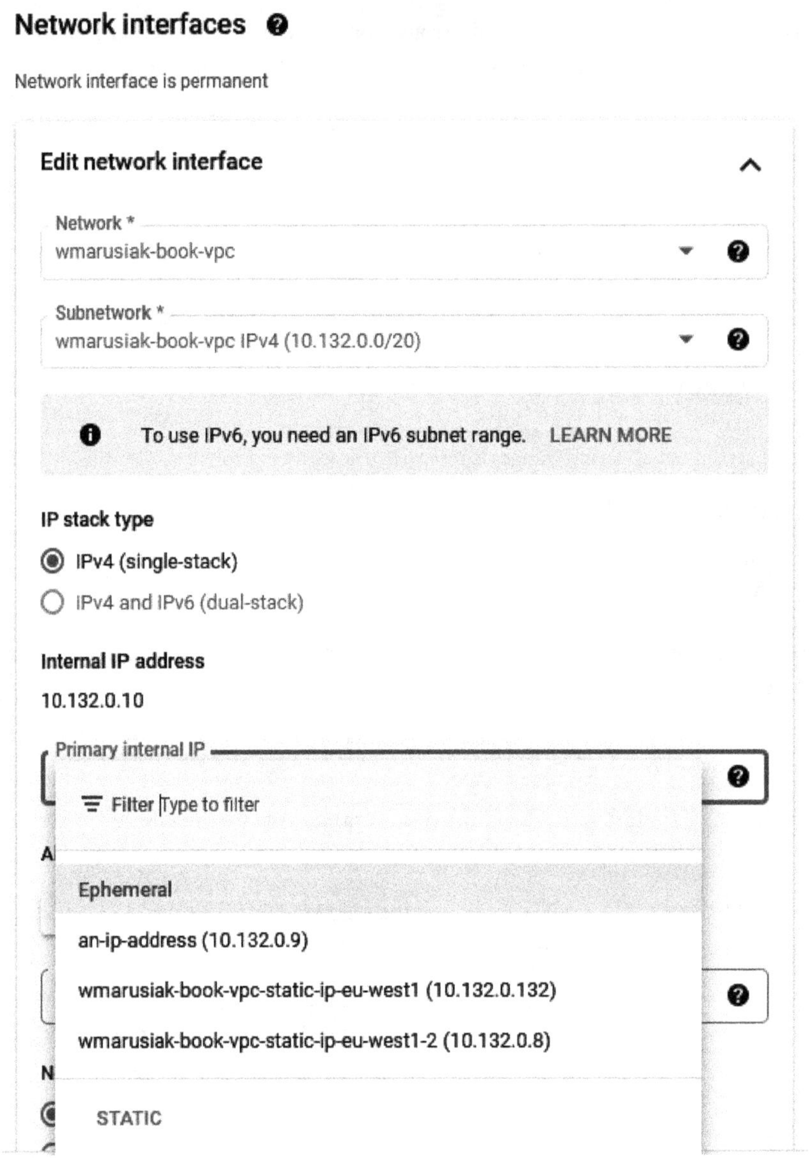

Network interfaces ❷

Network interface is permanent

Edit network interface   ⌃

Network *
wmarusiak-book-vpc   ▼   ❷

Subnetwork *
wmarusiak-book-vpc IPv4 (10.132.0.0/20)   ▼   ❷

❶   To use IPv6, you need an IPv6 subnet range.   LEARN MORE

IP stack type

◉ IPv4 (single-stack)

◯ IPv4 and IPv6 (dual-stack)

Internal IP address

10.132.0.10

Primary internal IP   ❷

☰ Filter Type to filter

A

Ephemeral

an-ip-address (10.132.0.9)

wmarusiak-book-vpc-static-ip-eu-west1 (10.132.0.132)   ❷

wmarusiak-book-vpc-static-ip-eu-west1-2 (10.132.0.8)

N

STATIC

Figure 4.59 – Adding a static IP address to the running instance

Once this task is done, your instance will have the static internal IP you previously configured.

Configuring the instance with the static external IP address

External IP address configuration is an essential piece of instance configuration. If you host a website or application or point it to the external domain name, it is desired to have a configured static IP address.

Once the instance is created with an external IP address, it is ephemeral. When your instance runs, it might have an IP address of 35.210.248.81, but it might be different after stopping it and starting again.

Therefore, for such use cases, we should reserve external IP addresses.

Console

In the **VPC** section of the Cloud console, we can reserve an external static IP address:

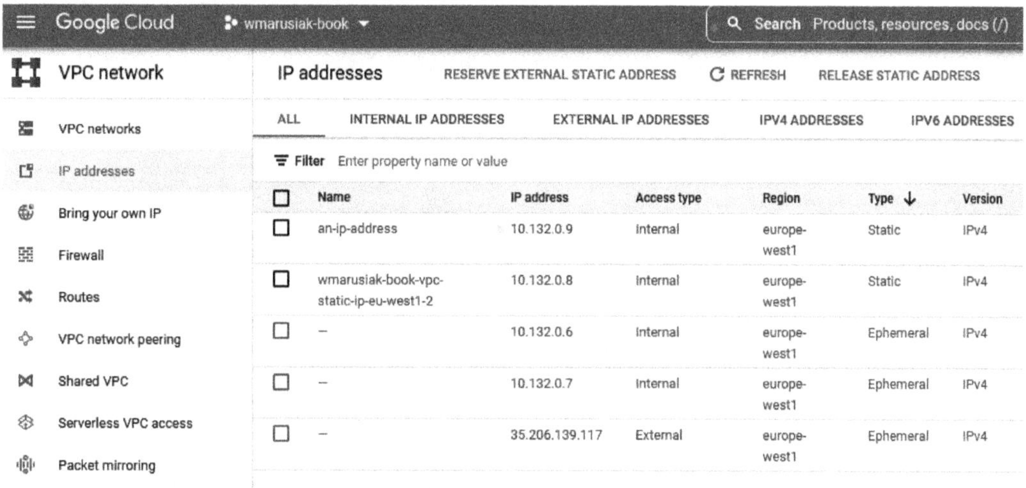

	Name	IP address	Access type	Region	Type ↓	Version
☐	an-ip-address	10.132.0.9	Internal	europe-west1	Static	IPv4
☐	wmarusiak-book-vpc-static-ip-eu-west1-2	10.132.0.8	Internal	europe-west1	Static	IPv4
☐	–	10.132.0.6	Internal	europe-west1	Ephemeral	IPv4
☐	–	10.132.0.7	Internal	europe-west1	Ephemeral	IPv4
☐	–	35.206.139.117	External	europe-west1	Ephemeral	IPv4

Figure 4.60 – The VPC section where the static external IP address can be configured

Once we click the **RESERVE EXTERNAL STATIC ADDRESS** button, we are navigated to a new page where we can provide information about the IP address.

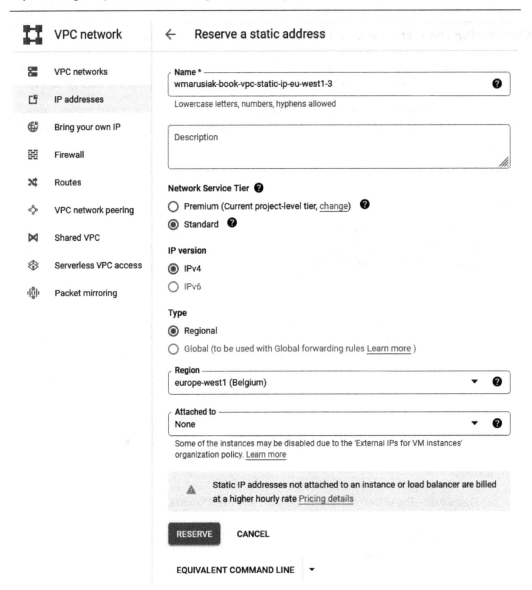

Figure 4.61 – The external static IP address reservation page

Once the **RESERVE** button is clicked, the IP address starts creating.

To attach the newly created external IP address to the running instance in the IP addresses section, we need to click the **Attach to** dropdown and select the desired instance:

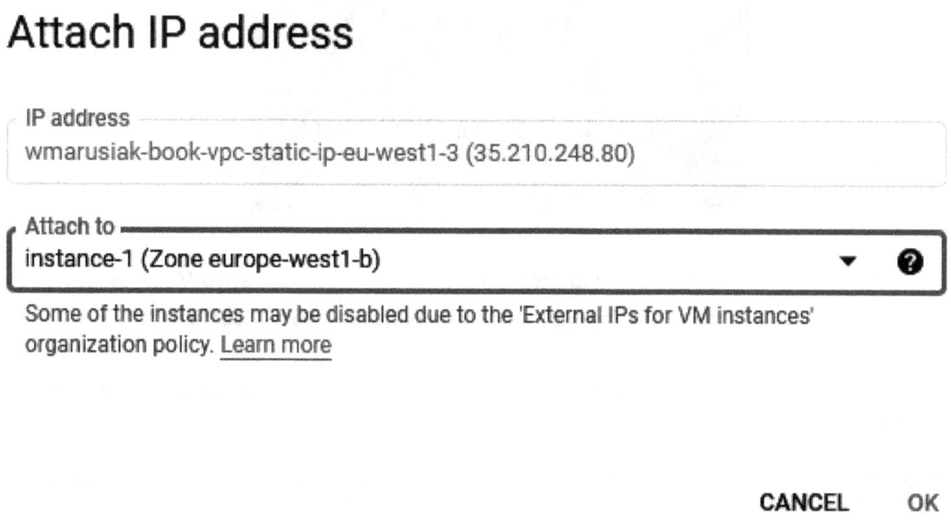

Attach IP address

IP address
wmarusiak-book-vpc-static-ip-eu-west1-3 (35.210.248.80)

Attach to
instance-1 (Zone europe-west1-b)   ▼   ❷

Some of the instances may be disabled due to the 'External IPs for VM instances'
organization policy. Learn more

CANCEL   OK

Figure 4.62 – The external static IP address attached to an instance

After a moment, IP address assignment to the running instance is completed.

Command line

To make the external static IP address reservation, we will use the `gcloud` command:

```
gcloud compute addresses create ADDRESS_NAME --region=REGION_NAME
--subnet=SUBNET --addresses=IP_ADDRESS
```

Once the IP address is created, we can change the instance's configuration to use the newly created
IP address.

The process requires us to get the instance details, remove the `accessConfigs` section of the
instance, and then update the config with the new IP address.

To retrieve accessConfigs, we run the `gcloud` command:

```
gcloud compute instances describe VM_NAME
```

```
networkInterfaces:
- accessConfigs:
  - kind: compute#accessConfig
    name: External NAT
    natIP: 35.205.122.231
    networkTier: PREMIUM
    type: ONE_TO_ONE_NAT
```

Figure 4.63 – The output of gcloud compute instances describes VM_NAME, with
a focus on the accessConfigs section where the IP address is defined

Before we can add a new accessConfigs section, we need to delete the existing one using the following command:

```
gcloud compute instances delete-access-config VM_NAME --access-config-
name="ACCESS_CONFIG_NAME"
```

The following screenshot shows the removal of the accessConfigs section from the instance:

```
admin_@cloudshell:~ (wmarusiak-book)$ gcloud compute instances delete-ac
cess-config instance-1 --zone=europe-west1-b --access-config-name="Exter
nal NAT"
Updated [https://www.googleapis.com/compute/v1/projects/wmarusiak-book/z
ones/europe-west1-b/instances/instance-1].
```

Figure 4.64 – accessConfig has been removed from the instance

Once the accessConfigs section is deleted, the previously associated IP address is removed. To attach the IP address, we need to use the following command:

```
gcloud compute instances add-access-config INSTANCE_NAME --access-
config-name="ACCESS_CONFIG_NAME" --address=ADDRESS_IP
```

Replace ADDRESS_IP with the actual IP address and not its name. We used the following command to attach the external IP to our instance:

```
gcloud compute instances add-access-config instance-1 --access-config-
name="External Static IP" --address=35.210.248.80
```

After a moment, the instance gets a new external IP address:

```
networkInterfaces:
- accessConfigs:
  - kind: compute#accessConfig
    name: External Static IP
    natIP: 34.79.5.162
    networkTier: PREMIUM
    type: ONE TO ONE NAT
  fingerprint: LbsjYej7o88=
  kind: compute#networkInterface
  name: nic0
  network: https://www.googleapis
  networkIP: 10.132.0.6
```

Figure 4.65 – The instance with a new external static IP

IP addresses in Google Cloud have the following essential characteristics:

- Used IPs can be version 4 and version 6

- There are two network tiers – a premium and a standard one

- IPs can be global and regional

We will discuss the networking section in upcoming chapters, but if you wish to learn more about network tiers, you can visit the Google Cloud documentation: `https://cloud.google.com/network-tiers/docs/overview`.

Changing an instance network

Google Cloud allows changes to the networking configuration of instances. Possible permitted modifications are as follows:

- From a legacy network to a VPC network in the same project

- From one VPC network to another VPC network in the same project

- From one subnet of a VPC network to another subnet of the same network

- From a service project network to the shared network of a shared VPC host project

All those actions must be performed when the instance is powered off, and it cannot be a part of a **managed instance group** (**MIG**) or **network endpoint group** (**NEG**).

Console

After stopping the VM instance, we need to edit its configuration. In the networking section, we need to perform network adjustments, as shown in the following screenshot:

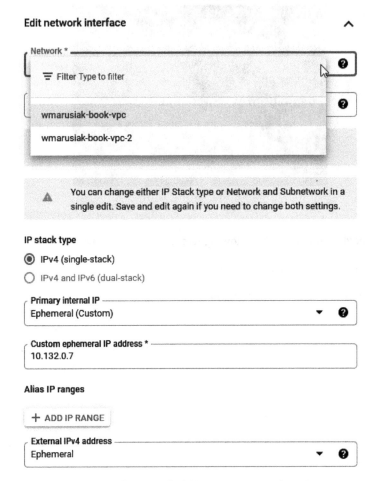

Figure 4.66 – Changing the VM instance network settings

In our case, we switched the instance to a different VPC in the same project.

Command line

The changes made through the console can also be done via the command line.

We need to stop the VM instance first:

```
gcloud compute instances stop INSTANCE_NAME --zone=ZONE_NAME
```

Once the instance is stopped, we can update its configuration:

```
gcloud compute instances network-interfaces update INSTANCE_NAME
--zone=ZONE_NAME --network-interface=NIC --network=NETWORK_NAME
--subnetwork=SUBNET_NAME
```

After a moment, the instance configuration is changed to the desired network.

This last activity concludes the networking-related activities. Those activities are vital to successfully managing Google Cloud and passing the ACE exam.

MIGs

An MIG is a group of VM instances treated as a single entity.

There are two kinds of instance groups to choose from:

- MIGs, which allow us to use applications on identical VM instances automatically
- Unmanaged instance groups, which allow us to load balance applications across instances managed by ourselves

There are many scenarios where an MIG can be used:

- Stateful applications or batch workloads
- Stateless batch or high-performance compute workloads
- Stateless workloads such as hosting a website

The following diagram illustrates the concept of an MIG with a Load Balancer:

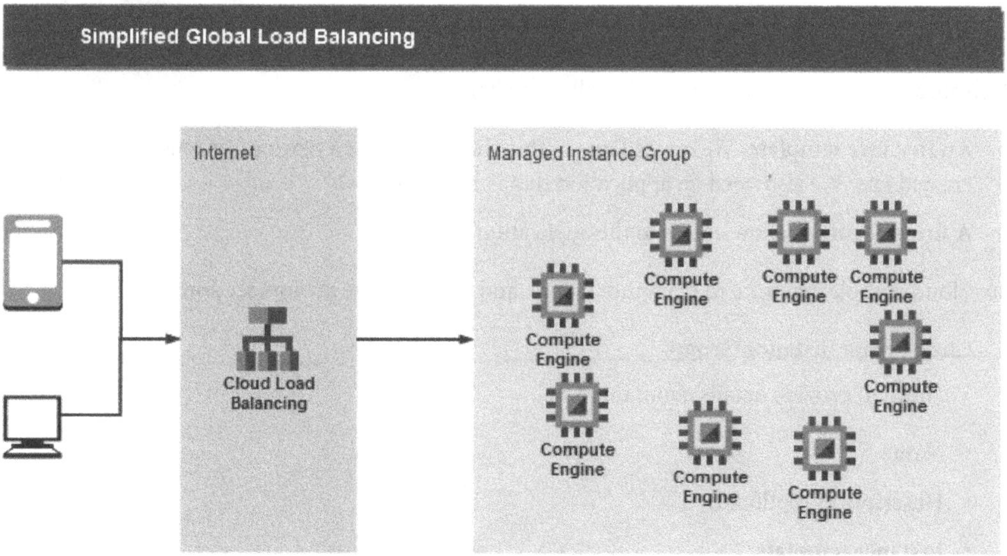

Figure 4.67 – A simplified view of Load Balancing with an MIG

The previous diagram shows simplified load balancing where an MIG receives network traffic from the Internet

There are several advantages of using MIGs:

- **High availability**: An MIG supports regional/multi-zone deployment. If there is zone failure, the application can still be served from the unaffected zone. One essential aspect is the load-balancing option for the application. Various load-balancing options with Cloud Load Balancing are supported with MIGs.

- **Scalability**: An MIG supports automatic scaling based on various metrics, so you no longer need to add servers manually. When the load on the servers is increased, more instances are added. When the load decreases, instances are automatically deleted.

- **Automated patching**: Whenever an application or configuration is changed, we have the option to update the underlying infrastructure. This allows for faster application shipment and updates.

- **Auto healing**: Instances in a group are monitored, and whenever an instance crashes, stops responding, or is deleted, it will be automatically replaced by a new instance from the template. Various health checks are available in the MIG and can be combined with Cloud Load Balancing health checks.

If your application or workload is stateless, you can benefit from using preemptible/spot instance VMs and lower your bill significantly.

Console

Let's create an MIG. To do so, we need the following items:

- **An instance template**: We created one in this chapter. Create a new one or reuse a previously created one. We also need an application that is configured.

- **A firewall rule** to allow access to the application.

In the Cloud console, navigate to Compute Engine and the **Instance groups** section:

1. Click **Create Instance Group**.
2. We need to provide details about our MIG:

   - **Name**
   - **Description** (optional)
   - **Instance template**

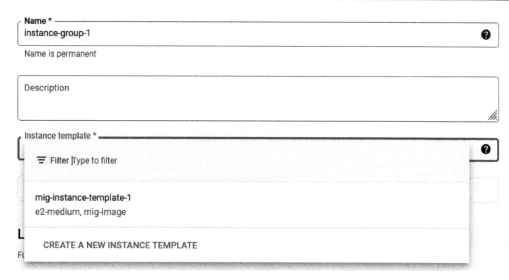

Figure 4.68 – The initial configuration section of the MIG

In the location section, we can choose single or multiple zones. If a single zone is selected, a target distribution shape is not possible. We have the option of **Even**, **Balanced**, and **Any**. Choose the desired configuration option:

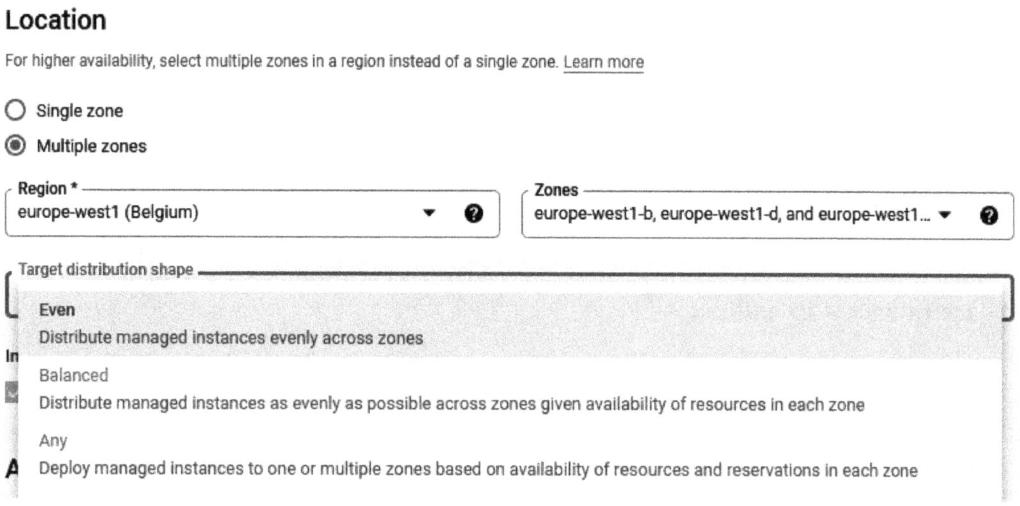

Location

For higher availability, select multiple zones in a region instead of a single zone. Learn more

○ Single zone

◉ Multiple zones

Region *
europe-west1 (Belgium)   ▼   ?

Zones
europe-west1-b, europe-west1-d, and europe-west1... ▼   ?

Target distribution shape

Even
Distribute managed instances evenly across zones

Balanced
Distribute managed instances as evenly as possible across zones given availability of resources in each zone

Any
Deploy managed instances to one or multiple zones based on availability of resources and reservations in each zone

Figure 4.69 – The MIG in a multiple-zone configuration

3. In the **Autoscaling** section, we can use autoscaling mode. We can choose from **On**, **Scale out**, and **Off**:

Autoscaling
Use autoscaling to automatically add and remove instances to the group for periods of high and low load. Learn more
Autoscaling mode
On: add and remove instances to the group
Scale out: only add instances to the group
Off: do not autoscale
DELETE AUTOSCALING CONFIGURATION

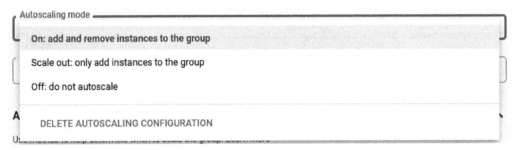

Figure 4.70 – Autoscaling options

4. There is also an option to define the minimum and maximum number of instances:

Autoscaling
Use autoscaling to automatically add and remove instances to the group for periods of high and low load. Learn more
Autoscaling mode
On: add and remove instances to the group
Minimum number of instances *
3
Maximum number of instances *
2000

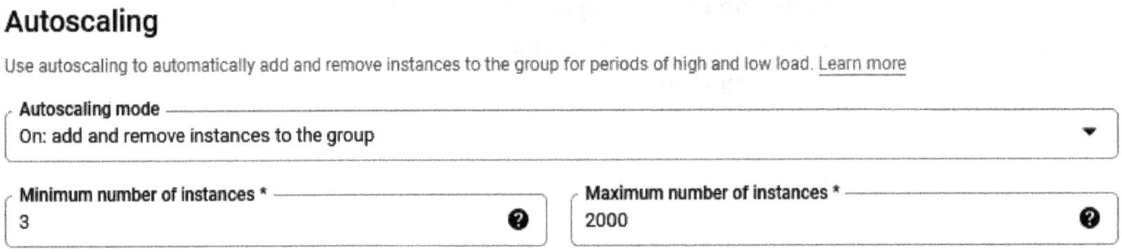

Figure 4.71 – Autoscaling mode with possibility to configure minimum and maximum amount of instances

In the **Autoscaling metrics** section, we can choose when the autoscaling event happens. As the metric type, we can choose from either **HTTP load balancing utilization** or **Cloud Monitoring metric** under **CPU utilization**:

Figure 4.72 – Autoscaling metrics

5. In the cool-down section, we can specify how long it takes for the application to initialize from boot time until it is ready to serve. This is a critical section, as some applications take a moment to start. If the application start exceeds the cool-down period, your monitoring metrics might detect that the application doesn't work and initiate an autoscaling event, deleting the monitored instance. We want to avoid this situation, and it is a general best practice to measure the application startup.

6. To better define scale-in controls, we can enable additional settings, as shown in the following screenshot:

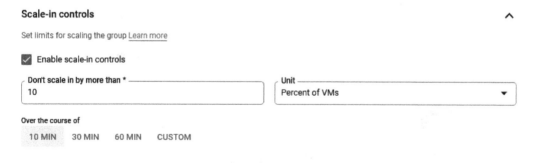

Figure 4.73 – Autoscaling metrics

7. In the **Autohealing** section, we can create detailed health checks for our application:

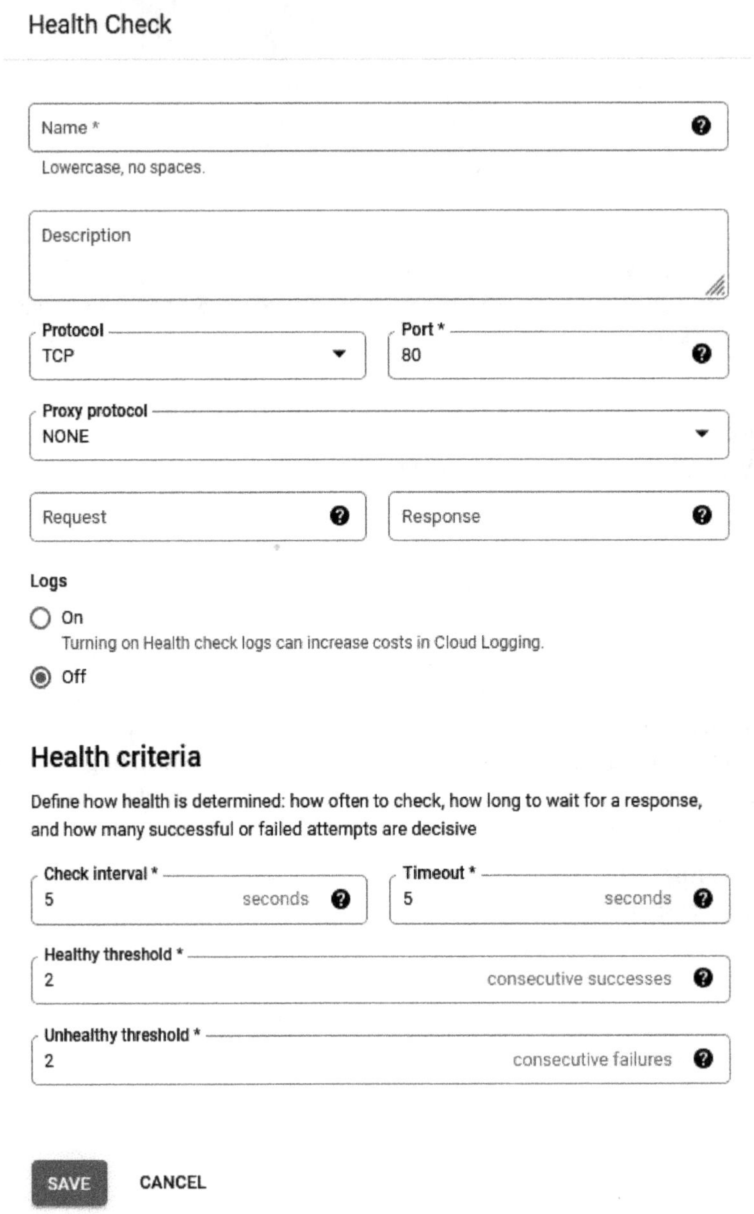

Health Check

Name *

Lowercase, no spaces.

Description

Protocol
TCP

Port *
80

Proxy protocol
NONE

Request

Response

Logs

○ On
   Turning on Health check logs can increase costs in Cloud Logging.

◉ Off

Health criteria

Define how health is determined: how often to check, how long to wait for a response, and how many successful or failed attempts are decisive

Check interval *
5   seconds

Timeout *
5   seconds

Healthy threshold *
2   consecutive successes

Unhealthy threshold *
2   consecutive failures

SAVE   CANCEL

Figure 4.74 – The Health Check configuration

8. The last section of the MIG is the **Port mapping** section. It is used to map the incoming traffic to a specific port number, together with HTTP load balancing:

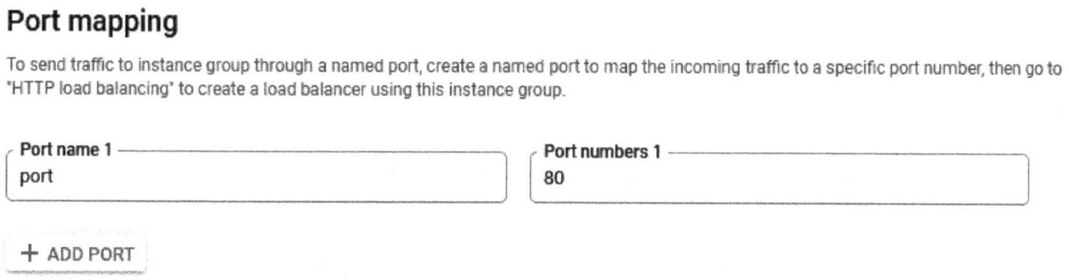

Port mapping

To send traffic to instance group through a named port, create a named port to map the incoming traffic to a specific port number, then go to "HTTP load balancing" to create a load balancer using this instance group.

Port name 1
port

Port numbers 1
80

+ ADD PORT

Figure 4.75 – The Port mapping options

It might take a moment to create all instances, depending on the number of instances configured. You can check how many of them have been made in the **Number of instances** section:

Figure 4.76 – Managed instance group created and ready for usage

In the **DETAILS** section, we can see the template information, update the parameters, and configure many options.

Command line

We need three steps to achieve the same configuration we did using the Cloud console.

The first section creates an MIG based on a pre-configured template:

```
gcloud beta compute instance-groups managed create INSTANCE_GROUP_
NAME --project=PROJECT_NAME --base-instance-name=INSTANCE_GROUP_NAME
--size=MINIMUM_SIZE --template=TEMPLATE_NAME --zones=ZONE_NAME_X,ZONE_
NAME_Y,ZONE_NAME_z --target-distribution-shape=EVEN
```

To create a named port, we need to execute the following command:

```
gcloud compute instance-groups managed set-named-ports INSTANCE_GROUP_
NAME --project=PROJECT_NAME --region=REGION_NAME named-ports=port:80
```

In the last section, we configure the autoscaling policy for our MIG:

```
gcloud beta compute instance-groups managed set-autoscaling INSTANCE_
GROUP_NAME --project=PROJECT_NAME --region=REGION_NAME --cool-down-
period=COOL-DOWN-PERIOD-IN-MIN --max-num-replicas=MAX_REPLICAS
--min-num-replicas=MIN_REPLICAS --mode=on --target-cpu-utilization=0.6
--scale-in-control=max-scaled-in-replicas-percent=10,time-window=600
```

In the next section, we will cover the autoscaling options for the existing running MIG.

Autoscaling

Autoscaling settings are visible in the **Details** section of the MIG:

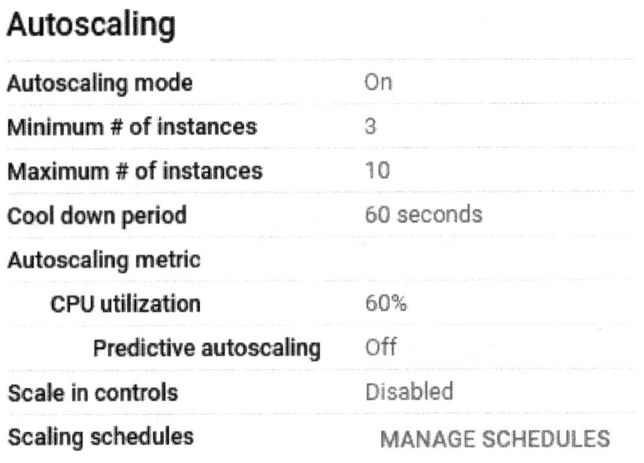

Autoscaling

Autoscaling mode	On
Minimum # of instances	3
Maximum # of instances	10
Cool down period	60 seconds
Autoscaling metric	
CPU utilization	60%
Predictive autoscaling	Off
Scale in controls	Disabled
Scaling schedules	MANAGE SCHEDULES

Figure 4.77 – Autoscaling information in the MIG

To change the autoscaling setting, we need to click the **EDIT** button, and then we will be redirected to the configuration window. It looks the same as when we created the MIG. If you wish, you can change the settings and confirm so by clicking the **SAVE** button:

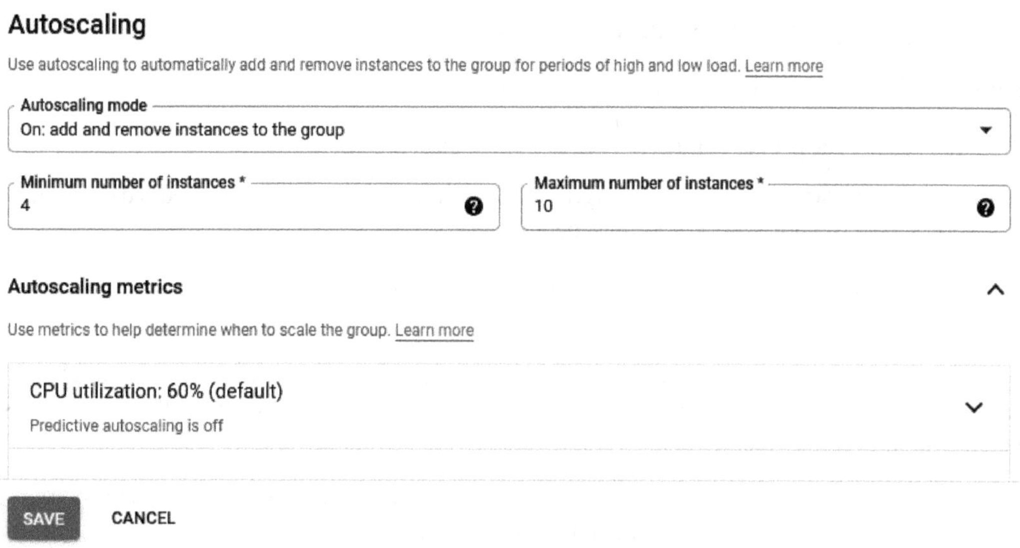

Autoscaling

Use autoscaling to automatically add and remove instances to the group for periods of high and low load. Learn more

Autoscaling mode
On: add and remove instances to the group   ▼

Minimum number of instances *
4   ❓

Maximum number of instances *
10   ❓

Autoscaling metrics   ⌃

Use metrics to help determine when to scale the group. Learn more

CPU utilization: 60% (default)   ⌄

Predictive autoscaling is off

SAVE   CANCEL

Figure 4.78 – The autoscaling changes for the MIG in the Cloud console

After clicking the **SAVE** button, the changes will be applied immediately to the MIG:

≡ **Filter** Enter property name or value

	Status	Name ↑	Zone	Recommendations	In use by	Internal IP
☐	✔	instance-group-1-2c6z	europe-west1-d		instance-group-1	10.132.0.19 (nic0)
☐	✔	instance-group-1-bh12	europe-west1-c		instance-group-1	10.132.0.20 (nic0)
☐	✔	instance-group-1-bjqp	europe-west1-b		instance-group-1	10.132.0.18 (nic0)
☐	↻	instance-group-1-pzvm	europe-west1-c			10.132.0.21 (nic0)

Figure 4.79 – A new instance is created after updating the autoscaling settings

The preceding screenshot shows the newly added example after changing the autoscaling settings.

In this section, we covered many topics about VM instances. We learned how to create a new instance, update its configuration, create snapshots, and create MIGs. The following section will focus on logging and monitoring agents and how to install them, and viewing base monitoring metrics.

Cloud logging and monitoring agents

Google Cloud's operations suite offers two monitoring agents:

- **Ops Agent**: The primary and preferred agent to collect metrics and logs
- **Legacy Monitoring agent**: Like Ops Agent, this can gather metrics from the supported operating systems but shouldn't be used for new deployments

Google's Ops Agent is a unified telemetry agent that uses Fluent Bit to collect logs and OpenTelemetry to collect metrics.

Fluent Bit is an open source log collector that is used to collect and process logs from a variety of sources. OpenTelemetry is an open source project that provides a unified way to collect telemetry data from applications and services.

By using Fluent Bit and OpenTelemetry, the Ops Agent can collect both logs and metrics from your applications and services. This data can then be used to monitor the health and performance of your applications, troubleshoot problems, and identify performance bottlenecks.

Installing the Ops Agent

The Ops Agent can be installed on many Linux- and Windows-based operating systems.

A complete and up-to-date list is available on the website, and installation will differ depending on the operating system: https://cloud.google.com/stackdriver/docs/solutions/agents/ops-agent#linux_operating_systems.

In this example, we will focus on installing Ubuntu Server 20.04.4 LTS:

1. To install the latest version of the Ops Agent, we need to run the following command:

    ```
    curl -sSO https://dl.google.com/cloudagents/add-google-cloud-
    ops-agent-repo.sh sudo bash add-google-cloud-ops-agent-repo.sh
    --also-install
    ```

Installation takes a moment, and after a while, in the monitoring section of the Cloud console, the Ops Agent will be detected:

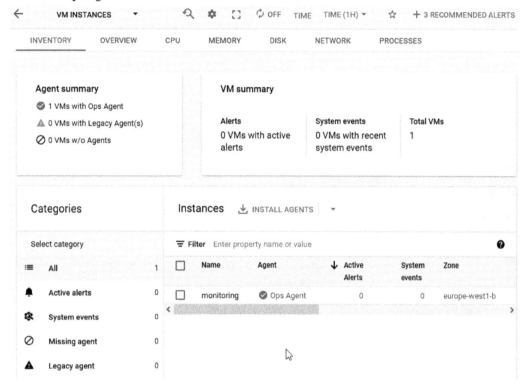

Figure 4.80 – The monitoring and logging Ops Agent installation was successful

To view the detailed metrics and logs from the instance, we need to click on its name:

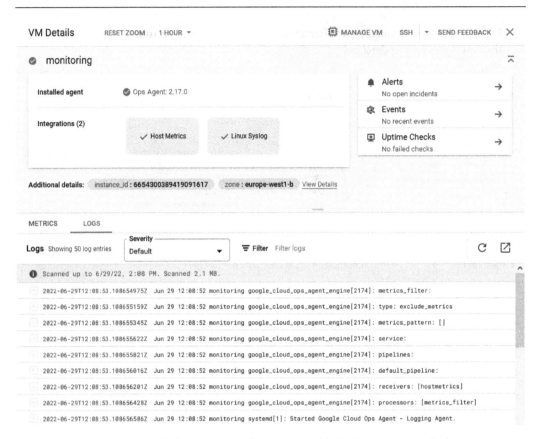

Figure 4.81 – The logging view of an instance with the Ops Agent installed

This concludes the installation of the Ops Agent on a Linux server. In the upcoming chapters, we will learn much more about logging and monitoring in Google Cloud.

Summary

Understanding GCE takes some time. We covered many topics, from the simplest one, VM creation, to the creation of an MIG. In between, we added and removed disk to instances and created snapshots, which aren't a backup solution but can be used if something happens and we need to roll back to the previous state of the instance quickly. We briefly touched on the networking of Compute Engine, which will have a dedicated chapter. We ended the chapter by installing cloud logging and monitoring agents, which is important in conjunction with MIGs and autoscaling.

In the next chapter, we will abstract VMs and move up the logical layers, where Kubernetes and Google Kubernetes Engine will play a leading role.

Questions

Answer the following questions to test your knowledge of this chapter:

1. You are deploying a production application on GCE and want to prevent anyone from deleting the data stored on its disk. How can you achieve this?

    A. Disable automatic restart on the instance.

    B. Disable perceptibility on the instance.

    C. Enable the `Delete boot disk when the instance is deleted` flag.

    D. Enable delete protection on the instance.

2. You are tasked to create a GCE instance using a command-line interface. What is the next step after creating a Google Cloud project?

    A. Create a VPC in the project.

    B. B. Grant yourself the Compute Admin IAM role.

    C. Configure an organizational policy.

    D. Enable the Google Compute API.

3. Your project and all its resources are deployed in the `europe-west4` region. You want to set the europe-west4 region as the default region for the `gcloud` command-line tool. How can you achieve this?

    A. It is not possible to set the default value of a region.

    B. B. Use the `gcloud` config set compute/region europe-west4.

    C. Use the `gcloud` config set compute/zone europe-west4.

    D. Use Cloud Shell where the region is predefined.

4. You were tasked to create a VM named `cloud-server-1` with four CPUs. Which of the following commands would you use to create the VM `cloud-server-1`?

    A. `gcloud compute instances create --machine-type=n1-standard-4 cloud-server-1`

    B. `gcloud compute instances create --cpus=4 cloud-server-1`

    C. `gcloud compute instances create --machine-type=n1-4-cpu cloud-server-1`

    D. `gcloud compute instances create --machine-type=n1-standard-4 -instancename cloud-server-1`

5. You created a new Linux instance on GCE. It is up and running, its status in the Cloud console is green, and it has assigned both internal and external IPs, but you still can't access it via the SSH protocol. What might be the possible issue? (Choose two answers):

   A. Check whether an SSH key has been added to the instance.

   B. Check whether the firewall rule has been created with port 22 and the TCP protocol has been created and assigned to the instance.

   C. Check whether the firewall rule has been created with port 22 and the UDP protocol has been created and assigned to the instance.

   D. Check whether the VPC network has been created.

6. You have deployed multiple Linux and Windows VM instances, and you have been tasked by your company's security team to access those instances using RDP and the SSH protocol. The security team forbids you to use publicly available IP addresses. Which solution can you use?

   A. Create a self-signed certificate and attach it to both Linux and Windows instances.

   B. Configure a Cloud IAP for HTTPS resources.

   C. Create an SSH key pair and add the public key to all instances.

   D. Configure a Cloud IAP for SSH and TCP resources.

7. As a cloud engineer, you have been tasked to deploy an application that must scale easily, be highly available, and be deployed as a VM. Which Google Cloud Engine feature will help you achieve those requirements?

   A. An instance image

   B. An MIG

   C. An instance with an internal load balancer

   D. An instance snapshot

8. Your manager asks you to prepare a list of all instances created in Google Cloud. Which gcloud command would you use to perform this task?

   A. The gcloud compute instance list

   B. The gcloud instances list

   C. The gcloud compute instances list

   D. The gcloud instance describe

9. An application owner contacts you to say that his server is running out of disk space. Which command will you use to increase the VM disk size by 50 GB?

A. `gcloud compute disks resize server1-disk1 --zone=europe-west1a --size=50GB`

B. `gcloud compute disk upgrade server1-disk1 --zone=europe-west1a --size=50GB`

C. `gcloud disks resize server1-disk1 --zone=europe-west1a --size=50GB`

D. `gcloud computes disks server1-disk1 --zone=europe-west1a --size=50GB upgrade`

10. A new team member is responsible for creating snapshots of VMs. Which role do you need to assign to his account following the principle of least privilege?

A. Storage instance admin

B. Compute snapshot admin

C. Compute storage admin

D. Compute admin

11. Your manager asks you to optimize cloud expenditure by shutting down development and test environment VMs that only used 8x5. How can you simply achieve this task?

A. Create a snapshot of VMs and start and stop them manually.

B. Write a script that automates the start and stops of the VMs.

C. Attach a startup and shutdown script to all VMs.

D. Create an instance schedule and attach it to desired VMs.

12. Which parameters can be used to scale an instance group up and down?

A. Average CPU utilization

B. An HTTP load balancing serving capacity, which can be based on either utilization or requests per second

C. Cloud Monitoring metrics

D. All of the preceding

13. The `cloud-server1` VM that you use daily is slow and sluggish. Which `gcloud` command would you use to reboot it?

A. `gcloud computes instance reset cloud-server1`

B. `gcloud instances reset cloud-server1 -region europe-west4`

C. `gcloud instance compute reset cloud-server1`

D. `gcloud compute instances reset cloud-server1`

14. Which Google Compute resource can be the source of an image?

    A. Snapshots and disks only

    B. Disks only

    C. Disk, snapshots, or other images

    D. Disks and instance templates

15. You work for a genomics company planning to conduct data analysis on around 100 TB of data. The data analysis would require 360 vCPUs and 240 GB of RAM. You need to recommend the cheapest option to conduct the research. Which of the following Google Cloud resources would you use?

    A. Preemptible instances

    B. Cloud Functions

    C. A committed use discount

    D. Sustained use discounts

16. Your colleague has been asked to increase the disk size on one of the servers by 200 GB. Accidentally, he increased it by 2,000 GB. He tried to downgrade the disk size but claimed he could not do it. What is the reason why?

    A. A VM disk can only be downgraded when the VM is powered off.

    B. A disk downgrade can be done only via a `gcloud` command or API request.

    C. You need to delete the VM snapshot first.

    D. It is not possible to downgrade the disk.

17. Which command would you use to delete an instance and preserve its disk boot?

    A. `gcloud compute instances delete cloud-server1 -keep-disks=boot`

    B. `gcloud disks delete cloud-server1 -keep-disks=boot`

    C. `gcloud compute instances delete cloud-server1 -keep-disks=boot`

    D. `gcloud delete compute instance cloud-server1 -keep-disks=boot`

    E. `gcloud compute instances delete cloud-server1 -keep-disks=all`

18. An application server runs on Compute Engine in the europe-west4-a zone. You must replicate the server to the europe-west6-c zone using the fewest steps possible. What should you do?

    A. Create a snapshot from the disk. Create a disk from the snapshot in the europe-west6-c zone and create a new VM from that disk.

    B. Copy the disk by using the `gcloud` command to the europe-west6-c zone. Create a new VM with that disk.

    C. Use the `gcloud compute instances disk clone server1-disk europe-west6-c` command to clone the disk.

    D. Create a template from the disk. Create a new disk from the template in the europe-west6-c zone, and then create a new VM from that disk.

19. Which command would you use to connect to the Compute Engine instance with a publicly available IP address, `30.40.50.60`, from Cloud Shell?

    A. `gcloud connect ssh username@30.40.50.60`

    B. `gcloud compute ssh username@30.40.50.60`

    C. `gsutil compute connect ssh username@30.40.50.60`

    D. `gcloud connect compute ssh username@30.40.50.60`

    E. None of the preceding

20. Which permissions are needed to manage SSH keys on a project when setting project-wide metadata to access an instance if the OS login doesn't work? (Choose two):

    A. `iam.configuresshMetadata.allInstances`

    B. `iam.serviceAccounts.actAs`

    C. `compute.instance.configureMetadata`

    D. `compute.projects.setCommonInstanceMetadata`

Answers

The answers to the preceding questions are provided here:

1C, 2D, 3B, 4A, 5AB, 6D, 7B, 8C, 9A, 10C, 11D, 12D, 13D, 14C, 15A, 16D, 17A, 18A, 19B, 20BD

5
Implementing Compute Solutions – Google Kubernetes Engine (Part 1)

This chapter aims to cover various compute solutions' implementation.

We are going to cover the following main topics:

- Traditional application deployment versus containerized deployment
- Kubernetes architecture
- **Google Kubernetes Engine** (GKE) architecture

We are very excited to introduce the concept of container orchestration as I'm seeing an everyday increase in traction toward containers. Kubernetes and its native Google Cloud implementation GKE is a very sophisticated and innovative product on the market. We hope you will enjoy the journey with me.

GKE

Kubernetes is an open source platform for managing containerized workloads declaratively for configuration and automation. The name *Kubernetes* originates from Greek and means helmsman or pilot.

Kubernetes is well known for its abbreviation—**K8s**. K8s stands for *K* in Kubernetes, 8 is the count between the letters *K* and *s*, and *s* is the last letter from the word *Kubernetes*.

Google open sourced Kubernetes in 2014, combining more than 15 years of Google experience running containerized workloads. Kubernetes originates from Borg, an internal tool for orchestrating containers at Google.

To learn more about the history of Borg and Kubernetes, visit the following link: `https://kubernetes.io/blog/2015/04/borg-predecessor-to-kubernetes/`.

GKE is a container orchestration platform. It is a managed service offered by Google Cloud that offers autoscaling and multi-cluster support.

The following section will talk about the differences between traditional, virtualized, and containerized deployments.

Traditional versus virtualized versus container deployment

This section is dedicated to understanding fundamental containerization concepts and how they differ from the previous deployment options:

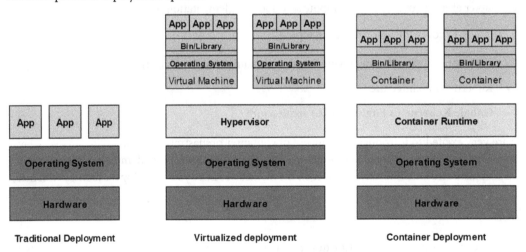

Figure 5.1 – Various application deployment types

Let's do a short review of different deployment types.

Traditional deployment

For forever, we used servers to deploy various types of applications. We could deploy multiple applications on a single server or spread them out to utilize only one dedicated server. Unfortunately, this led to two situations:

- A single server with just one application was most of the time underutilized, and resources such as the server itself, power, cooling, and storage were wasted and not utilized properly.

- A single server with multiple applications installed could be utilized much better, but overall server performance was quite often slow due to resource contention. Numerous applications had to fight over the CPU cycle, RAM allocation, or network bandwidth.

These issues increased the number of servers we needed to deploy, manage, and operate.

Virtualized deployment

Virtualization introduced many improvements in comparison to traditional deployment. It allowed the running of multiple **virtual machines** (**VMs**) on a single server with their operating system, securely isolating and deploying them faster than on the physical servers. Virtualization increased servers' utilization and ease of management and reduced hardware costs.

Container deployment

Containers are similar to VMs, but there is one significant difference. Containers don't require an entire operating system and all libraries to run even the smallest application.

Containers are lightweight packages of the application packed with all necessary libraries, are portable, and are easy to update and manage.

In the next section, we will focus on the GKE architecture, which containers are a part of.

GKE architecture

As we mentioned before, GKE is based on Kubernetes itself. We will briefly explain the core Kubernetes components and how they relate to GKE.

Because this book is aimed toward helping you ace the **Associate Cloud Engineer** (**ACE**) exam, we won't explain how to build a CI/CD pipeline and deploy it to GKE. If you wish to learn about Kubernetes in much more detail, there are many fantastic books on the market.

Kubernetes components

The central concept of Kubernetes is a cluster. As Kubernetes consists of multiple components, a diagram of Kubernetes architecture will allow us to understand its components and dependencies:

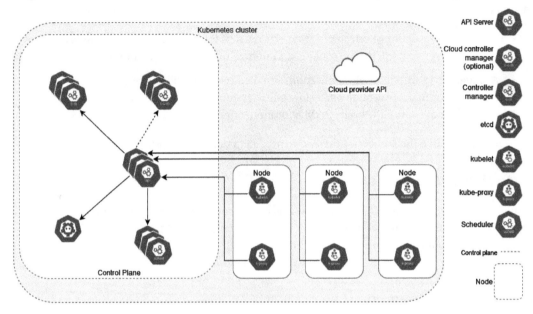

Figure 5.2 – Kubernetes architecture

A cluster consists of a few elements, as outlined here:

- **Nodes**—Worker machines where we deploy containerized applications. A node has multiple components that interact with each other, as follows:

  - **kubelet**—This is an agent that runs on each node and makes sure that containers are running in a Pod.

  - **kube-proxy**—This is a network proxy that runs on each node in the cluster. It maintains network rules on nodes that allow network communication to Pods.

  - **Container runtime**—Kubernetes supports multiple runtimes such as containers, CRI-O, or any other Kubernetes **Container Runtime Interface** (**CRI**).

- **Pods**—Pods are hosted on worker nodes. They are the smallest deployable units of computing that can be created and managed in Kubernetes. A Pod can be a single container or a group of containers with shared storage and network resources. The control plane has multiple components that interact with each other, as follows:

  - **kube-apiserver**—This is an API server that is the frontend for the Kubernetes control plane.

  - **etcd**—A highly available, strongly consistent, distributed key-value store where all configuration, data, or state is stored.

  - **kube-scheduler**—This is a component used to schedule containers to run on a node.

  - **kube-controller-manager**—This is a control plane component that runs controller processes. It has several controllers included: a node controller (responsible for node unavailability), job controller (creates Pods), endpoint controller (populates endpoint objects), service account and token controllers (create default accounts and API access tokens for new namespaces).

  - **cloud-controller-manager**—The cloud controller manager component allows us to link clusters into the cloud provider API and separate the components that interact with the cloud platform from those that only interact with your cluster. On-premises Kubernetes doesn't have this component.

To learn more about the Kubernetes concepts, please visit the following URL: `https://kubernetes.io/docs/concepts/overview/components/`.

Google Kubernetes components

Google Kubernetes components are based on Kubernetes, but Google Cloud fully manages the control plane for us. Essentially, GKE consumers must deploy applications and configure GKE according to their needs.

Storage in GKE

GKE offers several storage options for containerized applications running on GKE. On-disk files in containers are the simplest place for an application to write data, but it doesn't solve the main problem. When the container stops or crashes, the files and data are lost. Besides that, some applications might require shared storage or even need to access the data from different containers running in the same Pod.

Kubernetes abstract block-based storage to Pods by introducing volumes, **persistent volumes** (**PVs**), and storage classes.

Before we dive into different storage components, we need to understand dependencies and how they construct GKE storage:

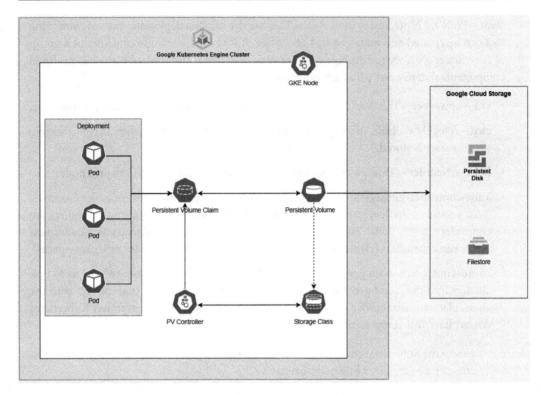

Figure 5.3 – Kubernetes storage architecture

On the right side of the diagram, we have persistent disks, which we know from **Google Compute Engine (GCE)**, and they are used as block storage for instances. Filestore, a managed Google Cloud **Network File System (NFS)** service, can be used as well as a storage option in GKE.

Volumes

Volumes serve as storage units that containers within a Pod can access. Certain volume types rely on ephemeral storage, meaning they do not persist once the Pod is terminated. Examples of such ephemeral storage types include `emptyDir`, which can be used as temporary storage for applications. Similar to CPU and memory resources, we can manage local ephemeral storage resources. On the other hand, other volume types are supported as durable storage, providing long-term data persistence.

In essence, a volume can be understood as a directory that is available to every container within a Pod. A Pod defines the volumes it includes and the specific location where containers can access and utilize those volumes.

Let's look at the different types of volumes:

- **emptyDir**—An `emptyDir` volume grants containers within a Pod access to an empty directory for reading and writing. It's important to remember that when the Pod is removed from a node, regardless of the cause, the data stored within the `emptyDir` volume is permanently deleted. The medium on which the `emptyDir` volume resides is determined by the underlying infrastructure of the node, which could be a disk, SSD, or network storage, depending on the configuration. Utilizing emptyDir volumes proves beneficial when temporary storage space is needed or when data needs to be shared among multiple containers within a Pod.

- **ConfigMap**—A ConfigMap resource is used to inject configuration data into Pods. This data, stored within a ConfigMap object, can be accessed through a volume of type ConfigMap and subsequently utilized by files running within a Pod. The files contained within a ConfigMap volume are defined by a corresponding ConfigMap resource.

- **Secret**—A Secret volume is used to securely expose confidential information—including passwords, OAuth tokens, and SSH keys—to applications. The data stored within a Secret object can be accessed via a volume of type Secret and utilized by files executing within a Pod.

- **downwardAPI**—A downwardAPI volume, in simple words, is information about the Pod and container in which an application is running. By utilizing the downwardAPI, our application can retrieve valuable information about the Pod without requiring any knowledge of Kubernetes. This is made possible through the utilization of environment variables and files, which are sources of information that any software can reuse.

- **PersistentVolumeClaim (PVC)**—Cluster operators have the ability to utilize a PVC volume to allocate long-lasting storage for applications. By employing a PVC, a Pod can mount a volume that is supported by this durable storage.

PVs

PV resources are used to manage durable storage in a cluster. In GKE, a PV is typically backed by a **persistent disk**. As an option, we can choose a managed NFS called Filestore.

Kubernetes manages the life cycle of a PV, and it can be dynamically provisioned; as resources, they exist independently of Pods.

PVC

A PVC is a user's request for storage, comparable to a Pod. While Pods consume resources on nodes, PVCs consume resources from PVs. Just as Pods can specify their desired resource levels, such as CPU and memory, PVCs can request specific sizes and access modes. Access modes determine whether the storage can be mounted as `ReadWriteOnce`, `ReadOnlyMany`, or `ReadWriteMany`.

Access modes

PV resources support the following access modes:

- `ReadWriteOnce`—The volume can be mounted as read-write by a single Kubernetes node.

- `ReadOnlyMany`—The volume can be mounted as read-only by many Kubernetes nodes.

- `ReadWriteMany`—The volume can be mounted as read-write by many Kubernetes nodes. PV resources that are backed by GCE persistent disks don't support this access mode.

Reclaim policies

PVs can have various reclaim policies, including `Retain`, `Recycle`, and `Delete`. For all dynamically provisioned PVs, the default reclaim policy is `Delete`.

Let's look at some reclaim policies and their actions:

- `Retain`—Manual reclamation

- `Recycle`—Data can be resorted after getting scrubbed

- `Delete`—Associated storage asset is deleted

We can take advantage of the reclaim policy and control how and when PVs are deleted.

Storage classes

Configuration of volume implementations, such as the Compute Engine persistent disk or **Container Storage Interface** (**CSI**) driver, is accomplished using StorageClass resources.

By default, GKE generates a StorageClass that utilizes the balanced persistent disk type (`ext4`). This default StorageClass is applied when a PVC does not explicitly mention a StorageClassName. However, we have the flexibility to substitute the default StorageClass with our own customized version. For instance, these custom classes can be associated with different **quality-of-service** (**QoS**) levels or backup policies. In other storage systems, this concept is occasionally referred to as "profiles."

Next, we will describe two GKE modes we can use—**GKE Standard** and **GKE Autopilot**.

GKE Standard

As with a pure Kubernetes architecture, a cluster is the foundation of GKE.

GKE clusters consist of one or more **control planes** and multiple worker machines where the workload runs, called **nodes**. The control plane and nodes are the main components of the container orchestration system:

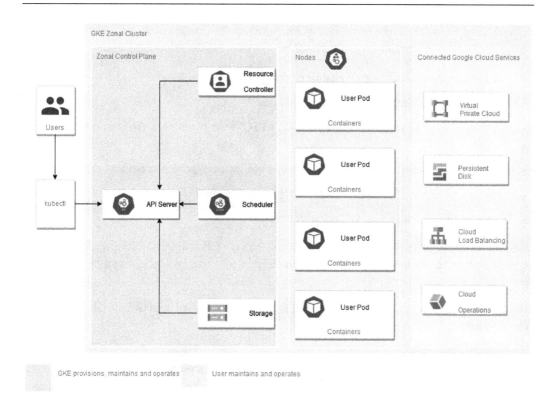

Figure 5.4 – GKE standard architecture

Control plane

The control plane has many roles, such as Kubernetes API server, scheduler, and resource controller. Its life cycle is managed by GKE when the cluster is created, deleted, or upgraded.

Nodes

Cluster nodes are called worker machines because the containers we schedule to run are deployed on worker nodes. Those worker nodes are Compute Engine VM instances managed by the GKE control plane.

Each worker node is managed by the control plane, receives updates, and reports its status to the control plane. Each node runs services that make up the whole cluster. For example, runtime and Kubernetes node agent **Kubelet**, which communicates with the control plane, starts and stops containers on the node.

The default node machine type is e2-medium, a cost-optimized machine type with shared cores that supports up to 32 vCPUs and 128 GB of memory. The default node type can be changed during the cluster creation process.

Each node runs a specialized operating system image to run the containers. At the time of writing, the following operating system images are available:

- Container-optimized OS with containerd (`cos_containerd`)

- Ubuntu with containerd (`ubuntu_containerd`)

- Windows **Long-Term Servicing Channel** (**LTSC**) with containerd (`windows_ltsc_containerd`)

- Container-Optimized OS with Docker (`cos`)—will be unsupported as of v1.24 of GKE

- Ubuntu with Docker (`ubuntu`)—will be deprecated as of v1.24 of GKE

- Windows LTSC with Docker (`windows_ltsc`)

To view the most current list of available images, please visit the following URL: `https://cloud.google.com/kubernetes-engine/docs/concepts/node-images#available_node_images`.

Starting from GKE version 1.24, Docker-based images aren't supported, and Google Cloud advises not to use them.

As the nodes themselves require CPU and RAM resources, it might be beneficial to check the available resources for the containers. The larger the node is, the more containers it can run. From the containers themselves, you can configure or limit their resource usage. To check available resources to run containers, we need to initiate the following command:

```
kubectl describe node NODE_NAME| grep Allocatable -B 7 -A 6
```

First, we need to get available nodes. This can be done by using the following command:

```
kubectl get nodes
```

The next screenshot shows the output of the previous command with details about the cluster, its version, and its age:

```
admin @cloudshell:~ (wmarusiak-book)$ kubectl get nodes
NAME                                        STATUS   ROLES    AGE   VERSION
gke-gke-cluster-1-default-pool-c9363098-x7sx   Ready    <none>   2d    v1.24.2-gke.1900
gke-gke-cluster-1-default-pool-c9363098-y11n   Ready    <none>   16d   v1.24.2-gke.1900
```

Figure 5.5 – Output of the kubectl get nodes command

Once we have a node name, we can check the resources available to run containers, as follows:

Figure 5.6 – Output of the command to check available resources to run containers on a node

This estimation doesn't take into account the eviction threshold. Kubernetes allows the triggering of eviction if the available memory falls below a certain point. It can be defined as `memory.available<threshold` in %, or as a quantity—for example, `memory.available<10%` or `memory.available<1Gi`.

More details about eviction can be found on the Kubernetes website at the following URL: `https://kubernetes.io/docs/concepts/scheduling-eviction/node-pressure-eviction/#eviction-thresholds`.

Tip

The total available memory for Pods can be calculated by using the following formula:

ALLOCATABLE = CAPACITY - RESERVED - EVICTION-THRESHOLD

Details about GKE reservations can be found at the following URL: `https://cloud.google.com/kubernetes-engine/docs/concepts/plan-node-sizes#memory_and_cpu_reservations`.

Now, let's learn how GKE Standard differs from GKE in Autopilot mode.

GKE Autopilot

Autopilot is a relatively new product from Google Cloud—it was released in February 2021.

Following this announcement, GKE now offers two modes of usage: Standard and Autopilot. We just discussed Standard mode, where we can configure multiple GKE options and fine-tune it to our liking. Autopilot mode, however, aims at delivering industry best practices and eliminates all node management operations, allowing a focus on application deployment:

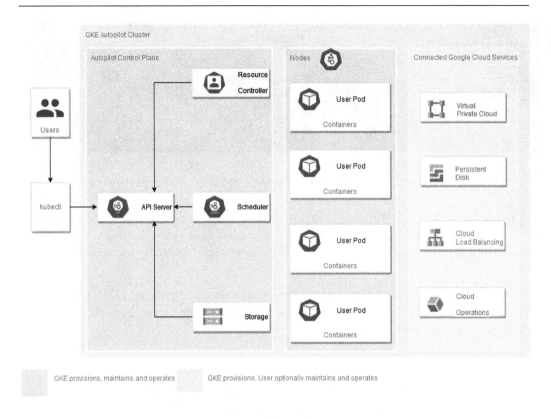

Figure 5.7 – GKE Autopilot architecture overview

In GKE Autopilot, there is no need to monitor the health of nodes or calculate the compute capacity of your cluster to accommodate workloads. You have the same Kubernetes experience as in Standard mode but with less operational overhead.

Google created a fantastic overview of features comparison between the two modes, and we highly encourage you to review the significant differences: https://cloud.google.com/kubernetes-engine/docs/resources/autopilot-standard-feature-comparison.

One big difference between the two modes is that Autopilot has a **service-level agreement** (**SLA**) that covers the GKE control plane (99.95%) and your Pods (99.9%), whereas GKE Standard has an SLA only for the control plane—99.5% SLA for zonal clusters and 99.95% for regional clusters. To gain insights into the GKE SLA, how various GKE deployment types influence the SLA, and which components it encompasses, please refer to the following URL: https://cloud.google.com/kubernetes-engine/sla.

While GKE Autopilot solves many operational burdens (monitoring, best practices, autoscaling, and many others), it has limitations that need to be considered when running workloads.

Some of GKE Autopilot's limitations are listed as follows:

- Hardened configuration of Pods that provides enhanced security isolation. This means that Pods cannot run with elevated privileges, such as root access.

- Revokes permissions for utilizing highly privileged Kubernetes primitives such as privileged Pods, thereby restricting the ability to access, modify, or directly control the underlying node VM.

- Most external monitoring tools will not work due to removing necessary access. Native Google Cloud monitoring must be used in that case.

- We cannot create custom subnets. Subnets are used to divide our cluster's network into smaller segments. In GKE Autopilot, subnets are created automatically based on the number of nodes in our cluster.

- We cannot use some Kubernetes networking features. Some Kubernetes networking features, such as NetworkPolicy and Ingress, are not supported in GKE Autopilot.

Those are just a few major limitations, and for production usage, we encourage you to visit the following link to read more: `https://cloud.google.com/kubernetes-engine/docs/concepts/autopilot-overview#security-limitations`.

GKE management interfaces

GKE offers multiple management interfaces we can interact with. Google Cloud offers full capabilities in each of the interfaces. Upcoming parts of the chapter will guide us through both the CLI and the Cloud console experience of cluster management and configuration.

Cloud Console

We already know Cloud Console from the previous chapter, where we worked heavily with Compute Engine and we worked with instances. The following screenshot shows two GKE clusters running in our project. The console looks familiar to GCE:

Figure 5.8 – GKE in Cloud Console

We will show you how to deploy GKE Standard and GKE Autopilot in the upcoming section.

Cloud Shell

Cloud Shell and its gcloud set of commands can be used to manage GKE together with Cloud Console. The gcloud command can be handy when you want to script and automate GKE-related tasks.

Cloud SDK

Cloud SDK provides Cloud Client Libraries, allowing you to interact with GKE resources. SDK libraries are available in the following programming languages: Java, Go, Python, Ruby, PHP, C#, C++, and Node.js.

kubectl

The primary tool for managing Kubernetes clusters is a tool called kubectl. It can be used on Windows, Linux, or macOS operating systems.

To install it on those operating systems, follow this guide: https://kubernetes.io/docs/tasks/tools/.

We are a big fan of Cloud Shell, which can be used directly from the browser, so we will show you how to use kubectl from Cloud Shell.

Here is the command we need to run to install it via the Google Cloud CLI component manager:

```
gcloud components install kubectl
sudo apt-get install kubectl
```

Once installed, we can interact with Kubernetes clusters.

Cluster management access configuration

As described in the *Kubernetes components* section, we interact with clusters using a YAML file called kubeconfig in the $HOME/.kube/config directory.

You can create a cluster using the following command:

```
gcloud container clusters create my-cluster
```

Then, kubeconfig is added automatically to the kubeconfig file. Similar to the gcloud commands in *Chapter 4,* about GCE, gcloud might require a zone parameter —for example, --zone=us-central1-a.

If you operate more than one Kubernetes cluster, you can check which cluster is currently in context and switch between them, like so:

```
kubectl config current-context
```

In this case, the current context is empty, so we need to configure it, as follows:

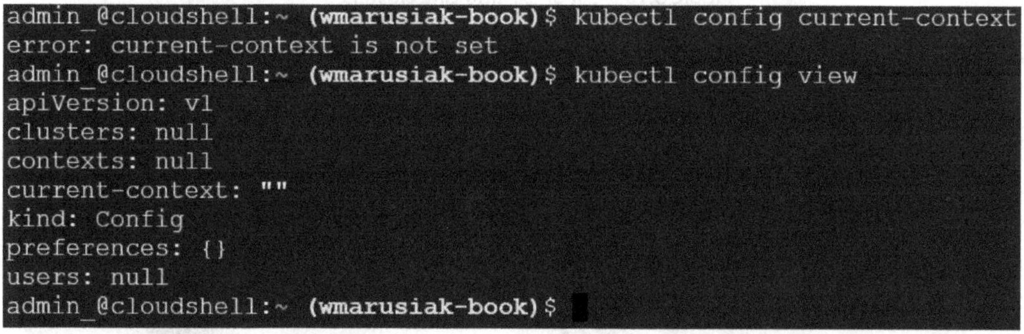

```
admin_@cloudshell:~ (wmarusiak-book)$ kubectl config current-context
error: current-context is not set
admin_@cloudshell:~ (wmarusiak-book)$ kubectl config view
apiVersion: v1
clusters: null
contexts: null
current-context: ""
kind: Config
preferences: {}
users: null
admin_@cloudshell:~ (wmarusiak-book)$ 
```

Figure 5.9 – Current kubectl context is not configured

To manage the Kubernetes cluster, we need to retrieve credentials. To receive them, we need to run the following gcloud command to list existing clusters:

```
gcloud container clusters list
```

The following screenshot shows us the output of the previous command:

```
admin_@cloudshell:~ (wmarusiak-book)$ gcloud container clusters list
NAME: gke-cluster-1
LOCATION: europe-west4-a
MASTER_VERSION: 1.22.8-gke.202
MASTER_IP: 34.90.230.99
MACHINE_TYPE: e2-small
NODE_VERSION: 1.22.8-gke.202
NUM_NODES: 3
STATUS: RUNNING

NAME: gke-cluster-2
LOCATION: europe-west6-a
MASTER_VERSION: 1.24.1-gke.1800
MASTER_IP: 34.65.13.158
MACHINE_TYPE: e2-micro
NODE_VERSION: 1.24.1-gke.1800
NUM_NODES: 3
STATUS: RUNNING
admin_@cloudshell:~ (wmarusiak-book)$
```

Figure 5.10 – List of existing GKE clusters

We need to retrieve the credentials if we want to manage the cluster.

Run the following command:

```
gcloud container clusters get-credentials --zone=europe-west4-a
CLUSTER_NAME
```

Once executed, we can finally list cluster components, as follows:

```
admin_@cloudshell:~ (wmarusiak-book)$ kubectl get pods --all-namespaces
W0717 17:59:49.668735   1265 gcp.go:120] WARNING: the gcp auth plugin is deprecated in v1.22+, unavailable in v1.25+; use gcloud instead.
To learn more, consult https://cloud.google.com/blog/products/containers-kubernetes/kubectl-auth-changes-in-gke
NAMESPACE     NAME                                              READY   STATUS    RESTARTS   AGE
kube-system   container-watcher-fg46p                           1/1     Running   0          48m
kube-system   container-watcher-lrhjk                           1/1     Running   0          48m
kube-system   container-watcher-z2bsh                           1/1     Running   0          48m
kube-system   event-exporter-gke-5479fd58c8-xs5t2               2/2     Running   0          49m
kube-system   fluentbit-gke-gtzvh                               2/2     Running   0          48m
kube-system   fluentbit-gke-rwlzk                               2/2     Running   0          48m
kube-system   fluentbit-gke-sqfqq                               2/2     Running   0          48m
kube-system   gke-metrics-agent-4xb71                           1/1     Running   0          48m
kube-system   gke-metrics-agent-6j7pm                           1/1     Running   0          48m
kube-system   gke-metrics-agent-9rrt8                           1/1     Running   0          48m
kube-system   konnectivity-agent-69cf7888d4-c5jq4               1/1     Running   0          48m
kube-system   konnectivity-agent-69cf7888d4-cq68x               1/1     Running   0          49m
kube-system   konnectivity-agent-69cf7888d4-kx2jm               1/1     Running   0          48m
kube-system   konnectivity-agent-autoscaler-555f599d94-nzkmv    1/1     Running   0          49m
kube-system   kube-dns-56494768b7-4cvx5                         4/4     Running   0          49m
kube-system   kube-dns-56494768b7-f2618                         4/4     Running   0          48m
kube-system   kube-dns-autoscaler-f4d55555-gxvx8                1/1     Running   0          49m
kube-system   kube-proxy-gke-gke-cluster-1-default-pool-3fbd4cb3-0n4s  1/1  Running  0       48m
kube-system   kube-proxy-gke-gke-cluster-1-default-pool-3fbd4cb3-8p2g  1/1  Running  0       47m
kube-system   kube-proxy-gke-gke-cluster-1-default-pool-3fbd4cb3-x25f  1/1  Running  0       48m
kube-system   l7-default-backend-69fb9fd9f9-xjgqs               1/1     Running   0          49m
kube-system   metrics-server-v0.4.5-bbb794dcc-7xnkw             2/2     Running   0          48m
kube-system   pdcsi-node-8mn9j                                  2/2     Running   0          48m
kube-system   pdcsi-node-m75sz                                  2/2     Running   0          48m
kube-system   pdcsi-node-xvatw                                  2/2     Running   0          48m
admin_@cloudshell:~ (wmarusiak-book)$
```

Figure 5.11 – kubectl command output with a listing of cluster resources

To view the current `kubectl` context, we run the command again:

```
kubectl config current-context
```

In this case, the current context was as follows:

```
gke_wmarusiak-book_europe-west6-a_gke-cluster-2
```

To switch context to another cluster, we need to run the following command:

```
kubectl config set-context CONTEXT_NAME
```

In our case, we ran the following:

```
kubectl config set-context gke-cluster-1
```

If we would like to rename the context, we can do this by executing the following command:

```
kubectl config rename-context OLD_CONTEXT_NAME NEW_CONTEXT_NAME
```

We used the following command:

```
kubectl config rename-context gke_wmarusiak-book_europe-west4-a
gke-cluster-1 gke-cluster-1
```

In the next section, we will learn how to create our first GKE cluster using Cloud Shell and the command line.

GKE Standard deployment

As with any other service in Google Cloud, the Kubernetes Engine API must be enabled before using the service. Once the API is enabled, we can proceed with our Kubernetes cluster creation. As mentioned, a GKE deployment can be created with two modes—Autopilot and Standard. We will choose the Standard mode, but we encourage you to try both ways during the learning phase.

Cloud Console

We start with Cloud Console in GKE:

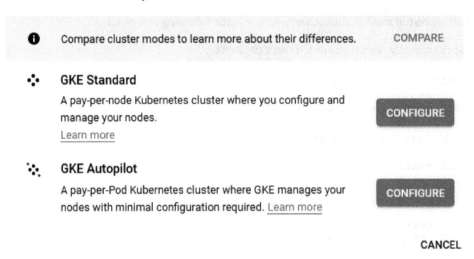

Figure 5.12 – Initial GKE cluster creation selection popup

If you are still unsure which GKE cluster mode you should choose, the following screenshot will help you decide:

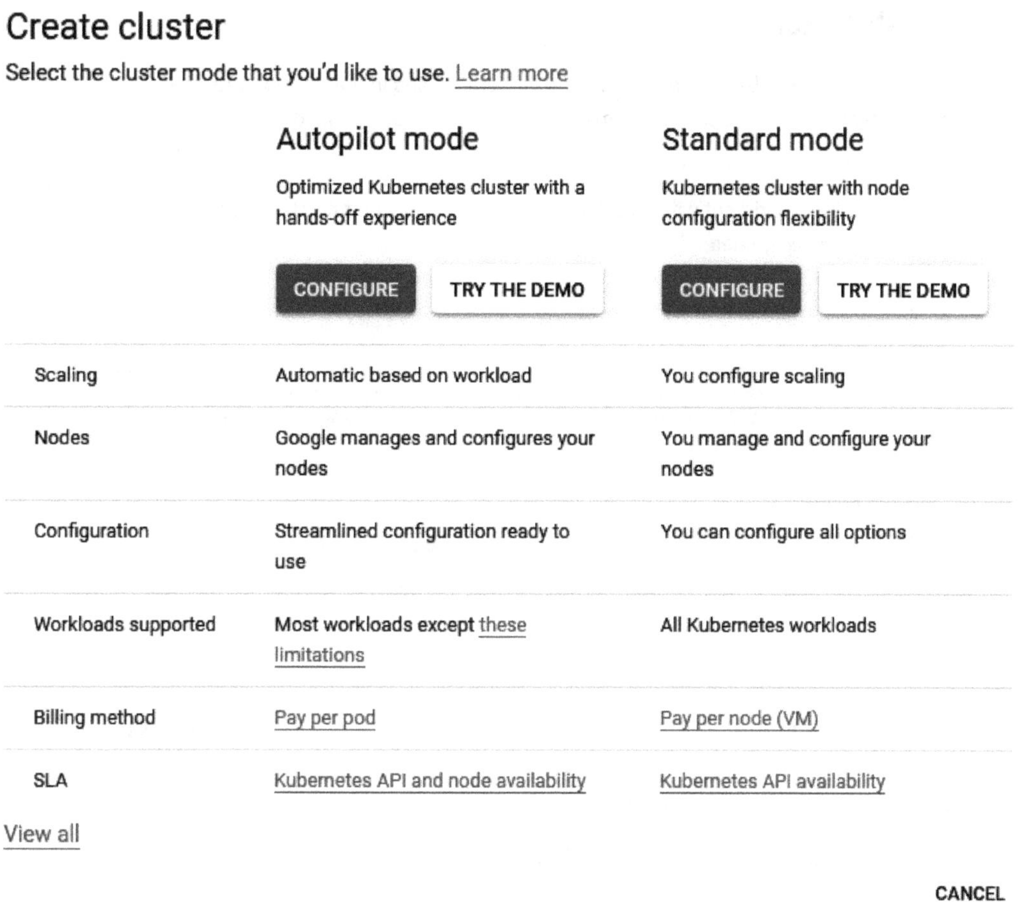

Create cluster

Select the cluster mode that you'd like to use. Learn more

	Autopilot mode Optimized Kubernetes cluster with a hands-off experience	**Standard mode** Kubernetes cluster with node configuration flexibility
	CONFIGURE TRY THE DEMO	CONFIGURE TRY THE DEMO
Scaling	Automatic based on workload	You configure scaling
Nodes	Google manages and configures your nodes	You manage and configure your nodes
Configuration	Streamlined configuration ready to use	You can configure all options
Workloads supported	Most workloads except these limitations	All Kubernetes workloads
Billing method	Pay per pod	Pay per node (VM)
SLA	Kubernetes API and node availability	Kubernetes API availability

View all

CANCEL

Figure 5.13 – Shortened GKE cluster comparison

Both architectures were described in the previous section about GKE architecture. Now, proceed as follows:

1. In Cloud Console, we need to provide the name of the cluster.
2. A quite important decision is whether the GKE cluster deployment is zonal or regional, as described in the *GKE architecture* section. We will proceed with the zonal deployment:

Cluster basics

The new cluster will be created with the name, version, and in the location you specify here. After the cluster is created, name and location can't be changed.

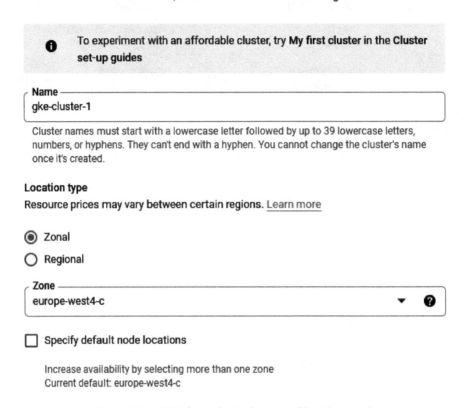

ℹ️ To experiment with an affordable cluster, try **My first cluster** in the **Cluster set-up guides**

Name
gke-cluster-1

Cluster names must start with a lowercase letter followed by up to 39 lowercase letters, numbers, or hyphens. They can't end with a hyphen. You cannot change the cluster's name once it's created.

Location type
Resource prices may vary between certain regions. Learn more

◉ Zonal

◯ Regional

Zone
europe-west4-c   ▼   ❓

☐ Specify default node locations

Increase availability by selecting more than one zone
Current default: europe-west4-c

Figure 5.14 – GKE cluster basics (name and location type)

3. In regional Standard GKE, we can specify default node locations. By selecting that field, we know where the control plane zone is:

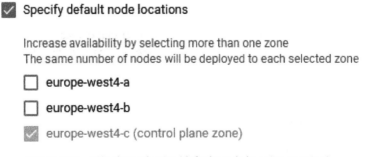

☑ Specify default node locations

Increase availability by selecting more than one zone
The same number of nodes will be deployed to each selected zone

☐ europe-west4-a

☐ europe-west4-b

☑ europe-west4-c (control plane zone)

Figure 5.15 – GKE cluster basics (default node locations setting)

4. In the **Control plane version** section, we can choose either the static or release channel control plane version:

Control plane version

Choose whether you'd like to upgrade the cluster's control plane version manually or let GKE do it automatically. Learn more.

○ Static version
   Manually manage the cluster's control plane version upgrades.

◉ Release channel
   Let GKE automatically manage the cluster's control plane version. Learn more.

┌ Release channel ─────────────────────────────────
│ Regular channel (default)   ▼
└──

┌ Version ───
│ 1.22.8-gke.202 (default)   ▼
└──

These versions have passed internal validation and are considered production-quality, but don't have enough historical data to guarantee their stability. Known issues generally have known workarounds. Release notes

Figure 5.16 – GKE cluster basics (control plane version section)

5. Once we provide all cluster basics values, we can proceed with the node pools section.

6. As described in the *GKE architecture* section, the pool is the actual part of our GKE where containers will be running. There are many options to choose from when creating a default node pool.

7. GKE allows us to pick many operating system images to run on cluster nodes:

Configure node settings

These node settings will be used when new nodes are created using this node pool.

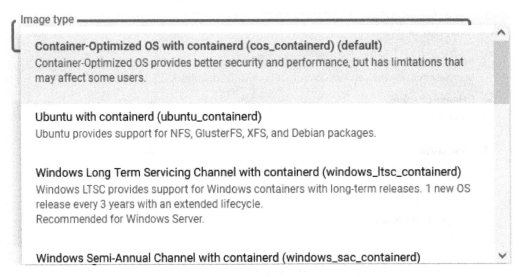

Figure 5.17 – GKE node pool (image type selection)

8. Machine configuration is an integral part of node pool creation. Once created, changing the node pool machine type is impossible. Creating a new node pool and migrating workloads is necessary to change the machine type:

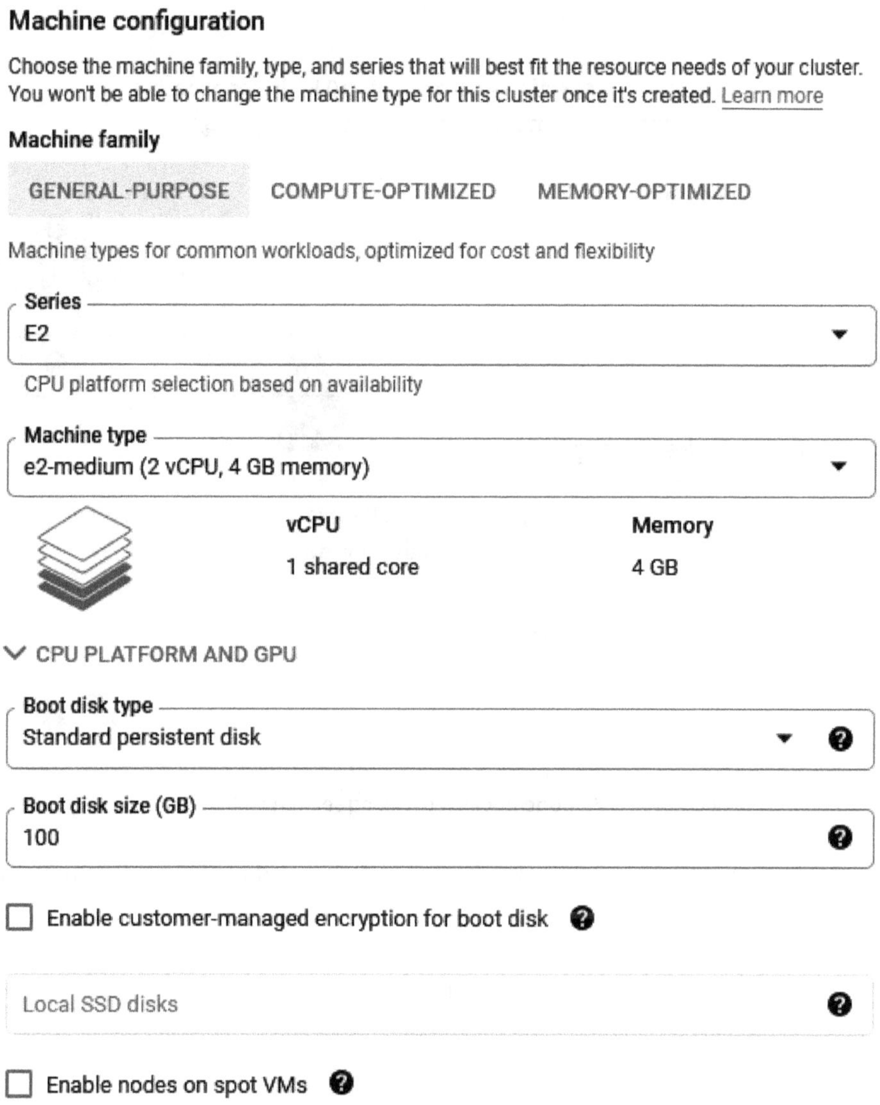

Machine configuration

Choose the machine family, type, and series that will best fit the resource needs of your cluster. You won't be able to change the machine type for this cluster once it's created. Learn more

Machine family

GENERAL-PURPOSE   COMPUTE-OPTIMIZED   MEMORY-OPTIMIZED

Machine types for common workloads, optimized for cost and flexibility

Series
E2 ▼

CPU platform selection based on availability

Machine type
e2-medium (2 vCPU, 4 GB memory) ▼

	vCPU	Memory
	1 shared core	4 GB

∨ CPU PLATFORM AND GPU

Boot disk type
Standard persistent disk ▼ ❷

Boot disk size (GB)
100 ❷

☐ Enable customer-managed encryption for boot disk ❷

Local SSD disks ❷

☐ Enable nodes on spot VMs ❷

Figure 5.18 – GKE node pool (Machine configuration section)

9. In the **Networking** section, we can specify the **Maximum Pods per node** setting, network tags, and a range of node pool Pod addresses:

Networking

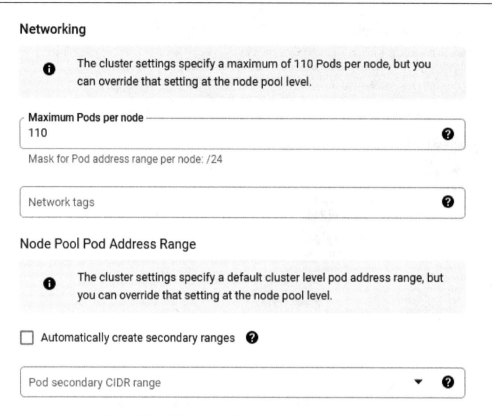

> ℹ️ The cluster settings specify a maximum of 110 Pods per node, but you can override that setting at the node pool level.

Maximum Pods per node
110   ❓

Mask for Pod address range per node: /24

Network tags   ❓

Node Pool Pod Address Range

> ℹ️ The cluster settings specify a default cluster level pod address range, but you can override that setting at the node pool level.

☐ Automatically create secondary ranges ❓

Pod secondary CIDR range   ▾   ❓

Figure 5.19 – GKE node pool (Networking section settings)

10. In the **Node security** section, we can specify the service account used by applications running on node pool VMs:

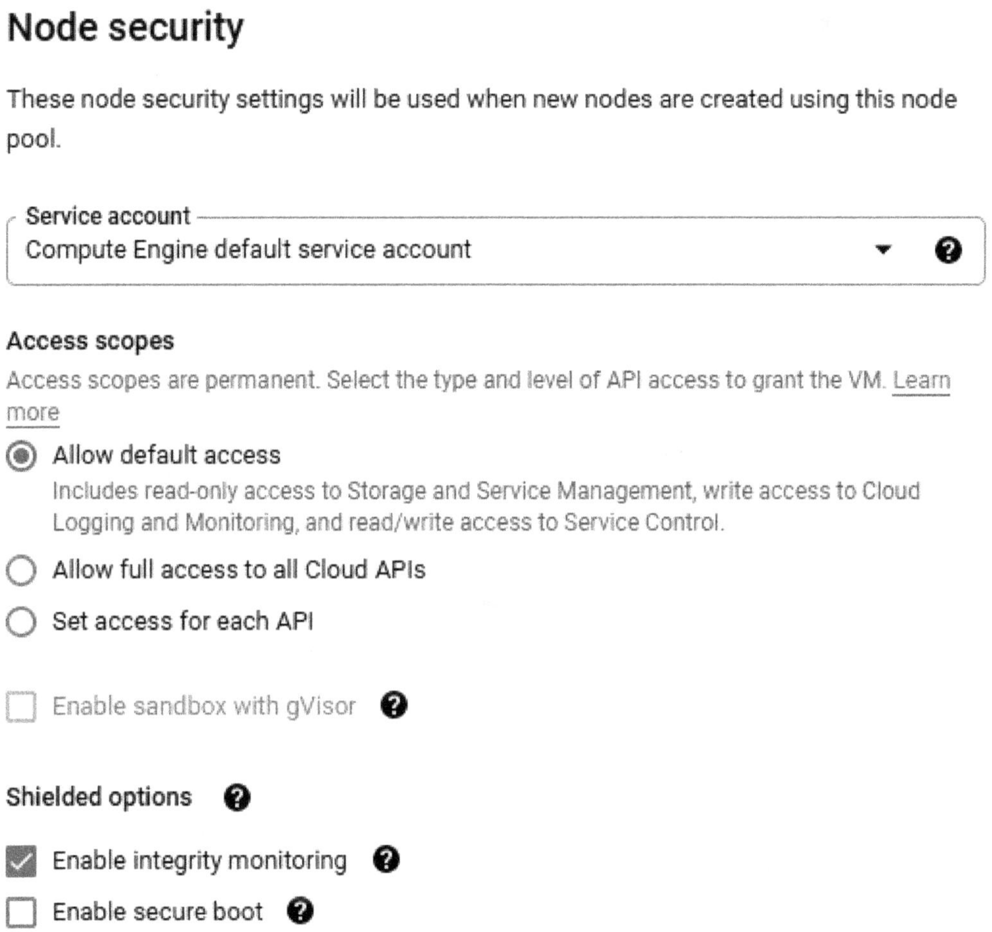

Node security

These node security settings will be used when new nodes are created using this node pool.

```
┌─ Service account ──────────────────────────────────────────────┐
│  Compute Engine default service account              ▼    ❓   │
└────────────────────────────────────────────────────────────────┘
```

Access scopes

Access scopes are permanent. Select the type and level of API access to grant the VM. Learn more

◉ Allow default access

   Includes read-only access to Storage and Service Management, write access to Cloud Logging and Monitoring, and read/write access to Service Control.

○ Allow full access to all Cloud APIs

○ Set access for each API

☐ Enable sandbox with gVisor ❓

Shielded options ❓

☑ Enable integrity monitoring ❓

☐ Enable secure boot ❓

Figure 5.20 – GKE node pool (security settings)

11. We can add labels and node taints in the **Node metadata** part of node pool creation:

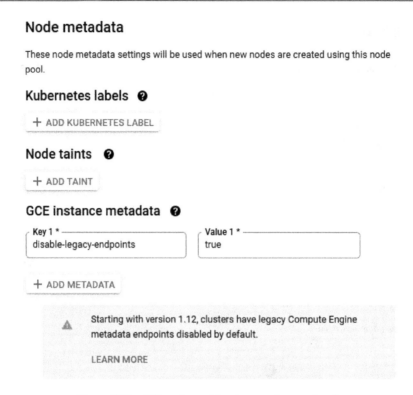

Figure 5.21 – GKE node pool (node metadata settings)

12. After a few minutes, the Standard GKE cluster is operational and ready to receive containerized workloads:

Figure 5.22 – GKE cluster successfully created

In the next section, we'll create GKE clusters using a CLI.

Command line

The simplest command to create a GKE cluster is shown here:

```
gcloud container clusters create-auto second-gke-cluster
--region=europe-west4
```

To use this command, you need a VPC with the default name, and the GKE cluster created using this command needs to be regional, not zonal, and be created in Autopilot mode.

The GKE cluster created with that simple yet effective command will have many default settings that can be changed later.

In the next section, we will learn how to deploy GKE using Autopilot mode.

GKE Autopilot deployment

We already know what differentiates GKE Standard and Autopilot, and we will focus on GKE deployment in Autopilot mode.

Cloud Console

Similar to standard GKE deployment, we need to click the **Create** button to start. As you will see in the screenshots and overall deployment flow, the deployment is much more simplified than with **Standard** mode, and this is a very good thing. We want an automated and simplified experience of running containerized applications in this mode. Follow these steps:

1.   The first two pieces of information we need to provide are the cluster name and desired region:

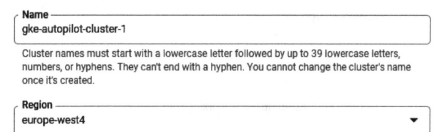

Figure 5.23 – GKE Autopilot initial configuration screen

2.   We can choose a network access option in the Networking section. It can be either a public or private cluster, and we already know the implications from the architecture overview. We will select a public cluster for this deployment:

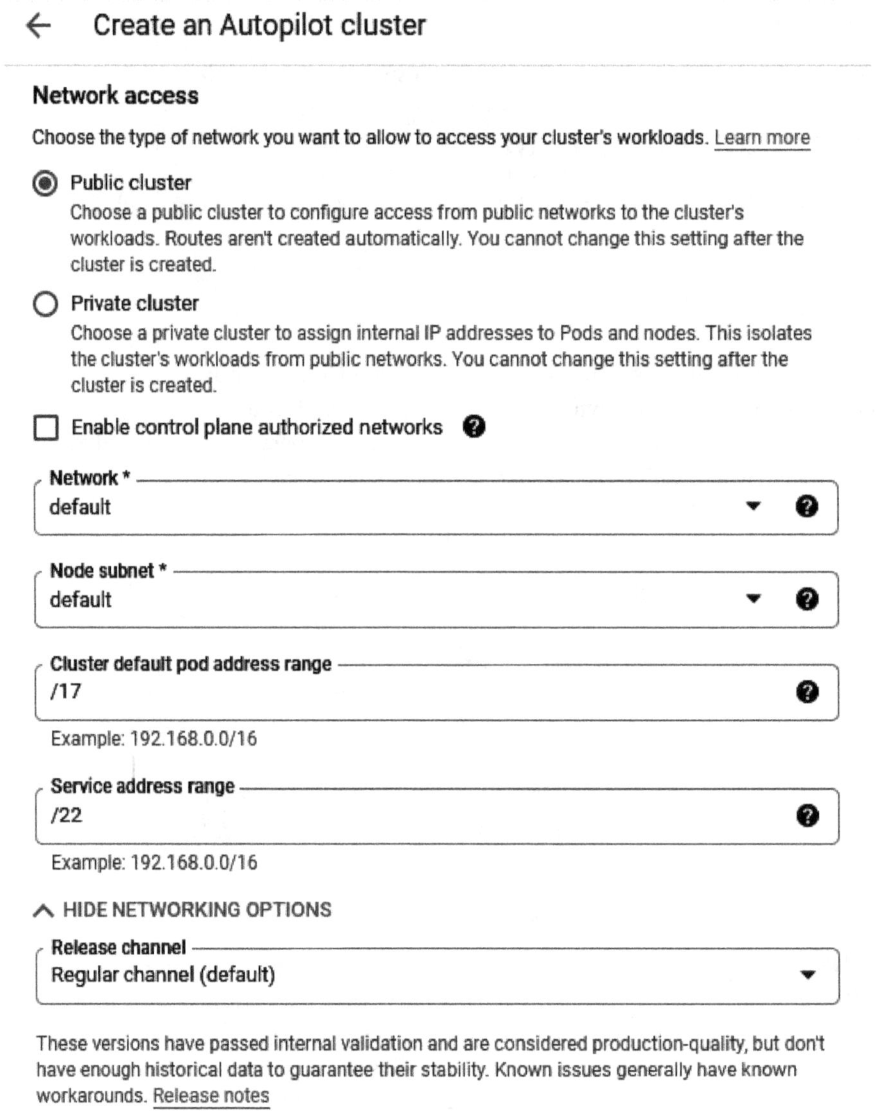

← **Create an Autopilot cluster**

Network access

Choose the type of network you want to allow to access your cluster's workloads. Learn more

◉ Public cluster
Choose a public cluster to configure access from public networks to the cluster's workloads. Routes aren't created automatically. You cannot change this setting after the cluster is created.

○ Private cluster
Choose a private cluster to assign internal IP addresses to Pods and nodes. This isolates the cluster's workloads from public networks. You cannot change this setting after the cluster is created.

☐ Enable control plane authorized networks ❓

Network *
default ▼ ❓

Node subnet *
default ▼ ❓

Cluster default pod address range
/17 ❓

Example: 192.168.0.0/16

Service address range
/22 ❓

Example: 192.168.0.0/16

∧ HIDE NETWORKING OPTIONS

Release channel
Regular channel (default) ▼

These versions have passed internal validation and are considered production-quality, but don't have enough historical data to guarantee their stability. Known issues generally have known workarounds. Release notes

Figure 5.24 – GKE Autopilot networking configuration screen

3.   In the **Automation** section, we can enable the maintenance window. If not selected, cluster maintenance might run at any time:

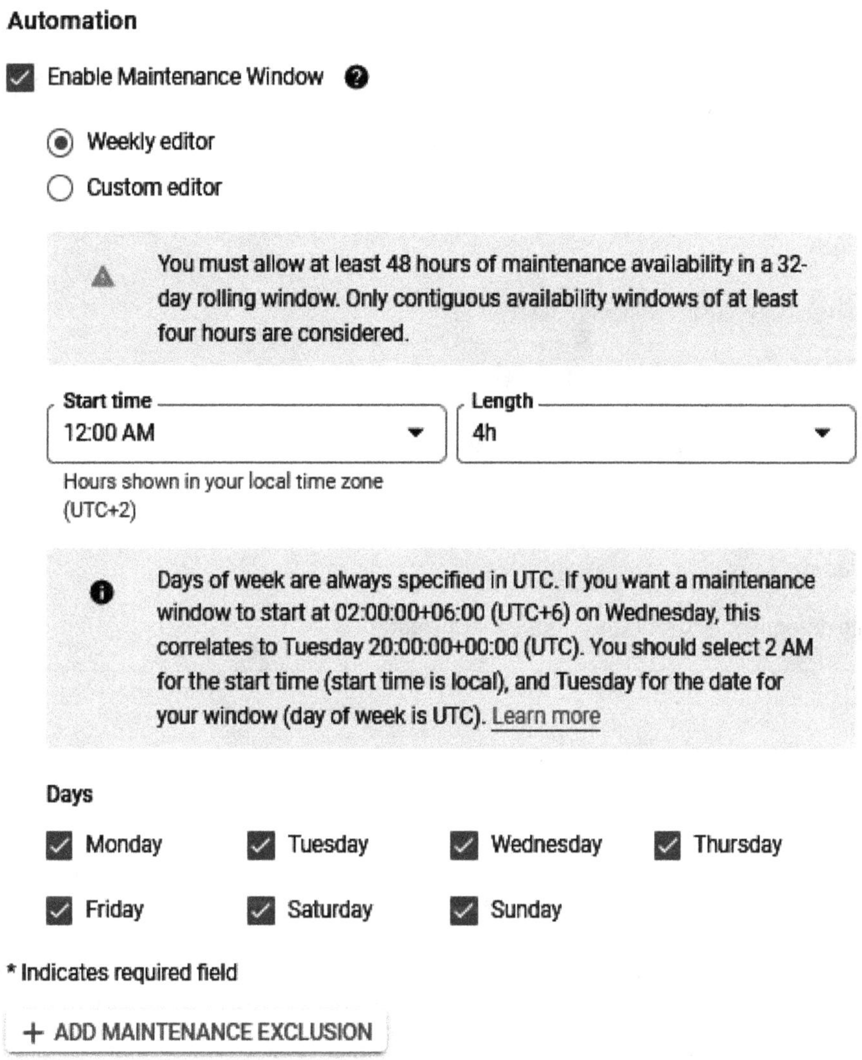

Automation

☑ Enable Maintenance Window ❷

    ◉ Weekly editor

    ◯ Custom editor

> ⚠ You must allow at least 48 hours of maintenance availability in a 32-day rolling window. Only contiguous availability windows of at least four hours are considered.

Start time	Length
12:00 AM ▼	4h ▼

Hours shown in your local time zone
(UTC+2)

> ❶ Days of week are always specified in UTC. If you want a maintenance window to start at 02:00:00+06:00 (UTC+6) on Wednesday, this correlates to Tuesday 20:00:00+00:00 (UTC). You should select 2 AM for the start time (start time is local), and Tuesday for the date for your window (day of week is UTC). Learn more

Days

☑ Monday   ☑ Tuesday   ☑ Wednesday   ☑ Thursday

☑ Friday   ☑ Saturday   ☑ Sunday

* Indicates required field

    + ADD MAINTENANCE EXCLUSION

Figure 5.25 – GKE Autopilot automation configuration screen

4.   We have options to enable Anthos Service Mesh, which is Google's implementation of the powerful Istio open source project, and enable additional security options:

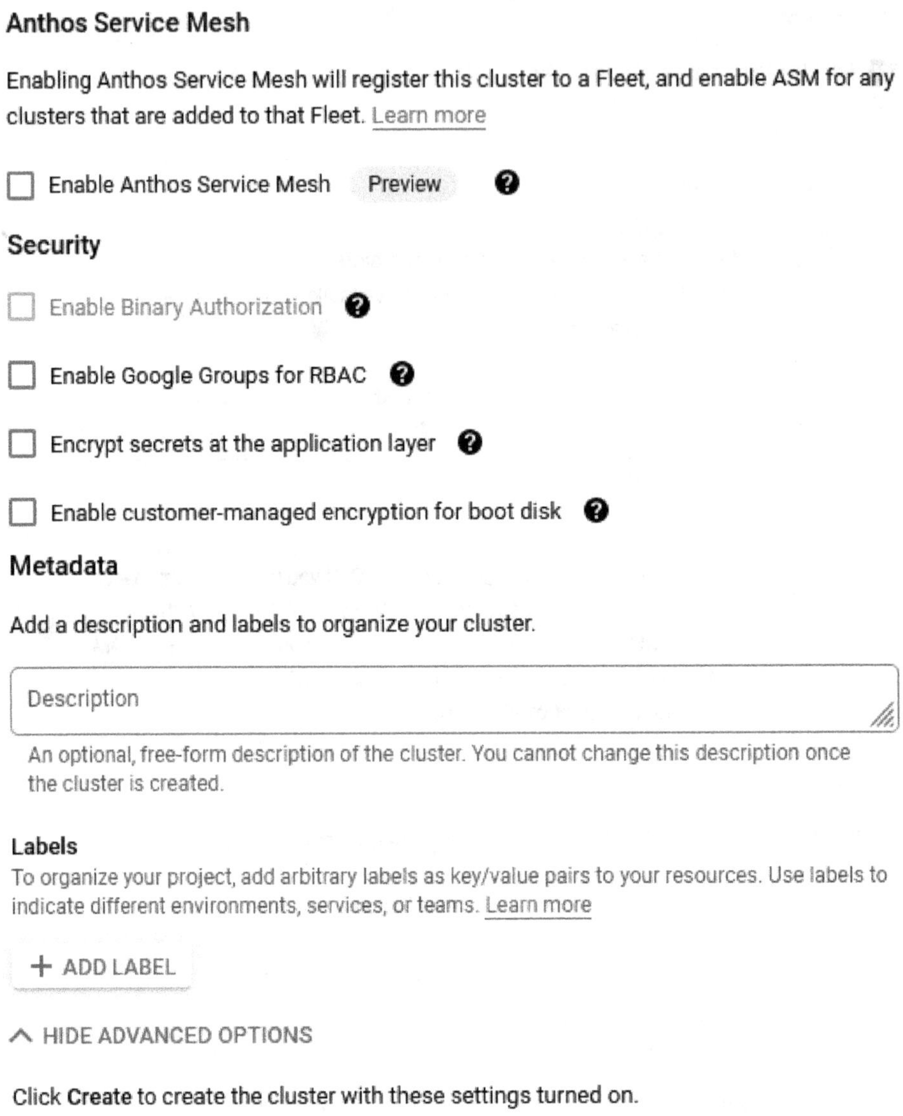

Anthos Service Mesh

Enabling Anthos Service Mesh will register this cluster to a Fleet, and enable ASM for any clusters that are added to that Fleet. Learn more

☐ Enable Anthos Service Mesh   Preview   ❷

Security

☐ Enable Binary Authorization   ❷

☐ Enable Google Groups for RBAC   ❷

☐ Encrypt secrets at the application layer   ❷

☐ Enable customer-managed encryption for boot disk   ❷

Metadata

Add a description and labels to organize your cluster.

```
Description                                                                    //.
```

An optional, free-form description of the cluster. You cannot change this description once the cluster is created.

Labels

To organize your project, add arbitrary labels as key/value pairs to your resources. Use labels to indicate different environments, services, or teams. Learn more

    + ADD LABEL

∧ HIDE ADVANCED OPTIONS

Click **Create** to create the cluster with these settings turned on.

Figure 5.26 – GKE Autopilot automation configuration screen (continued)

5.   After a moment, GKE in Autopilot mode creation completes, and we can consume resources:

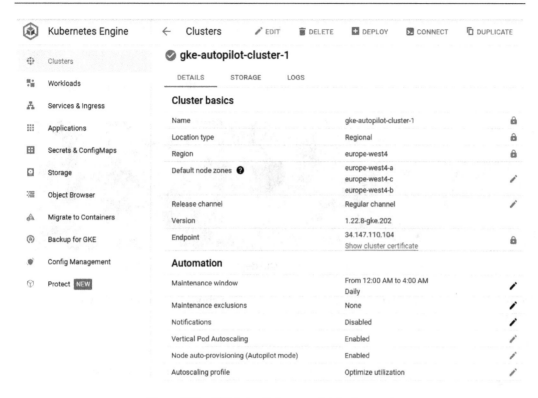

Figure 5.27 – GKE Autopilot successful deployment

Let's try deploying GKE in Autopilot mode using the CLI.

Command line

As the Autopilot clusters are, by default, regional clusters, we need to provide the region and not the zone in the command itself.

The simplest command to create a GKE Autopilot cluster would be this:

```
gcloud container clusters create-auto CLUSTER_NAME --region REGION
NAME --project=PROJECT_NAME
```

The command to create a cluster in the europe-west4 region in the wmarusiak-book project looks like this:

```
gcloud container clusters create-auto gke-cluster-autopilot-2 --region
europe-west4 --project=wmarusiak-book
```

Cluster creation takes a few minutes to deploy, and then we can immediately deploy an application.

We can run the following command to check whether the cluster was created:

```
gcloud container clusters list
```

After running the command, we receive information about the GKE cluster—its location, master version, master IP address, and much more:

```
admin_@cloudshell:~ (wmarusiak-book)$ gcloud container clusters list
NAME: gke-cluster-autopilot-2
LOCATION: europe-west4
MASTER_VERSION: 1.22.12-gke.2300
MASTER_IP: 35.204.144.64
MACHINE_TYPE: e2-medium
NODE_VERSION: 1.22.12-gke.2300
NUM_NODES: 2
STATUS: RUNNING
```

Figure 5.28 – GKE Autopilot successful deployment by using the CLI

The previous command provides more detailed information about the cluster itself. We know the GKE master, node version, machine type, and status.

To connect to the cluster, we need to use the following command:

```
gcloud container clusters get-credentials --region=REGION_NAME
CLUSTER_NAME
```

Once run, the kubectl configuration file will be updated with newly created cluster credentials. The Cloud Shell configuration file is located in the following path: .kube/config.

Naturally, it can be viewed or edited with your preferable command-line file editor.

The configuration file contains the cluster certificate, name, and more information:

```
    server: https://35.204.144.64
  name: gke_wmarusiak-book_europe-west4_gke-cluster-autopilot-2
contexts:
- context:
    cluster: gke_wmarusiak-book_europe-west4_gke-cluster-autopilot-2
    user: gke_wmarusiak-book_europe-west4_gke-cluster-autopilot-2
  name: gke_wmarusiak-book_europe-west4_gke-cluster-autopilot-2
current-context: gke_wmarusiak-book_europe-west4_gke-cluster-autopilot-2
kind: Config
preferences: {}
users:
- name: gke_wmarusiak-book_europe-west4_gke-cluster-autopilot-2
  user:
    exec:
      apiVersion: client.authentication.k8s.io/v1beta1
      command: gke-gcloud-auth-plugin
      installHint: Install gke-gcloud-auth-plugin for use with kubectl by following
        https://cloud.google.com/blog/products/containers-kubernetes/kubectl-auth-changes-in-gke
      provideClusterInfo: true
```

Figure 5.29 – Fragment of the kubectl configuration file with cluster details

Once the cluster is created, it is ready to host new applications. In the next section, we will create and deploy a new application to the cluster.

Working with applications

The beauty of Kubernetes is that applications developed, tested, and run on-premises can be moved to other Kubernetes environments without major refactoring. Of course, if you use a specific load balancer or storage type that isn't available in GKE, you will need to adjust those settings.

In the next section, we will learn what Artifact Registry is, its features, and how it can make our life easier.

Artifact Registry

Artifact Registry is a new product from Google Cloud that inherited features from **Google Container Registry (GCR)** and got some new features.

A container registry is a product that stores and manages Docker images and performs vulnerability analysis with fine-grained access control. You could easily integrate your CI/CD pipelines with it and store the images securely in a private repository.

Artifact Registry goes beyond GCR. Not only does it have the features of a container registry but also many others:

- Artifact storage from Google Cloud Build

- Artifact deployment to Google Cloud runtimes such as GKE, Cloud Run, Compute Engine, and App Engine flexible environments

- Software Delivery Shield offers end-to-end software supply chain security solutions

We have learned where we can store Docker images, so now it is time to deploy a sample application into our Google Kubernetes cluster.

Deploying applications

We will guide you through a sample application deployment from the Google Cloud samples Docker repository. The Artifact Registry URL is the URL that you use to access Artifact Registry repositories. The URL is of the following form: `https://<REGION>-docker.pkg.dev/<PROJECT_ID>/<REPOSITORY_NAME>`

For example, the Artifact Registry URL for the `my-repository` repository in the `my-project` project in the `us-central1` region would be this: `https://us-central1-docker.pkg.dev/my-project/my-repository`.

You can use the Artifact Registry URL to push and pull images from Artifact Registry repositories. You can also use the URL to browse the contents of a repository.

We will run the `hello-app` Docker image from the `us-docker.pkg.dev/google-samples/containers/gke/hello-app:1.0` repository.

To run this application, we can use the following command:

```
kubectl create deployment hello-server --image=us-docker.pkg.dev/
google-samples/containers/gke/hello-app:1.0
```

In the next screenshot, we can see the output of the previous command:

```
admin_@cloudshell:~ (wmarusiak-book)$ kubectl create deployment hello-
erver    --image=us-docker.pkg.dev/google-samples/containers/gke/hell
-app:1.0
Warning: Autopilot set default resource requests for Deployment defaul
/hello-server, as resource requests were not specified. See http://g.c
/gke/autopilot-defaults.
deployment.apps/hello-server created
admin_@cloudshell:~ (wmarusiak-book)$ 
```

Figure 5.30 – hello-app application deployed to GKE Autopilot cluster

The application is deployed, and to use it, we need to expose it to the internet so that we can access it. We can do this by using the following command:

```
kubectl expose deployment hello-server --type LoadBalancer --port 80
--target-port 8080
```

We can check running Pods by using this command:

```
kubectl get pods
```

After running the command, we receive information about running Pods and their name, status, and age:

```
admin_@cloudshell:~ (wmarusiak-book)$ kubectl get pods
NAME                          READY   STATUS    RESTARTS   AGE
hello-server-8444b8cdf-kt24d  1/1     Running   0          2m58s
admin_@cloudshell:~ (wmarusiak-book)$ 
```

Figure 5.31 – Pods running in the hello-app application

The last step is to find out the publicly accessible IP address of our application. To find this out, we should run the following command:

```
kubectl get service hello-server
```

In the next screenshot, we can see the output of the command with an external IP address that can be used to access the application:

```
admin_@cloudshell:~ (wmarusiak-book)$ kubectl get service hello-server
NAME            TYPE           CLUSTER-IP       EXTERNAL-IP     PORT(S)
    AGE
hello-server    LoadBalancer   10.43.128.38     35.204.28.39    80:30662/T
P    2m52s
```

Figure 5.32 – Publicly available IP address of the hello-app application

The last step to access the `hello-app` application is to insert an external IP address into the browser:

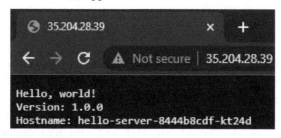

Figure 5.33 – hello-app application exposed on the internet

After confirmation that the `hello-app` application works as expected, the final step is to delete it. To do so, we can use the following command:

```
kubectl delete service hello-server && kubectl delete deployment
hello-server
```

After deleting the `hello-app` application with all its services, let's focus on the different types of deployments we can use.

Deployment

This is one of the easiest deployment types for an application, and it is mainly used for stateless applications or when we need a single Pod.

ReplicaSet

A ReplicaSet deployment type is used when we want multiple instances of a Pod with a specified number of running Pods.

StatefulSets

A StatefulSets deployment type is similar to Deployment because it uses a single image for Pods. StatefulSets, however, guarantees that when the application is scaled and when we add more Pods, each pod will be unique and have a unique identifier.

DaemonSet

Similar to other deployment types, Daemons manage a group of replicated Pods. A DaemonSet is mainly used for application deployment with ongoing background tasks that must be run on certain nodes.

To learn more and get sample deployment types, we recommend visiting the Kubernetes website for a more detailed overview: `https://kubernetes.io/docs/concepts/workloads/controllers/`.

Summary

The first chapter about GKE focused on the architecture, the main components, and how they work with each other. We learned about different types of GKE offerings in Google Cloud—GKE Standard and GKE Autopilot. Another important part of the chapter was about storage in GKE, which is very important to secure our data stored in Pods. An important lesson in this chapter was about the deployment of the two types of GKE clusters themselves and application deployment.

After learning which deployment types GKE and Kubernetes offer, we will learn how to view and manage GKE resources—clusters, node pools, Pods, and services in the next chapter.

Questions

Answer the following questions to test your knowledge of this chapter:

1. What are the primary components of GKE?

    A. Master nodes and worker nodes

    B. Master nodes

    C. Worker nodes

    D. Dedicated nodes, worker nodes, and master nodes

2. Which of the following statements about Kubernetes is true?

    A. A node is used to monitor GKE clusters

    B. A node is used to host the GKE API

    C. A node cannot be scheduled on demand

    D. A node is the smallest unit of computing hardware in Kubernetes

3. Which of the following statements describes a Pod in Kubernetes?

    A. Pods can only run one container

    B. Pods are static

C. Pods can be run on VMs

D. A Pod is a group of one or more containers

4. Which operating system image can you run on a node in GKE based on version 1.23 and upward?

A. Container-Optimized OS with containerd (`cos_containerd`)

B. Ubuntu with containerd (`ubuntu_containderd`)

C. Windows LTSC with containerd (`windows_ltsc_containerd`)

D. All of these

5. Which `gcloud` namespace can be used to create a GKE cluster?

A. `gcloud container clusters create`

B. `gcloud clusters container create`

C. `gcloud gke cluster create`

D. `gke cluster create`

6. You have been tasked with the creation of a GKE cluster that delivers industry best practices and eliminates all node management operations, allowing you to focus on application deployment. Which GKE mode will you choose?

A. GKE Standard

B. GKE Autopilot

7. Which command would you use to connect to a GKE cluster?

A. `gcloud clusters container get-credentials GKE_CLUSTER_NAME --region REGION_NAME --project PROJECT_NAME`

B. `gcloud connect gke get-credentials GKE_CLUSTER_NAME --region REGION_NAME --project PROJECT_NAME`

C. `gcloud container clusters get-credentials GKE_CLUSTER_NAME --region REGION_NAME --project PROJECT_NAME`

D. `kubectl connect GKE_CLUSTER_NAME`

8. Which product from Google Cloud can be used to store Docker images?

A. Cloud Run

B. Container Registry

C. Cloud Shield

D. Cloud Images

9. You have been tasked with deploying an application on GKE. You need to ensure that once the application is working, it will scale automatically, and the Pods will have unique identifiers. Which deployment type will you use?

    A. DaemonSet

    B. StatefulSet

    C. ReplicaSet

    D. Single Pod

10. Is it possible to change the node size from the node pool without recreating it?

    A. Yes

    B. No

Answers

The answers to the preceding questions are provided here:

1A, 2D, 3D, 4D, 5A, 6B, 7C, 8B, 9B, 10B

6

Implementing Compute Solutions – Google Kubernetes Engine (Part 2)

The second part of the chapter about implementing compute solutions using **Google Kubernetes Engine** (**GKE**) focuses on operations such as cluster, node pool, Pod, and Service management.

The following topics are covered:

- Cluster operations
- Node pool operations
- Pod management
- Service management
- GKE logging and monitoring

In the previous chapter about GKE, we learned how to create clusters in **Standard** and **Autopilot** modes. In this chapter, we will focus on the operational tasks of GKE.

Cluster operations

After the first containerized application deployment, we will focus on Google Kubernetes management. Not only will we modify our clusters, but we will view resources and delete them as well. By performing those operations, we learn and memorize the steps needed to perform those activities and prepare for future use of GKE and containers.

Viewing cluster resources

Before we can perform any operation on a GKE cluster, we need to gather information about the existing cluster state, its configuration, and the resources available to us. This information will help us to understand the cluster and ensure that our operations are successful.

There are a number of ways to gather information about a GKE cluster. One way is to use the `kubectl` command-line tool. The `kubectl get nodes` command will list all nodes in the cluster, and the `kubectl get pods` command will list all Pods in the cluster.

Another way to gather information about a GKE cluster is to use the Kubernetes Dashboard. The Kubernetes Dashboard is a web-based user interface that allows us to view and manage our GKE cluster.

Once we have gathered information about the existing cluster state, we can then begin to perform operations on the cluster. For example, we could add or remove nodes, change the Kubernetes version, or allocate more resources to certain Pods.

Cloud console

The initial Cloud console view of a cluster shows the following information located on the first tab, **OVERVIEW**:

- Cluster status
- Name
- Location
- Mode
- Number of nodes
- Total vCPUs
- Total memory
- Notifications
- Labels

More detailed information about the cluster is available when we click on a particular tab.

The second tab, **OBSERVABILITY**, contains summarized information about all clusters, and there is a possibility to drill down into a specific cluster if needed:

Figure 6.1 – OBSERVABILITY tab from the main GKE page

Finally, the third tab, **COST OPTIMIZATION**, lets us view cost optimization recommendations from Google Cloud:

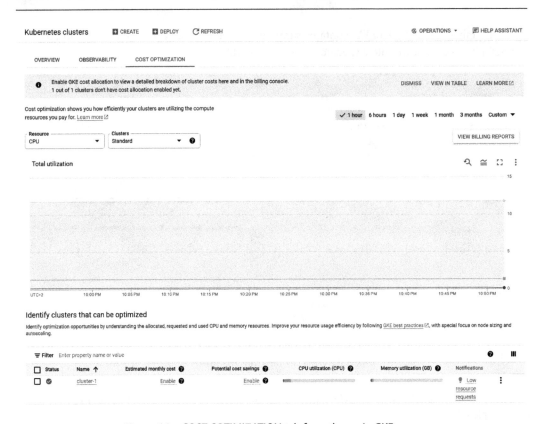

Figure 6.2 – COST OPTIMIZATION tab from the main GKE page

Having overall information, we can dig into existing clusters. To view detailed information, we need to click on the desired cluster. The information is split into four sections, as follows:

- **Details**
- **Nodes**
- **Storage**
- **Logs**

The **Details** section is dedicated to the whole cluster, where we can see information divided into the following sections:

- **Cluster basics**
- **Automation**
- **Networking**
- **Security**

- **Metadata**

- **Features**

We encourage you to check each section as the information is very detailed.

In the **NODES** tab of a specific cluster, we can drill down into **Node Pools** and **Nodes**. We see details about node performance metrics and a summary of node pools:

Figure 6.3 – Node pool summary overview

Command line

To list GKE clusters in use, we can use the `gcloud container clusters list` command in either Cloud Shell or your local computer, resulting in the following output:

```
admin_@cloudshell:~ (wmarusiak-book)$ gcloud container clusters list
NAME: gke-cluster-autopilot-2
LOCATION: europe-west4
MASTER_VERSION: 1.22.12-gke.2300
MASTER_IP: 35.204.144.64
MACHINE_TYPE:
NODE_VERSION:
NUM_NODES:
STATUS: RUNNING

NAME: gke-cluster-1
LOCATION: europe-west4-b
MASTER_VERSION: 1.24.2-gke.1900
MASTER_IP: 35.204.71.80
MACHINE_TYPE: g1-small
NODE_VERSION: 1.24.2-gke.1900
NUM_NODES: 2
STATUS: RUNNING
```

Figure 6.4 – Output of the gcloud container clusters list command with clusters listed

To drill down into a specific cluster, we can use the following command:

```
gcloud container clusters describe --zone=ZONE_NAME CLUSTER_NAME
```

The command's output is extensive, so you might consider filtering to shorten the output.

Adding clusters

In the previous section of the chapter, we deployed GKE in both Standard and Autopilot modes by using both Cloud console and the CLI. In this section, we will move directly onto modifying the cluster part.

Modifying clusters

Every person can perceive cluster modifications differently. For someone, it can be adding a node pool or modifying cluster settings; for another person, an upgrade is a cluster modification. Both can be correct, and it would be challenging to describe every possible modification of a GKE cluster.

One very important cluster modification is the GKE cluster version upgrade.

> **Note**
> By default, automatic upgrades are enabled for both GKE Standard and GKE Autopilot. There is the possibility to upgrade a GKE Standard cluster manually, but this option doesn't exist for GKE Autopilot.

Let's upgrade a GKE Standard cluster to a newer version.

Cloud console

To upgrade a GKE cluster in Cloud console, we need to click on the desired cluster. Then, proceed as follows:

1.   If a cluster upgrade is available, it will be visible in the **Cluster basics** section of Cloud console.

2. Click **UPGRADE AVAILABLE** and detailed information about possible upgrades will be displayed:

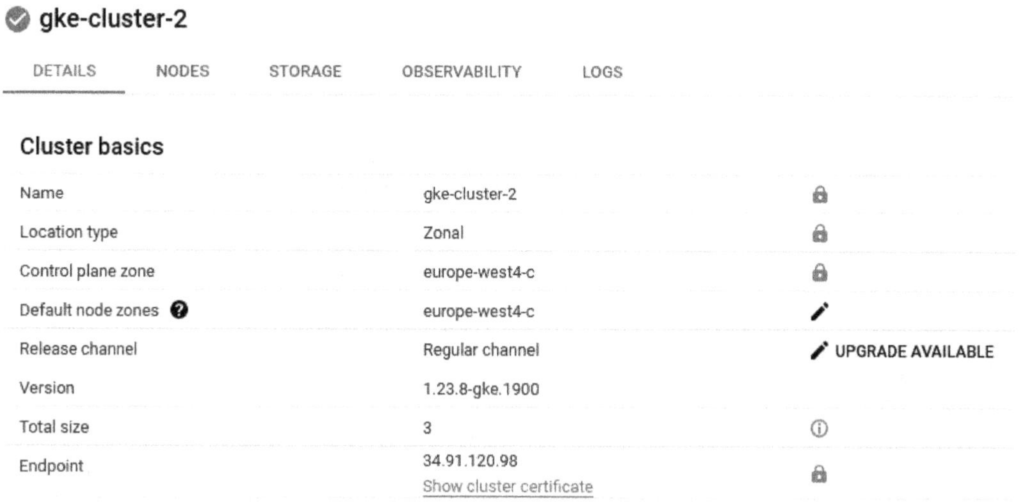

✅ gke-cluster-2

| DETAILS | NODES | STORAGE | OBSERVABILITY | LOGS |

Cluster basics

Name	gke-cluster-2	🔒
Location type	Zonal	🔒
Control plane zone	europe-west4-c	🔒
Default node zones ❓	europe-west4-c	✏️
Release channel	Regular channel	✏️ UPGRADE AVAILABLE
Version	1.23.8-gke.1900	
Total size	3	ⓘ
Endpoint	34.91.120.98 Show cluster certificate	🔒

Figure 6.5 – Cluster basics section with available upgrade

3. You can choose the static version or a release channel from the available options. The release channel has three options—**Stable channel**, **Regular channel**, and **Rapid channel**. You can choose the desired version depending on which channel you need:

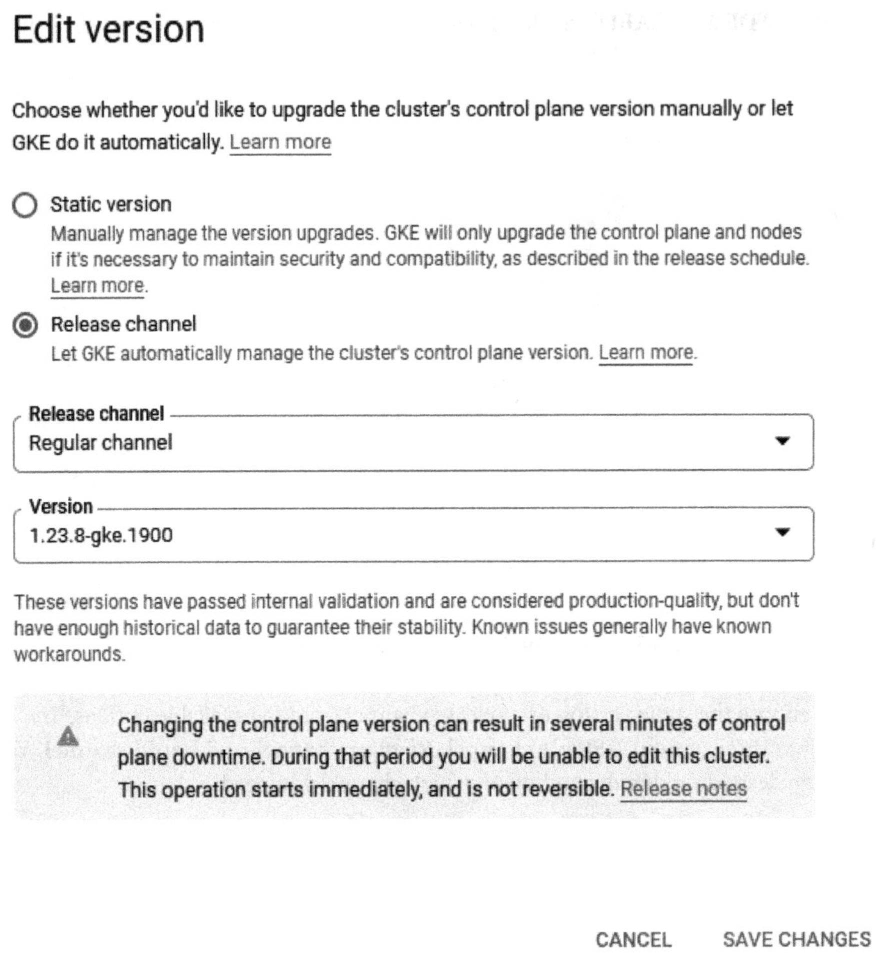

Edit version

Choose whether you'd like to upgrade the cluster's control plane version manually or let GKE do it automatically. Learn more

○ Static version
   Manually manage the version upgrades. GKE will only upgrade the control plane and nodes if it's necessary to maintain security and compatibility, as described in the release schedule. Learn more.

◉ Release channel
   Let GKE automatically manage the cluster's control plane version. Learn more.

┌─ Release channel ──┐
│ Regular channel   ▼ │
└──┘

┌─ Version ──┐
│ 1.23.8-gke.1900   ▼ │
└──┘

These versions have passed internal validation and are considered production-quality, but don't have enough historical data to guarantee their stability. Known issues generally have known workarounds.

> ⚠ Changing the control plane version can result in several minutes of control plane downtime. During that period you will be unable to edit this cluster. This operation starts immediately, and is not reversible. Release notes

                                            CANCEL   SAVE CHANGES

Figure 6.6 – Cluster basics section with available upgrade (continued)

4. After selecting the desired version, we need to click **SAVE CHANGES**, and the control upgrade starts. It might take a few minutes as all management components must be updated:

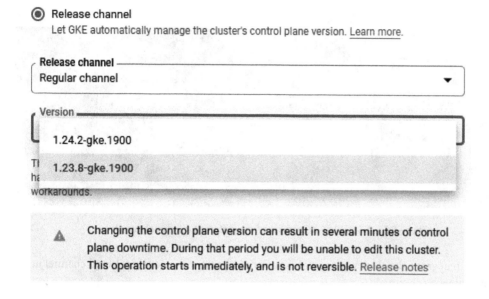

Figure 6.7 – Release channel version selection

5. After the control plane upgrade, you can proceed with the node pool upgrade to have the same version of GKE components.

With the upgrade in Cloud console complete, we move to the upgrade procedure using a CLI.

Command line

The procedure doesn't differ from the Cloud console procedure. The step we didn't have in Cloud console is retrieving available versions. Proceed as follows:

1. To retrieve available GKE versions, we need to run the following command:

```
gcloud container get-server-config --zone=zone_name
```

This results in the following output:

```
admin_@cloudshell:~ (wmarusiak-book)$ gcloud container get-server-config --zone=europe-west4-c
Fetching server config for europe-west4-c
channels:
- channel: RAPID
  defaultVersion: 1.24.4-gke.800
  validVersions:
  - 1.25.2-gke.1700
  - 1.25.1-gke.500
  - 1.24.6-gke.1500
  - 1.24.5-gke.600
  - 1.24.4-gke.800
  - 1.24.3-gke.2100
  - 1.23.12-gke.1600
  - 1.23.12-gke.100
  - 1.23.11-gke.300
  - 1.22.15-gke.1000
  - 1.22.15-gke.100
```

Figure 6.8 – Available GKE versions from different release channels

2. We can upgrade the cluster to the standard version per our previously selected channel using the following command:

    ```
    gcloud container clusters upgrade CLUSTER_NAME --zone=zone_name-
    -master
    ```

3. If we want to upgrade to a specific version, we can use the following command:

    ```
    gcloud container clusters upgrade CLUSTER_NAME --zone=zone_name-
    -master --cluster-version VERSION
    ```

4. In this case, we have a GKE cluster called gke-cluster-4 using a stable release channel. We will upgrade it from version 1.22.12-gke.2300 to the latest available—1.23.11-gke.300—and we will specify the cluster zone. If you want to upgrade to the latest version, it is possible to use the latest flag instead of the exact cluster version:

    ```
    gcloud container clusters upgrade gke-cluster-4 --zone=europe-
    west4-c --master --cluster-version 1.23.11-gke.300
    ```

This results in the following output:

```
admin_@cloudshell:~ (wmarusiak-book)$ gcloud container clusters
upgrade gke-cluster-4 --zone=europe-west4-c --master --cluster-v
ers
ion 1.23.11-gke.300

Master of cluster [gke-cluster-4] will be upgraded from version
[1.22.12-gke.2300] to version [1.23.11-gke.300]. This operation
is
long-running and will block other operations on the cluster (inc
luding delete) until it has run to completion.

Do you want to continue (Y/n)?  y
```

Figure 6.9 – Command to upgrade the GKE cluster to a specific version

5. After a few minutes, the cluster upgrade is finished. We can check the cluster version by running the `gcloud container clusters list --zone=europe-west4-c` command, which results in the following output:

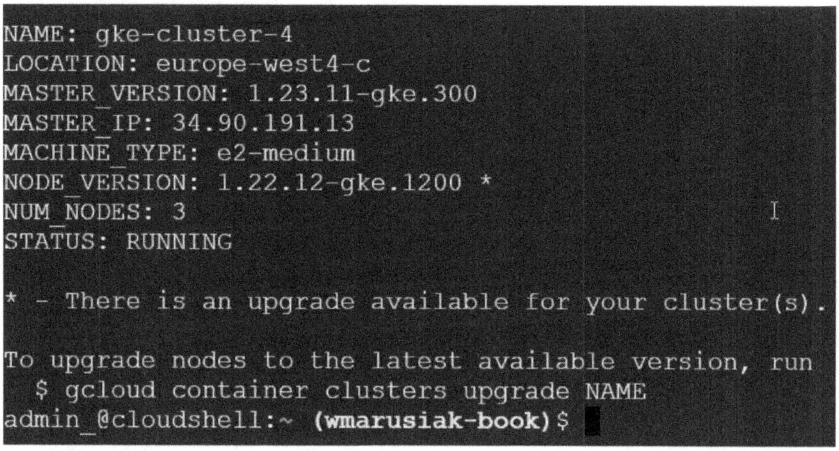

```
NAME: gke-cluster-4
LOCATION: europe-west4-c
MASTER_VERSION: 1.23.11-gke.300
MASTER_IP: 34.90.191.13
MACHINE_TYPE: e2-medium
NODE_VERSION: 1.22.12-gke.1200 *
NUM_NODES: 3
STATUS: RUNNING

* - There is an upgrade available for your cluster(s).

To upgrade nodes to the latest available version, run
   $ gcloud container clusters upgrade NAME
admin_@cloudshell:~ (wmarusiak-book)$
```

Figure 6.10 – The gke-cluster-4 cluster has been upgraded to a newer version

After successfully upgrading the cluster, our master GKE nodes have a new version, and the next step to complete the upgrade is to upgrade the node pool.

Now that we have a successful upgrade using the command line and Cloud console, we are ready to proceed with the next step in our learning—cluster removal.

Removing clusters

A cluster removal operation is irreversible, and all the resources within the cluster will be removed. This includes the following:

- Control plane resources
- All node instances in the cluster
- Any Pods that are running on those instances
- Any firewalls and routes created by GKE at the time of cluster creation
- Data stored in the hostPath host and emptyDir volumes

Cloud console

In Cloud console, choose the to-be-deleted cluster by selecting the three dots, as shown in the following screenshot:

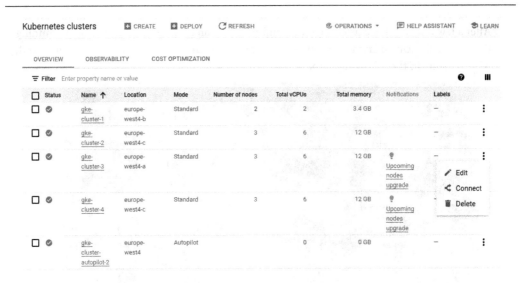

Figure 6.11 – GKE cluster deletion in Cloud console

We need to confirm cluster deletion by typing the name of the cluster, as follows:

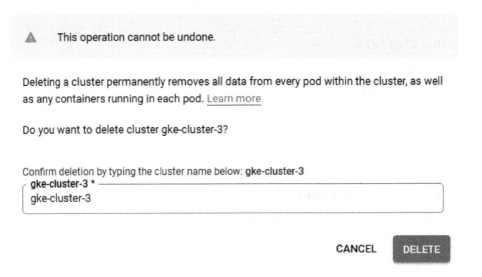

Figure 6.12 – Cluster deletion confirmation

Once the **DELETE** button is pressed, the cluster will no longer be accessible. After a moment, deletion completes, and the cluster with its resources no longer exists.

Command line

To delete a GKE cluster, we need to use the following command:

```
gcloud container clusters delete CLUSTER_NAME --zone=zone_name
```

In the next screenshot, we see the progress and output of the command that leads to cluster deletion:

```
admin_@cloudshell:~ (wmarusiak-book)$ gcloud container clusters delete gke-cluster-2 --zone=eu
rope-west4-c
The following clusters will be deleted.
 - [gke-cluster-2] in [europe-west4-c]

Do you want to continue (Y/n)?  y

Deleting cluster gke-cluster-2...done.
Deleted [https://container.googleapis.com/v1/projects/wmarusiak-book/zones/europe-west4-c/clus
ters/gke-cluster-2].
admin_@cloudshell:~ (wmarusiak-book)$ []
```

Figure 6.13 – Cluster deletion using CLI

By performing cluster operations, we have delved deeper into GKE management. Let's move on to node pool management.

Node pool operations

From the GKE architecture, we know that the node pool is the default place we host applications. As mentioned in the *GKE architecture* section in *Chapter 5*, you can't directly migrate applications from one node pool to another. What we need to do is to redeploy applications from one node pool to another.

As with every operation, we need to first know how many and what kind of node pools we currently have. In the next section, we start by listing existing node pools.

Viewing node pools

Before we start any pool activities, it is good to know how to list existing node pools.

Cloud console

To view existing node pools, we can view them in Cloud console by clicking on our cluster and then **NODES**:

Figure 6.14 – Node pool details in Cloud console

Command line

To list existing pools using the command line, we need to execute the following command:

```
gcloud container node-pools list --cluster CLUSTER_NAME
```

The next screenshot shows the output of the command with two available node pools— `default-pool` and `high-performance-pool`:

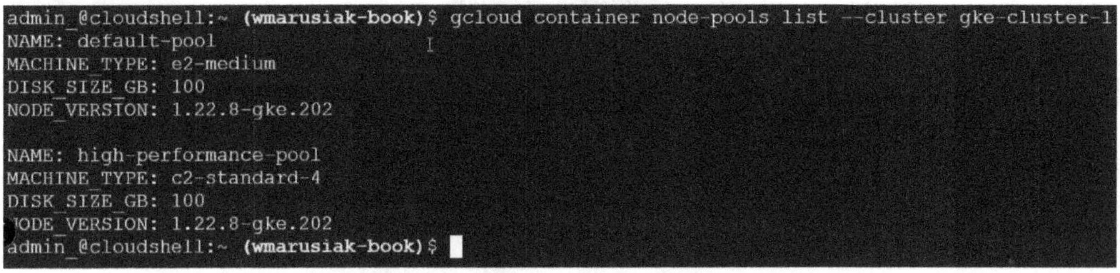

```
admin_@cloudshell:~ (wmarusiak-book)$ gcloud container node-pools list --cluster gke-cluster-1
NAME: default-pool
MACHINE_TYPE: e2-medium
DISK_SIZE_GB: 100
NODE_VERSION: 1.22.8-gke.202

NAME: high-performance-pool
MACHINE_TYPE: c2-standard-4
DISK_SIZE_GB: 100
NODE_VERSION: 1.22.8-gke.202
admin_@cloudshell:~ (wmarusiak-book)$
```

Figure 6.15 – Node pool details in Cloud Shell

Once we have information about existing pools, let's add a new node pool to the GKE cluster.

Adding node pools

We will also add a node pool in Cloud console using the CLI.

Cloud console

We start by adding an extra node pool in Cloud console, as follows:

1. Click the **ADD NODE POOL** button:

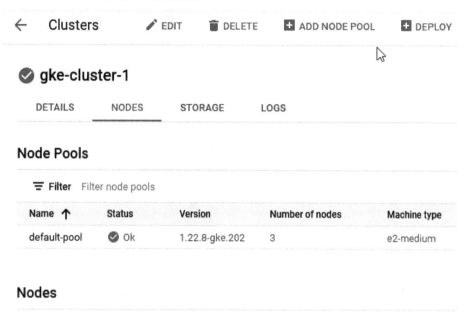

Figure 6.16 – ADD NODE POOL button in Cloud Shell

2.   We need to provide details such as node pool name, size, or upgrade configuration:

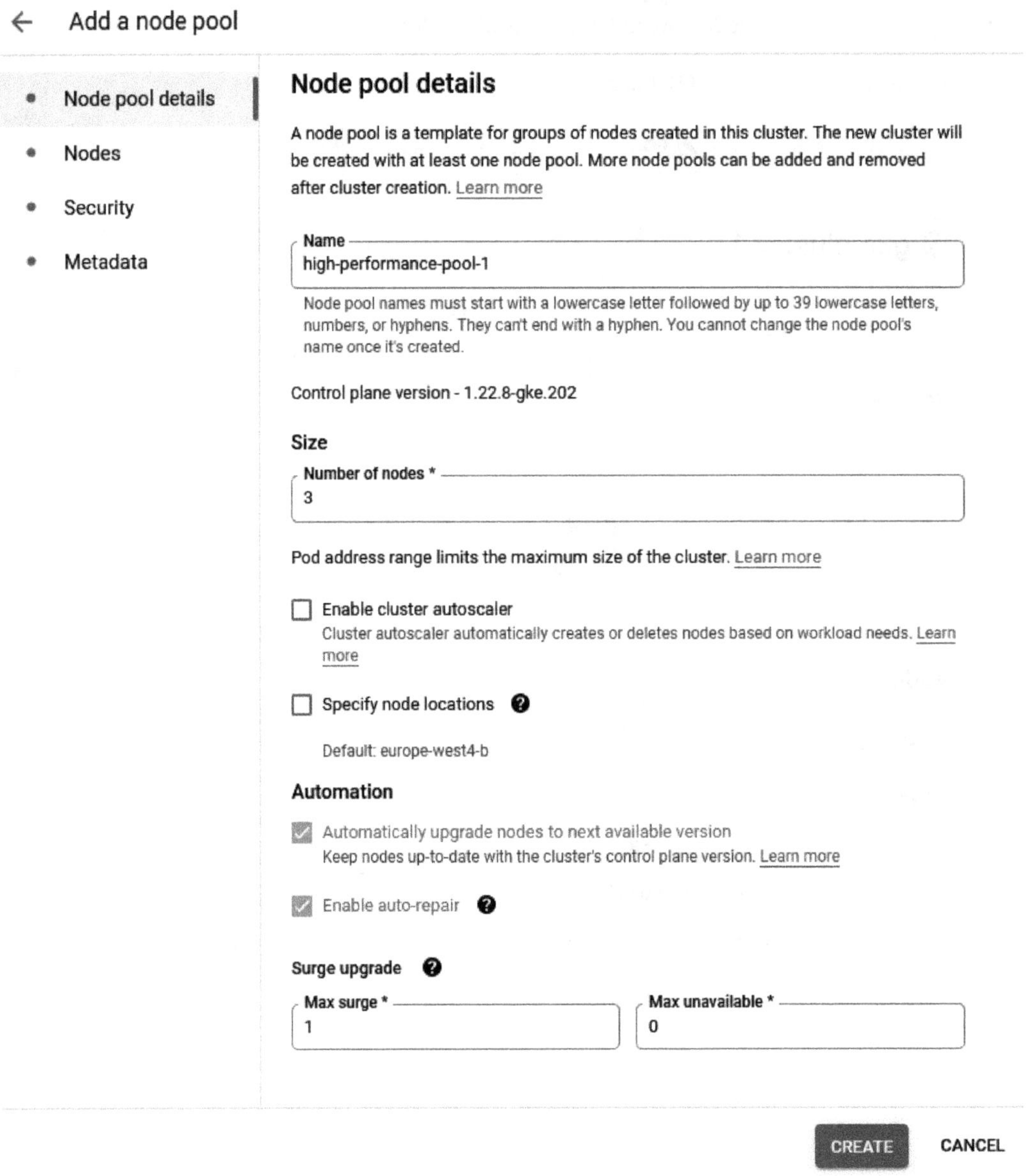

←   Add a node pool

Figure 6.17 – New node pool details

3. Select **Nodes** from the menu on the left, and let's choose a high-performance machine family:

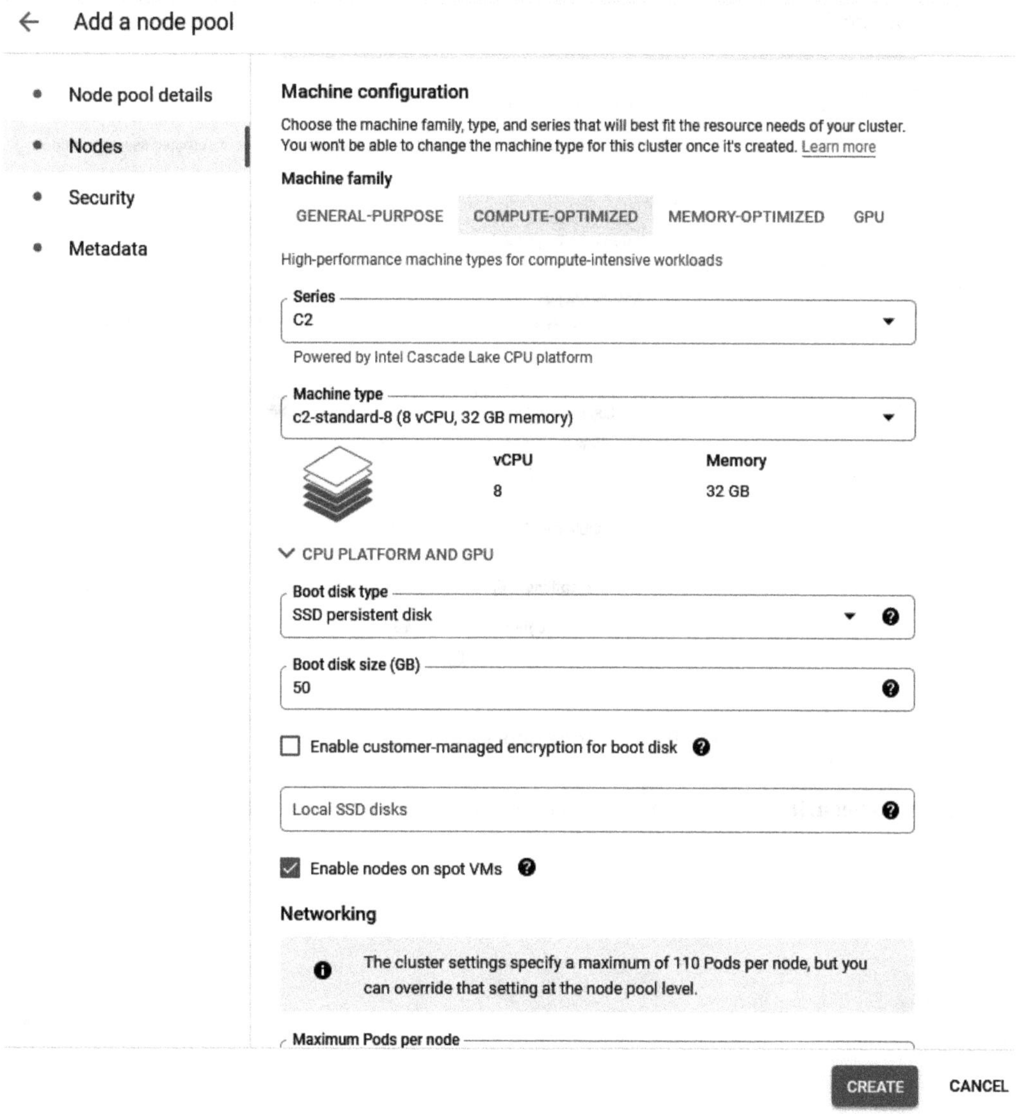

← Add a node pool

- Node pool details
- **Nodes**
- Security
- Metadata

Machine configuration

Choose the machine family, type, and series that will best fit the resource needs of your cluster. You won't be able to change the machine type for this cluster once it's created. Learn more

Machine family

GENERAL-PURPOSE   COMPUTE-OPTIMIZED   MEMORY-OPTIMIZED   GPU

High-performance machine types for compute-intensive workloads

Series
C2 ▼

Powered by Intel Cascade Lake CPU platform

Machine type
c2-standard-8 (8 vCPU, 32 GB memory) ▼

	vCPU	Memory
	8	32 GB

∨ CPU PLATFORM AND GPU

Boot disk type
SSD persistent disk ▼ ❓

Boot disk size (GB)
50 ❓

☐ Enable customer-managed encryption for boot disk ❓

Local SSD disks ❓

☑ Enable nodes on spot VMs ❓

Networking

🛈 The cluster settings specify a maximum of 110 Pods per node, but you can override that setting at the node pool level.

Maximum Pods per node

CREATE   CANCEL

Figure 6.18 – New node pool machine specification

4. We can change node security access scopes or enable shielded options:

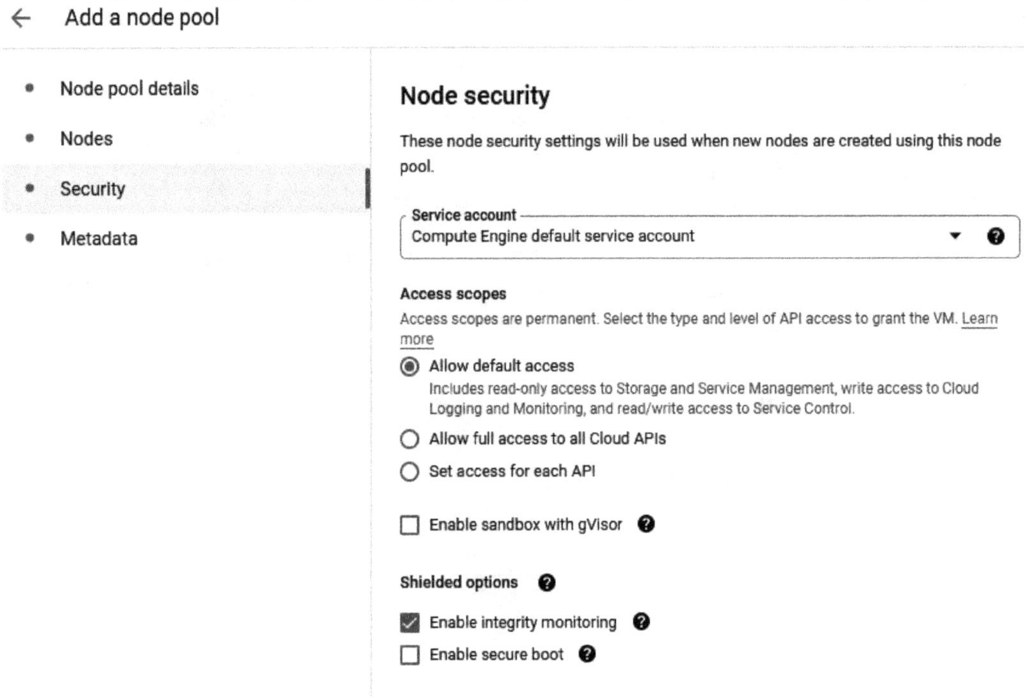

←   Add a node pool

- Node pool details
- Nodes
- Security
- Metadata

Node security

These node security settings will be used when new nodes are created using this node pool.

Service account
Compute Engine default service account ▼ ❓

Access scopes

Access scopes are permanent. Select the type and level of API access to grant the VM. Learn more

◉ Allow default access

Includes read-only access to Storage and Service Management, write access to Cloud Logging and Monitoring, and read/write access to Service Control.

◯ Allow full access to all Cloud APIs

◯ Set access for each API

☐ Enable sandbox with gVisor ❓

Shielded options ❓

☑ Enable integrity monitoring ❓

☐ Enable secure boot ❓

Figure 6.19 – New node pool security specification

5. Similar to **Security**, we can add Kubernetes labels in the **Metadata** section:

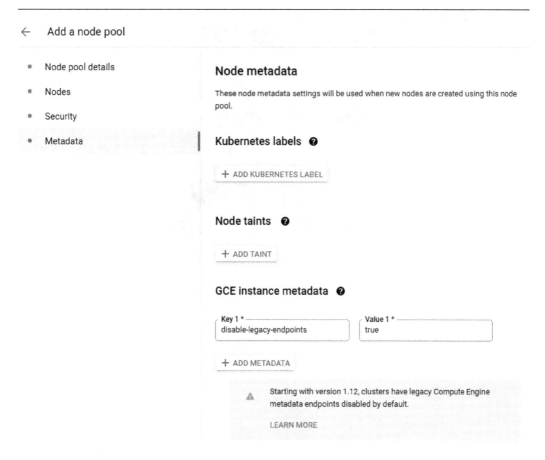

Figure 6.20 – New node pool metadata specification

6. Finally, when we click the **Create** button, the deployment will start.

7. After a moment, a new node pool is created and can be used to deploy workloads.

Command line

The creation of a minimalistic deployment pool (bare minimum without any extra settings) can be achieved by executing the following command:

```
gcloud container node-pools create POOL_NAME --cluster CLUSTER_NAME
--region=REGION_NAME
```

Execution of this command results in default settings configured for the node pool—three nodes with e2-medium as the machine type:

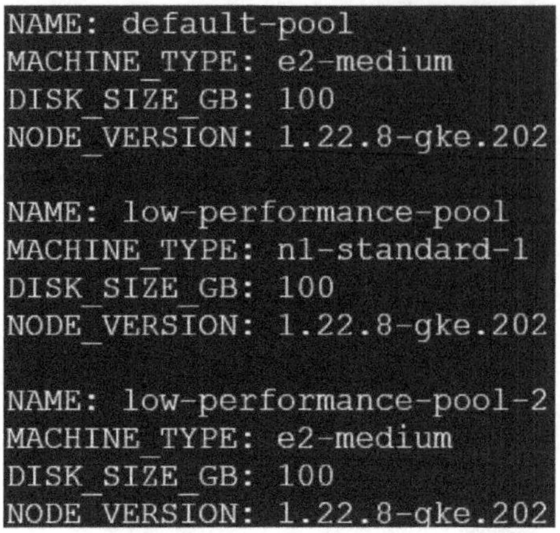

```
NAME: default-pool
MACHINE_TYPE: e2-medium
DISK_SIZE_GB: 100
NODE_VERSION: 1.22.8-gke.202

NAME: low-performance-pool
MACHINE_TYPE: n1-standard-1
DISK_SIZE_GB: 100
NODE_VERSION: 1.22.8-gke.202

NAME: low-performance-pool-2
MACHINE_TYPE: e2-medium
DISK_SIZE_GB: 100
NODE_VERSION: 1.22.8-gke.202
```

Figure 6.21 – Default and newly created node pool with default settings

In the next section, we will modify node pools.

Modifying node pools

After node pool creation, available operations that can be performed on the node pool are limited.

We can do the following:

- Change the number of nodes
- Enable the cluster autoscaler
- Change zones
- Choose a different image type
- Enable/disable surge upgrade
- Modify Kubernetes labels
- Modify node taints
- Modify network tags

As usual, we can modify the node pool using Cloud console, the CLI, or Cloud SDK.

Cloud console

Click on the desired cluster, navigate to **Nodes**, and choose and click the node pool you wish to edit.

Once you click **Edit**, make the desired changes and click **Save**:

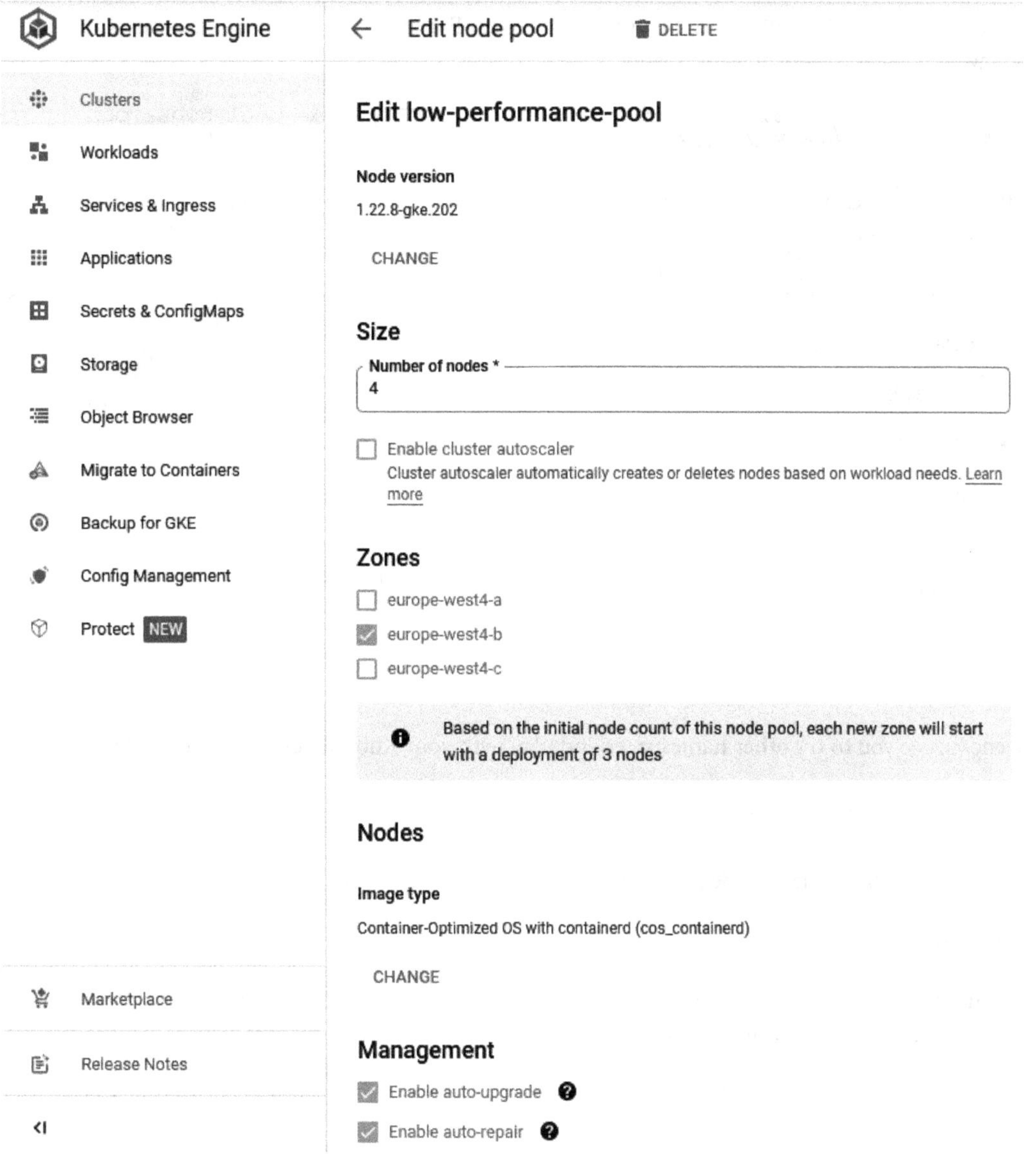

Figure 6.22 – Changes in node pool in Cloud console

Once the changes are done, the node pool will be updated with the desired settings.

Command line

We can also edit node pool details by utilizing the CLI. For example, if we want to resize the node pool, we can use the following command:

```
gcloud container clusters resize CLUSTER_NAME --node-pool NODE_POOL_
NAME --num-nodes NUM_NODES
```

In the `gcloud container clusters` namespace, other commands can be performed on clusters, as follows:

- `create`
- `create-auto`
- `delete`
- `describe`
- `get-credentials`
- `list`
- `resize`
- `update`
- `upgrade`

We encourage you to try other namespaces and play with your Kubernetes clusters while learning.

Deleting node pools

One of the final tasks that can be performed on a node pool is its deletion.

Cloud console

In Cloud console, we need to click on the desired GKE cluster, and then in the **Node Pools** section, we need to click on the "trash" icon to delete the desired node pool:

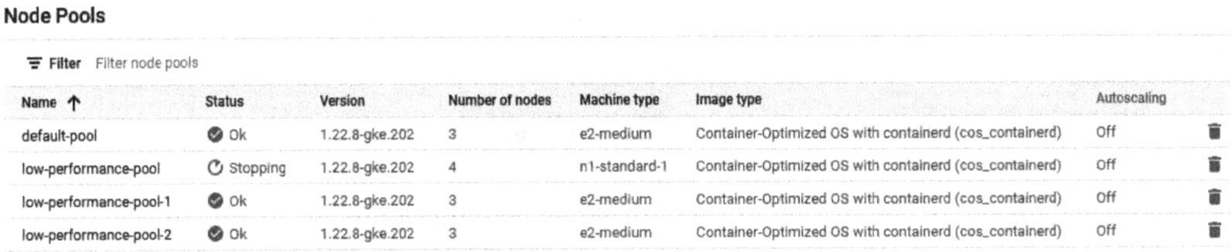

Node Pools

Name ↑	Status	Version	Number of nodes	Machine type	Image type	Autoscaling	
default-pool	✓ Ok	1.22.8-gke.202	3	e2-medium	Container-Optimized OS with containerd (cos_containerd)	Off	🗑
low-performance-pool	↻ Stopping	1.22.8-gke.202	4	n1-standard-1	Container-Optimized OS with containerd (cos_containerd)	Off	🗑
low-performance-pool-1	✓ Ok	1.22.8-gke.202	3	e2-medium	Container-Optimized OS with containerd (cos_containerd)	Off	🗑
low-performance-pool-2	✓ Ok	1.22.8-gke.202	3	e2-medium	Container-Optimized OS with containerd (cos_containerd)	Off	🗑

Figure 6.23 – Deleting a node pool in Cloud console

After a few moments, node pool deletion will be finished. We must remember that any node pool operation or changes will block other node pool changes. Only after the initial node pool activity change will we be able to conduct other changes.

Command line

We will finish our node pool activities with command-line deletion. To delete the node pool using the command line, we need to execute the following command:

```
gcloud container node-pools delete NODE_POOL_NAME --cluster CLUSTER_
NAME -zone=ZONE_NAME
```

After a moment, node pool deletion is successful.

After familiarizing ourselves with operations on node pools, we can proceed with learning about Pods, operations we can perform, and how to create, delete, and update Pods.

Pod management

Before we start managing Pods, we must learn what they are and how to deploy them.

Essentially, Pods are the smallest deployable units of computing that can be created and managed in Kubernetes. A Pod is a group of one or more containers, such as Docker containers. Pods share network and storage resources and represent an instance of a running process in the Kubernetes cluster.

Once clusters and node pools are ready, we will mainly work with Pods, and in the next sections, we will learn in detail about their lifecycle and possible operations.

Pod lifecycle

Pods go through a specific sequence of stages throughout their lifecycle. It begins with the Pending phase, progresses to the Running phase if at least one of its primary containers starts successfully, and ultimately transitions to either the Succeeded or Failed phase based on whether any container within the Pod terminates with a failure.

Pods can have the following statuses:

- Pending—The Kubernetes cluster has accepted the Pod but is not ready to be run yet. For example, an image is being downloaded.

- Running—The Pod is bound to a node, and all containers have been created.

- Succeeded—All containers in the Pod have been successfully terminated.

- Failed—All containers in the Pod have terminated, and at least one has terminated in failure.

- Unknown—The status of the Pod cannot be obtained.

Pod deployment

There are many ways in which Pods can be deployed. It depends on how the application is built and how we want to run it in Kubernetes.

Here are some of the most common methods:

- **Using the kubectl command-line tool**—This is the most common way to deploy Pods. You can use the `kubectl create` command to create a new Pod or the `kubectl apply` command to apply a YAML file that defines a Pod.

- **Using the Kubernetes Dashboard**—The Kubernetes Dashboard is a graphical user interface that you can use to deploy Pods. You can create new Pods or edit existing Pods from the dashboard.

- **Using a third-party tool**—There are a number of third-party tools that you can use to deploy Pods. These tools typically make it easier to deploy Pods, and they often provide additional features, such as automatic scaling and monitoring.

Here are some of the most popular third-party tools for deploying Pods:

- **Helm**—Helm is a package manager for Kubernetes. It makes it easy to deploy and manage complex applications on Kubernetes.

- **Argo CD**—Argo CD is a **continuous delivery** (**CD**) tool for Kubernetes. It can be used to automate the deployment of Pods, as well as the rollout of new versions of Pods.

- **Flux**—Flux is a CD tool for Kubernetes. It is similar to Argo CD, but it is designed to be more lightweight and easy to use.

Pod creation

The simplest Pod creation can be done by applying the following code example, where we name the Pod `nginx-deployment` and we use an image of `nginx 1.14.2` on port `80`:

```
apiVersion: apps/v1
kind: Deployment
metadata:
  name: nginx-deployment
spec:
  selector:
    matchLabels:
      app: nginx
  replicas: 2
  template:
    metadata:
      labels:
```

```
      app: nginx
  spec:
    containers:
    - name: nginx
      image: nginx:1.14.2
      ports:
      - containerPort: 80
```

We can also deploy this simple Pod by using the CLI. We saved the previous code into the `nginx.yaml` file:

```
kubectl apply -f nginx.yaml
```

This is the output after executing the command:

```
admin_@cloudshell:~ (wmarusiak-book)$ kubectl apply -f nginx.yaml
Warning: Autopilot set default resource requests for Deployment defaul
t/nginx-deployment, as resource requests were not specified.See http:/
/g.co/gke/autopilot-defaults.
deployment.apps/nginx-deployment created
```

Figure 6.24 – Successful deployment of nginx deployment

We can check the status of the Pod by using the `kubectl get pods` or `kubectl describe pod nginx` command from the CLI. The status of the Pod is also visible in Cloud console:

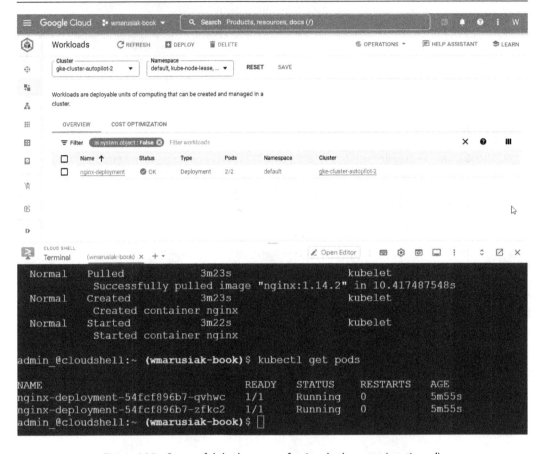

Figure 6.25 – Successful deployment of nginx deployment (continued)

Basic information about the Pods is displayed in both cases—Cloud Shell and the CLI.

In the next screenshot, we deployed multiple Pods into different GKE clusters and namespaces with the same Pod name:

	Name	Status	Type	Pods	Namespace	Cluster ↑	Location	Pods Running	Pods Desired	Is system object
☐	frontend	✅ OK	Replica Set	3/3	default	gke-cluster-1	europe-west4	3	3	false
☐	frontend	✅ OK	Replica Set	3/3	frontend	gke-cluster-1	europe-west4	3	3	false
☐	nginx-1	✅ OK	Deployment	3/3	default	gke-cluster-1	europe-west4	3	3	false
☐	frontend	✅ OK	Replica Set	3/3	default	gke-cluster-autopilot-2	europe-west4	3	3	false
☐	nginx-deployment	✅ OK	Deployment	2/2	default	gke-cluster-autopilot-2	europe-west4	2	2	false

Figure 6.26 – Workloads overview in Cloud console

We will now move to more advanced Pod deployment types such as ReplicaSet, StatefulSets, and others.

Namespace

By default, GKE creates several namespaces such as kube-node-lease, kube-public, and kube-system. When creating a GKE Autopilot cluster, the default namespace is created for our workloads. GKE Standard mode allows us to specify a node pool's newly created namespace manually.

Namespaces are used to isolate groups of resources within a single cluster. The name of the resources within a namespace must be unique but can be the same across all namespaces. Namespaces are primarily used in environments with many users, teams, or projects.

A namespace can be created with the kubectl create namespace YOUR_NAMESPACE command.

We can use the kubectl command to to view namespaces in a particular cluster.

Lastly, to delete a namespace, we need to use the kubectl delete namespaces YOUR_NAMESPACE command.

ReplicaSet

The ReplicaSet deployment type is used to maintain the desired set of Pods. It defines which image and how many Pods must be up and running.

In this sample Pod ReplicaSet deployment, we specify various information such as Pod name, labels, and how many replicas of the Pod we wish to have:

```
apiVersion: apps/v1
kind: ReplicaSet
metadata:
  name: frontend
  labels:
    app: guestbook
    tier: frontend
spec:
  replicas: 3
  selector:
    matchLabels:
      tier: frontend
  template:
    metadata:
      labels:
        tier: frontend
    spec:
      containers:
      - name: php-redis
        image: gcr.io/google_samples/gb-frontend:v3
```

The preceding code is available here: `https://raw.githubusercontent.com/kubernetes/website/main/content/en/examples/controllers/frontend.yaml`.

To test it out, we can deploy it using the `kubectl apply -f Filename` command or the preceding URL.

The preceding source code contains two important sections—the first is `kind: ReplicaSet` and the second is the `spec` section: `replicas` with value 3.

We can check ReplicaSets by running the `kubectl get ReplicaSet` command or viewing them in Cloud console.

Deployments

Deployment is the next possibility of how we can run the applications. We should use it to manage stateless applications where any Pod from the Deployment can be replaced if needed.

A Deployment provides declarative updates for Pods and ReplicaSets. It allows for a more sophisticated way to manage Pods.

We should use Deployments in the following cases:

- We want to have a rolling update where we phase out an old version of the application, and it will be replaced with a new version of the application.

- In Blue/Green deployments, where we can serve one version to a set of users, and once we are happy or unhappy with the results, it is possible to switch to the desired version of the application.

- When scaling up the deployment to accept more load.

To learn more about other deployment types, visit the Kubernetes documentation at `https://kubernetes.io/docs/concepts/workloads/controllers/deployment/#use-case`.

StatefulSets

Similar to Deployments, a StatefulSet creates Pods based on the container specification. One major difference is that a StatefulSet creates and tracks the identity of each Pod. Because Pods aren't interchangeable, the identifier will be persisted even if the Pod is rescheduled.

You might consider using StatefulSets in the following cases:

- You need to have stable and unique network identifiers.

- You require stable, persistent storage.

- Graceful and ordered deployment or scaling is needed.

- Ordered and automated rolling updates are needed.

DaemonSet

If we need to ensure that Pods will be scheduled on all or some GKE nodes, we can use the DaemonSet deployment type. When a new node is added to the cluster, Pods are scheduled on them.

The most typical use cases of a DaemonSet are outlined here:

- Using cluster storage daemon on nodes
- Using log collection daemon on nodes
- Using monitoring daemon on nodes

Jobs

A Job deployment type is used to track the successful completion of Pods. Once the specified number of completions is achieved, the job is complete, and it cleans created Pods.

One example of a Job deployment type can be π number computation up to the desired number of places, which in this case is 2000:

```
ApiVersion: batch/v1
kind: Job
metadata:
  name: pi
spec:
  template:
    spec:
      containers:
      - name: pi
        image: perl:5.34.0
        command: ["perl",  "-Mbignum=bpi", "-wle", "print bpi(2000)"]
      restartPolicy: Never
  backoffLimit: 4
```

Once a Job is created, we can check the Job status by using the `kubectl describe job pi` command, and to see the Job results, we need to check logs. The command to do that is `kubectl logs jobs/pi`.

The preceding code can be found at `https://kubernetes.io/examples/controllers/job.yaml`.

CronJob

A CronJob deployment type is useful when we execute a job based on a schedule written in Cron format.

After learning about different Pod deployment types, we will focus on the different operations we can do with Pods. Let's start with how to view Pods.

Viewing Pods

Depending on how the application is deployed, it is important to view details of the Pod, how it is configured, and how to troubleshoot some issues.

Cloud console

We have some Pods deployed into the GKE cluster, and we can see the status of workloads in Cloud console. Cloudconsole has a general overview of deployed workloads. The main screen allows us to view workloads by selecting a desired cluster or namespace:

Figure 6.27 – Workloads overview in Cloud console

Further on in the bottom section of the screen, we can apply more detailed filtering such as the following:

- **Name**
- **Status**
- **Type**
- **Pods**
- **Namespace**
- **Location**
- **Pods running**
- **Pods desired**
- **Is system object**

A detailed view of a workload is possible by selecting it from the main workload screen:

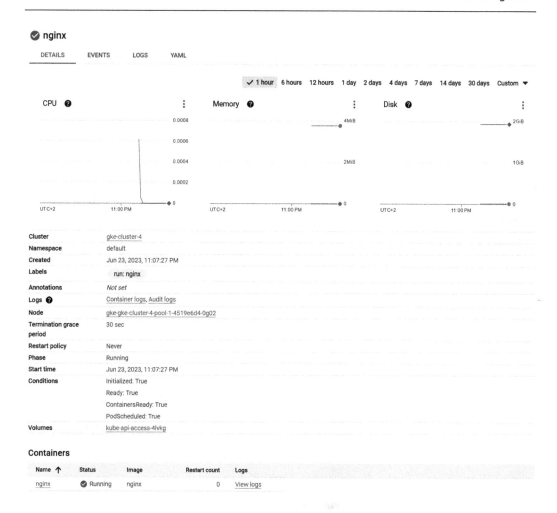

Figure 6.28 – Selected workload general overview

The top section of the workload allows us to see workload details, any events that might have occurred, container logs, and your workload represented in YAML format.

It is possible to go one level deeper and view the details of each of the Pods, which are part of the workload itself:

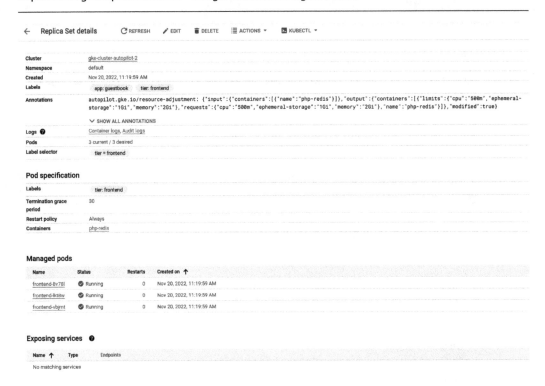

Figure 6.29 – Detailed view of Pods from the workload

After clicking on the Pod, similar to the general overview of the workload, we can check the Pod's details and see events, logs, and its YAML representation.

Command line

Now, after switching to the CLI, we will view the Pods' details using the kubectl utility.

To view all Pods in all namespaces, we need to use the following command:

```
kubectl get pods -A
```

However, the command output will show us all cluster resources alongside our deployed Pods.

To view Pods deployed into the default namespace, we need to use the following command:

```
kubectl get pods
```

If Pods were deployed into a dedicated namespace, we must append a --namespace YOUR_NAMESPACE parameter.

If we want to see the details of a specific Pod, we need to use the `kubectl describe pods MY_POD_NAME` command. This command is handy for seeing Pod events, especially if the Pod creation fails to troubleshoot the issue.

To list deployments, we can use the `kubectl get deployment MY_DEPLOYMENT` command.

It is possible to retrieve existing Pod or deployment configuration and save it as a file in YAML format using the `kubectl get pod my-pod -o yaml` command.

As you might have already seen, `kubectl` has multiple switches, each with multiple namespaces. To view the most common Kubernetes operations, it might be helpful to look at the following `kubectl` cheat sheet: `https://kubernetes.io/docs/reference/kubectl/cheatsheet/`.

In the next section, we will focus on adding Pods to the GKE cluster.

Adding Pods

Pod creation can be done by using Cloud console and the CLI. We will start with Cloud console.

Cloud console

In Cloud console, we need to select **Workloads** and click the **DEPLOY** button:

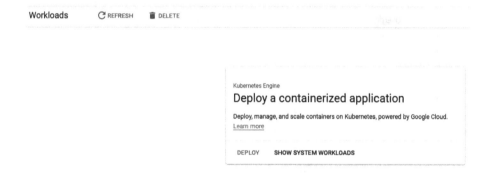

Figure 6.30 – Container deployment using Cloud console

We have the following options to choose from:

- **Existing container image**—The source of the image can be either a container registry or an artifact registry.

- **New container image**—The source image can be pulled from Cloud Source Repositories, GitHub, or Bitbucket:

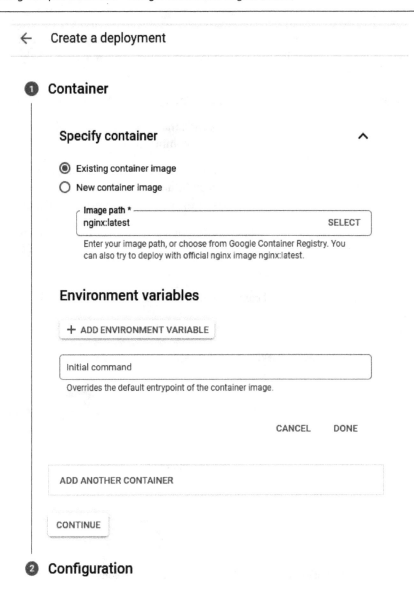

Figure 6.31 – Container selection for a new deployment

If needed, we can add multiple containers into one deployment. After clicking **CONTINUE**, we have the possibility to provide an application name, choose or create a namespace, add labels, view the configuration in YAML, and select which GKE cluster we want to deploy:

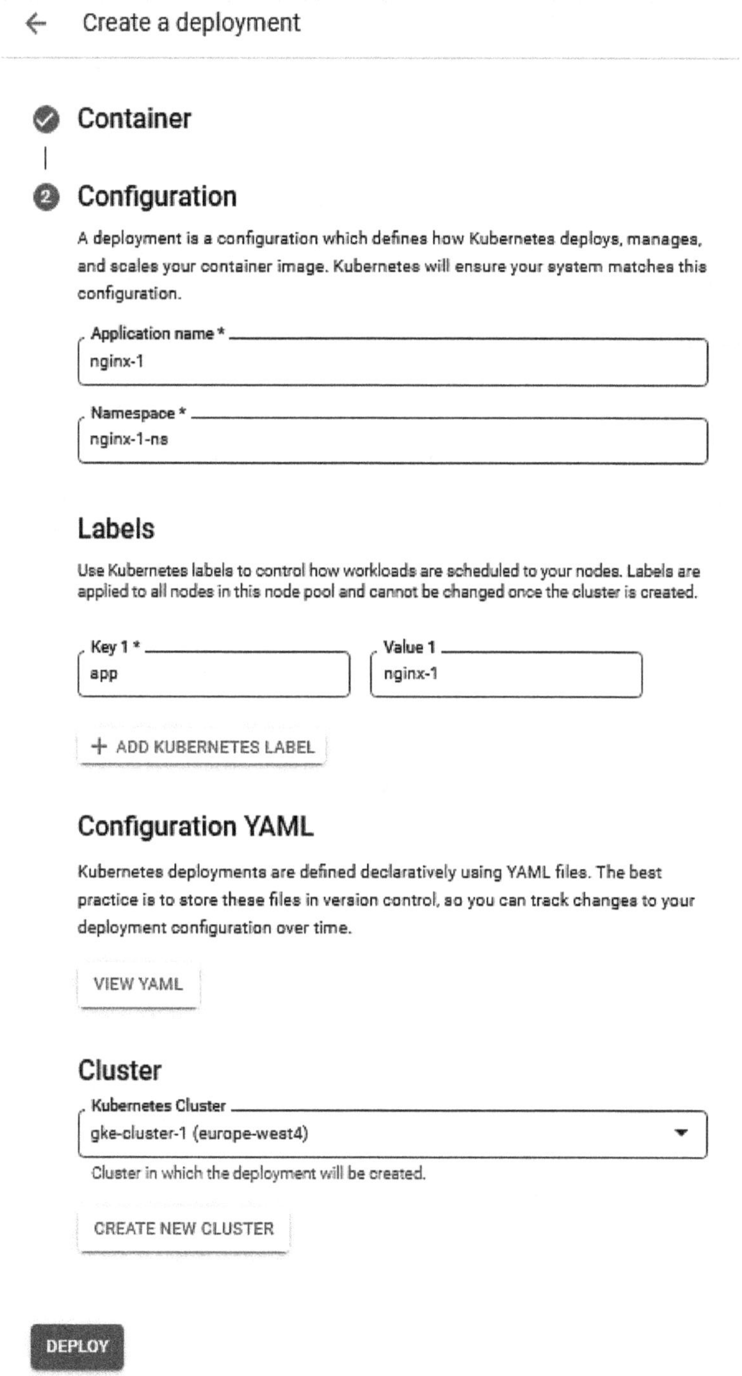

← Create a deployment

✓ **Container**

② **Configuration**

A deployment is a configuration which defines how Kubernetes deploys, manages, and scales your container image. Kubernetes will ensure your system matches this configuration.

Application name *
nginx-1

Namespace *
nginx-1-ns

Labels

Use Kubernetes labels to control how workloads are scheduled to your nodes. Labels are applied to all nodes in this node pool and cannot be changed once the cluster is created.

Key 1 *
app

Value 1
nginx-1

+ ADD KUBERNETES LABEL

Configuration YAML

Kubernetes deployments are defined declaratively using YAML files. The best practice is to store these files in version control, so you can track changes to your deployment configuration over time.

VIEW YAML

Cluster

Kubernetes Cluster
gke-cluster-1 (europe-west4)   ▼

Cluster in which the deployment will be created.

CREATE NEW CLUSTER

DEPLOY

Figure 6.32 – Final step to deploy the container using Cloud console

> **Note**
>
> If your target GKE cluster uses Standard mode, the application should be available within seconds (depending on the application size). If the target GKE cluster uses Autopilot mode, Pod scheduling might take a bit longer than in Standard clusters due to the necessity of node provisioning.

After the application is up and running, we can add extra Pods to the application. This can be done in the **ACTIONS** menu:

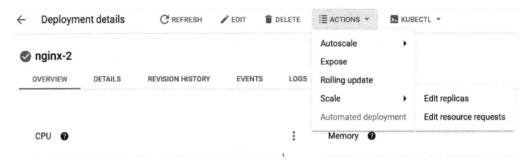

Figure 6.33 – Edit replicas menu in Deployment details

After changing the desired number of Pods, deployments of the additional Pods start immediately if there are enough resources in the node pool:

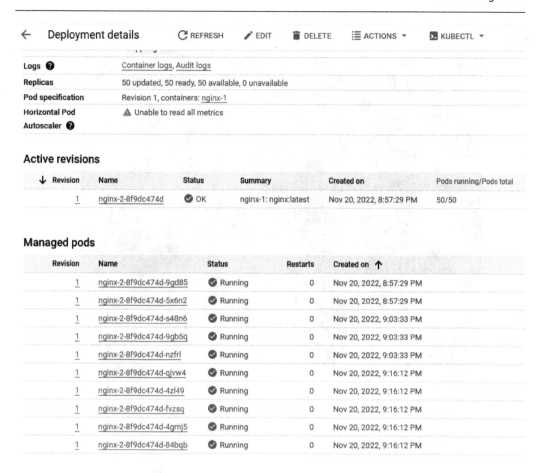

Figure 6.34 – Successful increase in Pods in deployment

In the next section, we will add a simple image to a GKE cluster.

Command line

The most popular option to create Pods using the command line is to use two main commands.

The first option is to use the `kubectl apply -f filename.yaml` command, where the YAML file contains all details of the Pod.

If you don't know how to create a Pod YAML file, you can use an example from the *Pod deployment* section of this chapter or use the following command:

```
kubectl create deployment dry_run_deployment --image=busybox
--dry-run=client --output=yaml
```

The output of the previous command shows ready-to-be-used YAML code:

```
admin_@cloudshell:~ (wmarusiak-book)$ kubectl create deployment
dry_run_deployment --image=busybox --dry-run=client --output=yam
l
apiVersion: apps/v1
kind: Deployment
metadata:
  creationTimestamp: null
  labels:
    app: dry_run_deployment
  name: dry_run_deployment
spec:
  replicas: 1
  selector:
    matchLabels:
      app: dry_run_deployment
  strategy: {}
  template:
    metadata:
      creationTimestamp: null
      labels:
        app: dry_run_deployment
    spec:
      containers:
      - image: busybox
        name: busybox
        resources: {}
status: {}
```

Figure 6.35 – Output of kubectl --dry-run command in YAML format

This generates a base deployment based on the selected image, which can be saved as a YAML file on a computer and edited to make changes. The most important section of that command is the `--dry-run=client --output=yaml` part, which previews the object that would be sent to the cluster without submitting it.

Now we've learned how to create deployments using saved YAML files on a computer, we can move on to creating Pods using `kubectl` to create deployment parameters. Simple Pod creation needs `name` and `image` parameters, as follows:

```
kubectl create deployment pod_name --image=image_name
```

A sample command to create a deployment with the name `nginx-gke-autopilot`, which uses nginx as a source image, is shown as follows:

```
kubectl create deployment nginx-gke-autopilot --image=nginx
```

This section concludes by adding both Cloud console and the CLI.

In the next section, we learn how to modify Pods.

Modifying Pods

Modification of Pods is possible by using different methods. Those methods may vary due to the different application deployment possibilities. Suppose we have an application deployed as a ReplicaSet and want to modify the number of usable Pods. In that case, we can edit the YAML deployment file, modify it, and redeploy it. We could get the existing workload YAML configuration file, save it as a local file, and redeploy it with changes.

Cloud console

Modifying running Pods in Cloud console is possible via the **Workloads** section in Cloud console. Our sample application, named frontend, is deployed as a ReplicaSet with three Pods as the desired state. To change the number of Pods, we need to click on the name of the workload:

Figure 6.36 – ReplicaSet deployment visible in the Workloads section of Cloud console

After selection, we are redirected to the workload details, where we can see the workload details and edit them.

When we click the **EDIT** button, the browser-based code editor allows us to edit the workload. In our case, we will replace the number of desired Pods from three to five:

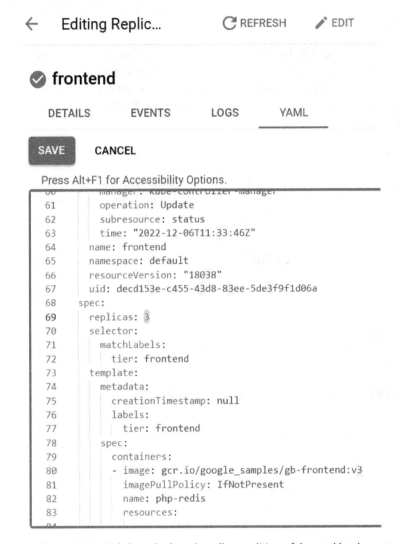

Figure 6.37 – Web-based editor that allows editing of the workload

If your GKE cluster has enough resources to run the desired number of Pods, they will be scheduled and available. After a moment, new Pods are created and ready to be used:

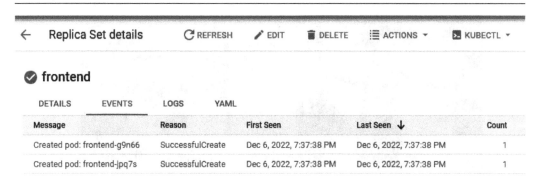

Figure 6.38 – Two new Pods added to the ReplicaSet

Of course, those aren't the only possible settings we can adjust, and we encourage you to experiment with them.

Command line

To modify deployed Pods, we have several possibilities, but it will depend on how the Pods are deployed. Let's try to modify the ReplicaSet deployment used in the previous section of the chapter.

We have a deployment with the name `frontend` with three replicas and we would like to change the number of replicas to seven. We can change the amount of the Pods in two different ways.

The first one is to simply use the `kubectl scale --replicas=7 -f https://kubernetes.io/examples/controllers/frontend.yaml` command, which results in the following output:

```
Every 2.0s: kubectl get pods

NAME             READY   STATUS     RESTARTS   AGE
frontend-7sg7z   0/1     Pending    0          2s
frontend-8kpcz   0/1     Pending    0          2s
frontend-8r4dd   0/1     Pending    0          2s
frontend-95644   1/1     Running    0          3m52s
frontend-k7jqt   1/1     Running    0          3m52s
frontend-qs5mz   0/1     Pending    0          2s
frontend-vnd59   1/1     Running    0          3m52s
```

Figure 6.39 – Modification of the ReplicaSet from three to seven replicas

We are using the `watch kubectl get pods` command, which allows me to see changes live. We can also use the `kubectl get pods -w` command, which doesn't require additional packages to be installed. After a few seconds, additional Pods are ready to be used:

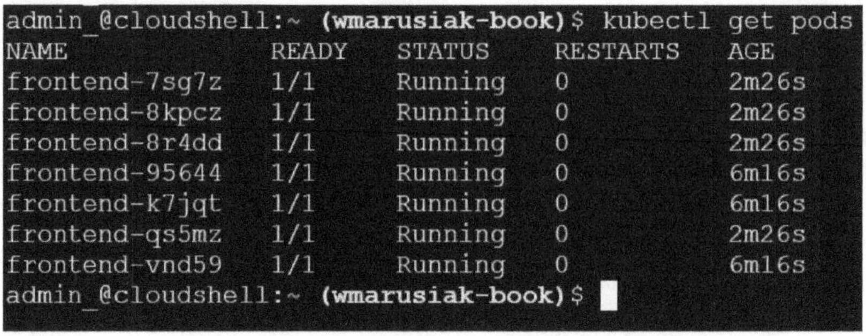

```
admin_@cloudshell:~ (wmarusiak-book)$ kubectl get pods
NAME              READY   STATUS    RESTARTS   AGE
frontend-7sg7z    1/1     Running   0          2m26s
frontend-8kpcz    1/1     Running   0          2m26s
frontend-8r4dd    1/1     Running   0          2m26s
frontend-95644    1/1     Running   0          6m16s
frontend-k7jqt    1/1     Running   0          6m16s
frontend-qs5mz    1/1     Running   0          2m26s
frontend-vnd59    1/1     Running   0          6m16s
admin_@cloudshell:~ (wmarusiak-book)$ ▋
```

Figure 6.40 – Modification of the ReplicaSet from three to seven replicas finished

We can also modify the code used to deploy Pods.

In our case, we will use a command-line file editor to change the value of replicas from 3 to 20:

```
apiVersion: apps/v1
kind: ReplicaSet
metadata:
  name: frontend
  labels:
    app: guestbook
    tier: frontend
spec:
  # modify replicas according to your case
  replicas: 20
  selector:
    matchLabels:
      tier: frontend
  template:
    metadata:
      labels:
        tier: frontend
    spec:
      containers:
      - name: php-redis
        image: gcr.io/google_samples/gb-frontend:v3
```

You can use your favorite file editor or web-based editor available in Cloud console:

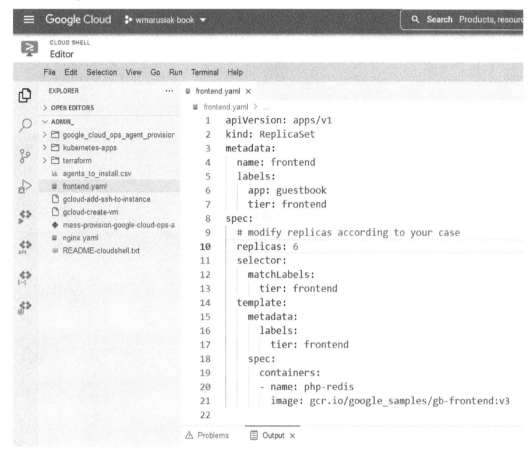

Figure 6.41 – YAML deployment definition file editing in the Cloud console web-based editor

Once the file is saved, we can use the YAML file to update the ReplicaSet from three to six Pods:

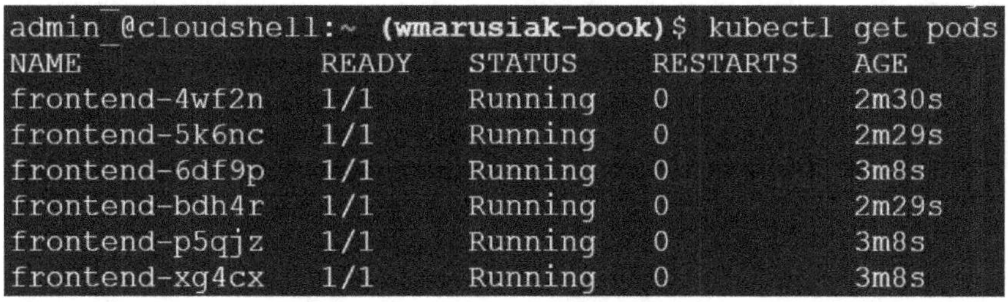

```
admin_@cloudshell:~ (wmarusiak-book)$ kubectl get pods
NAME            READY   STATUS    RESTARTS   AGE
frontend-4wf2n  1/1     Running   0          2m30s
frontend-5k6nc  1/1     Running   0          2m29s
frontend-6df9p  1/1     Running   0          3m8s
frontend-bdh4r  1/1     Running   0          2m29s
frontend-p5qjz  1/1     Running   0          3m8s
frontend-xg4cx  1/1     Running   0          3m8s
```

Figure 6.42 – YAML deployment definition file update from three to six Pods was successful

Now we've learned how to modify existing Pods, it is crucial to learn how to remove Pods from GKE clusters.

Removing Pods

Removal of Pods will depend on how you deployed them. If a single Pod has been deployed, then the removal of the Pod is a straightforward operation.

If the Pod is part of a ReplicaSet, then removal of the Pod itself will succeed, but the GKE control plane will run the desired number of Pods and create a new one. To remove Pods in such a case, we need to remove the deployment itself.

Cloud console

We have a ReplicaSet deployed and visible in the **Workloads** section of the GKE part of the Cloud console:

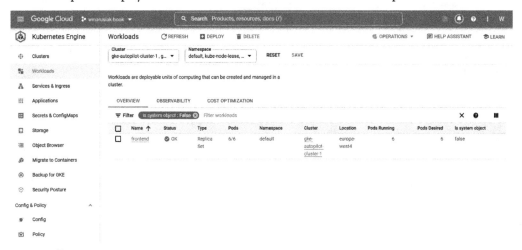

Figure 6.43 – Frontend ReplicaSet workload in Cloud console to be removed

To remove a single Pod or Pods from the GKE cluster, we need to click on the workload itself and scroll to the **Pods** section:

```
storage":"1Gi","memory":"2Gi"},"requests":{"cpu":"500m",
```

⌄ SHOW ALL ANNOTATIONS

Logs ❓	Container logs, Audit logs
Pods	6 current / 6 desired
Label selector	tier = frontend

Pod specification

Labels	tier: frontend
Termination grace period	30
Restart policy	Always
Containers	php-redis

Managed pods

Name	Status	Restarts	Created on ↑
frontend-fww5l	✅ Running	0	Dec 10, 2022, 8:52:01 AM
frontend-w6542	✅ Running	0	Dec 10, 2022, 8:52:01 AM
frontend-kksgl	✅ Running	0	Dec 10, 2022, 8:52:01 AM
frontend-2pn4p	✅ Running	0	Dec 10, 2022, 8:52:01 AM
frontend-926dm	✅ Running	0	Dec 11, 2022, 4:30:48 PM
frontend-w77qn	✅ Running	0	Dec 11, 2022, 4:31:16 PM

Figure 6.44 – Pods part of the ReplicaSet deployment

To remove a Pod from the ReplicaSet, click on the desired Pod and click the **DELETE** button:

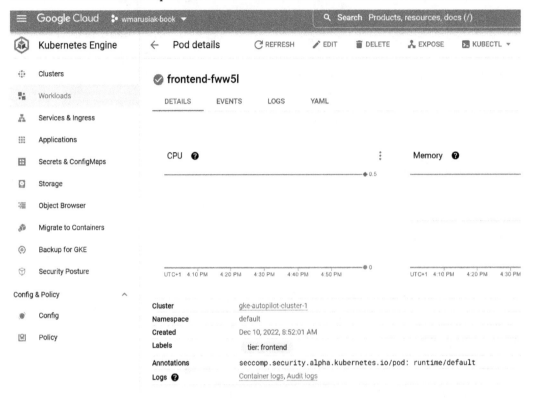

Figure 6.45 – Removal of a single Pod from the deployment

After clicking the **DELETE** button, we need to confirm the removal of the Pod:

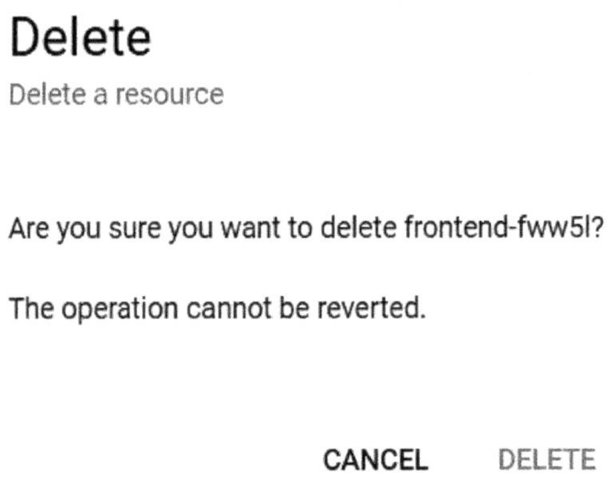

Delete
Delete a resource

Are you sure you want to delete frontend-fww5l?

The operation cannot be reverted.

CANCEL   DELETE

Figure 6.46 – Confirmation of Pod deletion in Cloud console

After a second, the old Pod is removed and a new one is created as part of the ReplicaSet deployment with the frontend.

Now, we will move on to complete deployment removal.

To remove a deployment, choose it from the **Workloads** section and click the **DELETE** button:

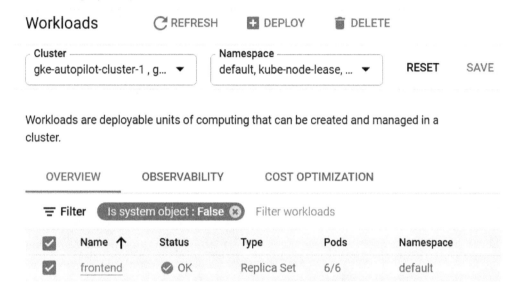

Figure 6.47 – Confirmation of Pod deletion in Cloud console

We need to confirm the deletion, and without any issues, the desired workload deletion starts:

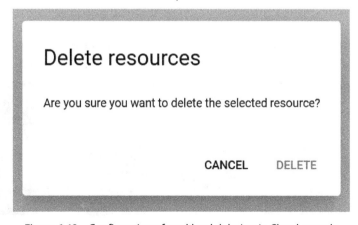

Figure 6.48 – Confirmation of workload deletion in Cloud console

In just a few seconds, the deletion process starts, and we can briefly observe all Pods' termination:

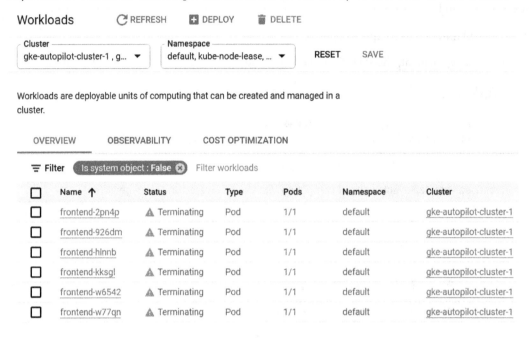

Figure 6.49 – Confirmation of workload deletion in Cloud console

If we hit **Refresh** in the browser, it will confirm the resource deletion.

Now, let's move on to command-line application removal.

Command line

Removal of Pods utilizes the `kubectl` command. Before we start with the removal of a single Pod, we need to list existing Pods. To list all Pods, we can use the `kubectl get pods` command:

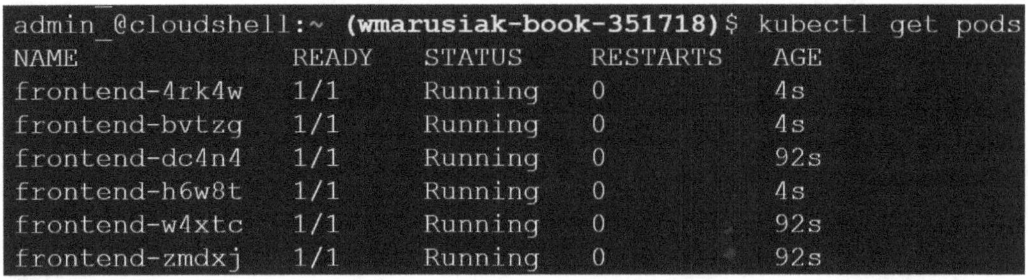

```
admin_@cloudshell:~ (wmarusiak-book-351718)$ kubectl get pods
NAME             READY    STATUS     RESTARTS     AGE
frontend-4rk4w   1/1      Running    0            4s
frontend-bvtzg   1/1      Running    0            4s
frontend-dc4n4   1/1      Running    0            92s
frontend-h6w8t   1/1      Running    0            4s
frontend-w4xtc   1/1      Running    0            92s
frontend-zmdxj   1/1      Running    0            92s
```

Figure 6.50 – Listing of existing Pods with kubectl command

To delete a single Pod, we can issue the `kubectl delete pod frontend-4rk4w` command. The Pod is deleted immediately, but we might ask ourselves the following: *How do I know if the Pod is part of the deployment or otherwise? How was the Pod deployed in the first place?*

To find this out, we can review the Pod configuration by using the `kubectl describe pod frontend-dc4n4` command.

The command output contains a lot of information, and we need to scroll to the `Controlled By:` section:

```
admin @cloudshell:~ (wmarusiak-book-351718)$ kubectl describe pod frontend-dc4n4
Name:              frontend-dc4n4
Namespace:         default
Priority:          0
Service Account:   default
Node:              gke-gke-cluster-1-default-pool-ff46b7f9-w92w/10.164.0.17
Start Time:        Sun, 11 Dec 2022 16:37:59 +0000
Labels:            tier=frontend
Annotations:       <none>
Status:            Running
IP:                10.4.2.4
IPs:
  IP:              10.4.2.4
Controlled By:     ReplicaSet/frontend
```

Figure 6.51 – Detailed information about the Pod

The `Controlled By:` section allow us to identify how a Pod or set of Pods deployment has been done. Once we know that the Pod is part of a ReplicaSet, we need to find the name of the ReplicaSet. To find this out, we can use the `kubectl get replicaset` command:

```
admin @cloudshell:~ (wmarusiak-book-351718)$ kubectl get replicaset
NAME        DESIRED    CURRENT    READY    AGE
frontend    6          6          6        3m24s
admin @cloudshell:~ (wmarusiak-book-351718)$
```

Figure 6.52 – Existing ReplicaSet deployments

So, we discovered that the ReplicaSet with the name `frontend` contains six replicas and Pods associated with it:

```
admin_@cloudshell:~ (wmarusiak-book-351718)$ kubectl get replicaset
NAME        DESIRED   CURRENT   READY   AGE
frontend    6         6         6       29m
admin_@cloudshell:~ (wmarusiak-book-351718)$ kubectl describe replicaset frontend
Name:         frontend
Namespace:    default
Selector:     tier=frontend
Labels:       app=guestbook
              tier=frontend
Annotations:  <none>
Replicas:     6 current / 6 desired
Pods Status:  6 Running / 0 Waiting / 0 Succeeded / 0 Failed
Pod Template:
  Labels:  tier=frontend
  Containers:
   nginx:
    Image:        nginx
    Port:         <none>
    Host Port:    <none>
    Environment:  <none>
    Mounts:       <none>
  Volumes:        <none>
Events:
  Type     Reason            Age    From                    Message
  ----     ------            ----   ----                    -------
  Normal   SuccessfulCreate  30m    replicaset-controller   Created pod: frontend-dc4n4
  Normal   SuccessfulCreate  30m    replicaset-controller   Created pod: frontend-w4xtc
  Normal   SuccessfulCreate  30m    replicaset-controller   Created pod: frontend-zmdxj
  Normal   SuccessfulCreate  29m    replicaset-controller   Created pod: frontend-4rk4w
  Normal   SuccessfulCreate  29m    replicaset-controller   Created pod: frontend-h6w8t
  Normal   SuccessfulCreate  29m    replicaset-controller   Created pod: frontend-bvtzg
```

Figure 6.53 – Detailed information about the frontend ReplicaSet

Finally, to delete it, we need to run the `kubectl delete replicaset frontend` command. After a moment, deletion completes.

We learned a lot about Pods, including how to deploy, manage and remove them. Our journey doesn't stop here. We will now move to the services section, where we will learn about different types of services and how we can use them in GKE.

Service management

Services are a crucial part of GKE. GKE uses services to group Pods into a single resource that is going to be accessed from outside of the GKE cluster. After the deployment of the application, we can choose different ways to access applications running in GKE.

Types of services

We have a handful selection of services to choose from, as follows:

- `ClusterIP`—This is a default service where clients' requests are sent to an internal IP address.

- `NodePort`—Clients send requests to the IP address of a node with a specific, configurable port value.

- `LoadBalancer`—Clients access the application by using the IP address of the load balancer.

- `ExternalName`—Clients access the application by using the DNS address.

- `Headless`—A headless service that can be used to group Pods without an IP address.

Both the Kubernetes and GKE documentation describe in detail services with all their options, and we recommend diving deep if you want to learn more beyond the scope of the book:

- `https://kubernetes.io/docs/concepts/services-networking/service/`

- `https://cloud.google.com/kubernetes-engine/docs/concepts/service`

Viewing services

By default, GKE creates services that are used by GKE itself. Those default services are set out here:

- `default-http-backend`

- `kube-dns`

- `kubernetes`

- `metrics-server`

The next screenshot shows these services in Cloud console, but as those are GKE core services, we should avoid interaction with them unless there is a clear reason to do so. Changing them might result in GKE cluster and workload downtime:

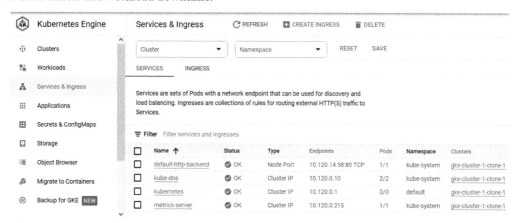

Figure 6.54 – Internal GKE services

Let's find out how to interact with services in GKE.

Cloud console

In Cloud console, we can view existing services deployed by clicking on the **Services & Ingress** menu. Once a service is created, we can view it in Cloud console:

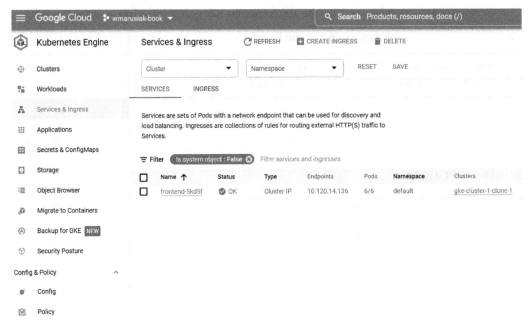

Figure 6.55 – Service visible in Services & Ingress section of GKE

To view service details, you need to click on the service name. In the **OVERVIEW** section, we can see service details with monitoring.

If we click on the **DETAILS** tab, we can see trimmed but still helpful information about the service:

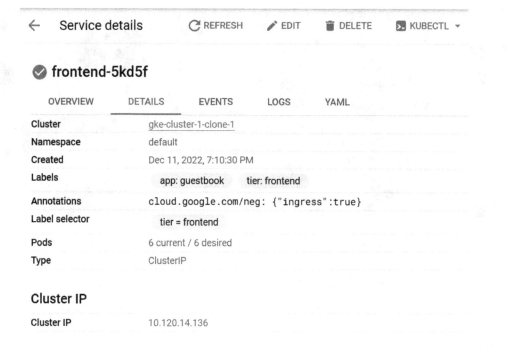

Figure 6.56 – Service visible in the Services & Ingress section of GKE

We can see service events, logs, and YAML configuration by clicking on the next tabs.

Command line

Once again, we utilize the `kubectl` command. This time, we will use the `kubectl get services` command to display available services:

```
admin_@cloudshell:~ (wmarusiak-book-351718)$ kubectl get services
NAME              TYPE        CLUSTER-IP      EXTERNAL-IP   PORT(S)    AGE
frontend-5kd5f    ClusterIP   10.120.14.136   <none>        80/TCP     7m
kubernetes        ClusterIP   10.120.0.1      <none>        443/TCP    46m
```

Figure 6.57 – Listing of services in the existing GKE cluster

To get details of a service, we can use the `kubectl describe service YOUR_SERVICENAME` command. This results in the following output:

```
admin_@cloudshell:~ (wmarusiak-book-351718)$ kubectl describe service frontend-5kd5f
Name:                frontend-5kd5f
Namespace:           default
Labels:              app-guestbook
                     tier=frontend
Annotations:         cloud.google.com/neg: {"ingress":true}
Selector:            tier=frontend
Type:                ClusterIP
IP Family Policy:    SingleStack
IP Families:         IPv4
IP:                  10.120.14.136
IPs:                 10.120.14.136
Port:                <unset>  80/TCP
TargetPort:          80/TCP
Endpoints:           10.116.0.6:80,10.116.0.7:80,10.116.1.4:80 + 3 more...
Session Affinity:    None
Events:              <none>
```

Figure 6.58 – Details of the frontend-5kd5f service by using the kubectl command

The same approach can be used to get details of other service types supported by GKE.

After learning how to view services, we can start creating and utilizing our own services.

Adding services

As mentioned at the beginning of the *Service management* section, we can define our services and control how applications can be accessed outside the GKE cluster.

We will combine the command line and Cloud console to add services to the GKE cluster.

Cloud console

First, we need to have the existing application deployed into the GKE cluster. We have the application named frontend prepared to be exposed outside the GKE cluster. Then, proceed as follows:

1. To create a service for an existing application, go to **Workloads** and select your workload.

2. From the workload detail, click the **ACTIONS** button and then **Expose**:

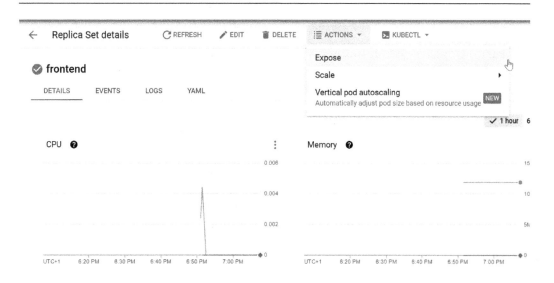

Figure 6.59 – Internal GKE services

3. We can choose the service type from **Cluster IP**, **Node port**, or **Load balancer**:

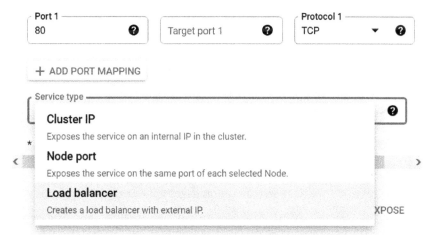

Expose

Expose a resource's Pods using a Kubernetes Service.

Port mapping

Port 1	Target port 1	Protocol 1
80		TCP

+ ADD PORT MAPPING

Service type

Cluster IP
Exposes the service on an internal IP in the cluster.

Node port
Exposes the service on the same port of each selected Node.

Load balancer
Creates a load balancer with external IP.

Figure 6.60 – Service type selection menu

4. We will choose the **Cluster IP** default from the selection.

5. Immediately after creation, we can see service metrics, the Cluster IP, and serving Pods:

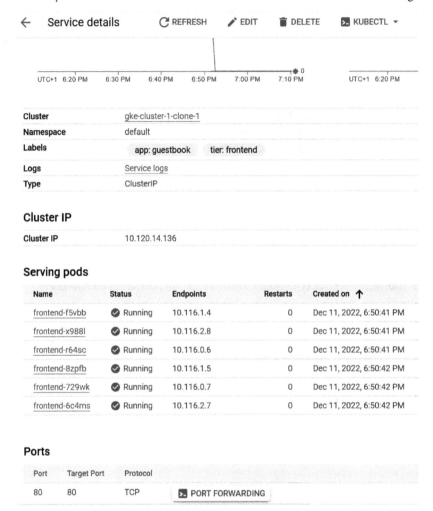

Figure 6.61 – Cluster IP service details

Command line

We have an application called my-nginx running as a deployment with two Pods. We want to create a service of type ClusterIP for the workload running under the name my-nginx.

To create a service of type ClusterIP, we can use the following code:

```
apiVersion: v1
kind: Service
```

```
metadata:
  name: my-nginx
  labels:
    run: my-nginx
spec:
  ports:
  - port: 80
    protocol: TCP
  selector:
    run: my-nginx
```

The preceding code can be downloaded from the following GitHub page: `https://raw.githubusercontent.com/kubernetes/website/main/content/en/examples/service/networking/nginx-svc.yaml`.

We recommend saving the file's content to the local disk so that we can use it as input for the `kubectl` command.

To create a service using the `kubectl` command-line tool, we need to run the following command: `kubectl apply -f YOUR_FILENAME.yaml`.

After applying the YAML file, a service of type `ClusterIP` is created. We can check if it is created by running the `kubectl get services` command and then `kubectl describe service SERVICE_NAME`:

```
admin_@cloudshell:~ (wmarusiak-book-351718)$ kubectl get services
NAME                TYPE        CLUSTER-IP       EXTERNAL-IP    PORT(S)    AGE
frontend-5kd5f      ClusterIP   10.120.14.136    <none>         80/TCP     46m
kubernetes          ClusterIP   10.120.0.1       <none>         443/TCP    86m
nginx-service       ClusterIP   10.120.15.20     <none>         80/TCP     44s
admin_@cloudshell:~ (wmarusiak-book-351718)$ kubectl describe service nginx-service
Name:                nginx-service
Namespace:           default
Labels:              run=my-nginx
Annotations:         cloud.google.com/neg: {"ingress":true}
Selector:            run=my-nginx
Type:                ClusterIP
IP Family Policy:    SingleStack
IP Families:         IPv4
IP:                  10.120.15.20
IPs:                 10.120.15.20
Port:                <unset>  80/TCP
TargetPort:          80/TCP
Endpoints:           10.116.0.9:80,10.116.1.7:80
Session Affinity:    None
Events:              <none>
admin_@cloudshell:~ (wmarusiak-book-351718)$ ▮
```

Figure 6.62 – Newly created ClusterIP service details

Now, let's learn how to modify services running on the GKE cluster.

Modifying services

Modifying services used in GKE will be similar to other parts of the GKE modification.

Cloud console

Modifying a service in Cloud console will rely on editing existing services available for us in GKE.

We have a `nginx-service` service from the previous section of the book available. To edit it, we will go to the **Services & Ingress** section, click on it, and then click the **EDIT** button:

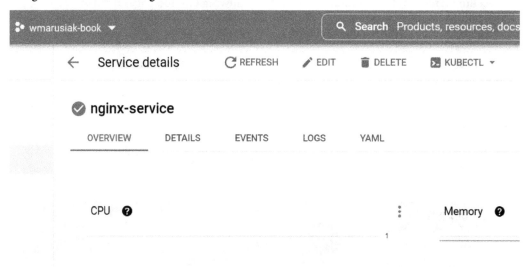

Figure 6.63 – Modification of a service in Cloud console

Depending on the service, your edit might look different than ours. In our case, we will change the port from `80` to `8080`. `Port` and `targetPort` are different ports where we must distinguish how we access the application. `Port` is the actual port on the Pod, and `targetPort` is the open port on the node or cluster level open to the requests:

```
 9    labels:
10      run: my-nginx
11    managedFields:
12    - apiVersion: v1
13      fieldsType: FieldsV1
14      fieldsV1:
15        f:metadata:
16          f:annotations:
17            .: {}
18            f:kubectl.kubernetes.io/last-applied-configuration: {}
19          f:labels:
20            .: {}
21            f:run: {}
22        f:spec:
23          f:internalTrafficPolicy: {}
24          f:ports:
25            .: {}
26            k:{"port":80,"protocol":"TCP"}:
27              .: {}
28              f:port: {}
29              f:protocol: {}
30              f:targetPort: {}
31          f:selector: {}
32          f:sessionAffinity: {}
33          f:type: {}
34      manager: kubectl-client-side-apply
35      operation: Update
36      time: "2022-12-11T18:56:42Z"
37    name: nginx-service
38    namespace: default
39    resourceVersion: "46693"
40    uid: a64ddd57-1e6f-45b1-9381-7f2179055bb6
41  spec:
42    clusterIP: 10.120.15.20
43    clusterIPs:
44    - 10.120.15.20
45    internalTrafficPolicy: Cluster
46    ipFamilies:
47    - IPv4
48    ipFamilyPolicy: SingleStack
49    ports:
50    - port: 80
51      protocol: TCP
52      targetPort: 8080
53    selector:
54      run: my-nginx
55    sessionAffinity: None
56    type: ClusterIP
57  status:
58    loadBalancer: {}
59
```

Figure 6.64 – Modification of the service by using Cloud console

After saving the file in the Cloud console editor, the service description is updated and reflects our changes:

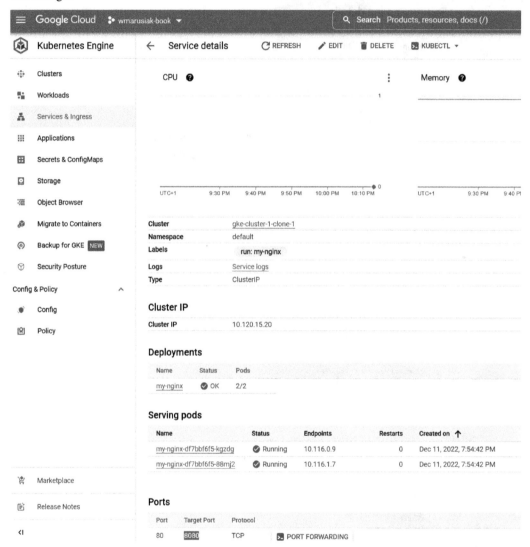

Figure 6.65 – Service update finalized by using Cloud console from target port 80 to 8080

After successfully modifying the service in Cloud console, we move on to the same task using the kubectl command-line tool.

Command line

Modification of the service by using the `kubectl` command-line tool allows us to change the service configuration easily.

We need to list services, get the service's configuration, modify it, and apply the new values to modify the service. Here's how we can do that:

1. To list all existing services, we can use the `kubectl get services` command:

```
admin_@cloudshell:~ (wmarusiak-book-351718)$ kubectl get services
NAME              TYPE         CLUSTER-IP       EXTERNAL-IP    PORT(S)     AGE
frontend-5kd5f    ClusterIP    10.120.14.136    <none>         80/TCP      3h11m
kubernetes        ClusterIP    10.120.0.1       <none>         443/TCP     3h51m
nginx-service     ClusterIP    10.120.15.20     <none>         80/TCP      145m
```

Figure 6.66 – Listing of existing services

2. Once we have the name of the service, we can get its configuration by using the `kubectl describe service SERVICE_NAME` command:

```
admin @cloudshell:~ (wmarusiak-book-351718)$ kubectl describe service nginx-service
Name:                nginx-service
Namespace:           default
Labels:              run=my-nginx
Annotations:         cloud.google.com/neg: {"ingress":true}
Selector:            run=my-nginx
Type:                ClusterIP
IP Family Policy:    SingleStack
IP Families:         IPv4
IP:                  10.120.15.20
IPs:                 10.120.15.20
Port:                <unset>  80/TCP
TargetPort:          8080/TCP
Endpoints:           10.116.0.9:8080,10.116.1.7:8080
Session Affinity:    None
Events:              <none>
```

Figure 6.67 – Detailed description of running the GKE service

3. To edit the configuration itself, we need to use the `kubectl edit service SERVICE_NAME` command, resulting in the following information:

```
spec:
  clusterIP: 10.120.15.20
  clusterIPs:
  - 10.120.15.20
  internalTrafficPolicy: Cluster
  ipFamilies:
  - IPv4
  ipFamilyPolicy: SingleStack
  ports:
  - port: 80
    protocol: TCP
    targetPort: 8089
  selector:
    run: my-nginx
  sessionAffinity: None
  type: ClusterIP
status:
  loadBalancer: {}
```

Figure 6.68 – Editing GKE service in a preferred text editor

4. After saving the file, the changes are applied immediately.

5. Execution of the `kubectl describe service YOUR_SERVICE_NAME` command shows the changes applied:

```
admin_@cloudshell:~ (wmarusiak-book-351718)$ kubectl describe service nginx-service
Name:              nginx-service
Namespace:         default
Labels:            run=my-nginx
Annotations:       cloud.google.com/neg: {"ingress":true}
Selector:          run=my-nginx
Type:              ClusterIP
IP Family Policy:  SingleStack
IP Families:       IPv4
IP:                10.120.15.20
IPs:               10.120.15.20
Port:              <unset>  80/TCP
TargetPort:        8089/TCP
Endpoints:         10.116.0.9:8089,10.116.1.7:8089
Session Affinity:  None
Events:            <none>
```

Figure 6.69 – Editing GKE service in a preferred text editor

6. The description of the service has changed—`TargetPort` has changed from port `8080` to `8089`.

Now that we have learned how to modify services, we need to learn how to remove them.

Removing services

Removal of services can be performed in Cloud console and by using the kubectl command-line tool.

Cloud console

In Cloud console, we need to navigate to **Services & Ingress**, select the desired service to be removed, and click the **DELETE** button:

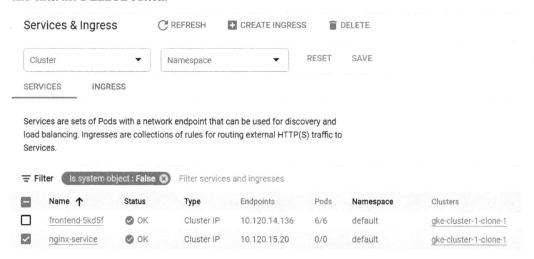

Figure 6.70 – Deleting services in Cloud console

After a moment, the service is deleted.

Command line

To remove a service in GKE, we need first to identify services running in the GKE cluster. To list all services, we can use the kubectl get services command:

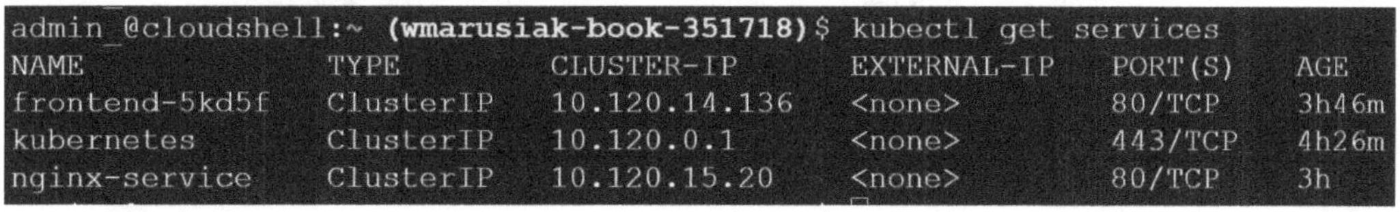

```
admin_@cloudshell:~ (wmarusiak-book-351718)$ kubectl get services
NAME             TYPE         CLUSTER-IP      EXTERNAL-IP    PORT(S)    AGE
frontend-5kd5f   ClusterIP    10.120.14.136   <none>         80/TCP     3h46m
kubernetes       ClusterIP    10.120.0.1      <none>         443/TCP    4h26m
nginx-service    ClusterIP    10.120.15.20    <none>         80/TCP     3h
```

Figure 6.71 – List of existing GKE services

To delete a service, we need to use the kubectl delete service YOUR_SERVICE_ NAME command:

```
admin @cloudshell:~ (wmarusiak-book-351718)$ kubectl delete service nginx-service
service "nginx-service" deleted
admin @cloudshell:~ (wmarusiak-book-351718)$
```

Figure 6.72 – Successful deletion of the service

After completing the section on services, we will move on to another important section of GKE—logging and monitoring.

GKE logging and monitoring

GKE includes, by default, native integration with Google Cloud Logging and Cloud Monitoring. If desired, you can use Managed Service for Prometheus as well.

When the GKE cluster is created, Cloud Monitoring and Cloud Logging are enabled by default and can be used to observe logs and view monitoring metrics:

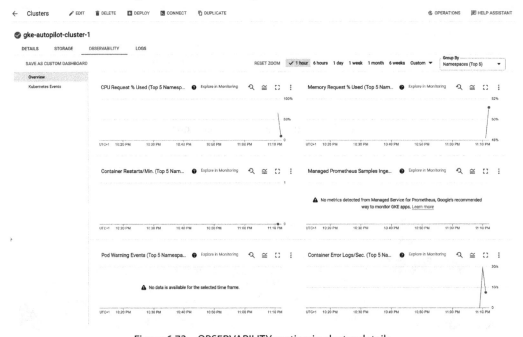

Figure 6.73 – OBSERVABILITY section in cluster details

As we will describe Cloud Logging and Cloud Monitoring in *Chapter 10*, we won't focus on those topics here.

Summary

Containerization of applications isn't something new; it is a fact. We need it not only to be successful when passing the **Associate Cloud Engineer** (**ACE**) certification but also to understand the future of the application deployment. Microservices, containerization, and micro-segmentation are "the now," and we can't avoid them. we hope the concept of containers, accompanying services, and various deployment types described in this chapter will help you not only scratch the surface but practically use them in real life as well.

Although we would have liked to dig deeper into some GKE sections, we had to focus on the overall target—passing the ACE cert. Kubernetes and GKE are such exciting topics that many books, blog articles, and videos have been created about them. Topics covered in this chapter are aligned with ACE requirements, but if you wish to dive deeper into GKE, we encourage you to follow up with detailed publications about it.

In the next chapter, we switch gears and move abstraction layers above, where we will learn and deploy containers in Cloud Run, create and run Cloud Functions, and familiarize ourselves with **Infrastructure as Code** (**IaC**) by using Terraform.

Questions

Answer the following questions to test your knowledge of this chapter:

1. Which of the following commands can be used to create a node pool?

    A. `gcloud container node-pools create POOL_NAME --cluster CLUSTER_NAME --region=REGION_NAME`

    B. `gcloud node-pools create POOL_NAME --cluster CLUSTER_NAME --region=REGION_NAME`

    C. `gcloud container node-pools add POOL_NAME --cluster CLUSTER_NAME --region=REGION_NAME`

    D. `kubectl node-pools add POOL_NAME --cluster CLUSTER_NAME --region=REGION_NAME`

    E. `kubectl container node-pool create POOL_NAME --cluster CLUSTER_NAME --region=REGION_NAME`

2. What are the main components of a GKE cluster

    A. `kube-apiserver`

    B. `etcd`

    C. `kube-scheduler`

D. `kube-controller-manager`

E. `cloud-controller-manager`

F. All of these

3. You have received a task to maintain a GKE cluster named `test-before-prod`. To save time, you would like to configure this cluster as your default GKE cluster. What should you do?

A. Create a file called `gke.default` in the `~/.gcloud` folder that contains the cluster name.

B. Use the `gcloud container cluster update test-before-prod` command.

C. Use the `gcloud config set container/cluster test-before-prod` command.

D. Create a file called `defaults.json` in the `~/gcloud` folder that contains the cluster name.

4. You have created an application and packaged it into a Docker image. You would like to deploy this Docker image as a workload on GKE. What do you need to do?

A. Upload the image to Container Registry and create a Kubernetes image.

B. Upload the image to Cloud Storage and create a Kubernetes image.

C. Upload the image to Container Registry and create a Kubernetes Deployment from the image.

D. Upload the image to Cloud Storage and create a Kubernetes Deployment from the image.

5. You have an application definition saved in a file called `application.yaml`. How can you run it on the GKE cluster?

A. Use the `kubectl apply -f application.yaml` command.

B. Use the `kubectl containers apply -f application.yaml` command.

C. Use the `gcloud containers apply -f application.yaml` command.

D. Use the `kubectl apply -e application.yaml` command.

6. What could be the reason that the Autopilot GKE cluster doesn't have any vCPU or memory used in the cluster overview?

A. The cluster is broken and needs to be recreated.

B. The cluster is healthy, but there are no applications running.

C. You don't have permission to view this information.

D. Autopilot GKE clusters don't display this information.

7. You have developed a new application with many microservices. The application will run on GKE, and you want to be sure that the cluster scales as more applications are deployed in the future. You want to avoid manual configuration as each new application is deployed. How can you ensure that the cluster will scale with new applications?

    A. Create a GKE cluster with autoscaling enabled on the node pool.

    B. Create a separate node pool for each new application and deploy it on the node pool.

    C. Deploy the application into GKE and enable **Vertical Pod Autoscaling (VPA)** to the deployment.

    D. Deploy the application into GKE and enable **Horizontal Pod Autoscaling (HPA)** to the deployment.

8. You want to create a sample Pod configuration file and save it in YAML format. How can you do this without writing the code yourself?

    A. Use the `gcloud containers describe application APPLICATION_NAME --dry-run=client -o yaml` command.

    B. Use the `kubectl APPLICATION_NAME --image=IMAGE_NAME --dry-run=client -o yaml` command.

    C. Use the `kubectl APPLICATION_NAME --image=IMAGE_NAME --run-dry=client -o yaml` command.

    D. Use the `kubectl APPLICATION_NAME --image=IMAGE_NAME -o yaml` command.

9. What are the default visible metrics in the deployment details located in the workload overview section?

    A. CPU and memory

    B. CPU, memory, and IOPS

    C. CPU, memory, and disk

    D. CPU, disk, and requests

10. You are being tasked with managing an application that runs on GKE. You need to find out which service is used with the application. Which command will you use?

    A. `kubectl describe service YOUR_SERVICENAME`

    B. `kubectl list service YOUR_SERVICENAME`

    C. `gcloud describe service YOUR_SERVICENAME`

    D. `gcloud list service YOUR_SERVICENAME`

Answers

The answers to the preceding questions are provided here:

1A, 2A, 3B, 4C, 5A, 6B, 7A, 8B, 9C, 10A

7

Implementing Compute Solutions – Cloud Run, Cloud Functions, and Infrastructure as Code

This chapter aims to familiarize ourselves with various compute solutions and how to implement them.

We are going to cover the following main topics:

- Cloud Run
- Cloud Functions
- Infrastructure as Code
- Marketplace solutions

We will start with IaC, a stateless computing service where we can run containerized code. The next topic will be IaC, where we will learn about running code in response to events without provisioning or managing servers. Lastly, we will look at **Infrastructure as Code (IaC)**, what benefits we can get by implementing it, and how to use IaC to deploy solutions.

Cloud Run

Cloud Run, a managed serverless compute platform, offers easy microservice deployment without service-specific configuration. It provides a simple and unified developer experience and uses container images as the unit of deployment. With scalable serverless execution, microservices automatically scale based on incoming requests, eliminating the need for Kubernetes cluster management. Additionally, Cloud Run supports code written in any language, thanks to its container-based architecture.

Before using Cloud Run, we must learn how it works, the use cases, and its benefits.

Cloud Run architecture

Cloud Run is a stateless computing environment where customers can run their containerized code on Google Cloud infrastructure. Cloud Run is a regional offering that benefits us with higher resiliency and availability. If one zone fails, Cloud Run could still provide the service. Higher availability is reflected by a service SLA of 99.95% a month.

Traffic to the services is automatically load-balanced across zones within a region, and container instances are automatically scaled up and down to meet incoming traffic.

To learn more about Cloud Run zonal redundancy, go to `https://cloud.google.com/architecture/disaster-recovery#cloud-run`.

Cloud Run services

The main component of the Cloud Run architecture is called a **service**. Each service is in a specific Google Cloud region where you use Cloud Run. Each service exposes a unique endpoint and automatically scales the Cloud Run infrastructure to handle load and requests.

A service is used to run code that responds to web requests or events. Some workloads that run extensively as Cloud Run services are as follows:

- Websites and web applications
- APIs and microservices
- Event-driven architectures and streaming data processing

The following diagram shows the Cloud Run services architecture:

Cloud Run services

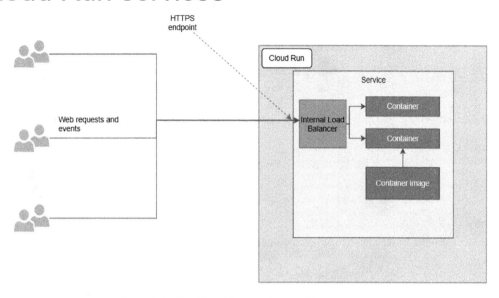

Figure 7.1 – The Cloud Run services architecture

A Cloud Run service includes an internal load balancer, which distributes requests to containers.

A service includes the following features by default:

- **HTTPS endpoint**: Every Cloud Run service has an HTTP endpoint and unique subdomain from the .run.app domain that supports custom domain configuration. It includes a TLS certificate and supports **WebSockets**, **HTTP/2,** and **gRPC**. All of these are end-to-end.

- **Autoscaling**: Cloud Run has built-in autoscaling, which allows the service to scale up from one to thousands of containers. If the service demand is decreased, the service scales down by removing idle containers. It is possible to limit the maximum number of instances.

- **Traffic management**: Every service deployment creates a new immutable version. Built-in traffic management allows you to route whole traffic to the latest revision, roll back a previous revision, or split traffic into multiple revisions. It allows you to test the new version and reduce the risk of deploying new, untested revisions.

Cloud Run revisions

Each deployment to service creates a **revision**. Once a revision has been created, it cannot be modified. If we wished to change the container image, we would need to create a new revision.

The following figure shows active requests connecting to **Service A** via **Revision A-3**. We have two older revisions of **Service A** that we can roll back to if needed. In parallel, we have two revisions of **Service B** that can be used to test the new version of the application:

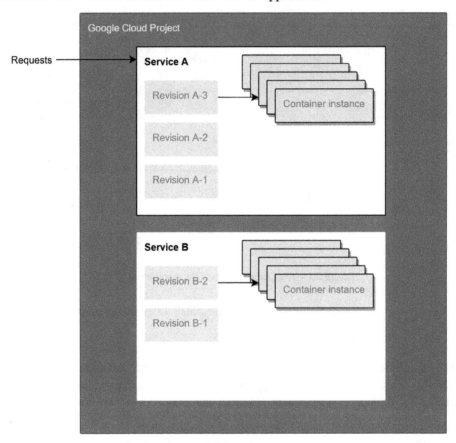

Figure 7.2 – Overview of the Cloud Run architecture

Now that we've learned about services and revisions, we can move on to Cloud Run jobs and how they can be used to host workloads.

Cloud Run jobs

A job is a collection of one or multiple independent tasks that are executed in parallel during the job execution. Each job is executed in a specific Google Cloud region and can run one or more containers until it is finished:

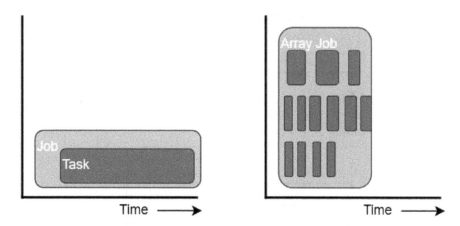

Figure 7.3 – Array of jobs in Cloud Run

The preceding figure shows us a comparison between a job that might have one task and can be executed longer and an array of jobs that can be parallelized and run faster than a job.

Using a single job to perform one task can take much longer than creating a job with many independent tasks. In Cloud Run, identical jobs may run independently, creating an array job.

An example of an array job in Cloud Run could be batch image processing stored in Cloud Storage.

Cloud Run jobs are best suited to be used when the code performs a job and then stops. Here are some examples:

- Scripts or other operational tasks
- Parallel jobs
- Saving the results of a query

Cloud Run for Anthos

We now know what use cases fit best when deploying on Cloud Run. Google Cloud has another offering for Cloud Run, called Cloud Run for Anthos. You might be wondering, what is Anthos? Anthos is a Google cloud-native platform that allows to deploy and manage applications consistently across on-premises environments, the edge, and multiple clouds. It is a unified platform that provides a consistent development and operations experience for all your applications, regardless of where they run. Anthos isn't part of the Associate Cloud Engineer certification, but if you want to learn more about Anthos, go to `https://cloud.google.com/anthos`.

The Cloud Run for Anthos architecture can be seen in the following diagram:

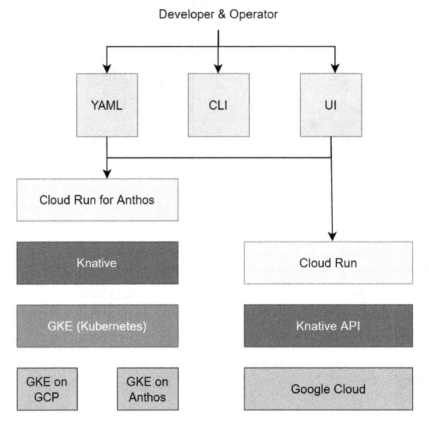

Figure 7.4 – Overview of Cloud Run for Anthos

Cloud Run for Anthos abstracts away the complexity of Kubernetes, allowing easy build and application deployment across hybrid and multi-cloud environments. Cloud Run for Anthos is a Knative open source project that enables serverless workloads on Kubernetes.

Cloud Run application deployment

Now that we've learned about the Cloud Run architecture and two possible application deployment types, it is time to deploy our first application – a service:

1. We will start by clicking the **CREATE SERVICE** button:

Google Cloud
wmarusiak-book
Search (/) for resources, docs, products, and more
Search
Cloud Run
Services
CREATE SERVICE
MANAGE CUSTOM DOMAINS
SERVICES
JOBS
PREVIEW
Run containers on a fully managed platform
Get started by creating a service - each Cloud Run service has a unique endpoint and autoscales deployed containers. Learn more
CREATE SERVICE
TAKE THE QUICKSTART

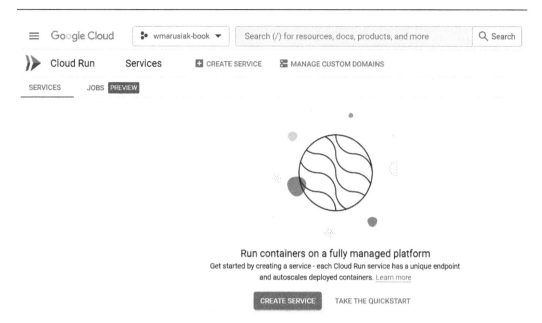

Figure 7.5 – Initial screen before deploying the Cloud Run application

2. We can choose from any container image we wish, but in our case, we will use a sample container provided by Google Cloud. To do so, we need to click the **TEST WITH A SAMPLE CONTAINER** button:

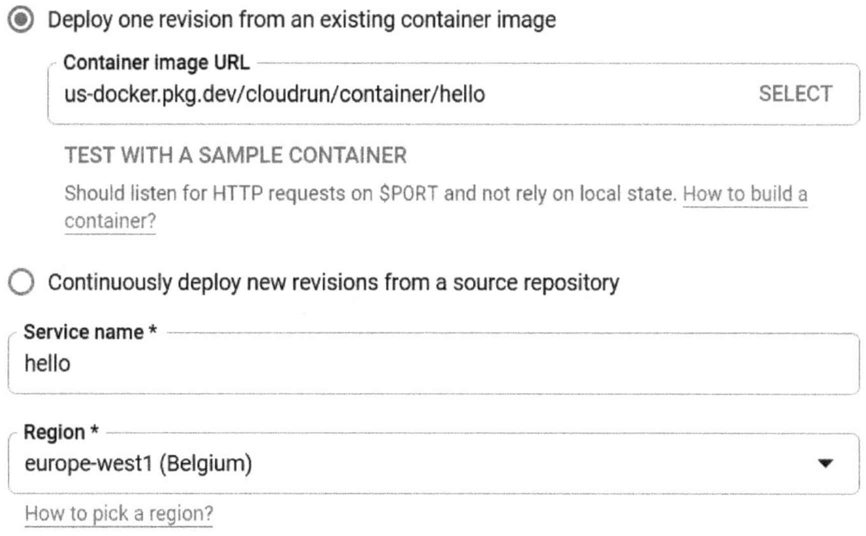

Deploy one revision from an existing container image
Container image URL
us-docker.pkg.dev/cloudrun/container/hello
SELECT
TEST WITH A SAMPLE CONTAINER
Should listen for HTTP requests on $PORT and not rely on local state. How to build a container?
Continuously deploy new revisions from a source repository
Service name *
hello
Region *
europe-west1 (Belgium)
How to pick a region?

Figure 7.6 – Cloud Run application deployment using a sample container provided by Google Cloud

3. We can allocate CPU where we are charged for the entire life cycle of the container instance or use CPU only when requests are processed.

4. In the **Autoscaling** section, we can choose the minimum and maximum number of instances. By default, the minimum is set to **0**. We must allocate at least one container to improve the application's latency. To learn more about **cold start** in Cloud Run, go to `https://cloud.google.com/run/docs/tips/general?authuser=4#start_containers_quickly`:

Autoscaling ❷

```
┌ Minimum number of instances * ──────────┐   ┌ Maximum number of instances ──────────┐
│ 0                                        │   │ 30                                      │
└──────────────────────────────────────────┘   └──────────────────────────────────────────┘
```
Set to 1 to reduce cold starts. Learn more

Figure 7.7 – The Autoscaling option of Cloud Run for specifying
the minimum and maximum number of instances

5. The next option is choosing service access from internal Google Cloud resources or from everywhere:

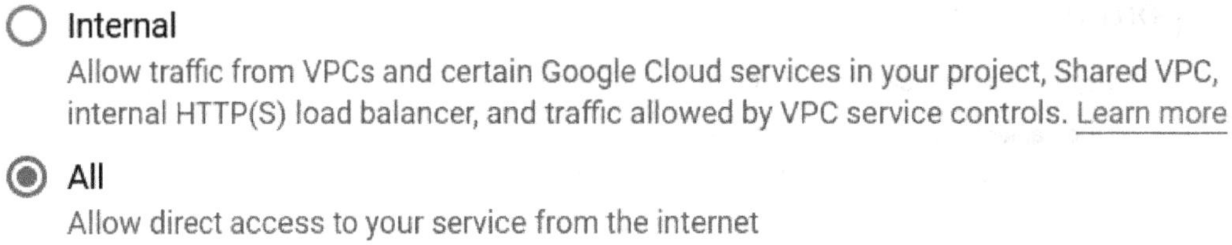

○ **Internal**
Allow traffic from VPCs and certain Google Cloud services in your project, Shared VPC, internal HTTP(S) load balancer, and traffic allowed by VPC service controls. Learn more

◉ **All**
Allow direct access to your service from the internet

Figure 7.8 – Cloud Run traffic configuration – internal traffic or direct traffic from the internet

6. We can allow unauthenticated service invocations or force authorization with Cloud IAM in the **Authentication** section. We will choose **Allow unauthenticated invocations**:

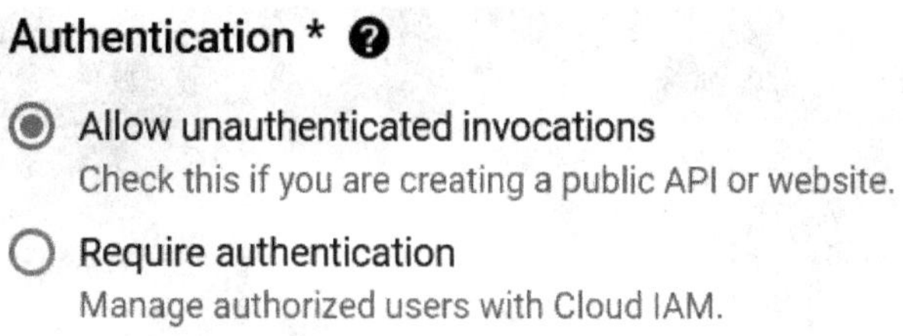

Authentication * ❓

⦿ **Allow unauthenticated invocations**
Check this if you are creating a public API or website.

○ **Require authentication**
Manage authorized users with Cloud IAM.

Figure 7.9 – Cloud Run authentication configuration

7. In the following sections – **Container**, **Networking**, and **Security** – we can fine-tune container deployment details such as capacity (the amount of memory, CPU, timeouts, or execution environment), HTTP2 or session configuration, and service account. We encourage you to try various options while learning Cloud Run. We will proceed with the default options.

8. We can access the application via its unique URL after deployment:

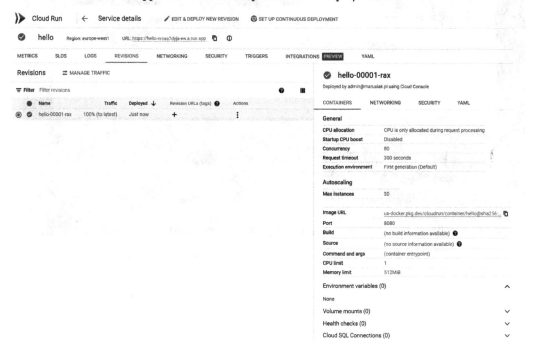

Figure 7.10 – The Cloud Run application is live

9. After visiting the URL in our browser, we can access the live application:

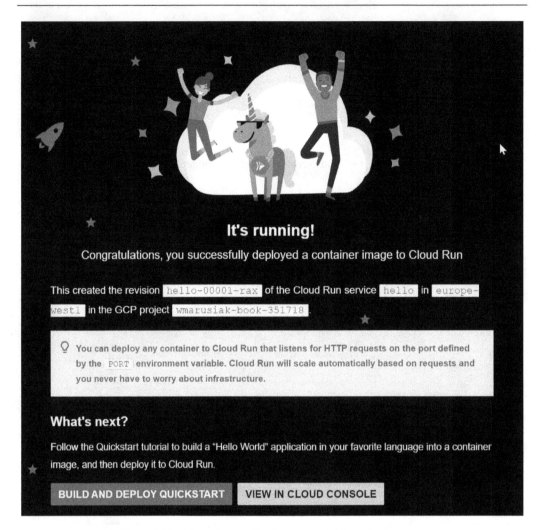

Figure 7.11 – Cloud Run application accessed from the browser

Now that we've successfully deployed our first service, it is time to dive deeper into revisions and traffic management.

Cloud Run application revisions

The following steps are based on the previously deployed sample container and look at the case where we want to update or change the container image we used previously. What do we do?

1. First, we need to find an image we can use to replace our existing container or change image content.

2. We will use several images to demonstrate revisions: Nginx and Apache HTTP Server images.

3. Let's start with Nginx. For this, we need to click the **EDIT & DEPLOY NEW REVISION** button:

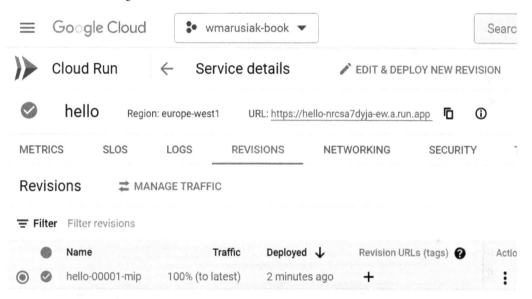

Figure 7.12 – New revision in Cloud Run

4. We will change the container image URL to a new one – nginx – and We will change the container port from 8080 to 80 while leaving all the other settings as-is:

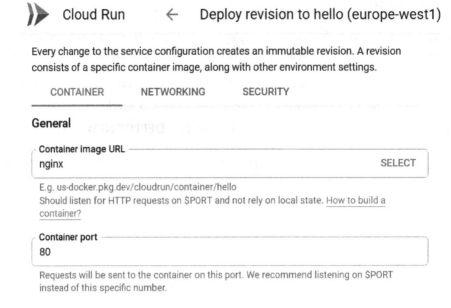

Figure 7.13 – New container image and container port in the new Cloud Run revision

5. Finally, we need to click the **Deploy** button.

6. In our case, as the image was small, the deployment took about 5 seconds. After revisiting the unique URL, we will see that the content has changed:

Figure 7.14 – The new container has been deployed as a new revision

7. In Cloud Console, we can see that a new revision has been deployed and that it's serving 100% traffic:

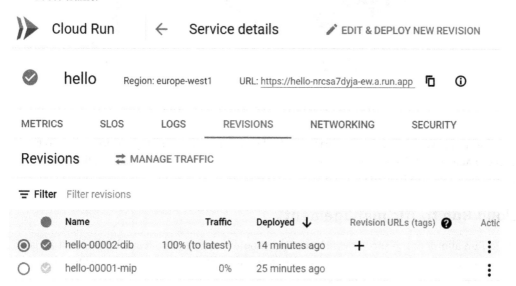

Figure 7.15 – New revision visible in Cloud Console

8. We deployed Apache HTTP Server with the **httpd** Docker image, where 100% of traffic is served:

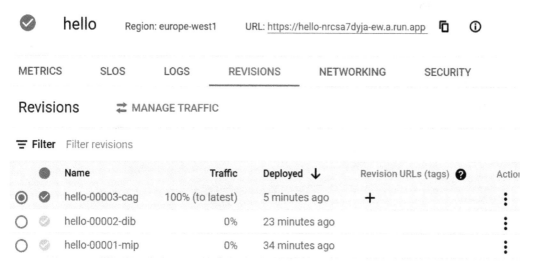

Figure 7.16 – HTTPD container created with a new version where 100% of traffic is served

9. When we visit the application URL, we'll see that the content has changed:

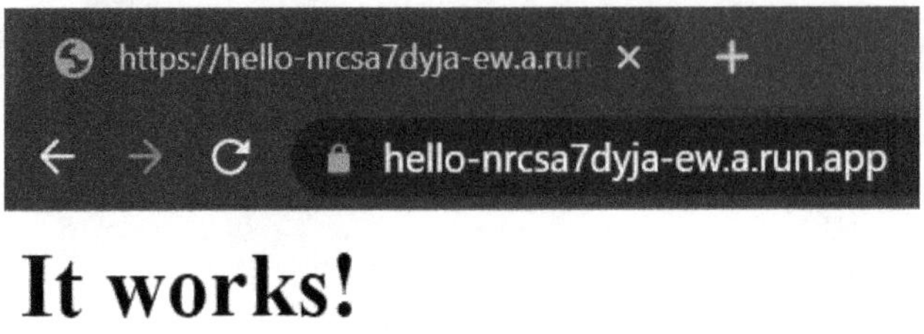

It works!

Figure 7.17 – HTTPD container in a browser

In this section, We showed you how easy it is to deploy new revisions of applications. It can be the exact container or a different one. We can do it very quickly and without any hassle. In the next section, we will show you how to manage traffic between revisions.

Cloud Run traffic management

Cloud Run allows you to specify which revision should receive traffic. It can be the latest revision, and you can split the traffic by percentages between different revisions. It is possible to use tags for testing, traffic migration, and rollbacks.

To manage the traffic in a service, we need to navigate to **Service** and click **REVISIONS**. Once we're in the **Revisions** section of the service, we can click the **MANAGE TRAFFIC** button:

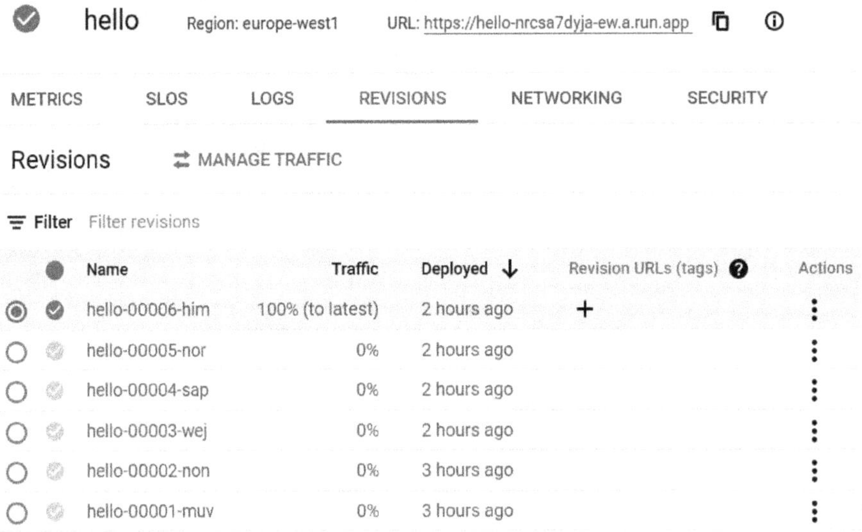

hello   Region: europe-west1   URL: https://hello-nrcsa7dyja-ew.a.run.app

| METRICS | SLOS | LOGS | REVISIONS | NETWORKING | SECURITY |

Revisions   ⇄ MANAGE TRAFFIC

≡ Filter   Filter revisions

	Name	Traffic	Deployed ↓	Revision URLs (tags) ❓	Actions
⦿ ✓	hello-00006-him	100% (to latest)	2 hours ago	+	⋮
○	hello-00005-nor	0%	2 hours ago		⋮
○	hello-00004-sap	0%	2 hours ago		⋮
○	hello-00003-wej	0%	2 hours ago		⋮
○	hello-00002-non	0%	3 hours ago		⋮
○	hello-00001-muv	0%	3 hours ago		⋮

Figure 7.18 – Overview of a service with multiple revisions

We will be presented with the **Manage traffic** window, where we can decide how network traffic flows:

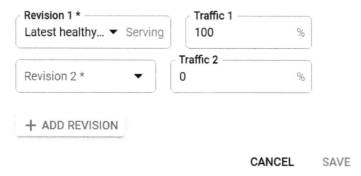

Figure 7.19 – Overview of a service with multiple revisions

We can decide how to distribute traffic between different revisions in this window.

For example, we can direct 50% of it to the latest healthy revision and the remaining 50% to another revision:

Figure 7.20 – Network traffic split between two revisions

After a moment, the internal load balancer will distribute network traffic as desired:

		Name	Traffic	Deployed ↓
◉	✔	hello-00006-him	50% (to latest)	2 hours ago
○	✔	hello-00005-nor	0%	2 hours ago
○	✔	hello-00004-sap	50%	2 hours ago
○	✔	hello-00003-wej	0%	3 hours ago
○	✔	hello-00002-non	0%	3 hours ago
○	✔	hello-00001-muv	0%	3 hours ago

Figure 7.21 – Network traffic split between two revisions in place

Similarly, we can roll back the changes or distribute traffic further across revisions of our application.

In the next section, we will focus on autoscaling and concurrent requests.

Cloud Run Traffic autoscaling

Before we start with the autoscaling concept in Cloud Run, we need to determine the limits of the Cloud Run instances. By default, Cloud Run services are configured to a maximum of 100 instances, and the default values for capacity are as follows:

- CPU: 1
- Memory: 512 MiB
- Request timeout: 300 seconds
- Maximum requests per container: 80
- Container instances: 30

At the time of writing, this book's maximums apply to Cloud Run:

- CPU: 8
- Memory: 34 GiB
- Request timeout: 3,600 seconds
- Maximum requests per container: 1,000
- Maximum container instances *(quota increase needed)*: 1,000

Cloud Run allows us to control the number of requests per instance precisely. Sometimes, you can lower the maximum concurrency to 1 if your code cannot process parallel requests; each request uses most of the available CPU and memory. Setting the maximum concurrency to 1 will likely negatively affect scaling performance due to the need to start many container instances before they can handle incoming requests.

To learn more about Cloud Run concurrency, go to `https://cloud.google.com/run/docs/about-concurrency`.

Cloud Run is a fantastic service, and we highly encourage you to try it out, explore its options, and have fun with it. To learn more about Cloud Run development tips, visit `https://cloud.google.com/run/docs/tips/general`.

The next section of this chapter will focus on another serverless product: Cloud Functions.

Cloud Functions

Cloud Functions, which falls under category of **Function-as-a-Service** (**FaaS**), is a serverless execution environment where we can run code without provisioning or managing any infrastructure. Cloud Functions is executed in a fully managed and serverless environment – you don't need to provision infrastructure or manage servers. Functions are triggered when an event being watched occurs.

Cloud Functions overview

The main advantage of Cloud Functions in Google Cloud is that you only need to write your code. Everything else will be done for you; there is no need to manage any infrastructure. Cloud Functions integrates very well within the Google Cloud products ecosystem. Functions listen and respond to various events – for example, when you upload an object to Cloud Storage, the function detects it and can invoke action.

Cloud Functions' use cases are most likely limited to our creativity, but I'd like to list just a few of the use cases used by Google Cloud customers:

- **Webhooks**: We can use HTTP triggers to respond to events from other systems such as GitHub, GitLab, Slack, or any software that sends HTTP requests. For example, we can create a Slack command that searches the Google Knowledge Graph API.

- **Data processing**: This involves listening and responding to Google Cloud Storage events – object creation, change, or deletion. For example, we can perform image processing, video transcoding, or data validation once data has been uploaded to Cloud Storage.

- **Lightweight APIs**: You can build your applications by combining different cloud functions.

- **Mobile backend**: You can use the Google Cloud mobile platform application product known as Firebase and write the backend in Cloud Functions.

- **IoT**: This is the ideal solution for a fleet of devices streaming data into Pub/Sub while invoking Cloud Functions to process, transform, and store data.

Events and triggers

Events are, generally speaking, things that happen in your cloud environment. The broadness of Google Cloud services allows users to interact when changes in databases, files, or virtual machines are made by responding to those events.

After an event, we have the option to respond to them. This response is called a trigger. By connecting the two, we can create sophisticated functions that can do some exciting work – fully automated and at scale.

Cloud Functions versions

Google Cloud offers two versions of Cloud Functions – 1st and 2nd generation. As anyone could expect, 2nd generation offers multiple improvements over the 1st generation.

To view a detailed comparison of the two generations, go to `https://cloud.google.com/functions/docs/concepts/version-comparison#comparison-table`.

Another essential feature is that the 2nd generation of Cloud Functions is built on Cloud Run, which was described earlier in this chapter. It also supports Eventarc – Google Cloud's approach to interacting with various services within Google Cloud.

To learn more about Google Eventarc, go to `https://cloud.google.com/eventarc/docs/overview`.

Google Cloud Functions example

Now that you've learned what Cloud Functions is, I'd like to show you how to implement a sample Cloud Function.

We will guide you through **optical character recognition** (**OCR**) on Google Cloud Platform with Cloud Functions.

Our use case is as follows:

1. An image with text is uploaded to Cloud Storage.
2. A triggered Cloud Function utilizes the Google Cloud Vision API to extract the text and identify the source language.
3. The text is queued for translation by publishing a message to a Pub/Sub topic.
4. A Cloud Function employs the Translation API to translate the text and stores the result in the translation queue.
5. Another Cloud Function saves the translated text from the translation queue to Cloud Storage.
6. The translated results are available in Cloud Storage as individual text files for each translation.

We need to download the samples first; we will use Golang as the programming language. Source files can be downloaded from – `https://github.com/GoogleCloudPlatform/golang-samples`. Before working with the OCR function sample, we recommend enabling the Cloud Translation API and the Cloud Vision API. If they are not enabled, your function will throw errors, and the process will not be completed.

Let's start with deploying the function:

1. We need to create a Cloud Storage bucket. Create your own bucket with unique name – please refer to documentation on bucket naming under following link: `https://cloud.google.com/storage/docs/buckets`. We will use the following code:

   ```
   gsutil mb gs://wojciech_image_ocr_bucket
   ```

2. We also need to create a second bucket to store the results:

   ```
   gsutil mb gs://wojciech_image_ocr_bucket_results
   ```

3. We must create a Pub/Sub topic to publish the finished translation results. We can do so with the following code: `gcloud pubsub topics create YOUR_TOPIC_NAME`. We used the following command to create it:

   ```
   gcloud pubsub topics create wojciech_translate_topic
   ```

4. Creating a second Pub/Sub topic to publish translation results is necessary. We can use the following code to do so:

   ```
   gcloud pubsub topics create wojciech_translate_topic_results
   ```

5. Next, we will clone the Google Cloud GitHub repository with some Python sample code:

   ```
   git clone https://github.com/GoogleCloudPlatform/golang-samples
   ```

6. From the repository, we need to go to the `golang-samples/functions/ocr/app/` file to be able to deploy the desired Cloud Function.

7. We recommend reviewing the included `go` files to review the code and understand it in more detail. Please change the values of your storage buckets and Pub/Sub topic names.

8. We will deploy the first function to process images. We will use the following command:

   ```
   gcloud functions deploy ocr-extract-go --runtime go119
   --trigger-bucket wojciech_image_ocr_bucket --entry-point
   ProcessImage --set-env-vars "^:^GCP_PROJECT=wmarusiak-book-
   351718:TRANSLATE_TOPIC=wojciech_translate_topic:RESULT_
   TOPIC=wojciech_translate_topic_results:TO_LANG=es,en,fr,ja"
   ```

9. After deploying the first Cloud Function, we must deploy the second one to translate the text. We can use the following code snippet:

```
gcloud functions deploy ocr-translate-go --runtime go119
--trigger-topic wojciech_translate_topic --entry-point
TranslateText --set-env-vars "GCP_PROJECT=wmarusiak-book-
351718,RESULT_TOPIC=wojciech_translate_topic_results"
```

10. The last part of the complete solution is a third Cloud Function that saves results to Cloud Storage. We will use the following snippet of code to do so:

```
gcloud functions deploy ocr-save-go --runtime go119 --trigger-
topic wojciech_translate_topic_results --entry-point SaveResult
--set-env-vars "GCP_PROJECT=wmarusiak-book-351718,RESULT_
BUCKET=wojciech_image_ocr_bucket_results"
```

11. We are now free to upload any image containing text. It will be processed first, then translated and saved into our Cloud Storage bucket.

12. We uploaded four sample images that we downloaded from the Internet that contain some text. We can see many entries in the `ocr-extract-go` Cloud Function's logs. Some Cloud Function log entries show us the detected language in the image and the other extracted text:

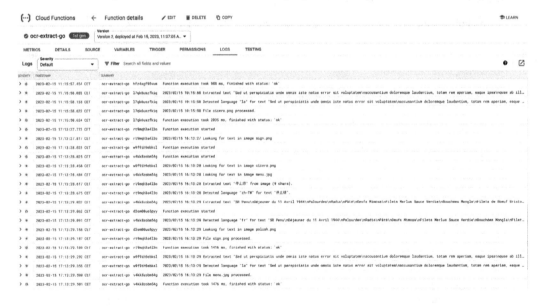

Figure 7.22 – Cloud Function logs from the ocr-extract-go function

13. `ocr-translate-go` translates detected text in the previous function:

Figure 7.23 – Cloud Function logs from the ocr-translate-go function

14. Finally, `ocr-save-go` saves the translated text into the Cloud Storage bucket:

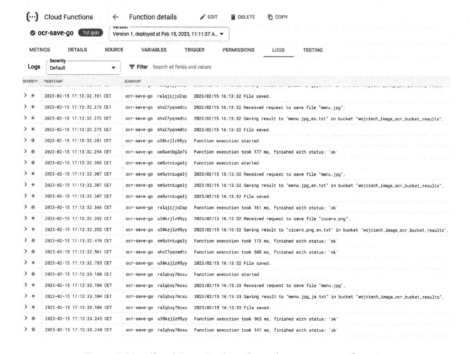

Figure 7.24 – Cloud Function logs from the ocr-save-go function

15. If we go to the Cloud Storage bucket, we'll see the saved translated files:

wojciech_image_ocr_bucket_results

Location	Storage class	Public access	Protection
us (multiple regions in United States)	Standard	Subject to object ACLs	None

OBJECTS   CONFIGURATION   PERMISSIONS   PROTECTION   LIFECYCLE   OBSERVABILITY `NEW`

Buckets > wojciech_image_ocr_bucket_results

UPLOAD FILES   UPLOAD FOLDER   CREATE FOLDER   TRANSFER DATA ▾   MANAGE HOLDS   DOWNLOAD   DELETE

Filter by name prefix only ▾   ⇶ Filter Filter objects and folders

	Name	Size	Type	Created	Storage class	Last modified
☐	cicero.png_en.txt	5.4 KB	text/plain; charset=utf-8	Feb 15, 2023, 5:13:33 PM	Standard	Feb 15, 2023, 5:13:33 PM
☐	cicero.png_es.txt	5.3 KB	text/plain; charset=utf-8	Feb 15, 2023, 5:13:31 PM	Standard	Feb 15, 2023, 5:13:31 PM
☐	cicero.png_fr.txt	6.2 KB	text/plain; charset=utf-8	Feb 15, 2023, 5:13:31 PM	Standard	Feb 15, 2023, 5:13:31 PM
☐	cicero.png_ja.txt	6.1 KB	text/plain; charset=utf-8	Feb 15, 2023, 5:13:31 PM	Standard	Feb 15, 2023, 5:13:31 PM
☐	menu.jpg_en.txt	339 B	text/plain; charset=utf-8	Feb 15, 2023, 5:13:32 PM	Standard	Feb 15, 2023, 5:13:32 PM
☐	menu.jpg_es.txt	363 B	text/plain; charset=utf-8	Feb 15, 2023, 5:13:32 PM	Standard	Feb 15, 2023, 5:13:32 PM
☐	menu.jpg_fr.txt	356 B	text/plain; charset=utf-8	Feb 15, 2023, 5:13:30 PM	Standard	Feb 15, 2023, 5:13:30 PM
☐	menu.jpg_ja.txt	504 B	text/plain; charset=utf-8	Feb 15, 2023, 5:13:33 PM	Standard	Feb 15, 2023, 5:13:33 PM
☐	polish.png_en.txt	3.9 KB	text/plain; charset=utf-8	Feb 15, 2023, 5:13:32 PM	Standard	Feb 15, 2023, 5:13:32 PM
☐	polish.png_es.txt	4.2 KB	text/plain; charset=utf-8	Feb 15, 2023, 5:13:32 PM	Standard	Feb 15, 2023, 5:13:32 PM
☐	polish.png_fr.txt	4.4 KB	text/plain; charset=utf-8	Feb 15, 2023, 5:13:32 PM	Standard	Feb 15, 2023, 5:13:32 PM
☐	polish.png_ja.txt	4.9 KB	text/plain; charset=utf-8	Feb 15, 2023, 5:13:32 PM	Standard	Feb 15, 2023, 5:13:32 PM
☐	sign.png_en.txt	9 B	text/plain; charset=utf-8	Feb 15, 2023, 5:13:31 PM	Standard	Feb 15, 2023, 5:13:31 PM
☐	sign.png_es.txt	16 B	text/plain; charset=utf-8	Feb 15, 2023, 5:13:31 PM	Standard	Feb 15, 2023, 5:13:31 PM
☐	sign.png_fr.txt	18 B	text/plain; charset=utf-8	Feb 15, 2023, 5:13:31 PM	Standard	Feb 15, 2023, 5:13:31 PM
☐	sign.png_ja.txt	9 B	text/plain; charset=utf-8	Feb 15, 2023, 5:13:31 PM	Standard	Feb 15, 2023, 5:13:31 PM

Figure 7.25 – Translated images saved in the Cloud Storage bucket

16. We can view the content directly from the Cloud Storage bucket by clicking **Download** next to the file, as shown in the following screenshot:

Figure 7.26 – Translated text from Polish to English stored in the Cloud Storage bucket

Cloud Functions is a powerful and fast way to code, deploy, and use advanced features. We encourage you to try out and deploy Cloud Functions to understand the process of using them better.

At the time of writing, Google Cloud Free Tier offers a generous number of free resources we can use. Cloud Functions offers the following with its free tier:

- 2 million invocations per month (this includes both background and HTTP invocations)
- 400,000 GB-seconds, 200,000 GHz-seconds of compute time
- 5 GB network egress per month

Google Cloud has comprehensive tutorials that you can try to deploy. Go to `https://cloud.google.com/functions/docs/tutorials` to follow one.

Now that we've covered the serverless products in Google Cloud, we will learn about IaC.

Infrastructure as Code

IaC is a new way to deploy and manage infrastructure. It doesn't only apply to cloud resources but to on-premises resources – for example, VMware vSphere. However, this book and this chapter will focus on IaC deployment in Google Cloud.

We briefly mentioned IaC in *Chapter 2*, where we discussed various ways of deploying resources in Google Cloud – Cloud Foundation Toolkit, Config Connector, and Terraform.

IaC aims to solve main issues from the past – lengthy time to deliver resources, errors during the deployment, ease of implementation, and the overall complexity of IT resource management.

Config Connector in Google Kubernetes Engine

In *Chapter 5* and 6 we learned how to create, configure, and use **Google Kubernetes Engine** (**GKE**) to deploy applications. We will use that knowledge to install, configure, and deploy Config Connector and Google Cloud resources. Config Connector is an open source Kubernetes add-on that allows us to manage Google Cloud resources in a Kubernetes way.

To use Config Connector, there are a few prerequisites that GKE needs to have:

- GKE version:

    - `1.15.11-gke.5` and later

    - `1.16.8-gke.8` and later

    - `1.17.4-gke.5` and later

- A Workload Identity Pool needs to be enabled

- GKE monitoring must be enabled

We will start by installing Config Connector on the newly created GKE cluster.

Installing Config Connector

As mentioned previously, Config Connector is an add-on to GKE. We can enable it during GKE cluster creation or reconfigure the existing GKE cluster to support it.

New GKE cluster

As mentioned previously, we must ensure that all the prerequisites have been met:

1. Go to GKE in Cloud Console.
2. Click **Create** and choose **GKE Standard**.
3. Provide the name of your GKE cluster.

4. Choose the supported GKE master version.

5. In the **Security** part of the cluster, select **Enable Workload Identity**:

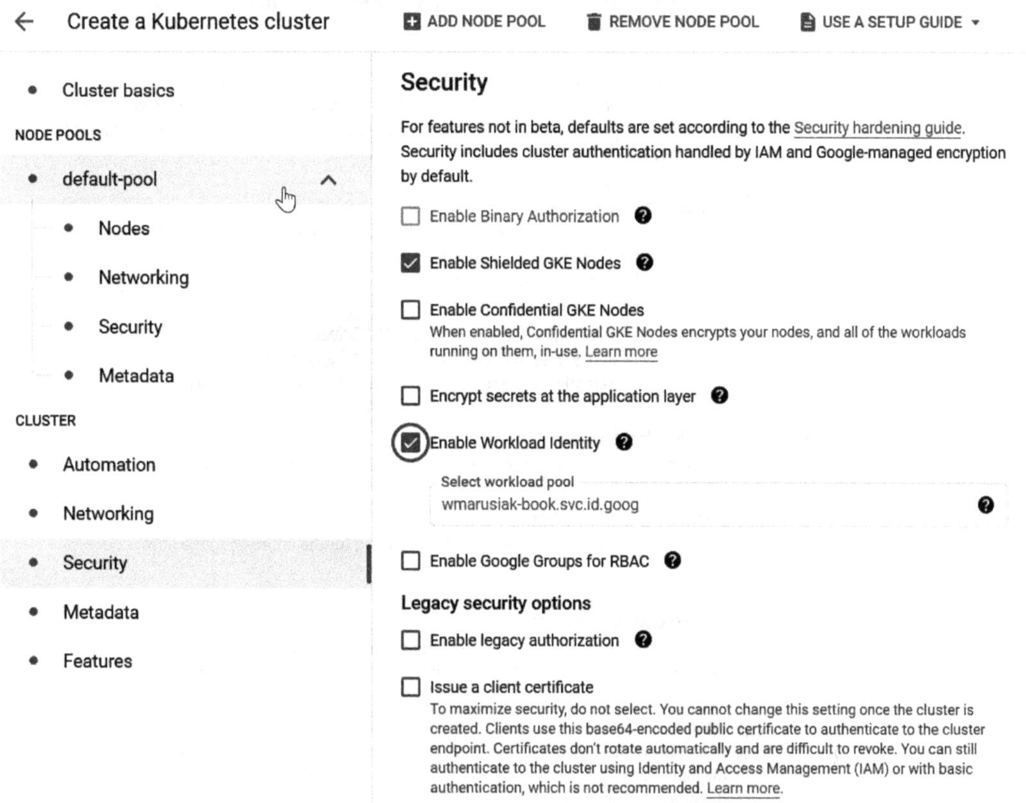

Figure 7.27 – Workload Identity configuration in the Security section of the newly created GKE cluster

6. In the **Features** section of the cluster, click **Enable Config Connector**:

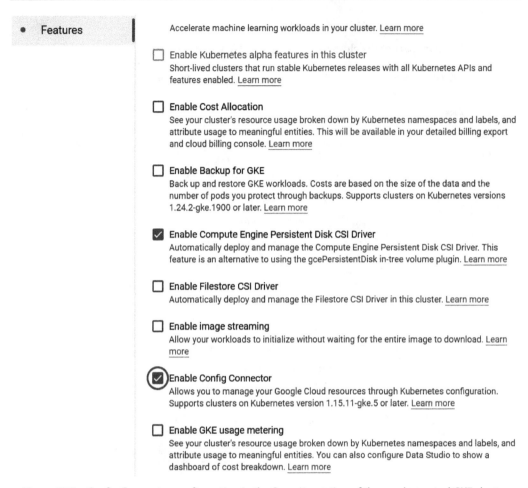

Figure 7.28 – Config Connector configuration in the Security section of the newly created GKE cluster

7. Monitoring must also be enabled and selected by default with newly created GKE clusters.

8. Now that we've created the cluster, Config Connector is ready to be used.

Next, we will enable Config Connector in the existing GKE cluster.

Existing GKE cluster

To enable Config Connector in the existing GKE cluster, we must enable the Config Connector add-on, enable Workload Identity, and create an Workload Identity:

1. Prior to doing any work with the existing GKE cluster, we need to authenticate with it to be able to run any command

2. We can use following command:

    ```
    gcloud container clusters get-credentials YOUR_CLUSTER_NAME
    --zone=ZONE --project=YOUR_PROJECT_NAMENAME
    ```

3. Once authenticated, we can enable Workload Identity on the existing cluster with the following
    command:

    ```
    gcloud container clusters update CLUSTER_NAME
        --region=COMPUTE_REGION \
        --workload-pool=PROJECT_ID.svc.id.goog
    ```

4. In our case, we used following code:

    ```
    gcloud container clusters update cluster-1 --region=us-
    central1-c --workload-pool=wmarusiak-book.svc.id.goog
    ```

5. Then, we need to enable Config Connector. To do this, we need to use following gcloud command:

    ```
    gcloud container clusters update CLUSTER_NAME --zone=YOUR_ZONE
    --update-addons ConfigConnector=ENABLED
    ```

After enabling the Config Connector add-on and Workload Identity in an existing GKE cluster, we
can proceed with IAM resources creation.

Config Connector creates and manages Google Cloud resources by using an **Identity and Access
Management** (**IAM**) service account to authenticate with Google Cloud. It then uses GKE's Workload
Identity to bind the IAM service account to a Kubernetes service account. This allows Config Connector
to access and manage Google Cloud resources on behalf of the Kubernetes cluster.

1. First, we need to create a workload identity. We need one because Config Connector authenticates
    with IAM to create and manage Google Cloud resources.

2. We will create a new service account using the following code:

    ```
    gcloud iam service-accounts create gke-workload-identity-sa
    ```

3. Next, we must grant elevated permission to the IAM service account in our project. Similar to
    the Pub/Sub section, please change the project and other values used in the following commands:

    ```
    gcloud projects add-iam-policy-binding wmarusiak-book
    --member="serviceAccount:gke-workload-identity-sa@wmarusiak-
    book.iam.gserviceaccount.com" --role="roles/editor"
    ```

4. The last step is to create an IAM policy binding between the IAM service account and the predefined GKE service account that Config Connector uses. To do so, we need to run the following command:

```
gcloud iam service-accounts add-iam-policy-binding
gke-workload-identity-sa@wmarusiak-book.iam.gserviceaccount.
com --member="serviceAccount:wmarusiak-book.svc.id.goog[cnrm-
system/cnrm-controller-manager]" --role="roles/iam.
workloadIdentityUser"
```

5. Now, we need to create the `configconnector.yaml` file with the following content. To apply it to the existing GKE cluster, we need to run the `kubectl apply -f configconnector.yaml` command:

```
# configconnector.yaml
apiVersion: core.cnrm.cloud.google.com/v1beta1
kind: ConfigConnector
metadata:
 # the name is restricted to ensure that there is only one
 # ConfigConnector resource installed in your cluster
 name: configconnector.core.cnrm.cloud.google.com
spec:
 mode: cluster
 googleServiceAccount: "gke-workload-identity-sa@wmarusiak-book.
iam.gserviceaccount.com"
```

6. After a moment, we can check if the Config Connector resources have been created. We can use the `kubectl get pods -A | grep config` command:

```
admin_@cloudshell:~ (wmarusiak-book)$ k g
et pods -A | grep config
configconnector-operator-system     configc
onnector-operator-0
             1/1     Running     0      8m49s
```

Figure 7.29 – Config Connector resources created in the kube-system namespace

7. We must configure the resource destination before creating any resource with Config Connector. Resources can be created at the project, folder, or organization level. But first, we must create a GKE namespace. we will use the following command:

```
kubectl create namespace config-connector
```

8. I will choose to organize resources at the project level. I will use the following command to configure this:

```
kubectl annotate namespace config-connector cnrm.cloud.google.
com/project-id=project_ID
```

If you wish, you can organize resources at the folder level by changing the annotation to `kubectl annotate namespace config-connector cnrm.cloud.google.com/folder-id=config_connector_folder` or `kubectl annotate namespace config-connector cnrm.cloud.google.com/organization-id=ORGANIZATION_ID`.

9. To verify the installation, we can run the following command:

```
kubectl wait -n cnrm-system --for=condition=Ready pod --all
```

We will get the following output:

```
admin_@cloudshell:~ (wmarusiak-book)$ kubectl wait -n cnrm-system \
    --for=condition=Ready pod --all
pod/cnrm-controller-manager-0 condition met
pod/cnrm-deletiondefender-0 condition met
pod/cnrm-resource-stats-recorder-66f6f9d9fc-pnhtb condition met
pod/cnrm-webhook-manager-659bfcc8c6-9rq6r condition met
pod/cnrm-webhook-manager-659bfcc8c6-xw5bf condition met
```

Figure 7.30 – Config Connector is correctly installed in the cluster

Now that we've learned how to configure Config Connector on the newly created GKE cluster and existing GKE cluster, we can create, modify, and delete Google Cloud resources.

Practical usage of Config Connector

Cloud Config supports many Google Cloud services. The complete list of supported services can be found at `https://cloud.google.com/config-connector/docs/reference/overview`.

We will create a Cloud Storage bucket using Config Connector as a sample resource.

Config Connector describes each resource well and provides some sample YAML code:

Sample YAML(s)

Typical Use Case

```yaml
# Copyright 2020 Google LLC
#
# Licensed under the Apache License, Version 2.0 (the "License");
# you may not use this file except in compliance with the License.
# You may obtain a copy of the License at
#
#     http://www.apache.org/licenses/LICENSE-2.0
#
# Unless required by applicable law or agreed to in writing, software
# distributed under the License is distributed on an "AS IS" BASIS,
# WITHOUT WARRANTIES OR CONDITIONS OF ANY KIND, either express or implied.
# See the License for the specific language governing permissions and
# limitations under the License.

apiVersion: storage.cnrm.cloud.google.com/v1beta1
kind: StorageBucket
metadata:
  annotations:
    cnrm.cloud.google.com/force-destroy: "false"
  labels:
    label-one: "value-one"
  # StorageBucket names must be globally unique. Replace ${PROJECT_ID?} with your project ID.
  name: ${PROJECT_ID?}-sample
spec:
  lifecycleRule:
    - action:
        type: Delete
      condition:
        age: 7
  versioning:
    enabled: true
  cors:
    - origin: ["http://example.appspot.com"]
      responseHeader: ["Content-Type"]
      method: ["GET", "HEAD", "DELETE"]
      maxAgeSeconds: 3600
  uniformBucketLevelAccess: true
```

Figure 7.31 – Config Connector sample YAML code

The code to create a Cloud Storage bucket looks like this:

```yaml
apiVersion: storage.cnrm.cloud.google.com/v1beta1
kind: StorageBucket
metadata:
  annotations:
    cnrm.cloud.google.com/force-destroy: "false"
  labels:
    label-one: "value-one"
```

```
   name: wmarusiak-cc-bucket
spec:
  lifecycleRule:
    - action:
        type: Delete
      condition:
        age: 7
  versioning:
    enabled: true
  uniformBucketLevelAccess: true
```

To create a resource, we need to save the code as a YAML file and apply it using the following command:

```
kubectl apply -f YOUR_FILENAME.YAML
```

After a moment, resource creation will be completed:

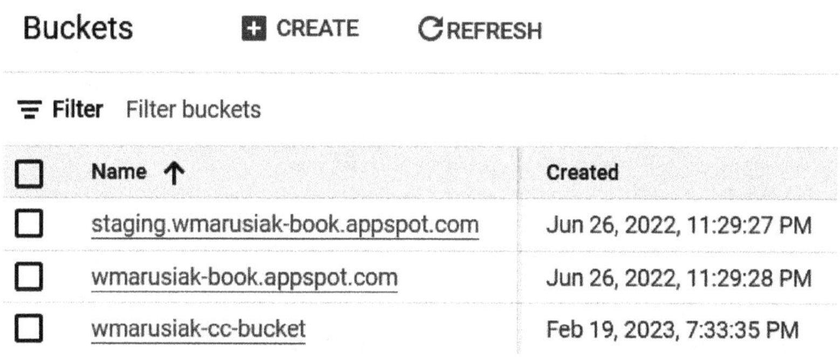

Figure 7.32 – Cloud Storage bucket created by Config Connector

We can edit the previous YAML file to change the Cloud Storage bucket configuration. Let's add additional labels and an additional life cycle rule:

```
apiVersion: storage.cnrm.cloud.google.com/v1beta1
kind: StorageBucket
metadata:
  annotations:
    cnrm.cloud.google.com/force-destroy: "false"
  labels:
    label-one: "value-one"
    label-two: "value-two"
  name: wmarusiak-cc-bucket
spec:
  lifecycleRule:
    - action:
```

```
        storageClass: NEARLINE
        type: SetStorageClass
      condition:
        age: 7
    - action:
        type: Delete
      condition:
        age: 365
  versioning:
    enabled: true
  uniformBucketLevelAccess: true
```

We must apply the file using the same command that we used previously:

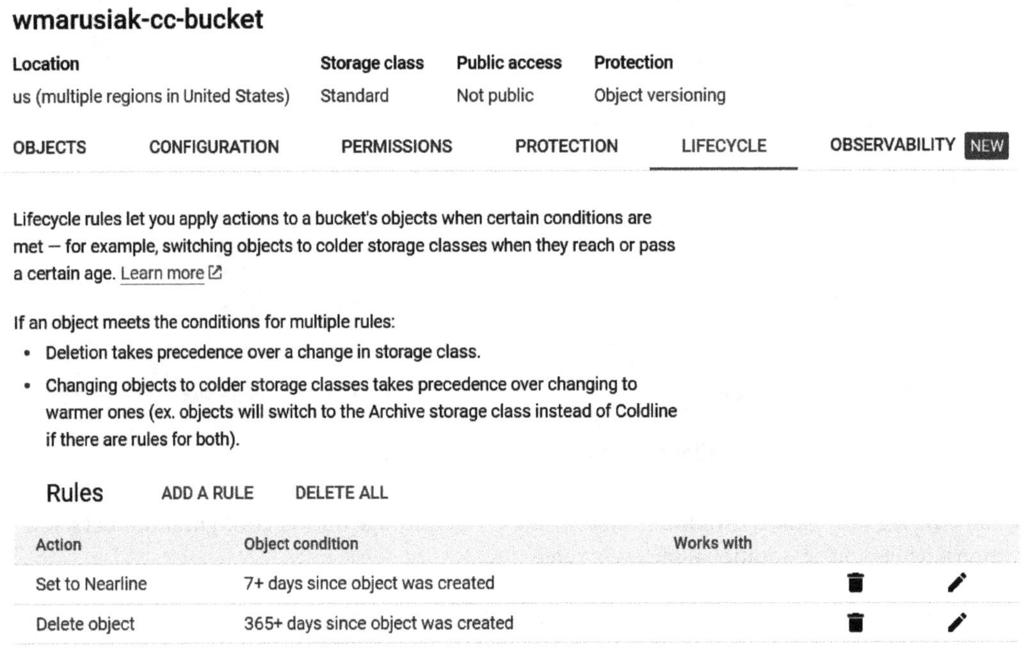

wmarusiak-cc-bucket

Location	Storage class	Public access	Protection
us (multiple regions in United States)	Standard	Not public	Object versioning

OBJECTS	CONFIGURATION	PERMISSIONS	PROTECTION	LIFECYCLE	OBSERVABILITY NEW

Lifecycle rules let you apply actions to a bucket's objects when certain conditions are met — for example, switching objects to colder storage classes when they reach or pass a certain age. Learn more ☑

If an object meets the conditions for multiple rules:

- Deletion takes precedence over a change in storage class.
- Changing objects to colder storage classes takes precedence over changing to warmer ones (ex. objects will switch to the Archive storage class instead of Coldline if there are rules for both).

Rules   ADD A RULE   DELETE ALL

Action	Object condition	Works with		
Set to Nearline	7+ days since object was created		🗑	✏
Delete object	365+ days since object was created		🗑	✏

Figure 7.33 – An additional life cycle rule has been added to the bucket

We can also see that an additional label was added to the bucket configuration:

wmarusiak-cc-bucket

Location	Storage class	Public access	Protection
us (multiple regions in United States)	Standard	Not public	Object versioning

OBJECTS   CONFIGURATION   PERMISSIONS   PROTECTION   LIFECYCLE   OBSERVABILITY `NEW`

Overview

Created	February 19, 2023 at 7:33:35 PM GMT+1
Updated	February 19, 2023 at 8:07:22 PM GMT+1
Location type	Multi-region
Location	us (multiple regions in United States)
Replication	Default ✏️
Default storage class	Standard ✏️
Requester Pays	● OFF
Tags	None ✏️
Labels	label-one : **value-one** label-two : **value-two** managed-by-cnrm : **true** ✏️
Cloud Console URL	https://console.cloud.google.com/storage/browser/wmarusiak-cc-bucket

Figure 7.34 – An additional label has been added to the bucket

After changing the resource, we can remove it. We can do this using `kubectl delete --namespace CC_NAMESPACE -f your_resource.YAML`. In our case, the command will be `kubectl delete --namespace config-connector -f config-connector-cloud-storage.yaml`.

To confirm that the Cloud Storage bucket was deleted, we can check the logs in Logs Explorer:

Figure 7.35 – Confirming that the Cloud Storage bucket has been deleted in Logs Explorer

Config Connector allows us to easily create and manage Google Cloud resources in a Kubernetes way. The following section focuses on managing Google Cloud resources using Terraform.

Terraform

In *Chapter 2* we briefly touched upon Terraform as part of the possible ways to manage Google Cloud resources. This book and its content focus on the Google Cloud Associate Cloud Engineer certification. We will briefly touch upon Terraform as one of the ways to deploy IaC. Many blog articles and books describe Terraform and other Hashicorp products in much greater detail; we recommend checking them out if you wish to use Terraform as your IaC deployment tool.

Fortunately for us, Cloud Shell includes Terraform as one of the base tools. Terraform is a tool that can be installed on many platforms, such as macOS, Windows, Linux, and many others. To install Terraform on your operating system, go to `https://developer.hashicorp.com/terraform/downloads`, which contains guides on various operating systems.

Practical Terraform implementation

There is no better way to learn than to get our hands dirty and implement the code. Let's get started:

1. We will start in Cloud Shell by creating the terraform directory.

2. Per Terraform's best practices, we will create a file called `main.tf`.

3. We will specify the Terraform provider as `hashicorp/google`:

```
terraform {
  required_providers {
    google = {
      source = "hashicorp/google"
      version = "4.51.0"
    }
  }
}

provider "google" {
  project = "wmarusiak-terraform-project"
  region  = "europe-west4"
  zone    = "europe-west4-c"
}

resource "google_compute_network" "vpc_network" {
  name = "terraform-network"
}
```

4. This section of the code deploys a new project (if one doesn't exist) and creates a VPC network named `terraform-network`.

5. Before we can use the code, we need to initiate the Terraform provider. To do so, we must use the `terraform init` command:

```
admin_@cloudshell:~/terraform (wmarusiak-book-351718)$ terraform init

Initializing the backend...

Initializing provider plugins...
- Finding hashicorp/google versions matching "4.51.0"...
- Installing hashicorp/google v4.51.0...
- Installed hashicorp/google v4.51.0 (signed by HashiCorp)

Terraform has created a lock file .terraform.lock.hcl to record the provider
selections it made above. Include this file in your version control repository
so that Terraform can guarantee to make the same selections by default when
you run "terraform init" in the future.

Terraform has been successfully initialized!

You may now begin working with Terraform. Try running "terraform plan" to see
any changes that are required for your infrastructure. All Terraform commands
should now work.

If you ever set or change modules or backend configuration for Terraform,
rerun this command to reinitialize your working directory. If you forget, other
commands will detect it and remind you to do so if necessary.
```

Figure 7.36 – Successfully initializing the Terraform provider

6. Before we implement the code, it is a good practice to validate our code and check which resources the code creates. We can use the `terraform apply` command to do this, which checks if we have permission to create specified resources and gives us an overview of the resources to be created. To validate the code, we can use the `terraform validate` command. To show changes that are required by the current configuration, we need to use the `terraform plan` command:

```
admin_@cloudshell:~/terraform (wmarusiak-book-351718)$ terraform plan

Terraform used the selected providers to generate the following execution plan. Resource action
 are indicated
with the following symbols:
  + create

Terraform will perform the following actions:

  # google_compute_network.vpc_network will be created
  + resource "google_compute_network" "vpc_network" {
      + auto_create_subnetworks          = true
      + delete_default_routes_on_create  = false
      + gateway_ipv4                     = (known after apply)
      + id                               = (known after apply)
      + internal_ipv6_range              = (known after apply)
      + mtu                              = (known after apply)
      + name                             = "terraform-network"
      + project                          = (known after apply)
      + routing_mode                     = (known after apply)
      + self_link                        = (known after apply)
    }

Plan: 1 to add, 0 to change, 0 to destroy.
```

Figure 7.37 – Terraform validates and shows the execution plan

7. Finally, we can use the `terraform apply` command to create the resources. As a final check, we will be asked if we want to create specified resources; we need to type `yes` to execute the code.

8. After a moment, the code will be implemented, and we can use the newly created resources:

```
  Enter a value: yes

google_compute_network.vpc_network: Creating...
google_compute_network.vpc_network: Still creating... [10s elapsed]
google_compute_network.vpc_network: Still creating... [20s elapsed]
google_compute_network.vpc_network: Still creating... [30s elapsed]
google_compute_network.vpc_network: Still creating... [40s elapsed]
google_compute_network.vpc_network: Creation complete after 42s [id=projects/wmarusiak-terrafor
-project/global/networks/terraform-network]

Apply complete! Resources: 1 added, 0 changed, 0 destroyed.
admin_@cloudshell:~/terraform (wmarusiak-book-351718)$ 
```

Figure 7.38 – Terraform code execution completed

9. After successfully implementing code with Terraform, we can delete the resources that were created using the `terraform destroy` command.

10. After a moment, the resources will be deleted:

```
Do you really want to destroy all resources?
    Terraform will destroy all your managed infrastructure, as shown above.
    There is no undo. Only 'yes' will be accepted to confirm.

    Enter a value: yes

google_compute_network.vpc_network: Destroying... [id=projects/wmarusiak-terraform-project/glob
l/networks/terraform-network]
google_compute_network.vpc_network: Still destroying... [id=projects/wmarusiak-terraform-projec
/global/networks/terraform-network, 10s elapsed]
google_compute_network.vpc_network: Still destroying... [id=projects/wmarusiak-terraform-projec
/global/networks/terraform-network, 20s elapsed]
google_compute_network.vpc_network: Still destroying... [id=projects/wmarusiak-terraform-projec
/global/networks/terraform-network, 30s elapsed]
google_compute_network.vpc_network: Still destroying... [id=projects/wmarusiak-terraform-projec
/global/networks/terraform-network, 40s elapsed]
google_compute_network.vpc_network: Still destroying... [id=projects/wmarusiak-terraform-projec
/global/networks/terraform-network, 50s elapsed]
google_compute_network.vpc_network: Destruction complete after 52s
```

Figure 7.39 – Resource deletion is finished

As this example has shown, using Terraform in Google Cloud is straightforward.

Terraform best practices

Google Cloud has published Terraform's best practices at `https://cloud.google.com/docs/terraform/best-practices-for-terraform`. These best practices cover topics such as the following:

- Module structure
- Naming conventions
- Using variables
- And many more

Similar cloud-agnostic Hashicorp-provided best practices for using Terraform are available at - `https://developer.hashicorp.com/terraform/cloud-docs/recommended-practices`

With the recent updates, Google Cloud introduced a possibility to view Terraform Code when we create a new virtual machine. You can view the Terraform code snippet after clicking the on **Equivalent Code** button in the Google Compute Engine section.

In the next section, we will build on the skills we've learned in this section and implement a sample template in the Google Cloud project.

Cloud Foundation Toolkit

Cloud Foundation Toolkit (**CFT**) is a set of reference templates that reflect Google Cloud best practices. CFT-provided templates can be used to quickly build repeatable enterprise-ready environments in Google Cloud. CFT can be deployed using Deployment Manager or Terraform. Google Cloud provides Terraform blueprints and modules that can be used immediately.

For the list of all blueprints, go to `https://cloud.google.com/docs/terraform/blueprints/terraform-blueprints`.

Let's check one of the templates and examine the settings we can configure in it. I've selected the Cloud VPN template available at `https://github.com/terraform-google-modules/terraform-google-vpn`.

As we learned in the previous section, the `main.tf` file will consist of the main code for our template:

```
resource "google_compute_router" "cr-uscentral1-to-prod-vpc" {
  name    = "cr-uscentral1-to-prod-vpc-tunnels"
  region  = "us-central1"
  network = "default"
  project = var.project_id

  bgp {
    asn = "64519"
  }
}

module "vpn-prod-internal" {
  source  = "terraform-google-modules/vpn/google"
  version = "~> 1.2.0"

  project_id          = var.project_id
  network             = "default"
  region              = "us-west1"
  gateway_name        = "vpn-prod-internal"
  tunnel_name_prefix  = "vpn-tn-prod-internal"
  shared_secret       = "secrets"
  tunnel_count        = 1
  peer_ips            = ["1.1.1.1", "2.2.2.2"]

  route_priority = 1000
  remote_subnet  = ["10.17.0.0/22", "10.16.80.0/24"]
}

module "vpn-manage-internal" {
```

```
    source   = "terraform-google-modules/vpn/google"
    version = "~> 1.2.0"
    project_id          = var.project_id
    network             = "default"
    region              = "us-west1"
    gateway_name        = "vpn-manage-internal"
    tunnel_name_prefix = "vpn-tn-manage-internal"
    shared_secret       = "secrets"
    tunnel_count        = 1
    peer_ips            = ["1.1.1.1", "2.2.2.2"]

    route_priority = 1000
    remote_subnet  = ["10.17.32.0/20", "10.17.16.0/20"]
}
```

This code can be adjusted to our needs and easily deployed with Terraform commands.

Google Cloud also offers a GitHub repository for creating an environment that is fully configured with best practices. The GitHub repository is available at `https://github.com/terraform-google-modules/terraform-example-foundation`.

It consists of many stages and is highly adjustable to our needs. Try various Google Cloud Terraform templates to build secure, enterprise-ready Google Cloud environments and resources.

The following section will focus on browsing and deploying Google Cloud Marketplace solutions.

Marketplace solutions

Google Cloud Marketplace is a catalog of third-party software that is integrated with Google Cloud Platform and ready to deploy in just a few clicks. The Google Cloud ecosystem is broad and consists of many products. However, some of them might not be available as native solutions. For example, let's say you have been using GitLab in the past and would like to use it in Google Cloud. Google Cloud offers its products with Git functionality, but you need to use certain features from GitLab and don't want to deploy it yourself.

In that case, Google Cloud Marketplace comes to the rescue:

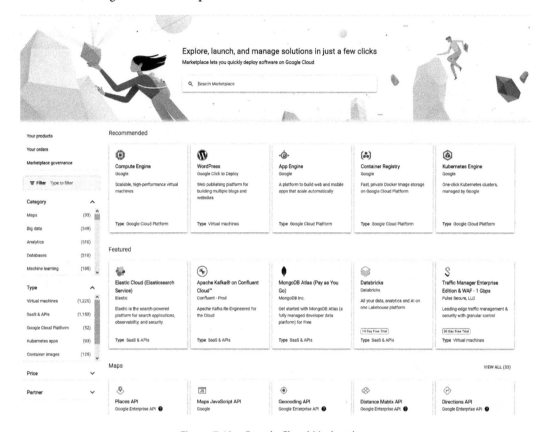

Figure 7.40 – Google Cloud Marketplace

The preceding screenshot shows that there are various options to choose from. In the search field, you can type in the product or solution you want to use, and within a few clicks, it will be up and running.

Marketplace solution deployment

Let's go through a sample Marketplace solution deployment. In Google Cloud Marketplace's search area, we will specify wordpress, one of the most popular blogging platforms, so that we can deploy WordPress automatically on Google Cloud:

Q   wordpress   ✕

77 results

openlitespeed-wordpress
LiteSpeed Technologies - Virtual machines

Blazing-fast WordPress with LSCache, 300+ times faster than regular WordPress. OpenLiteSpeed is the Open Source edition of LiteSpeed Web Server Enterprise and contains all of the essential features, including HTTP/3 support. OLS provides enormous scalability, and an accelerated hosting platform for WordPress. This solution gives you OpenLiteSpeed, PHP, MySQL Server, WordPress, LiteSpeed Cache, and other useful...

WordPress
Etrans Lab - Virtual machines

A WordPress publishing platform embedded with pre-configured LAMP, Webmin. You can set up your website in 1 minute.

WordPress with Redis
Etrans Lab - Virtual machines

A WordPress publishing platform embedded with pre-configured LAMP, Webmin, Redis. You can set up your website in 1 minute.

WordPress on CentOS 7
Cognosys Inc. - Virtual machines

WordPress is an open-source content management system based on PHP and MySQL. Features include a plugin architecture and a template system. It is most associated with blogging but supports other types of web content including more traditional mailing lists and forums, media galleries, and online stores. Enterprises planning to deploy WordPress for production on GCP can use this specially hardened image of...

WordPress Multisite
Google Click to Deploy - Virtual machines

WordPress is a software application used to create websites and blogs. WordPress Multisite allows users to create several WordPress sites under a single installation. New administrator roles in WordPress Multisite allow for plugins and themes to be shared across sites, and granular admin access to be granted on a per site level.

Wordpress With Ubuntu Server 20.04 LTS
Cognosys Inc. - Virtual machines

WordPress is a free and open-source content management system based on PHP and MySQL. WordPress is installed on a web server that is either part of an Internet hosting service or a network host in its own right. WordPress has a web template system using a template processor. Its architecture is a front controller, routing all requests for non-static URIs to a single PHP file which parses the URI and identifies the target page....

WordPress
Google Click to Deploy - Virtual machines

WordPress is a software application used to create websites and blogs.

Figure 7.41 – WordPress offering in Google Cloud Marketplace

From the 77 results, we will select one to be deployed in our Google Cloud project. After selecting the product, we are redirected to the **Product details** area:

Figure 7.42 – The openlitespeed-wordpress WordPress offering in Google Cloud Marketplace

After clicking **Launch**, we can proceed with the deployment. If some Google Cloud APIs aren't enabled, we can enable them via a pre-deployment check:

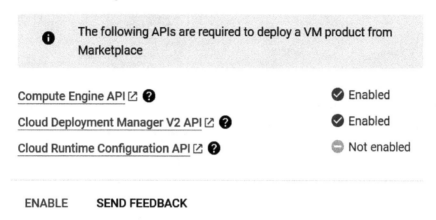

Enable required APIs

> ℹ The following APIs are required to deploy a VM product from Marketplace

Compute Engine API ↗ ❓   ✔ Enabled

Cloud Deployment Manager V2 API ↗ ❓   ✔ Enabled

Cloud Runtime Configuration API ↗ ❓   ⊖ Not enabled

ENABLE   SEND FEEDBACK

Figure 7.43 – Pre-deployment checks in Marketplace

After enabling missing APIs, we will be redirected to the offering configuration page, where we can adjust any settings and see the pricing summary:

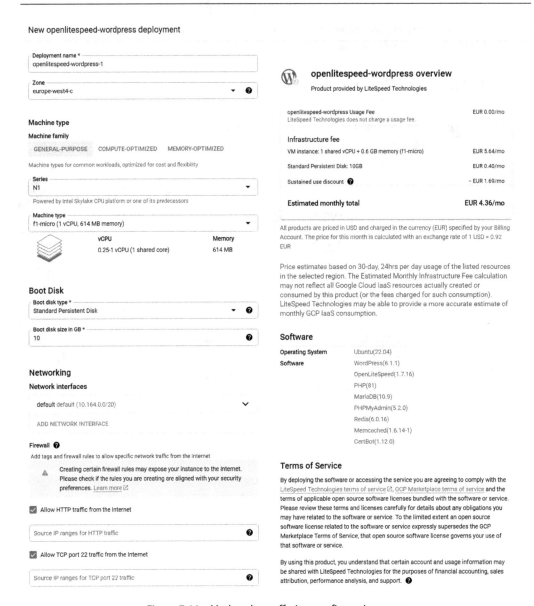

Figure 7.44 – Marketplace offering configuration page

Once we've configured everything, we'll be redirected to the **Deployment Manager** page, where we can track deployment progress:

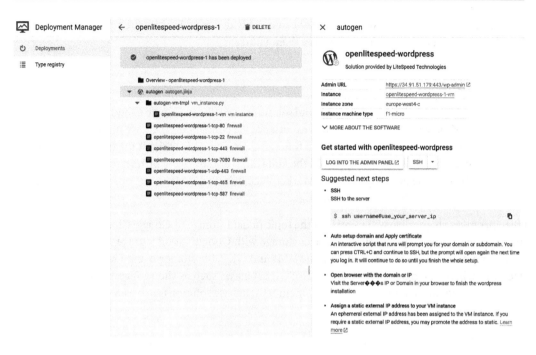

Figure 7.45 – Marketplace offering deployment progress

Once the deployment has been completed, we can start using the product. In our case, we can log in as a WordPress administrator and start blogging:

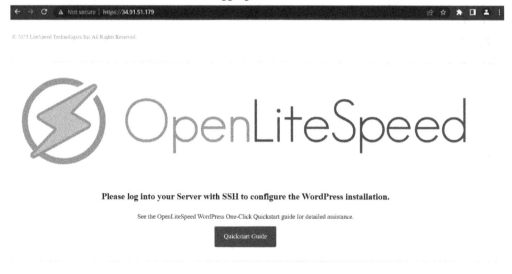

Figure 7.46 – Marketplace offering deployment progress

Once the resource is not needed anymore, we can quickly delete it. As there are many Marketplace offerings, we encourage you to try and deploy them yourself.

Summary

This chapter focused on the last of the compute solutions available in Google Cloud. We started with Google Cloud Run, which offers a serverless experience via containers. Then, we jumped into Cloud Functions, where serverless and event-based functions can run code without the need to provision or manage infrastructure. After, we explored the fantastic World of IaC with Terraform. We finalized this chapter by looking at Google Cloud Marketplace, which allows us to consume predefined, pre-configured, and tightly integrated offerings.

In the upcoming chapter, we will jump into the topic of data storage in Google Cloud. We will learn about different storage types, including object storage with Google Cloud Storage, block storage for local and persistent disks in Compute Engine VMs and GKE, file storage using Filestore, relational databases such as Cloud SQL and Spanner, NoSQL databases such as Cloud Bigtable and Firestore, data warehousing through BigQuery, and in-memory database solutions such as Memorystore.

Questions

Answer the following questions to test your knowledge of this chapter:

1. You have been tasked with deploying an application deployed as a Cloud Function. Which of the programming languages are supported? (Choose all that apply.)

   A. PHP

   B. Ruby

   C. Java

   D. Go

   E. Python

   F. Node.js

   G. PowerShell

   H. C++

   I. C#

2. What steps should you take to follow Google's recommended practices for efficiently deploying and managing the development, test, and production environments for your project deployment in Google Cloud while ensuring consistency? Your team is responsible for building these environments:

    A. Use Cloud Foundation Toolkit, create one deployment template that works for all environments, and deploy it with Terraform.

    B. Create one configuration for all environments in Terraform. Use parameters for different environments.

    C. Create a Cloud Shell script that uses `gcloud` commands to deploy all environments.

    D. Upload Cloud Foundation Toolkit in Marketplace

3. Which of the following use cases is not a good fit for Cloud Run jobs?

    A. APIs and microservices

    B. Running scripts to perform database migrations or other operational tasks

    C. Creating and sending invoices every month

    D. Parallelized processing of all files in the Cloud Storage bucket

4. What can be a trigger in Cloud Functions (2nd gen)? (Choose all that apply.)

    A. Firestore triggers

    B. HTTP triggers

    C. Pub/Sub triggers

    D. Eventarc triggers

5. To monitor Cloud Run job performance and metrics, it is necessary to configure Cloud Monitoring. (True or False?)

    A. True

    B. False

6. Which of the following use cases are best fit for Cloud Functions? (Choose all that apply.)

    A. Data processing/ETL

    B. Lightweight APIs

    C. IoT

    D. Running scripts or operational tasks

7. Choose the correct statement about Cloud Run revisions:

    A. Every new deployment creates an editable revision.

    B. You can only split traffic between the latest and previous revision.

    C. Cloud Run creates an HTTPS endpoint in a unique subdomain of the `*.run.app` domain.

    D. Cloud Run supports WebSockets, HTTP/2 (end-to-end), and gRPC (end-to-end).

8. By default, Cloud Run supports which amount of resources?

    A. CPU – 8, Memory - 34 GiB, Request timeout – 3,600 seconds, Maximum requests per container – 1,000

    B. CPU – 1, Memory – 512 MiB, Request timeout – 300 seconds, Maximum requests per container – 80, Container instances – 30

    C. CPU – 2, Memory – 1,024 MiB, Request timeout – 600 seconds, Maximum requests per container – 160, Container instances – 60

    D. CPU – 12, Memory – 3072 MiB, Request timeout – 1,800 seconds, Maximum requests per container – 480, Container instances – 180

9. Select every statement that is true about Cloud Run revisions:

    A. Each deployment to a service creates a revision.

    B. Each deployment to a revision creates a service.

    C. Once a revision has been created, it cannot be modified.

    D. If you want to change the container image, you must create a new service.

10. Which of the following is true about Cloud Run?

    A. Cloud Run jobs need to start a web server.

    B. If the Cloud Run task fails, the job continues until all tasks run, and the entire job is marked as failed.

    C. Tasks cannot be retried.

    D. Cloud Run jobs cannot use serverless VPC access, custom service accounts, or cloud SQL connections.

11. You have been tasked to manage Google Cloud resources through Kubernetes. Which tool can you use?

    A. Terraform

    B. Deployment Manager

    C. Cloud Functions

    D. Config Connector

12. You are trying to install Config Connector in your Google Kubernetes Cluster, but the installation is failing. Choose all components that might cause this issue:

    A. GKE with version 1.17.3.

    B. GKE monitoring is disabled.

    C. You haven't enabled a Workload Identity Pool.

    D. You haven't granted the `roles/iam.serviceAccountAdmin` permissions to Config Connector.

13. You are working with Terraform code to deploy resources into Google Cloud. Which command allows you to validate code for syntax errors?

    A. `terraform apply`

    B. `terraform init`

    C. `terraform validate`

    D. `terraform plan`

14. What is the name of the action that allows Cloud Functions to execute a response to various scenarios?

    A. A log entry

    B. A trigger

    C. An incident

    D. An event

    E. An occurrence

    F. A start

15. What is Google Cloud Marketplace?

    A. A software packaging offering

    B. A Google Cloud scripts marketplace

    C. A Google Cloud job market

    D. A collection of solutions that are fully integrated with Google Cloud and can easily be deployed with just a few clicks

16. How does Terraform differ from other IaC tools? (Choose all that apply.)

    A. Terraform can store local variables, passwords, and cloud tokens in the Terraform registry in an encrypted form.

    B. Terraform supports cloud and on-premises environments.

    C. Terraform can be deployed in a CI/CD way.

    D. Terraform doesn't require any agent deployments.

    E. All of the above.

17. What is the Cloud Function's 2nd generation memory limit?

    A. 64 GiB

    B. 2 GiB

    C. 16 GiB

    D. 32 GiB

18. Choose all serverless options from the Google Cloud portfolio:

    A. Google Kubernetes Engine

    B. Cloud Run

    C. Cloud Functions

    D. Google Compute Engine

    E. Google Cloud VMware Engine

19. Choose a product that provides a flexible serverless deployment platform for hybrid and multi-cloud environments:

    A. Google Kubernetes Engine

    B. Cloud Run

    C. Cloud Functions

    D. Cloud Run for Anthos

20. Choose the correct statement about Cloud Functions:

    A. In Cloud Functions (1st gen), the maximum timeout duration is 9 minutes (540 seconds).

    B. In Cloud Functions (2nd gen), the maximum timeout duration is 60 minutes (3,600 seconds) for HTTP functions and 9 minutes (540 seconds) for event-driven functions.

    C. In Cloud Functions (1st gen), the maximum timeout duration is 5 minutes (300 seconds).

    D. In Cloud Functions (2nd gen), the maximum timeout duration is 30 minutes (1,800 seconds) for HTTP functions and 4 minutes (240 seconds) for event-driven functions.

Answers

Here are the answers to this chapter's questions:

1ABCDEF, 2A, 3A, 4BCD, 5False, 6ABC, 7CD, 8B, 9AC, 10B, 11D, 12ABC, 13C, 14B, 15D, 16E, 17C, 18BC, 19D, 20AB

8

Configuring and Implementing Data Storage Solutions

This chapter will explore how to store data in Google Cloud. We are going to cover the following storage types:

- Object storage – Google Cloud Storage

- Block storage – local and persistent disks for Compute Engine VMs and GKE

- File storage – Filestore

- Different types of databases – Cloud SQL, Cloud Spanner, Bigtable, Firestore, BigQuery, and Memorystore

Google Cloud provides multiple fully managed services for different types of application needs. Each section will look into a specific type of storage and their features, security, and availability. We will also cover the use cases of each category. Designing a storage strategy for cloud workloads is critical to ensure every application's resiliency, performance, and response time.

Google's object storage – Cloud Storage

Google Cloud Storage is a Google-managed, highly available, and durable object storage for storing unstructured immutable data such as images, videos, and documents. Its common use cases are website hosting, content storage and delivery, analytics, and backup and archiving.

All data stored in Google Cloud Storage is encrypted with Google- or customer-managed keys. The service is globally available and consistent, making it visible to all entitled users after a file is uploaded. In addition, there is no limit on the objects you can store. Each object includes data, metadata, and a unique identifier used to interact with it.

Objects stored in Google Cloud Storage are organized in containers called **buckets**. **Buckets** belong to a **project** and help organize and control data access. We can configure buckets to match the desired performance, availability, and cost efficiency.

This section will focus on designing Google Cloud Storage and working with objects stored in buckets.

Location types

One of the essential decisions when creating a Google Cloud Storage bucket is to choose where to store objects. For example, if objects are critical to our business, we may want to replicate them across regions for higher availability. Alternatively, if we have a latency-sensitive application that reads from our bucket, we may want to deploy a bucket in the same region where the application is running.

Once a bucket is created, it is not possible to modify its location. Therefore, it is important to have a clear understanding of the advantages and disadvantages of each option before making a decision.

Let's look at the available location types for a Google Cloud Storage bucket to see how a geographic placement of a bucket determines its price, availability, and performance:

- A **regional** bucket is where objects are synchronously and automatically replicated between at least two zones in a single region. In the case of a zone failure, data is served from another zone. The failover and failback (once the region becomes available again) processes are transparent to users:

  - **Benefits**: Lower price per GB than other location types, as you only pay for data in a bucket in one region. Also, you benefit from low latency and higher throughput if you run your Google Cloud workloads in the same region as your bucket. Furthermore, regional buckets are the only way to meet a company's compliance policy to keep data within a particular country only

  - **Considerations**: This location type doesn't provide geo-redundancy (the distance between zones is less than 100 miles). Your objects won't be available in the case of a regional failure.

- A **dual-region** bucket is where you provide geo-redundancy (more than 100 miles distance between data center locations) for your objects by specifying a pair of regions within the same continent between which objects will be replicated asynchronously (not in real time) by Google Cloud. There are three geographic areas: **Asia**, **North America**, and **Europe**, where you can select two regions for your bucket. The target for a default replication is one hour, but usually, it takes less than that. **Turbo replication** enabled between regions in a dual-region bucket will shorten the guaranteed replication time for newly written objects to 15 minutes. In addition, a failure in one region will not affect the availability of your objects. Again, this process is transparent to users and requires no additional setup for the failover and failback:

  - **Benefits**: A dual-region bucket survives a failure in one of two regions. Also, you can define which regions out of the available ones you want to use for your bucket – for example, those closest to regions where you run your Google Cloud workloads or serve your content to users.

  - **Considerations**: Not all regions are available for this location type yet. Also, you must pay per GB for two copies of data located in two regions and the replication traffic for write operations between buckets. The **Turbo replication** option is also subject to an additional fee. Furthermore, if most of your objects exist for a short time, the dual-region type would be of no benefit because object existence would be shorter than the replication window.

- **Multi-region**: This also provides a geo-redundancy within two or more regions in the following geographical areas: **Asia**, **EU** (zones in the European Union), and the **US**. The difference between a multi-region and dual-region type is that you can't specify the regions for a multi-region bucket:

  - **Benefits**: The price for a multi-region bucket is lower than for a dual-region one. Also, if you are serving content from a bucket to users in a whole geographic region such as the US and you can't predict where your traffic is coming from, content served from a multi-regional bucket has the highest possibility of being close to users.

  - **Considerations**: We allow Google to store data in different regions in a specified area (**ASIA**, **US**, or **EU**), and we don't know which regions will be selected for each object. As a result, to access objects belonging to a multi-regional bucket, workloads running only in one region (for example, Compute Engine VMs in **us-west2**) will have to send requests across multiple US regions, impacting the service's latency.

The following diagram summarizes how a location type choice can affect the object's availability. There are three regions – **Region A**, **Region B**, and **Region C** – that belong to one geographical area, and three bucket locations – a regional bucket with one object (**cat.jpg**), a dual-region bucket with a replication set between **Region A** and **Region B** with a **dog.jpg** object, and a multi-region bucket with **dino1.jpg**, **dino2.jpg**, and **dino3.jpg** placed randomly across all regions, in two regions each:

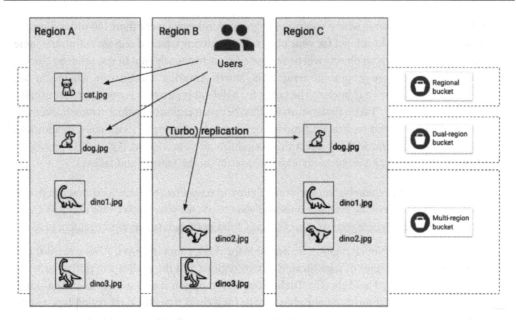

Figure 8.1 – A simplified diagram of an object placement for every Google Cloud Storage location type

When a disaster happens in **Region A**, users can still access objects in the dual-region and multi-region buckets, and they wouldn't even be aware of a failure if not for the **cat.jpg** object, which was in the regional bucket and is now unavailable.

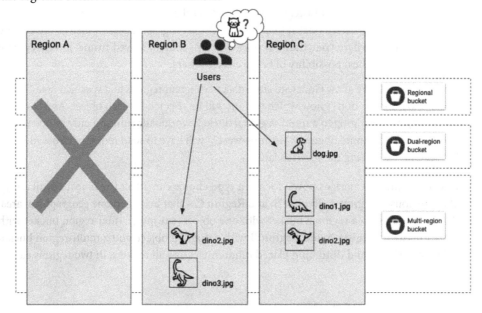

Figure 8.2 – A simplified diagram showing how Google Cloud Storage location
type choice affects object availability in case of a failure in a region

To conclude, the location type can give objects stored in a bucket the required availability. So, even if we access an object once in 5 years, we may still want it to be highly available on the day we need it, so we configure such a bucket, for example, as **dual-region**.

But once we start storing objects in buckets, we will notice that their access patterns differ. Some of the objects are accessed frequently while, on the other hand, some buckets store archival data that is rarely accessed. Do we have to pay the same price per GB for objects we download every day and those we do once in 5 years? In the next section, we will explore possible savings on the buckets for infrequently accessed data.

Storage classes

To optimize the cost of storing your data, based on the projected frequency of operations on objects in a bucket, you can choose one of the following storage classes as a default one for all of the objects in a bucket:

- **Standard** class is the default one if you don't make any choice. It is the best choice for frequent access to data, but it also has the highest price per GB. However, out of all the available classes, the price for operations such as *insert*, *list*, or *copy* is the lowest:

  - **Use case**: Hosting website content, media streaming and sharing, content storage for frequently accessed data, and serving data for gaming applications.

- **Nearline** will be the best if you access your objects less frequently than once per month. It has a lower price per GB than the Standard class, but if you decide to delete, replace, or move data sooner than 30 days, you will have to pay for early deletion, as if this object was actually stored for 30 days. Nearline also has higher operations charges than Standard:

  - **Use case**: Statistical data that is analyzed once per month, data archives, sporadically accessed multimedia content.

- **Coldline** is a good fit for data accessed less frequently than once a quarter. However, its minimum storage duration is 90 days, and, similar to Nearline, if you decide to delete, replace, or move data sooner, you will be charged the early deletion fee. In addition, making operation charges on objects costs more for Coldline than Nearline:

  - **Use case**: Archival storage, data accessed once a year, all rarely used data.

- **Archive** is designed for the least frequently accessed data but performs similarly to other storage classes. It is important to note that objects belonging to the Archive class are as easily accessible as ones from other classes. You don't have to restore them first to another class to be able to access them. However, data operations are the most expensive for the Archive class compared to other classes. Also, data deleted after a few months will incur the same cost as if it was stored for a whole year:

  - **Use case**: Data that is not expected to be accessed. It is a replacement for storing data on tapes but without weeks-long restores and with high durability for long-term storage requirements – for example, 3-7 years.

The following figure shows how the price and availability can differ depending on the storage class used for a Google Cloud Storage bucket with 1 TB of data. On the left, we have the **Standard** class, which is the most expensive but has the highest availability and no **early deletion** fees. On the right, we can see that an **Archive** class bucket can get expensive if data is retrieved earlier than expected in one year:

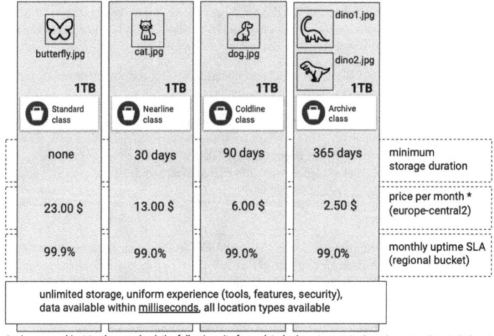

* prices are subject to change, check the following site for updated prices: https://cloud.google.com/products/calculator/

Figure 8.3 – An example of how price and availability values change for the same amount of data depending on a storage class for a regional bucket in europe-central2

Note that all storage classes offer similar performance and response times in milliseconds. They also have a consistent set of APIs and similar tooling. The difference is mainly in the cost metrics. Also, Standard storage provides the highest availability.

Data lifecycle

Storage classes work best when the frequency of operations on objects in a bucket can be predicted. But what about unpredictable access patterns? Although you can change the storage class of an individual object via a command line (a storage class is a metadata of an object), this could be unprofitable because the object will have to be rewritten, possibly incurring additional operation fees.

For such cases, Google Cloud Storage offers the following options to manage an object's class assignment:

- **Object Lifecycle Management** is a feature you can set at a bucket level that allows changing a class of an object without a rewrite operation and the cost that goes with it (although an early deletion fee could be applied). We can set the conditions such as an object's age and an automatic action that follows when this condition is met – for example, to move an object to a colder class (for example, from Standard to Nearline or from Nearline to Coldline, etc.) or delete it.

- The **Autoclass** feature is also a bucket-level setting configured during its creation. It automatically migrates infrequently accessed objects to colder classes without retrieval fees and class transition charges.

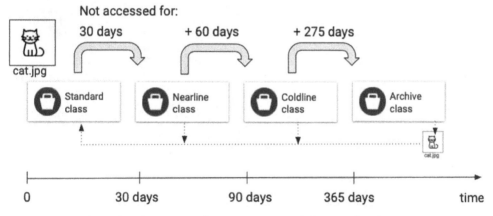

Figure 8.4 – Because an object is not accessed, the Autoclass feature
progressively transitions it to a less expensive storage class

The preceding figure presents how the Autoclass feature changes storage class metadata for a cat.jpg object. First, the original Standard class changes to Nearline after no one has accessed the object for 30 days. Next, after 60 days, the class changes to Coldline. When the object is moved to Coldline, it hasn't been accessed for *30+60=90* days. Still, if no one accesses it in the next 275 days, its class will change to Archive. But anytime someone accesses cat.jpg, regardless of its storage class, it will return to the Standard class.

Note that in both cases (**Object Lifecycle** and **Autoclass**), it is an individual object for which a storage class (its metadata) is changed. Buckets are not modified during this process, so there is no impact on your applications or users accessing data.

Working with buckets and objects

Now that we know how to design Google Cloud Storage buckets for availability and cost efficiency, let's see how we can upload and manage objects that go into our buckets.

Managing Google Cloud Storage via the Google Cloud console

The Google Cloud console is the easiest way for single-bucket operations and object uploads. You can access the **Buckets** section by selecting **Cloud Storage** in the main menu, as shown in the following screenshot:

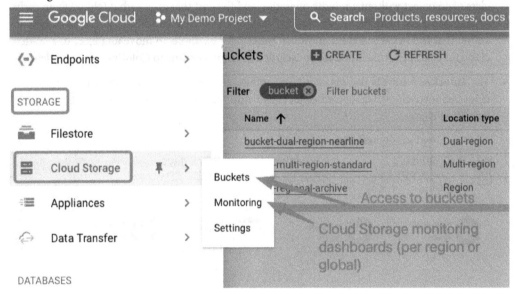

Figure 8.5 – The location of the Buckets section in the Google Cloud console

To create a bucket, use the **CREATE** button. This action will open a bucket creation wizard where you can name your bucket (a globally unique name is required), provide a location, and set an object class:

Figure 8.6 – Creating a bucket in the Google Cloud console

There are specific rules to follow when naming a bucket. For example, you can only use lowercase letters, numeric characters, dashes, and underscores. Dots are supported when a bucket contains a domain name but using a domain requires its ownership verification. Also, including "google" as a part of the name is not supported.

We will see the bucket creation process later in this section. Please note that once you create a bucket, you can't change its name.

As mentioned in the previous section, the only way to change most of the bucket's parameters is to create a new bucket with desired settings and move contents to this new bucket.

If you want to delete a bucket or multiple buckets with all content, select them in the same view as shown in the preceding screenshot; the **DELETE** button will appear at the top.

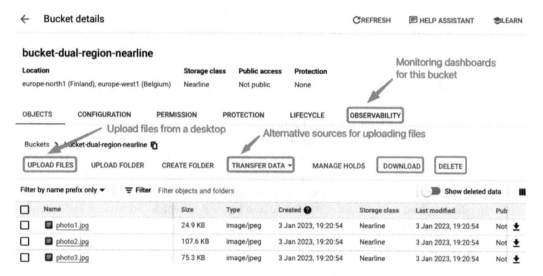

Figure 8.7 – Bucket details view

If you want to download or delete an object or a group of objects from a bucket in the Google Cloud console, use the **DOWNLOAD** or **DELETE** options, respectively. Both are available in the **Bucket details** view, as shown in *Figure 8.7*.

There are also alternatives to uploading and downloading data from a local workstation. For example, under the **TRANSFER DATA** option, you will find a wizard to create a transfer job, for example, from object stores belonging to other cloud providers or other Google Cloud Storage buckets.

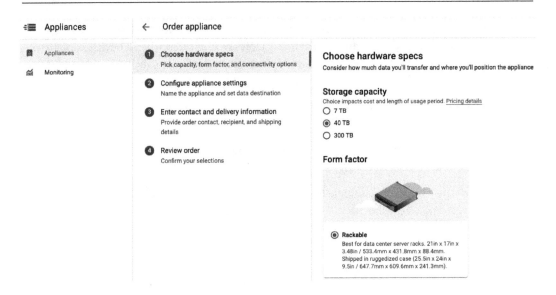

Figure 8.8 – Ordering Transfer Appliance for uploading large amounts of data

If you are planning to move a large amount of data from an on-premises data center to your Google Cloud Storage bucket, it is important to have a solid strategy in place. For example, if you have a deadline of one month to transfer 100 TB of data over your 1 Gbps bandwidth, it should be easily achievable. However, if you only have 100 Mbps bandwidth available, it could take several months to complete the transfer and you may not meet your deadline. In this scenario, it may be beneficial to consider an offline upload using Transfer Appliance (see *Figure 8.8*), which can have an end-to-end cycle time of less than a month.

Transfer Appliance is a high-capacity storage device that allows you to securely transfer your data to a Google upload facility, where it will be uploaded to Cloud Storage.

If your data is located in another cloud storage provider, you should consider using the **Storage Transfer Service**. This service automates the transfer of data between various object and file storage systems, such as Google Cloud Storage, Amazon S3, Azure Storage, or on-premises. It is a reliable and efficient way to transfer large amounts of data without requiring any coding skills.

Using the Google Cloud console is very convenient when learning to work with Google Cloud Storage. Later, when we use it in production, alternative ways to manipulate large amounts of objects are preferred. The following sections will describe how to work with Google Cloud Storage on a larger scale or programmatically.

Using gsutil as a command-line tool

Google Cloud Storage offers an automated command line tool, `gsutil`, to manage bucket and object level operations such as create, list, delete, move, and copy on a larger scale.

You can start by using `gsutil` from the Cloud Shell and practice the following commands:

- To create a `unique-name-of-the-bucket` bucket with a `standard` storage class in the `europe-central2` location, use the following command:

```
gsutil mb -c standard -l europe-central2 gs://unique-name-of-
the-bucket
```

- The following command is how you can list objects in a bucket:

```
gsutil ls -l gs://unique-name-of-the-bucket
```

You can find an example output of those two actions in the following screenshot:

```
admin_@cloudshell:~ (my-demo-project-   ■■)$ gsutil mb -c standard -l europe-central2 gs://agnieszka
Creating gs://agnieszka/...
admin_@cloudshell:~ (my-demo-project-  ▬▬)$ gsutil ls gs://agnieszka
admin_@cloudshell:~ (my-demo-project-▬▬)$ gsutil ls gs://agnieszka
gs://agnieszka/photo1.jpg
gs://agnieszka/photo2.jpg
gs://agnieszka/photo3.jpg
admin_@cloudshell:~ (my-demo-project-▬ ▬▬)$ gsutil ls -l gs://agnieszka
   25544  2022-12-29T19:59:14Z  gs://agnieszka/photo1.jpg
  110139  2022-12-29T19:59:14Z  gs://agnieszka/photo2.jpg
   77101  2022-12-29T19:59:14Z  gs://agnieszka/photo3.jpg
TOTAL: 3 objects, 212784 bytes (207.8 KiB)
```

Figure 8.9 – Creating a bucket and listing its content using gsutil

- To download a file from a bucket, use `gsutil cp`:

```
gsutil cp gs://unique-name-of-the-bucket/folder/file_name /
folder/destination_folder
```

Next, you can find an example of downloading a file to a Cloud Shell virtual machine directly and listing the folder's content to make sure the `photo1.jpg` file was downloaded successfully:

```
admin_@cloudshell:~/tmp (my-demo-project-▬▬)$ gsutil cp  gs://agnieszka/tmp/photo1.jpg /home/admin_/tmp
Copying gs://agnieszka/tmp/photo1.jpg...
/ [1 files][ 25.0 KiB/ 25.0 KiB]
Operation completed over 1 objects/25.0 KiB.
admin_@cloudshell:~/tmp (my-demo-project-▬▬)$ pwd
/home/admin_/tmp
admin_@cloudshell:~/tmp (my-demo-project-■ ■)$ ls -l
total 28
-rw-r--r-- 1 admin_ admin_ 25544 Dec 29 20:30 photo1.jpg
```

Figure 8.10 – A file copy from a bucket using gsutil

- If you are transferring or deleting many files, you can improve the performance of such an operation by using multi-threading with the `gsutil -m` option. For example, with the following command, you can delete all the content of the `tmp` folder on the `unique-name-of-the-bucket` bucket:

```
gsutil rm gs://unique-name-of-the-bucket /tmp/*
```

If you add the -m option, this operation (especially when the number of manipulated objects is significant) will be faster. Conversely, if you forget to use the -m option, you will be notified that the operation will be done sequentially, and that will take more time. Take a look at the following figure, which shows a notification about using the -m option for sequence operations:

```
admin_@cloudshell:~/tmp (my-demo-project-       )$ gsutil rm gs://agnieszka/tmp/*
Removing gs://agnieszka/tmp/...
Removing gs://agnieszka/tmp/my_demo_picture.jpg...
Removing gs://agnieszka/tmp/photo1.jpg...
Removing gs://agnieszka/tmp/photo2.jpg...
/ [4 objects]
==> NOTE: You are performing a sequence of gsutil operations that may
run significantly faster if you instead use gsutil -m rm ... Please
see the -m section under "gsutil help options" for further information
about when gsutil -m can be advantageous.

Removing gs://agnieszka/tmp/photo3.jpg...
/ [5 objects]
Operation completed over 5 objects.
```

Figure 8.11 – Deleting content of a folder in a bucket where we
got a note that the -m option could be used

If you want to practice more, you can find other examples of using gsutil here: https://cloud.google.com/storage/docs/gsutil/commands/help.

Client libraries and REST API access for developers

Google Cloud Storage offers client libraries for languages such as C++, C#, Go, Java, Node.js, PHP, Python, and Ruby so that you can interact with buckets directly from your code.

Furthermore, JSON and XML APIs are also available, so you can, for example, call APIs to upload data from your folder onto a Google Cloud Storage bucket.

Managing access to objects

There are two ways to control access to your objects in a bucket. You can select one of the following options when creating a bucket:

- **Uniform**, where you use **Identity and Access Management** (**IAM**) to define access permissions on a bucket level, so all objects inherit them. To grant access to a bucket, you need to select **Edit access**, as shown in the following screenshot:

Cloud Storage
Buckets
Monitoring
Settings
1 bucket selected
DELETE
PERMISSIONS
TAGS
LABELS
Filter
Filter buckets
Name
Location type
Location
Default storage class
Last modified
Multi-region
us
Standard
15 Dec 2022, 16:55:
bucket-dual-region-nearline
Dual-region
europe-north1, europe-west1
Nearline
3 Jan 2023, 19:13:0
bucket-multi-region-standard
Multi-region
eu
Standard
3 Jan 2023, 19:12:2
bucket-regional-archive
Region
europe-central2
Archive
Region
europe-central2
Region
europe-central2
Multi-region
us
Edit access
Edit tags
Edit labels
Edit website configuration
Edit default storage class

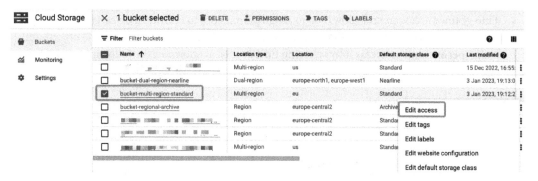

Figure 8.12 – Editing permissions for a bucket with uniform access control

In the next step, you provide a user and a role that you want to assign to this user – for example, a predefined role, **Storage Object Viewer**, that allows only viewing and listing an object and its metadata:

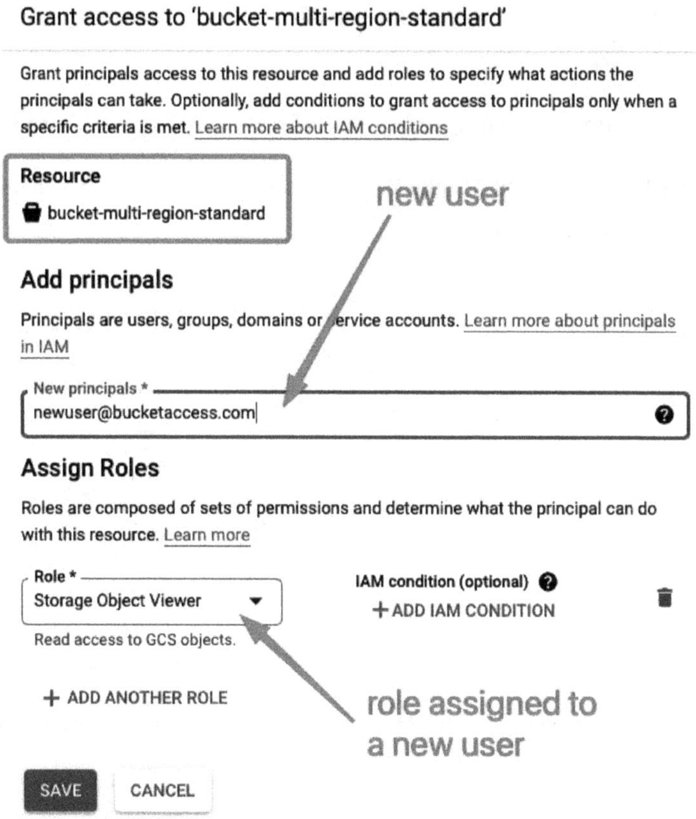

Grant access to 'bucket-multi-region-standard'
Grant principals access to this resource and add roles to specify what actions the principals can take. Optionally, add conditions to grant access to principals only when a specific criteria is met. Learn more about IAM conditions
Resource
bucket-multi-region-standard
new user
Add principals
Principals are users, groups, domains or service accounts. Learn more about principals in IAM
New principals *
newuser@bucketaccess.com
Assign Roles
Roles are composed of sets of permissions and determine what the principal can do with this resource. Learn more
Role *
Storage Object Viewer
Read access to GCS objects.
IAM condition (optional)
+ ADD IAM CONDITION
+ ADD ANOTHER ROLE
role assigned to a new user
SAVE
CANCEL

Figure 8.13 – Granting access to a bucket with uniform access control

Note that, in *Figure 8.13*, the **Resource** field shows a bucket, not an individual object.

- **Fine-grained** access control allows you to assign permissions to individual objects in conjunction with bucket-level permissions. Once the bucket is created, you can select individual objects and assign permissions to access it by selecting **Edit access**, as shown in the following screenshot:

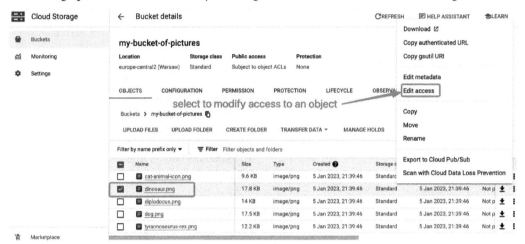

Figure 8.14 – Editing access permissions per object for a bucket with fine-grained access

Note that, in the following screenshot, the resource that we provide access to is an individual object:

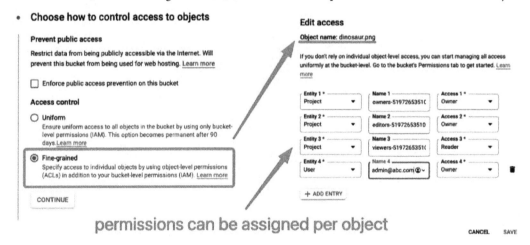

Figure 8.15 – Creating a fine-grained access level for a bucket with permissions applied on an object level

The **Fine-grained** access option also allows creating time-limited **signed URLs** for accessing an object through a link. You can give users a signed URL for temporary access to Cloud Storage objects without needing a Google account.

Alternatively, you can edit access to an object and set **Entity** as **Public**, **Name** as **all Users**, and **Access** as **Reader** to allow public access.

As shown in the following example, a public URL can be generated for an object so that everyone can download it:

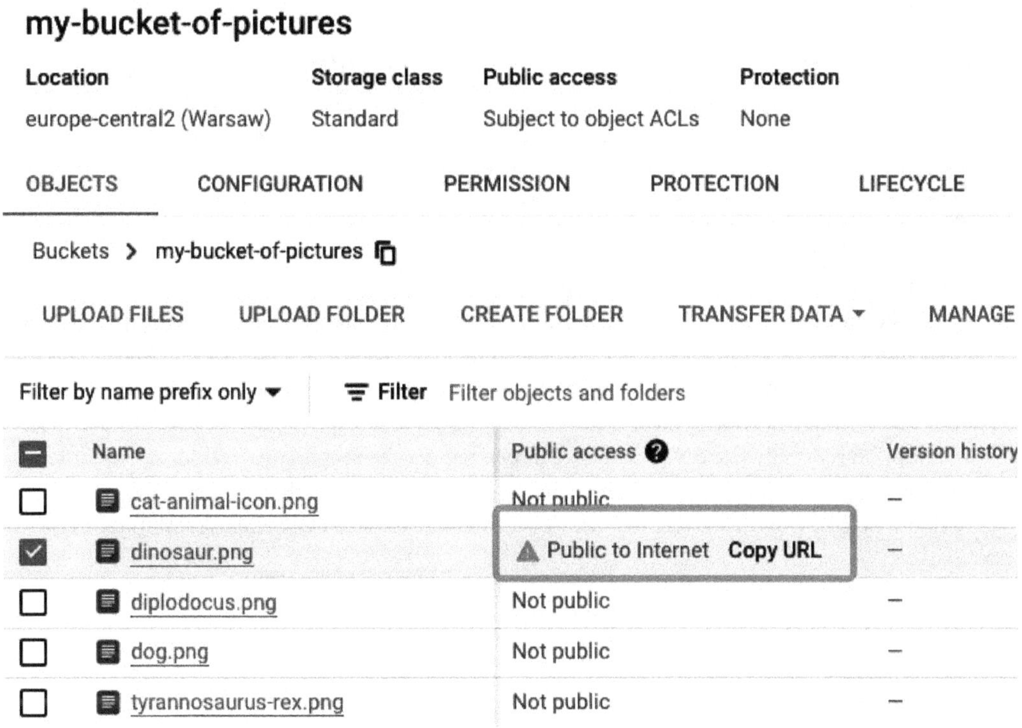

my-bucket-of-pictures

Location	Storage class	Public access	Protection
europe-central2 (Warsaw)	Standard	Subject to object ACLs	None

OBJECTS	CONFIGURATION	PERMISSION	PROTECTION	LIFECYCLE

Buckets > my-bucket-of-pictures 🗐

UPLOAD FILES   UPLOAD FOLDER   CREATE FOLDER   TRANSFER DATA ▾   MANAGE

Filter by name prefix only ▾   ☰ **Filter**   Filter objects and folders

	Name	Public access ❓	Version history
☐	🗐 cat-animal-icon.png	Not public	—
☑	🗐 dinosaur.png	⚠ Public to Internet Copy URL	—
☐	🗐 diplodocus.png	Not public	—
☐	🗐 dog.png	Not public	—
☐	🗐 tyrannosaurus-rex.png	Not public	—

Figure 8.16 – An object from a fine-grained access bucket that can be accessed by anyone

Let's put all this information from all the sections of this chapter together and use an example for summarizing what we have discussed in this chapter so far.

Creating a bucket in practice

Imagine setting up a Google Cloud Storage bucket for storing a copy of your backup data of the on-premises systems located in your data center in Frankfurt. You want your bucket to be the closest to your data center location and be available even if one of the Google regions fails. You expect the data will be accessed less than once a month, and you want to adjust the storage class to minimize costs. Also, the bucket can't be accessed from the internet. Furthermore, you might want to protect backups against malicious deletion and make sure no one deletes them for the next 5 years. Let's look at the possible steps you need to take to configure such a bucket:

1. In the **Cloud Storage** section, select **Bucket** and then **+CREATE**. Provide a bucket name, which must be unique globally across all Google Cloud projects. You should use a globally unique name that relates to the bucket's purpose, such as `my-backup-bucket-europe`

2. The next step is to decide where the backups should be stored. In this case, the requirement is for the bucket to be accessible even in the case of a region failure, so we can't select a regional bucket. On the other hand, we want to ensure minimal latency, so we also can't select a multi-regional option. In the multi-regional option, Google will decide where data is stored within a selected continent and possibly select one of the regions that are further compared to others. This choice can potentially introduce additional latency. For our needs, the best choice is dual-region placement. This allows us to select two regions that we want to use. In this case, we should keep data within the geographical area of Europe and select regions closest to our on-premises location. Moreover, in the case of a failure in one region, the second one will serve the content. As of writing this book, possible options in the bucket configuration page (see *Figure 8.17*) are Finland, Belgium, and Netherlands, with Belgium and Netherlands being closest to Frankfurt:

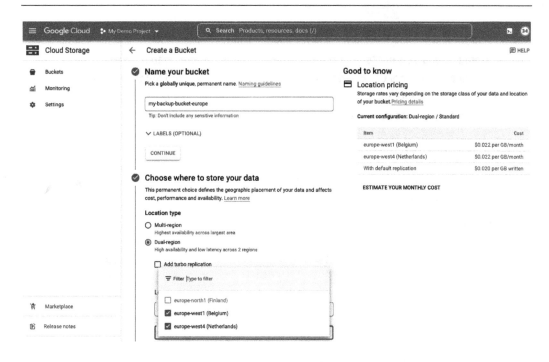

Figure 8.17 – Creating a bucket; selecting location type

3. Next, you can select the storage class based on planned data usage or use Autoclass. In our case, we will store backup copies that won't be frequently accessed. Therefore, Nearline is the optimal option as it is tailored for accessing data less than once a month. Also, it is good practice to verify with the backup vendor whether they support a storage class we want to use. For example, backup software may consolidate backups as a background task and read from a bucket more often than we think, and that will generate additional costs:

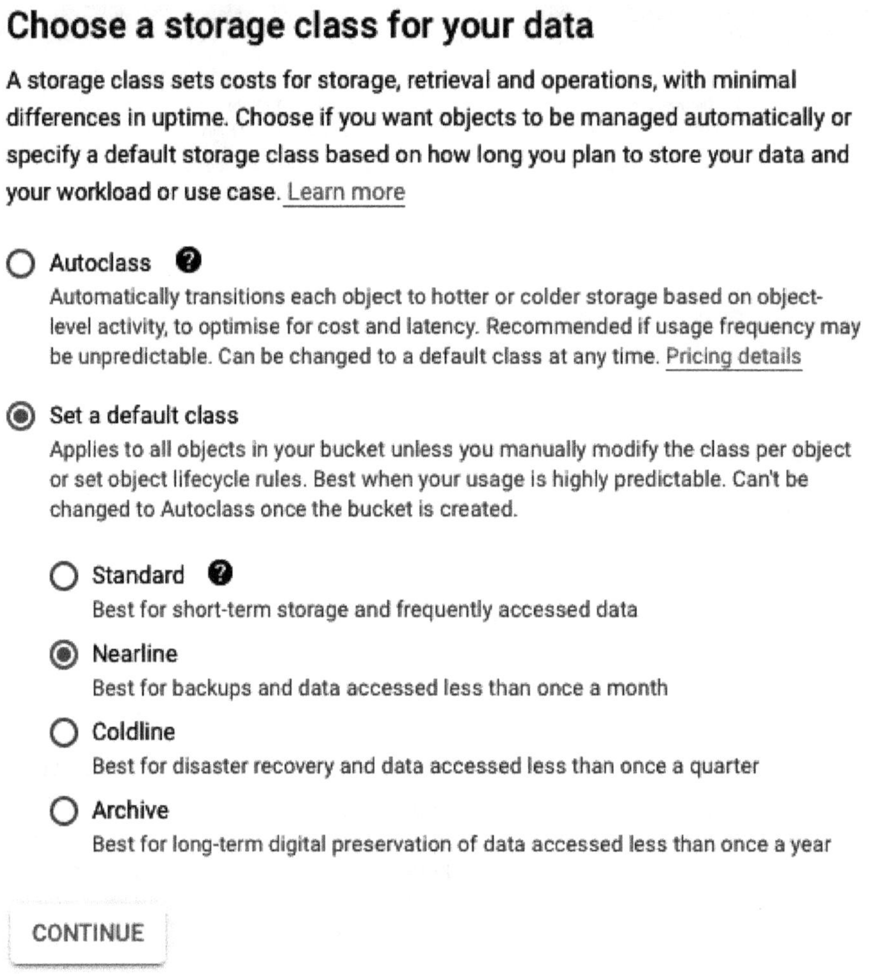

Choose a storage class for your data

A storage class sets costs for storage, retrieval and operations, with minimal differences in uptime. Choose if you want objects to be managed automatically or specify a default storage class based on how long you plan to store your data and your workload or use case. Learn more

○ Autoclass ❷

Automatically transitions each object to hotter or colder storage based on object-level activity, to optimise for cost and latency. Recommended if usage frequency may be unpredictable. Can be changed to a default class at any time. Pricing details

◉ Set a default class

Applies to all objects in your bucket unless you manually modify the class per object or set object lifecycle rules. Best when your usage is highly predictable. Can't be changed to Autoclass once the bucket is created.

   ○ Standard ❷

   Best for short-term storage and frequently accessed data

   ◉ Nearline

   Best for backups and data accessed less than once a month

   ○ Coldline

   Best for disaster recovery and data accessed less than once a quarter

   ○ Archive

   Best for long-term digital preservation of data accessed less than once a year

CONTINUE

Figure 8.18 – Creating a bucket; available storage classes

4. One of the requirements is to make sure backup files are not accessible from the internet. We can control it by selecting **Enforce public access prevention on this bucket**, ensuring no one can make those backup files public:

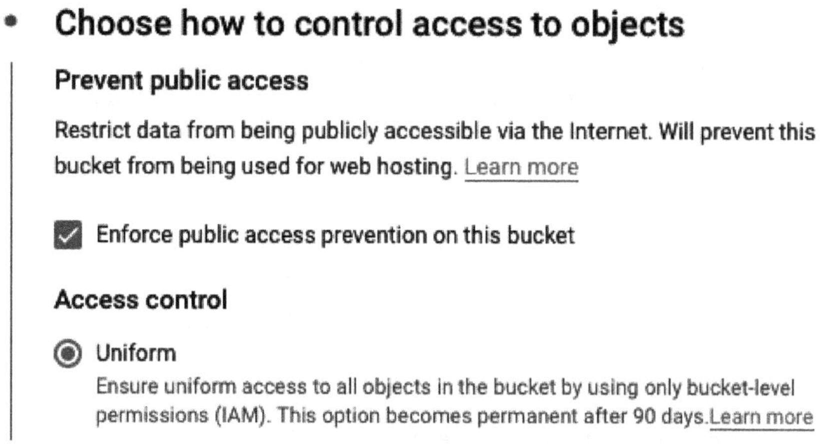

- ## Choose how to control access to objects

  ### Prevent public access

  Restrict data from being publicly accessible via the Internet. Will prevent this bucket from being used for web hosting. Learn more

  ☑ Enforce public access prevention on this bucket

  ### Access control

  ◉ Uniform

  Ensure uniform access to all objects in the bucket by using only bucket-level permissions (IAM). This option becomes permanent after 90 days. Learn more

Figure 8.19 – Creating a bucket; access control

5. The last requirement was to ensure that no one would delete backup files in five years. This can be configured by setting **Retention policy** to retain objects for five years. Please note that in real-life situations, depending on the backup solution vendor, the protection tools may have limited support:

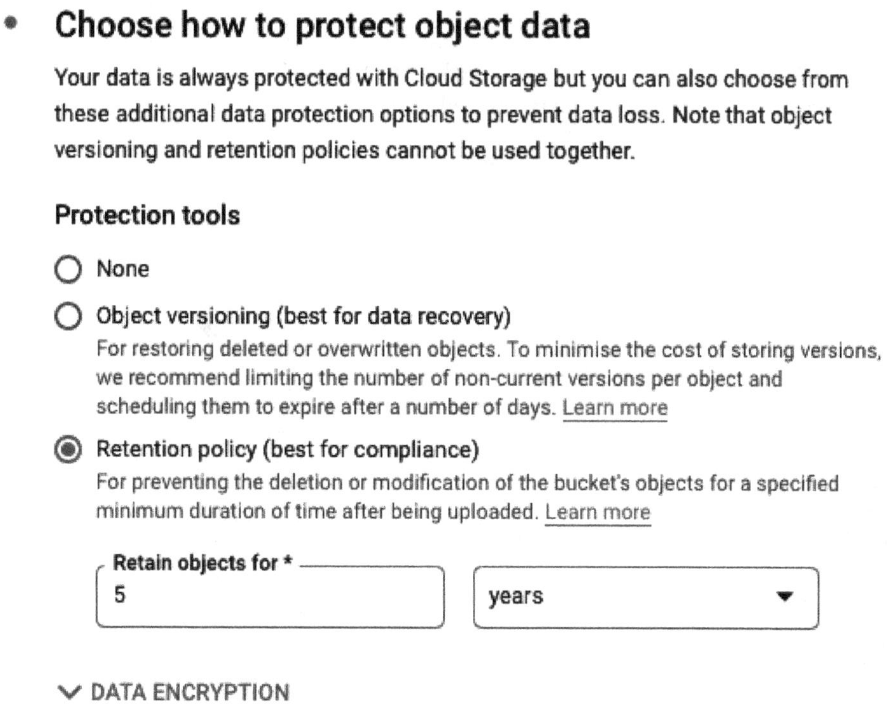

- ## Choose how to protect object data

  Your data is always protected with Cloud Storage but you can also choose from these additional data protection options to prevent data loss. Note that object versioning and retention policies cannot be used together.

  ### Protection tools

  ○ None

  ○ Object versioning (best for data recovery)

  For restoring deleted or overwritten objects. To minimise the cost of storing versions, we recommend limiting the number of non-current versions per object and scheduling them to expire after a number of days. Learn more

  ◉ Retention policy (best for compliance)

  For preventing the deletion or modification of the bucket's objects for a specified minimum duration of time after being uploaded. Learn more

Retain objects for *
5

  | years ▼ |

  ⌄ DATA ENCRYPTION

Figure 8.20 – Creating a bucket; retention policy

6. As a last step, we can also choose whether the files will be encrypted using the Google-managed encryption key or the **customer-managed encryption key** (**CMEK**). By utilizing CMEK, you gain greater control over various aspects of your key management and lifecycle such as using different types of keys (software or hardware-backed keys) and using keys managed externally.

7. To proceed with the setup, we need to hit **CREATE**. The bucket will be available in a few moments.

By following those steps, we created a Google Cloud Storage bucket that complies with our example task's requirements, and this way, we reviewed the most important features of Google Cloud Storage buckets.

Now that we have learned how the object store works, let's explore alternative ways to store data in Google Cloud.

Block storage – local and persistent disks

At Google Cloud, block storage in the form of disks emulating physical drives and attached to a compute layer is used by **Google Kubernetes Engine** (**GKE**) and **Google Compute Engine** (**GCE**). An operating system recognizes block storage as a volume that can be formatted so applications can use it.

Compute Engine instance has, by default, a single boot persistent disk where the operating system is running. However, you can add multiple **local** or **persistent** disks if you need additional storage space.

The step-by-step guide on configuring a Compute Engine VM, including persistent disks, was already presented in *Chapter 4*. Please look at *Figure 4.38*, which presents a table comparing available persistent disk types in Google Cloud: **Balanced**, **Extreme**, **SSD**, and **Standard**.

The following table summarizes the differences between available disks for Compute Engine VMs. Note that some disks can be replicated between zones. Also, a persistent disk can exist without a VM, whereas data on a local one will be discarded when a VM is stopped. Finally, you can expand a disk without powering off your VM.

Disk type	Characteristics	Backed By	Replication	Location and sharing	Encryption at rest
Standard	Persistent, cost effective	HDDs (Hard Disk Drives)	Single zone (several physical disks for redundancy) or a synchronous replication between two zones in a region	Exists separately from a VM, can be detached and attached to another VM or to more than one VM (read-only)	Yes, Google-managed or custom encryption keys
Balanced	Persistent, general purpose, a balance between performance and cost	SSDs (Solid-State Drives)		Exists separately from a VM, can be detached and attached to another VM or more than one VM (read-only and read-write)	
SSD	Persistent, best price per IOPS, suitable for high-performance databases				
Extreme	Persistent, highest performance, suitable for most demanding workloads, expected to be attached to largest VM types		Single zone (several physical disks for redundancy)	Exists separately from a VM, can be detached and attached to another VM	
Local	Low latency, temporary storage for cache or processing		No redundancy	Exists only with a VM, data is discarded when a VM stops	Yes, Google-managed keys

Figure 8.21 – Summary of available block storage options for Compute Engine VMs

Check out the following page for a more detailed comparison and performance characteristics for the block storage options: `https://cloud.google.com/compute/docs/disks`.

Data on zonal and regional persistent disks can be protected with snapshots. Snapshots can be manual or scheduled, and you can store them in a selected region or a multi-regional location. Refer to the *Creating instance snapshot* section in *Chapter 4* for more details on this topic.

Note that Google has also introduced a new type of block storage called **Hyperdisk**, which outperforms persistent disks. With Hyperdisk, each volume provides maximum IOPS and throughput, unlike in persistent disks where performance is shared across all attached volumes for a single virtual machine. Additionally, Hyperdisk volumes are independent of VMs, which means you can detach or move them to keep your data even after deleting your VMs. Furthermore, you can dynamically update the performance, resize existing Hyperdisk volumes, or add more volumes to a VM to meet your storage and performance needs, as Hyperdisk performance is not tied to size.

Although VMs can share disks among each other (for some disk types), the number of VMs that can be attached to a disk is limited, and such access is primarily suitable for applications and databases. However, if you are looking for shared storage for files that multiple applications or users can access, this will be covered in the next section.

File storage – Cloud Filestore

Cloud Filestore is a Google-managed, high-performance, network-attached storage for applications that require a (shared) filesystem interface to store files in a folder structure. Filestore's most common use cases are storing website content, users' home directories, images, or videos for editing, and storing data for batch jobs such as rendering.

Each created Filestore instance represents a single file share that can be mounted using the NFSv3 protocol (a networking protocol for distributed file sharing) to Compute Engine VMs, GKE, and even workstations on-premises, assuming they have network connectivity to such a Filestore instance.

To interact with Filestore, you can use the Google Cloud console, APIs, or `gcloud` commands. By default, Filestore automatically encrypts your data at rest. The access to a file share can be controlled based on the client's IP address. The following table presents the available service tiers.

Service tier	Min capacity [TiB]	Max capacity [TiB]	Capacity scaling	Read throughput for 10 TiB [MiB/s]	Write throughput for 10 TiB [MiB/s]	Availability	Backup solution	Availability during maintenance events	Monthly price*** for 10 TB in europe-central2 [USD]
Basic HDD	1	63.9	add capacity	180	120	Zonal	Backups	no	2,457.60
Basic SSD	2.5	63.9	add capacity	1 200	350	Zonal	Backups	no	3,686.40
High Scale SSD	10	100	add or remove capacity	2 600*	880**	Zonal	None	yes	3,686.40
Enterprise	1	10	add or remove capacity	1 200	1 000	Regional	Snapshots	yes	7,372.80

* for 100TB: 26 000   ** for 100TB: 8 800   *** prices are subject to change

Figure 8.22 – Filestore service tiers and their characteristics

The **Basic** tier is for general-purpose use such as file sharing and web hosting, with the **solid-state drive (SSD)** tier providing better read and write throughput than the **hard disk drive (HDD)**. The **High Scale** tier is designed for workloads with the highest capacity and performance demands, such as media rendering. The **Enterprise** tier has a regional redundancy to meet high availability requirements for mission-critical workloads. Note that the **Basic HDD** tier is the least expensive one. With High Scale and Enterprise, you can grow your instance and later shrink it. For the Basic tier, you can create a backup, and it will be a standalone copy of data. You can restore it to a source or another instance. The Enterprise tier offers snapshots that are a point-in-time view of a file share to which you can roll back your instance. They are stored on the instance and use its capacity.

In the next section, we will work on an example task to create a Filestore instance and mount its share to Compute Engine VMs.

Creating a file share in practice

Suppose you received a task to create a share so that the owner of vm-a and the owner of vm-b can work together on documents in a folder structure. Both VMs are deployed as Compute Engine VMs that run in the europe-central2 region with an NFS client already installed. The files take around 500 GB now, but the capacity can increase. Also, you need to set up a backup so that you can restore it if one of the owners deletes a file accidentally. The budget is limited. You decide to use a Filestore share and mount it to VMs. We assume you have a **Cloud Filestore Editor** role so you can create Filestore instances. Here are the steps you should follow to achieve it:

1. In the **Navigation** menu, go to the **Storage** section, select **Filestore**, and go to **Instances**. A **Create an instance** menu opens, as shown in the following screenshot:

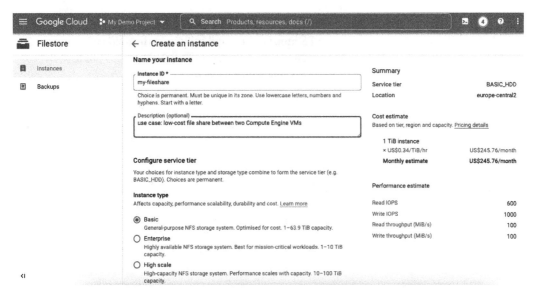

Figure 8.23 – Creating a Filestore instance

2. Provide a unique name for your instance (for example, `my-fileshare`) and a description.

3. Select **Basic** for **Instance type** because the budget is limited, and the workload (sharing documents) doesn't seem to require high performance or high availability. Under the **Instance type** section, you will find a **Storage type** section. Select **HDD** as we are looking for the lowest price. You can check the prices on the right-hand side in the **Cost estimate** section.

4. In the **Allocate capacity** section, provide a **1 TiB** value, as this is the minimal amount you can deploy with this storage type. Also, you can increase the instance capacity later up to 63.9 TiB as you already know that the owners plan to create more files.

5. In the **Choose where to store data** section, select the region where `vm-a` and `vm-b` run, so in this case, **europe-central2**. This way, you will ensure the lowest latency. Also, you will not be charged for ingress traffic to Filestore or egress traffic to a client if they are located within the same zone.

6. In the **VPC network section**, select a network that both VMs use to ensure network connectivity. The networking and VPCs will be explained in detail later in *Chapter 9*.

7. In the **Configure file share name** section, set the name for the share that VM owners will use to mount this share. In our case, it will be `documents`.

8. Note that you can also use the `gcloud` command line to create the instance:

```
gcloud filestore instances create my-fileshare --zone=europe-
central2-a --tier=BASIC_HDD --file-share=name="documents",capaci
ty=1TB --network=name="my-network"
```

9. Wait for the my-fileshare instance to be created and select it to view more details. Then, in the **OVERVIEW** section, look for **NFS mount point** and copy it. In the following screenshot, you can see that there is the 10.165.64.226:/documents NFS mount point:

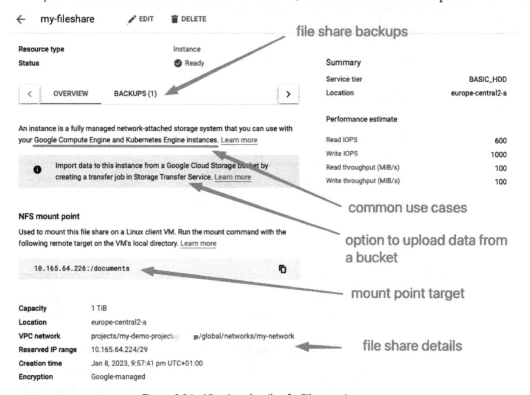

Figure 8.24 – Viewing details of a Filestore instance

10. Ask VM owners to SSH to their instances and create a folder under the /mnt directory (for example, /mnt/shared), and run the following command as a root:

```
mount 10.165.64.226:/document /mnt/shared
```

They can now go to /mnt/shared and see the files served from the my-fileshare instance, as shown in the following screenshot. You can also grant the owners **Cloud Filestore Viewer** roles, so they can check the mount point details themselves in the Google Cloud console:

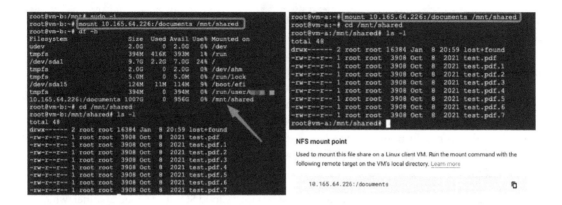

Figure 8.25 – Mounting the remote target on the VM's local directories

11. The last task is to run a backup task from time to time to be able to restore the files if someone deletes them. Edit the Filestore instance and select **Create a backup**. Provide a name and location and select **CREATE**.

Databases

Block, file, or object storage are not the only solutions to store data. Data can also be stored in databases: relational SQL databases and non-relational NoSQL databases. Both types will be covered in the next sections. Also, we will look into a data warehouse and in-memory database:

While looking for a database that will be the best fit for a solution, we consider the following requirements:

- **Availability**: Can an application accept that data is unavailable or available with a certain delay? Should it be regional (such as Cloud SQL), multi-regional, or span continents such as Spanner?

- **Scale**: How much data will be stored? For example, terabytes in a CloudSQL instance or petabytes with a Spanner instance.

- **Performance**: Is it a database for real-time systems or analytics? How fast should a database process read and write operations? How many regions will it have to serve? (If copies of a database are spread across regions, it may introduce some latency to write operations. This is a trade-off for maintaining strong consistency, like with Spanner). How can database performance be improved? For example, can we add more nodes?

- **Consistency**: In the case of database replication between regions, does the data written in one region have to be immediately available in another one?

- **Functions**: What are some additional features a database can offer? What form of a database backup is available?

- **Cost**: Does a solution need to be cost-optimized? For example, can it scale down when a larger capacity is no longer required?

In the next sections, we will look into database solutions offered by Google Cloud and discuss the requirements we just listed.

Relational databases

Data stored in relational databases is structured ahead of time and organized in tables with a static schema. Relational databases scale vertically by adding more compute and storage resources to the server where they run or by migrating to a larger server instance. To query and manipulate data in a relational database, a SQL programming language is used. The strength of relational databases is that they are designed for operations such as aggregations, sums, or multi-row transactions.

Google Cloud offers the following relational database services: Cloud SQL and Cloud Spanner, which we will cover in this section.

Cloud SQL

Cloud SQL is a relational database service that offers three engines – MySQL PostgreSQL, and Microsoft SQL Server. It has a built-in integration and can be used as a backend for other Google Cloud services such as Compute Engine, GKE, and Cloud Run. In addition, the integration with Google's serverless data warehouse, BigQuery (which will be covered later in this chapter), allows you to run federated queries to your Cloud SQL databases from BigQuery directly.

Each Cloud SQL instance is powered by a VM deployed in a Google-managed environment, and Google is responsible for its availability, updates, and patching. You can choose the amount of CPU, RAM, and storage for your instance according to the performance you need. CPU and RAM resources can be adjusted in time up to the maximum values a VM can offer, but it requires an instance shutdown. On the other hand, storage can be increased while an instance is running.

To handle more data or queries, you can increase the single VM capacity of your current instance by adding additional resources. This is called **vertical scaling**.

An instance is a resource pool for your databases. Once an instance is deployed, you can create databases that will run inside.

Assigning a **Public IP** to your instance will make it accessible from the outside of your environment. Alternatively, Cloud SQL can only connect to your internal network when it is configured with a **Private IP**. In addition, Cloud SQL has built-in encryption, both at rest and in transit.

Cloud SQL can be deployed in multiple zones within a selected region to achieve high availability. Furthermore, as data is replicated synchronously, when a failure occurs in a **primary zone**, a database will be served automatically from a **secondary zone** without data loss and the need to reconfigure applications connecting to an instance.

Use on-demand or scheduled backups to protect your Cloud SQL databases. Backups can run during a provided maintenance window. Also, there is an option to enable **point-in-time recovery** and recover data from a point in time, thanks to storing transaction logs.

In scenarios where you expect database traffic to come from different regions or need extra processing for analytics, leverage another Cloud SQL feature – **read replicas**. Read replicas are read-only copies of an original database that can be placed in the same or a different region, close to users. Read replicas can also be used to migrate a database to a different region or a larger instance.

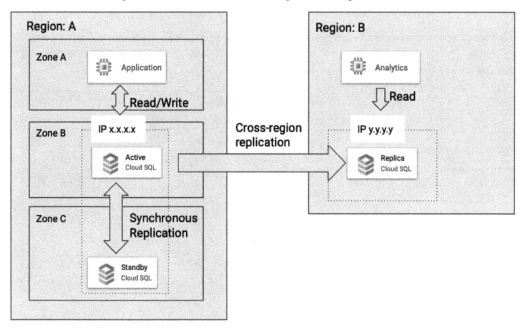

Figure 8.26 – Example use case of Cloud SQL high availability with a read replica located in another region

The preceding example presents how high availability and read replica features can be used together. An application in Region A and Zone A inserts data into a Cloud SQL database in Region A and Zone B; both run in the same region to minimize latencies. The SQL instance works in high availability mode, so the data is synchronously replicated to another zone, Zone C. In the case of Zone B failure, data will be served from the same IP (**x.x.x.x**) from the instance in Zone C. There is also a read replica instance in another region, Region B, where data is replicated. An analytics application, also located in Region B, reads data directly from a read replica served from a different IP, **y.y.y.y**. This approach offloads analytics traffic from the original instance and allows it to be served from a copy closer to the analytics application. In the case of a failure in Region A, the read replica in Region B can be promoted to a standalone primary instance.

Let's summarize what we have learned about Cloud SQL by going through the following example.

Working with a PostgreSQL database

Suppose you were asked to create a small but critical PostgreSQL database for an application that would run on a Compute Engine Linux VM, VM-a, in a my-subnet subnet in the europe-central2 region. The owner of the application is concerned about a potential latency between the database and their application. Also, although lightweight, the database needs to be highly available. In addition, the owner should be able to recover data from a specific time point within 7 days, and backups can only run within a 4-hour window during the night. Furthermore, the database can't be accessed from the internet.

The following diagram presents an example of how a Compute Engine VM can connect to a PostgreSQL database via a private network. We could use this approach to address the requirements of our task. Note that more information about networking will be presented in *Chapter 9*.

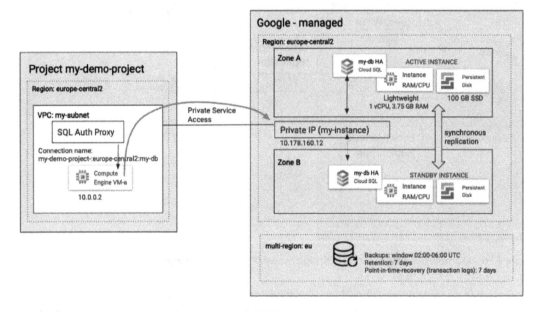

Figure 8.27 – Connecting to a PostgreSQL database from a VM via Private service access

Here are the steps that will guide you through the setup:

1. First, let's create a database. To create a SQL instance, go to the **DATABASES** section in the main menu of the Google Cloud console:

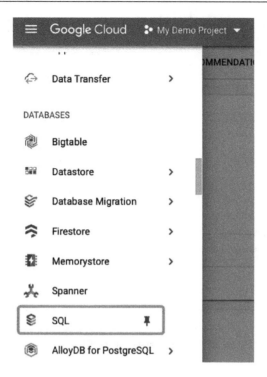

Figure 8.28 – The DATABASES section of the main menu

2. Out of the three available database engines, in this example, we will create a PostgreSQL instance by selecting **Create an instance** and then choosing **PostgreSQL**:

Figure 8.29 – Three database engines offered by Cloud SQL

3. In the next step, we provide the instance ID, my-instance, a password for the default postgres user, and the required version of the engine. Next, we select a predefined instance configuration (**Production** for critical workloads, or **Development**, a cost-optimized version). In our case, we need to provide high availability for the database, so we choose **Production**. Finally, note that on the right-hand side, there is a **Summary** section, which shows the most current setup and performance characteristics:

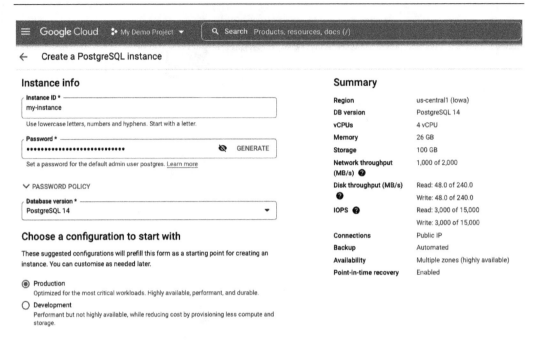

Figure 8.30 – Creating a PostgreSQL instance

4.   In the next step, we select a region where we want the instance to be deployed. For the minimal latency between the VM and the database, we select the same region where the VM is running: **europe-central2**. Also, as the database must be highly available, we select a multi-zonal availability:

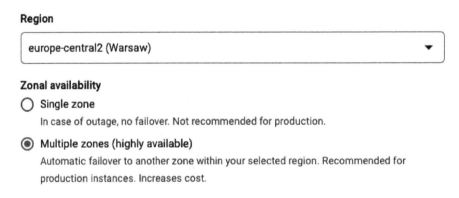

Figure 8.31 – Selecting a region and an availability type for a PostgreSQL instance

5. In the **Customize your instance** section, you can choose its machine type (*memory* and *cores*), storage type (**HDD** or **SSD**), and disk capacity. In our example, although the database needs to be highly available, it doesn't need high performance, so we will override the predefined settings and deploy a **Lightweight** machine type with 1vCPU and 3.75 GB of RAM, and set **Storage type** as SSD and **10 GB**.

6. In the **Connections** section, we configure the instance to be accessible only internally via **Private IP** and select the same VPC where the application is running – **my-network** for this connection. The private services access needs to be set up for the private communication to work, so we follow the **SET UP CONNECTION** wizard, selecting the default options. We will use **Cloud SQL Auth Proxy** installed inside VM-a to connect to the database:

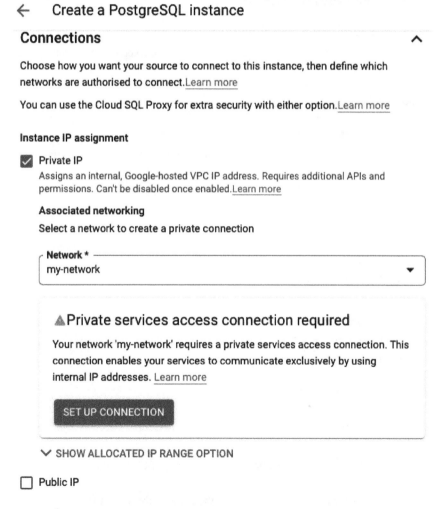

Figure 8.32 – Network configuration for a PostgreSQL instance

7. In the **Data protection** section, we select the 4-hour backup window to match the task's requirements and the default location where backups will be stored, which is the closest multi-region location to the database instance. The default retention is to keep 7 backups. We also need to enable point-in-time recovery and store 7 days of logs.

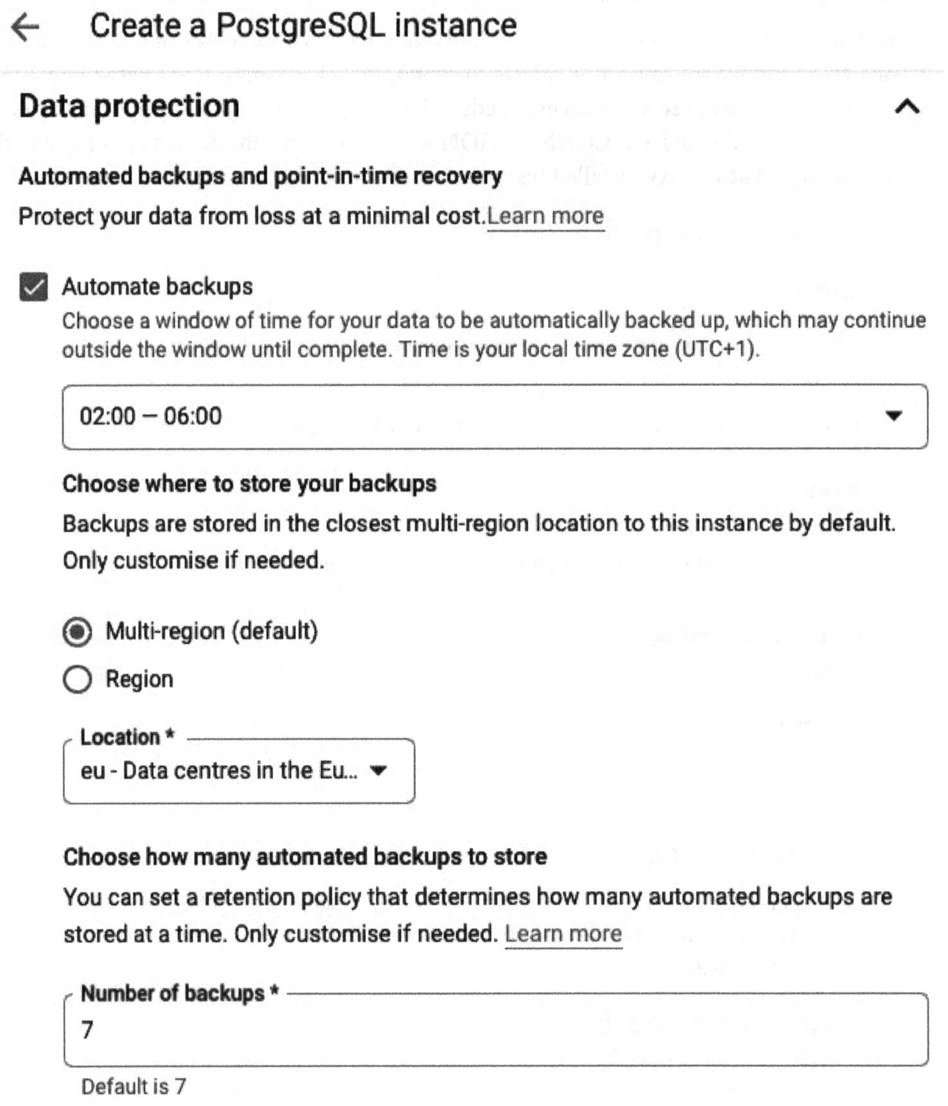

←   ## Create a PostgreSQL instance

Data protection   ⌃

Automated backups and point-in-time recovery
Protect your data from loss at a minimal cost.Learn more

☑ **Automate backups**
    Choose a window of time for your data to be automatically backed up, which may continue outside the window until complete. Time is your local time zone (UTC+1).

┌───┐
│ 02:00 – 06:00   ▼ │
└───┘

Choose where to store your backups
Backups are stored in the closest multi-region location to this instance by default. Only customise if needed.

◉ Multi-region (default)
○ Region

┌ Location * ──────────────────┐
│ eu - Data centres in the Eu... ▼ │
└──────────────────────────────┘

Choose how many automated backups to store
You can set a retention policy that determines how many automated backups are stored at a time. Only customise if needed. Learn more

┌ Number of backups * ──┐
│ 7   │
└───┘
Default is 7

Figure 8.33 – Configuring backups for PostgreSQL instance

8. Select **Create Instance** and wait till it is available. It usually takes a few minutes. Once the instance is ready, you can select it to view more details:

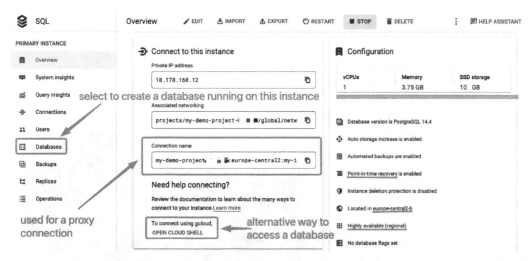

Figure 8.34 – Details of the PostgreSQL instance, my-instance

9. We need to create a PostgreSQL database that will run in my-instance. Select **Databases** from the menu and then **CREATE DATABASE**, providing its name: my-db. If you need to create additional users, you can do so in the **Users** section of the menu. To populate a database with data, you can use the **IMPORT** option to import data from a file uploaded to a Google Cloud Storage bucket:

Figure 8.35 – Importing data from a bucket

10. Enable **Cloud SQL Admin API** in the project where VM-a is running. Ensure that the service account that the VM is configured with has a **Cloud SQL Client** role. Both settings are needed to connect to the database from the VM.

11. SSH to VM-a and download **Cloud SQL Auth Proxy**:

```
wget https://dl.google.com/cloudsql/cloud_sql_proxy.linux.amd64
-O cloud_sql_proxy
```

12. Make it executable:

```
chmod +x cloud_sql_proxy
```

13. Start the proxy to my-instance:

```
./cloud_sql_proxy -instances=my-demo-project:europe-central2:my-
instance=tcp:5432 &
```

The application running on VM-a can use the local proxy to connect to the database, my-database. You can also connect to the database and access its content using the following command:

```
psql "host=127.0.0.1 port=5432 sslmode=disable dbname=my-
database user=postgres"
```

Figure 8.36 – Starting Cloud SQL Auth Proxy inside VM-a and accessing the my-db PostgreSQL database

In addition to the application's access to the database, the application owner could use integration with BigQuery to share database data with his analytics team. For example, if the instance was created with a Public IP instead of using a private service access communication, the analytics team could connect to Cloud SQL, not from a VM as in this example excercise, but from BigQuery directly and run federated queries on the PostreSQL database:

Figure 8.37 – Using BigQuery integration with Cloud SQL

The preceding figure shows an example of how a federated query in the BigQuery view looks once the **external connection** to Cloud SQL is created.

Cloud Spanner

There are limits to how much a relational database can expand. In most cases, it can only expand vertically. For example, you can grow Cloud SQL instances (described in the previous sections) by adding more storage or replicating to a larger instance up to the largest available type (vertical scaling), but to some point only, and not without performance sacrifices and downtime during migrations. Also, if a database needs to be reachable globally from applications requiring low latency, Cloud SQL can only provide regional read replicas for read-only operations.

Cloud Spanner is a Google-managed relational database service (with SQL schemas and querying) that can horizontally scale for reads and writes. **Horizontal scaling** is a method of increasing processing power and storage capacity by distributing the workload across multiple instances, unlike vertical scaling, which adds more resources to a single instance.

Furthermore, Cloud Spanner has global reachability as it can span across regions so that it can be accessed with low latency from all over the world. In addition, it meets the highest availability demands as it offers an SLA of up to 99.999% (roughly 5 minutes of downtime per year) for a multi-regional deployment. It doesn't failover to a **standby instance** like Cloud SQL, but it elects a new leader out of available read-write replicas.

Spanner is located in the **DATABASES** section of the main menu of the Google Cloud console. When configuring an instance, you can choose the following configurations:

- The **Regional** option, which will create three read-write replicas in three separate zones within a chosen region. Regional configurations have 99.99% availability (roughly 50 minutes of downtime in a year) and low write latency within their region.

- The **Multi-region** option:

  - Spans across the same continent, with two read-write replicas in two regions and one **Witness** location.

  - Spans across the globe; for example, two read-write replicas in two regions of the same continent (the US), with one Witness replica (the US) and two read-replicas in the other two continents (Europe and Asia).

Note that a Witness replica's role is not to serve reads but to form a majority quorum in case of a region's loss. Multi-region configurations have 99.999% availability and low read latencies in multiple regions. The trade-off is increased write latency compared to Regional configurations, as the replication is synchronous and read-write replicas in separate regions need to vote on each write. Once a transaction is committed, it is written to all databases.

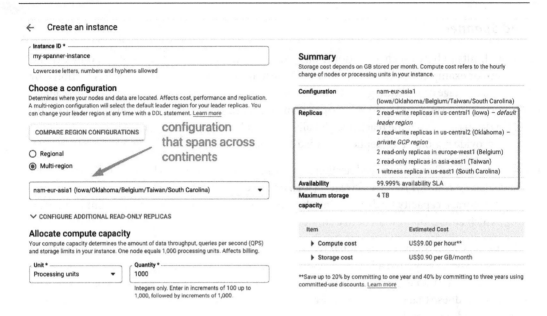

Figure 8.38 – Configuring a Spanner instance that spans globally

The following example presents how the replicas could be located when choosing the **nam-eur-asia1** configuration, which spans continents. The global consistency for Spanner databases is achieved by utilizing Google's low-latency global network and **TrueTime**, a global clock responsible for time synchronization across data centers:

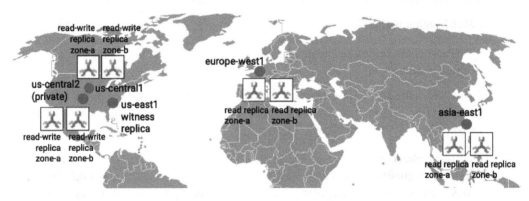

Figure 8.39 – Explanatory figure of Spanner node placements across
the globe for the nam-eur-asia1 multi-region setup

In addition to Spanner's location, you need to configure your instance compute and storage capacity by selecting either a required number of processing units or nodes (1 node equals 1,000 processing units). Each node equals 4 TB of storage with peak read and write performance per node being specific to a region. For example, for the `nam-eur-asial` setup, it is approximately 7,000 peak reads per region and 1,000 peak writes globally. Later, you can scale up or down your instance to add more resources or reduce the number of idle ones. This operation doesn't require a maintenance window.

Similarly to Cloud SQL, Spanner supports point-in-time recovery for up to seven days, protecting data against accidental deletion or corruption. For longer-term retention, Spanner offers backups in the form of a transactionally consistent full copy of a database that can be stored for one year.

Non-relational databases (NoSQL)

Non-relational databases store data in an unstructured format. In contrast to SQL databases with a fixed schema, NoSQL databases store data as documents (JSON), key-value pairs, graphs, or dynamic-sized tables. Non-relational databases scale horizontally by adding new servers, making them a good fit for big data. Let's look at the NoSQL database options that are offered by Google Cloud.

Cloud Bigtable

Imagine you need to design an application that continuously scans the state of millions of IoT sensors, or that the service you are designing will be responsible for keeping track of a few million users' behaviors and offering them recommendations based on their preferences. In such scenarios, you will have to store data in a low-latency database. Still, the data model must be flexible because data structures could change over time: upgraded IoT devices storing an additional set of parameters could be introduced, or a new service could be integrated with your recommendation engine. Therefore, such a database should be able to store large amounts of rapidly changing and constantly growing data. Also, it should retrieve data within single-digit milliseconds as everyone expects to get results in real time. On the other hand, high throughput demands could be seasonal, so such a database would have to be able to scale up and down based on load for cost optimization.

Cloud Bigtable is a good fit for such cases. It is a fully managed, key-value, and wide-column NoSQL database designed to store petabytes of data and scales well, offering low latency reads and writes. A Cloud Bigtable instance is a container that hosts clusters deployed in one or many regions. Clusters consist of nodes that define the performance of an instance. You can add or remove nodes manually via autoscaling without downtime. Inside an instance, we can create tables. With Bigtable, we manage tables, not a database itself.

The cost optimization of Cloud Bigtable comes not only from the ability to scale up and down. In addition, tables in Bigtable are sparse, which means they don't need to store entries in every cell. Because there is no charge for empty cells, savings can be significant, especially when such a database scales to an enormous number of rows and columns.

The IoT service or the recommendation engine from our example could also benefit from Cloud Bigtable's **versioning**, which can help, for example, with time series analysis. Cells in tables may not only be empty but they can also have different values at different time points. Each time data is written to a cell, it is timestamped, so when new data is written to the same cell, the old one is not overridden. You can enable a **garbage collection** to delete older versions when they are no longer needed and reclaim this space.

You can increase the availability of a Cloud Bigtable instance by replicating it to clusters in other regions. The replication in the same cluster within nodes is **strongly consistent**, but **eventually consistent** between clusters. This means that it can take some time between when data is written to one cluster and the time it can be read from another.

To protect data in tables, you can use backups stored on the cluster that owns a table and keep it for up to 30 days.

Cloud Bigtable is a non-relational database, so it might be not easy to use it for analytics operations as it doesn't support joins and aggregations. However, for analyzing data stored in Cloud Bigtable, leverage its integration with BigQuery.

You can work with an instance and create tables and backups in the Google Cloud console. But to interact with tables, you will have to use client libraries (HBase Java Client, Go, and Python Client), HBase Shell, or **cbt**, a command-line tool for performing operations on Cloud Bigtable. The cbt tool can be installed as a gcloud CLI component or launched from Cloud Shell.

Figure 8.40 –Creating a Bigtable table via the Google Cloud console

To download cbt to your workstation, use the following command:

```
gcloud components install cbt
```

You can configure cbt to use your project by editing the cbtrc configuration file:

```
echo project = my-demo-project-xxx >> ~/.cbtrc
```

A Bigtable instance can be created via the Google Cloud console or cbt. The user interface equivalent of creating an instance would be the following:

```
cbt createinstance <instance-id> <display-name> <cluster-id> <zone>
<number-of-nodes> <storage type: SSD or HDD>
```

To create a my-instance instance in the us-central1 region that runs on three nodes and uses SSD storage, use the following:

```
cbt createinstance my-instance "My instance" my-instance-c1
us-central1-b 3 SSD
```

Once my-instance is created, you need to update the cbtrc file for cbt to use this instance:

```
echo instance = my-instance >> ~/.cbtrc
```

The following figure shows the command-line output from the creation of a Bigtable instance using the aforementioned steps:

```
admin_@cloudshell:~ (my-demo-project-    )$ echo project = my-demo-project-   >> ~/.cbtrc
admin_@cloudshell:~ (my-demo-project-    )$ cbt help createinstance
cbt createinstance <instance-id> <display-name> <cluster-id> <zone> <num-nodes> <storage-type>
  instance-id      Permanent, unique ID for the instance
  display-name     Description of the instance
  cluster-id       Permanent, unique ID for the cluster in the instance
  zone             The zone in which to create the cluster
  num-nodes        The number of nodes to create
  storage-type     SSD or HDD

  Example: cbt createinstance my-instance "My instance" my-instance-c1 us-central1-b 3 SSD
admin_@cloudshell:~ (my-demo-project-    )$ cbt createinstance my-instance "My instance" my-instance-c1 us-central1-b 3 SSD
2023/01/18 17:50:51 -creds flag unset, will use gcloud credential
admin_@cloudshell:~ (my-demo-project-    )$ echo instance = my-instance >> ~/.cbtrc
admin_@cloudshell:~ (my-demo-project-    )$ cbt listinstances
2023/01/18 17:51:21 -creds flag unset, will use gcloud credential
Instance Name          Info
-------------          ----
my-instance            My instance
admin_@cloudshell:~ (my-demo-project-    )$ ▮
```

Figure 8.41 – Creating a Cloud Bigtable instance with the cbt tool

Let's use my-instance to create an example table that stores information about room temperature from sensors:

| | Column family: temperature | Column family: location | |
	temp	floor	room
s1	5 @date x | 10 @date y	1	1
s2	15	1	2
s3	15	1	3
s4	15	1	4
s5	15		
s6		1	6

Figure 8.42 – A table that stores the temperature and location of sensors

To create a table using cbt, run the following command:

```
cbt createtable sensors
```

Bigtable organizes data in **column families**, which are columns often used together, such as `location`, `floor`, and `room`. It helps to organize the data and limits the amount of pulled data. We will create two column families – `temperature` and `location`:

```
cbt createfamily sensors temperature
cbt createfamily sensors location
```

Then, we can provide values that match the values in the table in *Figure 8.42*. Note that you don't have to provide values for all the column families:

```
cbt set sensors s1 temperature:temp=5 location:floor=1 location:room=1
cbt set sensors s2 temperature:temp=15 location:floor=1
location:room=1
cbt set sensors s3 temperature:temp=15 location:floor=1
location:room=1
cbt set sensors s4 temperature:temp=15 location:floor=1
location:room=1
cbt set sensors s5 temperature:temp=15
cbt set sensors s6 location:floor=1 location:room=1
```

Use `cbt read sensors` to read the data from the table.

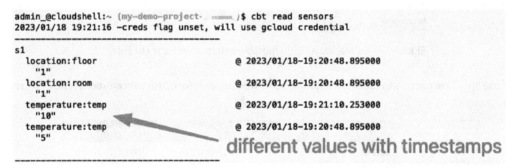

Figure 8.43 – A part of the output of the cbt read command that shows multiple values for the same cell

Now, let's say we update the temperature value for the `s1` sensor to `10`:

```
cbt set sensors s1 temperature:temp=10
```

We will see both `temperature` values with timestamps, as presented in *Figure 8.43*.

The following figure shows a screenshot of a section of a database output (for the `s4`, `s5`, and `s6` sensors) after we added values to columns for our sensors. Note that the table is sparse, so for the `s4` sensor, we have values for each of the columns (`floor`, `room`, and `temp`) but the `s5` sensor has only a value for `temp`, and the `s6` sensor only has values for `floor` and `room`.

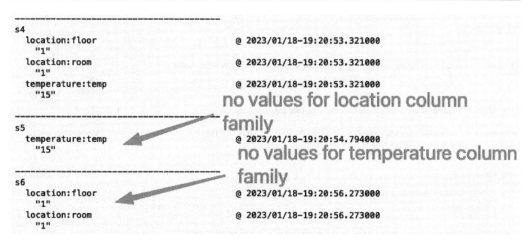

Figure 8.44 – A part of the output of the cbt read command showing that not all cells have values

Now that we looked into the key-value NoSQL database, let's see a different type of NoSQL type, which is a document store.

Firestore

Firestore is a serverless document database with all its underlying infrastructure components and complexity hidden from users. Compared to Cloud Bigtable, where we deploy an instance with nodes that define the performance, or Cloud SQL, where we configure CPU, RAM, and storage resources for an instance, there is no node provisioning and resource planning in Firestore. In consequence, Firestore scales horizontally and transparently to a user. Also, the pricing in Firestore is based on consumption (for example, on stored data and operations such as read, write, and delete), not on assigned resources.

Firestore operates in two modes:

- **Datastore mode**, which is compatible with a Datastore database and can be used by existing Datastore users. It has the same API but a new storage layer that provides strong consistency and high availability. Firestore is a new Datastore version optimized for writes and real-time updates.

- **Native mode**, which leverages a document model and integrates with third-party clients. It is optimized for concurrent connections.

In both cases, databases can be either multi-regional, with 99.999% SLA, or regional, with 99.99% SLA.

The first step of a Firestore setup is to select the mode. This selection is permanent. In this chapter, we will examine the **Native mode**. Selecting the location is the second and last step to configure Firestore:

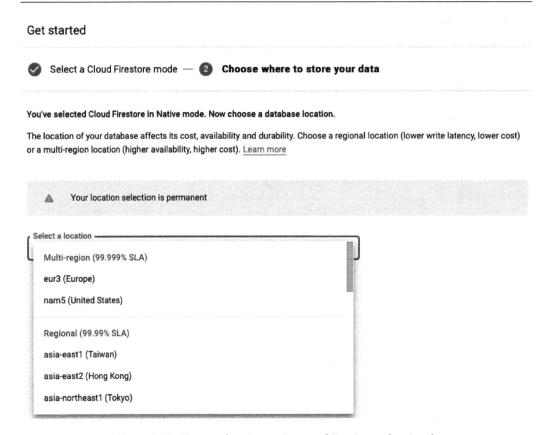

Figure 8.45 – Firestore location options: multi-region and regional

This document database stores **collections** of organized objects called **documents**. They consist of named string fields, numbers, and object data values in the form of JSON documents. There is no schema enforcement. Instead, documents are stored in a flexible tree-like structure:

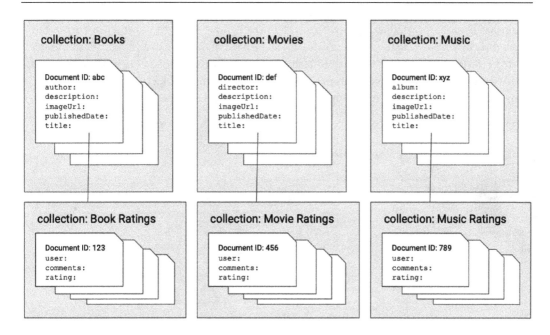

Figure 8.46 – Hierarchical structure of collections and documents

The preceding figure presents a simplified example structure of the Firestore database with collections named Books, Movies, and Music. In every collection, there is a set of documents with fields that describe features of books, films, and albums. Each collection has a **subcollection** that represents the ratings for some items.

In the following screenshot, we can see how the example **Book**, **Movies**, and **Music** collections could be implemented. For example, the **Book** collection consists of documents that contain fields describing the details of a book:

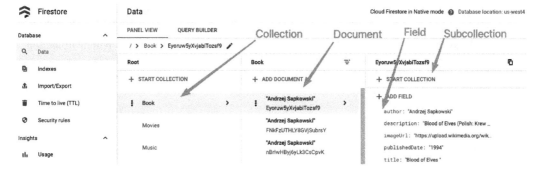

Figure 8.47 – The Data view in the Firestore panel with example collections

Firestore has libraries for popular languages such as Java or Python, and Android and iOS devices can access it directly via native SDKs. In most cases, it will be fixed in the code of an application, with an imported Firestore client library to query a database. But we can also use the Google Cloud console to query data. The following example shows a query run against the Book collection, where all the documents containing the defined author name in the author field are listed:

Figure 8.48 – Database query run from the Firestore panel

One of the most valuable features of Firestore that helps developers to build mobile-friendly applications is how it can handle data synchronization between a database and a client in real time: for example, when a user runs a query to see and rate books written by an author and, at the same time, a cover of one of the books changes, a client application is notified, and the changed data is sent to a device. Similarly, data can be synchronized across mobile devices that use the same application.

In addition to **real-time updates**, Firestore provides **offline support**. Imagine that a user from the preceding example temporarily loses access to the internet while looking at book ratings in the application. Assuming the application is leveraging the offline support functionality of Firebase, it will cache queries on a mobile device so a user can look at search results, even when a device is offline. Moreover, all the changes made when rating books are queued up on a device and will be uploaded after it goes online:

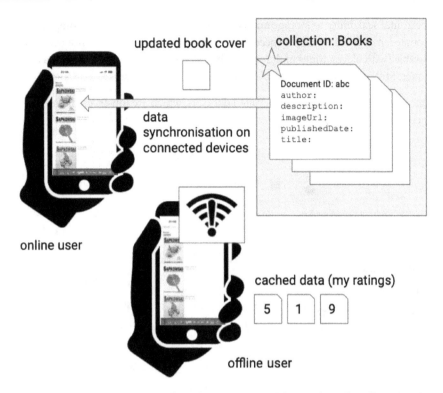

Figure 8.49 – Real-time updates for online devices and data caching for offline devices

Applications on mobile devices can directly interact with Firestore. Still, usually, there is a logic between a database and users, for example, to moderate uploaded data, send notifications to keep them engaged, or offload some functionality from a mobile application to limit battery usage on devices. Cloud Functions could be used for this purpose.

Looking at the way Firestore is structured, it won't be a good fit for offline analysis and queries across datasets. But Firestore data can be exported to BigQuery for more advanced queries, and BigQuery will be what we will cover next.

Warehouse and analytics – BigQuery

As data grows out of datasheets, it needs a more efficient system for its analytics – a data warehouse. However, scaling and managing such a platform on-premises can be challenging, especially when data grows from gigabytes to terabytes and petabytes. Such challenges are addressed by the Google-managed serverless data warehouse: BigQuery.

This is a query engine designed to handle massive amounts of data with no limit to the amount of data that can be stored. In addition, BigQuery supports SQL queries and is a good choice for table scan tasks and cross-database queries.

It owes its horizontal scalability to storage and compute separation. Although storage and compute layers are decoupled, it doesn't impact the speed of data access, thanks to Google's fast networking. Also, it is highly durable (with eleven nines of durability, the chance of data loss is almost 0) as it replicates data across zones. Still, its whole internal architecture is hidden from users as BigQuery is serverless.

Data in BigQuery is organized in containers called **datasets**, which are top-level folders that organize and control access to underlying tables:

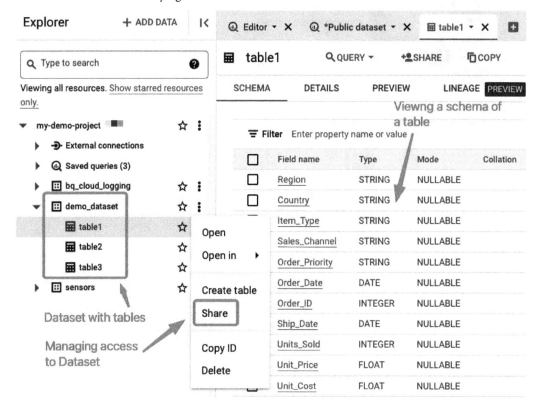

Figure 8.50 – BigQuery Explorer view in the Google Cloud console with example dataset with tables

BigQuery is integrated with Google's IAM service so you can manage read/write access to datasets for users and groups, enabling their collaboration on shared data. For example, a predefined **BigQuery Data Viewer** role lets you view a dataset's details. A **BigQuery Data Editor** role allows you to create, update, and delete dataset tables. A user with **BigQuery Job User** role has the ability to execute various jobs, such as running queries, within the whole project.

Data stored in BigQuery is encrypted before being written onto disks. The encryption is done using either Google-managed or customer-managed encryption keys.

You can import data to BigQuery in the following ways:

- If your data will not change, it can be loaded once as a batch operation. For example, you can use a file in a CSV format and let BigQuery auto-detect its schema. Data can be uploaded from a local machine, Google Cloud Storage, or Cloud Bigtable. You can also upload data from object storage from other cloud providers.

- If your data changes occasionally (for example, once a day), you can use the **Data Transfer** feature of BigQuery and load data on schedule from other Google services or external storage or warehouse providers.

- If data needs to be analyzed in real-time, some options would be to stream data to BigQuery via the **Storage Write API** or **Dataflow**, a Google Cloud serverless service for unified stream and batch data processing (for more information on Dataflow, check *Chapter 10*.

Once raw data is loaded, it can be used as staging data for further processing.

You can interact with BigQuery via the Google Cloud console or bq, a Python-based command-line tool from the gcloud CLI. It also supports client libraries for Python, Java, and Go. Alternatively, you can use the REST API or third-party tools for further integration.

The following screenshot presents the BigQuery **Explorer** view, where you can create datasets and tables, import data to a table, and run SQL queries:

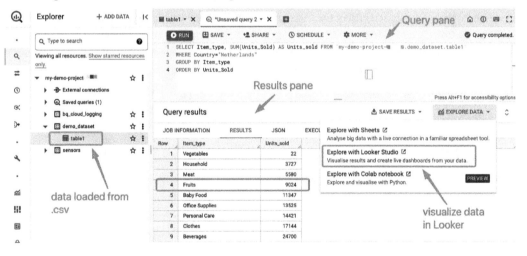

Figure 8.51 – Example SQL query on a table containing imported data from a CSV file

Data can be further visualized in **Looker Studio**, a platform where you can explore data and build charts based on various metrics and filters, narrowing down the dataset:

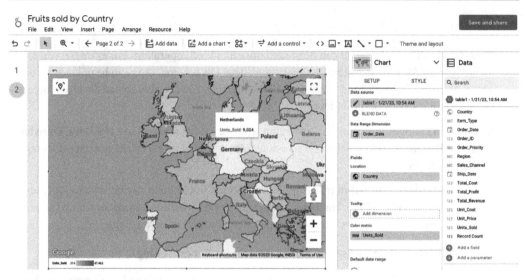

Figure 8.52 – Google Maps-style dashboard in Looker visualizing the query from Figure 8.51

You can practice SQL queries in BigQuery on a public dataset: `bigquery-public-data`. Please refer to the documentation for detailed instructions on how to use public datasets: `https://cloud.google.com/bigquery/docs/quickstarts/query-public-dataset-console`.

Please refer to the following screenshot for an example of how to query the public dataset's `bigquery-public-data.san_francisco_film_locations.film_locations` table to search for information regarding the filming locations of a popular movie that was shot in San Francisco:

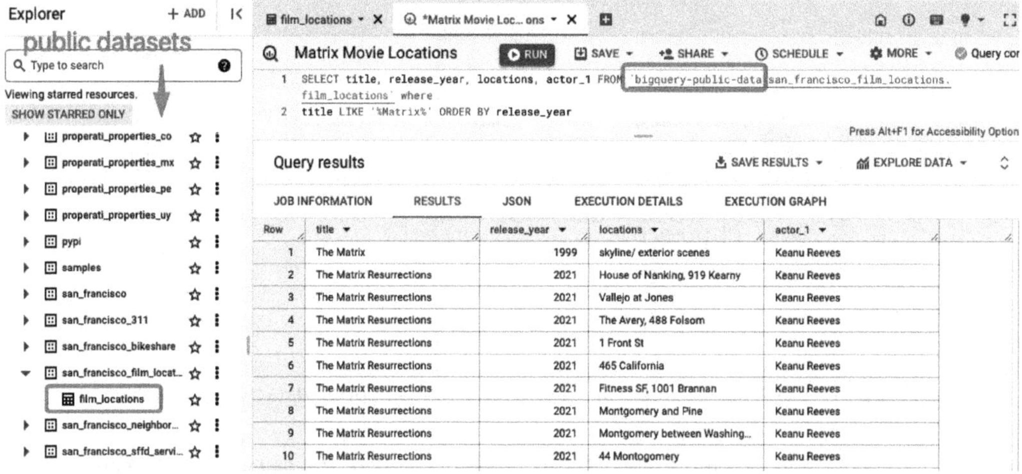

Figure 8.53 – Practicing SQL queries on the public dataset

To build queries, you can also use Cloud Shell, which has the bq command-line tool installed. In addition to the Google Cloud console, this is another option available to you. Simply run the bq ls command to list the available datasets. To construct your queries, use the following format:

```
bq query --use_legacy_sql=false 'SELECT title, release_year,
locations, actor_1 FROM `bigquery-public-data.san_francisco_film_
locations.film_locations` where title LIKE "%Matrix%" ORDER BY
release_year';
```

The following screenshot presents the Cloud Shell console view where the similar command is issued:

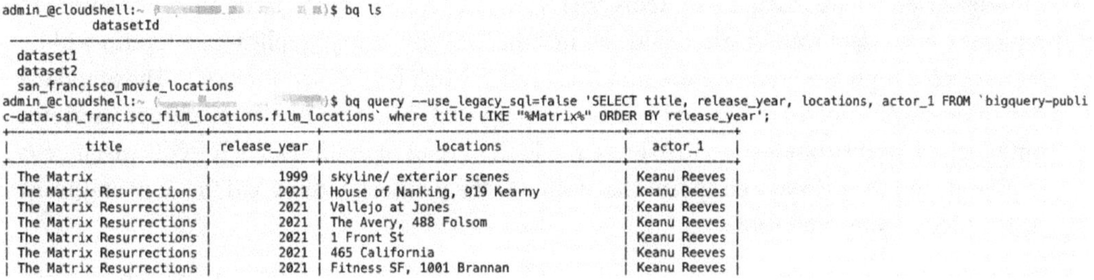

```
admin_@cloudshell:~ (                  )$ bq ls
           datasetId
--------------------------------------
  dataset1
  dataset2
  san_francisco_movie_locations
admin_@cloudshell:~ (                  )$ bq query --use_legacy_sql=false 'SELECT title, release_year, locations, actor_1 FROM `bigquery-publi
c-data.san_francisco_film_locations.film_locations` where title LIKE "%Matrix%" ORDER BY release_year';
+-------------------------+--------------+-------------------------------+--------------+
|        title            | release_year |          locations            |   actor_1    |
+-------------------------+--------------+-------------------------------+--------------+
| The Matrix              |      1999    | skyline/ exterior scenes      | Keanu Reeves |
| The Matrix Resurrections |     2021    | House of Nanking, 919 Kearny  | Keanu Reeves |
| The Matrix Resurrections |     2021    | Vallejo at Jones              | Keanu Reeves |
| The Matrix Resurrections |     2021    | The Avery, 488 Folsom         | Keanu Reeves |
| The Matrix Resurrections |     2021    | 1 Front St                    | Keanu Reeves |
| The Matrix Resurrections |     2021    | 465 California                | Keanu Reeves |
| The Matrix Resurrections |     2021    | Fitness SF, 1001 Brannan      | Keanu Reeves |
+-------------------------+--------------+-------------------------------+--------------+
```

Figure 8.54 – Practicing the bq command-line tool

Now, let's look into the last storage option of this chapter. It is a totally different kind of database than we have investigated so far. This one is optimized to provide the lowest response times.

In-memory datastore – Memorystore

Applications designed for real-time banking, online interactive gaming with player scores and profiles, or geospatial processing all need the fastest possible response times. Databases such as Cloud SQL or Spanner still rely on disk operations, although they provide high throughput. To reduce its response latency to an absolute minimum, a database could be stored in memory directly by a processor.

Google Cloud offers a fully managed in-memory data store service called **Memorystore** for two open source caching engines: **Redis** and **Memcached**. Both can be used to build a cache for an application for heavily accessed data with sub-millisecond access to a dataset. In this section, we will focus on Redis.

Reduced latency is a huge benefit, but it doesn't come without a trade-off. RAM is expensive and is available in smaller sizes compared to disks. That is why in-memory databases are kept closer to an application and used to accelerate an application response time, having a traditional, sizeable disk-based database at the backend.

Also, the in-memory database will not survive a node restart as memory is flushed in that process. Even though applications can be designed to populate cache from persistent disks to avoid downtime, Memorystore can be deployed with read replicas to which it can automatically failover. Also, Memorystore supports **Redis Database RDB snapshots**, which are point-in-time snapshots of a dataset.

When you provision a Redis instance, you provide the following: its name, location, the number of replicas, the VPC network that clients will use to connect to it, and its memory size. The more memory you provision, the higher throughput you will get.

There are two types of Memorystore for Redis:

- **Basic tier**, which you can deploy as a single Redis instance in a zone. It can serve as a simple cache, assuming an application that uses it can tolerate Redis data loss when this instance is restarted. The instance health is monitored, but there is no SLA.

- **Standard tier**, where instances of Redis are replicated across zones in a region. Up to five read replicas can be deployed. If you deploy an instance without a read replica, one replica will be deployed for high availability. Note that this replica won't be enabled for reads. The Standard tier offers an SLA of 99.9% (roughly 9 hours per year). Multiple read replicas are used not only for availability but also to distribute the load of read operations. Each Redis instance is deployed with the **primary endpoint** that points to the **primary replica** and the **read endpoint** distributed among read replicas.

The following figure presents an example of Memorystore deployment options, where, with the Basic tier, only one instance can be deployed and accessed via an endpoint, and with the Standard tier, we can have one or more instance replica(s) used for high availability accessed via a primary endpoint. Additionally, we can utilize multiple replicas for reads, accessed via a read endpoint.

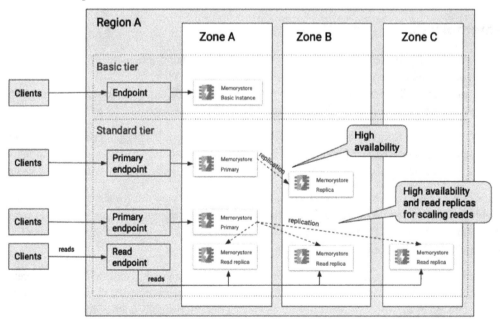

Figure 8.55 – Memorystore deployment options for the Basic and Standard tier

In the following screenshot, you can see the **Memorystore** section in the Google Cloud console. There is a Redis instance deployed in **europe-central2** with **5 GB** of capacity, a **Standard** tier with read replicas. It has two endpoints – **Primary endpoint** for read/write access and **Read endpoint** for scaling read operations:

Figure 8.56 – Memorystore dashboard with a Redis instance

You can manage a Redis instance in the Google Cloud console using `gcloud` commands or client libraries in your code. You can control access to an instance via IAM. To connect to a Redis instance, a client should be in the same VPC as the instance, as it uses an internal IP. Alternatively, to connect to the instance from another VPC, a VPN service could be used.

Let's assume you want to connect to an instance from a Compute Engine VM that uses the same VPC as your Redis instance. First, you need to deploy a `redis-tools` client:

```
sudo apt-get install redis-tools
```

To connect to an instance, use the following:

```
redis-cli -h 10.178.160.5
```

Here, the IP address is the one presented in the **Memorystore** dashboard for this instance.

You can run `redis-benchmark` to generate some workload:

```
redis-benchmark -h 10.178.160.5 -q
```

The following figure presents a monitoring chart of this instance with calls that the preceding `benchmark` command triggered to test the database performance. It's very convenient to have observability built into a database service because it allows for closer monitoring and troubleshooting of any issues that may arise:

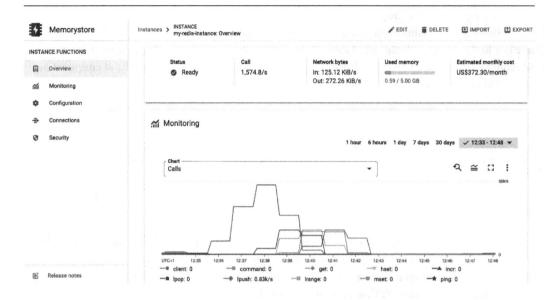

Figure 8.57 – A Redis instance dashboard with a monitoring chart

The preceding screenshot presents a **Monitoring** dashboard with client calls during `redis-benchmark` tests.

Summary

This chapter explored various ways that data can be stored in Google Cloud. Let's summarize what we have learned about storage.

For large amounts of unstructured data, we could use Google Cloud Storage. Applications installed inside Compute Engine VM will benefit greatly from performant local or persistent drives. If files need to be shared between users over a network, Filestore will be the best fit. If data that we store for an application is structured and can be organized in tables, relational databases such as Cloud SQL or Spanner will make a good choice, with Spanner being able to scale horizontally better. If the data is not relational but of the key-value type, Cloud Bigtable is a perfect use case. Firestore is the best fit if you are looking for a document database for mobile applications. BigQuery would be the best for analyzing large amounts of unchanged data.

Please refer to the following diagram, which will hopefully assist you in identifying the differences between the database solutions discussed in this chapter:

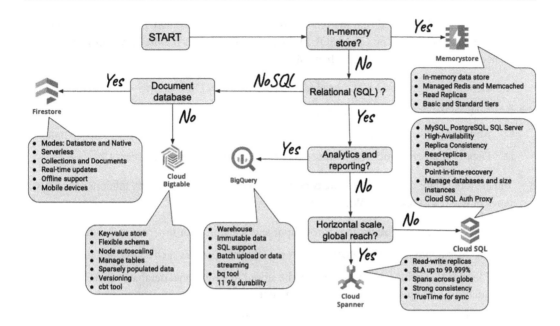

Figure 8.58 – Selecting the right database, a decision tree with keywords
that summarize features of databases in Google Cloud

As you may have noticed, we also briefly discussed networking when exploring accessing databases and storage. Moving forward, in the upcoming chapter, we will delve deeper into the world of networking and explore its intricacies.

Questions

Answer the following questions to test your knowledge of this chapter:

1. You are looking for a storage solution your global team could use for video editing collaboration. The current amount of data is 10 TB, but it is expected to grow to 80 TB. Which option should you choose?

    A. The Google Cloud Storage Standard tier as the price per operation on data is the lowest compared to other tiers.

    B. High Scale Filestore with a mechanism to backup edited videos to Google Cloud Storage for long-term storage.

    C. Compute Engine VM with a balanced persistent disk of 80 TB replicated between two zones in a region for better resiliency.

    D. Google Cloud Hyperdisk to ensure the highest performance.

2. Your company discovered that many users from the `europe-central2` region also use their application backed by Cloud SQL in the `europe-west3` region. How can you ensure all users get the same experience when using your application?

   A. Deploy another Cloud SQL instance (read-write replica) in `europe-central2`.

   B. Migrate the database to Cloud Spanner.

   C. Add more CPU and RAM resources to your Cloud SQL instance to handle increasing traffic.

   D. Deploy another Cloud SQL instance (read replica) in `europe-central2`.

3. You are looking for a database to store constantly changing data uploaded by millions of various types of sensors in real time. Which database should you choose?

   A. Bigtable, because it offers high throughput and scalability for unstructured data.

   B. BigQuery, because it is petabyte-scale storage that can process such a large amount of data.

   C. Cloud SQL, as this type of data should be stored in a relational database where advanced querying and operations on data are available.

   D. Only Cloud Spanner can handle such an amount of data.

4. Your team plans to deploy a Cloud SQL instance as a backend of their new gaming application. They expect massive traffic on the day the game is launched globally, but later, the number of users will most likely drop significantly. So, they asked you for advice on how to make the launch successful:

   A. Firebase is the most optimal database for gaming.

   B. Cloud SQL is a perfect fit. They should go with the largest machine type available and create a read replica in another region. Once the traffic decreases, to save costs, they can scale the database down by changing the machine type to a smaller one on the replica first (power off is required), promoting it to the primary instance, and downsizing the "new" replica in the next step.

   C. Cloud SQL is a perfect fit. They should use the medium-sized machine type and create a read replica in another region. Once the traffic increases, to adjust the throughput, they can scale the database up by changing the machine type to a larger one on the replica first (power off is required), promoting it to the primary instance, and changing the machine type for the "new" replica in the next step.

   D. They should use Spanner instead of Cloud SQL because its instances can span the globe so that all users will have the same experience (similar latency). Also, they can deploy the Autoscaler tool in Spanner, which could take care of increasing or reducing the number of nodes or processing units based on utilization.

5. Your manager is concerned about the Google Cloud Storage bill. He thought the Archive tier would be an inexpensive replacement to tape backups, but after running it for a month, it costs too much. Also, he is sure no backups were deleted. How can you explain it?

    A. It must be a mistake. You open a support ticket to have this sorted out.

    B. You investigate your billing report looking for early deletion charges, which must be the only reason for the increased Google Cloud Storage cost this month.

    C. You meet with the backup admin. It turns out backup copies weren't tagged as an archive, so the backup solution ran daily consistency checks on those objects, meaning operation charges were applied. You deactivate this option.

    D. You should activate Autoclass on the bucket and let it automatically adjust the storage class based on the access pattern.

6. Your team is working on a new application that will recommend nearby restaurants for mobile users in your city based on other users' ratings. Unfortunately, the mobile network coverage is poor in your city. The team worries users will lose interest if this application stops working when a mobile is offline. Your role is to help to overcome this issue:

    A. You recommend Firestore as it can handle caching application data on offline mobile devices.

    B. You suggest adding a mobile app code to monitor the network coverage. If it detects a drop in coverage, it will display random pictures of restaurants to keep the user engaged.

    C. You decide to use Memorystore, which is perfect for caching data.

    D. You propose adding a code to the mobile application to monitor the coverage. Once it detects it is dropping, it immediately pushes all changes to the Firestore database.

7. Your team selected Memorystore for Redis to keep player profiles for their gaming application. Your task is to protect the database against unexpected data loss in case of failure. What architecture should you recommend, assuming everyone is concerned about costs?

    A. The Basic tier would be sufficient as it costs less than the Standard tier. In addition, the underlying hardware and a Redis instance are monitored, so nothing should happen to the database.

    B. Standard tier deployed with no read replicas.

    C. Standard tier with three read replicas, one per zone in the region.

    D. The Basic tier would be sufficient as it costs less than the Standard tier. You can schedule continuous backups of the database to avoid data loss.

Answers

The answers to the preceding questions are as follows:

1B, 2D, 3A, 4D, 5C, 6A, 7B

9

Configuring and Implementing Networking Components

This chapter will explore how to build a network and configure network services for your workloads in Google Cloud. We are going to cover the following topics:

- Virtual Private Cloud

- Hybrid networking

- Securing cloud networks with firewall rules

- Cloud DNS

- Network load balancing

Networking is the foundation of every system architecture. However, connecting internal cloud workloads across projects, exposing services to the internet, or building a hybrid network between an on-premises location and Google Cloud can be challenging. Therefore, it is worth understanding how Google Cloud's network services portfolio could be used to build secure and reliable architectures.

Throughout this chapter, we will explore the concept of a **Virtual Private Cloud** (**VPC**) and its application in securing and connecting networks. Additionally, we will gain insight into the functioning of the DNS service in Google Cloud and identify the appropriate network load balancers for different types of workloads.

Virtual Private Cloud

A VPC is a networking service for your Google Cloud workloads, such as Compute Engine VMs or GKE. It is commonly referred to as a logical representation of a network in a cloud. Unlike a physical network in a data center, all its complex networking aspects are abstracted, allowing users to focus solely on consumption rather than configuration.

A VPC is a global service that consists of one or more subnets that can be created in the same or different Google Cloud regions. Google Cloud uses subnets to organize and manage resources in a VPC by dividing it into regional segments. A subnet is identified by a region and an IP range defined in **Classless Inter-Domain Routing (CIDR)** notation. CIDR can be described as a group of IP addresses used by a network (a subnet, in this case). It looks like a regular IP address but ends with a slash and a number. The number after the slash tells you how many addresses are within the range. For example, a CIDR IP address in IPv4 of `10.0.1.0/24` can be used by a subnet that needs 256 IP addresses (from `10.0.1.0` to `10.0.1.255`).

Regardless of their region, subnets in the same VPC are seamlessly connected without requiring any extra setup, such as VPN. Communication between workloads in the same VPC is internal and does not travel over the internet.

Please note that it is possible to create multiple VPCs for each project. However, they will be separated from each other by default.

The communication between workloads in the same VPC, but also to different VPCs or external environments, is always controlled by the firewall rules of a VPC. For example, even if VMs in different subnets of the same VPC should be able to communicate with each other, firewall rules that explicitly allow this communication must exist. We will cover firewall rules later in this chapter.

The following diagram shows an example of a project with two VPCs: VPC A and VPC B. Each VPC has three subnets configured in different regions, including Subnet1, Subnet2, and Subnet3 in VPC A, and SubnetA, SubnetB, and SubnetC in VPC B. Subnets within the same VPC are already connected and do not require any additional configuration. However, communication between workloads in different VPCs will require a VPN connection or VPC peering. In both cases, firewall rules must be in place to enable traffic between workloads:

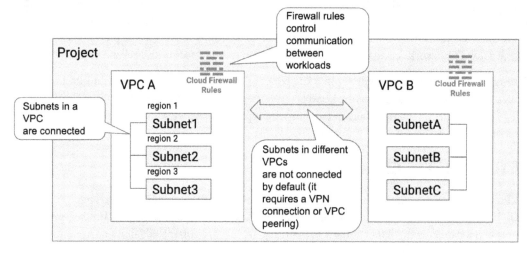

Figure 9.1 – Subnets in the same VPC can communicate with each other. Firewall rules control this communication. Subnets in different VPCs require additional setup to connect

You can create a VPC network, subnets, and firewall rules in Google Cloud Console or using `gcloud` `compute` commands. For example, to create `my-vpc-network` in the `my-demo-project` project, the following command could be used:

```
gcloud compute networks create my-vpc-network --project=my-demo-
project --subnet-mode=custom --mtu=1460 --bgp-routing-mode=regional
```

To create a `10.0.0.0/24` subnet called `my-first-subnet` in `my-vpc-network` in `europe-central2` region, you could use this command:

```
gcloud compute networks subnets create my-first-subnet --project=my-
demo-project --range=10.0.0.0/24 --stack-type=IPV4_ONLY --network=my-
vpc-network --region=europe-central2
```

To create a new VPC in Google Cloud Console, go to the **VPC networks** menu and select *Create VPC network* (shown in *Figures 9.2* and *9.3*). You can also add additional subnets to an existing VPC by editing an existing subnet.

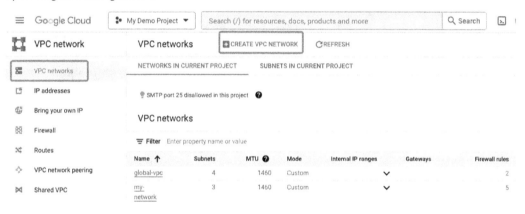

Figure 9.2 – Creating a VPC network in Google Cloud Console

It is important to note that subnets can be created either during the initial creation of a VPC network or at any point thereafter.

To connect to workloads in `my-first-subnet` or other subnets in `my-vpc-network`, firewall rules that allow this communication must exist. To create a firewall rule called `ssh-rdp-ping` that allows all users (from the default source range, `0.0.0.0/0`) to access all instances in `my-vpc-network` on TCP ports `22` (SSH) and `3389` (RDP) and to send a ping (ICMP), the following command could be used:

```
gcloud compute firewall-rules create ssh-rdp-ping  --network my-vpc-
network --allow tcp:22,tcp:3389,icmp
```

With the command from the preceding example, we created a subnet in `my-vpc-network` with an assigned IP address range in CIDR notation (`10.0.0.0/24`). The mode where you manually assign IP address ranges to subnets is called **Custom mode**. Alternatively, **Automatic mode** could be used.

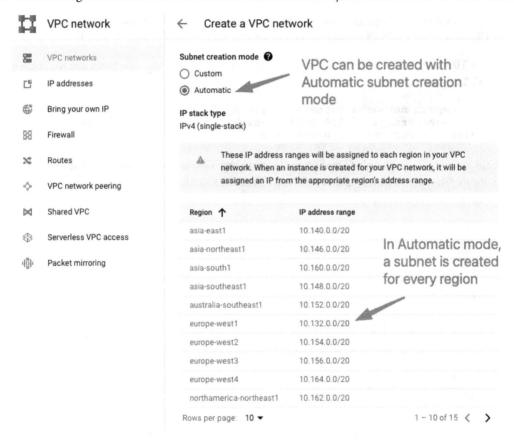

Figure 9.3 – Automatic subnet creation mode in VPC

Here are the differences between these modes:

- **Automatic mode**: This is where subnets are pre-populated for every region in a VPC network. There is a dedicated CIDR of `10.128.0.0/9` that is used for this purpose. Every region has a `/20` subnet, which allows up to 4,094 addresses to be created, excluding network, gateway, second-to-last, and broadcast addresses. In the preceding screenshot, you can see that `10.160.0.0/20` will be used by a subnet in the `asia-south1` region. When a new region is created, additional subnets are automatically added to a VPC in **auto mode**. Using auto mode doesn't prevent you from adding more subnets manually later. A VPC network configured with auto mode can transition to custom mode, but this action can't be reversed.

- **Custom mode**: This is where no subnets are automatically created. You control which regions you want subnets to be created in and what their IP ranges and mask length will be. The minimal range that can be configured is /29. You are responsible for planning ranges with custom mode, so there is no CIDR overlap. Custom mode can't be switched to **auto mode**. Also, you can expand a custom mode subnet, but a shrink operation is not allowed. The 10.0.0.0/24 subnet, my-first-subnet, from our example, can be expanded to /23 with the following command:

```
$ gcloud compute networks subnets expand-ip-range my-first-
subnet --region=europe-central2 --prefix-length=23
The IP range of subnetwork [my-first-subnet] will be expanded
from 10.0.0.0/24 to 10.0.0.0/23. This operation may take several
minutes to complete and cannot be undone.
```

In the following example, there are two VPCs – global-vpc, with three subnets deployed in three regions across the globe, and regional, with two subnets deployed in one region only. VPC is a global service, but with **custom mode**, you can choose where to create networks:

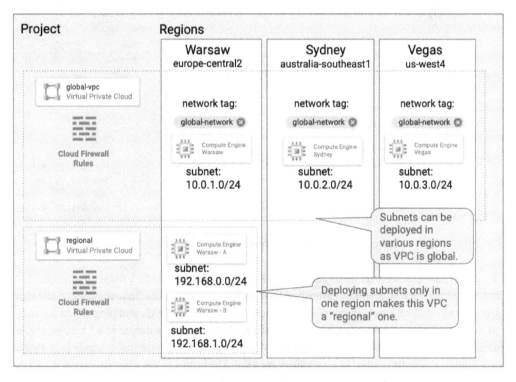

Figure 9.4 – Custom mode subnets in VPC

When managing a VPC, it is crucial to understand which roles are required to create networking resources and which roles allow you to assign resources to workloads. For example, a predefined IAM **Compute Network Admin** role provides full control over all network resources except firewall rules and SSL certificates. On the other hand, **Compute Security Admins** role can only manage firewall rules and SSL certificates. A **Compute Network User** role allows you to assign subnets from a **Shared VPC** to local workloads.

Networking for Compute Engine VMs

The *GCE network* section in *Chapter 4* describes what a Compute Engine VM creation task looks like. One of the demonstrated steps was assigning a VM to a VPC subnet and selecting a static/ephemeral public/private IP address for a VM. Once a VM has been created, it can communicate with other VMs in a VPC if firewall rules allow it. Note that a Compute Engine VM can only be deployed in a region where a local subnet exists.

In *Figure 9.4*, there are three VMs named `warsaw`, `vegas`, and `sydney` that have been deployed in different regions of `global-vpc`. The following screenshot provides a Google Cloud Console view of their deployment:

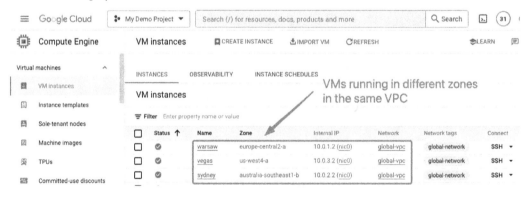

Figure 9.5 – Compute Engine VMs in global-vpc

Once a firewall rule has been set up to accept ICMP and TCP traffic within VMs with a `global-network` tag (network tags will be described later in this chapter in the *Securing cloud networks with firewall rules* section), we can open an SSH session to one of the VMs and ping the other two. The following screenshot shows a console view for the `sydney` VM. The output of a `traceroute` command to the `vegas` VM and the `warsaw` VM shows that they are just a single hop away. Although traffic crosses the globe (latency values are a good indicator of the distance between VMs), the network structure for subnets in regions in the same VPC is simple:

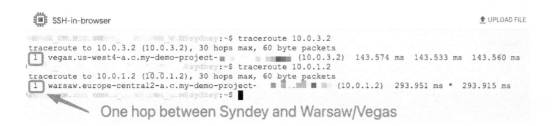

Figure 9.6 – Compute Engine VMs that belong to the same VPC are just one
hop away from each other, despite being deployed across the globe

To better understand the behavior of Compute Engine VMs, you can enable **VPC Flow Logs** on the
subnets in which they are deployed. The **VPC Flow Logs** feature is configured at the subnet level. It
takes samples of network flows that can be used for further security analysis or troubleshooting. For
example, the following screenshot shows a sample flow that's been captured between the `warsaw`
and `sydney` VMs when viewed in **Logs Explorer**:

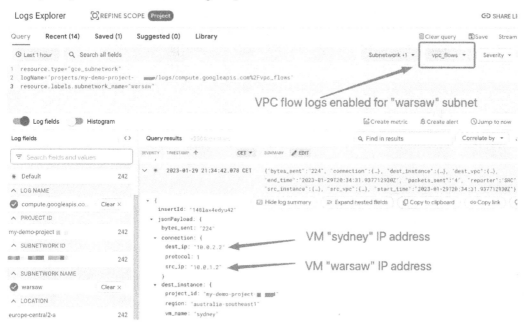

Figure 9.7 – The VPC flow logs of the "warsaw" subnet in Logs Explorer
showing the "warsaw" VM communicating with the "sydney" VM

Another useful feature that can be used to analyze and troubleshoot connectivity between VMs is
Connectivity Test from the **Network Intelligence** section:

Figure 9.8 – The Connectivity Test view with a test that verifies if the
ping sent from the "sydney" VM can reach the "warsaw" VM

When creating a **Connectivity Test** view, you must define the protocol that you want to test, such as
ICMP, TCP, or UDP. The source endpoint can be, among others, an IP address, a VM, App Engine,
Cloud SQL, a GKE cluster control plane or Cloud Run, a destination endpoint, or a port number.
Then, **Connectivity Test** checks the configuration between endpoints and sends packets to check if
the communication is working. As a result, you either get a confirmation that the test was successful
or a possible reason for failing. For example, the following screenshot presents a failed ping test, where
traffic was dropped because of a `block-traffic` firewall rule:

Figure 9.9 – The result of Connectivity Test shows it is a firewall
rule that blocks communication between VMs

Setting up connectivity for Compute Engine VMs can seem to be difficult, especially if you're just starting. With different subnets and multiple firewall rules to deal with, it's easy to feel overwhelmed. Thankfully, there are tools such as VPC Flow Logs and Connectivity Center that can provide valuable insights into any potential issues. This makes it much easier to troubleshoot any problems you may encounter.

Shared VPCs

Managing networking can be challenging when an organization owns multiple projects with multiple VPCs and subnets. For example, someone will have to track if users that create subnets don't use IP ranges that overlap (if some VPCs need to be connected in the future). In addition, someone will have to ensure that all projects have unified security settings and firewall rules. Also, if projects need access to an on-premises environment, each one will come with an additional dedicated VPN gateway or Interconnect and Cloud Router to manage.

To simplify network architectures, you can leverage a Shared VPC, where a **host project** shares a VPC with multiple **service projects** within the same organization. It is a centralized approach to multi-project networking. As a result, you get fewer networking components to manage, but you can still keep separate budgets for different projects. Service projects can continue to use their standalone VPC subnets. Still, the idea is only to use networking services such as subnets, routers, VPN gateways, and Interconnect links defined centrally in a host project. A single service project can only be attached to one host project. Usually, host projects are managed by networking and security admins, who prepare all network configurations and enforce firewall and security policies. Owners of service projects can then focus on their workloads.

The following diagram shows a host project that has a VPC and Interconnect to on-premises and regional subnets set up by a networking team with firewall rules created by a security team.

There are three service projects – **production**, **test**, and **analytics** – that have Compute Engine VMs with assigned subnets from the host project. With Shared VPC, users in these service projects don't have to worry about setting up or managing the network themselves; they can simply use it:

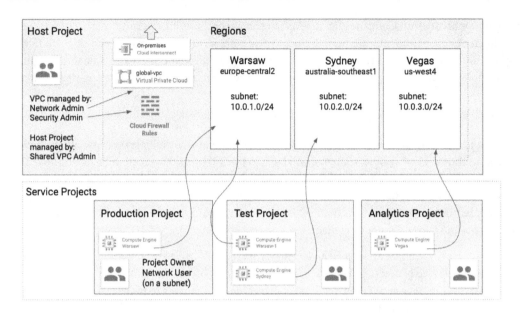

Figure 9.10 – Shared VPC concept where VPC subnets deployed in a host
project are used by Compute Engine VMs in a service project

To get a better understanding of how to set up a Shared VPC, let's take a closer look at the necessary configuration steps:

1. To provision a Shared VPC, you need to go to the **Shared VPC** page in the **VPC network** section. In addition to selecting a host project, you can choose to share all subnets in a VPC or select individual ones. Note that you need a **Shared VPC Admin** role (at the organizational level) to set up a host project:

Figure 9.11 – Setting up a Shared VPC where three individual subnets will be shared with service projects

2. In the next step, in the same **Shared VPC** view, with a **Shared VPC Admin** role, you can add projects from your organization that will be allowed to use subnets from a Shared VPC. Next, you must delegate access to selected or all subnets of the Shared VPC to Service Project Admins by assigning them a **Network User** role on selected subnets. Service Project Admins are usually owners of their projects, which allows them to create resources in service projects such as Compute Engine VMs.

3. Once the project becomes a service project, its VM instances, instance templates, or load balancers can have networks from a host project assigned to them. For example, the following screenshot demonstrates a VM instance creation view with the option to select a shared subnet:

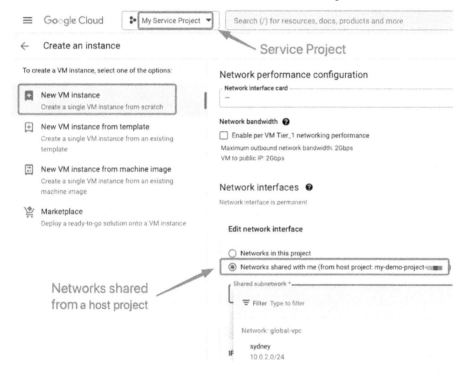

Figure 9.12 – Creating a Compute Engine VM with an interface in a shared subnet

In the next section, we will investigate another approach to multi-project networking: VPC network peering.

VPC network peering

VPC network peering allows private connectivity across two VPCs while keeping them administratively separated. Peered VPCs can either be in the same or different projects; they may even belong to different organizations. As opposed to a Shared VPC, managing VPC peering is decentralized. Network and security admins at both ends manage their routing and firewall tables without having access to a peer VPC.

VPC peering provides several advantages. First, it prevents VPC traffic from being exposed to the internet, resulting in increased security and reduced latency. It also offers cost savings compared to using public IP addresses for communication.

To configure VPC peering, you can use a predefined **Compute Network Admin** role. In the **VPC network** menu, there is a section for **VPC network peering**, as shown in *Figure 9.13*.

This is where a peering connection can be initiated. It's important to note that when you create a peering, unique IP ranges for subnets in both VPCs are required for the connection to be successfully established. A reminder of this requirement is given during the process:

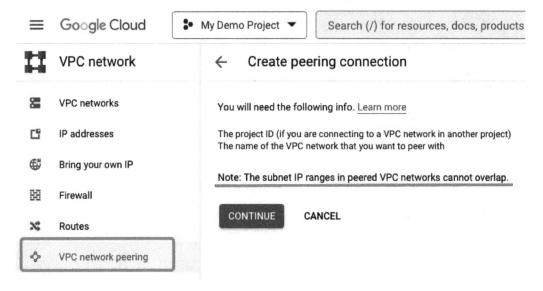

Figure 9.13 – Creating a peering connection between two VPCs

To establish a peering connection, you must indicate the VPC in your project that will be used for peering and the location of the destination VPC. Peering can occur within the same project or a different one. *Figure 9.14* is a follow-up to the peering connection setup depicted in *Figure 9.13*, where you can choose the network you wish to peer.

When the peering is ready, it will be in an **inactive** state because a peering needs to be configured at both ends. This means that once one side is done, a network administrator that manages the other side will have to go through similar steps for both ends to communicate. Either side can also remove the peering to stop communication.

Note that VPC peering is not transitive, and only directly peered VPCs can communicate. So, for example, if we have three VPCs called VPC-A, VPC-B, and VPC-C, and if VPC-A peers with VPC-B, and VPC-B peers with VPC-C, VPC-A won't be able to communicate with VPC-C.

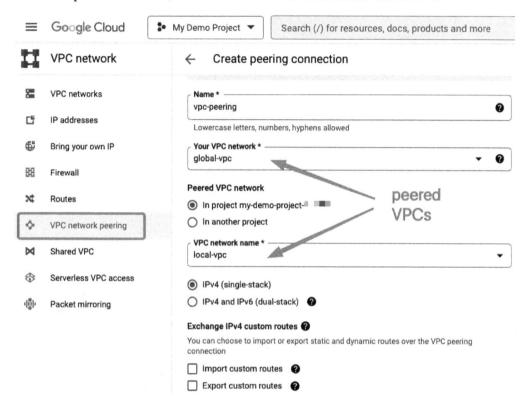

Figure 9.14 – Creating a peering connection between two VPCs in the same project

The following screenshot presents how routes are exchanged between VPCs. Take a look at the my-vpc-peering details of the local-vpc network. The local-vpc network peers with global-vpc. Both belong to the same project. On the right is a **global-vpc** view that lists subnets in this VPC. The peering connection details for my-vpc-peering on the left list all the routes imported from global-vpc. You can see that the subnets match those from the **global-vpc** subnet view. When a VPC peering finalizes, both sides exchange information about their local subnets so that the opposite side can use this information and route traffic toward these subnets:

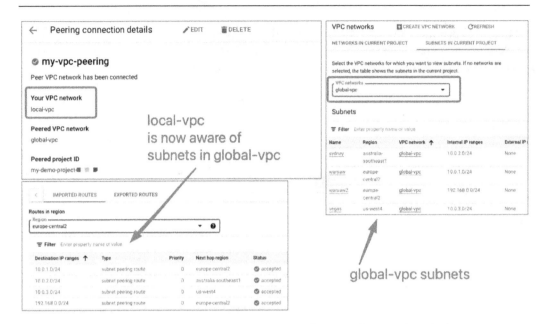

Figure 9.15 – Creating a Compute Engine VM with an interface in a shared subnet

VPC peers export all their subnet routes. There is no option to advertise routes selectively. If a VPC also has custom routes (such as a route to an on-premises subnet via a VPN tunnel or a static route), you can import/export such static and dynamic routes via a VPC peering connection. Similar to subnet routes, you can't select individual custom routes.

The following screenshot presents an example of a VPC peering between two VPCs under a single project. global-vpc has three subnets: in Warsaw (10.0.1.0/24) in europe-central2, in Sydney (10.0.2.0/24) in australia-southeast1, and in Vegas (10.0.3.0/24) in us-west4 region. There is also the custom route to the on-premises site in Zurich in the europe-west6 (10.99.99.0/24) region. local-vpc has one subnet in Zurich (172.16.0.0/24) in the europe-west6 region. When local-vpc peers with global-vpc, it exports its route, 172.16.0.0/24, and imports routes from global-vpc: 10.0.1.0/24, 10.0.2.0/24, and 10.0.3.0/24. Also, because importing custom routes is enabled, it receives a route to the on-premises site: 10.99.99.0/24. A Compute Engine VM located in Zurich in the europe-west6 region can communicate with VMs in the global-vpc region and on-premises subnet, assuming firewall rules allow it.

Note that although we cannot select which subnet routes are imported/exported over peering, we can leverage firewall rules to control this traffic.

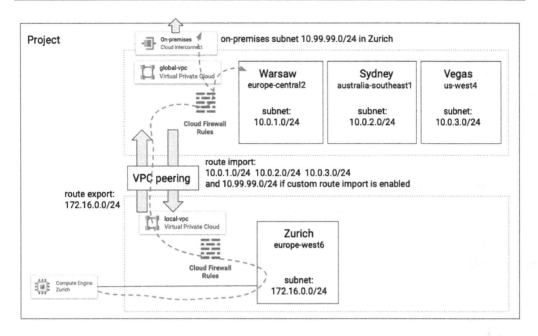

Figure 9.16 – Example of VPC peering between two VPCs

VPC peering and Shared VPC approach multi-project networking differently. Shared VPC is a centralized approach where network and security admins consolidate networking resources in a host project. Both host and service projects need to belong to the same organization. Shared VPC is often considered a concept that introduces less administrative work. But it cannot be used in scenarios where we want to connect two VPCs in the same project. Alternatively, VPC peering is a decentralized approach where administrators can only manage resources at their end. Connected VPCs can belong to the same project or a different one, even to a different organization.

Ultimately, the choice between Shared VPC and VPC peering will depend on your specific needs and goals for your network.

Now that we've explored how to establish a network connection between Google Cloud networks in different VPCs, let's look at how Google Cloud networks can be linked with on-premises networks.

Hybrid networking

This section will investigate how you can create a hybrid cloud by connecting your on-premises environment to Google. Note that similar mechanisms will allow you to build multi-cloud architectures by connecting your resources in another cloud with Google Cloud.

Cloud Router

When two networking environments are connected, they need a way to inform their peers about their local subnets. Furthermore, route propagation should be automatic, as new subnets can be added or old ones can be deleted at any time. Google Cloud uses the **Border Gateway Protocol** (**BGP**) protocol to exchange routing information with on-premises (or another cloud) devices.

Cloud Router is the service that speaks the BGP protocol in Google Cloud. It is a Google-managed, highly available service that advertises routes to VPC subnets via either Interconnect or VPN connection toward an on-premises site (or to other clouds). Cloud Router is a regional resource and belongs to a VPC. It uses a unique private or public **Autonomous System Number** (**ASN**) for BGP identification.

In the **Hybrid connectivity** section, there is a **Cloud routers** creation page. To create a new Cloud Router instance, you must provide its name, ASN number, the region where it will be configured, and the VPC where it will reside. Additionally, you need to select how it will advertise the routes of its VPC. See the following figure for reference:

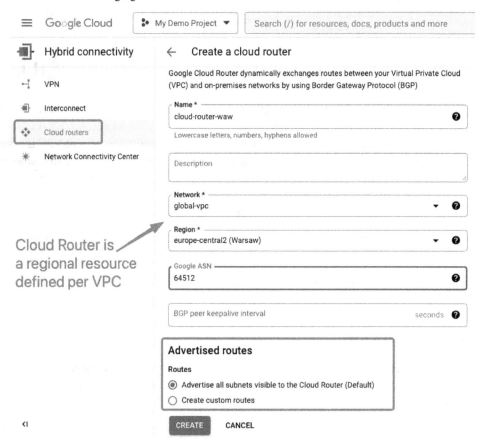

Figure 9.17 – Creating a Cloud Router instance that advertises all visible VPC subnets

There are two types of routes that Cloud Router can advertise:

- **Default route advertisement**: This is where Cloud Router dynamically advertises all subnet routes created in a VPC. If a VPC uses regional routing mode, Cloud Router will advertise only subnets from its region. Alternatively, if a VPC uses global routing mode, Cloud Router will advertise subnets from all regions.

- **Custom route advertisement**: This is where you can select which routes Cloud Router advertises. For example, this option can be used to advertise only a subset of local subnets or subnets outside a VPC.

In addition to being a BGP speaker, Cloud Router is also used as a control plane for a **Cloud NAT** service. Cloud NAT is a managed, regional service that allows workloads such as Compute Engine VMs and GKE to create outbound internet connections without the need for a public IP.

High availability VPN

VPN is often considered the fastest way to connect to Google Cloud. It uses a public network and doesn't require additional physical connection setup. Two types of Cloud VPN gateways at Google Cloud are **high availability (HA) VPN** and **Classic VPN**. Classic VPN doesn't offer high availability and BGP support. It only supports static routing. Google recommends using HA VPN whenever possible and Classic VPN only in cases where on-premises VPN devices don't support BGP. This section will focus on the HA VPN type of gateway.

A VPN gateway is a regional resource that uses IPSec tunnels with IKE encryption to establish a secure connection over the internet. It uses a pre-shared key to encrypt the traffic, so both sides of the connection need to know the key. Cloud VPN comes with external IP addresses that will be used to create tunnels over a public network. Although it is possible to set up only one tunnel, two or four (to another cloud provider) are required for 99.99% availability. Each Cloud VPN tunnel supports up to 3 Gbps together for ingress and egress traffic.

The following screenshot presents an example of a VPN tunnel configuration between the Google Cloud VPC `global-vpc` and `on-premises` devices. Although VPC is global and has subnets in the `europe-cental2` (`10.0.1.0/24`), `australia-southeast` (`10.0.2.0/24`), and `us-west4` (`10.0.3.0/24`) regions, VPN Gateway and Cloud Router are regional resources, which in this case are deployed in the `europe-central2` region only. The VPN gateway has two interfaces, each with a Public IP, that are used to set up two tunnels to the `on-premises` site. On the `on-premises` site, there are two VPN gateways, each with one interface with a public IP address. Behind the VPN gateways is a router that has a route to an `on-premises` subnet (`10.99.0.0/24`). Both sides are connected with two VPN tunnels. Two BGP sessions are established between Cloud Router (ASN `64512`) and the `on-premises` router (ASN `64513`). Assuming Cloud Router uses default route advertisement and the VPC uses global routing, routes to all VPC subnets are advertised by Cloud Router and visible to the `on-premises` router. Also, the `on-premises` route,

`10.99.99.0/24`, is visible to all subnets in `global-vpc`. Note that even if routes are visible, end-to-end communication between workloads in the cloud and `on-premises` is still controlled by firewalls that need to allow this external traffic:

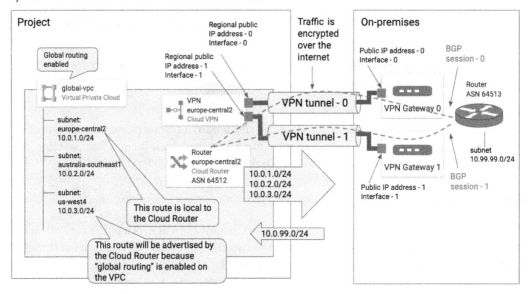

Figure 9.18 – Example of a VPN setup between a Google Cloud VPC and an on-premises environment

The following steps are required on the Google Cloud side to set up a VPN between Google Cloud and on-premises or another cloud:

1. Create a Cloud Router in a selected region, as presented in *Figure 9.17*.

2. Create a Cloud VPN gateway for the same region and VPC where the Cloud Router was configured. When a gateway is created, public IP addresses of its interfaces are generated and published so that they can be used to configure the tunnels on the other side.

3. Add a peer VPN gateway (on-premises/other cloud side) by providing a name and number of VPN interfaces, along with their public IP addresses.

4. It is also possible to create a VPN connection between two VPCs in the same or a different Google Cloud project. In this case, you need to have access to peer resources. Also, a Cloud VPN gateway and a Cloud Router in this project need to exist before this setup.

5. Add VPN tunnels between both ends. Each tunnel needs to have a unique name. In this step, you must also set up IKE encryption and generate a pre-shared key.

6. Configure peer tunnel endpoints on the on-premises/another cloud side.

7. Configure a BGP session for each tunnel, where you provide the name and ASN of a peer router. You can decide to set up BGP IP and peer BGP IP addresses manually or automatically. During the BGP session setup, you can choose to either advertise all routes visible to the Cloud Router or create custom routes.

8. The same BGP session setup needs to be created on the on-premises/other cloud side. It is recommended that you aggregate routes on-premises and ensure they don't overlap with the VPC subnet ranges.

Now that we've covered the steps to establish a VPN connection between on-premises and Google Cloud networks in a VPC, we can consider another option: creating Cloud Interconnect. We will also examine the differences between these two approaches

Interconnect

While VPN is considered the fastest way to connect to Google Cloud, **Cloud Interconnect** is the fastest connection to Google Cloud.

Like VPN, Cloud Interconnect enables communication based on internal IP addresses between workloads that are on-premises (or in another cloud) and created via a VPC. The difference between VPN and Interconnect is that Interconnect uses a dedicated physical connection and offers higher throughput. At the same time, VPN traverses the public network and offers from 1.5 to 3 Gbps per tunnel.

There are two types of Cloud Interconnect:

*   **Dedicated Interconnect**: This is a direct physical connection between your data center and Google Cloud network in a common colocation facility. The following capacities are supported: `1x 10` Gbps up to `8x 10` Gbps, `1x 100` Gbps up `to 2x 100` Gbps. Exchanging routes between two sites requires a BGP session to be set up.

> **Note**
>
> Check the following link to find a list of Google's collocation facilities where your network can meet Google's edge point of presence: `https://cloud.google.com/network-connectivity/docs/interconnect/concepts/choosing-colocation-facilities`.

*   **Partner Interconnect**: This is a direct physical connection between your data center and an authorized service provider's facility. It is then a partner's responsibility to establish connectivity to Google Cloud. The available capacity per link is smaller compared to Dedicated Interconnect; it starts from 50 Mbps up to 10 Gbps per connection. Partner Interconnect is used when Google's colocation facility is too far from a data center, or your workload's bandwidth needs are below 10 Gbps. Also, connecting to a partner's facility is preferred if you want to use a single physical connection to reach multiple cloud providers.

    With **Partner Interconnect**, you can either use a **Layer 2** connection, where you are responsible for establishing the BGP session between a Cloud Router and your router on-premises, or a **Layer 3** connection, where your service provider establishes a BGP session between a router in the service provider network and your Cloud Router:

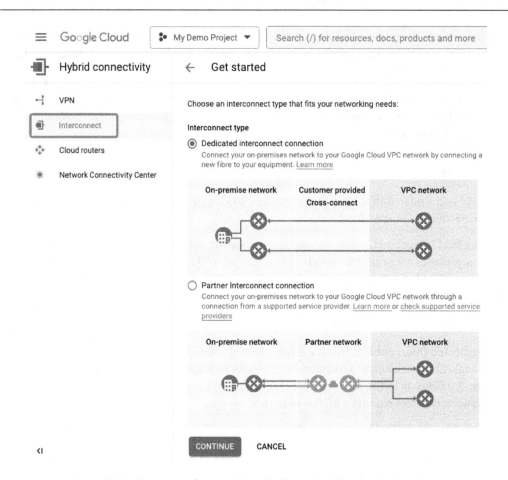

Figure 9.19 – Two types of connection – Dedicated and Partner Interconnect

> **Note**
> Check the following link to find a list of supported service providers that offer Layer 2 and Layer 3 connectivity to Google Cloud: `https://cloud.google.com/network-connectivity/docs/interconnect/concepts/service-providers`.

Securing cloud networks with firewall rules

As mentioned earlier in this chapter, even though subnets that belong to the same VPC are connected, it is the firewall's role to control communication between Compute Engine VM workloads. The same applies to networks connected via Interconnect/VPN or VPC peering. When routing information is exchanged, and connectivity is established, the next step is configuring firewall rules to allow a specific type of traffic to flow between Compute Engine instances.

By definition, a VPC is an isolated domain where almost every traffic type must be implicitly allowed. Firewall rules are applied at the VPC level. Because VPC is a global service, firewall rules are also global. With a single firewall rule, you can allow or block a specific communication that crosses regions or comes from an external network to instances in various zones.

Although firewall rules are defined at the VPC level, they are executed per VM instance. This is because firewalling in Google Cloud is distributed. As a result, there is no risk that a single firewall device could become a bottleneck when traffic increases. The following screenshot presents a section of the **VPC network** view while creating a new VPC network. The proposed initial firewall rules list is presented in the **Firewall rules** section:

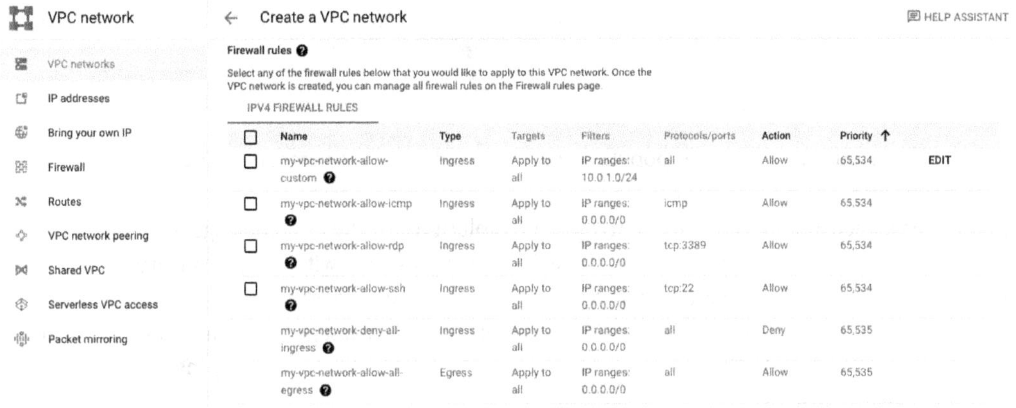

Figure 9.20 – The pre-populated list of firewall rules when creating a VPC

Note that two firewall rules on this list cannot be removed. Both have the lowest priority of 65535. The implied `deny-all-ingress` rule blocks all incoming connections to every VM instance in this VPC. The implied `allow-all-egress` rule allows all VM instances in this VPC to send traffic to any destination. Firewall rules are stateful, so the matching response can also be received by the source VM when a connection is allowed.

The following screenshot depicts an example situation where only two implied firewall rules were configured for the `my-vpc-network` VPC. When `vm-a` sends a ping to `vm-b`, even though they belong to the same subnet, `warsaw-subnet`, in the same `europe-central2` region, the firewall rules are evaluated for both individually. The ping message is allowed to egress a `vm-a` interface because of the `allow-all-egress` rule. And `vm-a` is allowed to receive a reply to the ping message because firewall rules are stateful in Google Cloud. On the other hand, `vm-b` is not allowed to receive any traffic because of the `deny-all-ingress` rule, so it will not receive the ping message. So, even though `vm-a` could receive a reply, it won't be sent. But if `vm-a` pings a responsive resource outside the VPC, such as on the public internet (via Cloud NAT), it should be able to get a reply:

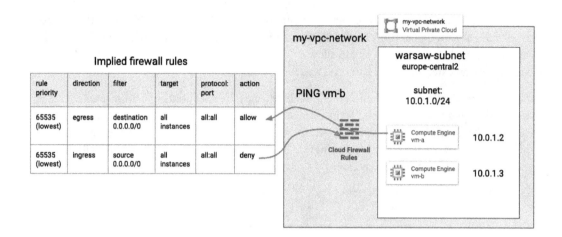

Figure 9.21 – The pre-populated list of firewall rules when creating a VPC

The following screenshot presents one of the possible solutions for the ping message to be received by vm-b. In addition to implied firewall rules, there is a new ingress rule with a higher priority of 65534 (the lower the number, the higher the priority) that takes precedence over the deny-all-ingress rule, and it allows all the instances in the VPC to receive ICMP messages when a sender IP address belongs to 10.0.1.0/24. This way, all VMs in the VPC will be able to receive ping messages from VMs in warsaw-subnet:

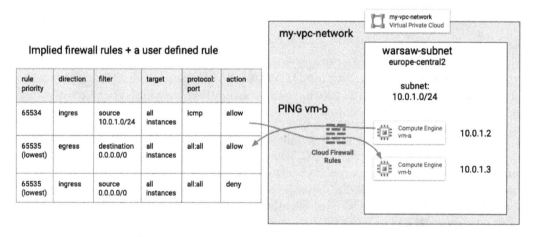

Figure 9.22 – A new firewall rule was added to allow vm-b to receive a ping message from vm-a

If instead of 10.0.1.0/24 (the whole warsaw-subnet IP address range), 0.0.0.0/0 was selected as a source, every source that can reach this VPC could ping all instances in my-vpc-network.

We can narrow down or broaden the possible sources that can access our workloads. However, a good practice is to follow the principle of least privilege and assign the minimum access required for an application to work. It is also recommended to keep the number of firewall rules to a minimum by combining similar flows and grouping VMs and port ranges.

Let's look at the possible options to adjust firewall rules so that only the necessary traffic can pass through.

Firewall rules can be added to a VPC at any time. The predefined **Compute Security Admin** role allows you to create, edit, and delete rules. **Compute Network Viewer** can be used to view rule details. When a new firewall rule is added, you need to give it a name and priority from 0 to 65535. Next, the source and target are defined based on the direction of the flow. Each rule applies to either ingress or egress traffic from the perspective of a target (the instance that receives packets). Also, each rule can either allow or deny access when matched.

A firewall rule can apply to the following targets:

- **All instances in a VPC network**: All Compute Engine VMs deployed in a VPC. GKE clusters and App Engine-flexible environments are also considered targets.

- **Specified target tag**: This allows you to make firewall rules applicable to specific VM instances. Look at *Figure 9.5*. It shows a list of VMs that have a network tag of global-network. This tag can be used if you want to create a firewall rule that applies to those VMs only.

- **Specified service account**: The rule applies only to instances with a specified service account.

The following source filters can be used for ingress rules:

- An IP address range, such as 0.0.0.0/0, which would mean any IP address.

- A source tag, where you can group VMs from which incoming traffic is either allowed or denied to your target.

- A service account (one or more), so the source would be all VMs with a specified associated service account.

- You can also specify a second source filter to build a more accurate firewall rule. Note that you cannot build a filter by combining source tags and service accounts as first and second source filters.

In the **VPC network** menu, there is a **Firewall** section; this is where you can create firewall rules. The following figure shows the available options for rule creation, such as **Direction of traffic**, **Action on match**, and **Targets**. Take a look to see how you can customize your firewall settings:

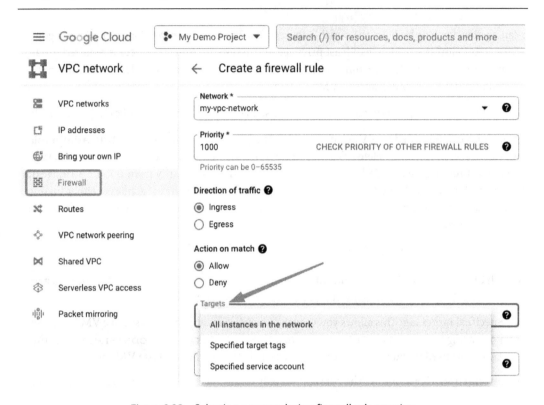

Figure 9.23 – Selecting a target during firewall rule creation

An IP address range, such as 0.0.0.0/0, which would mean any IP address, can be used as a destination filter for egress traffic.

All traffic rules can apply to the following ports and protocols:

- **Allow/Deny all**: All ports and protocols are allowed or denied

- **TCP**: All for all TCP traffic or selected ports, such as 443, or port ranges, such as 20-22

- **UDP**: All for all UDP traffic or selected ports, such as 53, or port ranges, such as 67-69

- **Other**: A protocol name, such as icmp or sctp, or a protocol number

Please take a moment to review the following figure, which shows the next step in creating a firewall rule. Here, you can select a source filter and specify the appropriate ports and protocols for your firewall rule:

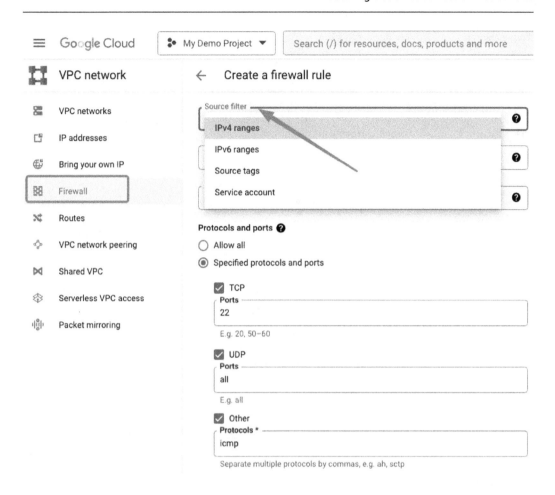

Figure 9.24 – Building a source filter for an ingress firewall rule

If you need to troubleshoot connectivity issues, you can temporarily disable a suspected firewall rule. Alternatively, you can enable firewall logs on a per-firewall rule basis and monitor the logs in **Logs Explorer**:

Name	Type	Targets	Protocols/ports	Action	Network ↑	Hit count ❓	Last hit ❓
my-vpc-network-allow-ssh	Ingress	Apply to ∨	tcp:22	Allow	my-vpc-network	11	2023-02-03 (20:31:00)

Figure 9.25 – When a rule has firewall logs enabled, it shows the rule hit count

One of the benefits of enabling firewall logs is that you can view the overall hit count, as presented in the preceding screenshot. Also, a hit count time graph is available when viewing firewall rule details. The following screenshot shows how firewall logs can be viewed in **Logs Explorer**:

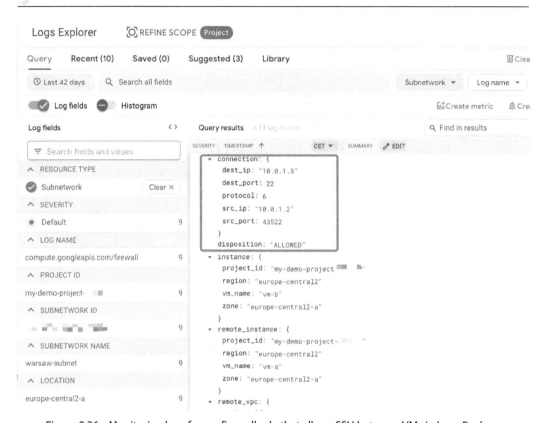

Figure 9.26 – Monitoring logs from a firewall rule that allows SSH between VMs in Logs Explorer

Firewall logs can generate large numbers of logs, so they should be enabled with care, such as during troubleshooting or traffic flow analysis.

Cloud DNS

Compute Engine VM instances use their **metadata servers** as internal DNSs to resolve the IP addresses of other VMs in the same network. A metadata server communicates with Google's public DNS for queries outside a local network. For example, the following figure shows an SSH session to a Compute Engine VM, vm-a, during which it resolves the external address, google.com, even though, as in this case, it doesn't have access to the internet. Also, it can resolve an address of another VM, vm-b, because it is in the same network and, in this case, the same subnet and zone. The **fully qualified domain name (FQDN)** of VMs is vm_name.zone.c.project_id.internal internally:

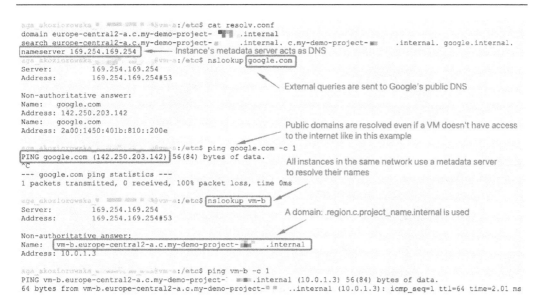

Figure 9.27 – Local metadata server acting as a DNS for a Compute Engine VM

As a metadata server can only resolve addresses for VMs in the same network and users can't edit their configuration, for more advanced architectures that scale outside a VPC network, Cloud DNS should be used.

Cloud DNS is a Google-managed DNS service that translates domain names into IP addresses with 100% availability. It is a global service that is defined at the project level. Cloud DNS is a database where you store the zone's DNS names of your systems and their IP addresses.

Cloud DNS supports two types of zones (where you store records for the same DNS name suffix):

- **Public zone**: This can be accessed from the internet. For example, if you want your application to be accessible by external users, a public zone such as my-external-app.com could be used. An existing domain can be transferred, and a new one can be registered in the **Cloud Domain** view of the **Network services** section.

- **Private zone**: This is accessible within private networks (in a VPC) and can be used in hybrid environments – for example, when a DNS on-premises is configured to forward queries for that zone to Cloud DNS.

Take a look at the following figure. It presents the **Cloud Domain** section of the **Networking services** menu on Google Cloud Console. If you want to configure a public zone for your Cloud DNS, you can use this section to search for an available public domain, check its price, and use Cloud DNS to publish it:

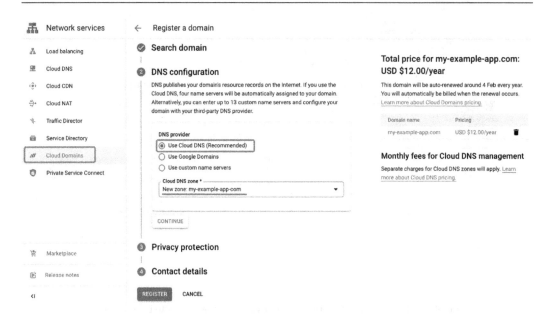

Figure 9.28 – Public domain registration in Google Cloud Console

Let's examine the necessary steps for creating a private DNS zone in Cloud DNS with an example.

Creating a zone in practice

Suppose you received a request to create a new zone called my-zone.com so that the vm-a (10.0.1.2) and vm-b (10.0.0.3) Compute Engine VMs that are deployed in my-vpc-network can communicate with each other using the vm-a.my-zone.com and vm-b.my-zone.com FQDNs. Follow these steps:

1. To create a new DNS zone, go to the **Cloud DNS** view in the **Network services** section. First, you need to specify **Zone type**, either **Private** or **Public**, and a zone name – that is, my-zone. com. In this case, it will be a private zone. Also, you need to specify which VPC is allowed to see my-zone.com. Both VMs use my-vpc-network, so this one should be selected:

Figure 9.29 – Creating a private zone my-zone.com

2. Once the zone has been created, you need to add the vm-a and vm-b Compute Engine VMs to **RECORD SETS**. A record set is a collection of DNS records in a zone that share the same DNS name and type:

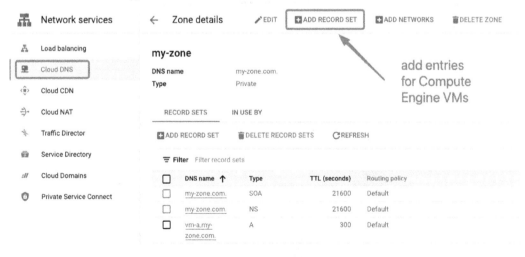

Figure 9.30 – Zone details view for Cloud DNS

3. When you create a record set for a Compute Engine VM, you only need to provide its name and IP address. As shown in the following screenshot, for vm-b, it will be 10.0.1.3. The DNS name for vm-b will be vm-b.my-zone.com:

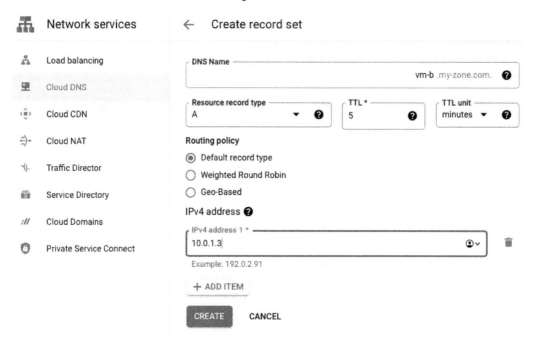

Figure 9.31 – Creating a record set for vm-b

4. When a record set is created, it is visible in the **Zone details** view:

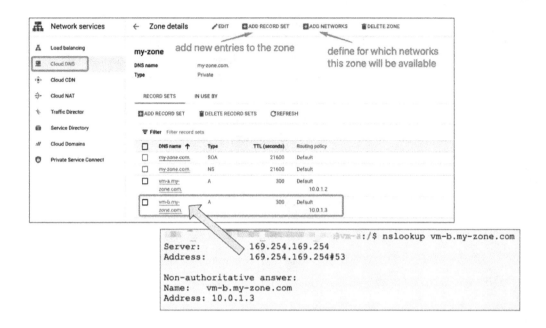

Figure 9.32 – Creating a record set for a Compute Engine VM

5. Once a zone has been set up, you can SSH to vm-a and check if vm-b.my-zone.com is resolved to 10.0.1.3, as presented in the preceding figure.

Now that we know how to set up a DNS zone for Google Cloud workloads, it's worth exploring the possibilities of using DNS services in hybrid cloud environments.

DNS forwarding for hybrid environments

In architectures where workloads that are on-premises and in Google Cloud need to communicate, along with VPN or Interconnect setup, DNS servers need to be configured so that on-premises sites can resolve Google Cloud zones and vice versa. A process where DNS queries are not handled by an initial server but are forwarded to another one is called **DNS forwarding**.

With Cloud DNS, you can configure the following:

*   **Outbound forwarding**: This is where queries are forwarded from Cloud DNS to a DNS on-premises for a specified private zone and a VPC.

*   **Inbound forwarding**: This is where queries are forwarded from a DNS on-premises to Cloud DNS for a specified private zone.

*   **Alternative DNS Server as a DNS policy**: This is where no zone is defined. All queries from a specified VPC are forwarded to an external DNS server.

Note that you cannot configure forwarding to another VPC. However, if you want VPC-A to forward queries for a specific zone defined in VPC-B, you can achieve this by setting up **DNS peering**. At this point, Cloud DNS in VPC-B can either resolve the address locally or have a forwarding set for this zone to send queries, for example, to a DNS on-premises. Also, **VPC peering** is not required for **DNS peering** to work.

Let's investigate the most popular case for hybrid environments: outbound forwarding. The following figure presents a Google Cloud project with a VPC called `my-vpc-network`:

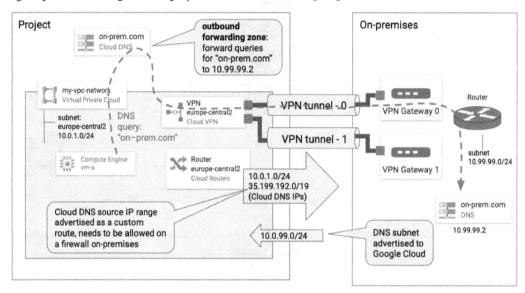

Figure 9.33 – Cloud DNS outbound forwarding for a zone, on-prem.com, for on-premises DNS

The VPC uses a Cloud DNS zone called `on-prem.com` that's been configured to forward queries outside Google Cloud to on-premises DNS `10.99.99.2`. This VPC is connected to an on-premises environment via a VPN connection. Both sides exchange routing information via BGP. When a VM, `vm-a`, in the `my-vpc-network` VPC queries `on-prem.com`, Cloud DNS forwards this query to DNS on-premises. For the DNS to respond to the query on-premises, Cloud Router needs to advertise a Cloud DNS IP range of `35.199.192.0/19`. Addresses from this range are used by Cloud DNS for communication. Although it is from a public IP space, it is not routable over the internet. Therefore, this communication is private and this range needs to be specifically allowed by a firewall on-premises. Once the DNS on-premises sends a reply to Cloud DNS, it will be forwarded to `vm-a`.

So far, we have covered creating and connecting VPCs, setting up firewall rules for workload protection, and ensuring cloud-to-on-premises connectivity. We've also explored the DNS service. However, to achieve optimal network efficiency, there is one important service remaining that we need to discuss – the load balancing service.

Network load balancing

When an application outgrows a single Compute Engine VM size, even of the largest type, it is time to use **managed instance groups** and load balancers to handle larger amounts of traffic.

Refer to *Figure 4.67* in *Chapter 4*, where this concept was initially introduced. A managed instance group is a set of identical Compute Engine instances deployed from a template in a zone or zones in a region. Thanks to the autoscaling feature, the group can dynamically grow or shrink depending on the load. When a health check detects that one of the instances has failed, it is recreated. When combined with a load balancer, a managed instance group can work as the backend of an application. The load balancer's role is, in this case, to distribute traffic to instances based on conditions such as CPU utilization or the number of requests.

A managed instance group is just one of the supported backend types for a load balancer in Google Cloud. Other possible backend workloads, depending on the load balancer's type, are, among others, unmanaged instance groups (instances configured individually and managed by a user) or serverless backends such as App Engine, Cloud Run, or Cloud Functions. Also, Google Cloud Storage can function as a backend that serves static content to users. This section will look into the selected load balancer types for managed instance groups. Note that all load balancer types are managed by Google and don't require installation, patching, and maintenance.

Global external HTTP(S) load balancer

A **global external HTTP(S) load balancer** distributes Layer 7 traffic from the internet to VMs or serverless services. It offers a single public anycast IP address that can be used across multiple backend instances in multiple regions. Requests that come from users are sent to the closest backend instances that can process them. This significantly improves the response time for globally available applications.

Because this type of load balancer faces the internet, it is often configured with **Cloud Armor**. Cloud Armor offers a **Distributed Denial of Service (DDoS)** defense service and **Web Application Firewall (WAF)** services. It can restrict access to an HTTP(S) load balancer closer to a source at the edge of the Google Cloud network to stop the unwanted traffic from flowing to a backend. In addition, with Cloud Armor, you can configure security policies to allow or deny traffic to a backend based on a source IP, an IP range, or the geographical location of a source client.

Also, an HTTP(S) load balancer is often paired with **Cloud Content Delivery Network (Cloud CDN)**. Cloud CDN uses Google's globally distributed points of presence to cache HTTPS content, providing faster delivery to users. When there is a request for specific content in a region and this content is not in a cache, it is forwarded to a load balancer and beyond for backend instances to retrieve it. Once retrieved, it is stored for future requests in the same location.

The following screenshot shows an example of a global external HTTP(S) load balancer serving content to users worldwide. It leverages Cloud Armour to deny traffic from unauthorized users and Cloud CDN to cache frequently requested content. Authorized users can access backend services via a single global public IP address. It is the load balancer's role to direct traffic to the closest backend that can process the request. On the backend side, there are regional managed instance groups with autoscaling enabled. Once the volume of the requests reaches a certain level, another instance is deployed up to a specified maximum value. In this example, users from Warsaw will be served by the backend in `europe-central2`, and the backend in `australia-southeast1` will receive traffic from users in Sydney:

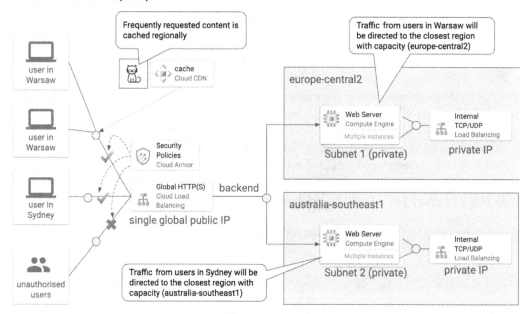

Figure 9.34 – Global external HTTP(S) load balancer example with Cloud CDN and Cloud Armor

If a managed instance group is full or inaccessible, the load balancer will forward traffic to another group with free capacity. Here, the following question may arise: What about users outside of those two regions? For example, what instance group would serve traffic coming from America?

To find an answer, let's look at the following screenshot. It presents an HTTP(s) load balancer configuration for `my-load-balancer` in the **Load balancing** view in the **Networking services** section of Google Cloud Console. The load balancer has been configured as an HTTP load balancer with a static global IP address:

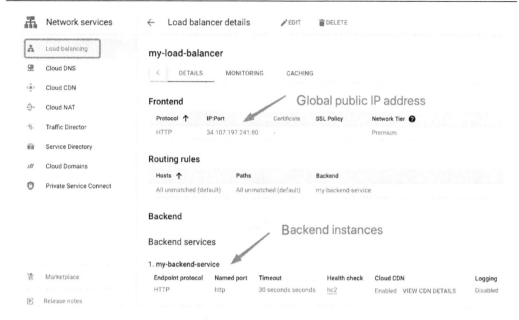

Figure 9.35 – Global external HTTP(S) load balancer view

On the backend side, there is a single backend service, `my-backend-service`; there are also two managed instance groups – `sydney-mig` with instances in `australia-southeast1` and `waw-mig` with instances in `europe-central2`. During the load balancer setup, a health check service called `hc2` is configured to monitor the instance's ability to receive new connections:

Backend

Backend services

1. my-backend-service

Endpoint protocol	Named port	Timeout	Health check	Cloud CDN		Logging
HTTP	http	30 seconds seconds	hc2	Enabled	VIEW CDN DETAILS	Disabled

∨ ADVANCED CONFIGURATIONS

Name ↑	Type	Scope	Healthy	Auto-scaling	Balancing mode	Selected ports ❓	Capacity
sygney-mig	Instance group	australia-southeast1	✓ 1 of 1	On: Target CPU utilisation 80%	Max backend utilisation: 80%	80	100%
waw-mig	Instance group	europe-central2	✓ 1 of 1	On: Target CPU utilisation 80%	Max backend utilisation: 80% Max. RPS: 50 (per instance)	80	100%

Figure 9.36 – The Backend section of the global external HTTP(S) load balancer view

Assuming the service is public and accessible from all over the globe, we can verify how the traffic flows to our backend in the **MONITORING** tab:

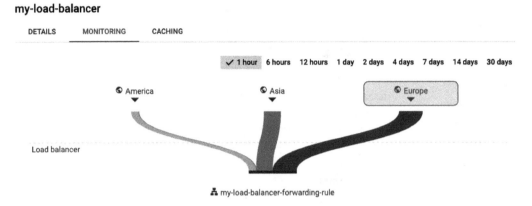

Figure 9.37 – The MONITORING tab of the global external HTTP(S) load balancer view

We can see it originates from America, Asia, and Europe. The stream from Asia lands in `sydney-mig`, the stream from Europe lands in `waw-mig`, and the stream from America also lands in `waw-mig`. In this case, `waw-mig` was selected as the closest instance group to users in America:

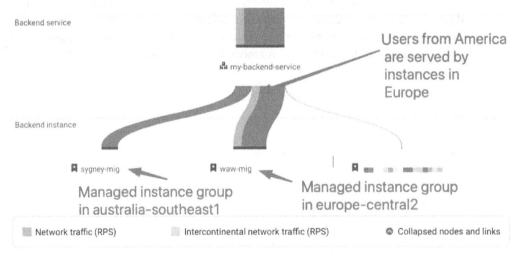

Figure 9.38 – The MONITORING tab of the global external HTTP(S) load balancer view showing traffic flowing to backend instances

There are other global services available besides the global external HTTP(S) load balancer. The next section will give more details about the two remaining global load balancers: SSL and TCP proxies.

Global external TCP/SSL proxies

A global external HTTP(S) load balancer works on Layer 7, balancing workloads across regions on ports 80 and 8080 for HTTP and port 443 for HTTPS. But in cases where an application uses TCP/SSL and runs on other ports, a TCP or SSL proxy could be used. Those load balancers also use a single public IP address to access backends globally, which minimizes latency between a user and a backend. Both support a multi-regional distribution of traffic and integrate with Cloud Armor to protect their backends. The difference is that they don't preserve a user's IP address. Instead, SSL or TCP connections are terminated by a load balancer and then proxied to an available backend in the closest region. A TCP proxy should be used when an application uses a TCP protocol and doesn't need SSL offloading. Alternatively, an SSL proxy offers SSL offloading so that instances on the backend don't have to decrypt SSL traffic, saving CPU cycles that can be used to serve more users.

External network TCP/UDP load balancers

With this load balancer configuration, you set up a regional public IP address that is still available from the internet but always points to a regional backend. Users (or Compute Engine VMs with access to the internet) from any location can access such services. Still, a load balancer can only distribute traffic between instances in the same region. For high availability, instances can be deployed in multiple zones of a region.

An external network TCP/UDP load balancer distributes traffic at the TCP/UDP (Layer 4) level on any port. It works in passthrough mode, which means it preserves the client's IP address, and the backend responses go directly to clients bypassing a load balancer:

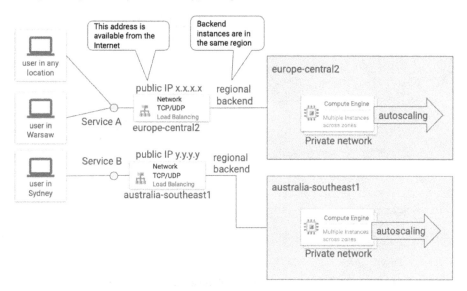

Figure 9.39 – External network TCP/UDP load balancer examples

The preceding figure presents an example with two load balancers, one used by `Service A` in `europe-central2` backed by an instance group in the same region and the second used by `Service B` in `australia-southeast1` backed by an instance group in the same region. Both represent different services that are globally accessible, just served from one region. As a result, users in different locations can access both services. Users who are closer to a configured load balancer will experience lower latency.

Internal TCP/UDP load balancing

The previous sections described load balancers that balance traffic that originates from the internet. Internal TCP/UDP (Layer 4) load balancers distribute traffic originating from internal clients or internal Compute Engine instances in internal networks. It protects an internal architecture from exposure as it hides behind a load balancer's internal IP address. It preserves the client IP (as a passthrough load balancer) and can balance on any TCP or UDP port.

You can access this load balancer from the same VPC network where it is running or from another VPC network via VPC peering or VPN. Also, it can be accessed from an on-premises location via VPN or Interconnect.

Although we call it a load balancer, there is no single box processing traffic. Instead, it is a service that's distributed at the lower layers of Google's software-defined networking. This provides scalability, high throughput, and low latency for balanced workloads. The following figure presents one of the use cases of an internal TCP/UDP load balancer:

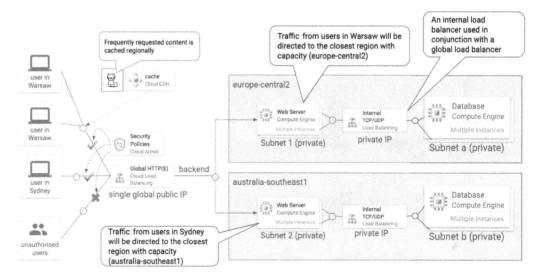

Figure 9.40 – Internal TCP/UDP load balancers used behind a global external HTTP(S) load balancer

In this tiered architecture, external users connect to an application available globally via a public IP address, served by a global external HTTP(S) load balancer. Behind it, we have a web server tier that's served from two regions. Users are directed to the closest available region. In every region, another load balancer – an internal TCP/UDP load balancer – distributes internal regional traffic from a web server tier to a database tier. The database tier is not accessible externally and consists of multiple instances deployed across zones in a region. In case of a failure in a zone, traffic is redirected to instances in another zone in the same region.

Selecting a load balancer

Selecting a particular load balancer depends mostly on your application architecture. Here are some examples:

- A global external HTTP (s) load balancer will be the best fit when a web-based application should be available from the internet and is expected to provide a good user experience (minimizing latency) and high availability by redirecting traffic to the closest operational regional backend

- A global external TCP/SSL load balancer should be used to allow access to an application from the internet on ports other than HTTP(S)

- An external network TCP/UDP load balancer will be a good choice for your internet-facing application if you need a client IP to be preserved or your service needs to load balance UDP traffic

- Use an internal TCP/UDP load balancer to distribute workloads in the same VPC and keep your backplane architecture hidden

> **Note**
> Check out the following link to the Google Cloud documentation on choosing the best load balancer for your workloads: `https://cloud.google.com/load-balancing/docs/choosing-load-balancer`.

Summary

In this chapter, we learned how to create global VPC networks for workloads that span multiple Google Cloud projects. We also explored how to connect Google Cloud with on-premises data centers. One of the most important topics we covered was how to protect workloads using firewall rules and Cloud Armor. Additionally, we delved into Google Cloud networking services such as Cloud DNS and different types of load balancers. We also learned how to use load balancers to improve the security and availability of globally available applications.

As we wrap up our discussion on networking, let's look ahead to the next chapter, where we'll continue to expand our knowledge by looking into the essential topic of data processing services.

Questions

Answer the following questions to check your knowledge of this chapter:

1. You are working on integrating Compute Engine workloads in a VPC with your on-premises data center. You have already configured and verified the VPN connectivity between the two environments. Also, Cloud DNS outbound forwarding was set for queries from the VPC to `my-on-prem-domain.com` to be sent to a DNS on-premises. However, while checking if the forwarding is working, you noticed that Compute Engine VMs in this VPC cannot resolve the `vm-1.my-on-prem-domain.com` address of `vm-1` on-premises. What could be the reason?

    A. The on-premises router is not advertising a `vm-1` subnet via BGP.

    B. Cloud DNS can only be configured to forward to zones in Google Cloud.

    C. Cloud Router needs to advertise the Cloud DNS IP range of `35.199.192.0/19` via BGP, which DNS on-premises uses to send a reply to Google Cloud.

    D. Firewall rules in the VPC block DNS queries on `port 53`.

2. You are meeting with a backup administrator to discuss how to set up backups of your Compute Engine VMs. The company has a separate project where a backup system is running (`backup project`). While preparing for the meeting, you investigate possible options for connecting those two existing projects. You are looking for a solution that doesn't require much administrative work. Also, your budget is limited. What would be the best approach?

    A. You should consider peering between a VPC in your project and a VPC in the backup project. This is an efficient way to connect two VPCs in different projects and exchange routing information.

    B. A Shared VPC is the best approach as it doesn't require any networking configuration on your end. Your project should be configured as a service project, with the backup project being a host project. This way, it can use the same networking that is used in the backup project.

    C. You should consider configuring a VPN between a VPC in your project and the backup project. This is an efficient way to connect two VPCs in different projects and exchange routing information.

3. Your team is investigating connectivity issues between Compute Engine VMs in VPC A in Project A and VPC B in Project B. VPC A and VPC B are peered, and the peering's state is Active. What could be the reason for the problem?

    A. Subnet routes are not exported by default. Therefore, you must enable the subnet routes to be imported/exported at both ends of the peering.

    B. Firewall rules block communication between Compute Engine VMs.

C. Peering needs to be configured for both VPCs. Most likely, peering was set at the VPC A side but has yet to be configured at the VPC B side.

4. As the first step of its multi-cloud strategy, your company has decided to move some of its workloads to Google Cloud. They also plan to move selected workloads to another cloud provider in the future. Your manager is asking you to investigate a cost-effective, forward-looking approach to connecting the on-premises site to the cloud, assuming the minimum required bandwidth at this moment is 2 Gbps. What would you recommend?

A. Partner Interconnect, because a single physical connection to a partner site can be used to reach multiple cloud providers.

B. VPN, as it can be configured on demand without the need for third parties.

C. Dedicated Interconnect, because the more workloads they migrate, the higher the demand for bandwidth will be. With this option, they can scale up to 200 Gbps.

5. You plan to deploy workloads in two regions: `europe-central2` (Warsaw) and `europe-west3` (Frankfurt). What would be the simplest way to provide connectivity between subnets in those two regions?

A. Use one VPC with two subnets, one in `europe-central2` and the second in `europe-west3`. Then, use firewall rules to enable communication on selected ports.

B. Use VPC peering between a VPC with a subnet in `europe-west3` and a VPC with a subnet in `europe-central2`. Then, use firewall rules to enable communication on selected ports.

C. Use VPN between a VPC with a subnet in `europe-west3` and a VPC with a subnet in `europe-central2`. Then, use firewall rules to enable communication on selected ports.

6. Would two Compute Engine VMs deployed in the same subnet be able to communicate with each other when only deny-all-ingress and allow-all-egress implied rules are configured?

A. Yes, because both are in the same subnet, and firewall rules are executed at the VPC level.

B. No, as firewall rules are executed at the VM level.

7. Which load balancer should offer the best user experience for a web application that requires high availability and will be accessed by users around the globe?

A. One external network TCP/UDP load balancer as it is accessible globally and distributes traffic to a backend in the same region, which guarantees the lowest latency.

B. Multiple external network TCP/UDP load balancers in multiple regions that are accessible globally and that distribute traffic to the backend in the same region, guaranteeing the lowest latency.

C. One global external HTTP(S) load balancer as it is accessible globally and can distribute traffic to the available backends in regions close to users.

Answers

Here are the answers to this chapter's questions:

1C, 2A, 3B, 4A, 5A, 6B, 7C

Part 3: Data Analytics, Security, Operations, and Cost Estimation in Google Cloud

The third part of the book covers data products, monitoring, logging, identity, and security. Once we learn how to store data in Google Cloud, we need to understand how to gain insights from it. After learning how to use data solutions, we will move on to an important part of Google Cloud: monitoring, logging, and estimating the cost of cloud solutions. One of the final chapters is about identity and security in Google Cloud, which allows us to cover the most important services and their usage. Finally, we can test our knowledge with two mock tests that cover all the aspects of what we have learned throughout our cloud journey.

This part of the book comprises the following chapters:

- *Chapter 10, Data Processing Services in Google Cloud*
- *Chapter 11, Monitoring, Logging, and Estimating Costs in GCP*
- *Chapter 12, Implementing Identity and Security in Google Cloud*
- *Mock Test 1 – First ACE Mock Test*
- *Mock Test 2 – Second ACE Mock test*

10

Data Processing Services in Google Cloud

For years, companies of all sizes have collected and stored vast amounts of data about their customers and business operations to enhance performance, achieve growth, and realize their goals. In 2006, Clive Humby, a renowned British mathematician, coined the phrase *Data is the new oil* to emphasize the growing importance of data in the modern business landscape. Google Cloud has a broad portfolio of data processing products.

In *Chapter 7*, we introduced some data-related services from the storage perspective. This chapter aims to familiarize us with the data processing services in Google Cloud. We discussed Cloud SQL, BigQuery, Firestore, Cloud Spanner, and Cloud Bigtable. To complete the story, we will cover the following topics in this chapter:

- Data processing point of overview – Pub/Sub, Dataproc, and Dataflow
- Initializing and loading data using the command line, API transfer, and loading the data from Cloud Storage and streaming it using Pub/Sub

Data processing services overview

Data processing in Google Cloud refers to the various tools and services provided by **Google Cloud Platform** (**GCP**) that enable organizations to process, store, and analyze large amounts of data in the cloud.

These services provide organizations with the necessary infrastructure and tools to collect, process, store, analyze, and visualize their data in the cloud, helping them discover meaningful insights and make better-informed business decisions.

Pub/Sub

Pub/Sub is a publish/subscribe service – a messaging service where the senders of messages are decoupled from the receivers.

Pub/Sub is a messaging service that is both scalable and asynchronous, allowing us to separate the message-producing services from the services that process those messages. It allows various Google Cloud services to communicate asynchronously with latencies of 100 milliseconds. The most common use case for Pub/Sub is streaming analytics and data integration pipeline with data ingestion and distribution.

Here are some other Pub/Sub use cases:

- **Ingestion user interaction and server events**: From your application or servers, you can forward events to Pub/Sub and process them with stream processing tools such as Dataflow.

- **Real-time event distribution**: Pub/Sub allows us to distribute events to multiple applications or databases.

- **Parallel processing and workflows**: When combined with Cloud Functions, Pub/Sub can distribute messages among multiple workers to be used in tasks such as file compression, sending email notifications, or processing images.

- **Enterprise event bus**: Pub/Sub is well suited to an enterprise-wide data sharing bus and distributing events.

There are two services – Pub/Sub and Pub/Sub Lite.

Pub/Sub is the default choice for most users and applications. Pub/Sub Lite, on the other hand, has a lower cost and offers lower reliability compared to Pub/Sub. Other differences are that Pub/Sub Lite topics are stored in only one zone and replicated asynchronously.

To learn more about the differences between the two services, go to `https://cloud.google.com/pubsub/docs/choosing-pubsub-or-lite`.

Pub/Sub architecture

To understand Pub/Sub, we need to list several key service components:

- **Message**: Data that flows through the service.
- **Topic**: A named entity that represents a feed of messages.
- **Subscription**: A named entity that receives messages on a particular topic.
- **Publisher**: Also called a producer, the publisher creates messages and publishes them to the messaging service on a specific topic.
- **Subscriber**: Also called a consumer, the subscriber receives messages on a specific subscription.

The following is a visual representation of the architecture:

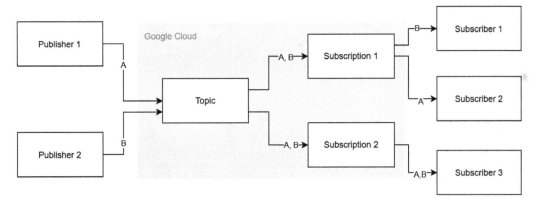

Figure 10.1 – Pub/Sub architecture

The preceding diagram shows two publishers – A and B – sending messages to a topic. The topic has two subscriptions that want to receive messages from the topic. On the right-hand side, subscribers receive messages from the specific subscription. We can also see that subscribers receive different messages. Some subscribers receive only message A or B, but **Subscriber 3** receives both A and B.

Pub/Sub combines the horizontal scalability of **Apache Kafka** and **Pulsar** with features found in traditional messaging middleware such as **Apache ActiveMQ** and **RabbitMQ**.

Pub/Sub integrates with other Google Cloud services such as **Dataflow**, **Logging** and **Monitoring**, triggers, notifications, and webhooks.

In the next section, we will learn about Dataproc – one of the next data processing services in Google Cloud.

Dataproc

Dataproc is a fully managed Google Cloud service that runs **Apache Hadoop**, **Apache Spark**, **Apache Flink**, **Presto**, and more than 30 other open source tools and frameworks. It can be used for data lake modernization, **Extract, Transform,** and **Load** (ETL) operations, and data science.

One advantage of using Dataproc is that there's no need to learn new tools or APIs. Dataproc allows us to start, scale, and shut down; each operation takes 90 seconds or less. Creating a cluster might take 5 to 30 minutes compared to on-premises deployments. Dataproc integrates with other Google Cloud services such as BigQuery, Cloud Storage, Cloud Bigtable, Cloud Logging, and Cloud Monitoring. This creates a data ecosystem that is easy to use, regardless of how you interact with it – the Google Cloud console, Cloud SDK, or REST API.

By default, Dataproc supports the following images:

- Ubuntu
- Debian
- Rocky Linux

To learn which exact versions of images are supported, go to `https://cloud.google.com/dataproc/docs/concepts/versioning/dataproc-version-clusters#supported_dataproc_versions`.

Dataproc architecture

Google Cloud allows you to run Dataproc on **Google Compute Engine** (**GCE**) or **Google Kubernetes Engine** (**GKE**). The main difference between Dataproc on GCE versus Dataproc on GKE is that Dataproc on GKE virtual clusters does not include separate master and worker VMs. In Dataproc on GKE, a node pool is created within the GKE cluster, and jobs are run as pods on these node pools:

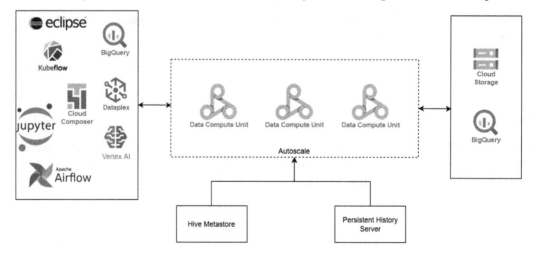

Figure 10.2 – High-level Dataproc architecture

The preceding diagram shows a high-level overview of the Dataproc architecture. On the left-hand side, we have possible sources of the data. In the middle section, we have data computing units that leverage autoscaling policies. If your job requires more compute units, you can configure autoscaling policies. You can store the results of the jobs in Cloud Storage or BigQuery.

The following section will discuss the next Google Cloud offering – the Dataflow data portfolio product.

Dataflow

Dataflow is a fully managed service that allows data modifications and enhancements in batch and stream modes. It provides automated provisioning and management of compute resources. Dataflow allows you to use **Apache Beam**, an open source unified model for defining batch and streaming data processing pipelines. You can use the Apache Beam programming model and Apache Beam SDK.

Dataflow provides templates that can accelerate product adoption.

Dataflow architecture

Dataflow provides several features that help you run secure, reliable, fast, and cost-effective data pipelines at scale. They are as follows:

- **Autoscaling**: *Horizontal* (scale out – the appropriate number of workers is selected) and *vertical* autoscaling (scale up – Dataflow dynamically scales up or down memory available to workers) allow you to run jobs in a cost-efficient manner.

- **Serverless**: Pipelines that use Dataflow Prime benefit from automated and optimized resource management, reduced operational costs, and improved diagnostics capabilities.

- **Job Monitoring**: Seeing and interacting with Dataflow jobs is possible. In the monitoring interface, you can view Dataflow jobs via a graphical representation of each pipeline, along with each job's status.

The following figure shows the Dataflow architecture, where we can see tight integration with core Google Cloud services and possibilities to interact with the service by using Dataflow SQL:

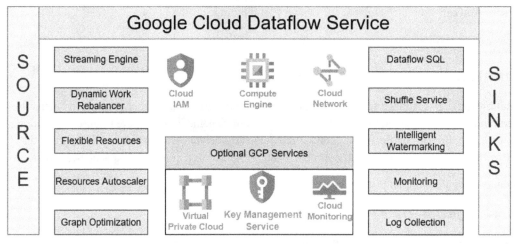

Figure 10.3 – High-level Dataflow architecture

You can also use **Customer Managed Encryption Keys (CMEKs)** to encrypt data at rest and specify networks or subnetworks with VPC Service Controls.

Now that we've learned about the architecture and use cases for each data processing product, we should learn how to initialize and load data into them.

Initializing and loading data into data products

In this practical part of the chapter, we will focus on initializing and loading data into the previously described data products. Covering such practical exercises and providing an architecture overview allow us to understand the products better.

Pub/Sub and Dataflow

The first example will combine the usage of three data products: Pub/Sub, Dataflow, and Cloud Storage. The Pub/Sub topic will read messages published to a topic and group the messages by timestamp. Ultimately, these messages will be stored in a Cloud Storage bucket:

1. Before we start, we need to enable a few APIs – Dataflow, Compute Engine, Cloud Logging, Cloud Storage, Google Cloud Storage JSON API, Pub/Sub, Resource Manager, and Cloud Scheduler.

2. In Cloud Shell, run the following command:

```
gcloud services enable dataflow.googleapis.com  compute.
googleapis.com  logging.googleapis.com  storage-component.
googleapis.com  storage-api.googleapis.com  pubsub.googleapis.
com  cloudresourcemanager.googleapis.com  cloudscheduler.
googleapis.com
```

Our solution will create a new service account and grant it several roles to interact with multiple services. Those roles have the `/dataflow–worker`, `roles/storage.objectAdmin`, and `roles/pubsub.admin` rights.

3. We must create a new service account with the following `gcloud` command:

```
gcloud iam service-accounts create data-services-sa
```

4. Once our service account has been created, we can grant roles to it. We can do so by executing the following command and specifying the previously mentioned roles – that is, `roles/dataflow. worker`, `roles/storage.objectAdmin`, and `roles/pubsub.admin`:

```
gcloud projects add-iam-policy-binding wmarusiak-book-351718
--member="serviceAccount data-services-sa@wmarusiak-book-351718
.iam.gserviceaccount.com" --role=roles/dataflow.worker
```

5. After adding these roles to the service account, we can grant our Google account a role so that we can use the previously created roles and attach the service account to other resources. To do so, we need to execute the following code:

```
gcloud iam service-accounts add-iam-policy-binding data-
services-sa@wmarusiak-book-351718.iam.gserviceaccount.
com --member="user:YOUR_EMAIL_ADDRESS" --role=roles/iam.
serviceAccountUser
```

6. Now, we must use service credentials to be configured as default application credentials. In Cloud Shell, run the following code:

```
gcloud auth application-default login
```

7. The next step involves creating a Cloud Storage bucket name. We must execute the `gsutil mb gs://YOUR_BUCKET_NAME` command in Cloud Shell. Please replace the bucket name with a unique name – we used `wmarusiak-data-services-bucket`.

8. Now that we've created the Cloud Storage bucket, we must create a Pub/Sub topic. We can use the `gcloud pubsub topics create YOUR_PUB_SUB_TOPIC_NAME` command to do so. We used `wmarusiak-data-services-topic` as our Pub/Sub topic name. Please replace the topic's name with a unique name.

9. To finish resource creation, we must create a Cloud Scheduler job in the working project. The job publishes a message to a Pub/Sub topic every minute. The command to create a Cloud Scheduler job is as follows:

```
gcloud scheduler jobs create pubsub publisher-job --schedule="*
* * * *" --topic=wmarusiak-data-services-topic --message-
body="Hello!" --location=europe-west1
```

10. To start the job, we need to run the following `gcloud` command:

```
gcloud scheduler jobs run publisher-job --location=europe-west1
```

The last step involves downloading a Java or Python GitHub repository to initiate the necessary code quickly.

11. We used Python code; you can use this instruction to download it:

```
git clone https://github.com/GoogleCloudPlatform/python-
docs-samples.git \ cd python-docs-samples/pubsub/
streaming-analytics/ pip install -r requirements.txt  #
Install Apache Beam dependencies
```

12. You can find the Python code by visiting the Google Cloud GitHub repository at `https://github.com/GoogleCloudPlatform/python-docs-samples/blob/HEAD/pubsub/streaming-analytics/PubSubToGCS.py`.

13. The last step is to run the Python code. We need to replace the constants with our actual data:

```
python PubSubToGCS.py --project=$PROJECT_ID --region=$REGION
--input_topic=projects/$PROJECT_ID/topics/$TOPIC_ID --output_
path=gs://$BUCKET_NAME/samples/output --runner=DataflowRunner
--window_size=2 --num_shards=2 --temp_location=gs://$BUCKET_
NAME/temp --service_account_email=$SERVICE_ACCOUNT
```

14. In our case, the code looks as follows:

```
python PubSubToGCS.py --project=wmarusiak-book-351718
--region=europe-west1 --input_topic=projects/wmarusiak-
book-351718/topics/wmarusiak-data-services-topic  --output_
path=gs://wmarusiak-data-services-bucket/samples/output
--runner=DataflowRunner --window_size=2  --num_shards=2 --temp_
location=gs://wmarusiak-data-services-bucket/temp --service_
account_email=data-services-sa@wmarusiak-book-351718.iam.
gserviceaccount.com
```

15. Our Dataflow job runs, and messages flow from Cloud Scheduler to Pub/Sub:

Figure 10.4 – Dataflow job execution graph

16. We can also see the code output in the Cloud Storage bucket, which contains stored messages:

wmarusiak-data-services-bucket

Location	Storage class	Public access	Protection
us (multiple regions in United States)	Standard	Subject to object ACLs	None

OBJECTS   CONFIGURATION   PERMISSIONS   PROTECTION   LIFECYCLE   OBSERVABILITY `NEW`

Buckets > wmarusiak-data-services-bucket > samples

UPLOAD FILES   UPLOAD FOLDER   CREATE FOLDER   TRANSFER DATA ▾   MANAGE HOLDS   DOWNLOAD   DELETE

Filter by name prefix only ▾   ☰ Filter   Filter objects and folders

	Name	Size	Type	Created	Storage class	Last modified
☐	output-21:54-21:56-0	67 B	application/octet-stream	Mar 21, 2023, 10:57:10 PM	Standard	Mar 21, 2023, 10:57:10 PM
☐	output-21:54-21:56-1	33 B	application/octet-stream	Mar 21, 2023, 10:57:10 PM	Standard	Mar 21, 2023, 10:57:10 PM
☐	output-21:56-21:58-0	67 B	application/octet-stream	Mar 21, 2023, 10:58:05 PM	Standard	Mar 21, 2023, 10:58:05 PM
☐	output-21:56-21:58-1	135 B	application/octet-stream	Mar 21, 2023, 10:58:06 PM	Standard	Mar 21, 2023, 10:58:06 PM
☐	output-21:58-22:00-0	34 B	application/octet-stream	Mar 21, 2023, 11:00:35 PM	Standard	Mar 21, 2023, 11:00:35 PM
☐	output-21:58-22:00-1	168 B	application/octet-stream	Mar 21, 2023, 11:00:35 PM	Standard	Mar 21, 2023, 11:00:35 PM
☐	output-22:00-22:02-1	202 B	application/octet-stream	Mar 21, 2023, 11:02:35 PM	Standard	Mar 21, 2023, 11:02:35 PM
☐	output-22:02-22:04-0	168 B	application/octet-stream	Mar 21, 2023, 11:04:36 PM	Standard	Mar 21, 2023, 11:04:36 PM
☐	output-22:02-22:04-1	34 B	application/octet-stream	Mar 21, 2023, 11:04:36 PM	Standard	Mar 21, 2023, 11:04:36 PM
☐	output-22:04-22:06-0	135 B	application/octet-stream	Mar 21, 2023, 11:06:36 PM	Standard	Mar 21, 2023, 11:06:36 PM
☐	output-22:04-22:06-1	67 B	application/octet-stream	Mar 21, 2023, 11:06:36 PM	Standard	Mar 21, 2023, 11:06:36 PM
☐	output-22:06-22:08-0	135 B	application/octet-stream	Mar 21, 2023, 11:08:36 PM	Standard	Mar 21, 2023, 11:08:36 PM
☐	output-22:06-22:08-1	67 B	application/octet-stream	Mar 21, 2023, 11:08:36 PM	Standard	Mar 21, 2023, 11:08:36 PM
☐	output-22:08-22:10-0	169 B	application/octet-stream	Mar 21, 2023, 11:10:05 PM	Standard	Mar 21, 2023, 11:10:05 PM
☐	output-22:08-22:10-1	33 B	application/octet-stream	Mar 21, 2023, 11:10:05 PM	Standard	Mar 21, 2023, 11:10:05 PM
☐	output-22:10-22:12-0	67 B	application/octet-stream	Mar 21, 2023, 11:12:06 PM	Standard	Mar 21, 2023, 11:12:06 PM
☐	output-22:10-22:12-1	135 B	application/octet-stream	Mar 21, 2023, 11:12:06 PM	Standard	Mar 21, 2023, 11:12:06 PM

Figure 10.5 – Saved job output in the Cloud Storage bucket

17. We can download objects to view the content of processed messages:

```
≡ samples_output-22 10-22 12-1 ✕

C: > Users > Wojciech Marusiak > Downloads >  ≡ samples_output-22 10-22 12-1
    1   Hello2,2023-03-21 22:10:01.013000
    2   Hello3,2023-03-21 22:10:01.014000
    3   Hello,2023-03-21 22:11:00.026000
    4   Hello3,2023-03-21 22:11:00.034000
    5
```

Figure 10.6 – Content of processed messages

18. To get a few more messages, we created two additional Cloud Scheduler services.

This example showed us the tight integration between Google Cloud products and how we can ingest incoming messages and process them in a few steps. In the next section, we will cover the Dataproc service.

Dataproc

It is one of the everyday use cases in data science and data engineering to read data from one storage platform, transform it, and use it elsewhere. Our Dataproc example will be based on a data processing pipeline that uses Apache Spark (Python API) with Dataproc (PySpark). We will run a sample pipeline to read data from Reddit posts stored in BigQuery and extract the title and body (raw text) with the timestamp that was created for each Reddit comment. This data will be converted into CSV format, compressed in ZIP format, and stored in a Google Cloud Storage bucket:

1. For our use case with Dataproc, we must enable three APIs – Dataproc, Compute Engine, and BigQuery. We can do this using the following `gcloud` command:

   ```
   gcloud services enable compute.googleapis.com dataproc.
   googleapis.com bigquerystorage.googleapis.com
   ```

2. We can default the Dataproc region by using the `gcloud config set dataproc/region YOUR_REGION`, command, where `YOUR_REGION` can be any available region. In our case, `YOUR_REGION` will be `europe-west1`.

3. To create a Dataproc cluster, we must provide its name and additional configuration:

   ```
   gcloud beta dataproc clusters create DATAPROC_CLUSTER_NAME
   --worker-machine-type n1-standard-2 --num-workers 6 --image-
   version 1.5-debian --initialization-actions gs://dataproc-
   initialization-actions/python/pip-install.sh --metadata 'PIP_
   PACKAGES=google-cloud-storage' --optional-components=ANACONDA
   --enable-component-gateway
   ```

We need to enter the Dataproc cluster's name, and we can choose different worker machine types. Pick a desired worker type from the available Google Compute Engine instance types. In our case, we changed it to `n1-standard-2` so that we don't exceed our CPU quota. We can also specify a different amount of worker nodes. After a moment, the Dataproc cluster will be operational and ready to accept incoming jobs:

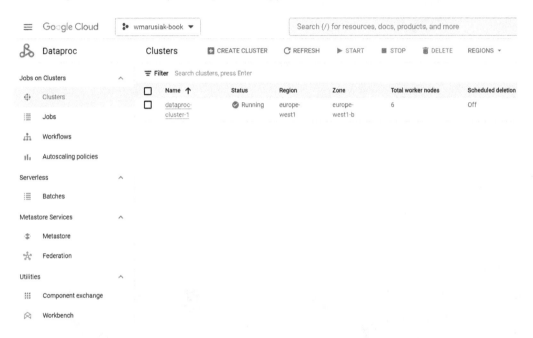

Figure 10.7 – The Dataproc cluster is operational

4. We will use the Google Cloud Python GitHub repository, which can be cloned with the following command:

```
git clone https://github.com/GoogleCloudPlatform/cloud-dataproc
```

5. Once we enter the repository with the `cd ~/cloud-dataproc/codelabs/spark-bigquery` command, we can execute the Dataproc job.

6. To execute the Dataproc job, we can use the following command:

```
gcloud dataproc jobs submit pyspark --cluster dataproc-cluster-1
--jars gs://spark-lib/bigquery/spark-bigquery-latest_2.12.
jar  --driver-log-levels root=FATAL counts_by_subreddit.py
```

7. The job's status can be viewed in the Google Cloud console or Cloud Shell once it's been accepted:

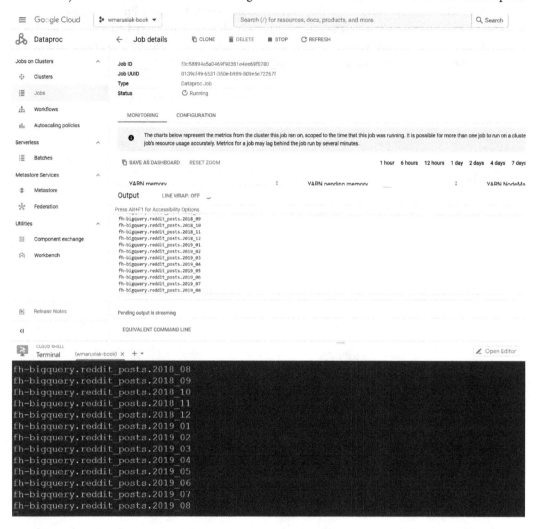

Figure 10.8 – Dataproc job visible in Cloud Shell and the Google Cloud console

Dataproc provides various components of the Dataproc cluster – **YARN ResourceManager**, **MapReduce Job History**, **Spark History Server**, **HDFS NameNode**, **YARN Application Timeline**, and **Tez**. This information is visible in **Cluster details** under the **WEB INTERFACES** tab:

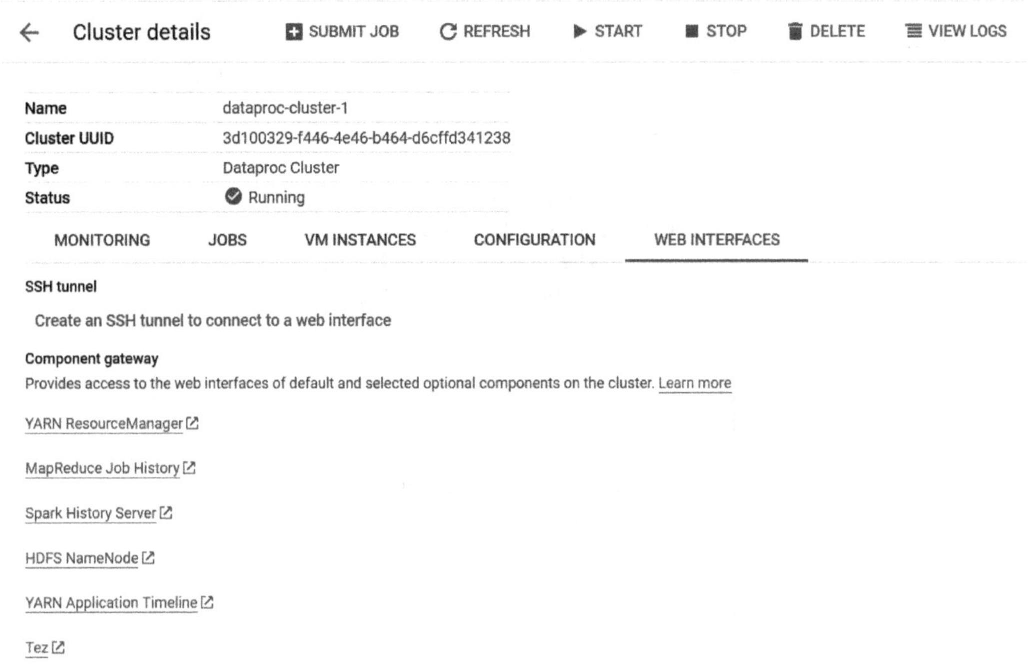

←   Cluster details   ➕ SUBMIT JOB   ⟳ REFRESH   ▶ START   ■ STOP   🗑 DELETE   ☰ VIEW LOGS

Name	dataproc-cluster-1
Cluster UUID	3d100329-f446-4e46-b464-d6cffd341238
Type	Dataproc Cluster
Status	✔ Running

MONITORING   JOBS   VM INSTANCES   CONFIGURATION   **WEB INTERFACES**

SSH tunnel

Create an SSH tunnel to connect to a web interface

Component gateway

Provides access to the web interfaces of default and selected optional components on the cluster. Learn more

YARN ResourceManager ↗

MapReduce Job History ↗

Spark History Server ↗

HDFS NameNode ↗

YARN Application Timeline ↗

Tez ↗

Figure 10.9 – Cluster details

8.   After a moment, the job will complete, and we can proceed with data transformation:

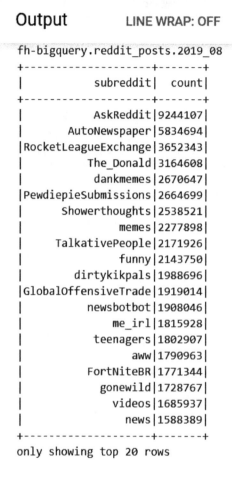

Output   **LINE WRAP: OFF**

```
fh-bigquery.reddit_posts.2019_08
+--------------------+-------+
|           subreddit|  count|
+--------------------+-------+
|            AskReddit|9244107|
|        AutoNewspaper|5834694|
|RocketLeagueExchange|3652343|
|          The_Donald|3164608|
|            dankmemes|2670647|
|PewdiepieSubmissions|2664699|
|       Showerthoughts|2538521|
|               memes|2277898|
|       TalkativePeople|2171926|
|                funny|2143750|
|          dirtykikpals|1988696|
|GlobalOffensiveTrade|1919014|
|          newsbotbot|1908046|
|              me_irl|1815928|
|            teenagers|1802907|
|                  aww|1790963|
|           FortNiteBR|1771344|
|            gonewild|1728767|
|               videos|1685937|
|                 news|1588389|
+--------------------+-------+
only showing top 20 rows
```

Figure 10.10 – Dataproc job results

9.   In BigQuery Web UI's Query Editor, we run the `select  *  from fh-bigquery.reddit_posts.2017_01 limit 10;` SQL query to view sample data output:

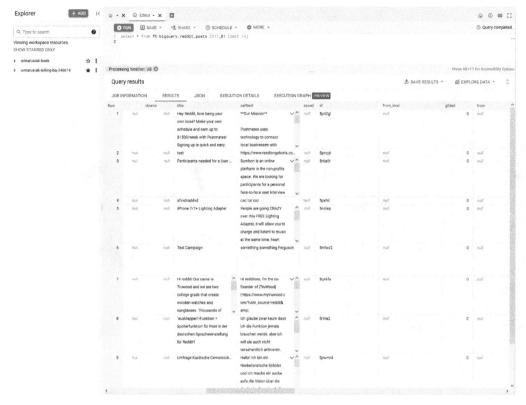

Figure 10.11 – SQL query output in BigQuery Web UI

10. We will see that different columns are available, but two columns – **title** and **selftext** – contain the information we will use later.

11. In the `cloud-dataproc/codelabs/spark-bigquery` folder downloaded in the previous steps repository, we run the `backfill.py` Python script. To do so, we can run the following `gcloud` command:

```
cd ~/cloud-dataproc/codelabs/spark-bigquery
bash backfill.sh dataproc-cluster-1 wmarusiak-dataproc-bucket-1
```

12. After a few minutes, the job will be completed, and the CSV files will be uploaded to the Google Cloud Storage bucket. We can list the bucket's content with the following command:

```
gsutil ls gs://YOUR_CLOUD_STORAGE_BUCKET/reddit_posts/*/*/food.
csv.gz
```

We will get the following output:

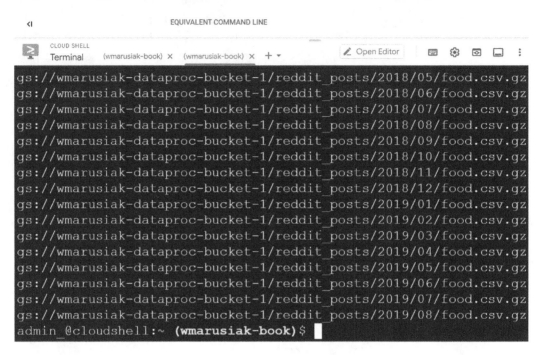

Figure 10.12 – SQL query output in BigQuery Web UI

13. So, what can we do with this data after processing it? One example could be building models on top of it.

14. Now that we've learned about and implemented Dataproc in Google Cloud, we will move on to the next section, where we will learn about APIs and their use cases and do a hands-on implementation of them.

Using Google Cloud APIs

API stands for **application programming interface**, a set of definitions and protocols for building and integrating applications. Google Cloud APIs are programmatic interfaces that interact with Google Cloud services. In *Chapter 3*, we learned how to enable and disable Google Cloud APIs with the gcloud command-line interface. In this part of this chapter, we would like to focus on working with Google Cloud APIs using REST/HTTP APIs. As mentioned in *Chapter 3*, Google Cloud offers many ways to interact with its services. For this chapter, we will show you how to interact with data-related products using REST/HTTP APIs.

Using Google Cloud APIs with REST/HTTP APIs

We can use various tools to work with REST/HTTP APIs. Depending on the operating system and our preferences, it can be a `curl` Linux command-line tool, or we can use desktop applications such as Postman, Swagger, or HTTPie. These tools are multiplatform, and you can try them out yourself. We will use Postman in this part of this book.

Before interacting with Google Cloud APIs, we need to authenticate ourselves with Google Cloud.

Authenticating using REST

Similar to the different choices Google Cloud offers us for interacting with APIs, we have different ways to authenticate with Google Cloud to work with its services. In our case, we will describe OAuth 2.0 authentication with Postman, as other authentication possibilities exceed Associate Cloud Engineer certification requirements.

If you wish to learn about different ways, go to `https://cloud.google.com/docs/authentication/client-libraries`.

OAuth 2.0

OAuth 2.0 is an open standard protocol that allows users to grant third-party application access to their resources without them revealing their credentials. It provides a secure and standard way for users to authorize access to their resources, such as social media profiles, email accounts, or online storage services.

In an OAuth 2.0 flow, the user authenticates with the resource provider (for example, Google, Facebook, or another provider) and then authorizes the third-party application to access their resources. The third-party application obtains an access token, which it can use to make requests on behalf of the user to access their resources.

To set OAuth 2.0, we must first create credentials in **APIs & Services** in Google Cloud:

1. In the desired project, go to **APIs & Services**.
2. Click **Credentials**. If this is the first time you're creating credentials, you must configure the consent screen. Click the **CONFIGURE CONSENT SCREEN** button:

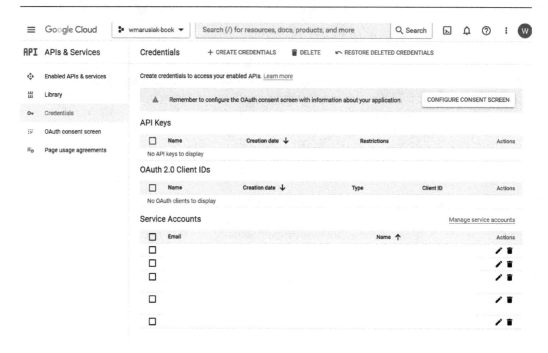

Figure 10.13 – The Credentials section in APIs & Services

3. In our case, we will set **User Type** to **Internal**. Click **Create**.

4. In the next section, we need to enter **App name** (the name of the app asking for consent) and **User support email** (for users to contact you with questions about their consent) details; optionally, we can add the app logo and more information about the app. We can also look at the app's home page, privacy policy, and terms of service:

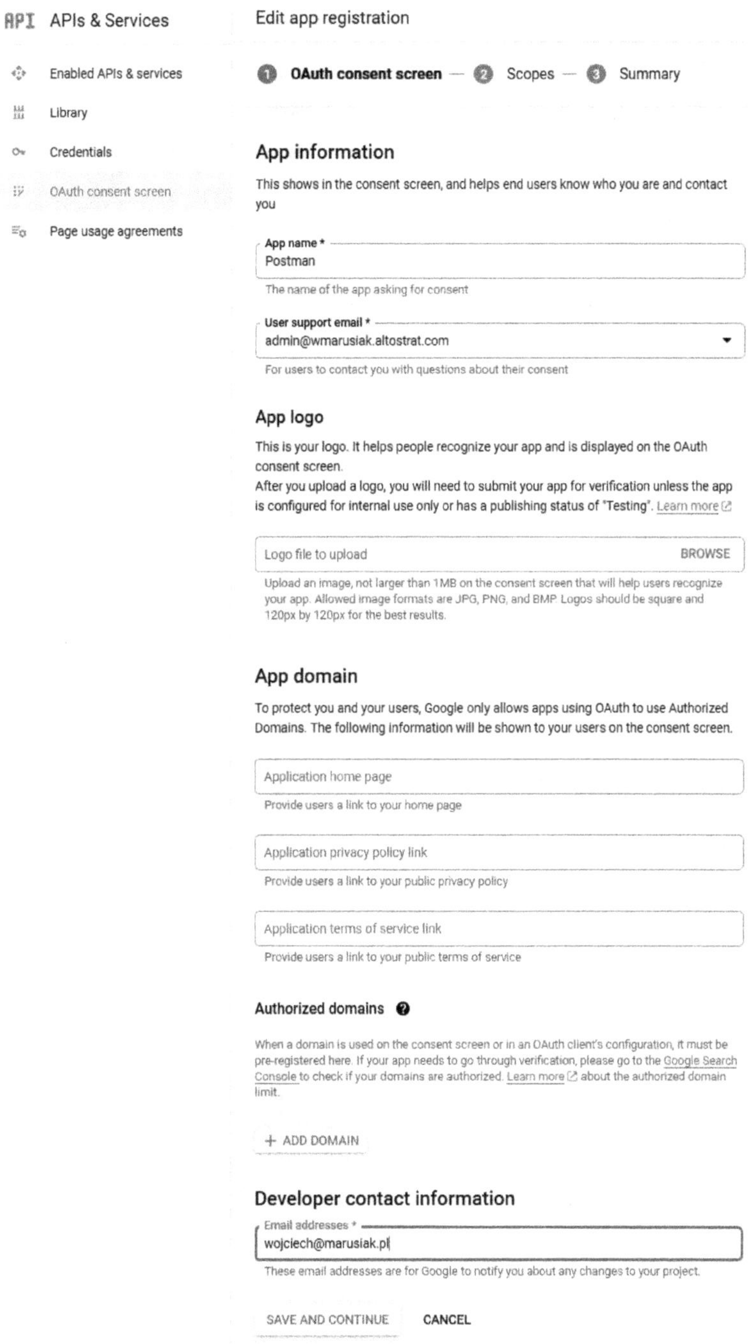

Figure 10.14 – OAuth consent screen creation

5. In the **Scopes** section, we can specify the permissions we want users to authorize for our app.

6. After saving the **Scopes** section, the OAuth consent section will be completed.

7. Back in the **Credentials** section, we can start creating credentials. Click the **CREATE CREDENTIALS** button to start this process. From the menu, choose **OAuth client ID**:

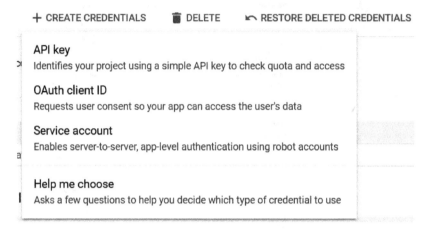

Figure 10.15 – The CREATE CREDENTIALS button and the possible choices

8. From the drop-down menu, choose **Web application**:

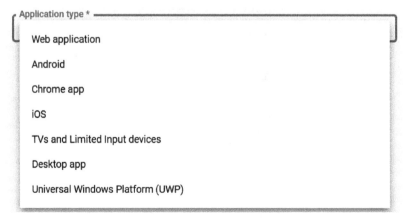

Figure 10.16 – Selecting an OAuth client ID application type

9. Enter the name of the web application and set **Authorized redirect URIs** to `https://oauth.pstmn.io/v1/callback` and `https://www.getpostman.com/oauth2/callback`, respectively:

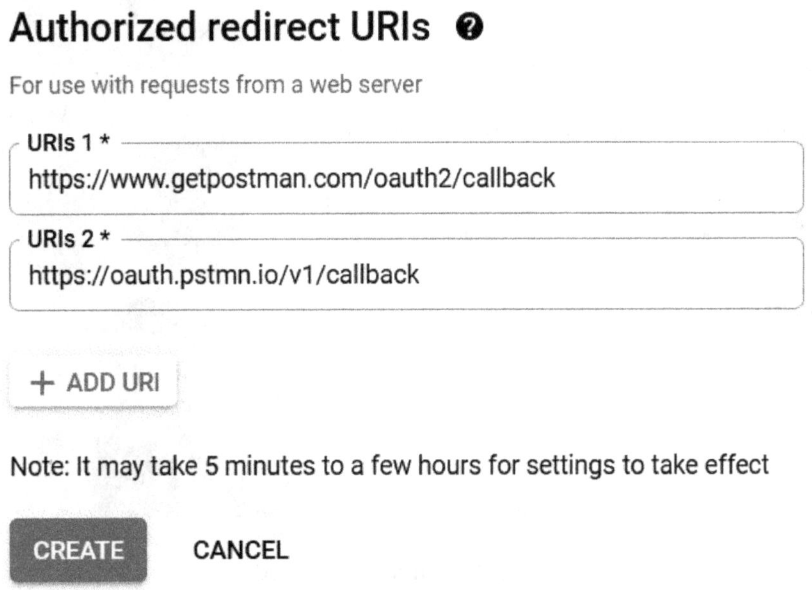

Authorized redirect URIs ❷

For use with requests from a web server

URIs 1 *

https://www.getpostman.com/oauth2/callback

URIs 2 *

https://oauth.pstmn.io/v1/callback

＋ ADD URI

Note: It may take 5 minutes to a few hours for settings to take effect

CREATE   CANCEL

Figure 10.17 – Authorized redirect URIs to work with Postman

10. Click **CREATE** to finalize the OAuth client ID creation process:

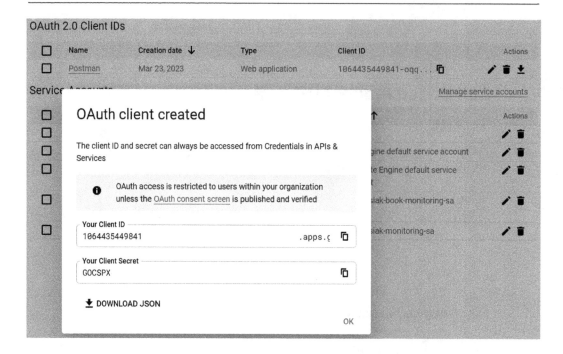

Figure 10.18 – OAuth client created

11. You will receive a client ID and client secret in the window. We will use these to authenticate our API request in Postman.

Now that we've retrieved the **Client ID** and **Client Secret** details, we must familiarize ourselves with API call types and response codes.

Popular API calls

To work with API calls, it is essential to understand which API calls we can make and what they do. Here is a list of the most popular ones:

- GET: A request to retrieve information from the server

- POST: A request to send information to the server

- PUT: A request to update existing data on the server

- DELETE: A request to delete data from the server

- PATCH: A request to update existing data on the server partially

- OPTIONS: A request to retrieve information about the communication options available on the server

- HEAD: A request to retrieve only the header information from the server

- CONNECT: A request to establish a network connection to the server

- TRACE: A request to retrieve a diagnostic trace of the actions performed by the server

- **Remote Procedure Call** (RPC): A request to execute a procedure on a remote server.

Now that we've learned what popular API calls we can make, it is essential to know what the most popular HTTP status codes are in response to API calls:

- 200 OK: The request was successful, and the response contains the requested data.

- 201 Created: The request has been fulfilled, and a new resource has been created.

- 204 No Content: The request was successful, but there is no data to return.

- 400 Bad Request: The request was malformed or invalid.

- 401 Unauthorized: Authentication is required and has failed or has not been provided.

- 403 Forbidden: The server has understood the request but refuses to authorize it.

- 404 Not Found: The requested resource could not be found.

- 500 Internal Server Error: The server encountered an error while processing the request.

- 502 Bad Gateway: The server received an invalid response from the upstream server.

- 503 Service Unavailable: The server cannot handle the request due to a temporary overload or maintenance.

In the next section, we will learn how to use Postman to make simple API calls in Google Cloud.

Postman configuration

"Postman is an API platform for building and using APIs. Postman simplifies each step of the API life cycle and streamlines collaboration so that you can create better APIs – faster".

This quote is from https://www.postman.com/product/what-is-postman/.

Postman can be used on any modern operating system – Windows, Linux, or macOS. To download it, go to https://www.postman.com/downloads/postman-agent/. If you do not wish to install Postman, you can use the web-based portal to interact with Google Cloud services using API calls:

1. Open Postman and click the + button to create a new API call.

2. We will start with a straightforward `GET` call to list instances in a particular Google Cloud zone: `GET https://compute.googleapis.com/compute/v1/projects/{project}/zones/{zone}/instances`. We will change the project and zone to the values that reflect our environment.

3. In Postman, we must enter the previous URL with the correct project name and zone:

Figure 10.19 – GET API call to query GCE instances in the europe-west4-a zone

4. Let's test whether we can retrieve any information by clicking **Send**.

5. As we can see in the **Body** section, there was an error with a status code of **401 Unauthorized**.

6. We authorized and previously created OAuth credentials in Google Cloud to authorize.

    In the **Authorization** tab of Postman, choose **OAuth 2.0**:

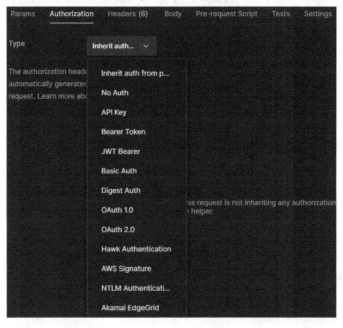

Figure 10.20 – The Authorization section of the API call

7. In the **Configure New Token** section, we need to configure the following information:

    A. **Type:** OAuth 2.0

    B. Add authorization data to request headers

    C. **Token Name:** Enter your desired name

    D. **Grant Type:** Authorization code

    E. **Callback URL:** We will use previously configured URLs in the **Credentials** section of **API & Services** – that is, `https://www.getpostman.com/oauth2/callback` and `https://oauth.pstmn.io/v1/callback`

    F. **Auth URL:** `https://accounts.google.com/o/oauth2/auth`

    G. **Access Token URL:** `https://accounts.google.com/o/oauth2/token`

    H. **Client ID:** Our previously created OAuth credential Client ID

    I. **Client Secret:** Our previously created OAuth credential client secret

    J. **Scope:** `https://www.googleapis.com/auth/cloud-platform`

8. Click the **Get New Access Token** button to retrieve a new token:

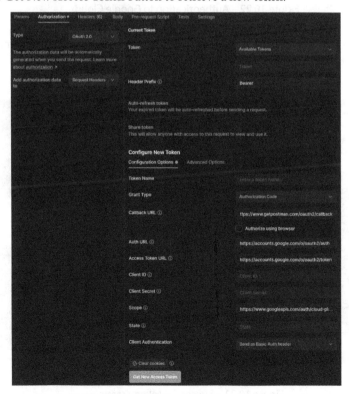

Figure 10.21 – New token filled with necessary information

9.   We need to authenticate using our email and password:

Figure 10.22 – Authentication to Google Cloud

10. We need to accept Postman permissions. If you are okay with Postman managing your Google Cloud data, proceed by clicking **Allow**.

11. The token will be successfully created and can be used with Google Cloud:

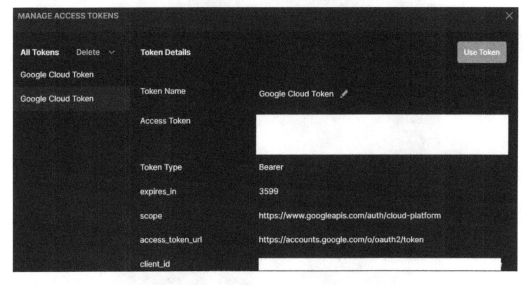

Figure 10.23 – Successful token creation

12. To finalize the token creation process, click the **Use Token** button.

13. Finally, after completing the authorization process, we can execute the GET call. Click the **SEND** button. In the response's **Body** section, we will see the response's output and Google compute instance details:

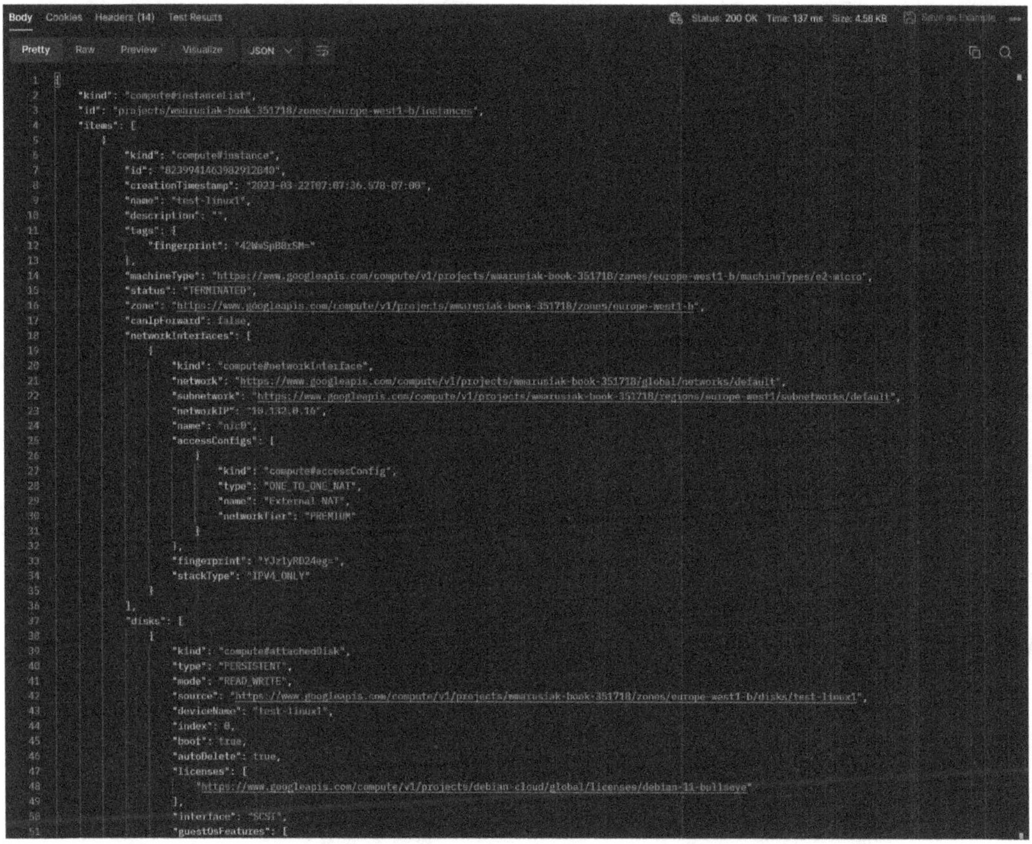

Figure 10.24 – Successful response and the compute instance details

Now that we've learned how to use Google Cloud APIs and retrieve information about compute instances, we will proceed with more hands-on examples.

Interacting with data services using API calls

Google Cloud offers comprehensive documentation about the usage of its APIs. We recommend several valid URLs that you should visit if you want to dive deeper:

- `https://cloud.google.com/apis/docs/overview`: General overview of the cloud APIs concept

- `https://developers.google.com/apis-explorer`: A tool that lets you try out Google API methods without having to write any code

- `https://cloud.google.com/apis/docs/getting-started`: A getting started guide for working with Google Cloud APIs

In this section, we will create a Pub/Sub architecture with one topic and two subscriptions based on the following diagram:

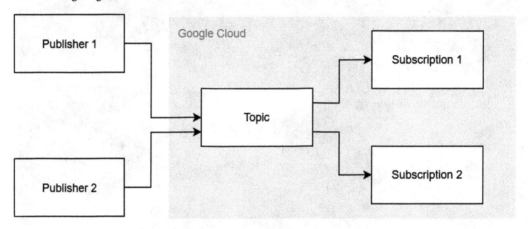

Figure 10.25 – Pub/Sub architecture

We will work with the REST APIs located at `https://cloud.google.com/pubsub/docs/reference/rest`.

We will start with topic creation and use **REST Resource: v1.projects.topics API**:

1. First, we will use a `PUT HTTP` request, `https://pubsub.googleapis.com/v1/projects/{project}/topics/{topic}`, where we need to replace `{project}` with our project ID and `{topic}` with a new topic name:

Figure 10.26 – Pub/Sub new topic creation with the REST API

2. We can check whether the topic exists via a REST API call. We can run a GET REST API call
    with the `https://pubsub.googleapis.com/v1/projects/{PROJECT_ID}/`
    `topics` URL. In our case, a topic was successfully created:

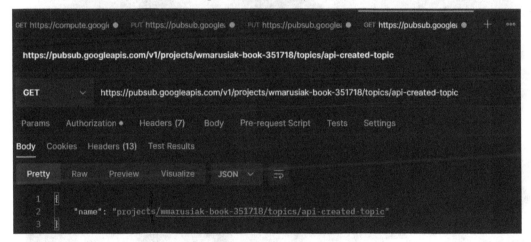

Figure 10.27 – Pub/Sub new topic was created

3. Now, we have two topics, called `api-created-subscription-1` and `api-created-subscription-2`. We will use the PUT method and send it to `https://pubsub.googleapis.com/v1/projects/{PROJECT_ID}/subscriptions/{SUBSCRIPTION_NAME}`. As usual, we need to replace PROJECT ID and SUBSCRIPTION NAME. In addition, we need to add the following JSON payload in the **Body** section. We need to replace `TOPIC_NAME` with the previously created topic and `SUBSCRIPTION_NAME` with the new name of the topic we want to create:

```
{
  "topic": "projects/{PROJECT_ID}/topics/{TOPIC_NAME}",
    "name": "{SUBSCRIPTION_NAME}"
}
```

We will get the following output:

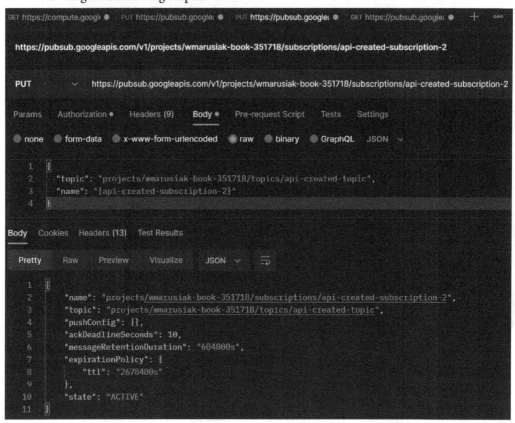

Figure 10.28 – Pub/Sub new subscription was created

4. These newly created subscriptions will also be visible in the Google Cloud console:

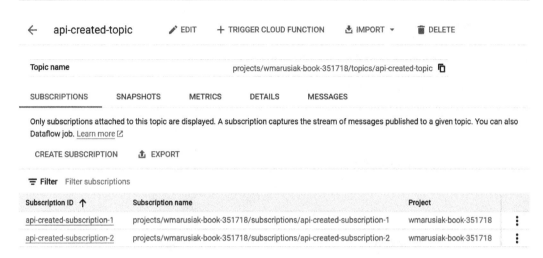

Figure 10.29 – Pub/Sub sample architecture visible in the Google Cloud console

As you can see, creating Google Cloud resources using APIs can be done much faster than in the Google Cloud console and they can easily be integrated into applications. This example focused on Pub/Sub, but more sophisticated architectures or applications can be created with all other Google Cloud services and their available APIs.

Summary

Google Cloud and its data processing services cover many problems. We started by looking at messaging and leveraging Pub/Sub and Pub/Sub Lite to integrate various Google Cloud products. We then learned about Dataproc, where we can quickly run fully managed Apache Hadoop, Apache Spark, or Apache Pig clusters and process massive amounts of data. Finally, Dataflow, a fully managed Apache Beam-based product, allows us to develop, execute, and process data pipelines in a simple, fast, and scalable way.

At the end of this chapter, we discovered another way to interact with Google Cloud services – REST APIs. We learned how to authenticate with Google Cloud using OAuth 2.0 and how to perform simple HTTP REST API calls. We leveraged our knowledge to create a Pub/Sub topic and attach it to its subscriptions.

The next chapter will discuss Google Cloud's operations suite (formerly Stackdriver), which provides a set of fully managed services for monitoring, logging, and tracing your applications and Google Cloud services. These services can help you improve the performance, reliability, and security of your applications.

Questions

Answer the following questions to test your knowledge of this chapter:

1. Choose the correct statement about Pub/Sub:

    A. Pub/Sub is a synchronous messaging service.

    B. Pub/Sub is an asynchronous messaging service.

    C. Pub/Sub is a message broker.

    D. Pub/Sub is a distributed messaging system.

2. Pub/Sub consists of which of the following components?

    A. Teams and subscribers

    B. Publishers and subscribers

    C. Subscribers and broadcasters

    D. Broadcasters and receivers

3. Choose the incorrect Pub/Sub use case:

    A. Enterprise event bus

    B. Real-time event distribution

    C. Refreshing static caches

    D. Parallel processing and workflows

4. Choose the correct statement:

    A. Pub/Sub is the only messaging service available in Google Cloud.

    B. Pub/Sub and Pub/Sub Lite are messaging services available in Google Cloud.

    C. Google Cloud offers Apache Kafka as a service.

    D. Pub/Sub cannot be used as a service-to-service communication service.

5. Choose the correct statement about a Pub/Sub topic:

    A. A topic is an application that creates and sends messages.

    B. A topic is an application with a subscription to a single or multiple events.

    C. A topic is a named resource to which publishers send messages.

    D. A topic requires acknowledgment to proceed with the message.

6. When a Pub/Sub message is not acknowledged before its acknowledgment deadline has expired, what does Pub/Sub do?

    A. Pub/Sub resends the message.

    B. Pub/Sub deletes the message.

    C. Pub/Sub keeps the message in the queue until it is acknowledged.

    D. Pub/Sub does nothing.

7. Dataproc provides out-of-the-box and end-to-end support for many of the most popular job types, including which of the following?

    A. Pidgeon jobs, PySpark, and MapReduce

    B. Spark, Spark SQL, PySpark, MapReduce, Hive, and Pig jobs

    C. PySpark, MapReduce, Hive, and Anaconda

    D. Spark, Spark SQL, and MySQL

8. What development languages are supported in Dataproc?

    A. Java

    B. Java and Scala

    C. Scala

    D. Java, Scala, Python, and R

9. Choose two correct statements about Dataproc:

    A. After submitting the job in the Dataproc cluster, it can't be stopped.

    B. It is possible to SSH into every machine from within the cluster.

    C. Dataproc only supports Debian and SUSE Linux distributions.

    D. Dataproc is billed on a per-second basis.

10. What is the main difference between Dataproc on GCE and Dataproc on GKE?

    A. Dataproc on GCE is faster.

    B. Dataproc on GKE requires an internal load balancer.

    C. Dataproc on GKE does not include separate master and worker VMs.

    D. Dataproc on GKE requires a separate GKE cluster and node pool.

11. Choose the correct statement about Dataproc web interfaces:

   A. Customers only have access to Spark History Server.

   B. Access to web interfaces costs additional fees.

   C. Customers can access YARN ResourceManager, MapReduce Job History, Spark History Server, HDFS NameNode, YARN Application Timeline, and Tez.

   D. To use additional Dataproc web interfaces, it is necessary to configure a site-to-site VPN.

12. Single-node Dataproc clusters are best suitable for which use cases? (Choose all that apply.)

   A. Trying out new versions of Spark and Hadoop

   B. Building a proof of concept

   C. Small-scale non-critical data processing

   D. Large-scale parallel data processing

   E. High-availability workloads

13. Choose the correct statement about Dataflow:

   A. Dataflow is a fully managed Apache Spark service.

   B. Dataflow is a fully managed Apache Kafka service.

   C. Dataflow is a fully managed Apache Beam service.

   D. Dataflow is a fully managed Apache Airflow service.

14. To use the Dataflow service, which API is needed to be enabled?

   A. `dataflew.googleapis.com`

   B. `dataflow.gogleapis.com`

   C. `dataflow.googleapis.com`

   D. `dataflow.googleapis.net`

15. Which `gcloud` command can be used to configure the default Dataproc region?

   A. `gcloud set config dataproc/region YOUR_REGION`

   B. `gcloud config set region/dataproc -r YOUR_REGION`

   C. `cloud config set dataproc -n YOUR_REGION`

   D. `gcloud config ser dataproc/region YOUR_REGION`

16. When configuring an OAuth client ID in **APIs & Services** under the **Credentials** section, what can you use to restrict the domains to which the application can send requests?

    A. Authorized JavaScript origins and authorized redirect URLs

    B. Authorized redirect URLs

    C. Authorized domains

    D. Authorized JavaScript origins

17. Google Cloud offers many ways to authenticate with APIs. Choose the correct ones:

    A. Authentication using client libraries

    B. Authenticate using REST

    C. Authenticate using API keys

    D. All of the above

18. Which API calls are valid?

    A. GET, POST, REMOVE, UPDATE

    B. POST, REMOVE, TRACE, CONNECT

    C. TRACE, PATCH, GET, PUT

    D. SPOT, PUT, PATCH, TRACE

19. Choose the correct statement:

    A. When making HTTP calls, we always receive a client and server response.

    B. 404 Not Found means that the requested resource could not be found.

    C. 200 OK means the request was successful, and the API call succeeded.

    D. 404 Bad Request means the request was malformed or invalid.

20. Which API call can be used to check whether a Pub/Sub topic exists?

    A. GET https://pubsub.googleapis.com/v1/projects/{PROJECT_ID}/topics

    B. PUT https://pubsub.googleapis.com/v1/projects/{PROJECT_ID}/topics

    C. GET https:// googleapis.com/pubsub/v1/projects/{PROJECT_ID}/topics

    D. TRACE https://pubsub.googleapis.com/v1/projects/{PROJECT_ID}/topics

Answers

The following are the answers to this chapter's questions:

1B, 2B, 3C, 4B, 5C, 6A, 7B, 8D, 9BD, 10C, 11C, 12A, B, and C, 13C, 14C, 15C, 16A, 17D, 18C, 19BC, 20A

11
Monitoring, Logging, and Estimating Costs in GCP

At first look, the observability services don't appear to be the most critical topic. It is possible to run workloads without monitoring them. But soon, after you start deploying services at scale, you will look for a monitoring service to optimize or plan the usage of Google Cloud resources. You will want to investigate logs once the first issues appear. Then, you will need to build customized dashboards and alerts to get notified of the status of your services.

This chapter will help you better understand what kind of observability tools Google Cloud offers and how to use them for your workloads.

We will focus on Google Cloud's operations suite (formerly Stackdriver), which consists of the following fully managed services – **Cloud Monitoring** for visibility into the health of your applications and Google Cloud services, **Cloud Logging** for real-time log management, and application-level diagnostic tools such as **Trace** and **Profiler** to reduce the latency and cost of your services.

In this chapter, we will also learn how to estimate costs in Google Cloud.

We are going to cover the following main topics:

- Monitoring
- Logging
- Diagnostics
- Estimating costs with Google Cloud Pricing Calculator

As a beginner, learning about monitoring and logging can be difficult since you usually need a deployed real-life application to access more interesting statistics and logs. If you're up for a challenge, you can try following the steps in the *Getting started with Python* documentation (check the following link) and deploy a real-life web application called **Bookshelf**. This application uses Cloud Run and Google Cloud Storage and can be accessed from the internet, giving you the chance to collect some interesting logs and metrics: `https://cloud.google.com/python/docs/getting-started`.

Cloud Monitoring

If you have ever worked as an on-premises system administrator, you have probably physically inspected or logged in to your server's management console in response to various alerts that have fired in your monitoring console. For example, a fan or a disk failure, a power outage, or a network port flap can happen in any data center and can be easily detected thanks to monitoring systems.

Although moving to Google Cloud means you don't have to monitor the underlying network and physical infrastructure anymore, you are still responsible for your applications in a similar way as you were responsible for them on-premises.

Google offers a highly efficient service called Cloud Monitoring, which is avaiable by default once you create your project. This service provides many tools for collecting, analyzing, and presenting real-time monitoring data for both Google Cloud services and user workloads. Most Google Cloud services are already connected to the monitoring system when you set them up and start using them. Cloud Monitoring is not limited to Google Cloud; it can also be used to collect metrics from other solution providers, such as those available on-premises or on AWS. This makes it a versatile tool for monitoring hybrid-cloud environments.

If you plan to have multiple Google Cloud projects and on-premises workloads, you might assume you must log in to various places to monitor everything. However, that is not the case. Instead, you can create a dedicated monitoring project to gather data from the entire setup and view it all in one place. To expand the scope of your metrics, use the **+ ADD GCP PROJECTS** option to include other projects in your monitoring project. Refer to the accompanying screenshot for guidance:

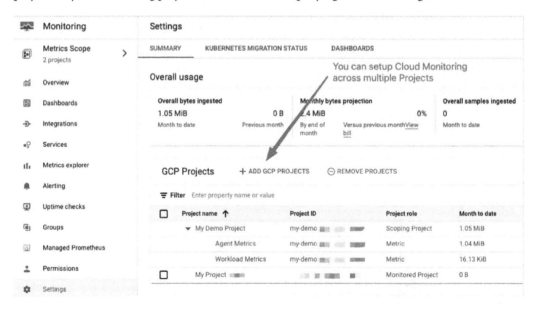

Figure 11.1 – Increasing the monitoring scope by adding more projects to Cloud Monitoring

An excellent way to start learning about Cloud Monitoring is by exploring what your service's default dashboards can offer and creating your personalized dashboards in the next step. For example, if you create a Compute Engine VM or start using Google Cloud Storage or GKE, a service-specific dashboard will be added in the **Dashboards** section under the **GCP** category, as shown in the following screenshot. This is the section where you can start discovering the default metrics:

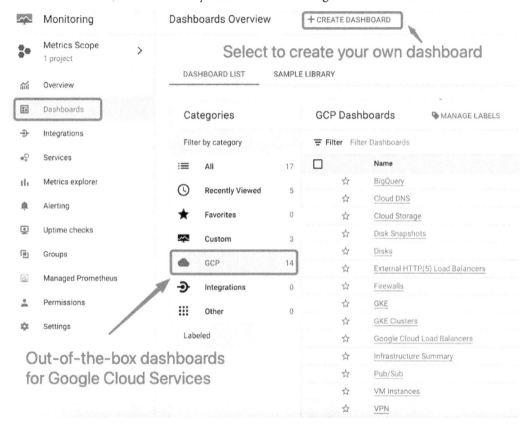

Figure 11.2 – Default dashboards for GCP services

To help you easily understand what can be monitored without any extra setup, here is a table showing some Google Cloud services and their corresponding pre-built metric parameters:

Service	Selected out-of-the-box metrics
Compute Engine VM	CPU utilization, network traffic, disk operations, and uptime
Google Cloud Storage	Number of requests per bucket, network traffic sent/received per bucket, total number of objects stored in a bucket, and size of the objects

Service	Selected out-of-the-box metrics
GKE	Container restarts, CPU utilization, and memory utilization
Cloud Run	Container CPU utilization, container memory utilization, request count, request latencies, sent bytes, and received bytes

Table 11.1 – Examples of pre-build metrics for selected Google Cloud workloads

You can also use built-in charts and out-of-the-box metrics to build customized views to have all the services that build your application in one dashboard.

In the **Dashboards** overview, select **+ CREATE DASHBOARD**, provide its name, and as a next step, drag and drop a metric you need and rearrange or resize it to fit nicely into your dashboard. You can later edit and adjust your dashboard after observing the metrics for some time, so they show only the relevant data.

Let's look at the example of such a customized dashboard. Its purpose is to have a single dashboard to view resource usage, alerts, and logs for Compute Engine VMs. It consists of four charts – a stacked bar chart to present their CPU utilization, a small text chart that could be used to add more details about monitored objects, an alert chart that shows whether a preconfigured threshold for CPU is exceeded, and a large logs panel showing recent logs from the VMs:

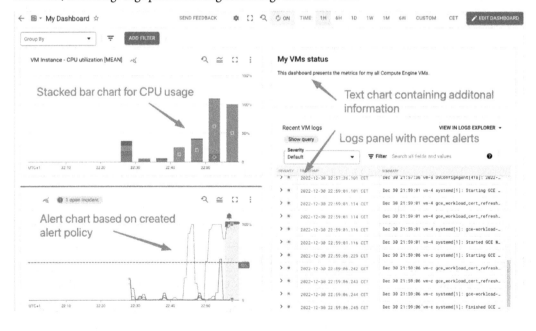

Figure 11.3 – Example of a customized monitoring dashboard based on out-of-the-box metrics

Once you start exploring various charts, you will soon notice that although all the data seems to be presented for services such as GKE or App Engine, some of the Compute Engine charts are empty.

Specifically, you won't find memory metrics for your VMs unless you install an additional component called **Ops Agent**. Keep in mind that this only applies to Compute Engine VMs; GKE and App Engine already have built-in agents for collecting metrics, so you don't need to install anything extra for those services.

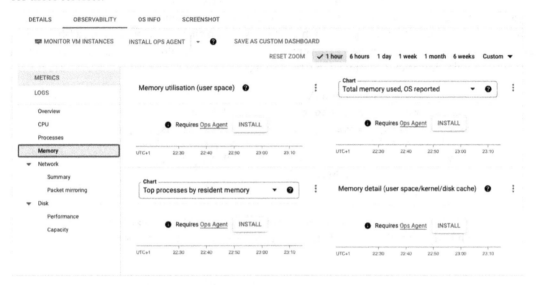

Figure 11.4 – Some of the metrics require Ops Agent installation

Ops Agent is a collectd-based daemon that collects telemetry data from Compute Engine VMs for cloud monitoring and logging services. It collects data for supported operating systems and applications from the inside of a VM. You can install it via the Google Cloud console or a command line.

The command to install the agent on the Linux VM is as follows:

```
curl -sSO https://dl.google.com/cloudagents/add-google-cloud-ops-
agent-repo.sh
sudo bash add-google-cloud-ops-agent-repo.sh --also-install
```

You can check whether it is running using the following command:

```
sudo service google-cloud-ops-agent status
```

When you create a Compute Engine VM, you have the option to attach either a default or a dedicated service account to it.

The Ops Agent uses this service account to interact with the Logging and Monitoring services, so it requires permission. To ensure proper functionality, assign the service account the following roles:

- For Monitoring, use Monitoring Metric Writer
- For Logging, use Logs Writer

To install the agent on multiple VMs, use Agent Policies. This feature automates the installation and upgrading of a fleet of Ops Agents. For instance, if you have a large number of Debian v10 Compute Engine instances, you can create a policy to install Ops Agent on all of them by attaching a label such as env: production to the instances in your project and enabling automated upgrades. To execute this, use the following gcloud command in Cloud Shell:

```
gcloud beta compute instances \
    ops-agents policies create ops-agents-debian \
    --agent-rules="type=ops-agent,version=current-major,package-
state=installed,enable-autoupgrade=true" \
    --os-types=short-name=debian,version=10 \
    --group-labels=env=production\
    --project=my-project
```

Once the policy is in use, any existing or newly created compliant VM with the env: production label, as shown in the following screenshot, will trigger the Ops Agent installation:

Figure 11.5 – An example of a VM with an env:production tag running on
Debian v10, compliant with the "ops-agents-debian" policy

Let's explore how the Agent Policy can be implemented in practice. The preceding screenshot is taken from the **VM instances** section in the **Compute Engine** menu. Clicking on any of the VMs will take you to a new page with more specific information about that particular VM. On the left-hand side, there is the **DETAILS** tab view, where you can see that this VM has the necessary label: env: production. On the right-hand side, the **Basic info** view shows that the required version of the Debian operating system is 10, which should trigger the Ops Agent installation through the Agent Policy.

The following screenshot shows a log extract (Cloud Logging will be discussed later in this chapter) confirming that `ops-agent-policy` was activated for this VM and that the Ops Agent was installed successfully.

Figure 11.6 – The Agent Policy installs Ops Agent on compliant VMs

Once Ops Agent is installed, Google Cloud Monitoring detects it and collects more detailed information, such as information about memory usage and running processes. For example, the following screenshot shows previously empty dashboards that are now populated with data once Ops Agent is installed:

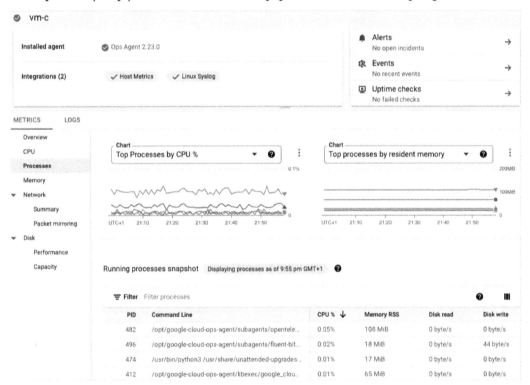

Figure 11.7 – VM processes metrics available after Ops Agent installation

Now that we know how to set up and adjust monitoring of our services, we can look at the dashboards and analyze, for example, how many resources they are using. But do we have to watch dashboards constantly? In the next section, we will see how this process can be automated.

Creating Cloud Monitoring alerts based on resource metrics

Monitoring dashboards alone, even the most sophisticated ones, wouldn't be enough for system administrators as they would have to monitor them 24/7 looking for various anomalies. That is why Google Cloud Monitoring provides alerting capabilities for the following use cases:

- **User notifications** – Used to notify admins when metrics exceed a certain threshold or when certain conditions are met. Administrators can use this feature to prevent potential issues proactively. For instance, if the CPU usage of a VM instance increases unexpectedly, it's advisable to investigate it as it could be due to a coding bug or ransomware attack. This preemptive approach can help avoid problems before they occur.

- **Autoscaling** – You can use metrics exported from your application to auto-scale its underlying **Managed Instance Group** (**MIG**). The autoscaling feature will adjust the number of instances in response to a signal (such as CPU usage or latency) from your metrics. This feature automatically adjusts the number of instances based on metrics such as CPU usage or latency, eliminating the need for manual monitoring and modifications.

- **Uptime checks** – With uptime checks, you can monitor the availability of internet-accessible URLs, VMs, APIs, or load balancers. Probes placed around the globe continuously send requests to a target that you can configure and report its responses. As a result, you can create alerts based on failed uptime checks and get paged when your service is down.

Let's take a closer look at the first use case and examine the various ways in which a user can receive alerts and how to configure a CPU-usage-based alert for selected VM instances.

To create alerts based on metrics, you need to specify how Google Cloud Monitoring should notify you. You can configure it under the **Alerting** section by selecting the **Edit Notification Channels** option. You can use the following options for your notifications: **email**, **SMS**, **webhook**, **Pub/Sub**, **Slack**, and **PagerDuty**. If you are using the Cloud Console mobile app to manage Google Cloud resources from your iOS or Android device directly, you can also use it as your notification channel.

Notification channels are not mandatory, but the alternative is that alerts will only be displayed in the Google Cloud Console, and you will have to monitor the **Alerting** dashboard continuously.

When notification channels are set, you need to complete the following steps to create your alert:

1. In the **Alerting** section, select + **CREATE POLICY**.

2. Create your first alert condition by selecting a metric from the metrics explorer. For example, to create an alert based on CPU usage for VM instances, you can select **VM Instance** and from the **Instance** section, select **CPU usage**, as shown in the following screenshot:

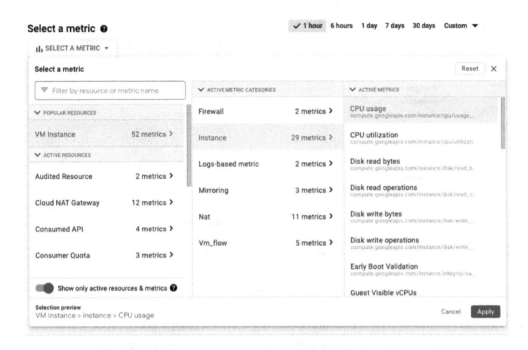

Figure 11.8 – Example view on VM Instance metrics explorer

3. Add a filter if you want to create an alert for a specific subset of resources – for example, for VMs with a particular name or running in a specific region. This setting is optional.

4. Select the **minutes** or **hours** option in the rolling window or provide a custom value. This parameter and the rolling window function describe how the threshold will be calculated. For example, when we set the rolling window to **10 minutes** and the function to **mean**, a mean value for the duration of 10 minutes will be calculated. Other possible functions are, among others, *min*, *max*, *count*, *sum*, and *percentage*. Click **Next** to confirm your selection.

5. The next step is to configure the trigger for the alert. For the threshold-based triggers, you can specify whether the alert should be fired for the following:

- Every violation

- A percentage of violations

- A number of violations

   You must also specify whether the threshold position is above or below the threshold value. Once you select the threshold, it will appear on the chart on the right-hand side, and you will be able to verify how the value you provided corresponds to the situation from the selected time.

   An alternative option to the threshold value is the absence of a metric. It gets triggered when metrics are absent for a selected period.

The last step in this section is to provide the condition name (if you want to use multiple conditions, a name would be beneficial) and confirm the settings by clicking **Next**:

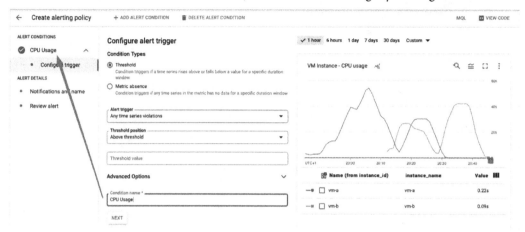

Figure 11.9 – Alert condition's view

6. You can create more alert conditions by selecting **+ADD ALERT CONDITION**. It is possible to create advanced scenarios with a multi-condition trigger, where you get a single alert when a subset of conditions happens simultaneously – for example, the VM CPU value exceeds 50%, and at the same time, the memory utilization reaches 80%:

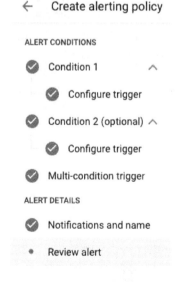

Figure 11.10 – Multi-condition view

In the **Notifications and name** section, select your notification channels. After the alert is triggered, you will not only be notified via selected channels but an alert will also be shown in the **Alerting** section in the Google Cloud Console. You can specify how long an unattended alert should be visible in your Console in the **Incident autoclose duration** section:

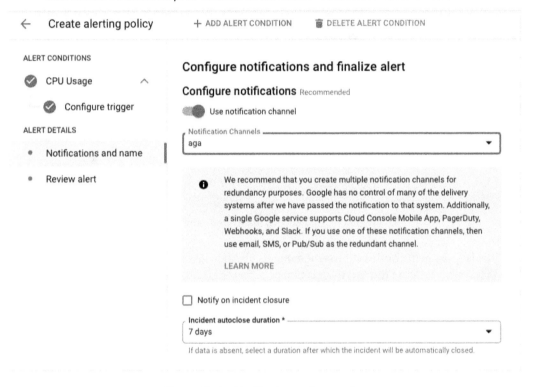

Figure 11.11 – Notification and name view

7. The **Notifications and name** section also includes an optional text field to provide instructions and the steps an operator can follow once this alert is triggered:

Figure 11.12 – Additional instructions that can be provided for an alert

8. The last step in the **Notifications and name** section is to give the name for this alerting policy that will be visible in the **Alerting** section once an alert is fired.

9. When you review your policy, save it. It will be enabled by default.

Figure 11.13 – An example of an email notification for an alerting policy

When an alert is triggered, Google Cloud Monitoring will notify you of the issue through the designated notification channels. As shown in *Figure 11.13*, you may receive a similar email notification about the CPU utilization of a VM.

Creating and ingesting Cloud Monitoring custom metrics

In addition to monitoring native GCP services and operating systems of your VMs (via Ops Agent), Cloud Monitoring provides you with options to closely monitor your applications. If your application runs on a Compute Engine VM and is listed as a supported third-party application in the Google Cloud Monitoring documentation (`https://cloud.google.com/monitoring/agent/ops-agent/third-party`), you can leverage Ops Agent to monitor it. For example, Ops Agent supports nginx (a web server app) integration to collect connection metrics and access logs. If your VM has Ops Agent installed and you follow the Ops Agent nginx configuration instructions published on the aforementioned URL, Cloud Monitoring will start ingesting new metrics related to web server traffic.

The following screenshot shows the **Dashboard list** section with an **Integration Dashboards** category in which **Nginx Overview** was added automatically after the Ops Agent configuration:

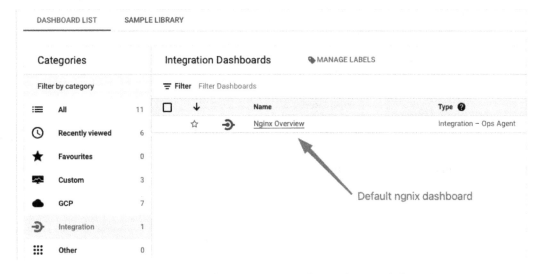

Figure 11.14 – Once the nginx service is detected, a new dedicated
dashboard is shown under the Integration section

If you look for more customized dashboards for your nginx service, you can set them up the same way we do later in the *Custom metrics* section. **VM Instance** metrics will have new additional nginx-related metrics such as Nginx request count.

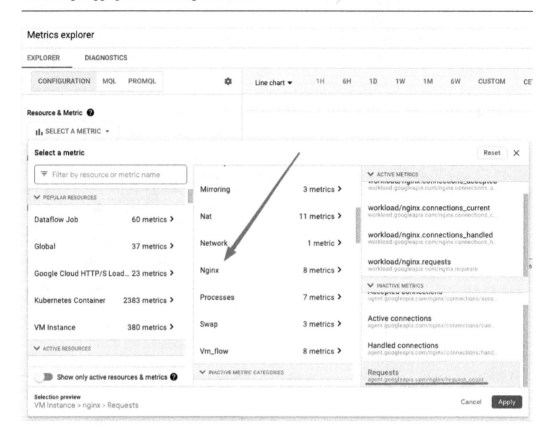

Figure 11.15 – Metrics available for nginx

The following is an example of a customized dashboard built using dedicated nginx metrics:

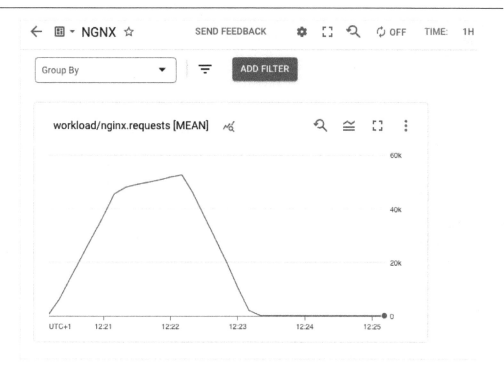

Figure 11.16 – Example dashboard with nginx requests

It shows the number of incoming requests that can be tracked thanks to the nginx-specific Ops Agent configuration. Similarly, we can leverage dedicated metrics for all other supported third-party applications.

Custom metrics ingestion

What if your application doesn't run inside a Compute Engine VM, built-in metrics don't collect what you need, or a more customized approach to monitoring your app is required? For such scenarios, Google Cloud provides custom metrics and log-based metrics.

Custom metrics

Suppose you want to collect application-specific metrics that the built-in Cloud Monitoring doesn't offer. In that case, you can capture those by using the client library for the monitoring APIs directly in your code and send the metrics to Cloud Monitoring. It is the lowest possible layer at which you can control and collect data. The downside to this approach is that you will have to manage the entire setup in your code.

The alternative would be to use the OpenCensus metrics instrumentation library to define custom metrics. It is an open source framework for collecting metrics used in Google Cloud as a default ingestion mechanism. If you don't want to use instrumentation libraries, there is another possibility – to use Google Cloud Managed Service for Prometheus. Prometheus is a standard for monitoring in the open source ecosystem and offers a wide range of system integrations in multi-cloud environments. In Google Cloud, it can be used to monitor Kubernetes and VM workloads.

Log-based metrics

With log-based metrics, you can configure metrics based on log entries from Cloud Logging (this service will be the subject of the next section) without any additional instrumentation. For example, if you want to monitor a specific behavior of your application and you know how this behavior is represented in logs, there is no need to use a monitoring API; you can configure a dashboard where the specific occurrence of a log entry is parsed and monitored.

Let's look at an example application. It creates a log entry, `Application Restarted`, every time a specific process fails and is reloaded. We can create a simple query in **Logs Explorer** to list this specific entry. The following figure shows that the restart incident happens quite frequently.

You can create log-based metrics from **Logs Explorer** directly. There is a **Create metric** option in the same line as **Histogram**. Alternatively, you will find **Log-based Metrics** in the **Logging** section in the menu on the left:

Figure 11.17 – Logs Explorer showing selected log entries

The log-based metrics feature allows you to create metrics that will be later visible in **Metrics Explorer** in the **Monitoring** section. There are two types of metrics:

- **Counter metrics**: These are used to track the number of events occurrences, and can be used to count how many times a particular error occurred.

- **Distribution metrics**: These are used to extract numeric values from logs, and can be used to extract regular expressions and numeric values such as the latency of an application.

In our example, we will select the option to count the number of entries matching a chosen filter. We will also provide the metric's name, description, and units.

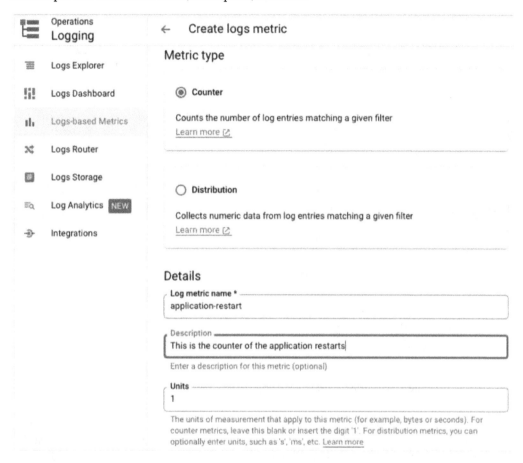

Figure 11.18 – Logs-based metrics configuration

In the **Filter** section, we need to specify what logs we want to monitor and how we want to parse them. We will use the instance name, type, and text from the log entry in this example:

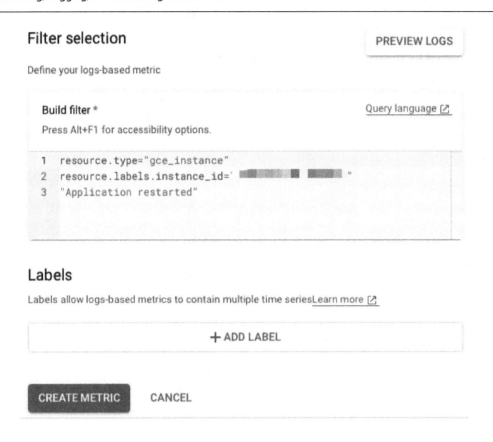

Figure 11.19 – The continuation of logs-based metrics configuration

You can build complex filters that count certain text occurrences and parse the logs to ingest certain values or array types. More information on the Logging query language that is used for building such filters can be found at the following link: https://cloud.google.com/logging/docs/view/logging-query-language.

Once our metric is created, it can be found in **Metrics Explorer** (initially introduced in *Figure 11.8*) under the /logging/user section:

Figure 11.20 – Logs-based metrics in Metrics Explorer

The next step is to create a dashboard using the newly created metric. The parameters we need can be defined in the **ADVANCED** section – no preprocessing and grouping, **count** as an alignment function, and a 1-minute period:

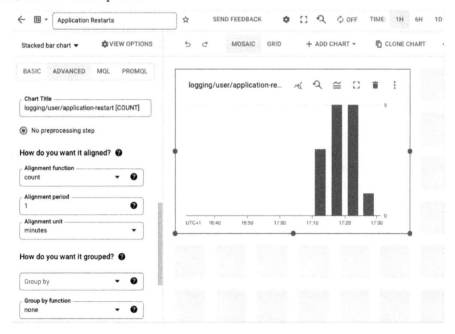

Figure 11.21 – Creating an advanced chart that counts log entry occurrences

Once the dashboard is saved, it can also be used to create alerts when the counters exceed a certain threshold. The alert configuration was explained earlier in this chapter. In the following screenshot, there is an example of an alert configured every time an application has two restarts in a minute:

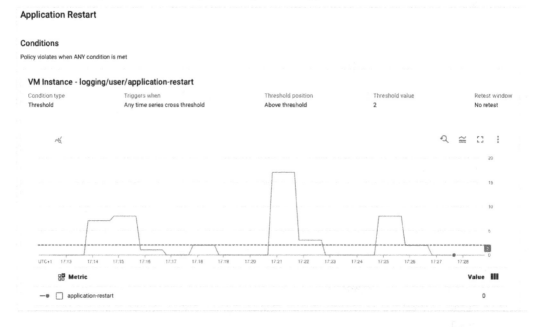

Figure 11.22 – Alert threshold set up on log-based metrics

When creating a log-based alert, consider that there can be a delay between when an error happens for your application and when enough errors are aggregated in the metrics to trigger a notification.

Cloud Logging

Cloud Logging is a comprehensive solution for managing logs generated by your applications, the platform they run on, and the underlying infrastructure, whether it's on Google Cloud, other cloud providers, or on-premises systems. This fully managed service allows you to easily store, search, analyze, monitor, and receive alerts on logging data and events from all of these environments.

Logs are one of the most important sources of information when it comes to day-to-day admin activities and troubleshooting. Google Cloud services are capable of generating various types of logs, including the following:

- **Platform logs**: These are, in most cases, enabled by default and can't be disabled; they are logs from Google Cloud services such as Compute Engine VMs or Google Cloud Storage.

- **Component logs**: These are similar to platform logs but come from the Google software components that run on user-owned systems.

- **Security logs**: These logs are collected for auditing and compliance purposes. In *Chapter 12*, detailed information about security logs will be provided.

- **User-written logs**: These are enabled and controlled by a user. They are logs collected by Ops Agent, APIs, client libraries, and third-party applications.

- **Multi-cloud and hybrid-cloud logs**: These come from other cloud providers and on-premises environments.

The Logging service, by default, encrypts the ingested logs using Google-managed encryption keys. But it is possible to use customer-managed keys to control the encryption process altogether.

When designing system architecture, you may want to have control over where your logs are streamed and for how long they are stored. To route logs to specified destinations, Google Cloud uses **log sinks**. All logs are stored in `_Required` and `_Default` log buckets, but it is also possible to keep them in other destinations, such as the following:

- Google Cloud Storage
- BigQuery
- Pub/Sub, which can be used for third-party integrations such as Splunk
- Customer-owned cloud logging buckets

When your project is created, there are two sinks defined:

- `_Required`, which sends logs to a global audit log bucket where the logs are stored for 400 days. You can't delete a `_Required` sink or edit it to change the log destination. Logs that are stored in an audit log bucket are related to the following:

  - Admin activities related to modifying configuration or metadata, for example, when a VM instance is created

  - System events from Google Cloud Platform

  - Access transparency related to a justified Google's access to your resources

- `_Default`, which sends the remaining part of logs to a global default log bucket where logs are stored for 30 days. A user can change the retention period. You can also delete the `_Default` sink and create your sinks if you don't want your logs to be stored in a global bucket.

The following diagram is based on *Routing and storage overview* from Google's documentation, which you can read here: `https://cloud.google.com/logging/docs/routing/overview`. It covers how logs are routed via default, customized sinks, and the default and customized destinations to route them:

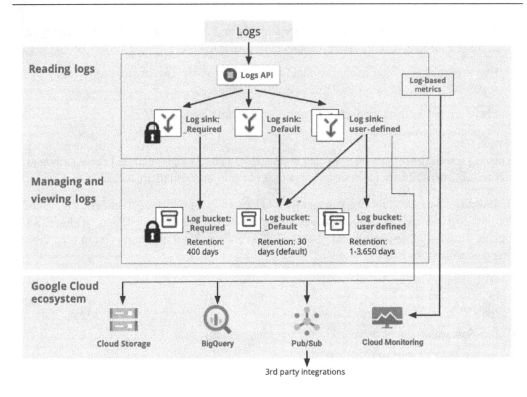

Figure 11.23 – Routing and storing Cloud Logging entries

In addition to _Required and _Default sinks, users can define their own sinks and send data to other locations, also customizing the retention time to adjust to their company's policy. In the upcoming sections, we will learn how to customize such **log sinks**, but first, let's look at how logs are presented in Cloud Logging dashboards and how to filter logs before we send them to a new destination.

Viewing and filtering logs in Cloud Logging

We already had a sneak peek into Cloud Logging when we built log-based metrics in the *Cloud Monitoring* section. Now, it's time to explain how to view logs with **Logs Explorer**.

The upper section of **Logs Explorer** includes a **Query** pane with a time-range selector, an editor to build queries, a filter to narrow down a scope, and a search box where you can search across all log fields:

Figure 11.24 – Logs Explorer Query pane

On the left-hand side, a **Log fields** pane is updated according to the fields shown in log entries. It has a **SEVERITY** section, a **RESOURCE TYPE** or service section, and others that help narrow down the logging scope.

In terms of severity, each log entry is categorized based on the seriousness of the issue. The **SEVERITY** levels include **Emergency**, **Alert**, **Critical**, **Error**, **Warning**, **Notice**, **Info**, **Debug**, and **Default**. You can utilize these levels to refine your search.

For example, only **Error** logs will be listed if you select an **Error** severity level. If you select the **VM instance** resource type, the log output will be limited to Compute Engine VMs.

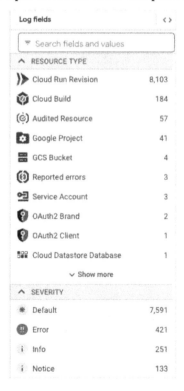

Figure 11.25 – Logs Explorer Log fields pane

In the center pane, you will find a **Histogram** section where the distribution of logs over time is visualized, as can be seen in the following screenshot. It will help you to look for trends in your system's behavior or detect when a specific issue started.

Figure 11.26 – Logs Explorer Histogram and Query results section

Under **Histogram**, there is a **Query results** pane where logs are listed. You can expand all nested fields in a selected log entry, show or hide similar ones, download logs, or save them to Google Drive.

Viewing specific log message details in Cloud Logging

If you are looking for a specific message in Cloud Logging to examine its content, you can start by listing logs of a certain severity coming from a specific resource in the **Log fields** pane. Once you select a time range in the **Query** pane to narrow your search, you can inspect the **Query results** pane. When you expand a log entry and select a field, you will see an option to show/hide matching entries:

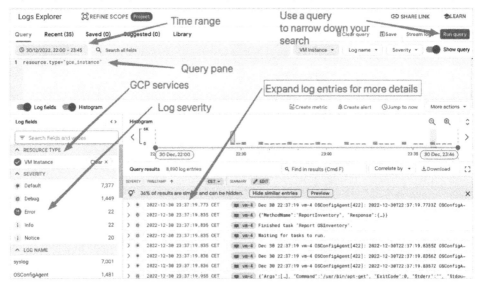

Figure 11.27 – Logs Explorer sections that help to narrow down a log search

Selecting **Show/hide similar entries** will populate a **Query** pane with a query that matches your request. The **Query** pane is where you can build more sophisticated logic that will narrow down your log search:

Figure 11.28 – Using a Query pane to narrow down a log search

Let's look at the following screenshot. In the **Query** pane, there is a query that limits the log search to the Cloud Run service, showing only entries with the severity level of WARNING in the us-east4 zone and only the HTTP request with status of 400:

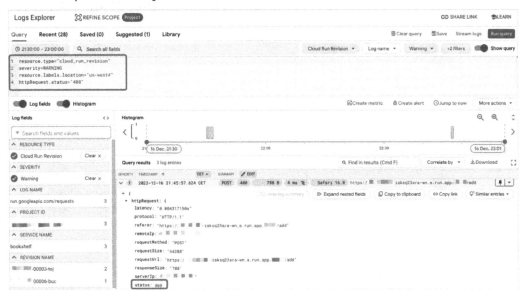

Figure 11.29 – Example query for logs related to HTTP service

Narrowing down a search scope will make your troubleshooting easier. But you may also want to limit the scope before sending logs to other destinations. In the next section, where we will learn how to configure log sinks; building filters to include specific logs will prove useful.

Please keep in mind that Logs Explorer is the ideal tool for troubleshooting and exploring log data. However, if you need assistance in creating insights and identifying trends, Google provides Log Analytics specifically for this purpose.

You can learn more about Log Analytics from this link:

`https://cloud.google.com/logging/docs/log-analytics#analytics`.

Configuring log routers

Imagine a situation where you have a policy in your company that requires you to keep all logs coming from your workloads in a specific geographic region. Because the `_Default` log bucket is global (logs generated in a particular region are stored in this region), you must change this default behavior.

To modify the destination of logs in your project, you need to change the configuration settings in the **Logs Router**. The Logs Router is responsible for receiving logs, filtering them based on user-defined criteria, and forwarding them to specified destinations. Let's see how we can adjust the Logs Router settings to send logs to a different location.

First, you will need to create a new log bucket by selecting **CREATE LOG BUCKET** in the **Logs Storage** section:

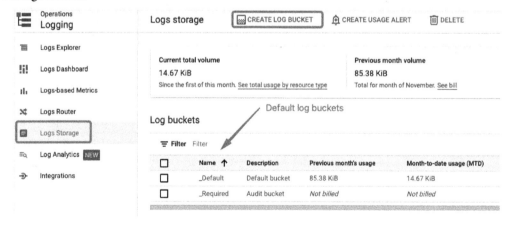

Figure 11.30 – Configuring a new log bucket

For the log bucket region, you can select a single region, global region, or multi-region such as the EU or US. The retention can be set between 1 and 3,650 days (around ten years) and modified later.

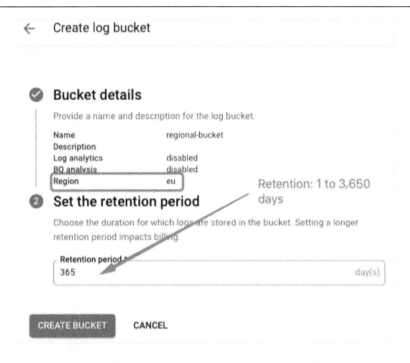

Figure 11.31 – Configuring a region and a retention period for a log bucket

Once a regional log bucket is created, you can either configure a new sink by selecting **CREATE SINK** in the **Cloud Router** section or edit an existing default one and point it to the new log bucket. If you create a new sink to replace the default one, you may want to build a new inclusion filter to include a specific subset of logs. Otherwise, all available logs will be routed to this new log bucket.

Figure 11.32 – Editing a default sink

To modify an existing `_Default` sink to send logs to a new log bucket, edit the sink and replace the existing bucket with your bucket in the **Select a log bucket** section and save the configuration:

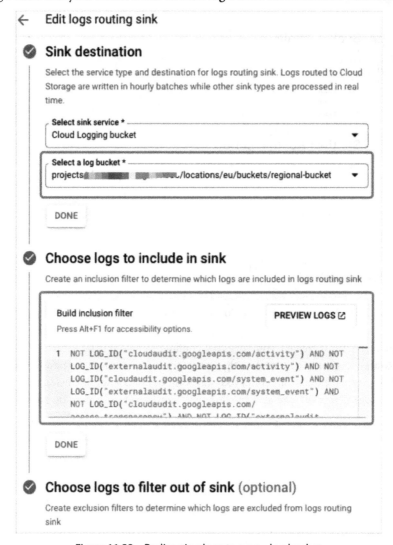

Figure 11.33 – Redirecting logs to a new log bucket

After the sink has been modified, the last step is to check that logs are now stored in the new log bucket. To ensure the sink works, go to **Logs Explorer** and select **REFINE SCOPE**. Then, in **Scope by storage**, select the new bucket.

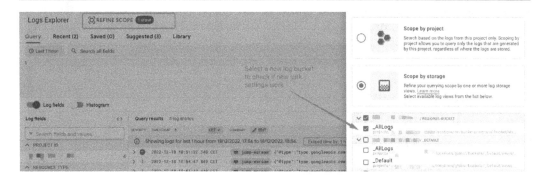

Figure 11.34 – Verifying that logs are stored in a new logs bucket

You should be able to see new logs appearing in the **Query results** section, as illustrated in the preceding screenshot.

Configuring log sinks to export logs to external systems

We configured a sink to route logs to a new log bucket in the previous section. Log buckets are the default choice for storing logs. It is also possible to route all or a subset of logs to alternative locations for longer retention (Google Cloud Storage), in-depth analysis (BigQuery), or third-party applications (in the cloud or on-premises).

When creating an alternative sink destination, one of the possible options is to send logs to a Cloud Storage bucket. Please note that a Cloud Storage bucket is a different destination from a Cloud Logging bucket. It is also not a real-time service because logs are written in hourly batches to Cloud Storage buckets.

If you want to export the logs to a third-party application that runs in the cloud or on-premises, you should use a Google Cloud Pub/Sub topic as the destination for your log sink. If there is network reachability between your application and your project and the required permissions, log files will populate in the configured Pub/Sub topic. Once you configure your application to pull messages from the Pub/Sub subscriptions, logs will be ingested to their final destination:

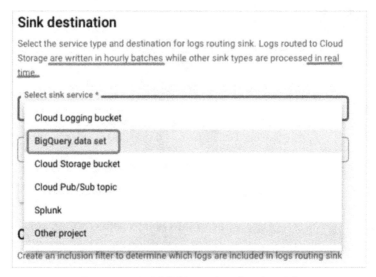

Figure 11.35 – Available services for a log sink

Let's configure a sink to export logs to an external system for further analysis. In this example, we will export them to BigQuery, so we need to create a data set in the **BigQuery** section, as illustrated in the following screenshot:

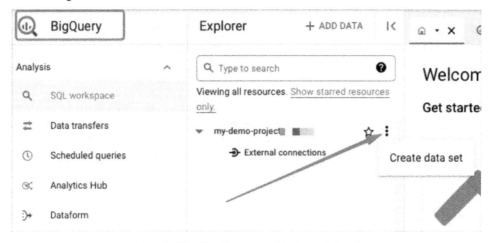

Figure 11.36 – Creating a new BigQuery data set

Creating a new data set includes providing its ID and preferred location. We will reference the ID when creating a new log sink:

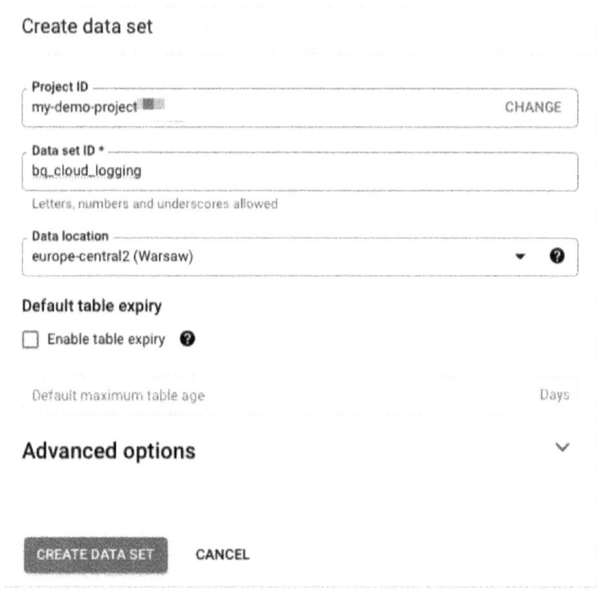

Figure 11.37 – Set up a name and location for a new BigQuery data set

We created a log sink for a log bucket in the previous section. In a similar way, we can create a log sink for a BigQuery data set:

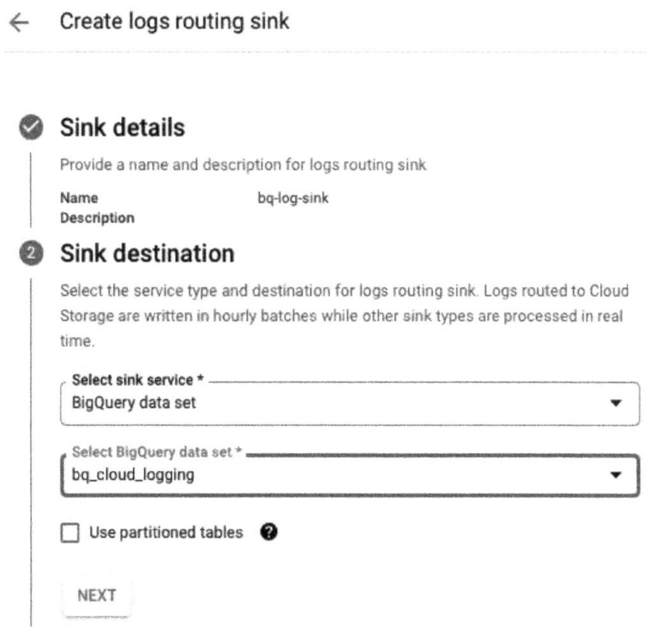

Figure 11.38 – Configuring a BigQuery data set as a log destination

We don't want to send all the logs to a data set, so we build an inclusion filter. The example filter will send only the logs related to a startup of a Compute Engine VM to Big Query. You can practice creating inclusion filters by building queries in **Logs Explorer**. If the query returns correct log entries, it can be copied and used as an inclusion filter:

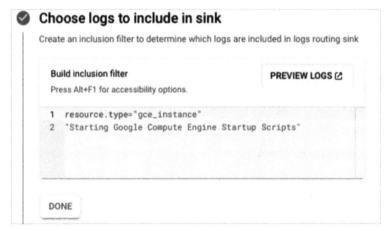

Figure 11.39 – Example inclusion filter that includes only logs related to a VM startup

After creating the sink, we can check whether logs are sent to the BigQuery data set. If you don't know how to start a query, select the data set and then **Query**.

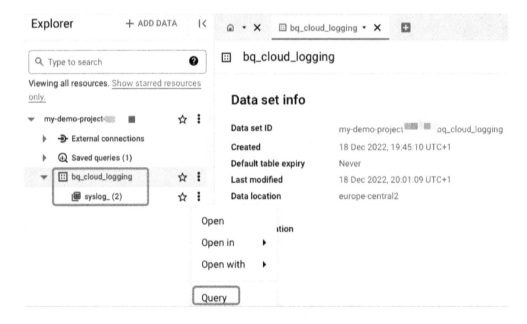

Figure 11.40 – How to query a data set

It will open an editor with a simple query that will look like this one:

```
SELECT * FROM `my-demo-project-xxx.bq_cloud_logging.syslog_20221219`
LIMIT 1000
```

You can run it to see how the data set is organized and create a more precise one later:

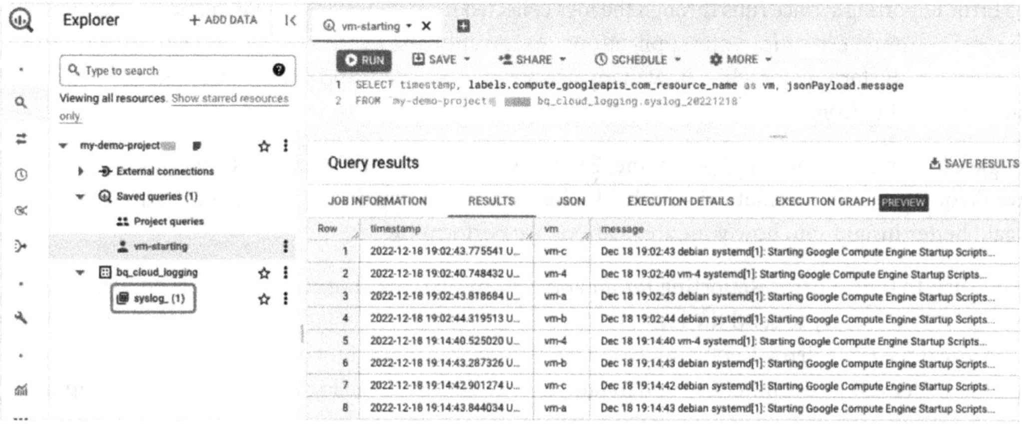

Figure 11.41 – A query that lists imported VM startup entries

In *Figure 11.41*, we can see a screenshot of the Big Query Explorer view that confirms the successful routing of logs to BigQuery and correct filtering. Only entries related to Compute Engine startup operation are displayed, as intended. Cloud Logging is a highly effective tool for in-depth troubleshooting of workloads. In the upcoming section, we will explore other tools that can aid in troubleshooting.

Diagnostics

Google Cloud Monitoring and Logging will help you to make data-driven decisions to shape your application. Knowing how many underlying resources it uses, its current health state, and what type of errors it generates is critical for service availability and future improvements.

But there is more to what the Google Cloud operations suite can offer. This section will describe the additional operations suite services that help with application diagnostics for further improvements and troubleshooting. This is essential, particularly for serverless applications. For this type of system, monitoring the underlying platform is challenging, and browsing through platform logs to understand a user's experience can also be tricky. Tools such as Trace and Profiler can help immensely here.

Using cloud diagnostics to research an application issue

It is possible to diagnose an issue caused by a code in your application using Cloud Monitoring alone. Still, you will have to somehow go from metrics to the request and logs that generated that metric's data point. Also, examining logs from a web service in Logs Explorer to track the most common errors would be doable but time-consuming. Therefore, this section will focus on dedicated Google Cloud observability tools that address those issues.

Error Reporting

The Error Reporting service runs through the logs collected from your systems, automatically identifying the most common errors for your applications. As a result, just by looking at a dashboard, you can tell when errors started emerging, how many users were impacted, and which part of the code those issues are coming from.

Google Cloud services such as App Engine, Compute Engine, Cloud Functions, Cloud Run, and GKE have Error Reporting automatically enabled. This means that you do not have to configure anything to gain better insight into how your applications are performing.

If you wish to utilize Error Reporting for an application that does not run on any of the mentioned services, it is necessary to send the logs to Cloud Logging in a particular format. Cloud Logging will automatically enable Error Reporting when a user log that meets any of the supported patterns is ingested. Refer to this document to understand how to structure the log entry for your application:

```
https://cloud.google.com/error-reporting/docs/formatting-error-
messages
```

Figure 11.42 – Error reporting view for an example application

The preceding screenshot shows the **Error reporting** section for a Cloud Run application. Cloud Run is integrated with Error Reporting, so there is no need for any additional configuration. You can see which revision of Cloud Run is causing errors, when they occurred, and how many errors there were, and the corresponding code is presented at the bottom of this view.

Trace

If you want to improve the performance of your applications and provide your users with a better experience, you can use Google Cloud Trace. This tool helps you identify the areas of your application that cause delays, so you can focus on optimizing those components and reducing overall latency.

It works by default with Google-managed services such as Cloud Run, Cloud Functions, and App Engine, but it is also available as a Trace API and SDK for Java, Node.js, Ruby, and Go to be used inside a Compute Engine VM or even outside Google Cloud. By using Trace, you can track potential bottlenecks and issues in your applications:

Figure 11.43 – Trace view for an example application

Trace will help you understand your service's topology and its flow of requests. In addition, it is responsible for monitoring calls to services and measuring the time it takes for each call to finalize.

Profiler

Google Cloud Profiler helps developers to understand their code's performance characteristics and identify what parts of their application consume the most resources. It continuously collects CPU usage and memory-allocation information from applications with a low-overhead Profiler package imported into their code (Java, Go, Node.js, and Python are supported). Profiler data can be sent to a Google Cloud project, even from another cloud or on-premises. The results of code performance analysis can be used to improve the speed and reduce the costs of an application.

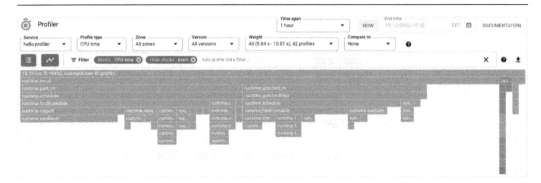

Figure 11.44 – A flame graph in the Profiler view

The preceding screenshot shows a Profiler view with a flame graph. Each frame in the graph represents a function in the code, and its relative size shows this function's resource consumption proportion. Looking at the graph, you can see the resource usage patterns and potential hotspots of library functions in this demo application.

Debugger

Cloud Debugger (unfortunately planned to shut down in the middle of 2023 and be replaced by an open source CLI tool called Snapshot Debugger: `https://github.com/GoogleCloudPlatform/snapshot-debugger`) allows you to inspect what is happening in the code of a running application. For example, suppose you located an error in your production application thanks to Error Tracking and examined the corresponding logs in Logs Explorer. Now you have precise information on what line of your code should be examined. As a next step, you can use Debugger to take a snapshot of what is happening in the code in this position and check the details of variables without pausing this service.

Predefined roles for Google Cloud's operations suite services

When working with Google Cloud's operations suite products described in this section (Debugger, Profiler, and Trace, but also Logging and Monitoring, which were presented earlier in this chapter), it is essential to know what the permissions model looks like. For example, what role can be assigned to a user that wants only to view dashboards?

In the following table, you can find predefined roles that a user can leverage to access and edit dashboards and logs for each service described in this chapter:

Service	Role	Description
Cloud Monitoring	Monitoring Viewer	Read-only access to get and list information on monitoring data and configuration
	Monitoring Editor	Read/write access to all monitoring data and configuration
	Monitoring Admin	All monitoring permissions
Cloud Logging	Logs Viewer	Access to view logs
	Logging Admin	Full access to Logging
Error Reporting	Error Reporting Admin	Full access to Error Reporting
	Error Reporting User	List errors, update error metadata, delete error events
	Error Reporting Viewer	Read-only access
	Error Reporting Writer	For service accounts, send error events
Cloud Debugger	Cloud Debugger Agent	For service accounts, register and provide debug snapshot data
	Cloud Debugger User	Create, delete and view snapshots and log points
Cloud Trace	Cloud Trace Admin	Full access to the Trace console
	Cloud Trace Agent	For service accounts, write traces by sending data to Trace
	Cloud Trace User	Access to Trace console, view traces, insights and statistics
Cloud Profiler	Cloud Profiler Agent	Register and provide profiling data
	Cloud Profiler User	Query and view profiling data

Table 11.2 – Predefined IAM roles for Google Cloud's operations suite services

Note that the mentioned observability services usually have a predefined **Viewer** role that allows for read-only access to dashboards, and an **Admin** role that provides full access to resources.

Viewing Google Cloud status

You can monitor, in real-time, the status of Google Cloud services organized by by-products or regions at the following address: `https://status.cloud.google.com`.

The following screenshot shows the status dashboard of Google Cloud services. You can see that at the time of taking the screenshot, additional status information was published for the Cloud Firestore service in all regions.

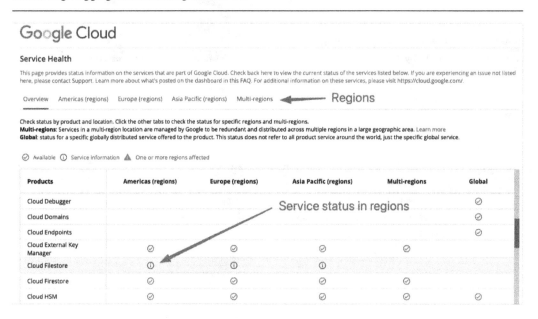

Figure 11.45 – Viewing the Google Cloud Service Health dashboard

Your Cloud Console dashboard also has a Google Cloud Platform status card. If an issue you are experiencing is listed there, monitor the dashboard for incoming messages. Otherwise, if all services are operational, your issue is most likely related to your environment and is not global, so you should open a support case to get help.

Figure 11.46 – Viewing the Google Cloud Platform status in the Cloud Console dashboard

The preceding screenshot shows the Google Cloud Platform status with potential issues with the Google Cloud Console. This section is located by default in the top-right corner of the **DASHBOARD** view although this view can be customised, if needed.

Estimating costs with the Google Cloud Pricing Calculator

Suppose your project team needs to determine the cost of an application that utilizes Compute Engine, GKE, Google Cloud Storage, and Interconnect to your on-premises data center. This is to secure a budget for the project. Instead of studying the pricing documentation for each service, you can quickly calculate the estimate using the Google Cloud Pricing Calculator.

You can access the Google Cloud Pricing Calculator web app through this link: `https://cloud.google.com/products/calculator`.

The calculator is designed to simplify estimating a monthly bill for even very complex architectures that utilize various Google Cloud services. It is organized by product, starting with Compute Engine and GKE, moving on to databases such as CloudSQL and Cloud Bigtable, networking options such as Interconnect and VPN, serverless services such as Cloud Run, and storage options such as Google Cloud Storage or Filestore. Users can customize each product's components and provide detailed configurations, including class, tier, size, and estimated traffic. Once the configuration of every service is complete, you simply click **ADD TO ESTIMATE** and the calculator will instantly provide a monthly cost for all the included services.

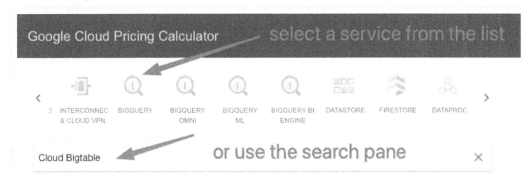

Figure 11.47 – Google Cloud Pricing Calculator supports various Google Cloud services

Here's an example of calculating the monthly cost for a Compute Engine VM that will be used for a web service running on Ubuntu in the `europe-central-2` region, 24/7. This VM requires a 100-GB boot drive and needs to be available from the internet.

In the **SERVICE SELECTION** pane of the Pricing Calculator, shown in *Figure 11.48*, find a **Compute Engine** service and provide details such as the number of VMs (1), an operating system (**Debian**), an instance type (depending on the web server requirements – in this case, we will leave the default **E2** type).

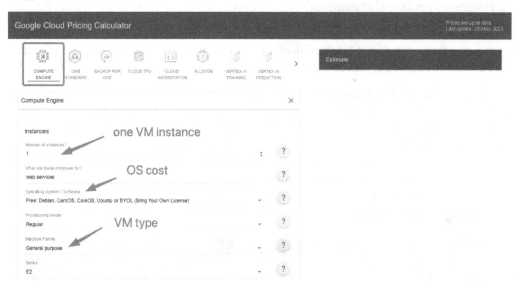

Figure 11.48 – Preparing a price estimate for a VM instance

Select **europe-central2** as the region and choose the **Balanced persistent disk** option for the boot disk with **100** GB of storage, as shown in *Figure 11.49*. Additionally, specify the duration for which you plan to run the VM as **24** hours, and **7** days per week. Also, add one public IP address. Leave all other values as their defaults.

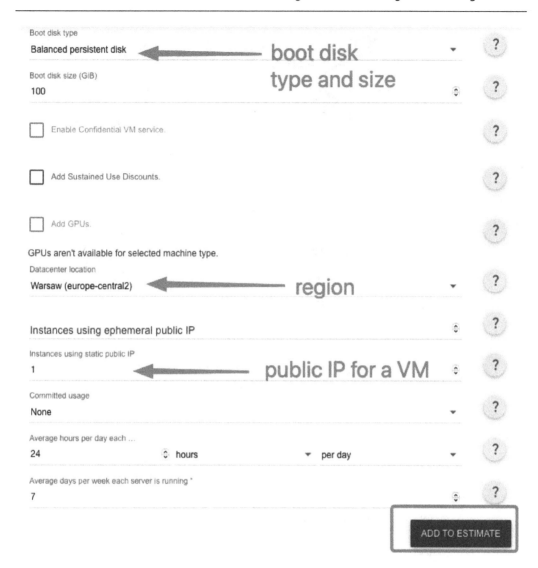

Figure 11.49 – Preparing a price estimate for a VM instance (continuation)

Once you have entered all your required details, simply click on the **ADD TO ESTIMATE** button shown in *Figure 11.49* to receive an accurate estimate of your monthly operating costs for the VM.

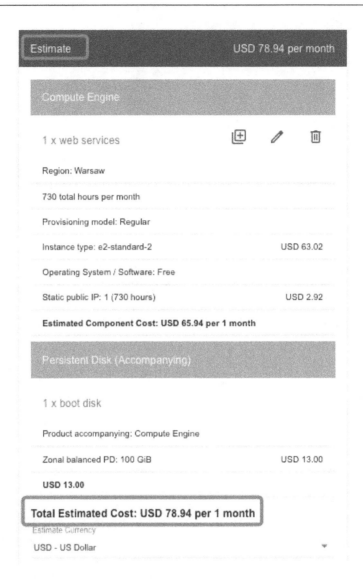

Figure 11.50 – Google Cloud Pricing Calculator final estimate for running a VM instance

Considering the settings provided, the Pricing Calculator generated two estimates for our Compute Engine VM. The first estimate is for the VM itself, which will be billed at a monthly rate of $65.94. The additional boot drive will also be charged at $13.00 per month. Consequently, the monthly cost to keep the web application running will be $78.94. Please note that the Pricing Calculator will automatically update the estimate if any changes or new services are added. You can add more Google Cloud services to this estimate to reflect the architecture you plan to run on Google Cloud.

If you're interested in understanding the pricing for a particular service, you can find a comprehensive pricing list for Google Cloud services at `https://cloud.google.com/pricing/list`. Additionally, if you anticipate using services for a minimum of one year, you may be eligible for Committed Use Discounts (CUDs). For more information on CUDs, please visit `https://cloud.google.com/docs/cuds`.

Summary

Even though you may get fewer observability-related questions compared to the other services on the ACE exam, the Monitoring and Logging services are essential areas in your hands-on experience with Google Cloud. Initially, observability helps you better understand how Google Cloud services work. Later, when you run your applications in production, it will help you to improve customer experience and reduce costs.

To get the most out of observability, start with out-of-the-box dashboards, add agents for Compute Engine VMs to collect additional metrics, and create logs-based metrics and alerts. Next, centralize monitoring into a dedicated project or logs by aggregating sinks. Finally, use Trace, Profiler, and Debugger to optimize your application.

Questions

Answer the following questions to test your knowledge of this chapter:

1. While looking at the **Cloud Monitoring** dashboard, you noticed that the Compute Engine VM memory consumption chart is empty. What can you do to fix the problem?

    A. Edit the **VM Instances** dashboard in the **Cloud Monitoring** section and change a memory chart to **VM Memory Total** instead of **VM Memory Used**.

    B. Verify whether Ops Agent runs inside this VM using `sudo service google-cloud-ops-agent status`.

    C. Restart the VM.

    D. Make sure Cloud Monitoring is enabled in this project and your account has a **Monitoring Viewer** role.

2. Users are complaining that the response time of your web app has increased. You want to use the Google Cloud suite to investigate the issue. Which service will help you to track latencies?

    A. Trace

    B. Profiler

    C. Cloud Logging

    D. Debugger

3. Your company's policy is to only deploy workloads in low-carbon Google Cloud locations. How can you ensure that all your logs are stored in a location compliant with this policy?

   A. It is impossible to choose where logs are stored as they are always stored in the same region as the system generating them.

   B. You need to create a log bucket in a low-carbon location and point the log sinks to this new bucket.

   C. You need to create a log bucket in a low-carbon location. Cloud Logging will detect the new bucket and redirect logs automatically.

   D. You need to edit the existing log bucket and change its location to a low-carbon one.

4. You are looking for inexpensive storage to keep your logs long-term. Which approach would be the best?

   A. Edit an existing sink and send logs to BigQuery.

   B. Create a new sink and send logs to Google Cloud Storage.

   C. Edit a `_Default` log bucket to change its retention to 3,650 days.

   D. Both bucket types can be a good choice because there is no difference between keeping logs in a log bucket or a Google Cloud Storage bucket.

5. You got a task to configure monitoring for a new project. The team owning this project wants to deploy services running on Compute Engine, Google Cloud Storage, and GKE. What steps should you follow to collect metrics from those services?

   A. Go to the **Cloud Monitoring** section and enable monitoring. All metrics for the services that your team wants to deploy will be automatically collected.

   B. Go to the **Cloud Monitoring** section and enable `Monitoring`. Select +**CREATE DASHBOARD** and create dashboards for the required services.

   C. Cloud Monitoring is enabled by default, and once services are deployed, service-specific metrics will automatically appear in the **Monitoring** dashboard. For a Compute Engine VM, you will need to install Ops Agent for better OS and applications observability.

   D. Cloud Monitoring is enabled by default, and once services are deployed, service-specific metrics will automatically appear in the **Monitoring** dashboard. No additional configuration is required.

Answers

The answers to the preceding questions are provided here:

1B, 2A, 3B, 4B, 5C

12
Implementing Identity and Security in Google Cloud

In the previous chapters, topics such as roles, users, and service accounts often appeared in the context of what permissions are needed to access or configure a specific Google Cloud service. This chapter will provide more visibility on identity and access in Google Cloud. In addition, we will focus on the security aspter and learn about preventing unauthorized access and auditing user actions on Google Cloud resources.

Furthermore, the *Google Cloud setup checklist* section in *Chapter 3* briefly mentioned a checklist that guided users through the initial setup of Google Cloud foundation in order to run enterprise ready workloads.The first points on this list were Cloud Identity users and groups, and administrative access. As those topics are important from the identity and security perspective, we will cover them in detail.

In this chapter, we will explore the following main topics:

- Creating a cloud identity for an organization
- Providing access to Google Cloud resources
- Managing service accounts
- Using Cloud Audit Logs for security and compliance

Creating a Cloud Identity

Suppose you use a Google Cloud free trial, as described in the *Billing and budgets* section in *Chapter 3*, to learn about the platform or use Google Cloud for small personal projects. To keep things simple, as you are the only user, you probably use your @gmail account, assigning it a **Project Owner** role for every project you create. The following figure shows an example of such a configuration:

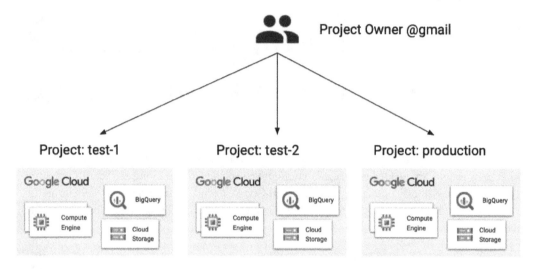

Figure 12.1 – Multiple personal projects owned by a single user

This approach is a good fit for small projects owned by a single user or just a few users, but a more scalable solution is needed for an enterprise. First, to manage access for multiple users and groups, and second, to provide a hierarchy of resources to match a large organization's structure – departments, teams, or applications. This is where Google's identity service comes into play as an alternative to using individual @gmail.com accounts.

Google's Identity as a Service platform allows for centralized management of users and groups. The platform includes security features such as password management, two-step verification, and single sign-on for SAML applications or third-party identity providers. Additionally, there is an option to synchronize identities from Active Directory or OpenLDAP to a Google directory.

There are two ways to configure an identity:

- Cloud Identity, which is available in both free and premium versions
- Workspace, which includes extra services such as Gmail, Google Drive, Docs, and Sheets

A company using a different identity provider still needs an identity account in Cloud Identity or Workspace. However, they can federate their provider to their Google identity account to access Google Cloud with existing credentials.

Let's look at the example process of creating a free Cloud Identity account. To start the configuration, a company needs a domain. If it doesn't own a domain, one can be purchased at `https://domains.google.com`, as presented in the following figure:

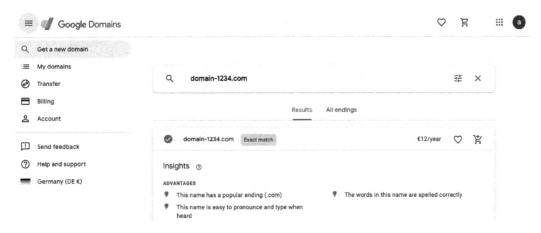

Figure 12.2 – Google Domains portal, where you can purchase and manage domains

Note that a domain doesn't necessarily have to come from the Google Domains platform. Next, a domain will be used to set up Cloud Identity. One domain can be associated with only one Cloud Identity

If logged in to the Google Cloud console as a @gmail user, you can set up your organization and Cloud Identity in the **Identity & Organization** section of **IAM & Admin**, as shown in the following screenshot:

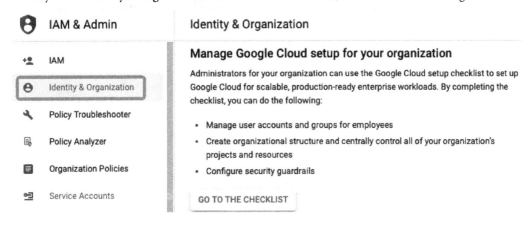

Figure 12.3 – Set up a Google Cloud organization in the console

If you select **GO TO THE CHECKLIST**, you will directly access the Cloud Identity setup from the Google Cloud console:

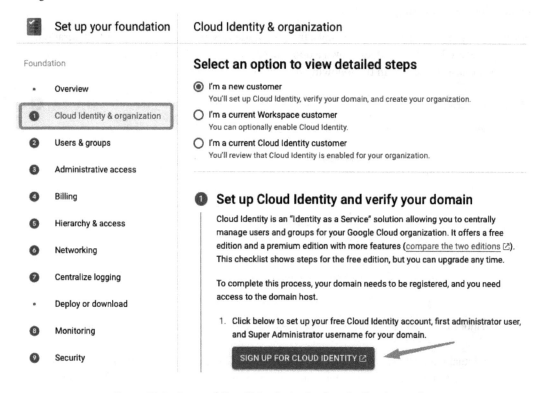

Figure 12.4 – Setup of Cloud Identity in the Google Cloud console

Alternatively, if you haven't logged in to the Google Cloud console before but you own a domain, you can start setting up Cloud Identity using the following link: `https://workspace.google.com/gcpidentity/signup/welcome?sku=identitybasic`.

During the Cloud Identity setup, you provide a company name, contact info with an email from a different domain that will be used as a recovery email, a new or existing domain, and login details. A user created during the identity setup will have a **Super Admin** role, which is an administrator seed role with all permissions:

Figure 12.5 – Selected screenshots from initializing Cloud Identity for a domain

Once the setup is done, you can further configure your Cloud Identity in the Google Admin console at `https://admin.google.com` using a new administrator account. Note that this is a different portal from the Google Cloud console.

Before you start creating users, Google must verify your domain ownership. For that reason, you will be asked to add a new TXT record to your domain on your host's website:

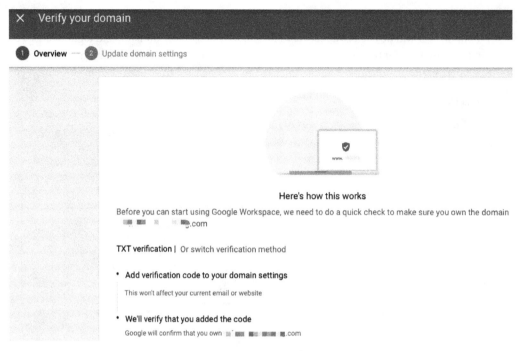

Figure 12.6 – Domain verification for Cloud Identity

Google recommends using a **super admin** account only when necessary; for example, for account recovery scenarios. For day-to-day activities, separate accounts with fewer permissions should be created. Once your domain is configured and verified, you can proceed with creating users that will access Google Cloud resources.

Users and groups

You can create accounts for each user to be managed by Cloud Identity manually in the **Users** tab in the **Directory** section of the Google Admin console by selecting **Add new user** as shown in *Figure 12.7*. Alternatively, you can upload user accounts via a CSV file, sync users with your existing LDAP directory, such as Active Directory, or use the Admin SDK Directory API to create and manage users programmatically.

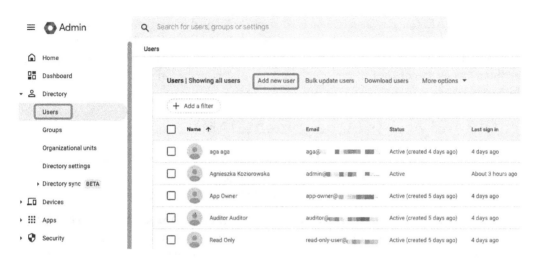

Figure 12.7 – Adding users in the Google Admin console

Next, you can create groups and add users to groups in the **Groups** section. For example, as presented in the following screenshot, one of the first groups that should be created is the `gcp-organization-admins` group (the name is only a suggestion), which consists of users that, in the next step, obtain permissions to create and manage a Google Cloud **organization**, a root node in the Google Cloud resource hierarchy:

Figure 12.8 – Groups in the Google Admin console

The necessary permissions to manage an organization in Google Cloud are not set in the Google Admin console but in the Google Cloud console. Users with Cloud Identity accounts will be able to log in to the Google Cloud console and create and access resources according to their assigned roles and permissions. The following section will provide more details on managing an organization, users, and resources.

Note that although in Google Console, you can't create individual users, there is still an option to create service accounts and Google groups. Permissions in Google Cloud can be granted to a Cloud Identity user, a Cloud Identity group, a Google Cloud service account, and a Google group. Find out more about Google Groups at `https://cloud.google.com/iam/docs/groups-in-cloud-console`.

Identity and Access Management (IAM)

When you log in to the Google Cloud console with a newly created **super admin** user, right after its Cloud Identity is configured, a Google Cloud **organization** resource will be automatically created once you accept the terms and conditions. In addition, the organization will be linked to your billing.

As a first step after logging in as a **super admin**, you should go to the **IAM** section of **IAM & Admin** and assign the **Organization Administrator** role to the previously created `gcp-organization-admins` group, as shown in the following screenshot. Next, you can log in as a member of this group, start configuring resources, and provide other users with permissions. This way, you will avoid using a **super admin** account to manage Google Cloud resources. The role and permissions assignment process will be explained in detail in the following sections.

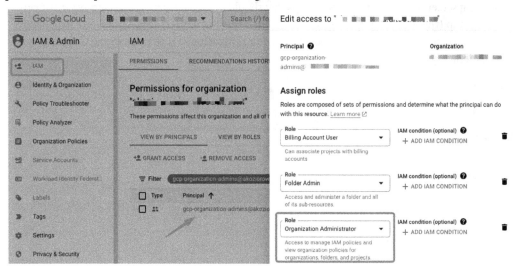

Figure 12.9 – Assigning the Organization Administrator role to the gcp-organization-admins group

Identity and Access Management (IAM) is where you centrally control who can do what type of activities on which Google Cloud resources. Note that *resources* are not only Google Cloud services such as Compute Engine VMs or Google Cloud Storage. IAM can control access to a project, folder, or even organizational level. It helps to adopt the security principle of least privilege as it allows building fine-grained access to resources. Let's investigate a hierarchy of Google Cloud resources to better understand how permissions are applied across all levels.

Building a resource hierarchy

In the Google Cloud resource hierarchy, an organization is provisioned automatically and it is the top-level node above all other folders, projects, and resources. Any policies or restrictions set at the organization level will apply to the folders, projects, and resources that fall under it.

The hierarchy helps to manage access to resources, so there is no need to work with resource owners individually. For example, if a resource owner leaves an organization, the resource can be assigned to another user or team.

Following the **Cloud Identity and organisation** setup wizard introduced earlier in this chapter, you will be presented with various examples of how a resource hierarchy can be configured in the **Hierarchy and access** section:

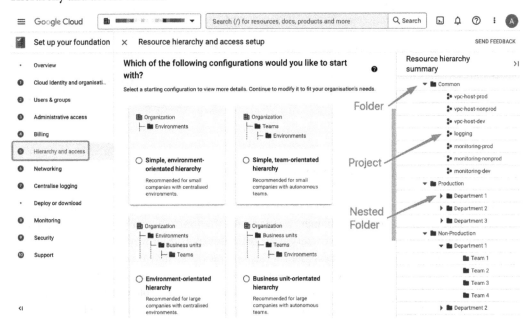

Figure 12.10 – "Hierarchy and access" step of the "Cloud Identity and organization setup" checklist

Folders will help you to organize a hierarchy so it matches the structure of your company. For example, you can create folders for each department, nest additional folders for each team in a department, and set up permissions so that users can only access their team's resources. The folder structure will also provide security isolation and separate workload types such as production and development.

Google Cloud **projects**, which are containers where you run workloads, can be attached directly to an organization or placed in folders or nested folders.

The following diagram presents an example of a simple resource hierarchy. Under **Organization: example.com**, there are two folders: `test` and `production`. In the `test` folder, there are two projects: `test-1` and `test-2`, with various Google Cloud services. There is one project in the `production` folder: `production`, also with various Google Cloud services:

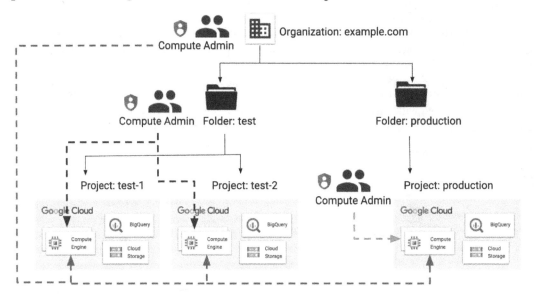

Figure 12.11 – Example of an organization hierarchy

IAM controls access to resources at different levels of a resource hierarchy. Permission to create, modify, or view a resource can have various attachment points – organization, folder, or project. For example, if a Compute Admin role was assigned to users at the organization level, it would be inherited by all projects. If a Compute Admin role was assigned at the folder level, as shown in *Figure 12.11*, where the Compute Admin role is assigned to users at the `test` folder level, it would be propagated only to projects `test-1` and `test-2` in the `test` folder. If a Compute Admin role was assigned to users at the project level (the `production` project in this example), it would be propagated only in this one project. In some cases, permissions can even be assigned to an individual resource in a project.

Note that a policy for a resource is a union of what is set on a resource directly and what is inherited as a project, a folder, and an organization policy. But if access is allowed higher in a hierarchy, it can't be restricted at a lower level.

IAM roles

In Google Cloud, permissions are not assigned to users and groups directly. Instead, users have roles assigned to them. Roles are a collection of permissions. Permissions usually match API methods that describe which operations are allowed on a resource and have the following form: `<service>.<resource>.<action>`.

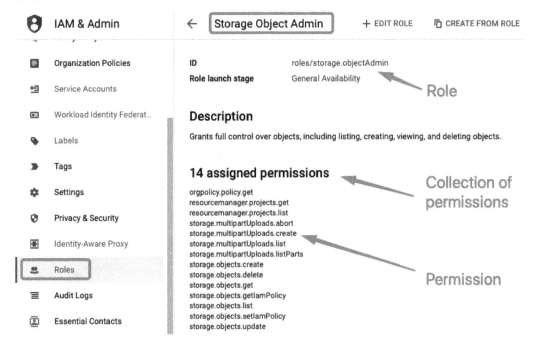

Figure 12.12 – Example of a role, which is a set of permissions

For example, as the preceding screenshot illustrates, the **Storage Object Admin** role is a collection of permissions such as `storage.objects.create` or `storage.objects.delete`.

There are three types of IAM roles:

- **Basic** roles, with very broad access that spans multiple Google services:

  - **Viewer**, a role that allows viewing all resources.

  - **Editor**, a role that allows viewing, creating, and deleting all resources.

  - **Owner**, a role that allows viewing, creating, and deleting all resources and managing roles and permissions. Also, it allows setting up billing for a project.

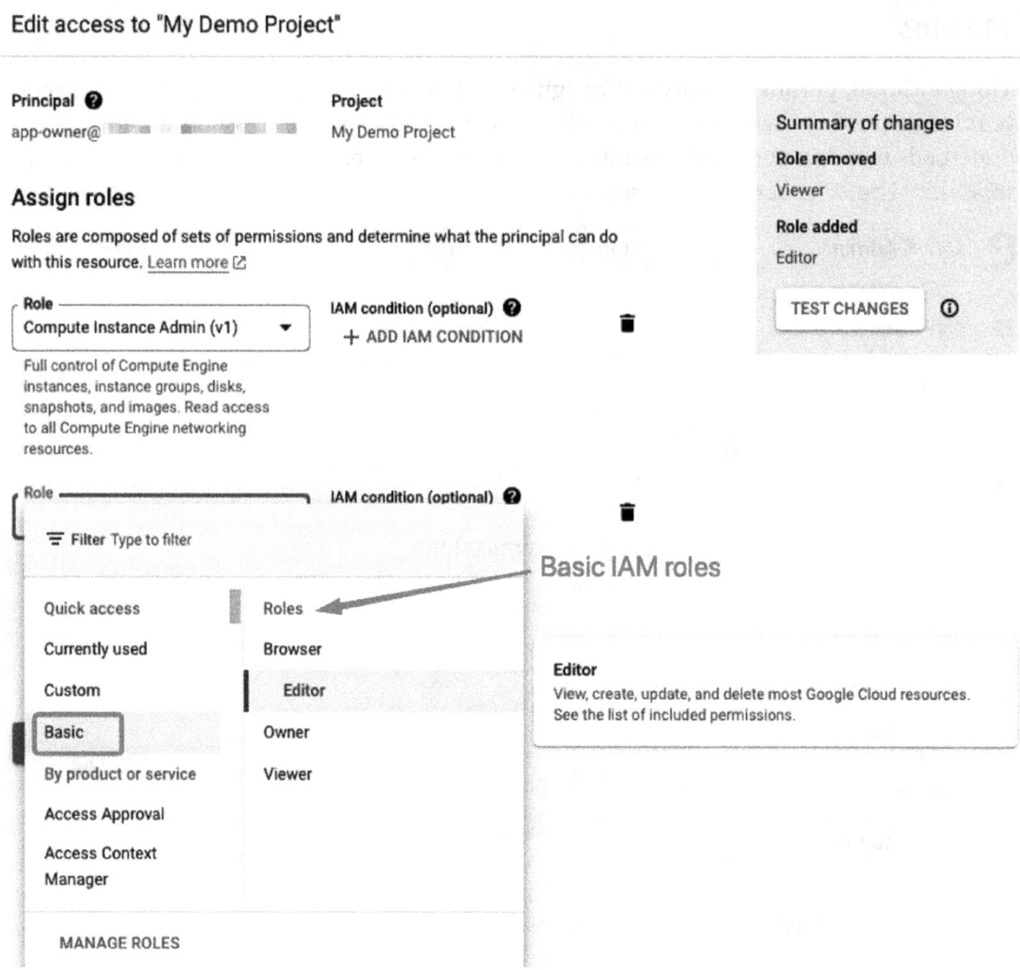

Edit access to "My Demo Project"

Principal ❓
app-owner@ ░░░░░░░░░░░░░░░░

Project
My Demo Project

Summary of changes

Role removed
Viewer

Role added
Editor

TEST CHANGES ⓘ

Assign roles

Roles are composed of sets of permissions and determine what the principal can do with this resource. Learn more ↗

Role
Compute Instance Admin (v1)   ▾

Full control of Compute Engine instances, instance groups, disks, snapshots, and images. Read access to all Compute Engine networking resources.

IAM condition (optional) ❓
+ ADD IAM CONDITION   🗑

Role   **IAM condition (optional)** ❓   🗑

☰ Filter Type to filter

Quick access	Roles
Currently used	Browser
Custom	Editor
Basic	Owner
By product or service	Viewer
Access Approval	
Access Context Manager	

Basic IAM roles

Editor
View, create, update, and delete most Google Cloud resources. See the list of included permissions.

MANAGE ROLES

Figure 12.13 – Basic IAM roles in the Google Cloud console

- **Predefined** roles, that offer finer-grained access to resources. Those roles have permissions bundled together and usually have sufficient scope for working with a specific service. Administrators can choose from multiple options such as an admin of a service, a user of a service, or a viewer of a service. Multiple roles can be combined to provide necessary access. For example, the **Compute Engine Instance Admin** role has a set of permissions to manage Compute Engine VMs. Still, a user will need the `compute.networks.create` permission, which belongs to the **Compute Network Admin** role, to create a subnet for a VM:

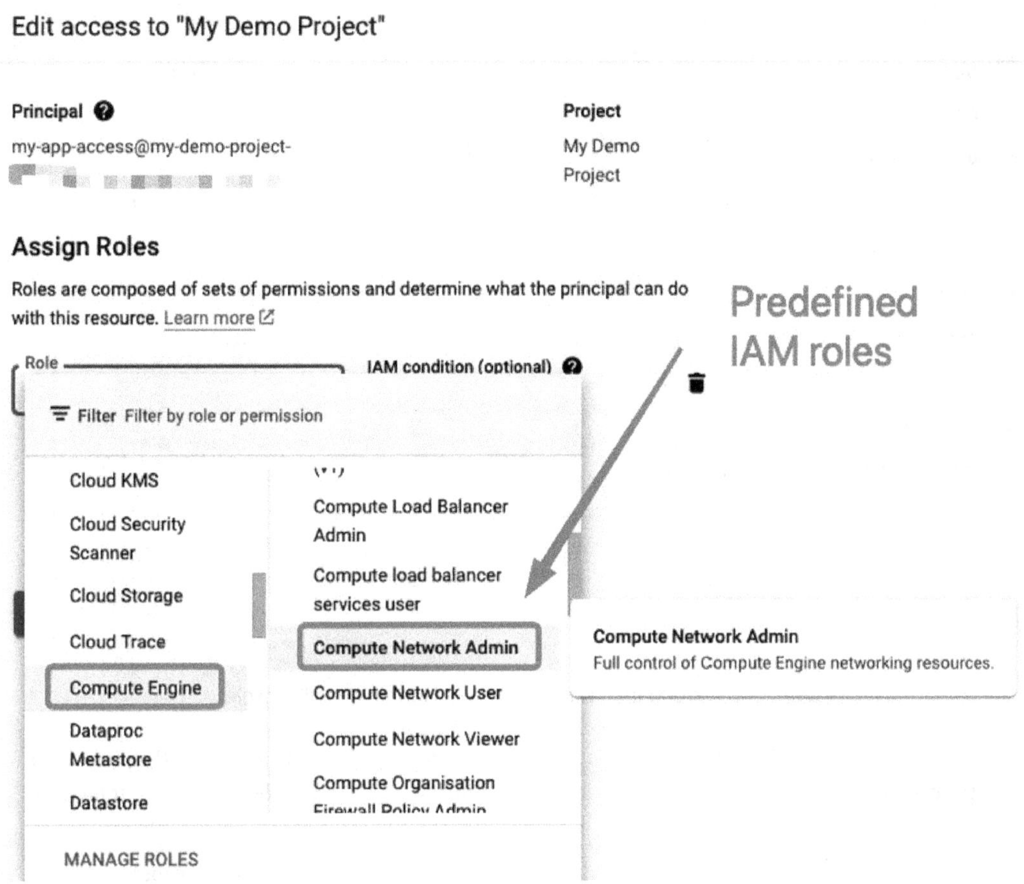

Edit access to "My Demo Project"

Principal ❓

my-app-access@my-demo-project-
▓▓ ▓▓▓▓▓ ▓▓

Project

My Demo
Project

Assign Roles

Roles are composed of sets of permissions and determine what the principal can do
with this resource. Learn more ↗

Figure 12.14 – Predefined IAM roles in the Google Cloud console

- **Custom** roles can be created from scratch by manually putting the required permissions together. Also, a custom role can be created out of an existing role or from existing roles. Custom roles require more administrative work to keep them up to date than predefined roles, as Google can introduce modifications to Google Cloud permissions from time to time.

To create a custom role, go to the **Roles** section in **IAM & Admin** and select **CREATE ROLE**. Next, you need to provide a descriptive name and set of permissions you want to be included in this role:

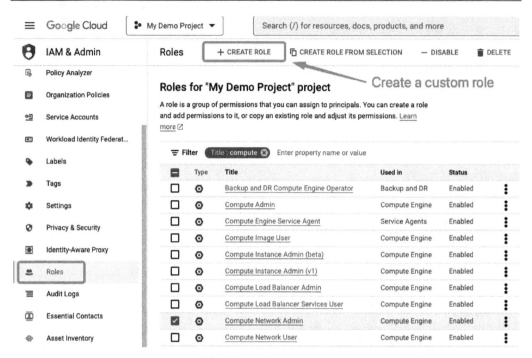

Figure 12.15 – Predefined IAM roles in the Google Cloud console

Building a role from scratch could be a trial-and-error process before completing the list of permissions. Creating a new role by cloning and modifying existing ones that best match the desired permissions would be easier.

Suppose you want to create a role with almost all Cloud Storage administrative permissions except the one for deleting objects. To achieve it, you should select the **Storage Admin** role in the **Roles** section and choose **CREATE FROM ROLE** option as presented in the following screenshot:

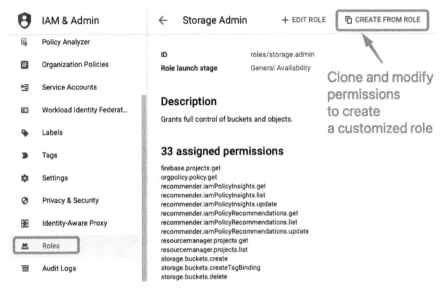

Figure 12.16 – Creating a new role from an existing one

Next, you need to select a name (`Custom Storage Admin - Can't Delete Objects` in this case) and a description and remove permissions you don't need for this role from the list. In our case, it will be `storage.objects.delete`:

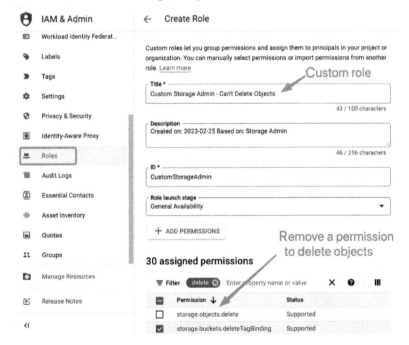

Figure 12.17 – Selecting permissions for a custom role

Once the role is created, it will be available for assignment, as presented in the following screenshot:

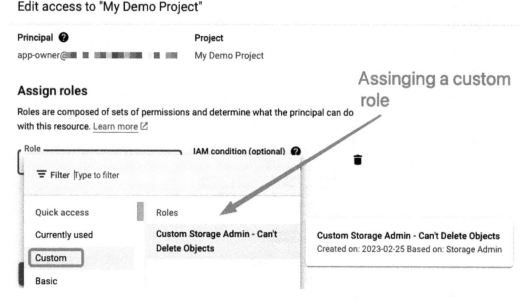

Figure 12.18 – Custom role assignment for a user

It is advised to test a role before assigning it to users. In this case, a role was assigned to the `app-owner` user. When trying to delete an object in a Google Cloud Storage bucket, this user was presented with an error that permission was missing for deleting an object, as can be seen in the following screenshot. Errors often describe what permission is missing for the task to be completed, simplifying troubleshooting:

Figure 12.19 – A user needs the storage.object.delete permission to delete Google Cloud Stroage objects

Note that it is possible to copy custom roles between projects. The `gcloud` command can be used to copy a role created as in the preceding example (where we used `CustomStorageAdmin` as the source role ID, as shown in *Figure 12.17*) to another project:

```
gcloud iam roles copy --source=CustomStorageAdmin --source-
project=<source-project> --destination=CustomStorageAdmin
--dest-project=<destination-project>
```

IAM policies

Now that we have learned how to create accounts, build a resource hierarchy, and set up roles, we will look into IAM policies that connect all of those items to allow users to access resources in a fine-grained way within a hierarchy.

In IAM, Cloud Identity users, Cloud Identity groups, service accounts, and, for some services, a Cloud Identity organization or all (authenticated) users are called **principals**. **Principals** are granted roles on resources via IAM policy binding.

Note that a recommended practice for IAM policies is not to grant roles to individual users but to groups. Groups help manage users at scale because each member inherits roles assigned at the group level.

The following figure presents how IAM access to resources is set up. It is the result of assigning a principal (such as a group or a user) an IAM role (a set of permissions) on a resource (such as a project, folder, or – in some cases – a particular service). Note that the higher a resource in a hierarchy, the broader the access scope. For example, all projects under a folder will inherit permissions assigned at the folder level.

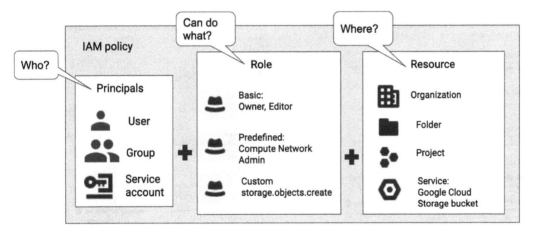

Figure 12.20 – An IAM policy consists of a principal, a role, and a resource

Now, let's take a look at how IAM access can be assigned to resources in the Google Cloud console:

1. To grant access to resources, select **GRANT ACCESS** in the **IAM** section in **IAM and admin**. In the **IAM** section, you can also find a list of existing permissions at the project level or, if a folder or organization was selected, at higher levels in a hierarchy:

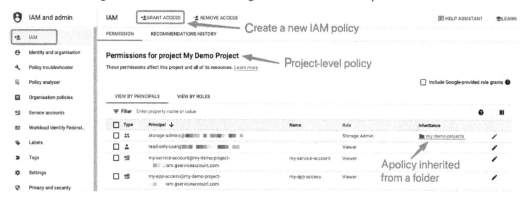

Figure 12.21 – Granting access to resources in IAM in the Google Cloud console

2. In the next step, you provide a principal and a role. A principal can have multiple roles assigned. The following screenshot presents the **GRANT ACCESS** view for different scenarios. On the left-hand side, an organization is a resource on which a basic role, **Viewer**, is assigned to a single user. On the right-hand side, a folder is a resource on which a predefined role, **Storage Admin**, is assigned to a group of users:

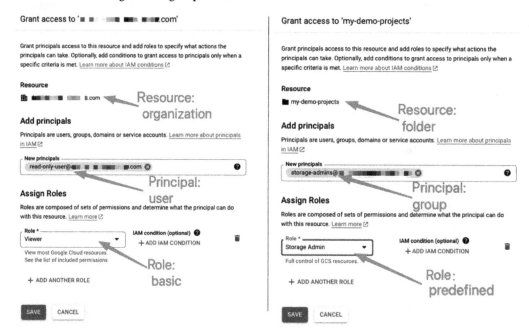

Figure 12.22 – Comparing different IAM policies at an organization and a folder level

The following is another example where two roles are assigned to a single user at the project level. To add more roles, as in this case, select **ADD ANOTHER ROLE** in the **GRANT ACCESS** view of the **IAM** section:

Figure 12.23 – Adding multiple roles to a principal

Note that in the **IAM** section, you can view permissions for each principal and modify them as presented in the following screenshot:

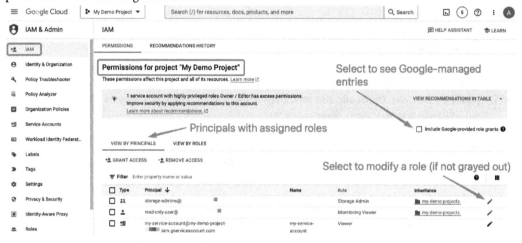

Figure 12.24 – Viewing and editing IAM permissions

When permissions are assigned higher in a hierarchy, such as at the folder level, you can't modify them at a lower (project) level. In such cases, the edit option is grayed out.

Organization policies

One of the additional benefits of building a resource hierarchy is the ability to centrally set constraints on what users can configure on a Google Cloud service. Applying organization policies to a resource hierarchy at the root level helps to comply with a company's security policies across all projects.

Let's look at the following example. Suppose one of the outcomes of a security audit in your company is a request to limit external access to Compute Engine VMs. It was discovered that users create VMs with a public IP, and firewall rules allow access from the internet to VMs on certain ports. As your company has multiple projects, controlling how VMs are configured would be challenging. Although organization policies don't enforce policies retrospectively, they can control how new resources are configured. To help the company to improve its security posture, you can configure the **Define allowed external IPs for VM instances** policy at your organization level.

You can set this policy up by selecting your organization as the scope and editing the policy in **Organization Policies** in **IAM & Admin**, as presented in the following screenshot:

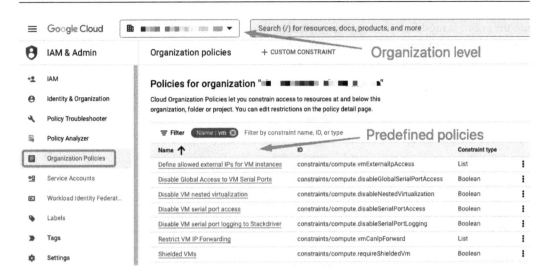

Figure 12.25 – Listing policies for an organization

In the **Rules** section of the **Edit policy** view, you can define on which resources a policy will be enforced (for example, a specific VM name or a tag). In our example, it will be denied for all VMs:

✕   Edit policy

Define allowed external IPs for VM instances

This list constraint defines the set of Compute Engine VM instances that are allowed to use external IP addresses. By default, all VM instances are allowed to use external IP addresses. The allowed/denied list of VM instances must be identified by the VM instance name, in the form: projects/PROJECT_ID/zones/ZONE/instances/INSTANCE

Applies to

Organisation {resourceName}

○ Inherit parent's policy ❓
○ Google-managed default ❓
◉ Customise ❓

Policy enforcement ❓

○ Merge with parent   ❓
   Rules are combined at all levels regardless of hierarchy. 'Deny' overrides 'allow'.
◉ Replace   ❓
   Ignore the parent's policy and use these rules.

Rules

Rules define the values that are enforced by an organisation policy constraint. For a Boolean constraint, you can set the enforcement of the constraint on or off. For a list constraint, you can create a list of values that should be allowed or denied by the policy, or set enforcement to deny or allow all values.

Any rule can be made conditional based on Tags by clicking 'Add condition'. This allows you to fine-tune the enforcement of your organisation policy. Learn more about policy conditions.

┌─────────────────┐
│ Deny all   │   ⌄
└─────────────────┘

Figure 12.26 – Customizing a policy that limits assigning a public IP to VMs

Once the policy is modified, you can verify whether it works as expected. The following screenshot shows the **Create an instance** view, where a user is presented with a warning that a specific organization policy is in place and that it is not allowed to add an external address to a VM:

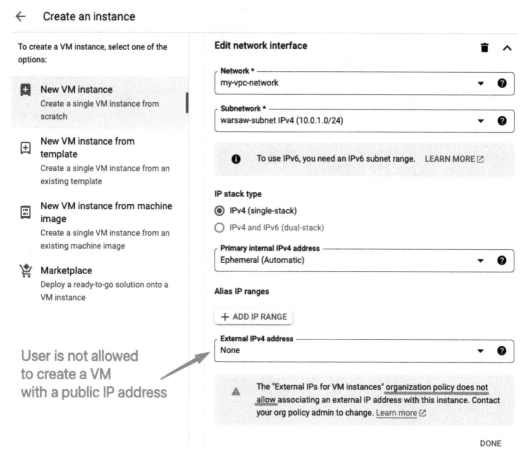

Figure 12.27 – Verifying that an organization policy takes effect,
and a user cannot assign a public IP to a VM

Suppose another audit revealed that users create resources outside of their home country. As your company has a regulatory obligation to keep workloads and data within a country, you need to prevent this from happening. In this case, you can use the **Google Cloud Platform – Resource Location Restriction** policy at the organization level to enforce all new resources only to be created in a specific Google Cloud region, for example, only in `europe-central2` (Warsaw). You can define the scope of the policy in the **Rules** section, creating an `allow` entry with the following condition: `in:europe-central2-locations` (all zones in the `europe-central2` region), as presented in the following screenshot:

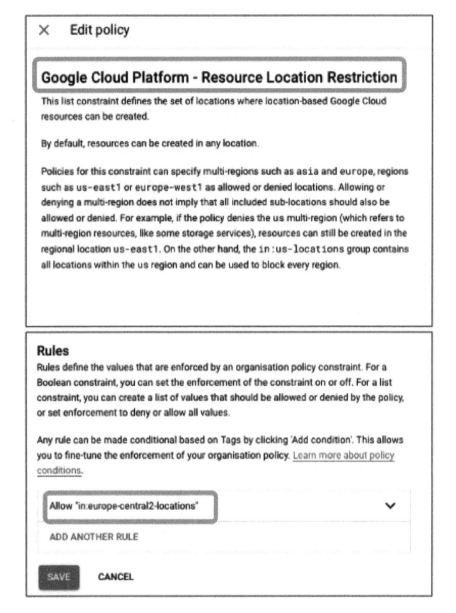

Figure 12.28 – Creating an organization policy rule to allow
creating resources only in europe-central2 zones

Now, if users want to create resources, depending on the service, either only the `europe-central2` region will be available for selection or an attempt to create a resource in another region will fail. The following figure shows that a user wants to create a Google Cloud Storage bucket and Warsaw is the only region available. This proves that the policy is working as expected.

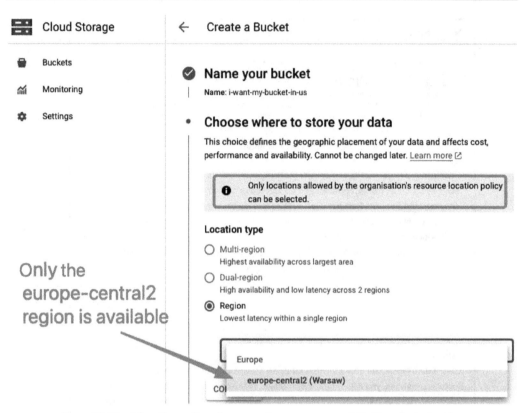

Figure 12.29 – A location policy allows creating resources only in the selected region

Check the list of all available policies that you can apply to your organization at `https://cloud.google.com/resource-manager/docs/organization-policy/org-policy-constraints`.

Up to this point, we have focused on providing access or restricting it for users or groups at the organization, folder, or project level. A similar approach can also be applied to service accounts, the special accounts that are used not by humans but by applications. In the next section, we will provide more insights into this topic.

Managing service accounts

A service account is an identity that an application or a Compute Engine VM uses to run authorized API calls to Google Cloud services such as Google Cloud Storage, BigQuery, and so on. Contrary to a user account, this account type is not created in the Google Admin console as a Cloud Identity, but in a Google Cloud project. It doesn't have a password and can't be used for interactive login to a console. Service accounts can be used by applications running in Google Cloud and on-premises. Also, users can use service accounts in certain scenarios.

There are the following types of service accounts:

- **Google-managed service accounts** (service agents) are created automatically so that Google Cloud services that you enable can interact with your resources. You can find the complete list of service agents at `https://cloud.google.com/iam/docs/service-agents`.

- **User-managed default service accounts** are created automatically when an API for a service is enabled. They help to get started with a service but can be modified or replaced later. For example, Compute Engine comes with a default service account: `<project-number>-compute@developer.gserviceaccount.com`.

- **User-managed service accounts** are created in IAM by a user with permissions: `iam.serviceAccounts.create`. A predefined role, **Service Account Admin**, or **Create Service Accounts** can be used for this task. User-defined accounts use the following format: `<service-account-name>@project-id.iam.gserviceaccount.com`.

Service accounts authenticate via short-lived credentials or associated public/private RSA key pairs.

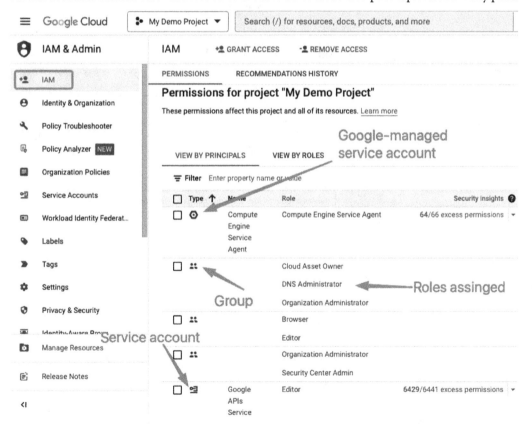

Figure 12.30 – Users, groups, and service accounts listed in the IAM section

You can view the list of service accounts in the **IAM** section, as shown in the preceding screenshot. Alternatively, you can use the `gcloud` command:

```
gcloud iam service-accounts list
```

Now, having introduced the concept of a service account, in the next section, we will look into how to create and manage permissions for this type of account.

Creating and granting permissions

As service accounts are not a part of Cloud Identity, there is a dedicated section, **Service accounts** in the **IAM & Admin** view, where you can create and configure them. For example, the following screenshot presents a service account created in the console:

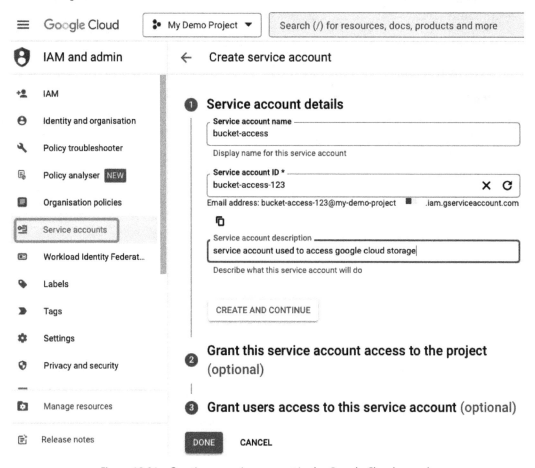

Figure 12.31 – Creating a service account in the Google Cloud console

After selecting **CREATE SERVICE ACCOUNT** in the **Service accounts** section, you need to provide a descriptive name, such as bucket-access in this example, and either add roles and users that can impersonate the account or skip this step and assign them later. The gcloud command equivalent would be the following:

```
gcloud iam service-accounts create bucket-access
--description="account used to access google cloud storage" --display-
name="bucket-access"
```

For the role assignments for a service account, go to the **IAM** section and select **GRANT ACCESS**, as presented in the following figure. Provide your service account in the **Add principals** section and select required roles in the **Assign roles** section. Role assignment for service accounts is similar to user role assignment. Using service accounts with minimum permissions is recommended, so even though it is possible to assign basic roles to a service account, it would be better to use predefined or customized roles.

In the example that follows, a bucket-access service account is granted the **Storage Admin** role. This means that whoever has access to this account (a user, a Compute Engine VM, or a service) can use it to interact with Google Cloud Storage to create or delete buckets and objects:

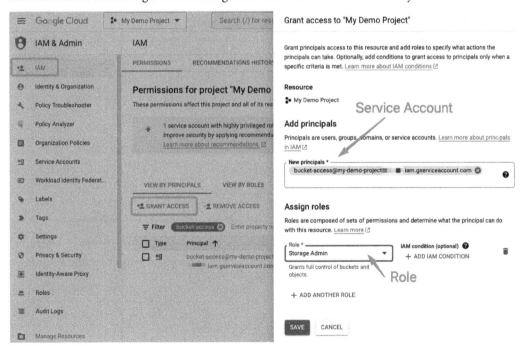

Figure 12.32 – Assigning a role to a service account

Users that use **basic roles** have access to service accounts by default. If you don't use basic roles, you need to explicitly grant a user access to a service account in the **Service Accounts** view by selecting a service account and then selecting **GRANT ACCESS** in the **PERMISSIONS** tab:

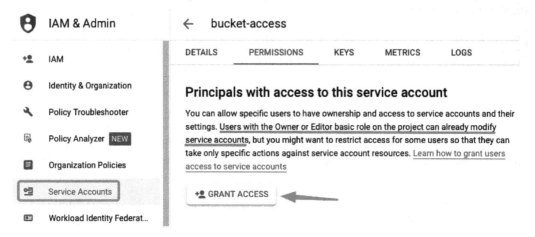

Figure 12.33 – Granting access to a service account for a user

By granting access, you use a service account not as an *account* anymore. It becomes a resource, meaning you grant a user a specific role on a service account. For example, when you create a Compute Engine VM, you can provide a service account that this VM will use to access services such as Google Cloud Storage.

Note that if you don't have a **Service Account User** role on this service account, you won't be able to create a VM with this service account assigned.

Attaching service accounts to resources

As mentioned in the previous section, a resource such as a Compute Engine VM can use a service account to interact with a Google Cloud API. Note that it is also possible to attach a service account to a resource that is deployed in a different project.

When a VM is created, it uses a default service account that you can replace with a new one assuming you have at least a **Service Account User** role on this new account:

Figure 12.34 – Adding a service account to a Compute Engine VM

Once a VM is created, you can access it via ssh and check what credentials it uses to authenticate to Google Cloud services with the following command: `gcloud auth list`.

In the following figure, a `vm-a` Compute Engine VM uses the `bucket-access` service account. This service account has a **Storage Admin** role in this project. This means a VM using this service account can access and interact with Google Cloud Storage. For example, it can create and list buckets as shown in the following screenshot:

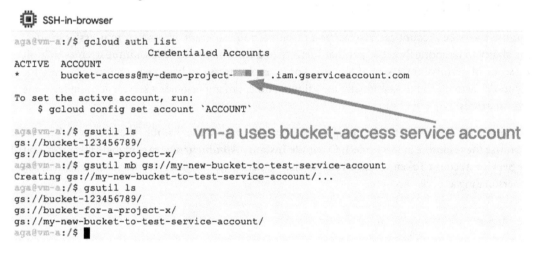

Figure 12.35 – Using a service account to interact with Google
Cloud Storage from a Compute Engine VM directly

To confirm what type of account was actually used for a `my-new-bucket-to-test-service-account` creation (shown in *Figure 12.35*), we can look into the Cloud Logging log entry for the **GCS Bucket** type and confirm that the `bucket-access` user account was used:

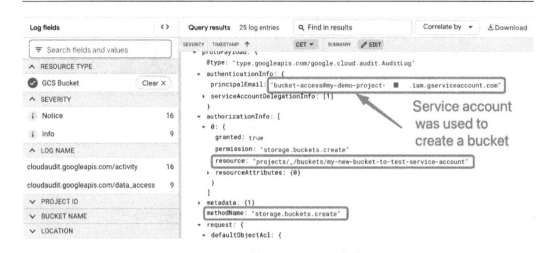

Figure 12.36 – Cloud Logging log entry showing the account used for a bucket creation

Check the following link to see what other Google Cloud services besides Compute Engine VMs use service accounts: `https://cloud.google.com/iam/docs/attach-service-accounts`.

Impersonating a service account

Because a service account can also act as a resource, you can grant access to it to users or groups. The ability to temporarily act as another identity in a controlled way helps administrators to limit the scope of permissions assigned to users. For example, users can have permissions necessary for day-to-day activities, and occasionally, for a limited time, can impersonate a service account for some extra activities.

Let's look at the example in the following figure. The `app-owner` user has the following roles: **Viewer**, to browse the resources in this project, **Compute Instance Admin,** to manage compute instances, and the **Service Account Token Creator** role (on the `bucket-access` service account), which allows impersonating a service account.

Figure 12.37 – Impersonating a service account by a user

In the CLOUD SHELL section of the screenshot, you can see the `app_owner` user trying to create a storage bucket. This task fails, as the user doesn't have the required permissions. However, once the same command is issued with `--impersonate-service-account=bucket-access@`, the command succeeds and the bucket is created because `bucket-access` is a service account with a **Storage Admin** role.

Short-lived service account credentials

If you are building an application outside Google Cloud, a service account will be used to interact with Google Cloud services. You will need a way to authenticate with this account. It doesn't come with a password, so an alternative could be to generate an RSA public/private key pair. The following screenshot shows how to achieve this in the Google Cloud console:

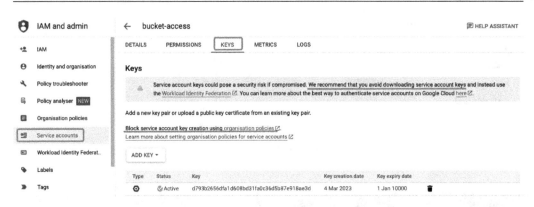

Figure 12.38 – Creating a key pair for a service account

Service account key details are presented in the **KEYS** tab when selecting a service account. You can create a new pair by selecting **ADD KEY**. Note that you can download a private key only during the key pair's creation.

Access to a file with a key is sufficient to authenticate as a service account that owns the key. In the example that follows, the gcloud auth activate-service-account <service account> --key-file=<path/key> --project=PROJECT_ID command is used in vm-a that could even be running on-premises, followed by a command that creates a storage bucket. The service account – bucket-access – is the one that interacts with the Google Cloud Storage service from outside of a project:

Figure 12.39 – Using a service account with a key

As a downloaded key could be easily shared between users and possibly exposed, it is recommended to consider alternative options. When there is no other option, rotating keys frequently is highly recommended. One of the alternatives would be to use workload identity federation and give external identities permission to impersonate a service account and generate short-lived credentials for the application. You can find more information on workload identity federation at https://cloud. google.com/iam/docs/workload-identity-federation.

Let's examine the other alternative, the token generation process, to better understand the benefits of short-lived credentials.

The `gcloud auth print-access-token` command returns a short-lived OAuth 2.0 access token that can be used for API calls on behalf of this user. In particular, the `gcloud auth print-access-token –impersonate-service-account=<service_acount>` command (assuming the **Service Account Token Creator** role is granted for the requester on a privilege-bearing service account) will return a short-lived (one hour by default) access token for a service account. Like a `bucket-access` account, a service account can have fine-grained permissions required for controlled interaction with a single service only, like Google Cloud Storage. In addition, the limited lifetime of a token minimizes the threat of it falling into the wrong hands, as could happen to a key.

Look at the following example. Details of a token generated by `gcloud auth print-access-token` can be validated using an HTTPS POST request: `https://oauth2.googleapis.com/tokeninfo?access_token=<ACCESS_TOKEN>`.

Figure 12.40 – Checking details about a token via HTTPS POST

An application can use a new token for an hour to interact with Google Cloud Storage as the token generated for a `bucket-access` service account, the one with the **Storage Admin** role assigned:

Figure 12.41 – Creating a bucket via API using an access token

The logic described is usually implemented programmatically and embedded into the code of an application. Client libraries handle token management.

Note that the number of service accounts for a project is limited by quotas. By default, you can create up to 100 service accounts. A good security practice is to remove any unused accounts. Since the number of service accounts can increase over time, it can become challenging to manage them, especially when multiple applications use them only occasionally. In case you are unsure if an application still uses a service account that you are about to delete, disable it first and ensure it is not used before deleting it.

Now that we have learned how to create users, groups, and service accounts and control their access to various Google Cloud resources, it is important to highlight that those tasks are just the first step in securing your environment. The next step is to find a way to make sure all permissions are assigned correctly and the desired setup is preserved. Also, if certain permissions are assigned, it is still important to know whether they were used with good and justified intentions. The next section will introduce the audit logging concept, which helps to track access and changes to your Google Cloud environments.

Using Cloud Audit Logs

In *Chapter 11*, in the *Cloud Logging* section, we explored various types of Google Cloud logs and learned how to view, filter, and store them. The concept of Cloud Audit Logs was briefly introduced as well. This section aims to provide more visibility into the Cloud Audit Logs topic.

Cloud Audit Logs are a part of Cloud Logging. Still, contrary to logs generated by workloads, they record user actions providing details on who did what activity (for example, created or deleted a resource) from where (such as from a local computer, browser etc.)and when this happened. This type of log is mainly collected for auditing, troubleshooting, and compliance.

There are the following audit log types:

- **Admin Activity** logs that log users' creation and deletion of Google Cloud resources. The log collection is enabled by default and can't be disabled. We also can't delete such logs. Google will store them for 400 days in the `_Required` log bucket for free. You can retain them longer by creating a parallel log sink to another destination. Refer to the *Configuring log routers* section in *Chapter 11* to review how this can be achieved.

    A simplified view of Admin Activity logs can can be found (at the time of writing this chapter) on the Google Cloud console home page in the **ACTIVITY** tab.

    The following screenshot presents example log entries generated when the `app-owner` user created and deleted buckets:

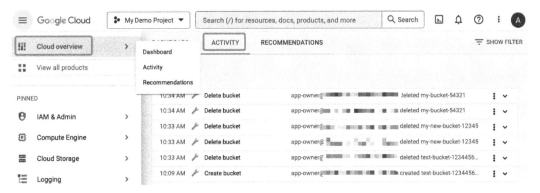

Figure 12.42 – The ACTIVITY tab presenting a simplified version of Admin Activity logs

Logs Explorer in the **Cloud Logging** section provides detailed insight into Cloud Audit Logs. If you select **CLOUD AUDIT: activity** for **Log name**, you will see all the Admin Activity entries, as presented in the following screenshot:

Figure 12.43 – Admin activity audit log in Log Explorer generated
during a Google Cloud Storage bucket creation

- **Data Access** logs are generated when users read or write to Google Cloud resources or read metadata information. For example, when a user creates a Google Cloud Storage bucket, an Admin Activity log is generated. When users upload or access objects in this bucket, this activity generates Data Access logs. Multiple users or applications could access those objects, generating a high volume of logs, which is why Data Access logs are disabled by default. You can enable log generation per service in the **Audit log** view of the **IAM & admin** section. The following figure presents how Data Access logs can be enabled for a selected service.

Three types of Data Access logs can be enabled separately (see *Figure 12.44*): **Admin Reads** (for reading metadata and configuration information), **Data Read** (for reading user data), and **Data Write** (for writing user data). By default, those logs are chargeable, have 30 days of retention, and are stored in the _Default log bucket.

To limit the number of generated logs, you can "exempt principals," meaning logs will not be generated for selected user or service accounts, even if the log collection is enabled. For example, suppose you have an application that constantly reads from a Google Cloud Storage bucket using a service account. This service account could be added as an exempted principal, so its actions won't generate Data Access logs. On the other hand, you can set up an organization policy to disallow Audit Logging exemptions to enforce logging for all accounts.

Figure 12.44 – Enabling audit logs for data access to Google Cloud Storage

- **System Event** logs are automatically generated by Google systems and stored for free in the `_Required` log bucket. You can't disable or delete them. They record actions driven by the Google Cloud platform and can be viewed in the Logs Explorer. For instance, the following screenshot shows `system_event` logs generated during a server maintenance action when a Compute Engine VM was migrated to another server. System Event logs could be a good source of information for troubleshooting. For example, if you want to understand why a VM was rebooted, you can check whether a host error caused this by verifying System Event log entries:

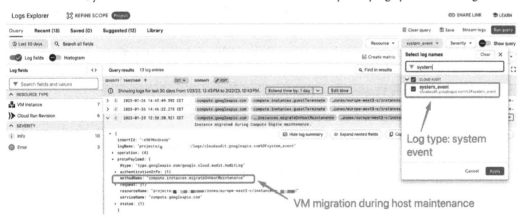

Figure 12.45 – System Event log entry generated during a host maintenance event

- **Policy Denied** logs are generated when a user or service account is denied access to a Google Cloud service because of a security policy violation. The logs are generated and stored in the `_Default` log bucket and can't be disabled. Policy Denied logs are chargeable, but you can exclude them from ingestion.

For security reasons, only certain users should have access to audit logs, which may contain sensitive data. The **Logs Viewer** role grants access to Admin Activity and System Event logs, but to view Data Access audit logs, a separate **Private Log Viewer** role is required.

Summary

This chapter explored setting up an organization and building a resource hierarchy to match a company's structure. We learned how to control access to Google Cloud resources on a project, folder, and organizational level. One of the most important topics we investigated was working with service accounts used by Google Cloud services and external applications. Lastly, we looked into Cloud Audit Logs that need to be collected to meet an enterprise's security and compliance needs.

Questions

Answer the following questions to test your knowledge of this chapter:

1. Suppose you have just created a new Google Cloud project and want to follow the best practices for granting access to its resources. How can you provide view permissions to all resources in the project for your team members?

    A. Grant each user a basic Viewer role.

    B. Create a group and add all team members to this group. Assign a basic Viewer role to this group.

    C. Create a group and add all team members to this group. Assign a basic Editor role to this group.

    D. Grant each user a basic Editor role.

2. What would be a good use case for basic roles?

    A. Basic roles could be used in a test environment only, or if, a project has just one owner.

    B. Basic roles can't be used as they are being deprecated.

    C. You should always use basic roles because they are easy to manage and kept up to date by Google.

    D. Basic roles should only be used with service accounts.

3. How can a user create a service account?

    A. In the Google Admin console at `https://admin.google.com`.

    B. In the Cloud Identity console.

C. There is no need to create service accounts. They are created automatically when an API for a service is enabled.

D. Service accounts can be created in IAM in the Google Cloud console.

4. What is the difference between the following roles: Service Account User and Service Account Token Creator?

A. Service Account User role allows to attach a service account to a resource and Service Token Creator role allows to create access tokens for a service account.

B. You need a Service Account User role to be able to assign a Service Token Creator role to a service account.

C. There is no difference. You can use them interchangeably.

D. You need a Service Account User role to be able to create tokens.

5. What is a recommended approach to granting an application outside Google Cloud administrative access to Google Cloud Storage?

A. Create RSA keys for a service account with a Storage Admin role assigned. Store the private key on-premises. The application can leverage `gcloud auth activate-service-account <service account> --key-file=<path/key> --project=PROJECT_ID` for authentication.

B. You can't grant an application outside Google Cloud access to Google Cloud Storage.

C. Use Service Token Creator permissions to generate access tokens for a service account with a Storage Admin role assigned.

D. Impersonate a service account in the application with `--impersonate-service-account=bucket-access`, where `bucket-access` is a service account with a Storage Admin role assigned.

6. You made a mistake and accidentally deleted a Cloud Storage bucket with rarely accessed archive data. You managed to restore the bucket and objects from a backup. Is there a way to hide this embarrassing accident from your team?

A. There is no way to hide it. Deleting and creating a resource will be logged in Admin Activity.

B. Deleting and creating a resource will be logged in Admin Activity and retained for 400 days. If no one checks the logs within that time, the log entry will eventually be deleted.

C. Deleting and creating a resource will not be logged at all without an additional setup.

D. Deleting and creating a resource will be logged. You can delete the log entry in Cloud Logging, having the Logging Admin role, so no one discovers what happened.

7. During a team meeting, you discuss simplifying permissions management for multiple projects your team created. All projects are configured directly under your organization, and all users have Editor roles on projects. What approach would you recommend to improve management and security?

    A. Create a folder resource under the organization and move all your team's projects under this folder. Use organization policies to enforce better security, such as disallowing public IP usage and creating RSA keys for service accounts.

    B. Create a folder resource under the organization and move all your team's projects under this folder. Create one group account for your team and add users to the group. Assign predefined roles to the group on a folder level. Use organization policies to enforce better security, such as disallowing public IP usage and creating RSA keys for service accounts.

    C. Create a folder resource under the organization and move all your team's projects under this folder. Create group accounts for your team and add users to the groups according to their needs. Assign predefined roles to the groups at the folder level. If needed, assign additional predefined roles on a project level. Delete permissions assigned to individual users in projects.

    D. Once the projects are created under an organization, you can't introduce any changes to the hierarchy.

Answers

The answers to the preceding questions are provided here:

1B, 2A, 3D, 4A, 5C, 6B, 7C

Mock Test 1

Questions

Answer these questions to practice for the exam:

1. You want to use Google Cloud free credits to explore Google Cloud's services and prepare for your ACE exam. You plan to stay within the limits of the free tier whenever possible so that you won't run out of credits too soon. However, you are asked to provide a payment method during the free trial signup. Why do you think this happened?

    A. It was a mistake. There is no need to provide credit card details because you will receive $300 in credits from Google. You need to contact the support team.

    B. Google will transfer $300 to your bank account, so you need to share your credit card details during the signup process.

    C. Providing payment details is required for the billing account setup, regardless of whether you plan to use a paid account or free credits. This is also how your identity is verified. You will need to monitor your spending because you will be charged once you run out of free credits.

    D. Providing payment details is required for the billing account setup, regardless of whether you plan to use a paid account or free credits. This is also how your identity is verified. You won't be charged, even if you run out of free credits. You need to explicitly upgrade your account to a paid account for Google to be able to charge you.

2. The CFO has just informed you that the company has decided to switch banks, and as a result, a new billing account must be configured and attached to all existing and new Google Cloud projects. She is asking you, the administrator of the resources, whether this can be achieved without downtime for production workloads and what happens to all pending charges. What applies here?

    A. Changing a billing account for a project shouldn't impact running services. You can attach a new active billing account to a project at any time by going to the **My Project** page of the **Billing** section. Pending charges will be billed to the former billing account, and all new charges will be billed to a new billing account.

    B. Changing a billing account for a project shouldn't impact running services. You can attach a new active billing account to a project at any time by going to the **My Project** page of the **Billing** section. Pending and new charges will be billed to a new billing account.

    C.   Changing a billing account for a project causes downtime to all running services. Therefore, you need to schedule a maintenance window to switch the billing accounts on the **My Project** page of the **Billing** section. Pending charges will be billed to the former billing account, and all new charges will be billed to a new billing account.

    D.   Changing a billing account for a project causes downtime to all running services. You need to schedule a maintenance window to switch the billing accounts on the **My Project** page of the **Billing** section. Pending and new charges will be billed to a new billing account.

3.   Your team is preparing to migrate their on-premises workloads to Google Cloud. However, it is worried about the bill and anticipate that it might be higher than they initially calculated. What can you recommend to them to better control its cloud spending?

    A.   They should monitor their projects' total and forecasted monthly costs in billing account reports to ensure only necessary services are generating costs.

    B.   They should create a budget for the cloud billing account that includes all their services in all their projects and set a fixed monthly budget amount and alert thresholds. If their spending exceeds one of these thresholds, billing admins will receive an email notification. No resources will be stopped. Also, they will still be able to create new workloads.

    C.   They should create a budget for the cloud billing account that includes all their services in all their projects and set a fixed monthly budget amount. If their spending exceeds the target amount, they won't be able to create new workloads.

    D.   They should set a limit on the company's credit card so that they won't be charged more than the allowed amount.

4.   What mechanism prevents users from creating unlimited resources for a specific service type while keeping existing workloads unaffected?

    A.   Quotas

    B.   Disabling APIs

    C.   Cloud billing budgets

    D.   Limits on a credit card used by cloud billing

5.   After installing some patches for the operating system in a Compute Engine VM, you noticed the application running on the VM stopped working. After lengthy troubleshooting, you decide to rebuild the VM and reinstall the application on a clean operating system. The problem is that the new VM was assigned a different private IP, and users cannot access the application. How can you fix this issue?

    A.   You must reserve the initial internal IP as the static IP address in this VPC. Then, you shut down the VM, edit the network interface, select the reserved address, and start the VM.

B. Private IP addresses are automatically assigned. You can't assign a private IP manually by selecting the one you need. Instead, users need to change the IP that they are using to a new one. You must send an email to all users that share a new IP address.

C. You must reserve the initial internal IP as the static IP address in this VPC. Then, you must recreate the VM one more time, this time, selecting the reserved address for a network interface.

D. You must shut down the VM, edit the network interface, change the IP to the initial one, and start the VM.

6. You have to run a batch job and have a limited budget for this task. To save costs, you are considering creating a managed instance group with VMs in a spot provisioning model. But first, you need to verify that your script handles the preemption correctly. How can you achieve this?

A. You can use spot VMs in a managed instance group and use `gcloud compute instances simulate-maintenance-event` on VMs to test the unexpected termination.

B. You can't use spot VMs in a managed instance group.

C. You can use spot VMs in a managed instance group, but no mechanism is available to help simulate the unexpected termination.

D. You can only use preemptive VMs in a managed instance group, but no mechanism is available to help simulate the unexpected termination.

7. You want to run a daily backup to prevent Compute Engine VM data from being accidentally deleted. Which option should you choose?

A. Scheduling `gcloud compute images create` to run daily so that a new VM image will be created every day.

B. Scheduling `gcloud compute instance-templates create` to run daily so that a new VM instance template will be created every day

C. Use the Google Cloud console to create a VM similar to an existing one via the **CREATE SIMILAR** option in the **VM instances** view

D. Create a daily snapshot schedule for the disks attached to the VM

8. Your organization has two teams: team 1 creates the frontends, while team 2 creates backends for applications. The teams often share projects and always use the same billing account. How can the finance department calculate the organization's spending on frontend and backend resources separately?

A. By using filters in the **Cost breakdown** section of the **Billing** view. Each team can select the services it uses each month and share the report with the finance department.

B. By using folders. Each team should keep its workloads in a dedicated folder in every project. The finance department can verify spending by filtering the cost per folder in the **Cost breakdown** section of the **Billing** view.

C. By using labels. The teams should label their resources as `team:team-1` or `team:team-2`. Billing data should be exported to BigQuery for analysis. Queries that return the overall spending for both teams can be exported to Looker Studio and shared with the finance department.

D. By using tags. The teams should tag their resources as `team-1` or `team-2`. Billing data should be exported to BigQuery for analysis. Queries that return the overall spending tagged as `team-1` and `team-2` can be exported to Looker Studio and shared with the finance department.

9. Which storage volume for a Compute Engine instance is protected against a failure in a zone and provides the best balance of performance and cost?

A. Regional balanced Persistent Disk volume

B. Zonal balanced Persistent Disk volume

C. Regional Cloud Storage bucket

D. Zonal standard Persistent Disk volume

10. What are the advantages of using a managed instance group?

A. High availability – it supports multi-zone deployments, scaling based on various metrics, built-in mechanisms for automatically patching instances, and auto-healing, which creates a new instance in case the old one crashes

B. High availability – it supports multi-zone deployments, built-in mechanisms for automatically patching instances, and auto-healing that reboots instances in case of a crash

C. High availability – it supports multi-zone deployments, scaling up based on various metrics, built-in mechanisms for automatically patching instances, and auto-healing, which reboots instances in case of a crash

D. High availability – it supports multi-zone deployments, scaling down based on various metrics, built-in mechanisms for automatically patching instances, and auto-healing, which reboots instances in case of a crash

11. Which instance group type would you choose to set up automatic management for a group of VMs with persistent data?

A. Managed instance group (stateless)

B. Managed instance group (stateful)

C. Unmanaged instance group

D. All of the above

12. Which compute model should you choose if you want to run a simple event-driven serverless service that processes images right after they are uploaded to Google Cloud Storage? You also don't want to worry about the execution environment.

    A. Cloud Run

    B. A managed instance group

    C. GKE

    D. Cloud Functions

13. Which compute model should you choose if you want to run a stateless web-based service that scales based on the number of incoming requests and uses no resources when there are no requests? Also, your developers want to use their custom build for this service.

    A. Cloud Functions

    B. Cloud Run

    C. GKE

    D. Kubernetes

14. Which of the following is true about regional GKE clusters?

    A. They can't be deployed in Autopilot mode

    B. They contain multiple replicas of the control plane, running in multiple zones in a region and nodes in multiple or a single zone

    C. They can be changed to zonal at any time

    D. They have one replica of the control plane running in a selected zone and nodes in multiple zones

15. How can you isolate a GKE cluster so that it can't be accessed from the internet and at the same time allow outbound internet access for the nodes?

    A. Deploy a public cluster

    B. Deploy a private cluster with **Access control plane using its external IP address** option enabled

    C. Deploy a private cluster and use Cloud NAT for outbound internet traffic

    D. Deploy a private cluster with Private Google Access enabled on a VPC

16. Which sentence about GKE Autopilot is not true?

    A. It can be configured with regional or zonal availability

    B. Resources are provisioned based on workloads

C. You pay for the resources that are consumed by workloads (per pod)

D. It's deployed with a hardened configuration

17. How can you configure Cloud Monitoring and Logging for GKE standard cluster mode?

A. No configuration is required as Cloud Monitoring and Logging are enabled by default during cluster creation

B. You need to install the Ops Agent inside the nodes and enable FW rules to allow incoming traffic on ports 20201 and 20202

C. You need to install Ops Agent inside the nodes and modify the config.yaml file by adding gke to the list of monitored systems

D. Cloud Monitoring and Logging for GKE is supported only for GKE autopilot cluster mode

18. You are writing an application and you want to focus on code, without having to manage infrastructure. That is why you want to use Cloud Functions. But you also want to experiment with some code and send just a subset of traffic to every new revision. How can you achieve this with Cloud Functions?

A. You must use Cloud Run to split traffic between revisions. This can't be achieved with Cloud Functions.

B. Traffic splitting between various versions of your code is a Cloud Functions second-generation feature, so you need to use this version.

C. Cloud Functions (first- and second-generation) support the traffic-splitting mechanism by default. It doesn't matter which version you use.

D. You can configure an HTTP(S) load balancer to distribute traffic between revisions of Cloud Function deployments.

19. Which sentence does not describe Cloud Functions?

A. It supports languages such as Python, Java, Go, and Node.js

B. You can trigger Cloud Function execution with HTTP/S requests, Pub/Sub messages, and Cloud Storage changes, such as a new object being created or deleted.

C. You are billed only for the time your function is executed

D. It supports network protocols beyond HTTP/S

20. Select the sentence that is not true about Cloud Run.

A. It runs code in response to events

B. It runs containers in a fully managed environment

C.   It allows you to use any language and any library

D.   It scales automatically

21. What are the minimum steps required to deploy a Cloud Run service?

A.   Build a container with code that listens to HTTP requests on a predefined port. Then, create a service endpoint and deploy the container by selecting its image and providing a name for a service and a region where it should run. Finally, configure Cloud Logging for the Cloud Run service.

B.   Build a container with code that listens to HTTP requests on a predefined port. Then, create a source repository and upload the image before creating a service endpoint. Finally, deploy the container by selecting its image from the source repository and providing a name for a service.

C.   Build a container with code that listens to HTTP requests on a predefined port, then deploy the container by selecting its image and providing a name for a service and a region where it should run.

D.   Build a container with code that listens to HTTP requests on a predefined port, then deploy the container on a previously created GKE cluster in a selected region.

22. You are an instructor who delivers Associate Cloud Engineer exam preparation courses. Every time a course starts, you must deploy labs for your students. To simplify troubleshooting, all deployments must be the same. After the course, labs need to be destroyed to avoid costs. How can you prepare your labs efficiently?

A.   Use Infrastructure as Code. You can use Google Cloud Platform Provider in Terraform to provision your projects and create resources. Later, you can use `terraform destroy` to remove the provisioned workloads.

B.   You should prepare a deploy script and use Cloud Client Libraries to access the Google Cloud API programmatically to set up your projects. Later, by detaching your billing account from projects, you can ensure resources will be deleted.

C.   Use Infrastructure as Code. You can use Google Cloud Platform Provider in Terraform to provision your projects and create resources. Later, you can delete each project manually to ensure no services are running.

D.   You should prepare a deploy script and use Cloud Client Libraries to access the Google Cloud API programmatically to set up your projects and delete them later.

23. What is a good use case for running Cloud Run on Anthos instead of using a fully managed Cloud Run?

    A. Incorporating Kubernetes' best practices and creating a better bridge between the Dev and Ops teams

    B. Running a flexible serverless platform to deploy workloads in hybrid and multi-cloud environments

    C. Simplifying the application deployment and management experience for Kubernetes

    D. Ability to scale down to zero

24. Your team is designing a business-critical application that is expected to go from a small to a massive scale. Which managed relational database would you recommend, knowing they need the ability to scale the instance without downtime and require strong consistency?

    A. Cloud SQL

    B. Cloud BigTable

    C. Cloud Firestore

    D. Cloud Spanner

25. While building a truck tracking application for a global logistics company, you look for a scalable, low-latency database to store the GPS position of thousands of vehicles at a given timestamp. Which database should you choose?

    A. Cloud SQL

    B. Cloud BigTable

    C. Cloud Firestore

    D. Cloud Spanner

26. You are designing a serverless system to analyze real-time data streamed by people counting appliances in stores so that your analytics team can better understand consumers' behavior. What would be the most critical components of such a system?

    A. Real-time data should be streamed to Pub/Sub first so that no event is lost in the case of processing bottlenecks. Then, data should be parsed through Dataflow and sent to BigQuery, where it will be available to the analytics team.

    B. Real-time data should be streamed directly to BigQuery, where it will be available for the analytics team.

    C. Real-time data should be streamed to Pub/Sub first so that no event is lost in the case of processing bottlenecks. Then, data should be parsed through Dataproc and sent to BigQuery, where it will be available for the analytics team.

D.   Real-time data should be streamed to Pub/Sub first so that no event is lost in the case of processing bottlenecks. Then, data should be parsed through Dataproc and sent to BigTable, where it will be available for the analytics team.

27. Which CLI command can be used to create a Google Cloud Storage bucket called `my-awesome-bucket`?

A.   `cbt mb my-awesome-bucket`

B.   `bq mb gs://my-awesome-bucket`

C.   `gsutil mb gs://my-awesome-bucket`

D.   `gcloud buckets create gs://my-awesome-bucket`

28. You are working on an application to help studio photographers share session photos with their customers. You have decided to use Google Cloud Storage buckets to store photos, but you are worried that storing a large number of high-resolution images can be expensive. To limit the storage bill, you decided that photos will be available for download for 30 days only. How can you achieve this?

A.   Use Google Cloud SDK in your application's code to interact with Google Cloud Storage, query the objects' lifetimes, and delete ones that are older than 30 days.

B.   List bucket details in the Google Cloud console in the Google Cloud Storage view, order objects by date, and delete the oldest every month.

C.   Use the Google Cloud Storage Autoclass feature to automatically detect access patterns and move objects to the Archive storage if they are not accessed for 30 days.

D.   Use Object Lifecycle with **Action** set to `delete` and **Condition** set to `age=30`.

29. Which of the following storage systems would be the best fit for storing users' home directories?

A.   Google Cloud Storage

B.   Persistent Disk

C.   Filestore

D.   Local Disk

30. You are designing a standalone application that must survive a failure in a Google Cloud region. You decide to create resources in two regions, europe-west3 and europe-central2, and build a replication mechanism between them. Which network design would be the most optimal for this case?

A.   One VPC with a subnet in the europe-west3 and europe-central2 regions

B.   Two VPCs with a subnet in the europe-west3 and europe-central2 regions

    C. One shared VPC with a subnet in the europe-west3 and europe-central2 regions

    D. There is no need to create two redundant subnets since the VPC is a global, highly available service

31. You used Google Cloud SDK in your code to spin up 500 Compute Engine VMs in the same subnet. However, in the Google Cloud console, you noticed that only around half of them were successfully deployed. What could be the reason for this?

    A. Your application ran out of memory

    B. Your subnet was created with a /24 mask and you used all of the IP addresses

    C. Using Google Cloud SDK is not supported for creating a large number of resources

    D. Your Organization Policy only allows you to create 250 VMs per user

32. How can you provide internet access to a Compute Engine VM with only a private IP assigned?

    A. Internet access will only be available for a VM with a public IP assigned

    B. Use Cloud NAT

    C. You need to add a default route of 0.0.0.0/0 to the internet in the VPC where a VM is running

    D. You need to add a DNS entry of 8.8.8.8 to the VM's networking configuration

33. Which load balancer type would best fit a globally accessible external non-HTTPS application?

    A. An external network TCP/UDP load balancer

    B. A global external TCP/SSL Proxy

    C. A global external HTTP(S) load balancer

    D. None of them

34. You are connecting your on-premises environment with Google Cloud. However, your on-premises router doesn't support BGP for exchanging routes. Which option can you choose to connect to Google Cloud?

    A. Dedicated Interconnect

    B. Partner Interconnect

    C. HA VPN

    D. Classic VPN

35. You are working on an application that will be running inside a Compute Engine VM. The application will index files uploaded to a Google Cloud Storage bucket, searching for specific text patterns. How can the application access the bucket?

   A. The service account that is assigned to the VM needs to have Google Cloud Storage access permissions such as Storage Admin for interacting with the bucket

   B. The VM can access the objects in the same project as the bucket if Private Service Access is enabled on a VPC

   C. If a user who creates the VM has the Compute Admin role, the VM will be able to access the objects

   D. The default service account that's assigned to a VM during deployment has Google Cloud Storage access permissions by default, so the VM can interact with the bucket

36. Starting next year, your company must comply with regulatory requirements to store data in the European Union. How can this be achieved?

   A. By using the `gcloud asset search-all-resources` command to search for assets outside the EU.

   B. By creating VPC subnets only in EU regions. Here, resources can only be created in regions where a subnet exists.

   C. By using an organization policy to limit the regions where resources can be deployed to the EU ones. This will apply to new resources only, so an audit needs to be conducted to identify which existing resources need to be migrated.

   D. By using an organization policy to limit the regions to which resources can be deployed to the EU ones. This will apply to existing and new resources, so it has to be done during a maintenance window to ensure there's no impact on existing services.

37. You are working as a networking administrator in a global company. Your current assignment is to plan networking for all new Google Cloud projects to simplify its management overhead. However, you want to address the following problem with existing projects: every time Google launches a new region, developers contact you and ask for a subnet in a new region. As a result, you log in to existing projects one by one and manually add a new subnet. How can you simplify this process?

   A. Use a Shared VPC in the custom mode

   B. Use a Shared VPC in auto mode

   C. Use a VPC in custom mode

   D. Use a VPC in auto mode

38. Your organization still uses legacy tools that require service account keys. You must ensure the keys are used only by the entitled tools. Which option will help you to achieve this?

    A. Cloud Logging

    B. Service Account Insights

    C. Cloud Monitoring

    D. Cloud Audit Logs

39. You supervise three teams of developers: team a, team b, and team c. Those teams create and use multiple Google Cloud projects for their workloads. Following Google's recommendations, how can you ensure you have view access to all of them?

    A. Create a root folder for your teams and add individual folders for each team under the root folder. Ensure team members only have a Project Creator role at their team's folder level. The Project Viewer role needs to be assigned to you at the root folder level.

    B. The Project Viewer role needs to be assigned to you in every project individually.

    C. The Project Viewer role needs to be assigned to you at the organization level.

    D. Create a root folder for your teams and add individual folders for each team under the root folder. Ensure team members only have a Project Creator role at their team's folder level. The Project Viewer role needs to be assigned to you at every team's folder level.

40. Which is not the recommended best practice for providing access to Google Cloud resources?

    A. Attaching IAM roles to groups instead of individual users

    B. Using the principle of least privilege

    C. C. Using Basic roles

    D. Using Predefined roles

41. You deployed an application on a Compute Engine VM, which generates unstructured logs that must be stored for 7 years. After a few weeks, you notice that the log volume it generates is too high to be stored locally on a Persistent Disk. To reduce spending, you decide to send logs to an external system. Which option would be the best fit?

    A. Add functionality to your application's code to send logs to the Google Cloud Storage archive class bucket. Set Object Lifecycle on the bucket to delete data after 7 years.

    B. Add functionality to your application's code to send logs to a syslog appliance on-premises, backed by a storage array that can be used for archiving.

    C. No code changes are required. Install Ops Agent, which will collect and process logs and send them to Cloud Logging without additional setup. Create a log sink to send the application logs to a log bucket and set its retention to 7 years.

D. Add functionality to your application's code using client libraries to structure and send logs to the Cloud Logging API. Create a log sink to send the application logs to a log bucket and set its retention to 7 years.

42. The security team in your organization contacted you, the application owner, and asked you to troubleshoot their access to Audit Logs for your project. They wanted to examine logs from Google Cloud Storage for object upload and deletion on your buckets. But when they accessed Cloud Logging, they could only see logs related to bucket creation. How can you fix this?

A. The security team needs a Logging Admin role to be able to see Audit Logs.

B. You need to enable Data Access Logs for the Google Cloud Storage service. Also, the security team needs to be added to "exempted principals" in the Google Cloud Storage data audit log configuration.

C. You need to enable Data Access Logs for the Google Cloud Storage service. Also, the security team needs a Private Log Viewer role to be able to see Data Access logs.

D. The security team needs a Private Log Viewer role to be able to see Admin Activity logs.

43. You want to configure a VPC in a newly created project. What is the first step you need to do to be able to create a VPC?

A. Enable the Compute Engine API

B. Go to **VPC Networks**, select **CREATE VPC NETWORK**, and start configuring the VPC

C. Enable the Cloud Networking API

D. You don't need to do anything – the default VPC is ready to use once a new project is created

44. Your team wishes to consolidate the monitoring of all Compute Engine VMs deployed in multiple projects in one place. However, they also want to be able to view VM metrics per individual project. How can they achieve this most effectively?

A. They should decide which of the existing projects will become a new scoping project and add all existing projects to this one.

B. They should create a new project dedicated to monitoring and add other projects to the scoping project.

C. This can only be achieved by exporting metrics to a third-party monitoring tool.

D. They should decide which of the existing projects will become a new scoping project and add all existing projects to this one. They should use filters and customized charts to monitor VMs for individual projects.

45. How can you create a group that includes both users and service accounts?

    A. In the Google Cloud console, at the organization level, go to the **Groups** section of IAM, create a group, and add all members and their roles.

    B. Log in to the Admin console as a superadmin at `https://admin.google.com`, go to **Directory | Group**, create a new group, and add its members. Next, add the group members.

    C. Log in to the Admin console as a superadmin at `https://admin.google.com`, go to **Directory | Group**, create a new group, and add its members. Next, add the group members. Finally, log in to the Google Cloud console and verify that the group exists.

    D. You can't create a group that consists of both users and service accounts.

46. A support team should only be able to view monitoring dashboards without access to other resources in all projects under the `production` folder. What option would follow Google's recommendation in this scenario?

    A. Create a group for the support team and assign a Project Viewer role to the group at the `production` folder level.

    B. Assign a Project Viewer role to individual users at the `production` folder level.

    C. Create a group for the support team and assign a Project Viewer role to the group at the `production` folder level. In the individual projects, assign the Monitoring Viewer role to the group.

    D. Create a group for the support team and assign a Monitoring Viewer role to the group at the `production` folder level.

47. You accidentally applied the `gcloud projects delete project1` command instead of `gcloud projects delete project2`. How can you revert this action?

    A. `gcloud projects undelete project1`

    B. `gcloud projects restore project1`

    C. `gcloud projects revert project1`

    D. There is no option to undo this action

48. Which method would be the most optimal for creating 15 independent Compute Engine VMs with the same settings?

    A. In the **Compute Engine** view, go to the **VM instances** section and select the **BULK CREATE VMs** option

    B. Create an instance template and use a managed instance group to deploy the required number of VMs

C. Use bulk creation in the CLI – for example, `gcloud compute instances bulk create --name-pattern=vm## --count=15 --zone=europe-central2-a --network=my-vpc-network --subnet=warsaw-subnet`

D. Use bulk creation in the CLI – for example, `gcloud compute instances bulk create --predefined-names=vm1,vm2,vm3,vm4,.. --zone=europe-central2-a --network=my-vpc-network --subnet=warsaw-subnet`

49. In which case is using a Pub/Sub Push subscription type as a delivery mechanism for an application the best option?

A. When you're dealing with a large volume of messages

B. When high message throughput is expected

C. When Google Cloud credentials can't be used

D. When a public HTTPS endpoint with a non-self-signed certificate can't be used

50. You want to provide internet access to your Compute Engine VMs, which are deployed in two zones – europe-west3 and europe-central2 – in the same VPC (my-vpc) in a newly created project called my-project. Which set of commands should you run?

A. `gcloud compute routers create router-waw --project=my-project --network=my-vpc --region=europe-central2`

`gcloud compute routers create router-fra --project=my-project --network=my-vpc --region=europe-west3`

`gcloud compute routers nats create nat-waw --router=router-waw --region=europe-central2 --auto-allocate-nat-external-ips --nat-all-subnet-ip-ranges`

`gcloud compute routers nats create nat-fra --router=router-fra --region=europe-west3 --auto-allocate-nat-external-ips --nat-all-subnet-ip-ranges`

B. `gcloud compute routers create router my-router –project=my-project --network=my-vpc`

`gcloud compute routers nats create nat –router=my-router --auto-allocate-nat-external-ips --nat-all-subnet-ip-ranges`

C. `gcloud compute routers create router my-router --project=my-project --network=my-vpc`

`gcloud compute routers nats create nat-waw --router=my-router --region=europe-central2 --auto-allocate-nat-external-ips --nat-all-subnet-ip-ranges`

```
gcloud compute routers nats create nat-fra --router=my-
router --region=europe-west3 --auto-allocate-nat-external-
ips --nat-all-subnet-ip-ranges
```

D. Compute Engine VMs are always created with a public IP, allowing internet egress with no additional configuration

Answers

Here are the answers to this mock test's questions:

1D, 2A, 3B, 4A, 5C, 6A, 7D, 8C, 9A, 10A, 11B, 12D, 13B, 14B, 15C, 16A, 17A, 18B, 19D, 20A, 21C, 22A, 23B, 24D, 25B, 26A, 27C, 28D, 29C, 30A, 31B, 32B, 33B, 34D, 35A, 36C, 37B, 38D, 39A, 40C, 41D, 42C, 43A, 44B, 45A, 46D, 47A, 48C, 49C, 50A

If you liked reading this book, *Google Cloud Associate Cloud Engineer Certification and Implementation Guide*, you can join this book's dedicated GitHub repository to ask questions about this book, or just to stay up to date on the latest changes. The repository is located at https://github.com/PacktPublishing/Google-Cloud-Associate-Cloud-Engineer-Certification-and-Implementation-Guide.

Figure 13.1 – QR code to this book's GitHub repository

You can also join this book's Slack channel if you want to interact with this book's authors and other readers. The channel is located at bit.ly/ace-gcp-book-slack.

Figure 13.2 – QR code to this book's Slack channel

Mock Test 2

Questions

Answer the following questions to test your knowledge of this chapter:

1. Your team of developers received their own Google Cloud project to use as their sandbox environment. You would like to be notified if any developers exceed $1,000 per month of their Google Cloud spending. What should you do?

   A. Set up individual billing accounts for each developer and manually check their monthly spending.

   B. Ask the developers to report their monthly Google Cloud spending to you.

   C. Set up a budget alert in Google Cloud that notifies you if any individual developer exceeds $1,000 per month of their Google Cloud spending.

   D. Monitor the spending every quarter and meet with the developers to discuss their usage.

2. Employees in a single physical location use your internal facing application exclusively. It requires strong consistency, fast queries, and multi-table ACID transactional updates. It is based on PostgreSQL, and you received a requirement to deploy it in Google Cloud with minimal code changes. Which database solution is most suitable for this?

   A. Google Cloud Spanner

   B. Google Cloud SQL for PostgreSQL

   C. Google Cloud Firestore

   D. Google Cloud Bigtable

3. Which Google Cloud product is best suited to storing sensor data from construction equipment with high data throughput, consistent time-based data retrieval, and atomic storing and retrieving signals?

   A. Google Cloud Spanner

   B. Google Cloud SQL for PostgreSQL

   C. Google Cloud Storage

   D. Google Cloud Bigtable

4. Which of the following Google Cloud Compute Engine features can prevent the accidental deletion of a VM?

    A. **Deletion protection**: This feature prevents a VM from being deleted unless the user explicitly confirms the deletion.

    B. **Snapshots**: Snapshots are point-in-time copies of a VM. They can be used to restore a VM to a previous state if it is accidentally deleted.

    C. **Backups**: Backups are copies of a VM that are stored off-site. They can be used to restore a VM to a previous state if it is accidentally deleted or if the underlying hardware fails.

    D. **IAM permissions**: IAM permissions can be used to control who has access to delete a VM. This can help to prevent accidental deletions by unauthorized users.

5. What is the first step to take when preparing to create a Google Cloud Spanner instance for a new project that will be used to deploy a globally distributed application?

    A. Set up a Cloud Storage bucket to store backups.

    B. Install the Cloud Spanner client libraries on your local machine.

    C. Configure a firewall to allow access to the Cloud Spanner instance.

    D. Create a Google Cloud Spanner instance configuration and select a multi-region or regional instance.

6. When configuring a VPC firewall for an application, how should you limit data egress to the fewest open ports?

    A. Set up a default deny egress rule, and then create allow rules only for necessary ports and destinations.

    B. Configure an allowlist of allowed egress IP addresses and ports.

    C. Use a proxy server to restrict outbound traffic to approved destinations.

    D. Use Cloud Audit Logging to monitor egress traffic and block any suspicious activity.

7. Which steps should you take to ensure that future CLI commands, by default, address the specific GKE cluster named `development`?

    A. Run the following command – `gcloud config set container/cluster development`.

    B. Run the following command – `gcloud config set cluster/development`.

    C. Run the following command – `gcloud config set container/development`.

    D. Run the following command – `gcloud config set development/cluster`.

8. Which of the following options would be the best approach to reducing the cost of running a fault-tolerant batch workload that runs every night on many **VMs** in Google Cloud Platform?

   A. Reducing the size of the VMs to reduce the cost.

   B. Using preemptible or spot VMs to reduce cost.

   C. Using standard persistent disks instead of SSD persistent disks.

   D. Using larger VMs to handle the workload more efficiently.

9. Your company operates in a strongly regulated environment. An auditor wants to review who accessed data in Cloud Storage buckets. Which options to audit access data in Google Cloud Storage buckets would you choose?

   A. Using Cloud Asset Inventory to view access logs for Cloud Storage buckets.

   B. Enabling Cloud Audit Logs for Cloud Storage buckets to view activity logs.

   C. Using the Export Logs API.

   D. Using Cloud Storage reports to view the access logs for Cloud Storage buckets.

10. Which of the following options would you use to investigate whether a former employee accessed sensitive customer information in Google Cloud after leaving the company?

   A. Using Cloud Audit Logs to view the access history of the former employee's Google Cloud account.

   B. Using Google Cloud DLP to scan for sensitive information in the Google Cloud projects and storage buckets accessed by the former employee.

   C. Using Google Cloud's operations suite to view the former employee's activity logs in Google Cloud.

   D. Using Cloud Identity and Access Management to check the former employee's access to Google Cloud and revoke it if necessary.

11. Which command can grant a user the `editor` role for a specific Google Cloud project using the `gcloud` command-line tool?

   A. `gcloud projects add-iam-policy-binding`

   B. `gcloud iam roles create`

   C. `gcloud iam service-accounts create`

   D. `gcloud compute firewall-rules create`

12. Which statement about Google Cloud VPN in **high availability** (**HA**) mode is correct?

    A. Google Cloud VPN in HA mode is designed to provide HA by replicating VPN gateways across multiple regions.

    B. Google Cloud VPN in HA mode is only available for use with Google Cloud Compute Engine instances.

    C. Google Cloud VPN in HA mode is not recommended for production use, as it can cause connectivity issues.

    D. Google Cloud VPN in HA mode is a paid service that requires a separate subscription.

13. Imagine that you have an application hosted on a bare-metal server situated in your data center, which needs access to cloud storage. However, your security policies prevent the servers that host the application from having public IP addresses or accessing the internet. In such a case, you must abide by Google's recommended guidelines to facilitate the application's access to cloud storage. What actions should you take?

    A. Use the `nslookup` or `dig` command to get the IP address of `storage.googleapis.com`. Negotiate with the security team to provide public IP addresses to bare-metal servers. Allow only egress traffic from bare-metal servers to the IP addresses of `storage.googleapis.com`.

    B. Use Cloud VPN or Cloud Interconnect to create a tunnel to your VPC in Google Cloud. Use Cloud Router to create a custom route advertisement for `199.36.153.4/30` and `2600:2d00:0002:1000::/64`. Announce that network to your on-premises network through the VPN tunnel. In your on-premises network, configure the DNS server to resolve `*.googleapis.com` as a CNAME to `restricted.googleapis.com`.

    C. Use Migrate for Compute Engine to migrate bare-metal servers to Compute Engine. Create an internal Load Balancer that uses `storage.google.com` as a backend. Configure new Compute Engine instances to use Internal Load Balancer as proxy.

    D. Use Cloud VPN, and create a VPN tunnel to your VPC in Google Cloud. In the VPC, create Compute Engine with a Squid proxy. Configure your server to use the Squid proxy to access Cloud Storage.

14. What steps should be performed as a prerequisite before creating a new Compute Engine instance using the CLI, and after creating a new project in Google Cloud with the `gcloud` command-line tool and linking a billing account to the project?

    A. Set the default project using the `gcloud config set project [PROJECT_ID]` command.

    B. Enable the Compute Engine API for the project using the `gcloud services enable compute.googleapis.com` command.

C. Install the Google Cloud SDK on the machine where the CLI will be run.

D. Create a new service account with the necessary permissions to create Compute Engine instances.

15. What is the command to create a new Kubernetes Engine cluster in Google Cloud using the `gcloud` CLI?

A. `gcloud kubernetes clusters create`

B. `gcloud compute instances create`

C. `gcloud container clusters create`

D. `gcloud compute kubernetes create`

16. What steps can be taken to automate the installation of Jenkins for efficient and streamlined application building and deployment from source code during the development of a new application?

A. Create an instance template with Jenkins already installed. Create a managed instance group from the template.

B. Create a new Kubernetes Engine cluster and create a deployment from the Jenkins image.

C. Create a new Compute Engine instance and install Jenkins manually.

D. Deploy Jenkins from Google Cloud Marketplace.

17. What steps should you take to deploy additional pods that require **n2-highmem-32** nodes on GKE, without causing any downtime, given that your existing application already runs on multiple pods across eight GKE **n2-standard-8** nodes?

A. Create a new GKE cluster with `n2-highmem-32` nodes and redeploy the pods. After that, delete the old cluster.

B. Use the `gcloud container clusters upgrade` command and deploy new pods.

C. Create a new cluster with both n2-highmem-32 and `n2-standard-8` nodes. Redeploy the pods and delete the old cluster.

D. Create a new node pool, specify the machine type as n2-highmem-32, and deploy the new pods.

18. What steps must you take to deploy a Docker image of your application as a workload on GKE?

A. Upload the image to Cloud Storage and create a GKE service, referencing the image.

B. Upload the image to Cloud Storage and create a GKE deployment, referencing the image.

C. Upload the image to Artifact Registry and create a GKE deployment, referencing the image.

D. Upload the image to Container Registry and create a Kubernetes Service, referencing the image.

19. Which programming languages are supported by Google Cloud Functions?

    A. Java

    B. Python

    C. Ruby

    D. All of the preceding.

20. Which of the following statements is true about Google Cloud Functions?

    A. It allows developers to write and deploy code without worrying about server infrastructure.

    B. It is only compatible with Google Cloud Platform services.

    C. It requires developers to manage their servers and infrastructure.

    D. It is a platform to manage cloud storage and data processing.

21. What **database management systems (DBMs)** can be hosted on Google Cloud SQL?

    A. Only MySQL

    B. Only PostgreSQL

    C. Only Microsoft SQL Server

    D. MySQL, PostgreSQL, and Microsoft SQL Server

22. What is the main benefit of using Shared VPC in Google Cloud?

    A. It allows you to share VMs between multiple projects.

    B. It allows you to share billing information between multiple projects.

    C. It allows you to share VPC networks and subnets between multiple projects.

    D. It allows you to share IAM roles and permissions between multiple projects.

23. What is the main difference between Google Cloud Internal Load Balancer and Google Cloud HTTPS Load Balancer?

    A. Google Cloud Internal Load Balancer is used for internal traffic within a VPC, while Google Cloud HTTPS Load Balancer is used for external traffic over the internet.

    B. Google Cloud Internal Load Balancer supports only HTTP traffic, while Google Cloud HTTPS Load Balancer supports both HTTP and HTTPS traffic.

    C. Google Cloud Internal Load Balancer is a software-based load balancer, while Google Cloud HTTPS Load Balancer is a hardware-based load balancer.

    D. Google Cloud Internal Load Balancer is a Layer 4 load balancer, while Google Cloud HTTPS Load Balancer is a Layer 7 load balancer.

24. What is the main difference between jobs and services in Google Cloud Run?

    A.   Jobs are used for short-lived tasks, while services are used for long-running applications.

    B.   Jobs are used for batch processing, while services are used for real-time applications.

    C.   Jobs are used for background tasks, while services are used for frontend tasks.

    D.   Jobs and services are the same things in Google Cloud Run.

25. You have been tasked with the life cycle configuration of the Google Cloud Storage bucket. The life cycle rule should change the object's class from Standard to Coldline. Choose the correct rule in JSON format:

    A.
```json
{
    "rule": [
        {
            "action": {
                "storageClass": "COLDLINE",
                "type": "SetStorageClass"
            },
            "condition": {
                "age": 30
            }
        }
    ]
```

    B.
```json
{
    "rule": [
        {
            "action": {
                "storageClass": "NEARLINE",
                "type": "SetStorageClass"
            },
            "condition": {
                "age": 60
```

```
            }
          }
        ]
      }
C.  {
      "rulesToSet": [
        {
          {
            "storageClass": "COLDLINE",
            "type": "SetStorageClass"
          },
          "condition": {
            "age": 30
          }
        }
      ]
    }
D.  {
      "rule": [
        {
          "execute": {
            " SetStorageClass ": "COLDLINE",
            "type": "StorageClass"
          },
          "condition": {
            "age":
          }
        }
      ]
    }
```

26. You have been tasked with uploading many files from an on-premises fileserver into a Google Cloud Storage bucket. You want to leverage a parallel multithreaded copy mechanism. Choose the correct `gsutil` command:

    A. `gsutil cp -r -M dir gs://my-bucket`

    B. `gcloud -m cp -r dir gs://my-bucket`

    C. `gsutil cp -r dir gs://my-bucket`

    D. `gsutil -m cp -r dir gs://my-bucket`

27. You are planning the migration of 200 VMs running on VMware vSphere from on-premises, with a total size of 280 GiB of data. Your internet provider agreed to increase the speed of your internet connection to 1 Gbps. What is the fastest way to migrate the VMs to Google Cloud?

    A. Use the `gsutil` command-line utility with the `-m` option.

    B. Use the Migrate to VMs service to migrate directly into Google Compute Engine.

    C. Order Transfer Appliance TA300, and copy all the VMVM files onto it. Once data is uploaded to the Cloud Storage bucket, use the `gcloud compute images import my-imported-image --source-file gs://your_gcs_bucket/my_server.vmdk` command.

    D. Convert VMware VMs into the RAW format and upload them to the Cloud Storage bucket. Use the `gcloud compute images import my-imported-image --source-file gs://your_gcs_bucket/my_server.raw` command.

28. An application owner has informed you that app performance is degraded. After checking the application performance metrics in Cloud Monitoring, the bottleneck has been identified – the PostgreSQL database. Cloud Monitoring points to insufficient CPU capacity and slow read performance from the database. What steps can be taken to improve the performance of the PostgreSQL database? (Select four correct answers):

    A. Increase the CPU capacity of the database instance.

    B. Add more memory to the database instance.

    C. Optimize the database schema and indexes.

    D. Use a different database management system.

    E. Create read replicas to offload read queries from the primary instance.

29. As an operations team member, you have been tasked with creating a notification channel in Google Cloud's operations suite. What are the valid options for delivering notifications?

    A. Email, mobile app, SMS, and Pub/Sub

    B. Email, mobile app, Pub/Sub, and Webhooks

    C. Email, PagerDuty, and SMS

    D. Email, mobile app, PagerDuty, SMS, Slack, Webhooks, and Pub/Sub

30. Choose correct identities where IAM roles can be granted:

    A. A Google account and a Service account

    B. A Google group and a Cloud Identity domain

    C. A Google account, a service account, a Google group, a Google Workspace domain, and a Cloud Identity domain

    D. A Google Workspace domain and a Cloud Identity domain

31. Which of the following options is a way to provide a group of data scientists with access to a 10-GB dataset acquired from a third-party research firm, minimizing the steps they will have to take to access it from their statistics programs written in R, while also giving each scientist their dedicated VM with the data available in the VM's filesystem?

    A. Load the dataset into BigQuery.

    B. Use Cloud Storage to store the dataset.

    C. Use a disk with the data to create a source image, and then create VMs from the source image.

    D. Store the dataset in Google Drive.

32. Which command can be used to create a VPC?

    A. `gcloud compute create networks`

    B. `gcloud compute networks create`

    C. `gsutil networks vpc create`

    D. `kubectl compute networks create`

    E. `gcloud vpc networks create`

33. After a successful proof of concept with Google Cloud, you have been tasked with creating a production Cloud SQL database. As a precaution, you want to enable deletion protection on your production Cloud SQL database. Which command can be used to perform this task?

    A. `gcloud sql instances create INSTANCE_NAME --deletion-protection`

    B. `gcloud compute sql create instances INSTANCE_NAME --deletion-protection`

C. `gsutil compute sql instances create INSTANCE_NAME --no-delete`

D. `gcloud sql instances patch [INSTANCE_NAME] --no-deletion-protection`

34. Which roles are necessary to check quotas for a project?

A. Project Owner (roles/owner), Project Editor (roles/editor), and Quota Viewer (`roles/servicemanagement.quotaViewer`)

B. Project Owner (`roles/owner`)

C. Quota Viewer (`roles/servicemanagement.quotaViewer`)

D. Quota Administrator (`roles/servicemanagement.quotaAdmin`)

E. Project Owner (`roles/owner`) and Quota Administrator (`roles/servicemanagement.quotaAdmin`)

F. All of the preceding

35. What are the options for batch-loading data into BigQuery?

A. Avro

B. CSV and JSON

C. ORC

D. PHP

E. AVRO, CSV, JSON, and ORC

36. Which of the following is an appropriate use case for Google Dataflow?

A. Running a web server and serving HTTP requests

B. Generating interactive visualizations of large datasets

C. Processing streaming data in real time

D. Storing and querying data in a distributed data warehouse

37. Choose the correct statement about Google Cloud VPCs and CIDR ranges:

A. You can create one CIDR range for each VPC.

B. You can create a CIDR range for each subnet.

C. You can create a CIDR range for each region.

D. You can create a CIDR range for each zone.

38. You want to implement an infrastructure-as-code approach regarding infrastructure deployment in your company. Terraform was brought to your attention, and you would like to try it out. Which order of Terraform command(s) allows you to deploy your code successfully?

    A. `terraform create`

    B. `terraform apply, terraform init`

    C. `terraform init, terraform plan, terraform apply`

    D. `terraform configure, terraform apply, terraform init`

39. Before migration to Google Cloud, your developer's team used RabbitMQ as a message broker. After successfully migrating all applications, you want to use cloud-native technologies. Choose the correct product that will allow you to use messaging services in Google Cloud.

    A. Dataflow

    B. Dataproc

    C. Pub/Sub

    D. BigQuery

40. You are considering using managed instance groups in Compute Engine, configured with an autoscaling policy. What are valid autoscaling policy metrics?

    A. The average CPU utilization

    B. An HTTP load-balancing serving capacity

    C. Cloud Monitoring metrics

    D. All of the preceding

41. What are potential use cases for Google Cloud Functions? (Select two correct answers):

    A. Triggering real-time data processing tasks

    B. Building and deploying web applications

    C. Automating infrastructure management tasks

    D. Running long-term, resource-intensive computations

42. Which of the following are features of Google Cloud Spanner? (Select two correct answers):

    A. It is a NoSQL database that allows for flexible schema designs.

    B. It is a fully managed relational database service.

    C. It provides strong consistency and HA across multiple regions.

    D. It is designed for low-latency, high-throughput workloads.

43. You have been asked to create a firewall rule to allow TCP traffic destined for VM1, with the IP 192.168.1.2 on port 80. Choose the correct command to perform this task:

A. gcloud compute firewall-rules create firewall-rule-1 --network NETWORK_NAME --action deny --direction egress --rules tcp --destination-ranges 192.168.1.2/32 --priority 1000

B. gcloud compute firewall-rules create firewall-rule-1 --network NETWORK_NAME --action allow --direction egress --rules tcp:80 --destination-ranges 192.168.1.2/32 --priority 60

C. gcloud compute firewall-rules create firewall-rule-1 --network NETWORK_NAME --action allow --direction egress --rules tcp:443 --destination-ranges 192.168.1.2/32 --priority 70 --target-tags webserver

D. gcloud compute firewall-rules firewall-rule-1 --network NETWORK_NAME --action allow --direction ingress --rules tcp:22 --source-tags database --priority 80 --target-tags webserver

E. gcloud compute firewall-rules firewall-rule-1--network NETWORK_NAME --action deny --direction egress --rules tcp --destination-ranges 192.168.1.2/32 --priority 1000

44. Choose the correct statement about Google Cloud Dataproc. (Select two correct answers):

A. Dataproc is managed by Apache Spark and the RabbitMQ service.

B. Dataproc supports Windows Server and Ubuntu images.

C. Dataproc allows you to run it on Google Compute Engine or Kubernetes Engine.

D. Dataproc on Google Kubernetes Engine doesn't have separate master and worker nodes.

E. Dataproc is billed on a per-minute basis.

45. You would like to analyze logs stored in Cloud Logging in external systems. What are the valid external sink destinations?

A. A Cloud Logging bucket

B. A BigQuery dataset

C. A Cloud Pub/Sub topic

D. Splunk

E. All of the preceding

46. What are the three types of roles in Google Cloud IAM? (Select three correct answers):

    A. Basic roles

    B. Special roles

    C. Admin roles

    D. Custom roles

47. What is true about a VPC created in auto mode? (Select two correct answers):

    A. When an auto-mode VPC network is created, one subnet from each region is automatically created within it.

    B. Those automatically created subnets use a set of predefined IPv4 ranges that fit within the 10.128.0.0/9 CIDR block.

    C. When new Google Cloud regions become available, you have to create new subnets in those regions manually.

    D. You cannot add more subnets manually to VPC networks in auto mode.

48. Which of the following statements about the type of applications deployed on Kubernetes are true?

    A. A ReplicaSet ensures that a specified number of pod replicas run at any given time.

    B. A Deployment provides declarative updates for pod replicas and allows for rollbacks if necessary.

    C. A StatefulSet is used to manage stateful applications that require stable network identities and ordered deployment and scaling.

    D. A DaemonSet ensures that a pod runs on every node in a cluster.

    E. All of the preceding.

49. What types of service accounts are available in Google Cloud IAM? (Select more than two correct answers):

    A. User-managed service accounts

    B. Default service accounts

    C. Google-managed service accounts

    D. Service-specific service agents

    E. None of the preceding

50. What statements about Kubernetes Services are true regarding exposing a containerized application outside a GKE cluster? (Select two correct answers):

A. A Service can expose a containerized application to the internet using a static IP address and a LoadBalancer type.

B. A Service can only expose a containerized application to other applications running inside the GKE cluster.

C. A Service can expose a containerized application to the internet using an Ingress resource.

D. A Service cannot expose a containerized application outside a GKE cluster.

Answers

The answers to the preceding questions are provided here:

1C, 2B, 3D, 4A, 5D, 6A, 7A, 8B, 9B, 10A, 11A, 12A, 13B, 14A, 15C, 16D, 17D, 18C, 19D, 20A, 21D, 22C, 23A, 24A, 25A, 26D, 27C, 28A, B, C, and E, 29D, 30C, 31C, 32B, 33A, 34A, 35E, 36C, 37B, 38C, 39C, 40D, 41A and C, 42B and C, 43B, 44C and D, 45E, 46A, B, and D, 47A and B, 48E, 49A, B, C, and D, 50A and C

If you liked reading *Google Cloud Associate Cloud Engineer Certification and Implementation Guide*, you can join its dedicated GitHub repository to ask questions about the topics covered in it, or just to stay up to date with the latest changes. The repository is located at `https://github.com/PacktPublishing/Google-Cloud-Associate-Cloud-Engineer-Certification-and-Implementation-Guide`.

Figure 14.1 – The QR code for the GitHub repository

You can also join the book's Slack channel if you want to interact with the authors and other readers. The channel is located at `bit.ly/ace-gcp-book-slack`.

Figure 14.2 – The QR code for the Slack channel

Index

Packtpub.com

Subscribe to our online digital library for full access to over 7,000 books and videos, as well as industry leading tools to help you plan your personal development and advance your career. For more information, please visit our website.

Why subscribe?

- Spend less time learning and more time coding with practical eBooks and Videos from over 4,000 industry professionals

- Improve your learning with Skill Plans built especially for you

- Get a free eBook or video every month

- Fully searchable for easy access to vital information

- Copy and paste, print, and bookmark content

Did you know that Packt offers eBook versions of every book published, with PDF and ePub files available? You can upgrade to the eBook version at packtpub.com and as a print book customer, you are entitled to a discount on the eBook copy. Get in touch with us at customercare@packtpub.com for more details.

At www.packtpub.com, you can also read a collection of free technical articles, sign up for a range of free newsletters, and receive exclusive discounts and offers on Packt books and eBooks.

Other Books You May Enjoy

If you enjoyed this book, you may be interested in these other books by Packt:

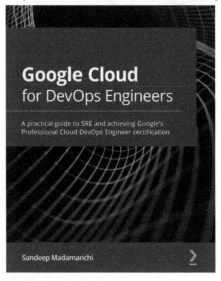

Google Cloud for DevOps Engineers

Sandeep Madamanchi

ISBN: 9781839218019

- Categorize user journeys and explore different ways to measure SLIs
- Explore the four golden signals for monitoring a user-facing system
- Understand psychological safety along with other SRE cultural practices
- Create containers with build triggers and manual invocations
- Delve into Kubernetes workloads and potential deployment strategies
- Secure GKE clusters via private clusters, Binary Authorization, and shielded GKE nodes
- Get to grips with monitoring, Metrics Explorer, uptime checks, and alerting
- Discover how logs are ingested via the Cloud Logging API

Official Google Cloud Certified Associate Cloud Engineer Study Guide

Dan Sullivan

ISBN: 9781119564416

- Plan a cloud solution using one or more GCP services
- Create a cloud environment for an organization
- Manage Kubernetes and VMs
- Deploy applications and infrastructure
- Use monitoring and logging to ensure availability of cloud solutions
- Set up identity management, access controls, and other security measures

Packt is searching for authors like you

If you're interested in becoming an author for Packt, please visit `authors.packtpub.com` and apply today. We have worked with thousands of developers and tech professionals, just like you, to help them share their insight with the global tech community. You can make a general application, apply for a specific hot topic that we are recruiting an author for, or submit your own idea.

Share Your Thoughts

Now you've finished *Google Cloud Associate Cloud Engineer Certification and Implementation Guide*, we'd love to hear your thoughts! Scan the QR code below to go straight to the Amazon review page for this book and share your feedback or leave a review on the site that you purchased it from.

https://packt.link/r/1803232714

Your review is important to us and the tech community and will help us make sure we're delivering excellent quality content.

Download a free PDF copy of this book

Thanks for purchasing this book!

Do you like to read on the go but are unable to carry your print books everywhere? Is your eBook purchase not compatible with the device of your choice?

Don't worry, now with every Packt book you get a DRM-free PDF version of that book at no cost.

Read anywhere, any place, on any device. Search, copy, and paste code from your favorite technical books directly into your application.

The perks don't stop there, you can get exclusive access to discounts, newsletters, and great free content in your inbox daily

Follow these simple steps to get the benefits:

1. Scan the QR code or visit the link below

https://packt.link/free-ebook/978-1-80323-271-3

2. Submit your proof of purchase

3. That's it! We'll send your free PDF and other benefits to your email directly